Wissenschaftliche Untersuchungen
zum Neuen Testament

Herausgeber/Editor
Jörg Frey

Mitherausgeber/Associate Editors
Friedrich Avemarie · Judith Gundry-Volf
Martin Hengel · Otfried Hofius · Hans-Josef Klauck

196

Pieter W. van der Horst

Jews and Christians in Their Graeco-Roman Context

Selected Essays on Early Judaism, Samaritanism, Hellenism, and Christianity

Mohr Siebeck

Pieter W. van der Horst, born 1946, studied Classical Philology and received a PhD in Theology (1978); from 1969–2006 he was firstly research assistent, then junior and later senior lecturer, and finally full professor in New Testament, Early Christian Literature, and the Jewish and Hellenistic world of Early Christianity at the Faculty of Theology of Utrecht University.

BM
176
. H576
2006

ISBN 3-16-148851-2
ISBN-13 978-3-16-148851-1
ISSN 0512-1604 (Wissenschaftliche Untersuchungen zum Neuen Testament)

Die Deutsche Bibliothek lists this publication in the Deutsche Nationalbibliographie; detailed bibliographic data is available in the Internet at *http://dnb.ddb.de.*

© 2006 Mohr Siebeck Tübingen.

This book may not be reproduced, in whole or in part, in any form (beyond that permitted by copyright law) without the publisher's written permission. This applies particularly to reproductions, translations, microfilms and storage and processing in electronic systems.

The book was typeset by Martin Fischer in Tübingen, printed by Gulde-Druck in Tübingen on non-aging paper and bound by Großbuchbinderei Spinner in Ottersweier.

Printed in Germany.

Preface

The author wishes to express his sincere thanks to the following persons: To Professors Martin Hengel and Jörg Frey for their willingness to accept this collection of essays for publication in their series WUNT; to Dr. Henning Ziebritzki of Mohr Siebeck's publishing house for his care in seeing the book through the press; to Dr. Gerard Mussies and Professor Martien Parmentier for their permission to have the two articles of which they were co-authors reprinted; and especially to my friend Dr. James N. Pankhurst for his unfailing readiness during so many years to emend the English of almost all my essays.

The author also thanks the following publishing houses for their permission to reprint the essays in this volume: Bar Ilan University Press, Brill Academic Publishers, Cambridge University Press, T. & T. Clark International (Continuum), Librairie Droz, Mohr Siebeck, Neukirchener Verlagshaus, Edizioni dell' Orso, Oxford University Press, Peeters Publishers, Kluwer Academic Publishers (Springer Verlag), Scholars Press, and Sheffield Academic Press.

Utrecht, Sept. 2005   PWvdH

Table of Contents

Abbreviations

ANRW	Aufstieg und Niedergang der Römischen Welt
ARW	Archiv für Religionswissenschaft
BAGD	Bauer-Arndt-Gingrich-Danker, *Greek-English Lexicon of the NT*, 2nd ed.
BDAG	Bauer-Danker-Arndt-Gingrich, *Greek-English Lexicon of the NT*, 3rd ed.
BZ	Biblische Zeitschrift
CBQ	Catholic Biblical Quarterly
CCSG	Corpus Chistianorum Series Graeca
CIJ	Corpus Inscriptionum Judaicarum (ed. Frey)
CPJ	Corpus Papyrorum Judaicarum (edd. Tcherikover & Fuks)
CSCO	Corpus Scriptorum Christianorum Orientalium
DDD	Dictionary of Deities and Demons in the Bible
GLAJJ	Greek and Latin Authors on Jews and Judaism (ed. Stern)
GMA	Greek Magical Amulets (ed. Kotansky)
HTR	Harvard Theological Review
HUCA	Hebrew Union College Annual
ICS	Illinois Classical Studies
IG	Inscriptiones Graecae
IJO	Inscriptiones Judaicae Orientis (edd. Noy *et al.*)
JBL	Journal of Biblical Literature
JECS	Journal of Early Christian Studies
JIGRE	Jewish Inscriptions of Graeco-Roman Egypt (edd. Horbury & Noy)
JIWE	Jewish Inscriptions of Western Europe (ed. Noy)
JJS	Journal of Jewish Studies
JNES	Journal of Near Eastern Studies
JQR	Jewish Quarterly Review
JSJ	Journal for the Study of Judaism
JSNT	Journal for the Study of the New Testament
JTS	Journal of Theological Studies
LCL	Loeb Classical Library
LSJ	Liddell-Scott-Jones, *Greek English Lexicon*
Mnem.	Mnemosyne

NP	Neue Pauly
NT	Novum Testamentum
NTS	New Testament Studies
OLD	Oxford Latin Dictionary (ed. Glare)
OLZ	Orientalistische Literaturzeitung
PG	Patrologia Graeca
PGM	Papyri Graecae Magicae (ed. Preisendanz)
PL	Patrologia Latina
PW	Pauly-Wissowa
RAC	Reallexikon für Antike und Christentum
RB	Revue biblique
REJ	Revue des études juives
SC	Sources chrétiennes
TLZ	Theologische Literaturzeitung
TRE	Theologische Realenzyklopädie
TSAJ	Texts and Studies in Ancient Judaism
TUGAL	Texte und Untersuchungen zur Geschichte der altchristlichen Literatur
VC	Vigiliae Christianae
ZNW	Zeitschrift für die neutestamentliche Wissenschaft
ZPE	Zeitschrift für Papyrologie und Epigraphik

Introduction

This volume is the ninth, and probably the last, in a series of volumes with essays that I have written over the years.[1] It is published on the occasion of my 60th birthday in mid 2006, which happens to coincide with my retirement as a professor at Utrecht University. That retirement is early, and sudden, and not wholly voluntary; it is due partly to drastic financial measures taken by the Faculty of Theology and partly to the drastic deterioration of my eyesight. Even so, it seemed to be a good opportunity to collect several of my most recent contributions (and some of the earlier ones, on which see more below).

As the subtitle indicates, the essays cover a rather wide range of subjects, and the reader is entitled to know what the underlying unity of all this is, if indeed there is any such unity. One will find studies on subjects as far apart as the origins of Greek atheism in 5th century BCE Athens and aspects of rabbinic anthropology in Talmudic sources of almost a millennium later. One will find a study of the curious phenomenon of subtractive numerals in various ancient languages but also a contribution on a newly discovered early Christian poem on the sacrifice of Isaac. One will find a study of the meaning of the Greek words *hoi de* in Matthew 28:17 but also one on the famous Huguenot Jacques Basnage's view of the Samaritans. And so one could go on, but what is the focus in this variety? The focus is the cultural milieu of early Christianity in the widest sense of the word.

As a student of classical Greek and Roman antiquity in the sixties of the previous century, I developed a strong interest in the religious mentality of

---

[1] The eight volumes that were published previously are partly in Dutch, partly in English. They are (in chronological order): *De onbekende God. Essays over de joodse en hellenistische achtergrond van het vroege christendom* (Utrechtse Theologische Reeks 2), Utrecht 1988; *Essays on the Jewish World of Early Christianity* (Novum Testamentum et Orbis Antiquus 14), Fribourg-Göttingen 1990; (with Gerard Mussies) *Studies on the Hellenistic Background of the New Testament* (Utrechtse Theologische Reeks 10), Utrecht 1990; *Studies over het jodendom in de oudheid*, Kampen 1992; *Hellenism – Judaism – Christianity. Essays on Their Interaction* (Contributions to Biblical Exegesis and Theology 8), Kampen 1994 (a second, much enlarged edition appeared in Leuven in 1998); *Mozes, Plato, Jezus. Studies over de wereld van het vroege christendom*, Amsterdam 2000; *Japheth in the Tents of Shem. Studies on Jewish Hellenism in Antiquity* (Contributions to Biblical Exegesis and Theology 32), Leuven 2002; *Joden in de Grieks-Romeinse wereld*, Zoetermeer 2003. These volumes contain some 130 essays (160 if those in the present volume are included), which is about half of the articles I have written; those not reprinted are mostly encyclopedia articles and contributions for a wider audience.

ancient men and women, including the early Christians. Soon I found out that it is not possible to understand early Christianity if one does not know its Jewish heritage, so I also began to study biblical and rabbinic Hebrew, and later on Palestinian and Babylonian Aramaic as well, in order to enable myself to read the Hebrew Bible and also the Jewish interpretations of this Bible as an essential part of that heritage. And this turned out to be a crucial step for the future direction of my academic career.

It was in the summer of 1968 that I happened to read an article by Willem C. van Unnik, the New Testament professor at Utrecht University (whom I did not yet know at that time), which further opened my eyes to the importance of knowing both the ancient Graeco-Roman and the Jewish literature from the centuries around the turn of the era in order to elucidate difficult passages in the New Testament.[2] After that summer I started to follow a course in Syriac and much to my pleasure the teacher turned out to be the very same Willem C. van Unnik. Since I was the only student in that course, we developed a close relationship and by the end of that academic year he offered me a job as a research assistant in his department. It was van Unnik who emphasized time and again that, however important a thorough knowledge of Graeco-Roman culture is for the understanding of the developments in early Christianity, knowledge of Jewish culture is even more important in order to understand this new religion in its initial phases. His classic *dictum* was that after his birth, Jesus was not carried around the hearth (as was the Roman custom) but circumcised, and that anyone who forgot that fact would never understand the New Testament. His own work was, and still is, an impressive example of how one can bring to bear a wide-ranging knowledge of the literature and religions of antiquity in its broadest sense on the study of early Christianity. I say 'wide-ranging' knowledge because van Unnik also emphasized that it is myopic to confine oneself to study of first-century sources; one should cast one's nets as widely as possible: Plato's *Timaeus* is as important as the rabbinic midrash, and the Dead Sea Scrolls are as important as the patristic interpretations of the Bible. He himself roamed widely in the ancient world, and even went as far as publishing studies on medieval Syrian church history.[3] His view was that a broad knowledge of the cultural surroundings of early Christianity would always have, if not a direct, at least an indirect impact on the way one views the manifestations of this religion in its early phases. Van Unnik was my great paragon and he had a formative influence on my subsequent

---

[2] The article was '"Den Geist löschet nicht aus" (1 Thessalonicher V 19),' *Novum Testamentum* 10 (1968) 255–269.

[3] For bibliographical details see my 'Einleitung des Herausgebers' in Willem Cornelis van Unnik, *Das Selbstverständnis der jüdischen Diaspora in der hellenistisch-römischen Zeit*, aus dem Nachlaß herausgegeben und bearbeitet von Pieter Willem van der Horst, Leiden 1993, 13–50.

scholarly career. No wonder that under his guidance I wrote a dissertation on a Jewish author who was very much at home in the Greek world.[4]

Another major impetus came in the same period, when Martin Hengel published his magisterial *Judentum und Hellenismus* in 1969.[5] This work had a deep and lasting influence on many who worked in the fields of early Jewish and Christian studies and was, of course, 'gefundenes Fressen' for a young classical philologist who was also engaged in Jewish studies. It inspired me not only to pursue further the line of research that van Unnik had already put me on but also to pay much closer attention to the many forms of interpenetration between the classical world of Greece and Rome and the Jewish (and Christian) world around the beginning of the Common Era. Eventually my research in this field (and also my long-standing friendly relationship with Martin Hengel) led to a publication on the position of Greek as a language spoken by Jews in Palestine on the occasion of the celebration of the 30th anniversary of Hengel's book (or rather, of the 25th anniversary of its English translation) in 1999.[6] Hengel's insights into the thorough hellenization of Judaism, not only in the Diaspora but also in the Jewish homeland, even in the pre-Christian period, has opened many eyes to the contributions Hellenistic culture has made to the changing face of Judaism in this formative period and to the implications this has for our study of 'Hellenistic elements' in early Christianity.

Van Unnik put me to work on the *Corpus Hellenisticum Novi Testamenti* project.[7] Many of my early publications, for that reason, focus on the Hellenistic background of the New Testament. Some 15 of them have been reprinted in the volume I published in 1990 in collaboration with my long-time colleague, Dr. Gerard Mussies (see note 1). The reason that I have decided to reprint here two of these essays is simply that the book unfortunately never had any wide circulation and has, therefore, largely been ignored (it was a publication by the Faculty of Theology in Utrecht, but since this institute had no distribution apparatus, the book reached very few people and was never reviewed anywhere). The only two studies from that volume which are reprinted here, however, are my very first article, written in 1969 and published in 1970,[8] and the rather provocative piece

---

[4] *The Sentences of Pseudo-Phocylides*, Leiden 1978. Unfortunately, van Unnik died a couple of months before the public defense of my doctoral thesis in the spring of 1978.

[5] Tübingen 1969 and many reprints; English translation (*Judaism and Hellenism*), London 1974. See also his later books *Juden, Griechen und Barbaren. Aspekte der Hellenisierung des Judentums in vorchristlicher Zeit*, Stuttgart 1976, and *The 'Hellenization' of Judaea in the First Century after Christ*, London 1989.

[6] See my 'Greek in Jewish Palestine in Light of Jewish Epigraphy,' in J.J. Collins & G.E. Sterling (eds.), *Hellenism in the Land of Israel*, Notre Dame 2001, 154–174, reprinted in my *Japheth in the Tents of Shem* 9–26.

[7] On the history of this project see my article 'Corpus Hellenisticum' in the *Anchor Bible Dictionary* 1 (1992) 1157–1161.

[8] It was published in German under the title 'Drohung und Mord schnaubend (Acta IX 1)' in *Novum Testamentum* 12 (1970) 257–269, but is presented here in an English translation.

written by both Mussies and myself on the subtractive numerals in antiquity.[9] In my opinion, both articles deserve a wider circulation than they have received hitherto because there is much new and relevant material in them. Now the relevance of a study of subtractive numerals may not be readily apparent, but once the reader realizes that Paul uses such a numeral in 2 Cor. 11:24 ('forty strokes less one'), the importance of putting this expression in as wide a linguistic context as possible will become clear.

Most of the other contributions are more recent and they reflect my increased interest and research in ancient Judaism. There is a comparative study of the closely related questions which both Philo of Alexandria and the rabbis asked about difficult verses in the book of Genesis, where their different answers are also put into perspective.[10] Apart from other *Philonica*, on which more below, there is a further study of rabbinic materials in the article on the tension between God's positive commandment to procreate (*peru u-revu*) in Gen. 1:28 on the one hand, and the often less than positive view the rabbis had of sexual desire, which they regarded as a manifestation of the evil inclination (*yester ha-ra'*) in humans.[11] There is also a recent contribution on the subject of my dissertation, the *Sentences* of Pseudo-Phocylides, in which I cross swords with the American scholar John Collins on this Jewish poet's views on afterlife.[12] As in the previous volumes, the reader will once again notice that there is also material on the ancient Samaritans. Here a third scholar is to be mentioned for his influence upon me, Alan D. Crown from Sydney. Twenty years ago, in 1985/86, he was my guest at the Utrecht Faculty for a couple of guest lectures, and he opened my eyes to the degree to which the Samaritans had unduly suffered from neglect by scholars in Judaic research. The Samaritans formed a substantial part of the Jewish population of Palestine (even though they would never call themselves 'Jews' but rather 'Israelites') and also had their own large diaspora.[13] It is mainly due to the great efforts of Alan Crown that Samaritan studies have come to flourish of late[14] and thanks to him I have been involved in these developments, albeit on a modest scale. Again, I focused initially mainly on the interaction be-

---

[9] It was originally published in *Illinois Classical* Studies 13 (1988) 183–202.

[10] 'Philo and the Rabbis on Genesis: Similar Questions, Different Answers,' in: A. Volgers & C. Zamagni (eds.), *Erotapokriseis. Early Christian Question-and-Answer Literature in Context* (Contributions to Biblical Exegesis and Theology 37), Leuven 2004, 55–70.

[11] 'A Note on the Evil Inclination and Sexual Desire in Talmudic Literature,' in U. Mittmann-Richert, F. Avemarie & G.S. Oegema (eds.), *Der Mensch vor Gott. Forschungen zum Menschenbild in Bibel, antikem Judentum und Koran (Festschrift für Hermann Lichtenberger zum 60. Geburtstag)*, Neukirchen 2003, 99–106.

[12] 'Pseudo-Phocylides on the Afterlife: A Rejoinder to John J. Collins,' *Journal for the Study of Judaism* 35 (2004) 70–75.

[13] See my 'The Samaritan Diaspora in Antiquity' in my *Essays on the Jewish World of Early Christianity* 136–147.

[14] See, e.g. A.D. Crown (ed.), *The Samaritans*, Tübingen 1988, the most extensive reference work to date.

tween Samaritans and Hellenistic culture,[15] but later I widened the scope of my investigations as may be apparent from the two essays included in this volume. My recent book *De Samaritanen*[16] is the long-term result of this involvement in samaritanological research.

Again another scholar who has exerted influence on my scholarly career is David T. Runia of Melbourne, one of the great Philonic scholars of our time. After reading his magisterial 1983 dissertation on Philo's creative use of Plato's *Timaeus* in his biblical exegesis,[17] I became much more aware of the importance of this paragon of Jewish Hellenism from Alexandria. Runia also made very clear to me how great the impact of Philo had been on the theology of many Church Fathers.[18] Some of the fruits of my fascination with Philo are to be found in this volume,[19] although half of them are no more than *parerga* to my recent commentary on Philo's *In Flaccum* which David Runia and Gregory Sterling invited me to write for their new Philo of Alexandria Commentary Series (PACS).[20]

It was the work on this commentary, and especially the investigation of the complicated backgrounds of the serious conflict in Alexandria in the year 38 CE described by Philo that led me to further research the situations in which various Jewish diaspora communities had lived. Not only my earlier study on the Jews of ancient Crete, but also the recent ones on the Jews of Cyprus, of Sicily, and of the city of Sardis have been included here.[21] They show the great variety in degrees of integration and acculturation in these diaspora communities and they demonstrate how difficult it is to say with any certainty why in some places the various religious groups lived in harmony, or at least not in conflict, while elsewhere things derailed completely. A special case is the story of the conflicts,

---

[15] See my study of the Samaritan diaspora mentioned in note 13 and the one on 'The Samaritan Languages in the pre-Islamic Period,' *Journal for the Study of Judaism* 32 (2001) 178–192, reprinted in my *Japheth in the Tents of Shem* 235–249. See also my 'Samaritans and Hellenism' in my *Hellenism – Judaism – Christianity* 49–58.

[16] Kampen 2004 (the book is in Dutch).

[17] Published as *Philo of Alexandria and the* Timaeus *of Plato*, Leiden 1986.

[18] See his *Philo and Early Christian Literature*, Assen-Minneapolis 1993.

[19] The article on 'Philo of Alexandria on the Wrath of God' was originally published in Dutch as 'Philo Alexandrinus over de toorn Gods,' in A. de Jong & A. de Jong (eds.), *Kleine encyclopedie van de toorn*, Utrecht 1993, 77–82. For the present volume I have translated it into English.

[20] See my *Philo's* Flaccus: *The First Pogrom*, Leiden 2003. The *parerga* reprinted here are 'Common Prayer in Philo's *In Flaccum* 121–124,' *Kenishta: Studies of the Synagogue World*, ed. J. Tabory, vol. 2, Bar Ilan 2003, 21–28; and 'Philo's *In Flaccum* and the Book of Acts,' in: R. Deines & K.-W. Niebuhr (eds.), *Philo und das Neue Testament. Wechselseitige Wahrnehmungen* (Wissenschaftliche Untersuchungen zum Neuen Testament 172), Tübingen 2004, 95–105.

[21] The study of Cretan Jewry had already been republished in 1990 in my *Essays on the Jewish World* 148–165, but it is included here again – albeit in an abbreviated form – in order to retain the character of a trilogy on the Jewish communities of the three great islands in the Mediterranean Sea (Crete, Cyprus, Sicily). About the Jews of the great island of Euboia we know next to nothing (see Philo, *Legat.* 282, and *IJO* I, Ach57).

throughout the period of the Roman and early Byzantine Empire, between Jews and Greens, a notorious hooligan-like circus faction active in the great cities, and of the seemingly strange alliance between Jews and Blues, the opponents of the Greens. Here social psychology turned out to be very helpful in solving an anomaly.[22] All these studies of details concerning diaspora communities fill in the background against which we have to understand the lives and activities of the early Christians who, as a minority, had to maintain their position between these parties.[23]

Related to this area of research is another field in which I have done work over the past 15 years, early Jewish epigraphy. In an attempt to fill a lacuna, I published in 1991 an introductory work to the study of Jewish epitaphs (which form the bulk of the epigraphic material).[24] The book received a very warm welcome since there existed no such work for students of ancient Judaism.[25] When I was writing the book (during a sabbatical spent at the Hebrew University in Jerusalem), I could not foresee how quickly the situation in this field of research would change in terms of the availability of new critical editions of the epigraphic material and of in-depth studies. In a high tempo, between 1992 and 2004, most of this material was published again in much better editions than the old and outdated *Corpus Inscriptionum Judaicarum* (CIJ) by Frey,[26] upon which I still had to rely by and large in 1990/91, and very much new material was added in these publications. In a long review article on the three recent volumes *Inscriptiones Judaicae Orientis* (IJO), reprinted in this volume, I sketch these developments and show how dramatically the situation has improved. The study of Jewish epitaphs, honorary inscriptions, and other epigraphic material is of great importance to the student of early Judaism and Christianity since these sources quite often provide us with information about Jewish life and thought that we do not find in the literary documents (for instance, data about age at death and onomastics).

---

[22] Published as 'Jews and Blues in Late Antiquity,' in D. Accorinti & P. Chuvin (edd.), *Des Géants à Dionysos. Mélanges de mythologie et de poésie grecques offerts à Francis Vian*, Alessandria 2003, 565–572.

[23] See also I. Levinskaya, *The Book of Acts in Its First Century Setting,* vol. 5: *Diaspora Setting*, Grand Rapids-Carlisle 1996. Diaspora studies have come of age in recent decades; see John Barclay's Introduction to J.G.M. Barclay (ed.), *Negotiating Diaspora. Jewish Strategies in the Roman Empire*, London – New York 2004, 1–7.

[24] *Ancient Jewish Epitaphs. An Introductory Survey of a Millennium of Jewish Funerary Epigraphy (300 BCE – 700 CE)*, Kampen 1991.

[25] Even the otherwise excellent book by B.H. McLean, *An Introduction to Greek Epigraphy of the Hellenistic and Roman Periods from Alexander the Great down to the Reign of Constantine*, Ann Arbor 2002, deals very insufficiently with Jewish material.

[26] J.-B. Frey, *Corpus Inscriptionum Judaicarum. Recueil des inscriptions juives qui vont du IIIe siècle avant Jésus-Christ au VIIe siècle de notre ère*, 2 vols, Rome 1936–1952. Vol. I was reprinted in 1975 with an extensive Prolegomenon containing many corrections and additions by Baruch Lifshitz.

The interpretation of biblical texts in ancient Judaism and early Christianity is also a field that has been blossoming in the past decades.[27] My first steps in this field were taken some 15 years ago in an article written for Adam van der Woude's *Festschrift* on the widely diverging interpretations, by ancient Jews and Christians, of the enigmatic words in Ezek. 20:25 where God says that he gave Israel 'laws that were not good!'[28] The text in Ex. 22:28 as rendered in the Septuagint, "Thou shalt not revile the gods," also evoked a wide variety of exegeses in Jewish and Christian circles, which I charted briefly.[29] In the present volume there are two further examples, albeit on a modest scale, namely, a study of the way in which the limitation of the human life span to 120 years by God in Gen. 6:3 was variously interpreted by Jews and Christians in antiquity, and one on the way Jewish interpreters viewed what was for them the amazing activity of the prophetess Huldah in 2 Kings 22 and how their views relate to the rabbinic traditions about the presence of Huldah's tomb in Jerusalem, quite close to the Temple, of all places. Both studies show how passages in the Bible that were regarded as problematic by the ancient readers were creatively dealt with.[30]

Again another subject that has witnessed an upsurge in scholarly interest[31] and has fascinated me intensely since the beginning of the nineties was that of ancient prayer cultures. It resulted *inter alia* in a booklet in Dutch in which I presented an annotated translation of 60 ancient prayers, 20 Graeco-Roman, 20 Jewish, and 20 Christian,[32] and also in an article on the uncommon and suspect phenomenon of silent prayer,[33] in a study of one of the few ancient thematic treatises on prayer, especially on the question of whether one should pray at all, and if so, what for,

---

[27] Among the innumerable publications I mention – *honoris causa* – only James Kugel's magisterial *Traditions of the Bible. The Bible as It Was at the Start of the Common Era*, Cambridge MA-London 1998.

[28] "'I Gave Them Laws That Were Not Good." Ezekiel 20:25 in Ancient Judaism and Early Christianity,'in J.N. Bremmer & F. García Martínez (eds.), *Sacred History and Sacred Texts in Early Judaism. A Symposium in Honour of A.S. van der Woude*, Kampen 1992, 94–118, repr. in my *Hellenism – Judaism – Christianity* 135–156.

[29] "'Thou shalt not revile the gods." The LXX-translation of Ex. 22:28 (27), its background and influence, ' *Studia Philonica Annual* 5 (1993) 1–8, reprinted in my *Hellenism – Judaism – Christianity* 125–134.

[30] The first study appeared in the new annual *Zutot* (2002, 18–23), the second was published in Dutch in *Nederlands Theologisch Tijdschrift* 55 (2001) 91–96, and translated by me into English for the present volume.

[31] See, e.g., J.H. Charlesworth, M. Harding & M. Kiley (eds.), *The Lord's Prayer and Other Prayer Texts from the Greco-Roman Era*, Valley Forge 1993; M. Kiley (ed.), *Prayer from Alexander to Constantine*, London-New York 1997; J.H. Newman, *Praying by the Book. The Scripturalization of Prayer in Second Temple Judaism*, Atlanta 1999; H. Löhr, *Studien zum frühchristlichen und frühjüdischen Gebet*, Tübingen 2003. Many other works could be mentioned as well.

[32] *Gebeden uit de antieke wereld*, Kampen 1994.

[33] 'Silent Prayer in Antiquity,' *Numen* 41 (1994) 1–25, reprinted in my *Hellenism – Judaism – Christianity* 293–316.

namely the fifth oration of Maximus of Tyre,[34] as well as in an investigation of whether or not a forgotten prayer text in one of the Egerton papyri is Jewish or Christian.[35] In this volume, the readers will find a short contribution on a remarkable prayer by the Jews of Alexandria after their persecution by the Roman governor Flaccus, as reported by Philo in his *In Flaccum.*[36]

As far as the New Testament is concerned, some of the contributions in this volume intend to shed light on long-standing translation problems (although often not even seen as problematic) from insights won in classical philology. The question of whether the words οἱ δὲ ἐδίστασαν in Matt. 28:17 mean 'but they doubted' or 'but some doubted' or 'but others doubted' (which makes quite a difference!) is solved on the basis of strictly philological considerations: it means 'but some doubted.' In a second contribution, the same kind of philological considerations, but now of a more lexical nature, lead to the suggestion that in the parable of the rich man and the poor Lazarus the words ἐγένετο δὲ ἀποθανεῖν τὸν πτωχὸν καὶ ἀπενεχθῆναι αὐτὸν ὑπὸ τῶν ἀγγέλων εἰς τὸν κόλπον ᾿Αβραάμ do not just mean that the poor man was carried away to Abraham's bosom but that he was carried to a place he deserved or where he belonged, the bosom of Abraham (*apo-* in composita often has this force). The striking expression ἐμπνέων ἀπειλῆς καὶ φόνου in Acts 9:1 is studied in the light of expressions in Greek literature that circumscribe strong emotions or passions with verbs of breathing or snorting.[37] Finally, in a philological study of the expression καὶ οὕτως πᾶς Ἰσραὴλ σωθήσεται in Rom. 11:26, I argue that the words καὶ οὕτως in this context do not mean 'and so [or 'thus'] all Israel will be saved,' but '*only then* will all Israel be saved.' That καὶ οὕτως can have this sense, although it is not registered in the standard Greek lexicons, is well-known among classical philologists, but hardly familiar among theologians (a justly renowned commentator even says that a temporal meaning of this word is *never* found in Greek!).[38] These proposals are not shattering innovations but they do prove that detailed knowledge of the Greek language can help solve New Testament exegetical problems, which sounds like a truism but unfortunately still needs to be said over and over again. It may be added here that the article on the Hellenistic popular beliefs about the power of the shadow[39] was ultimately inspired by the silence of the NT commentaries on

---

[34] 'Maximus of Tyre on Prayer. An Annotated Translation of Εἰ δεῖ εὔχεσθαι (Dissertatio 5),' in H. Cancik, H. Lichtenberger & P. Schäfer (eds.), *Geschichte – Tradition – Reflexion: Festschrift für Martin Hengel zum 70. Geburtstag,* 3 vols., Tübingen 1996, Vol. 2: 323–338.

[35] 'Neglected Greek Evidence for Early Jewish Liturgical Prayer,' *Journal for the Study of Judaism* 29 (1998) 278–296.

[36] Originally published as 'Common Prayer in Philo's *In Flaccum* 121–124,' *Kenishta: Studies of the Synagogue World,* ed. J. Tabory, vol. 2, Bar Ilan 2003, 21–28.

[37] Since this was my very first publication, written when I was 23, the reader is asked to exercise a certain clemency as regards the woodenness of the presentation.

[38] This note appeared in the *Journal of Biblical Literature* 119 (2000) 521–525.

[39] Originally published in German as 'Der Schatten im hellenistischen Volksglauben,' in M. J. Vermaseren (ed.), *Studies in Hellenistic Religions,* EPRO 78, Leiden 1979, 27–36.

Acts 5:15, where Luke says that the people of Jerusalem 'even carried out their sick into the streets and laid them on beds and pallets, hoping that as Peter came by at least his shadow might fall on some of them.' And, finally, the study on Philo's *In Flaccum* and the Book of Acts highlights the importance of each of these two works for the study of the other.[40]

My early interest in patristic literature may be seen in an article of 1971, not reprinted here, on Augustine's view of suicide as compared to that of his pagan contemporary, the philosopher Macrobius.[41] A later study dealt with the interesting motif of Plato's fear of telling the (supposedly Christian) truth in apologetic patristic literature.[42] Although not at all a patristic scholar myself, in this volume I have yet again included some studies of the works of Church Fathers. The first is a by-product of my Dutch book *De Woestijnvaders* (The Desert Fathers),[43] in which I also translated large parts of Cyril of Scythopolis' work on the Palestinian monks in the desert of Judaea. In this chapter, which was originally presented as a paper at a Jerusalem conference about Sabas, the famous founder of the Mar Saba monastery in the Judaean desert,[44] I investigate various aspects of Cyril's use of Scripture and compare these to the other monastic authors from the 4th to 6th century. Another undeservedly less known author is Macarius Magnes, whose work *Monogenês* (or *Apokritikos*) is a long refutation of the attacks on Christianity by an unnamed opponent whose identity has always been an object of much speculation (was he Porphyry?). It is a fascinating work which had long awaited a new critical edition. The recent one by Richard Goulet gave me the opportunity to discuss some of the issues in a review article that is reprinted here. Further the reader will find a study, co-authored by my colleague Martien Parmentier, on a recently published papyrus, Pap. Bodmer 30, which contains a very interesting 4th century poem on the sacrifice of Isaac. The article includes the first English translation of the Greek text and a study on both the Jewish and the Christian backgrounds of the many non-biblical elements in this text.[45] Finally, as far as

---

[40] 'Philo's *In Flaccum* and the Book of Acts,' in: R. Deines & K.-W. Niebuhr (eds), *Philo und das Neue Testament. Wechselseitige Wahrnehmungen* (Wissenschaftliche Untersuchungen zum Neuen Testament 172), Tübingen 2004, 95–105.

[41] 'A Christian Platonist and a Pagan Platonist on Suicide,' *Vigiliae Christianae* 25 (1971) 282–288.

[42] 'Plato's Fear as a Topic in Early Christian Apologetics,' *Journal of Early Christian Studies* 6 (1998) 1–14, repr. In *Hellenism – Judaism – Christianity* 257–268.

[43] Amsterdam 1998.

[44] 'The Role of Scripture in Cyril of Scythopolis' *Lives of the Monks of Palestine*,' in J. Patrich (ed.), *The Sabaite Heritage in the Orthodox Church from the Fifth Century to the Present*, Leuven 2001 [published in 2002], 127–145.

[45] Published as 'A New Early Christian Poem on the Sacrifice of Isaac,' in A. Hurst & J. Rudhardt (eds.), *Le Codex des Visions* (Recherches et rencontres 18), Geneva 2002, 155–172. This batch of papyri contains several more early Christian poems that deserve much more attention from patristic scholars; see A. Hurst & J. Rudhardt (eds), *Papyri Bodmer XXX–XXXVII: Codex des Visions, poèmes divers*, München 1999. For one of my earlier publications (with

Christian sources are concerned, we move to quite a late document, the seventh-century Ἐπαπορητικὰ κεφάλαια κατὰ τῶν Ἰουδαίων, 'Arguments to corner the Jews,' a short Byzantine manual in the form of 25 questions which should enable Christians in their disputations with Jews to drive them into a corner from which they could not escape (note ἐπαπορητικά). In this contribution I present the document in a first English translation and add some comments to place the document in its historical context.[46]

As to the pagan Graeco-Roman part of this volume, I already mentioned the studies on the shadow in Hellenistic folklore and the one on subtractive composite numerals. Apart from these, the reader will find an article on a recently found new fragment of the great philosophical inscription in the city of Oenoanda (Asia Minor), in which the Epicurean thinker Diogenes sets out his view of life according to Epicurus (the text is from the early 2nd century CE). The fragment also chides the Jews as 'the most superstitious and disgusting of all nations,' a statement that I try to put into the context of the tradition of ancient Judaeophobia[47] and of contemporary history. Jews and Christians were often charged with atheism in the ancient world because they did not worship the generally accepted gods, but they were no atheists in the strict sense, and there were very few atheists in antiquity in general, as far as we know. Nevertheless, atheism did originate in ancient Greece, but why and when and where? That is the topic of another article (originally published in Dutch but here presented in an English translation) in which I argue that even though the well-known Diagoras (5th century BCE) was the first outspoken atheist, it was in all probability Critias, a nephew of Plato's mother, who first invented a theory that the origin of religion was based on a cynical lust for power.

Finally, there are two pieces on magic, an interdenominational or syncretistic phenomenon of which the documents are often hard to categorize as pagan, Jewish or Christian. How difficult it often is to take such a decision (if possible at all) is demonstrated in the article on the great magical papyrus in the Bibliothèque Nationale in Paris (PGM IV) and the Bible, as well as in the contribution on the exorcistic formula 'the God who drowned the king of Egypt,' which is of course of Jewish origin but was also in use among pagan magicians.[48]

A.H.M. Kessels) on a Bodmer papyrus see 'The Vision of Dorotheus (Pap. Bodmer 29). Edited with Introduction, Translation and Notes,' *Vigiliae Christianae* 41 (1987) 313–359.

[46] Originally published as 'Twenty-Five Questions to Corner the Jews: A Byzantine Anti-Jewish Document from the Seventh Century,' in E.G. Chazon, D. Satran & R.A. Clements (eds.), *Things Revealed. Studies in Early Jewish and Christian Literature in Honor of Michael E. Stone* (Supplements to the Journal for the Study of Judaism 89), Leiden 2004, 289–302.

[47] See P. Schäfer, *Judeophobia. Attitudes towards the Jews in the Ancient World*, Cambridge MA-London 1997.

[48] Originally published as "The God Who Drowned the King of Egypt.' A Short Note on an Exorcistic Formula,' in: A. Hilhorst & G.H. van Kooten (eds.), *The Wisdom of Egypt. Jewish, Early Christian, and Gnostic Studies in Honour of Gerard P. Luttikhuizen*, Leiden 2005, 135–140.

These brief remarks hopefully suffice to put these essays not only into the context of the individual 'Werdegang' of an old-fashioned scholarly recluse, but also into that of the developments in both Jewish, classical, and early Christian studies in the second half of the 20th century. I have left out of account my work on ancient Jewish mysticism, which was only published in Dutch and intended for a non-academic audience.[49] I had to be selective, as the subtitle of this volume indicates. Even so the author hopes that these essays will inspire in many readers a desire to widen their horizons and try to enjoy the fascinating panoramas to be seen in the multifaceted world of the religions of late antiquity.[50]

---

[49] E. g., my annotated translation of *3 Enoch* or *Sepher Hekhaloth* published as *Het boek der hemelse paleizen (3 Henoch), een joods mystiek geschrift uit de late oudheid* (Joodse Bronnen 2), Kampen 1999.

[50] The essays have only slightly been updated, mainly in places where it seemed essential (e. g., references to important new editions of texts or documents). These updating additions are always put between square brackets […]. Typographical errors have been removed as much as possible. One essay (the one on Cretan Jewry) has been abridged.

The Jews of Ancient Crete

The history of Cretan Jewry in antiquity is largely unknown to us. This is due not only to the scarcity of our sources, but also to the fact that this history seems to have been a rather uneventful one. This is in keeping with the history of the island itself, for it can be said that from the late Hellenistic period to the early Middle Ages Crete enjoyed a unique period of peace and had practically no 'history' inasmuch as until the seventh century CE 'nothing regarded as worthy of note by the ancient authors happened.'[1] Although the scarce literary and epigraphical data[2] do not grant us more than occasional glimpses of the Jewish communities in Crete, it is nonetheless worthwhile assembling the material available in order to try to make a dossier as complete as possible, something that has not been done so far.[3]

Before surveying the evidence, let us ask how and when the Cretan diaspora originated. We can only guess at the answer to this question but it may be an educated surmise. We know that during the Maccabaean revolt many Jews fled from Palestine to other countries like Egypt and Syria. It is not improbable that some of them may have taken refuge in Crete since that would tie in very well with a passage in *1 Maccabees* to be discussed presently. Some may have come by way of Egypt, for an inscription from Crete reveals that Ptolemy VI Philometor (180–145 BCE) sent troops to Gortyn in Crete[4] in the middle of the sixties of the second century BCE, and it is well known from various sources that Philometor used a great many Jews in his military operations, often in leading positions.[5] Admittedly, this does not constitute compelling proof that the Cretan

---

[1] I.F. Sanders, *Roman Crete. An Archaeological Survey and Gazetteer of Late Hellenistic, Roman and Early Byzantine Crete*, Warminster 1982, 1.

[2] There are no remains of ancient synagogues in Crete.

[3] For incomplete and summary statements on Cretan Jewry see Sanders, *Roman Crete* 43; M. Stern, 'The Jewish Diaspora,' in S. Safrai & M. Stern (eds.), *The Jewish People in the First Century* (CRINT I 1), Assen 1974, 160; S. Marcus, 'Crete,' *Enc. Jud.* 5 (1972) 1088–89; U. Baumann, *Rom und die Juden*, Bern & Frankfurt 1983, 240 n. 12; E. Schürer, G. Vermes, F. Millar and M. Goodman, *The History of the Jewish People in the Age of Jesus Christ* III 1, Edinburgh 1986, 69.

[4] M. Guarducci (ed.), *Inscriptiones Creticae*, 4 vols., Rome 1935–1950, IV no. 195. Ptolemy probably sent his troops to assist Gortyn in its war against Cnossos.

[5] P.M. Fraser, *Ptolemaic Alexandria*, 3 vols., Oxford 1972, I 83 with notes in II 163–4. For other Ptolemaic officials in Crete see *ibid.* I 66, 101. It is notable that there were also many

diaspora started in the sixties of the second century BCE, but it is a hypothesis that gains some support from *1 Macc.* 15:22–23.

This passage immediately follows upon a letter written in 140 BCE by Lucius, consul of Rome, to Ptolemy VIII Euergetes in which he asks him to refrain from waging war upon the Jews whom he calls 'our friends and allies' (15:17). After having quoted the letter, the author of *1 Maccabees* adds:

> (22) He wrote the same letter to king Demetrius and to Attalus, Ariarathus and Arsaces, (23) and to all the following countries: to Sampsame and the Spartans, Delos, Myndos, Sicyon, Caria, Samos, Pamphylia, Lycia, Halicarnassus, Rhodos, Phaselis, Cos, Side, Aradus, Gortyn, Cnidus, Cyprus, and Cyrene.

These lines form an interesting document for the spread of the Jewish diaspora in the middle of the second century BCE.[6] For our purpose it is remarkable that, whereas in the case of other islands the name of the whole island is mentioned (Delos, Samos, Rhodos, Cos, Cyprus), only in the case of Crete is the name of one single city mentioned, which happens to be Gortyn, where Ptolemy VI had sent his troops a quarter of a century before. This adds probability to my hypothesis that the military operation of Philometor may have marked the beginning of Jewish settlement in Crete, especially in Gortyn, which was also the birthplace or residence of one of the very few Cretan Jews about whom more is known than just the name, as will be seen later (see below on Sophia).[7]

Although we will reserve the epigraphical evidence for Cretan Jewry for the latter part of this study, it seems appropriate to deal at this point with an inscription which may indicate that in approximately the same period there were also Samaritans in Crete. It is a recently published inscription from the island of Delos and runs as follows:[8]

> The Israelites of Delos who contribute their offerings to the temple (of) Argarizin (or: to the sacred mountain of Garizin) crown with a golden crown Sarapion, the son of Iason, from Cnossos, for his benefaction towards them.

Cretans in Ptolemaic service in Egypt (*ibid.* 66, 70, 81, 88–9, 101, 180, 614–5), which indicates the strong ties between Egypt and Crete.

[6] See the commentary on this passage by J.A. Goldstein, *I Maccabees*, Garden City 1976, 496–500. It is obvious that these lines list not just names of allies, but countries and cities where Jews were living and in danger of being attacked.

[7] In a private communication, Professor Martin Hengel suggested that Jewish settlement in Crete may have started as early as the third century BCE, in view of the fact that elsewhere in Greece (Attica, Cyprus) there is evidence of Jewish presence from *ca.* 300 BCE onwards (see the references in his *Juden, Griechen und Barbaren*, Stuttgart 1976, 121) and that there is also a third century BCE epitaph (in Gaza) of a Cretan officer in Ptolemaic service (*SEG* 8, 269; see Hengel's *Judentum und Hellenismus*, Tübingen 1969, 26 with n. 77), which may be indicative of contacts between Crete and Jewish Palestine in that period.

[8] Ph. Bruneau, 'Les Israélites de Délos et la juiverie délienne,' *Bulletin de correspondence hellénique* 106 (1982) 465–504. At pp. 468–9 Bruneau presents a photo and a transcription with translation of the inscription.

There is no doubt that the Israelites who pay their temple taxes to the *hieron Argarizin*[9] are the religious community of the Samaritans, who describe themselves as Israelites in order to distinguish themselves from those called *Ioudaioi* who had their own synagogue nearby on Delos.[10] These Samaritans honour Sarapion from Cnossos in Crete for his benefactions to the community. An earlier Samaritan inscription, built into the same wall of what may have been a Samaritan synagogue, records the honouring of a certain Menippus of Heraclea for having erected and dedicated at his own cost a building, probably for the Samaritan community.[11] What Sarapion's gift to the community was, we do not know, but the relevant point is that he was most likely a Samaritan believer from Crete, whether he was only born in Cnossos or still lived there when he acted as a benefactor to the Delan Samaritans.[12] That he had a very pagan-sounding name is no proof that he cannot have been a Samaritan believer. The Jewish prosopography of Ptolemaic and Roman Egypt shows that several Jews bore theophoric names containing the elements 'Isis' and 'Horus,'[13] so a Samaritan name with the element 'Sarapis' need not be surprising. Of course, the possibility can never be ruled out that the Samaritans honoured pagan benefactors, but it is much more probable that a religious community honours a co-religionist. In that case, we may assume that in the second century BCE there were Samaritans in Crete, which should cause no astonishment in view of the extent of the Samaritan diaspora in antiquity.[14] Since the editor dates the inscription between 150 and 50 BCE on palaeographical grounds, and since it was most probably written before the destruction of the Samaritan sanctuary on Mount Garizim in *ca.* 110 BCE, it is plausible to suppose that Sarapion lived in Cnossos around the middle of the second century BCE.

---

[9] For *Argarizin* = *har Garizim* = the mountain of Garizim or mount Garizim, see also Pseudo-Eupolemus, fragm. 1, *ap.* Eusebius, *Praep. Ev.* 9.17.5. It is written as one word in Samaritan sources (e. g., *argarizim* in the Greek translation of the Samaritan Pentateuch). Cf. also the use of *Argarizin* in Josephus, *Bell.* 1.63, which derives from a Samaritan source; see R. Egger, *Josephus Flavius und die Samaritaner*, Fribourg – Göttingen 1986, 294–6. See further C.R. Holladay, *Fragments from Hellenistic Jewish Authors*, vol. 1, Chico 1983, 183 n. 21, and R. Pummer, 'Argarizin: A Criterion for Samaritan Provenance?,' *JSJ* 18 (1987) 18–25, who fails to discuss *Bell.* 1.63. Bruneau, 'Les Israélites' 477, refers to *TOURGARIZIN* on the Madaba map (*tur* being Aramaic for 'mountain').

[10] See Bruneau, 'Les Israélites,' *passim.*

[11] See Bruneau, 'Les Israélites' 471–2. The inscription is damaged so that we do not know what Menippus built and dedicated.

[12] See Bruneau, 'Les Israélites' 481: 'Le plus probable est que Sarapion et Ménippos soient eux-mêmes Samaritains.' This is doubted by A.T. Kraabel, 'New Evidence of the Samaritan Diaspora Has Been Found on Delos,' *Biblical Archaeologist* 47 (1984) 44–6.

[13] See V.A. Tcherikover, A. Fuks & M. Stern (eds.), *Corpus Papyrorum Judaicarum*, vol. 3, Cambridge MA 1964, 167–196.

[14] See A.D. Crown, 'The Samaritan Diaspora to the End of the Byzantine Era,' *Australian Journal of Biblical Archaeology* 2 (1974/75) 107–123; and my article 'The Samaritan Diaspora in Antiquity,' in my *Essays on the Jewish World of Early Christianity*, Fribourg – Göttingen 1990, 136–147.

The next piece of evidence in chronological order dates from more than a century and a half later. In the early fourties of the first century CE, the Jewish philosopher Philo of Alexandria wrote his *Legatio ad Gaium* where he quotes at length a letter from Agrippa I to the Emperor Caligula, in which the former says that Jerusalem has settled colonies in almost every country of the world:

And not only are the mainlands full of Jewish colonies, but also the most highly esteemed of the islands: Euboia, Cyprus, and Crete (*Legat.* 282).

The difference from the earlier testimonies is striking. Here it is no longer a few cities that are mentioned, like Gortyn or Cnossos: it is stated that the greater islands, Crete included, are *full of Jewish settlements*. That the Cretan diaspora had expanded considerably in the meantime is confirmed by a few other testimonies from the last quarter of the first century CE.

In one of his many stories about Jews who had been deceived by an impostor, Josephus tells about a Jewish fraud who pretended to be the prince Alexander whom king Herod had put to death (*Bell.* II 101–116). This man gave out that the executioners sent to kill both him and Aristobulus had stolen them away out of compassion, substituting in their stead the corpses of persons who resembled them. So, contrary to the rumours, he was still alive.

'With this tale he completely deceived the Jews in Crete, and, being magnificently furnished with supplies, he sailed across to Melos (*Bell.* II 103).

In Melos and elsewhere, and finally in Rome, the Pseudo-Alexander succeeded in gathering a large following among the Jews, but the Emperor Augustus unmasked him as an impostor.[15]

Whereas this history took place at the beginning of the first century, the same Josephus tells us in his autobiography that in the second half of the seventies he divorced his wife and took another:

Thereafter I married a woman who was Jewish by birth and had settled in Crete. She came of very distinguished parents, indeed the most illustrious people in that country (*Vita* 427).

These two passages demonstrate that Cretan Jewry had not only become numerous, as Philo had already shown, but also that some of them were probably well-to-do and belonged to the upper class of the island.

Contemporary with Josephus' testimonies, two passages in the New Testament, though not very illuminating, nevertheless offer corroborative evidence. In a text comparable to *1 Macc.* 15 and Philo's *Legat.* 282 (discussed above), the author of Acts enumerates a large number of countries from which diaspora Jews went on pilgrimage to Jerusalem, where they witnessed the manifestations of the Holy Spirit. Acts 2:9–11:

---

[15] The same story is also found in Josephus, *Ant.* XVII 324–338.

Parthians and Medes and Elamites and residents of Mesopotamia, Judea and Cappadocia, Pontus and Asia, (10) Phrygia and Pamphylia, Egypt and the parts of Libya belonging to Cyrene, and visitors from Rome, both Jews and proselytes, (11) Cretans and Arabs, we hear them telling in our own tongues the mighty works of God (RSV).

In spite of Otto Eissfeldt's theory that the placing of 'Cretans and Arabs' after the summarizing 'Jews and proselytes' indicates that these two words should not be interpreted literally but as a general statement meaning '(Jews and proselytes) from West to East,'[16] I still think it legitimate to take the sentence at its face value as meaning that Jews lived in Crete, too. This is what is implied in the second New Testament text, in the pseudo-Pauline letter to Titus, written to a Christian community in Crete, where we read in 1:10–14;

There are many insubordinate men, empty talkers and deceivers, especially the circumcision party; (11) they must be silenced, since they are upsetting whole families by teaching for base gain what they have no right to teach. (12) One of themselves, a prophet of their own, said: 'Cretans are always liars, evil beasts, lazy gluttons.' (13) This testimony is true. Therefore, rebuke them sharply, that they may be sound in faith (14) instead of giving heed to Jewish myths or to commands of men who reject the truth (RSV).

Although the passage concerns Jews who have become Christians, it is also an indirect testimony to Jewish presence in Crete. The author of the epistle accuses what he calls literally 'those of the circumcision,' *i. e.*, Jewish converts, of perverting the truth of the gospel by taking notice of Jewish fables or myths and human commandments, and he tries to blacken them by applying to them a quote from a poem by Epimenides of Cnossos about the objectionable character of the Cretans.[17] This shows that, as in Asia Minor and Syria, tensions sometimes ran high between Christians of Jewish and Gentile origin. For the present purpose it is not necessary to enter into the details of this controversy. We should, however, record the appearance around the turn of the first to the second century CE of the first signs that Christianity made converts among Cretan Jews. This is the beginning of a process of which we find the sad apogee in the final literary document concerning Cretan Jewry.

But before discussing that last testimony, we will – by way of interlude – look at a curious text from the beginning of the second century CE. In the famous fifth book of his *Historiae*, Tacitus relates the fall of Jerusalem in 70 CE, but before doing so he makes the following remark:

As I am now to record the final days of a famous city, it seems appropriate to inform the reader of its origins. The Jews are said to have been refugees of the island of Crete who

---

[16] O. Eissfeldt, 'Kreter und Araber,' *Kleine Schriften,* vol. 3, Tübingen 1966, 28–34. See also G. Schneider, *Die Apostelgeschichte* I, Freiburg 1980, 253, and R. Pesch, *Die Apostelgeschichte* I, Neukirchen 1986, 106.

[17] On the problem of the attribution of this verse see esp. C. Spicq, *Les Epitres Pastorales* II, Paris 1969, 608–9 (there lit.), and M. Dibelius & H. Conzelmann, *Die Pastoralbriefe*, Tübingen 1966, 101–3.

settled in the coastal area of Africa in the stormy days when, according to the story, Saturn was dethroned and expelled by the aggression of Jupiter. This is a deduction from the name Iudaei: that word is to be regarded as a barbarous lengthening of Idaei, the name of the people dwelling around the famous mount Ida in Crete (*Hist.* V 2, 1–3).

This curious passage seems to be the product of a mixture of blurred historical reminiscences, folk etymology, the equation of Shabbath with the day of Saturnus, and fantasy. The reminiscences may concern the very early contacts between Palestine and Crete in the age of the so-called Sea Peoples (ca. 1200 BCE), when most probably the Philistines invaded Palestine from Crete.[18] It is not improbable that the Philistines were expelled from Crete (*Creta insula profugos*, says Tacitus) and that therefore until late antiquity the god Marnas in the originally Philistine city of Gaza was identified with *Zeus Cretagenes* (Zeus who was born in Crete).[19] This unhistorical identification of Philistines with 'Judaeans' induced the folk-etymological equation of *Iudaei* and *Idaei*, a well-known type of 'aetiological' etymology of which a famous other but similar example is Vergil's derivation of *Iulus* from *Ilus*, the founder of Troy (Ilium), which is meant to link the founding of Rome with that of Troy.[20] On the connection between Saturnus and the Jews and especially the Jewish Sabbath, the 'day of Saturnus,' several ancient authors make their comments. Since these can easily be found in Stern's *GLAJJ*,[21] they need not detain us here. All these elements, perhaps with the admixture of the story that Cretans – like Jews – abstained from eating pork,[22] may have created this fanciful theory of the Cretan origin of the Jews. It does not add anything to our knowledge of Jewish history in Crete, however.

From the period between the beginning of the second to that of the fifth century CE we have no literary evidence on Cretan Jewry. Rabbinic literature yields no data nor do Christian sources. It is possible only to speculate. Thus a considerable influx of Jews into Crete from Cyrene (ancient Libya) may have occurred in the years 115–117 CE, when the great revolt erupted there and elsewhere in North Africa. There had been close connections between Crete and Cyrene ever since Rome united the two administratively to form one province in the sixties of the first century BCE. It is known that during the revolt many Jews fled to the islands, and it is probable that many of them went to Crete.[23]

---

[18] On this problem see W. Fauth in H. Heubner & W. Fauth, *P. Cornelius Tacitus: Die Historien*, vol. 5, Heidelberg 1982, 20–2 (there lit.). On the Sea Peoples E. Noort, *Die Seevölker in Palästina*, Kampen 1994.

[19] See G. Mussies, 'Marnas, God of Gaza,' *ANRW* II 18, 4, Berlin & New York 1990, 2412–2457.

[20] Vergil, *Aen.* I 267–8. See A.M.A. Hospers-Jansen, *Tacitus over de Joden*, Groningen 1949, 112. Other instances in M. Stern, *Greek and Latin Authors on Jews and Judaism* (= GLAJJ), vol. 2, Jerusalem 1980, 33.

[21] See the references in *GLAJJ*, vol. 3, Jerusalem 1984, 147.

[22] See the references in *GLAJJ*, vol. 1, Jerusalem 1974, 559.

[23] See S. Applebaum, *Jews and Greeks in Ancient Cyrene*, Leiden 1979, 292–3, and H.Z. (J.W.) Hirschberg, *A History of the Jews in North Africa*, vol. 1, Leiden 1974, 39.

Now we turn to the final and most dramatic piece of relevant literary evidence extant: the *Historia Ecclesiastica* of Socrates, composed in about 440, a work designed to continue the story of Eusebius' *Historia Ecclesiastica*,[24] and covering the events from the accession of Constantine to the year 438/9. In one of the final chapters of the book (VII 38) he writes the following:[25]

At about the same time, many of the Jews in Crete became Christians because of the following incident. A Jewish impostor pretended to be Moses. He said he had been sent from heaven in order to evacuate the Jews who lived on the island by leading them through the sea. For he said he was the same person who also saved Israel through the Red Sea long ago. During a whole year he went around along every town of the island, and he tried to persuade the Jews who lived there to believe such things. He exhorted them to leave behind all their money and possessions. For he promised to lead them through the dry sea to the land of promise. Those who let themselves be cheated with such hopes began to neglect all their tasks. And they also despised what they possessed and let it be taken away by any chance person. When the day designated by the Jewish impostor arrived, he himself led the way and all the others followed with their wives and little children. He brought them to a promontory that stood as a precipice above the sea and ordered them to plunge into it. Those who first reached the edge did so, and they died straight away, partly because they dashed against the cliffs, partly also because they drowned in the water. And more people would have been killed if not by God's providence some Christian fishermen and merchants would have been there. These saved some who were drowning by dragging them up. Only then, when they were suffering so badly, they realized their folly. They kept the others off from throwing themselves down by telling them about the deaths of those who threw themselves down before. Then they too realized the fraud and blamed themselves for their uncritical belief. But when they eagerly wanted to kill the pseudo-Moses, they could not lay their hands on him, for he had disappeared. And this raised in many the suspicion that he had been an avenging demon who had taken on human disguise in order to outrage their people there. By this incident many of the Jews who then lived in Crete took leave of Judaism and embraced the Christian faith (*Hist. Eccl.* VII 38).[26]

Several elements in this passage need to be discussed.[27] As regards the reliability of the story, it should be said that, although on the one hand Christian bias may

---

[24] See G.F. Chesnut, *The First Christian Histories*, Paris 1977, 167–189.

[25] The text translated is that from Migne's *Patrologia Graeca* 67, 825–8 (with minor corrections). Unfortunately, the new edition by P. Périchon for the *Sources Chrétiennes* series, although announced long ago (see his article 'Pour une edition nouvelle de l'historien Socrate: les manuscrits et les versions,' *Recherches de science religieuse* 53 (1965) 112–120), has not appeared so far. See also the old three-volume edition by R. Hussey, *Socratis Scholastici Ecclesiastica Historia*, Oxford 1853, text in vol. 2, 822–4; Hussey has no annotations to this chapter. [In 2004, finally, Périchon published, in collaboration with P. Maraval, the first volume in the *Sources Chrétiennes,* containing only book 1. Also the new edition by G.C. Hansen and M. Sirinjan, published in 1995 in the *GCS* series, was not yet available when this article was written. Their new text does not make any difference for the translation.]

[26] For Latin versions of the same story see, *inter alios*, Cassiodorus, *Historia tripartita* XII 9 (*PL* 69, 1210–11 or *CSEL* 71, 677–8). Several other Latin authors are listed by B. Blumenkranz, *Juifs et chrétiens dans le monde occidental 430–1096*, Paris – La Haye 1960, 244 n. 139.

[27] Very brief discussions of this passage are given by M. Seligsohn in *Jew. Enc.* 9 (1905)

be responsible for some exaggeration (e. g., *many* of the Jews following the impostor), especially in the happy ending (*many* of them becoming Christian), on the other hand it was to be expected exactly in this period, as we shall see presently, that messianic hopes would run high. So there can be little doubt that the kernel of the story is historical. The period in question can be fixed fairly exactly. The *terminus ante quem* is 438/439 CE, the final year dealt with by Socrates in this work; the *terminus a quo* is 431/432, since the immediately preceding story recounts events which took place during the consulship of Bassus and Antiochus, who became consuls in 431. So most probably the time can be placed in the first half or the middle of the thirties of the fifth century CE. Strikingly enough, this is the first messianic movement known since the Bar Kochba revolt exactly three centuries before. That messianic risings no longer occurred after the shattering defeat of the second revolt (132–5 CE) is not surprising, but why did they recur, in both pacifistic-quietistic and in belligerent ways, from *ca.* 430 onwards? For this movement was only the first in a long series ranging from our pseudo-Moses to Shabbetai Zwi.[28]

There are clear reasons for the resurgence of messianic expectations in this period. First, ever since the destruction of the Temple in 70 CE, Jews had prayed for and expected the defeat of Rome and the ascendancy of the Jewish people consequent upon it.[29] 'In the fifth century these hopes reached their fever point. The Empire was breaking up; the long-anticipated collapse was about to take place.'[30] The city of Rome had been conquered and sacked by the Visigoths in 410. The years following saw other invasions in Italy and elsewhere. In 430 North Africa was overrun by the Vandals. And in 433 Attila's rise to power in the Hunnish kingdom was the beginning of a new and tremendous threat to the power of Rome. Second, there was an enormous deterioration in the conditions of life for the Jews in the first third of the fifth century. Roman, *i. e.* Christian, oppression intensified. Theodosius II (408–450) abolished the Jewish patriarchate and closed the few remaining rabbinic schools. This emperor, who deposed the patriarch Gamliel VI, also forbade the construction of new synagogues and ordered the destruction of existing ones. In 438 he even issued a decree in which

---

64; S.W. Baron, *A Social and Religious History of the Jews*, vol. 5, New York 1957, 168, 367; B. Blumenkranz, *Juifs* 244.

[28] For a list of messianic movements from the fifth through the twelfth centuries see K.H. Bernhardt, 'Zur Eigenart und Alter der messianisch-eschatologischen Zusätze im Targum Jeruschalmi I,' in *Gott und die Götter. FS E. Fascher*, Berlin n.d. (1958?), 79. For the same period see further A.H. Silver, *A History of Messianic Speculation from the First through the Seventeenth Centuries*, Boston 1959 (repr. of the 1927 ed.), 25–80; H. Ben Sasson, 'Messianic Movements,' *Enc. Jud.* 11 (1972) 1420–22. Both Silver and Ben Sasson wrongly date the appearance of the Cretan Moses to the middle of the fifth century.

[29] See Silver, *History* 27–9 for references. For a general survey of Jewish attitudes toward Rome in antiquity see G. Stemberger, *Die römische Herrschaft im Urteil der Juden*, Darmstadt 1983.

[30] Silver, *History* 29.

Jews, defined as enemies of the Roman laws and of supreme majesty, were forbidden to hold any high office. Thus in the twenties and thirties of the fifth century, their civil inferiority and discrimination were legally sanctioned. This in itself would have been already enough to kindle messianic sentiments.[31]

But quite apart from these factors, older traditions predicted that the messiah would come sometime in the fifth century. As may be observed in Talmud Bavli (*Avoda Zara* 9a-b; *Sanhedrin* 97a-b and 99a, and parallel passages), calculations varied from 365 to 400 (or more) years after the destruction of the Temple, that is to say, somewhere from *ca.* 435 onwards. Rav Ashi, who lived in the beginning of the fifth century, even sought to avert any evil consequences which might follow upon the failure of this messianic hope by saying that before the eighty-fifth jubilee, i. e. 440–490 CE, one should *not* expect the messiah (*Sanh.* 97b).[32] It was inevitable that the worsening circumstances fertilized these messianic speculations exactly in the thirties of the fifth century CE. No wonder, too, that in an age of eschatological ferment someone claiming to be a new God-sent Moses found a ready audience.

The next point to be noted is that the event described follows a pattern well-known from similar messianic movements in the first century CE.[33] A constitutive element in it is the idea that the eschatological liberation will be similar to the exodus from Egypt. 'Jewish prophecy – and particularly Jewish eschatological prophecy – foresees the future as re-creation of the past.'[34] Already the prophet Micah had said: 'As in the days when you came out of the land of Egypt, I will show them marvellous things' (7:15, RSV). This 'exodus' motif in eschatological expectation recurs in most messianic movements of the Imperial period and later times, and of course the figure of a new Moses was integral to

---

[31] For the text of the imperial decrees see A. Linder, *The Jews in Roman Imperial Legislation*, Detroit & Jerusalem 1987, 295–337. See further J. Juster, *Les Juifs dans l'Empire Romain*, 2 vols., Paris 1914, I 162–7, II 101–3; M. Simon, *Verus Israel. A Study of the Relations Between Christians and Jews in the Roman Empire*, Oxford 1986, 224–33; A.M. Rabello, 'Theodosius II,' *Enc. Jud.* 15 (1972) 1101–2. It should be added that Theodosius' measures sometimes had only regional application or were later mitigated.

[32] Silver, *History* 26–7. See on these passages also E.E. Urbach, 'Redemption and Repentance in Talmudic Judaism,' in R.J. Zwi Werblowski & C.J. Bleeker (eds.), *Types of Redemption*, Leiden 1970, 190–206.

[33] P.W. Barnett, 'The Jewish Sign Prophets 40–70 AD: Their Intentions and Origins,' *NTS* 27 (1980/81) 679–97; R.A. Horsley, 'Popular Messianic Movements Around the Time of Jesus,' *CBQ* 46 (1984) 471–95; *idem*, 'Popular Prophetic Movements at the Time of Jesus,' *JSNT* 26 (1986) 3–27; M. Hengel, *Die Zeloten*, Leiden 1976 (2nd ed.), *passim*. See now also R.A. Horsley and J.S. Hanson, *Bandits, Prophets and Messiahs: Popular Movements in the Time of Jesus*, New York 1986. Horsley's careful distinction between messianic and prophetic movements is relevant for the study of the various first-century charismatic types, but not for our passage from the fifth century.

[34] H. Jacobson, 'Visions of the Past: Jews and Greeks,' *Judaism* 35 (1986) 468; cf. *ibid.* 479: 'Jews consistently saw themselves, both in large (i. e., the Jewish nation) and in small (individuals), as re-experiencing, re-creating or re-living the history of earlier Jews.' Jacobson argues that in this respect there is a striking difference between Jews and Greeks.

this expectation.[35] 'It was perfectly natural that a people whose very identity had been forged in the recitation of the exodus deliverance should treasure the memory of Moses and look for rescue in their own periods of crisis in terms of a repetition of the exodus events.'[36] A second element that played a role here is the prediction in Deut. 18:15–18 of the appearance of a prophet like Moses, although this motif is less explicit in our sources.[37] If the evidence is studied, especially in Josephus,[38] it will be seen that recurring traits of these first-century movements are the exodus into the desert, the usually sizeable following, and the expectation of miracles promised by the messianic pretender. Now since there is no desert in Crete, the first could not play a part in our story. It was therefore replaced by the theme of being led dryshod through the sea to Palestine. The miracle of deliverance is present in the form of the exodus miracle *par excellence*, the passage through the sea. The large following is also included. As these movements in the first century appeared to re-enact the great divine act of liberation from biblical history, so our pretender and his followers acted out this pattern of liberation according to the historical-eschatological typology and thus participated in the new and anticipated divine action.[39] Hence we see that after four centuries the pattern is still essentially unchanged, the only real new element being that the pretender called himself Moses. Another difference is, of course, that the movement did not end in massacre by the ruling authorities, which was the common disastrous ending of the first-century movements according to Josephus. The recurrence of this ancient pattern in the story under discussion suggests that the Cretan Jews fostered the old traditions of their people.

The final question to be raised in this connection is whether the event recorded by Socrates implied the end of Cretan Jewry, as the author seems to suggest. As a matter of fact, apart from an inscription which may derive from the same period and which will be discussed presently, no reports whatsoever exist on Jews or Judaism in Crete between the first half of the fifth century and the eleventh century.[40] Furthermore, reports from *ca.* 1000 CE onwards suggest that Cretan Jews formed only a very small group by then. What had happened in the intervening five or six centuries, we do not know. The only Cretan Church father of some significance, Andrew of Crete, who worked in the first half of the eight century, makes very negative and scathing remarks concerning the Jews, but these are so

---

[35] See J. Jeremias, 'Moses,' *TWNT* 4 (1942) 852–78, esp. 860–8; D.L. Tiede, *The Charismatic Figure as Miracle Worker*, Missoula 1972, 178–207.

[36] Tiede, *Charismatic Figure* 178–9.

[37] Jeremias, 'Moses' 860–1.

[38] E.g., *Bell.* II 258–263; VI 285; VII 437–441; *Ant.* XVIII 85–87; XX 97–98, 167–172, 188.

[39] This formulation is borrowed from Horsley, *JSNT* 26 (1986) 7–8.

[40] For the later Middle Ages see, e.g., I. Lévi, 'Les juifs de Candie de 1380 à 1485,' *REJ* 26 (1893) 198–208; S. Schwarzfuchs, 'A propos des juifs de Crète et de Nègrepont,' *REJ* (3rd ser.) 2 [119] (1961) 152–8; L.J. Weinberger, *Jewish Poets in Crete*, Cincinnati 1985.

much the stock invectives known from other Christian writers that Andrew probably borrowed them from his predecessors. They cannot be used to shed light on
the situation of the Cretan Jews of that time.[41] Whether or not the events related
by Socrates marked the ending of ancient Cretan Jewry, we have to record that
it constitutes the last piece of extant evidence for a very long period.

To turn lastly to the epigraphical material, one piece of inscriptional evidence,
the recently published Samaritan inscription from Delos, has already been discussed above, and we will now limit ourselves to evidence from Crete itself. A
search of the 1936 edition of vol. I of J.-B. Frey's *Corpus Inscriptionum Judaicarum* yields nothing. In the 1975 reprint, however, Baruch Lifshitz has added a
Prolegomenon with quite a number of new inscriptions, three of which are from
Crete.[42] Before presenting these, we first have to discuss briefly the difficult
problem of how to tell a Jewish from a non-Jewish inscription. In his *Corpus Papyrorum Judaicarum*, Victor Tcherikover lists the following criteria:[43] a papyrus
is Jewish (a) if the word *Ioudaios* or *Hebraios* occurs in it; (b) if technical terms
like 'synagogue' or 'sabbath' appear in it; (c) if it originates from what is known
to have been a place of exclusively Jewish settlement; (d) if it contains Jewish
names. Now, unfortunately, the first three criteria cannot be applied to any Cretan
inscription, with one exception, and in applying the fourth criterion we move
on extremely slippery ground. As Ross Kraemer reminds us, there are very few
names 'which can be demonstrated to have been used only by Jews, and never by
Christians or pagans, whether in the same or other geographic areas.'[44] As will be
seen, both Bandy (see n. 42) and Lifshitz designate inscriptions as Jewish only
on the basis of a name which could as well be regarded as Christian or pagan,
whereas they do not mention some inscriptions from the corpus of *Inscriptiones
Creticae* which on the same principle could have been included as Jewish.

To begin with the first category, Bandy's first 'Jewish' inscription (from the
fifth century CE) runs as follows (*Inscr. Cret.* IV no. 509):

[This burial place belongs] to lord Satyros, son of Theodoulos, a priest, (and) to Moses, a
ruler who (both?) sought salvation with many toils.[45]

---

[41] See Andreas Cretensis, *Homiliae* 2 (PG 97: 821C), 3 (845C-D0, 8 (964B), 10 (1024C)
etc.

[42] In the forty years in between both Margareta Guarducci's *Inscriptiones Creticae* (4 vols.,
Rome 1935–1950) and Anastasios C. Bandy's *Greek Christian Inscriptions from Crete* (Athens
1970; with an appendix on Jewish inscriptions) were published. [Now we have D. Noy, A.
Panayotov & H. Bloedhorn, *Inscriptiones Judaicae Orientis I: Eastern Europe*, Tübingen 2004,
where on pp. 249–253 three Jewish inscriptions from Crete are published, one of which is a
very dubious case.]

[43] V.A. Tcherikover & A. Fuks, *Corpus Papyrorum Judaicarum*, vol. 1, Cambridge MA
1957, xvii–xx.

[44] R.S. Kraemer, 'Hellenistic Jewish Women: The Epigraphical Evidence,' *SBL Seminar
Papers 1986*, Atlanta 1986, 191 (183–200).

[45] Bandy, *Greek Christian Inscriptions* 140. I correct his translation where I do not agree
with him.

Bandy regards the inscription as Jewish because of the occurrence of the name Moses and the mention of the offices of priest, *hiereus*, and ruler, *archôn*, which he suggestively translates as 'head of the synagogue.' As Lifshitz aptly remarks, however, 'the name of Moses is extremely rare in Jewish inscriptions and very frequent in Christian epigraphy.'[46] It should be added that *hiereus* could be the title of a Christian official, and that *archôn*, although it can designate a Jewish official, may be a secular ruler of some kind.[47] That is to say, Bandy may be right and Lifshitz may be right; we just do not know.[48]

Curiously enough, the critical sense that Lifshitz displayed in this case seems to leave him in another case. For his own first inscription, on a tombstone regarded by him as Jewish, runs as follows (*Inscr. Cret.* II no. 8):

Sanbathis (set up this stone) for Hermes for the sake of memory.[49]

Lifshitz assumes that the inscription is Jewish because of the occurrence of the name Sanbathis, which is one of the Hellenized forms of the Hebrew name Shabbetai. He is certainly right in stating that this name was very common among Jews. But he could have known the very instructive excursus on 'The Sambathions' by Menachem Stern in the *Corpus Papyrorum Judaicarum*,[50] where it is proved beyond any doubt that, whereas in the Hellenistic period this name was by and large a typically Jewish name, in the Roman and Byzantine periods a great many non-Jews adopted it without being aware of its original connotations.[51] Stern's evidence is from Egypt, but it is attested from Crete as well that the names Sanbathion and Sanbathis were used by pagans and Christians.[52] If Lifshitz would have been as critical in this instance as in the case of Bandy's first inscription, he would have omitted it, for the inscription is not from the Hellenistic period. However, it should be said once more that there is no way of attaining any certainty regarding inscriptions which do not exhibit, in addition to names, explicitly Jewish symbols like the menorah or Christian

---

[46] Prolegomenon to the CIJ reprint, New York 1975, 89.

[47] See *BAGD* 114.

[48] Except Lifshitz, also B. Nystrom, '*Inscr. Cret.* IV 509: An Ancient Christian Priest?,' *ZPE* 50 (1983) 122, regards this inscription as non-Jewish. [And so does Noy, *Inscr. Jud. Orient.* I, 341–3, where this inscription is relegated to an appendix with material not considered Jewish.]

[49] [This inscription is also published by Noy c.s., *Inscr. Jud. Orient.* I, 343–4, but again regarded as probably Christian.]

[50] *CPJ* III, Cambridge MA 1964, 43–56.

[51] In the Hellenistic period the usual Greek form of the name was Sabbathai/Sabbathaios or Sambathaios; in Imperial times it often became Sambat(h)iôn and Sambathion or Sambathis or Sabbatis (fem.); later hypocoristic forms are Sambas (masc.) and Sabbê (fem.). Details in Stern (see n. 50).

[52] E.G., *Inscr. Cret.* II.xxiv.12. For more evidence of the non-Jewish use of the names Sambathis etc. see H. Solin, 'Juden und Syrer im westlichen Teil der römischen Welt. Eine ethnisch-demographische Studie mit besonderer Berücksichtigung der sprachlichen Zustände,' *ANRW* II 29, 2, Berlin & New York 1983, 587–789, esp. 645 n. 145 and 679.

symbols like the cross or alpha and omega. That is to say, Guarducci's large corpus of Cretan inscriptions may well include a number of Jewish ones which we cannot recognize as such. What, for instance, is one to say of graffiti with names such as *Avdias*, which is almost certainly the transcription of Ovadia (*Inscr. Cret.* II.xxiii.28.34.52); or of inscriptions containing the name *Zaulos*, which can hardly be other than a scribal variant of *Saulos* (*Inscr. Cret.* II.xii.23 and IV 223b); or of inscriptions with names like *Simon* and *Ioannes* (*Inscr. Cret.* II.xv.4 and 5; I.xxv.8); or of the numerous inscriptions in which names such as *Eirena* or *Theodoros* or *Dositheos* are found (*Inscr. Cret.*, Index s.vv.)? They may be Jewish, but some, or all, may be Christian or pagan, like the inscriptions with names such as Moses and Sanbathis. We have to reconcile ourselves to the fact that there are no means of distinguishing between Jewish and non-Jewish inscriptions on the basis of names alone, when other indicators are absent. This sad conclusion leaves us with only two inscriptions regarded as Jewish by both Bandy and Lifshitz and by other scholars as well.[53]

The first is a tombstone and is not very revealing. The accumulation of three typically Jewish names in three successive generations makes it highly probable that it is a Jewish inscription. It runs as follows:

Josephus, son of Theodorus, (set up this stone) for Judas his son as a memorial. (He lived) one year (*Inscr. Cret.* I.v.17).[54]

This inscription from the third or fourth century CE was found in an area at Kassanoi called *Hebroi* (= *Hebraioi*), 'where there was reputed to be a Jewish cemetery.'[55] But it is not only this element that makes it probable that we have to do with a Jewish inscription. An additional factor is that although, as we have seen, 'Jewish' names need not in themselves indicate a Jewish origin, in this case a Jewish origin is made extremely probable by the fact that the father's name is recorded, which is an element lacking in all Christian inscriptions of Crete.[56]

Although I am convinced that this inscription is Jewish, it must be admitted that it leaves room for doubt to the extreme sceptic. Fortunately, the final piece of epigraphic evidence does not. Again, it is a sepulchral inscription, from Kastelli Kissamou, which was dated by Bandy to the first or second century CE, but by the great epigrapher Louis Robert to the fourth or fifth century CE.[57] The latter

---

[53] There is a possibility that *Inscr. Cret.* IV no. 518 (Bandy's no. 35) is Jewish, but it may be Christian, and the interpretation is highly uncertain because the text is seriously damaged.

[54] See Bandy, *Greek Christian Inscriptions* 142, for a photo of the inscription.

[55] Bandy, *ibid.*

[56] Bandy, *ibid.*

[57] This inscription is not included in *Inscr. Cret.* It was first published by Bandy in *Hesperia* 32 (1963) 227–9, and afterwards also in his *Greek Christian Inscriptions* 143. Jeanne and Louis Robert discussed it in their 'Bulletin épigraphique' in *Revue des études grecques* 77 (1964) 413, and Lifshitz in the Prolegomenon to *CIJ*, at I 88, where the text is printed as no. 731c. [It is now no. Cre3 in *Inscr. Jud. Orient.* I 252–3.]

dating is also defended by Lifshitz and by Bernadette Brooten in her dissertation.[58] The text runs as follows :

Sophia of Gortyn, elder and leader of the synagogue of Kissamos, lies here. The memory of the righteous one be for ever. Amen.[59]

There is an illuminating difference between the interpretation of this inscription by Bandy and the one by Brooten. Bandy adopts the traditional theory that 'elder' (*presbytera*) and 'leader of the synagogue' (*archisynagôgissa*) are 'honorary titles' (143), bestowed upon Sophia because her husband – not she herself – held the offices of elder and head of the synagogue. It was Brooten who was the first to break through this traditional androcentric interpretation.[60] She convincingly interpreted a whole series of inscriptions concerning Jewish women in such a way that it became obvious that titles like *presbytera* and *archisynagôgissa* were not honorary titles but indicated real functions.[61] She writes on our inscription: 'There is no *internal* reason for believing that Sophia of Gortyn received the titles through her husband. If her husband were the source of her titles, why is she not called Sophia the wife of X? The image of Sophia of Gortyn emerging from the inscription (…) is of a very important figure in the Jewish community of Cissamos. She was not only an elder, but also head of the synagogue. There is no evidence that she was married.'[62] 'Important for the interpretation of *presbytera* is its parallelization with *archisynagôgissa*, which makes it unlikely that *presbytera* is simply a term to distinguish Sophia the elder from a Sophia the younger.'[63] Brooten's research has made several things clear. First, a number of inscriptions leave no doubt that in some communities, especially in the diaspora, there were female elders. They probably had financial, possibly also educational responsibilities. Second, there are a number of inscriptions that mention women as head of a synagogue. In these, no husbands are mentioned; and it is highly significant that in those instances where wives of (male) *archisynagôgoi* are mentioned, they do *not* bear this title. That is to say, the traditional theory that regards this title as honorific when a woman is the bearer has no leg to stand on. *Archisynagôgissai* were indeed female leaders of a

---

[58] B.J. Brooten, *Women Leaders in the Ancient Synagogue*, Chico 1982, 11–2, 41.

[59] *CIJ* 731c = *Inscr. Jud. Or.* Cre3.

[60] It should be said, however, that in the same year (1982) the late I.F. Sanders adopted the same interpretation of the inscription as Brooten by taking it at face value; see his *Roman Crete* 43: 'One of these [inscriptions] includes the only evidence for the organization of the faith, the dead person, Sophia of Gortyna, being an elder and leader of the synagogue at Kissamos.'

[61] It is very much to the point when Susanne Heine writes: 'Wer, wie bewußt oder unbewußt immer, Frauen in höheren Ämtern und Funktionen nicht wahrhaben will, neigt nicht nur dazu, weibliche Vornamen zu übersehen, sondern auch dazu, das Amt dann, wenn eine Frau es bekleidet, abzuwerten' (*Frauen der frühen Christenheit*, Göttingen 1986, 98).

[62] *Women Leaders* 12.

[63] *Women Leaders* 41. See now also R.S. Kraemer, 'A New Inscription from Malta and the Question of Women Elders in the Diaspora Jewish Communities,' *HTR* 78 (1985) 431–8.

synagogue. They were probably active in administration and exhortation. 'They could have worked in a team of two or three synagogue heads, for we have seen that the number was not necessarily restricted to one. Or perhaps they served alone. (…) Sophia of Gortyn, both elder and head of the synagogue, must have been very actively involved in the affairs of the synagogue. Was it her long years of work that convinced even the most sceptical that a woman was capable of filling that office? Family ties, long years of involvement, largesse – these have often played a role in attaining various offices and seem as likely in the case of women as of men.'[64]

Brooten has been quoted at length because her conclusions shed a striking light on Cretan Jewry in late antiquity. The comparable inscriptions she adduces make very probable indeed that in diaspora situations women could rise to high positions and even to leadership in Jewish communities.

Independently from her, my own research has led me to identical conclusions along very different lines.[65] Needless to say, it is not possible to draw generalizing conclusions for the whole of Crete from one sepulchral inscription in Kastelli Kissamou, but it can at least be asserted that in some quarters of Cretan Jewry in the later Roman period emancipatory tendencies made the most of their chances so that women were able to attain to positions of leadership. That such women were at odds with strict rabbinic rules is obvious.[66]

Some final remarks. It is self-evident that the material at our disposal does not allow for a history of Cretan Jews in antiquity to be written. Although it can never be excluded that new documents may emerge, it has to be recognized that the chances are small. New literary sources can hardly be expected and papyrological evidence from Crete itself will not be found; only a few fresh inscriptions (an epitaph or two) may reasonably be expected. The small corpus of evidence will in consequence probably remain small and not allow us to arrive at general conclusions. A recent historian of Crete observes of the Jews that 'the literary references depict a peaceful, rich community, if somewhat gullible,'[67] solely on the basis of two passages in Josephus and Socrates. That is too sweeping a statement when in fact all that can be deduced from these passages is that in the first century there were rich Jews living in Crete and that in the first and fifth centuries many (?) Jews put their unthinking trust in an impostor. Similarly, the inscription

---

[64] Brooten, *Women Leaders* 32–3.

[65] P.W. van der Horst, 'Images of Women in the Testament of Job,' in M.A. Knibb & P.W. van der Horst (eds.), *Studies on the Testament of Job*, Cambridge 1989, 93–116. Idem, 'Portraits of Biblical Women in Pseudo-Philo's *Liber Antiquitatum Biblicarum,*' *Journal for the Study of the Pseudepigrapha* 5 (1989) 29–46.

[66] See, e. g., L. Swidler, *Women in Judaism. The Status of Women in Formative Judaism*, Metuchen 1976. M. Küchler, Schweigen, *Schmuck und Schleier. Drei neutestamentliche Vorschriften zur Verdrängung der Frauen auf dem Hintergrund einer frauenfeindlichen Exegese des Alten Testaments im antiken Judentum*, Freiburg & Göttingen 1986.

[67] Sanders, *Roman Crete* 43.

of Sophia of Gortyn does not permit us to conclude that Jewish women in Crete found it easy to reach leading positions; the case of Sophia was probably exceptional. When the afore-mentioned historian says that the Jewish community was peaceful, we can more easily agree with him since there is no evidence to the contrary. The fact that we have no reports on Cretan Jewry between say 100 and 430 CE may indicate that in the second through fourth centuries the Jews reached a high degree of integration in Cretan society, a situation that was probably only disrupted by the legal measures of Theodosius II.[68] As was said in the beginning, the evidence yields no more than occasional glimpses of the history of this community, but these are without doubt interesting and fascinating.[69]

---

[68] Compare the situation of several Jewish communities in Asia Minor, e. g. Sardis, on which see A.T. Kraabel, 'Paganism and Judaism: The Sardis Evidence,' in A. Benoit *et al.* (eds.), *Paganisme, Judaïsme, Christianisme. Mélanges offerts à Marcel Simon*, Paris 1978, 13–33.

[69] This article is the expanded version of a paper read at the July 1987 meeting of the European Association for Jewish Studies in Berlin. It may be added here that I have left out of account all legendary material from the Christian apocrypha such as the story that after Jesus' execution, the emperor Tiberius had Annas and Caiaphas arrested and brought to Rome, but on the way Caiaphas died. When they wanted to bury him in Crete, the earth refused to receive his body and they had to cover it with stones; see, e. g., M.R. James, *The Apocryphal New Testament*, Oxford 1924, 153. Until the nineteenth century there was near Cnossos a site called 'the tomb of Caiaphas'; for details see N.A. Bees, *Die griechisch-christlichen Inschriften des Peloponnes*, Athens 1941, 41 with n. 2.

The Jews of Ancient Cyprus

Jews lived on the Greek islands in the Mediterranean Sea from as early as the third or second century BCE. Best known are the communities of Crete[1] and Delos,[2] much less known are those of Euboia, Cos, Rhodes, and Samos.[3] In this contribution I will briefly present the most relevant evidence for Jewish presence on the important island of Cyprus.[4] Scarce though it may be, this evidence does make clear that there was indeed a relatively large and vital Jewish community on this ancient island. I will first discuss the literary evidence, thereafter the epigraphic material.

The earliest evidence is a passage in *1 Maccabees* 15, describing Simon the Maccabee's rule, during which he forged close contacts with the Romans in his struggle against the Seleucids. About 140 BCE, Numenius was sent as his envoy to Rome and came back with "letters to the kings and countries" (15:15), in which the consul of Rome warned them not to harm the Jews anywhere. Copies were sent "to all the countries (...), and to the Spartans, and to Delos, and to Myndos, and to Sicyon, and to Caria, and to Samos, and to Pamphylia, and to Lycia, and to Halicarnassus, and to Rhodes, and to Phaselis, and to Cos, and to Side, and to Arados, and to Gortyna, and to Cnidos and Cyprus and Cyrene" (15:23).[5] This list no doubt implies that in all these places or regions Jewish communities were to be found. For Cyprus this implies that the Jews had been residents there for a considerable time previous to 140 BCE. In order to understand why the rulers of Cyprus received a letter warning them not to harm the interests of the Jews, one

---

[1] P.W. van der Horst, 'The Jews of Ancient Crete,' *JJS* 39 (1988) 183–200, reprinted in my *Studies on the Jewish World of Early Christianity*, Fribourg & Göttingen 1990, 148–165 [see the previous chapter].

[2] Ph. Bruneau, *Recherches sur les cultes de Délos*, Paris 1970, 480–493, and idem, '"Les Israélites de Délos" et la juiverie délienne,' *Bulletin de correspondence hellénique* 106 (1982) 465–504.

[3] See the survey by Fergus Millar in E. Schürer, *The History of the Jewish People in the Age of Jesus Christ*, rev. ed. by G. Vermes a.o., vol. III.1, Edinburgh 1986, 68–72.

[4] Very brief and incomplete surveys are A. Reifenberg, 'Das antike zyprische Judentum und seine Beziehungen zu Palästina,' *Journal of the Palestine Oriental Society* 12 (1932) 209–215; G. Hill, *A History of Cyprus*, 4 vols., vol. I, Cambridge 1940, 241–243; and T.B. Mitford, 'The Cults of Roman Cyprus,' *Aufstieg und Niedergang der Römischen Welt* II.18.3, Berlin – New York 1990, 2204–2206.

[5] For the problems relating to this letter (e.g., its displacement in the present text of *1 Macc.*) see J.A. Goldstein, *1 Maccabees* (Anchor Bible 41), Garden City 1976, 492–494.

must assume that their numbers were not insignificant, which would be possible only if the Jews had lived there already for a longer period, perhaps from as early as the third cent. BCE, like on Crete and Delos.[6] That Jews were present on the island at least in Maccabaean times is indicated also by the Hasmonaean coins found in Paphos.[7] It should be borne in mind that Cyprus was attractive from an economic point of view since it was "admirably situated for commerce between Asia Minor, Syria, Judaea and Greece."[8] Especially by the end of the first cent. BCE, "when Herod the Great obtained the concession of half the Cypriot copper-mines from Augustus in 12 B.C.E., the commercial prospects thus opened up will have encouraged Jewish immigration."[9]

The impression of there being a large and significant community is corroborated by an important passage in Josephus. In *Ant. Jud.* 13.284, Josephus, speaking about the reign of Ptolemy IX Soter II (142–80 BCE), says that "at this time not only were the Jews in Jerusalem and in the country-side (of Judaea) in a flourishing condition, but also those who lived in Alexandria and in Egypt and Cyprus." He adds, in a quote from Strabo,[10] that Ptolemy's mother, Cleopatra III, who was at war with her son, sent Jewish troops with Chelkias and Ananias as generals to Cyprus (287).[11] Again, the fact that the Jews of Cyprus are mentioned in one breath with the large communities in Jerusalem, Alexandria, and Egypt is telling enough. The fact that the Egyptian queen sent Jewish troops to Cyprus only helps to confirm the impression that this island had a large Jewish presence in the last decades of the second century BCE. In *Ant. Jud.* 18.131, Josephus tells us that one of Herod's granddaughters, Alexandra, married an important man from Cyprus called Timios, probably a Jew as well.[12] Finally, in *Ant. Jud.* 20.142 we read that in the middle of the fifties of the first century CE, the Roman governor of Judaea, Felix, fell in love with Agrippa's sister, Drusilla. She was married to Azizus, but with the aid of a Jewish magician from Cyprus called Atomus, he successfully induced her to marry him. Here for the first time

---

[6] It is not clear to me how Lea Roth can confidently state that the beginning of the third century BCE was "the period at which a Jewish settlement on the island apparently began to develop on a large scale" (L. Roth, 'Cyprus,' *Enc. Jud.* 5 [1972] 1181), although, of course, it is not impossible to surmise that "under Ptolemy I there seems to have been a considerable exodus from Palestine of Jews who settled in many places in the Eastern Mediterranean, and Cyprus must have had its share of such settlers" (Hill, *History of Cyprus*, vol. I, 241 note 4).

[7] See D.H. Cox in *Numismatic Notes and Monographs* 145 (1959) 25–26 (nos. 191–200, including Herodian coins [non vidi]); also Reifenberg, 'Das antike zyprische Judentum' 213.

[8] Sh. Applebaum, 'The Social and Economic Status of the Jews in the Diaspora,' in S. Safrai & M. Stern (eds.), *The Jewish People in the First Century*, vol. 2, Assen 1976, 711.

[9] M. Smallwood, *The Jews Under Roman Rule*, Leiden 1976, 412. The reference for Herod is Josephus, *Ant. Jud.* 16.128–129.

[10] See M. Stern, *Greek and Latin Authors on Jews and Judaism*, vol. 1, Jerusalem 1974, 268–270.

[11] For the sequel see *Ant. Jud.* 13.324–333.

[12] Though that is not as certain as Lea Roth claims it to be ('Cyprus' 1181).

we come across the motif of Jewish magicians from Cyprus which, as we will presently see, will occur more often.

Philo is another witness to Jewish presence on Cyprus when around 40 CE, in *Legatio ad Gaium* 282, he has king Agrippa I list the many countries where Jews have established 'colonies,' and goes on to say that many such colonies are also to be found on "the most highly esteemed of the islands, Euboea, Cyprus, and Crete."

Further evidence comes from the New Testament. The Book of Acts mentions several Jews from Cyprus.[13] First, in Acts 4:36 it is said that to the earliest Christian community in Jerusalem, consisting exclusively of Jews, belonged a Levite of Cypriot origin called Joseph, whom the apostles surnamed Barnabas. This Barnabas is later said to have become the most important companion of the apostle Paul during his early missionary activity. This partnership, however, soon broke up: Acts 15:39 says that in Antioch they became so embroiled in conflict with each other that Barnabas sailed away to Cyprus, apparently returning to his original homeland. Before that rupture, however, the two had visited Cyprus together and proclaimed the Christian message in Salamis, the main city on the east coast of the island, where there were several synagogues (13:5 says so explicitly). Thereafter they travelled to the West, and in Paphos "they met a certain magician, a Jewish false prophet, named Bar-Jesus" (13:6), who opposed them and tried to turn the proconsul, in whose service he was, away from the faith, says the author. Paul cursed the magician so that he became blind. This is our second encounter with a Jewish magician from Cyprus. Another indication of Jewish presence at Cyprus is given in Acts 11:19–20 where we are told that, after a persecution of Christians in Jerusalem (in the middle of the thirties), some of the persecuted Jewish Christians "travelled as far as Phoenicia, Cyprus, and Antioch, and they spoke the word to no one except Jews; but among them were some men of Cyprus and Cyrene who, on coming to Antioch, spoke to the Greeks also." This might imply that even before Paul's first visit to Cyprus there were Jewish Christians on that island, but it is more probable that the reference is to Cypriot Jews who had moved to Palestine and become members of the early Christian community in Jerusalem. So even if the New Testament does not testify to the size and importance of the Cypriot Jewish community, its existence is taken for granted. Maybe one could even speculate that, in view of Paul's custom of preaching first in the synagogues of the major diaspora centres, the fact that his very first missionary trip brings him to Cyprus is an indirect indication of the importance of the Jewish community there.

For the period after 70 we have little literary evidence, but the Roman historian Cassius Dio (beginning of the third cent. CE) tells us that at the time of

---

[13] A. Nobbs, "Cyprus," in D.W.J. Gill & C. Glempf (eds.), *The Book of Acts in Its First-Century Setting. Volume 2: The Book of Acts in Its Graeco-Roman Setting,* Grand Rapids – Carlisle 1994, 279–289.

Trajan, in 115–117 CE, the Jews of Cyprus revolted against the Romans (and Greeks) under the leadership of a certain Artemion, and massacred 240.000 non-Jews (*Historia Romana* 68.32). According to Eusebius, they even destroyed the whole city of Salamis and massacred all its inhabitants (*Chronicon*, Trajan XIX, p. 219 ed. Karst = p. 164 ed. Schoene = Jerome, *Chron.* p. 196 ed. Helm).[14] This revolt was part of a larger Jewish uprising that started in the Cyrenaica (i. e., Libya), where the Jews attacked the Greeks and Romans and killed 220.000 of them after having committed undescribable atrocities (says Dio), and the revolt spread to nearby Egypt and Cyprus.[15] Even though these numbers of casualties are improbably high,[16] they do indicate that the Jewish population of Cyprus must have been large. There is also a notice in Eusebius to the effect that the Cypriot Jews came to the rescue of the Egyptian Jews and "continued to plunder the country of Egypt" (*Historia Ecclesiastica* 4.2). The war was devastating, and the Romans ruthlessly quelled the revolt, almost totally annihilating the Jewry of Egypt and of the Cyrenaica.[17] About the fate of the Cypriot Jews in the suppression of the revolt we know little, but, as Cassius Dio reports, because of their role in the war "no Jew may set foot on this island [Cyprus] anymore, but if one of them is driven upon its shores by a storm, he is put to death" (*Hist. Rom.* 68.32). This again is an exaggeration, but it does indicate that the magistrates took extreme measures against the Jews there. The fact that the Romans tried to kill as many insurgents as possible and were successful in that respect implies that by 117 CE Cypriot Jewry was at least decimated, if not worse.[18]

It is probably because of its (near) extinction that the literary sources are silent about this community for a long time.[19] We have to wait till the early seventh century when Sophronius, bishop of Jerusalem, tells us a story about a Christian on Cyprus who had fallen ill but was healed by two Christian saints, Cyrus and John, who found out that the poor man had been made ill by a Jewish magician who lived on the island (here we meet a Jewish magician for the

---

[14] The same information is repeated by Orosius, *Hist.* 7.12.8 and Syncellus, *Chron.* 657. See M. Hengel & A.M. Schwemer, *Paul Between Damascus and Antioch*, London 1997, 347 note 240.

[15] See M. Smallwood, *The Jews* 389–427, esp. 412–415; Schürer, *History*, vol. I, Edinburgh 1973, 529–534.

[16] Reifenberg, 'Das antike zyprische Judentum' 211: "eine starke Übertreibung."

[17] See J. Mélèze-Modrzejewski, *The Jews of Egypt*, Philadelphia 1995, 198–205.

[18] Rabbinic literature seems, according to some interpreters (e. g. S. Krauss in his entry on Cyprus in the *Jewish Encyclopedia*), to confirm this when in Talmud Yerushalmi, *Sukka* 5.1, 55b, it is said that the blood of the Jews slaughtered by Trajan flowed into the sea as far as Cyprus (he passage is repeated in *Lamentations Rabbah* 1.16.45), but here it is rather the Jews of Egypt or Palestine who are meant. See M. Stern, *Greek and Latin Authors on Jews and Judaism*, vol. 2, Jerusalem 1980, 389.

[19] I refer here only in passing to the fifth-century *Acts of Barnabas* (ch. 23) which mentions the synagogue of Salamis and tells the legendary story of a Jewish uprising against Barnabas' preaching organized by the Jewish magician Bar-Jesus, resulting in the death of Barnabas.

third time).[20] Shortly afterwards (in the thirties or fourties of the seventh cent. CE), bishop Leontius of Neapolis (on Cyprus) wrote a work *Contra Judaeos*,[21] which writing may be taken to point towards a Jewish presence on the island.[22] This is confirmed by the report of Eutychius Alexandrinus (first half of the tenth century) that during the reign of Heraclius (610–641), Cypriot Jews joined their Palestinian coreligionists in a series of raids of Christian monasteries.[23] As we will see in the next section, epigraphical sources indicate that in the centuries after 117 CE the Jewish community of Cyprus seems indeed to have recovered from the blow.

We now turn to the epigraphic evidence.[24] The earliest piece is an inscription from the (probably late) Hellenistic period found in Kourion that mentions the Jew Onias.[25] Unfortunately it does not yield any other information. From the Roman period, more specifically from the third and fourth centuries CE, derive the following: From the third century is *CIJ* 736 = *DF* 83, an inscription on a column from Lapethos that reads: 'Ex-voto of rabbi Atticus.'[26] This inscription need not imply that as early as the third century CE the Jewish community of Cyprus had come under rabbinic sway, for that would be both improbable and exceptional. From the circa 60 'epigraphical rabbis'[27] it is very difficult to ascertain in which cases the word *rabbi* designates an ordained Rabbi and in which cases it

---

[20] *Laudatio sanctorum martyrum Cyri et Johannis* 55 (=PG 87/3: 3625). J. Starr, *The Jews of the Byzantine Empire*, New York 1939, 85–86, mentions medieval sources reporting that a Jewish sorcerer from Salamis was burnt there at the stake ca. 635 CE.

[21] PG 93:1597–1612. On this treatise see H. Schreckenberg, *Die christlichen Adversus-Judaeos-Texte und ihr literarisches und historisches Umfeld (1.–11. Jh.)*, Frankfurt 1990, 445.

[22] This is, of course, not necessarily the case. It is also unwarranted to conclude from the fact that Epiphanius, bishop of Salamis, wrote a refutation of the ideas of a great number of Jewish (and Christian) groups, that all these groups were represented on Cyprus, in spite of what is suggested by S. Krauss-W. Horbury, *The Jewish-Christian Controversy I: History*, Tübingen 1996, 43.

[23] *Annales* 2.220–223 (PG 111:1084–5 = CSCO 45:101–2). See K.L. Noethlichs, *Die Juden im christlichen Imperium Romanum (4.–6. Jahrhundert)*, Berlin 2001, 48 with note 111.

[24] Some of it was collected by J.-B. Frey, *Corpus Inscriptionum Judaicarum*, vol. 2, Rome 1952, 6–7, and B. Lifshitz, *Donateurs et fondateurs dans les synagogues juives*, Paris 1967, 73–76. See also T.B. Mitford, "Some New Inscriptions from Early Christian Cyprus," *Byzantion* 20 (1950) 105–175, here esp. 110–116. The corpora of Frey and Lifshitz will be referred to in the main text as *CIJ* and *DF*. [For a new edition of the Jewish inscriptions from Cyprus see the Addendum.]

[25] T.B. Mitford, *The Inscriptions of Kourion*, Philadelphia 1971, 133–134 (no. 70). Another late Hellenistic inscription mentioned as Jewish by Mitford, 'Cults' 2204, is much too fragmentary to warrant his conclusion that it "appears to concern the construction in cedar wood of the doorway of a synagogue at Amathus" (*ibid.*).

[26] For a discussion of this inscription see Reifenberg, "Das antike zyprische Judentum" 211–212.

[27] S. J. D. Cohen, 'Epigraphical Rabbis,' *JQR* 72 (1981/82) 1–17. For an addendum see P. W. van der Horst, "'Lord, Help the Rabbi'. The Interpretation of SEG XXXI 1578b," *JJS* 38 (1987) 102–106, now also in my *Essays on the Jewish World* 182–186.

means just an individual of rank or an important person, a well established meaning of *rabbi*, also in rabbinic literature.[28] 'Rabbi' was not a protected title and there was no central registry of persons who were ordained Rabbis. "Who could prevent various communities from bestowing the title 'rabbi' on their prominent citizens regardless of their practices and beliefs? Hence it makes no sense to assume that all rabbis in antiquity were Talmudic scholars."[29] Other inscriptions make clear that the real leaders of the communities were the *archontes*, the *archisynagôgoi*, the *gerousiarchai*, etc.[30] Most of the epigraphical rabbis were not rabbis in our sense of the word, and most synagogues in both Israel and the diaspora were not led by rabbis. Nowhere do the inscriptions support the notion of rabbinic dominance. Epigraphical rabbis "appear as *donors*, not as leaders of the synagogues."[31] This is probably what we see here: the marble column may very well have been a gift of 'rabbi' Atticus, who on the basis of a vow (the text has *euchê* = *neder*) donated it to his synagogue. Of course the more important aspect of this inscription is that one century, or a century and a half, after the destructive war of 115–117 we again see Jewish presence on Cyprus and even the presence of synagogue buildings.

Probably also from the third century CE is *DF* 85,[32] again an inscription on a marble column, from Constantia. It is heavily damaged and very incomplete, but according to the most probable reading it says: "… of [NN?] who was five times *archisynagôgos*, the son of Ananias, who was two times *archôn*."[33] Another possibility is that Ananias' son was five times *archisynagôgos* and two times *archôn*. These two titles are widely attested as designations of synagogue officials in Jewish inscriptions. Both were leading figures with tasks and responsibilities that are still relatively unclear but nonetheless important.[34] Even though the inscription is not very informative in itself, it does again testify to Jewish presence in Cyprus after the revolt.

From the fourth century (but possibly later) is *CIJ* 735 = *DF* 82, again an inscription on a marble column, this time from the town of Golgoi: "Jose the elder, son of Synesius, has restored the whole construction of the synagogue." For 'synagogue' the inscription has *hebraïkê*, a very exceptional term to designate a synagogue building. As far as I know, there is no other instance of this

---

[28] See L. I. Levine, *The Rabbinic Class of Roman Palestine in Late Antiquity*, Jerusalem – New York 1989, 15: "In antiquity this title was applied to anyone of high standing in the community".

[29] Cohen, 'Epigraphical Rabbis' 13.

[30] See P.W. van der Horst, *Ancient Jewish Epitaphs*, Kampen 1991, 85–98; L.I. Levine, *The Ancient Synagogue*, New Haven-London 2000, 387–428.

[31] Cohen, 'Epigraphical Rabbis' 14 (italics added).

[32] It is not in *CIJ* because Mitford published the inscription only in 1950, after the death of Frey; see Mitford, 'New Inscriptions' 110–116.

[33] I here follow Lifshitz's reconstruction with some modifications, not the more speculative one by Mitford.

[34] See van der Horst, *Epitaphs* 89–93; Levine, *Synagogue* 390–404 (the best discussion).

usage[35] (the first further occurrence being from the eleventh century). Obviously its meaning here is 'the place where the Hebrews gather.' The designation 'Hebrews' for Jews is found more often in ancient inscriptions.[36] The inscription implies that Jose paid for the costs of the restoration of the local synagogue, so he must have been well to do.[37]

From the fifth or sixth century is an inscription from Lapethus listed by Lifshitz, but I find it a dubious case.[38] *DF* 84 runs as follows: "God, help (us)! We, Entolios the elder and Enkairios the son of the late Isaak, who was also called Sindouros, offer you what is yours from what is yours. In the fifth month of the fifth indiction. Lord, save (us)!. Amen." The inscription definitely has a Christian ring about it ('we offer you what is yours from what is yours'), but Lifshitz argues that the names Entolios (N.B.: *entolê* = *mitswah*) and Isaac are typically Jewish and hence assumes that the inscription is of Jewish provenance. He himself must concede, however, that both names are found also among Christians in late antiquity. Names, morever, are never a sure criterion for the determination of the Jewishness of inscriptions for there are very few names (if any) "which can be demonstrated to have been used only by Jews, and never by Christians or pagans, whether in the same or other geographic areas."[39] It cannot be excluded that this inscription is Jewish, but it is one of those cases where certainty is impossible. Finally, the only Hebrew evidence we have is a gem inscribed with the name 'Benayahu ben Hur' (*CIJ* 737), but it is hard to date.[40] It does attest, however, to Jewish presence. We may further point to Jewish oil lamps decorated with menorot from the third – fifth cent. CE. and a glass medalion with a menorah, lulav and ethrog, from the same period.[41]

We have observed references to Jewish magicians recurring in the evidence. Here it should be kept in mind that in antiquity quite often the words 'magician' or 'magic' were used as terms of abuse and reveal to us nothing more than the negative attitude of the users of these words towards the beliefs and practices of their opponents or enemies. Even so it is striking that not only Christian but also

---

[35] See also C. Claußen, *Versammlung, Gemeinde, Synagoge. Das hellenistisch-jüdische Umfeld der frühchristlichen Gemeinde*, Göttingen 2002, 145.

[36] For instances from Rome, Corinth, and Lydian Philadelphia see van der Horst, *Epitaphs* 87.

[37] *Pace* S. Krauss, *Synagogale Altertümer,* Berlin 1922 = Hildesheim 1966, 307.

[38] The first editor thinks it is Christian; see Mitford, 'New Inscriptions' 141–143.

[39] R. S. Kraemer, 'Hellenistic Jewish Women: The Epigraphical Evidence,' *SBL 1986 Seminar Papers*, Atlanta 1986, 191.

[40] Although J. Juster, *Les Juifs dans l'Empire Romain*, vol. 1, Paris 1914, 189 note 5, thinks it is 'tres ancien.'

[41] Reifenberg, 'Das antike zyprische Judentum' 213 (with photos opposite p. 212). T.B. Mitford, 'Further Contributions to the Epigraphy of Cyprus,' *American Journal of Archaeology* 65 (1961) 1118–119, publishes the text of a Cypriot horoscope of Flavian date in which one of the months is given the Jewish name Shebat (if that reading is correct!), but it is hard to draw conclusions from that.

Jewish authors (see Josephus, above) speak about Jewish magicians on Cyprus. In that light it may be interesting to note that in a well near Paphos a large cache of more than two hundred lead tablets with so-called *defixiones* (curses to 'bind' people, *i. e.*, to render them incapable of speaking or acting) from the early Christian period was discovered.[42] Several elements in these texts betray Jewish influence. It is a well-known fact that Jews played a major role in the development and practice of magic in late antiquity,[43] but as far as Cyprus is concerned it is noteworthy that in the first century CE Pliny the Elder writes: "There is yet another branch of magic, derived from Moses, Jannes, Lopates, and the Jews, but living many thousand years after Zoroaster. And much more recent is their branch in Cyprus" (*Naturalis Historia* 30.11).[44] Unclear though this passage may be, it does suggest Jewish prominence in circles of Cypriot magicians, nicely dovetailing with the various texts we have already seen about Cypriot Jewish magicians (in Josephus, the Book of Acts, Sophronius). There can be little doubt that magic was part and parcel of the Jewish religion on Cyprus, as elsewhere.

Finally another kind of indirect evidence has to be mentioned briefly, namely, the 23 inscriptions for the *Theos Hypsistos* ('God Most High') at Cyprus.[45] This cult, 'a convenient meeting ground for Jew and judaizer, Christian and pagan,'[46] was certainly a product of 'cross-fertilization between Jews and pagans,'[47] and may for that reason be regarded as a sign of Jewish presence, although that is not an unavoidable conclusion. We have to leave that matter aside, however.

On the basis of this short survey we may conclude that evidence for Jewish settlements on ancient Cyprus exists for six towns and villages: Salamis, Paphos, Kourion, Golgoi, Constantia, and Lapethos.[48] There were certainly more places where Jews lived of which we know nothing. The literary evidence combined with the epigraphical material shows that throughout the Hellenistic, Roman, and early Byzantine periods, Jews lived on Cyprus. For the first centuries we have to reckon with ever increasing numbers, although there is no way of being more precise. In none of the references to the Cypriot Jews during the last two centuries BCE and the first century CE is there any hint of friction at any time between them and the Greeks (and Romans) of the island, and Josephus does

---

[42] See J.G. Gager, *Curse Tablets and Binding Spells from the Ancient World*, Oxford 1992, 132–136. The more important of these *defixiones* were published as nos. 127–142 in Mitford, *The Inscriptions of Kourion* 246–283.

[43] See e. g. M. Simon, *Verus Israel. A Study of the Relations Between Christians and Jews in the Roman Empire*, Oxford 1986, 339–368.

[44] Stern, *Greek and Latin Authors* I, 498–499.

[45] See the convenient list and the texts in S. Mitchell, 'The Cult of Theos Hypsistos Between Pagans, Jews, and Christians,' in P. Athanassiadi & M. Frede (eds.), *Pagan Monotheism in Late Antiquity*, Oxford 1999, 144–145.

[46] Mitford, 'Cults' 2207.

[47] Mitchel, 'Cult' 114

[48] For their location see Map B VI 18 of the Tübinger Atlas des Vorderen Orients: *Die jüdische Diaspora bis zum 7. Jahrhundert n. Chr.*, Wiesbaden 1992.

not mention any anti-Roman agitation there after 70 comparable to the trouble in Egypt and Cyrenaica at that time.[49] For reasons that by and large still remain unexplained, that peaceful situation changed drastically, however, when in 115 CE "the Jews of Cyprus made their sole, and fatal, incursion into recorded political history."[50] In spite of the devastating blow they received from the Romans, it is certain that the Jews were able to re-establish themselves on the island after some time (as they did as well in Egypt and the Cyrenaica). The evidence from the third through seventh centuries CE leaves no doubt about that.

[*Addendum*: The collection of Jewish inscriptions from Cyprus in D. Noy & H. Bloedhorn, *Inscriptiones Judaicae Orientis, vol. III: Syria and Cyprus*, Tübingen 2004, 213–226, was published only after the completion of this article. For the minor differences between this collection and mine see my review of this work elsewhere in this volume.]

---

[49] Smallwood, *Jews* 412–3.
[50] Smallwood, *Jews* 412.

The Jews of Ancient Sicily

The evidence for a Jewish presence in Sicily in antiquity is as scarce as the attestation for it is plentiful in the Middle Ages.[1] Unlike the other large islands in the Mediterranean Sea, Crete and Cyprus,[2] for Jews in Sicily we do not have any literary evidence before the late sixth century CE (but see the Appendix). We do have, however, some 20 Jewish inscriptions from this island, conveniently collected by David Noy,[3] which make clear that Jews had been present in Sicily well before medieval times. In addition to that, we have a fascinating document in the form of an ancient Jewish amulet, published by Roy Kotansky.[4] Chronologically this material (both inscriptions and amulets) ranges from the third to the fifth century CE. What can we learn from these scant testimonies?

Let us begin with a rapid survey of the inscriptions. From Taormina we have a curious Greek inscription (JIWE 143) stating that the day of the sabbath is good or that the sabbath is a good day (*hêmera agathê*, cf. *yom tov*). The context and purpose of this inscription is unclear. From Acireale we have a seal with the Greek name Heuresis and a menorah and shofar (JIWE 144). JIWE 145, from Catania, is interesting in that the inscription is bilingual: it is an epitaph with the first line in Hebrew followed by nine lines in Latin. The Hebrew says: *Shalom 'al Yisra'el, Amen Amen. Shalom Shmu'el.* The Latin part says that Aurelius Samohil (= Samuel) bought this tomb for himself and his wife Lassia Irene, who died at the age of 23.[5] He adds the adjuration that nobody should open the tomb and 'put someone else's body on top of our bones.' This adjuration is solemnized by referring to the victories of the rulers, the honours of the patriarchs (certainly the influential Jewish leaders in Palestine), and the Law which the Lord gave the

---

[1] For the Middle Ages see the massive collection of documents in S. Simonsohn, *The Jews in Sicily*, 7 vols., Leiden 1977–2005. Still valuable is C. Roth, 'Jewish Intellectual Life in Medieval Sicily,' *Jewish Quarterly Review* 47 (1956/57) 317–335.

[2] See P.W. van der Horst, 'The Jews of Ancient Crete,' *Journal of Jewish Studies* 39 (1988) 183–200; and *idem*, 'The Jews of Ancient Cyprus,' *Zutot: Perspectives on Jewish Culture* 2003, 110–120.

[3] D. Noy, *Jewish Inscriptions of Western Europe. Vol. 1: Italy (excluding the City of Rome), Spain and Gaul*, Cambridge 1993, 184–220; henceforth JIWE.

[4] R. Kotansky, *Greek Magical Amulets. The Inscribed Gold, Silver, Copper, and Bronze Lamellae*, vol. 1, Opladen 1994, 126–154; henceforth GMA.

[5] A not unusual age at death for a woman; see my *Ancient Jewish Epitaphs. An Introductory Survey of a Millennium of Jewish Funerary Epigraphy (300 BCE–700 CE)*, Kampen 1991, Ch. 5 ('Age at Death').

Jews. JIWE 146, again from Catania, is a Greek epitaph for two girls, Leontia who died at the age of 3 and Kalliope who died at the age of 18. Two menorahs have been incised on this marble plaque. A menorah is also incised on nr. 147, again a Greek epitaph from Catania, which is almost impossible to decipher due to damage. Nr. 148 (Catania) is a marble plaque on which Irenaeus, an elder (*presbyteros*), states (in Greek) that he has bought the burial place without offending the commandment. Since it is unclear what commandment Irenaeus is referring to, the Jewishness of the inscription is debated (since sometimes *entolê* is also used for Jesus' precepts). Also another marble plaque from Catania recording the acquisition of a tomb (JIWE 149, in Greek) says that the owner (again an elder, *presbyteros*, called Jason) in no way infringed the commandment. JIWE 150, again from Catania, states that Zosimianus bought this tomb; a menorah is added after the text. From Syracuse there is a Greek epitaph (JIWE 151) in which Irene Nymphe (or: Irene the bride) says that no one should open the grave where she lies, but the Jewishness of the inscription is again a matter of some debate. Another Syracusan epitaph in Greek (JIWE 152) threatens anyone who opens the tomb with 'the future' (*to mellêtikon*), which most probably refers to the final judgement. The Jewish character is ensured by the closing formula 'Blessing to the pious here' (*eulogia tois hosiois hôde*). JIWE 153 is a Samaritan inscription from Syracuse. It is written on a marble column in Samaritan Hebrew and cites the text of Num. 10:35: 'Rise, YHWH, may your enemies be scattered,' a text found more often in Samaritan inscriptions and on amulets.[6] JIWE 154 (from Noto Vecchio) contains only menoroth as tomb decoration. Nr. 155 is a Greek epitaph from Acrilla for 'Jason the child' (with a menorah). JIWE 156 is a Hebrew amulet on a gold sheet from Comiso. It is heavily damaged but contains twice the line 'He shall save by the name that is in the height and He shall spare the lowly.' The often garbled Hebrew suggests that the copyist did not really understand what he was writing. From Sofiana we have Greek epitaphs for Attinis (= Atinius), an elder, with a menorah and for Judas Sabatias (JIWE 157 and 158). From probably the same place there is a bronze sheet with an amulet text in Greek and transliterated Hebrew containing mostly names of angels, both well-known and unknown (JIWE 159).[7] The final items are two epitaphs in Greek, one on a very damaged stone from Agrigento with the word *Ioud[aios]* in final position (JIWE 160), the other (161, from Terme Imerese) calling the deceased, Gaius Seius Ptolemaeus, a *Samareus*, the meaning of which is uncertain: Was

---

[6] R. Pummer, 'Inscriptions,' in A.D. Crown (ed.), *The Samaritans*, Tübingen 1989, 192; Pummer, 'Samaritan Rituals and Customs,' *ibid.* 652.

[7] The same text was published simultaneously as no. 33 in Kotanksky, GMA. Among the well-known names we find the four archangels Michael, Gabriel, Raphael, and Uriel; among the many unknown we find names such as Delko and Gibitiba.

the man a Samaritan (a member of the Samaritan religious community) or a Samarian (an inhabitant of Samaria)?[8]

The amulet from Acre published by Kotansky (GMA 32) is a copper tablet found in the early 19th century and published several times since.[9] It is usually called 'the phylactery of Moses,' since the amulet identifies itself as such in the opening lines: "A phylactery which Moses used to protect himself in the Holy of Holies (and) to lead him in the glory of the divine." And in line 8 it says: "A phylactery of Moses (to protect himself) when he went up on Mount Sinai … to receive the amulet," and this is repeated again in line 23. The amulet also states three times that whoever carries it will not have to fear sorcerers or binding spells or evil spirits. The protecting charm itself begins with the words, "Iaô Sabaôth Adônaie Seilam Ablanathanalba, O world of the world,[10] protect so-and-so, Abrasax," followed by *nomina barbara*. This is a familiar mix of Jewish and Greek elements that one finds so often in magical papyri, including those of non-Jewish origin.[11] The surprise comes in lines 19–22, where we find a previously unidentified fragment of Aquila's translation of Deuteronomy 32:1–3: "The heaven will be darkened, and I will speak, and let the earth hear the words of my mouth, as fine dew upon the grass, and as gentle showers upon the herb, because I have called the name of the Lord."[12] The text on the tablet is rather corrupt but according to the careful and convincing study by Kotansky there are several Aquilan elements in these lines (*inter alia*, the reading 'will be darkened'), but for our purposes it is unnecessary to go into these details.[13] The important point is that this particular quotation in the amulet's text is not without its purpose. As Kotansky observes, Deuteronomy 32 and 33 preserve the last words of Moses before his death. Both chapters "contain poetic compositions that effectively close the whole of the Mosaic Pentateuch" (144). In the verses quoted,

---

[8]   On this problem see my 'The Samaritan Diaspora in Antiquity,' in my *Essays on the Jewish World of Early Christianity*, Fribourg – Göttingen 1990, 136–147.

[9]   For publication details see GMA 126. It is unclear to me why Noy, who knows this amulet (see p. 213), did not include this text in JIWE, whereas he did so with GMA no. 33.

[10]   The strange phrase *kosme kosmou* is probably a wooden translation of the Hebrew words *'olam le-'olam*.

[11]   M. Smith, 'The Jewish Elements in the Magical Papyri,' in his *Studies in the Cult of Yahweh*, vol. 2, Leiden 1996, 242–256.

[12]   On Aquila see N. Fernández Marcos, *The Septuagint in Context. Introduction to the Greek Versions of the Bible*, Leiden 2000, 109–122. For the sake of comparison I also give Deut. 32:1–3 according to the NRSV translation of the Masoretic version: "Give ear, O heavens, and I will speak, let the earth hear the words of my mouth. May my teaching drop like the rain, my speech condense like the dew, like gentle rain on grass, like the showers on new growth. For I will proclaim the name of the Lord." The JPS translation runs as follows: "Give ear, O heavens, let me speak; let the earth hear the words I utter! May my discourse come down like the rain, my speech distill like the dew, like showers on young growth, like droplets on the grass. For the name of the Lord I proclaim."

[13]   See for a detailed study of this Aquilan quote Kotansky, GMA 149–154.

"Moses sings his song to the whole assembly of Israel, with his own words likened to a divine utterance that even heaven and earth must hear. The words not only represent a distillation of all Moses' divine teaching as given on Sinai, they serve as a sort of incantation in themselves, for the words appropriately end, 'I will proclaim the name of the Lord.' That name, and its proclamation, represents the very essence of the magic 'Phylactery of Moses' – it is the 'Sabaoth' of the inscribed golden leaf (line 6), the Divine Names and Tetragrammaton (lines 14–18, 29 f.) that Moses acquires on his ascent to Sinai" (144).

Much more should be said about this curious amulet, but we leave it here in order to return to our main question: What does all this teach us about the Jews of ancient Sicily?

To begin with, we can see from the places where the materials were found that in the later Roman Empire Jews lived all over Sicily, although there seems to be a certain concentration of evidence in Catania (JIWE 145–150). Further, in contrast to Crete and Cyprus, all of the evidence is late: Whereas for the other two large islands, Jewish inhabitants are attested as early as the last centuries BCE, for Sicily they are not attested before the third century CE. That is not to say they were not there before; we simply have no evidence, but no evidence does not imply absence. In view of the fact that many other islands in the Mediterranean Sea had Jewish diaspora communities from much earlier times, it is hard to believe they did not exist in Sicily, but we will have to wait for new evidence before we can be sure about that. Thirdly, not surprisingly, the Jews of Sicily spoke Greek, like almost all other diaspora Jews (at least in the West). We saw three inscriptions in Hebrew, but one of them was no more than some stock phrases of a liturgical character (like *shalom 'al Yisra'el*) and a greeting; moreover the rest of this inscription was in Latin (JIWE 145). The second one was a Samaritan inscription with a biblical quote in Hebrew (JIWE 153), but Samaritan inscriptions with such quotes tend to be always in Hebrew so that we cannot use such evidence for determining the spoken language – as a matter of fact, like the Jews, all diaspora Samaritans spoke Greek.[14] The third one is a Hebrew amulet (JIWE 156) the text of which is in large parts so unintelligible that its first editor suggests that "the copyist did not understand it and copied it purely for magical purposes."[15] So none of these three inscriptions entitles us to assume that Sicilian Jews knew more than minimal Hebrew. The only Latin inscription (JIWE 145) is an exception and as such an indication of an exceptionally high degree of integration into Roman society; even in the city of Rome, Latin inscriptions by Jews are a rarity (although increasing over time).[16] Finally, again not surprisingly, Jews in Sicily tended to indulge in magic, as we also see elsewhere (for instance in Cyprus; see my article mentioned in note 2).

---

[14] See my 'The Samaritan Languages in the Pre-Islamic Period,' in my *Japheth in the Tents of Shem. Studies on Jewish Hellenism in Antiquity*, Leuven 2002, 235–250.

[15] Noy, JIWE 208.

[16] See L.V. Rutgers, *The Jews of Late Ancient Rome*, Leiden 1995, 176–7.

No synagogues have been excavated in Sicily. Even so, the evidence reviewed suggests that there were Jewish communities with their own organizations. Some of the inscriptions mention elders (*presbyteroi*), a well-attested designation for dignitaries of Jewish communities (JIWE 148, 149, 157); they were probably members of a council of elders (*gerousia*).[17] Rabbis are not mentioned at all, but the reference to the honor of the patriarchs in JIWE 145 suggests that contacts with the Jewish leadership in Palestine were maintained. And the use of Aquila's Bible translation in the amulet discussed above (GMA 32) is at least an indication that this rabbinically inspired Greek version had influence and prestige among (some) Sicilian Jews. Almost the only setting in which they could have heard this version is that of a synagogue service, so this is another indication that there must have been Jewish synagogues in Sicily. In this connection it is to be noticed that JIWE 143 stresses the importance of the sabbath. Also the frequent occurrence of the menorah as a Jewish symbol is indicative of an outspoken Jewish self-awareness and identity.

Another interesting feature of the evidence is the presence of Samaritans. To be sure, the *Samareus* of JIWE 161 need not have been a Samaritan at all (see above), but the presence in Syracuse of a marble column with a Samaritan inscription (JIWE 153) cannot but indicate that the city harbored a community of Samaritans. We know from a literary source that there was indeed a Samaritan community in Sicily in the sixth century: Pope Gregory the Great wrote to the bishops of the islands that the Samaritans there should not be allowed to circumcise their Christian slaves (*Epist.* 6.33) and that these slaves should be redeemed (*Epist.* 8.21).

The same Gregory also attests to Jewish presence in Sicily by the end of the sixth century: He ordered the bishops to give the Jews of Palermo full indemnification for the damage suffered by the expropriation of the synagogue by Christians (*Epist.* 9.38). As Salo W. Baron aptly remarks in this context, "This protection of Jewish religious institutions, while in keeping with the accepted Roman law, was particularly significant in Italy in so far as there the conflict between Saint Ambrose and the emperor over the illegal expropriation of the synagogue of Callinicum in 388 had helped create the illusion that the church favored such mob action."[18] Be that as it may, these papal documents make clear that by the end of antiquity there must have been sizeable Jewish and Samaritan communities in Sicily. And this growth continued in the Middle Ages: In the

---

[17] See my *Ancient Jewish Epitaphs* 91; esp. L.I. Levine, *The Ancient Synagogue. The First Thousand Years*, New Haven-London 2000, 407–408.
[18] S.W. Baron, *A Social and Religious History of the Jews*, vol. 3, New York-Philadelphia 1957, 30. At pp. 28–33 Baron also mentions other letters of pope Gregory concerning things Jewish.

12th century, Benjamin of Tudela counted no less than 1500 Jewish families in Palermo.[19]

Appendix: Caecilius of Calacte

In the entry on Sicily in the *Encyclopaedia Judaica* (14:1493), S.J. Sierra mentions the first-century CE Greek orator Caecilius of Calacte (*i. e.,* Kalê Aktê on the north coast of Sicily) as the first Sicilian Jew known to us, although he spent most of his life in Rome. This opinion is also adhered to by Martin Goodman in the revised English edition of Schürer's *History*.[20] Actually the only evidence for Caecilius' Jewishness is a remark to that effect in the muddled entry on this orator in the 10th century Byzantine encyclopedia called the *Suda*. This is very weak evidence, the more so since all other data about Caecilius, to be found in much earlier and therefore more reliable authors, do not give us the slightest hint of his Jewishness. Also the topics of his books do not suggest in the least that the writer was a Jew. I would therefore submit that, for reasons of methodological strictness, in a study of Sicilian Jews in antiquity Caecilius of Calacte should be left out of account.

[Note: The volume edited by N. Bucaria, *Ebrei e Sicilia* (Palermo 2003), came to my notice only after the completion of this article.]

---

[19] *Sefer ha-Massa'ot* 108 (p. 78 in Adler's edition).
[20] E. Schürer, *The History of the Jewish People in the Age of Jesus Christ*, vol. 3, Edinburgh 1986, 701–703. Cf. also M. Stern, *Greek and Latin Authors on Jews and Judaism*, vol. 1, Jerusalem 1974, 361–363, 566.

The Synagogue of Sardis and its Inscriptions

Introduction

Forty years ago, in 1962, American archaeologists unearthed the greatest ancient synagogue ever in a large-scale excavation in the city of Sardis, capital of ancient Lydia in Asia Minor.[1] The colossal basilica-shaped building measures almost 20 x 100 meters and could accommodate some 1000 people.[2] This richly decorated basilica is an integral part of a huge bath-and-gymnasium complex in the city centre and as such it is also a monument to the integration of the Jewish community in this Graeco-Roman city. This spectacular discovery provided a strong stimulus to scholarly research on the Jewish diaspora in antiquity, especially as regards problems of acculturation, assimilation, and identity formation.[3] The more than eighty inscriptions that were found inside the synagogue are obviously of the greatest importance for the study of these issues, but unfortunately we have had to wait very long for their publication. To be fair, the greatest epigraphist of the 20th century, the French scholar Louis Robert, had published some of these inscriptions as early as 1964,[4] but that was less than 10% of the material. At last we now have the long awaited publication of this dossier in the form of a special issue of the *Harvard Theological Review,* in which John Kroll presents the material.[5] In this modest contribution, I first want to briefly say something about what was known about the Jews of Sardis before the discovery

---

[1] A.R. Seager & A.T. Kraabel, 'The Synagogue and the Jewish Community,' in G.M.A. Hanfmann (ed.), *Sardis from Prehistoric to Roman Times*, Cambridge (MA) 1983, 169–178. For a concise survey of the archaeological data see also P.R. Trebilco, *Jewish Communities in Asia Minor*, Cambridge 1991, 40–43.

[2] In the scholarly literature one finds sometimes other measures (e. g., a length of 60 meters) but these are the interior measures of the basilica, especially of the great hall in which the meetings took place, and that room is of course considerably smaller than the total complex which encompassed not only the great assembly hall but also the large forecourt with provisions for ritual washings and a number of other rooms. For information about the details of these adjacent rooms the reader is referred to the publications mentioned in note 1.

[3] See, e. g., J.M.G. Barclay, *Jews in the Mediterranean Diaspora*, Edinburgh 1996.

[4] *Nouvelles inscriptions de Sardes*, Paris 1964, 37–58.

[5] J.H. Kroll, 'The Greek Inscriptions of the Sardis Synagogue,' *HTR* 94 (2001) 5–127. Pp. 57–127 contain photos of the inscriptions. [After the original publication of this article the inscriptions were published anew by Walter Ameling in *Inscriptiones Judaicae Orientis II: Kleinasien*, Tübingen 2004, 209–297.]

of the synagogue, and then devote some words to the importance of the inscriptions for our knowledge of Judaism in the ancient diaspora.

Jews in Sardis

It was only after the middle of the third century CE that the great basilica was converted into a synagogue; thereafter it served the Jewish community for several centuries until the city was destroyed by the Sassanids in 616 CE. Jews, however, had been living in Sardis some centuries before they had this synagogue. How many centuries before is uncertain, however, because of a problem in the interpretation of a word in Obadiah 20. The prophet says there that the exiles of Jerusalem who live in Sepharad will possess the towns of the Negev. Sepharad (only in later Hebrew the designation for Spain) is a name that occurs nowhere else in the Hebrew Bible and it is uncertain which place or region the prophet has in mind here.[6] That uncertainty is also reflected in the ancient versions: the Septuagint renders it Ephratha (or Sephratha), the Vulgate Bosporus, and the Peshitta and the Targum read Spain. According to some modern scholars, however, the city of Sardis is meant here.[7] Why? In 1916 an Aramaic inscription from the Persian period (KAI no. 260) was found on the ancient necropolis of Sardis. In that text the name Sepharad (in the same spelling as in Obadiah 20: sprd) is used for the capital of the Persian satrapy Sparda = Sardis. And fifty years later, in 1966, another Aramaic inscription from the Persian period (ca. 450 BCE) was published from which it became apparent that in Daskyleion, not far from Sardis, a Jewish family had settled.[8] That is to say that it is not impossible that the prophet indeed does have in mind here Jewish exiles in the Lydian capital, Sardis. But that cannot be strictly proved, and it is understandable that some scholars remain skeptical.[9]

The Jewish historian Flavius Josephus mentions a letter by the Seleucid king Antiochus III from 205 BCE in which this ruler states that he has transferred two thousand Jewish families from Mesopotamia to the most important cities of Lydia and Phrygia (*Antiquitates Judaicae* XII 148–152). So there can be little

---

[6] See the survey in J.D. Wineland, 'Sepharad,' *Anchor Bible Dictionary* 5 (1992) 1089–90.

[7] See, e.g., E. Lipinski, 'Obadiah 20,' *Vetus Testamentum* 23 (1973) 368–370; H.W. Wolff, *Dodekapropheton 3: Obadja und Jona* (BKAT XIV/3), Neukirchen 1977, 47–48. Also Wineland (see n. 6) is inclined to see a reference to Sardis here..

[8] For details the reader is referred to the publications mentioned in the previous note.

[9] E.g., Trebilco, *Jewish Communities* 38; and F. Millar in E. Schürer, *The History of the Jewish People in the Age of Jesus Christ*, rev. ed. by G. Vermes, F. Millar & M. Goodman, vol. III 1, Edinburgh 1986, 20–21.

doubt that by the end of the third century BCE, Sardis, as capital of Lydia, had Jewish inhabitants.[10]

Furthermore, Josephus cites some decrees of Julius Caesar and the Roman Senate from the middle of the first century BCE which stipulate the rights of the Jews in a number of cities in Asia Minor. The Roman governor of Asia Minor had in general granted the Jews freedom from military service as well as permission to live fully in accordance with the Jewish ancestral laws and customs (*Ant. Jud.* XIV 223–227), but apart from that there was also a special decree concerning the situation of the Jews in Sardis:

Lucius Antonius, son of Marcus, proquaestor and propraetor, to the magistrates, council and people of Sardis, greeting. Jewish citizens of yours have come to me and pointed out that from the earliest times they have had an association of their own in accordance with their native laws and a place of their own in which they decide their affairs and controversies with one another.[11] Upon their request that it be permitted them to do these things, I decided that they may be maintained and permitted them so to do (*Ant. Jud.* XIV 235).[12]

Slightly further on Josephus quotes a decree of the people of Sardis:

The following decree was passed by the council and people on the motion of the magistrates. Whereas the Jewish citizens living in our city have continually received many great privileges from the people and have now come before the council and the people and have pleaded that, as their laws and freedom have been restored to them by the Roman senate and people, they may, in accordance with their accepted customs, come together and have a communal life and adjudicate suits among themselves, and that a place be given to them in which they may gather together with their wives and children and offer their ancestral prayers and sacrifices to God, it has therefore been decreed by the council and the people that permission shall be given them to come together on stated days to do these things which are in accordance with their laws, and also that a place shall be set apart by the magistrates for them to build and inhabit, such as they may consider suitable for this purpose, and that the market officials of the city shall be charged with the duty of having suitable food for them brought in (*Ant. Jud.* XIV 259–261).

From these decrees several things become clear. The privileged position of the Jews in the city did not come to them automatically. They had had to struggle for it and they apparently had sufficient influence and goodwill to get things done as they wanted. They got their own piece of land for the building of a synagogue (not the one now excavated), the right to have their own meetings and to decide on their own affairs there, and it was even taken care of by the city magistrates

---

[10] There are scholars who doubt the authenticity of the letter of Antiochus III; see Barclay, *Jews* 261 with note 8.

[11] This almost certainly refers to a synagogue. For the multifunctionality of ancient synagogues see now esp. L.I. Levine, *The Ancient Synagogue*, New Haven 2000, 124–134 *et passim*.

[12] Translation by Ralph Marcus in LCL VII 575.

that kosher food would be available.[13] We thus get a picture of a Jewish community that is keen on the maintenance of its own identity in the midst of a pagan society, but that is also enabled by that very same society to do so without serious problems. We also have information from other cities in Asia Minor that makes clear that the Jewish communities there were in a relatively safe and secure position and could develop a high degree of integration in city life in such a way that they could also maintain their identity, The city of Aphrodisias, situated in the South-Western part of Asia Minor, is a fine example of that kind of integration, as I have argued elsewhere.[14]

The synagogue

This picture is now confirmed in a striking way by the excavation of the great synagogue in Sardis and its inscriptions. As was already noted, the synagogue was an integral part of a centrally located complex consisting of a public bath, a gymnasium, and a shopping mall. The building is 'one of the most prominent features of the city's ruined urban landscape,'[15] as every modern visitor can now easily see. Even apart from the enormous size, this points to the fact that the Jewish community of Sardis was definitely not a 'quantité négligeable.' Minorities in a city do not usually get hold of a central and prestigious building if they do not have any clout and influence there. In my view, therefore, Thomas Kraabel is completely right when he says: 'The importance of the discovery of the Sardis synagogue is simply that it reveals a Jewish community of far greater wealth, power, and self-confidence than the usual views of ancient Judaism would give us any right to expect.'[16] The Jewish community in Sardis was a minority, 'but a powerful, even a wealthy one, of great antiquity, in a major city of the Diaspora,

---

[13] See T. Rajak, 'Jews, Pagans and Christians in Late Antique Sardis: Models of Interaction,' in her *The Jewish Dialogue with Greece and Rome. Studies in Cultural and Social Interaction*, Leiden 2001, 447–462, esp. 448. The enigmatic remark that the Jews were also allowed to bring their sacrifices to God in their own communal building must be left out of account here. Sacrifices to the God of Israel outside the Jerusalem temple were of course strictly forbidden according to the priestly rules, but that does not imply that everyone agreed with and stuck to these rules. It is known that there were other Jewish temples outside of Jerusalem. See, e. g., M. Smith, *Palestinian Parties and Politics that Shaped the Old Testament*, New York 1971, ch. 4, esp. p. 97; M.E. Stone, *Scriptures, Sects and Visions. A Profile of Judaism from Ezra to the Jewish Revolts*, London 1980, 77–82. But see also the discussion of the problem by J. Leonhardt, '*Euchai kai thusiai* (A 14:260) – Opfer in der jüdischen Synagoge von Sardes?,' in J.U. Kalms (ed.), *Internationales Josephus-Kolloquium Amsterdam 2000*, Münster 2001, 189–203, who argues that this passage cannot be interpreted as a break with the Jerusalem temple by the Jews of Sardis.

[14] P.W. van der Horst, 'Jews and Christians in Aphrodisias in the Light of Their Relationships in Other Cities of Asia Minor,' in my *Essays on the Jewish World of Early Christianity*, Fribourg-Göttingen 1990, 166–181.

[15] Rajak, 'Jews, Pagans and Christians in Sardis' 449.

[16] Kraabel in *Sardis* (n. 1) 178.

controlling a huge and lavishly decorated structure on 'Main Street' and able to retain control of it as long as the city existed.'[17] Here one does not find Jews who keep a 'low profile' but influential and self-conscious people. The inscriptions that have now been published add an extra confirmation to this picture.

The inscriptions

Apart from the Greek inscriptions there are a handful of Hebrew epigraphic remains, but I will leave these out of account, not only because they have not yet been published,[18] but also because these five or six fragments yield little more than the word *shalom* and the proper names Jochanan and Severus. These few Hebrew fragments can certainly not be used as proof that the Jews in Sardis were still able to speak Hebrew for they prove no more than that one or two people knew the characters of the 'sacred language,' or one or two words in that language, as a sign of belonging to the history of the Jewish people. The fact that more than 90% of the inscriptions are in Greek makes abundantly clear that the daily language of this Jewish community was Greek. The eighty or so Greek inscriptions offer us an interesting window on various aspects of this diaspora community.

To begin with, it should be said that most of the inscriptions in this synagogue 'commemorate members of the congregation who contributed the many elements of interior decoration: the mosaics on the floor, the marbling of the walls, and a number of architectural and ritual furnishings.'[19] That is a type of inscription that we also find in other ancient synagogues and of which more than one hundred were already known.[20] This corpus is now expanded considerably by these new inscriptions, which – like the others of this type – all date from the period of ca. 300–600 CE.

It is often mentioned that the generous donor made his donation 'in fulfillment of a vow' (*kat' euchên, hyper euchês, eplêrôsa euchên, euchên etelesa, euxamenos* etc.). Once the donation was made out of gratitude for the health of the giver (63), possibly an act of thanksgiving for recovery from a serious illness because the donation consisted of nothing less than a monumental marble Torah shrine (the *'aron ha-qodesh*), here designated with a word that has not been previously attested with this meaning, viz. *nomophylakion*, lit. that in which the

---

[17] Kraabel, 'The Diaspora Synagogue: Archaeological and Epigraphic Evidence Since Sukenik,' in *Aufstieg und Niedergang der Römischen Welt* II 19,1, Berlin-New York 1979, 488.

[18] F.M. Cross from Harvard University is preparing an edition. [In the meantime Cross has published them in *Harvard Theological Review* 95 (2002) 3–19.]

[19] Kroll, 'Greek Inscriptions' 5.

[20] For a (now outdated) collection of these inscriptions see B. Lifshitz, *Donateurs et fondateurs dans les synagogues juives*, Paris 1967. At pp. 24–31 Lifshitz deals with the inscriptions from Sardis that had been published by Louis Robert in 1964 (*Nouvelles inscriptions de Sardes*).

law is guarded.[21] With due piety it is often stated that the gift was donated 'from the gifts of Providence' (12, 16–17, 19–24, 58, 66). It is striking that the God of Israel is designated no less than 11 times by the non-biblical term *Pronoia*, something that we know primarily from the writings of several Church Fathers.[22] Graeco-Jewish authors such as Philo and Josephus, too, use the term *pronoia* dozens of times, but always as an attribute or quality, never as the equivalent of God. In antiquity, *pronoia* was initially used primarily for the impersonal *providentia* in Stoic philosophy. Later on this concept was also employed in a wider sense in the philosophical debates of the Hellenistic and Roman period (think of the various tractates *Peri pronoias* from the Imperial time[23]). It is not improbable that this striking use of *pronoia* as a designation of God in these inscriptions was influenced by the religio-philosophical debates about providence in later antiquity. As was the case with Philo (albeit in a very different way), these Hellenized Jews, too, were influenced in their ways of thinking and speaking by debates in contemporary philosophy; no wonder if one realizes how many centuries they had already lived in the thoroughly Greek city that Sardis was. 'They took over an important gentile word in the same way that they had appropriated gentile sculpture, hauling Roman eagles and Lydian lions into their building to adorn it, boldly making them Jewish in the process.'[24]

Six times the donors are called 'God-fearers' (*theosebeis*, 8, 9, 22, 57, 59, 66). This is of importance since we almost certainly have to do here with the *terminus technicus* for non-Jewish sympathizers with Judaism (the *sebomenoi* of the Book of Acts).[25] It is the great donor inscription from Aphrodisias that had already made impressively clear that in that Carian city non-Jews had contributed generously (and in great numbers) to the financing of a Jewish building (or burial place), and, in addition to that, those many 'God-fearers' (almost half of the more than 120 donors belonged to that category of pagan 'affiliates of some sort'[26]) turned out to belong to the higher strata of society.[27] Although in Sardis the numerical ratio is quite different from that in Aphrodisias, here again one can see unmistakably that till long after Constantine pagans of the higher echelons

---

[21] This rare word is used elsewhere in the sense of 'office of the guardian of the laws.'

[22] A.T. Kraabel, 'Pronoia at Sardis,' B. Isaac & A. Oppenheimer (eds.), *Studies on the Jewish Diaspora in the Hellenistic and Roman Periods* (= Te'uda XII), Tel Aviv 1996, 75–96. Only inscription no. 29 has the formula 'from the gifts of the Almighty God.'

[23] Kraabel, 'Pronoia at Sardis' 82–84. See esp. M. Dragona-Monachou, 'Divine Providence in the Philosophy of the Empire,' *Aufstieg und Niedergang der Römischen Welt* II 36, 7, Berlin-New York 1994, 4417–4490.

[24] Kraabel, 'Pronoia' 95.

[25] The most comprehensive and recent study of the phenomenon of 'Godfearers' is B. Wander, *Gottesfürchtige und Sympathisanten*, Tübingen 1998.

[26] Rajak, 'Jews, Pagans and Christians' 449.

[27] J. Reynolds & R. Tannenbaum, *Jews and Godfearers at Aphrodisias* Cambridge 1987.

tended to sympathize with Judaism rather than with Christianity.[28] One of these 'gentile sympathizers' even donated the large menorah to the synagogue (66)!

When donors mention their occupation or function, secular professions are mentioned much more often than religious ones. Only in three cases are positions or functions in the Jewish community mentioned, whereas in no less than twenty cases secular professions and functions are mentioned (among which three goldsmiths!). What is especially striking is that no less than nine persons are *bouleutai*, i. e., members of the city council (*boulê*), the highest administrative body of the city. Here we see Jews who have climbed up to the highest rung on the social ladder, for 'the councils of Greek cities under the Late Empire were open only to the wealthier families, with membership, once purchased, being hereditary and held for life.'[29] So distinguished and well-to-do Jewish families participated in the government of the city. No wonder that here, unlike elsewhere in the fifth and sixth century, the synagogue was not expropriated by the Christians in order to be converted into a church building. This basilica could have been a magnificent church, but what happened in fact was that during the fifth and sixth century the Christians in Sardis had to make do with a much smaller building than the synagogue. A striking difference from the famous Aphrodisias inscription, which also mentions nine *bouleutai*, is that there the city councilors are all gentiles whereas here they are Jews!

As far as religious functions are concerned, an elder (*presbyteros*, 52 and 75) is mentioned twice. Elders are found more often in other Jewish inscriptions.[30] They were members of the council of elders (often called *gerousia*) who formed the governing body of the religious community. Furthermore, someone is called *hiereus kai sophodidaskalos* (4). 'Priest,' *hiereus*, is here almost certainly not the designation of an official temple priest, which seems very unlikely after the destruction of the Jerusalem temple in 70 CE (although it can never be ruled out completely; think of the reference to sacrifices by Jews in Sardis in *Ant. Jud.* XIV 259–261 [quoted above]). Cases like these most probably concern descendants of former priestly families who 'were accorded the privilege of pronouncing certain benedictions during services' and were regarded as 'preferred readers of the Torah.'[31] The prestige of these *kohanim* was still so great, even centuries after the destruction of the temple, that in the rabbinic catacombs of Beth She'arim (in the Galilee) a special burial chamber had been reserved for them.[32] *Sophodidaskalos* is a teacher of wisdom. The word looks like a variant of the more usual *nomodidaskalos*, teacher of the Law. Since the Torah was widely regarded as

---

[28] See my study 'Jews and Christians in Aphrodisias in the Light of Their Relations in Other Cities of Asia Minor' (n. 14).

[29] Kroll, 'Greek Inscriptions' 10.

[30] For a list see P.W. van der Horst, *Ancient Jewish Epitaphs*, Kampen 1991, 91.

[31] Kroll, 'Greek Inscriptions' 18.

[32] P.W. van der Horst, *Ancient Jewish Epitaphs* 96.

the compendium of all divine wisdom in ancient Judaism,[33] it seems very probable that the term is a designation of a Torah scholar (not necessarily a rabbi), something that fits in well with the priestly descent of the man.

Most of the gifts mentioned in the inscriptions are the marble wall decorations and floor mosaics of the synagogue, but some are of a different nature. Two persons donated each a menorah (66, 69; in no. 66 the menorah is called *heptamyxion*, lit. 'sevenburner'); another donated the marble for the Torah shrine (63); and Samoe possibly donated the *bima*, the elevated structure from which the Torah was read (4?). This Samoe is one of the very few with a biblical name (it is a rendition of Shamuʻa); further we only find one instance of Samuel (34, 56). All other names are familiar Greek and Latin names, except Eulogios (9), a name derived from *eulogia = berakha*, blessing.[34] This Eulogios happens to be a 'God-fearer,' as were his parents, who gave him this name as they probably already felt attracted to Judaism.

The lions and the Torah

Finally, I will briefly discuss some inscriptions that are interesting for reasons other than the ones mentioned so far, to begin with no. 10. There we read the following text:

I, Aurelios Olympios of the tribe of the Leontii, fulfilled a vow with my wife and children.

The fact that a Jew is named after the Greek mountain of the gods (Olympus) is not so strange in the light of the fact that we know quite a number of names of Jews (and Christians[35]) with theophoric elements (till the present day there are Jews called Isidore = 'gift of Isis').[36] 'Leur sens était apparamment oblitéré chez les Juifs comme chez les chrétiens.'[37] Of greater interest is the fact that Aurelius Olympius says that he belongs to 'the tribe of the Leontii.' Louis Robert was convinced that this is not a tribe of the city of Sardis but of the Jewish community. He points out that not only does the name Leontios occur more frequently among Jews (also in Sardis), but that in addition to that the lion is used frequently as a symbolic decorative element in the synagogal mosaics and reliefs.[38] For that

---

[33] See, e. g., E.J. Schnabel, *Law and Wisdom from Ben Sira to Paul,* Tübingen 1985.

[34] Robert, *Nouvelles inscriptions* 40: 'Il [ce nom] convient de façon excellente à un Juif, puisqu'il évoque l'*eulogia*, la bénédiction, cette prière qui figure sur les tombes juives comme dans les synagogues.' For other Jews with the name Eulogios or Eulogia see the indices in J.B. Frey, *Corpus Inscriptionum Iudaicarum*, 2 vols, Rome 1935–52, and in D. Noy, *Jewish Inscriptions of Western Europe*, 2 vols., Cambridge 1993–95.

[35] Think of Origenes = son of Horus!

[36] On Jewish names with pagan theophoric elements see the fine essay by G. Mussies, 'Jewish Personal Names in Some Non-Literary Sources,' in J.W. van Henten & P.W. van der Horst (eds.), *Studies in Early Jewish Epigraphy*, Leiden 1994, 242–276, esp. 245–249.

[37] Robert, *Nouvelles inscriptions* 46 n. 2.

[38] Robert, *Nouvelles inscriptions* 46 with nn. 6–8.

reason he regards the tribe of the Leontii as 'une adaptation hellénisante' of the tribe of Judah. Indeed, in Jacob's blessing (Gen. 49:9) Judah is called a young lion and this symbolic designation is still used in Apoc. 5:5 and in later Jewish and Christian writings. Jews from the tribe of Judah for that reason had a preference for the name Leontios, says Robert. Baruch Lifshitz disagrees and objects that this self-designation would make little sense since most Jews (*Ioudaioi*) were descendants of the tribe of Judah; he takes the expression *phylê Leontiôn* to mean 'the family of the Leontii'[39] since in the Septuagint *phylê* is often used to render the Hebrew word for family, *mishpachah*. Kroll, however, agrees with Robert. He points out that another part of the wall decoration to which Aurelios Olympios contributed was donated by God-fearers, or non-Jews. It may well be the case that Aurelius Olympius wanted to distinguish himself as a Jew by advertising himself explicitly, and not without pride, as a member of the tribe of young lions, the tribe of Judah: he is a Leontios and hence a real *Ioudaios*! Besides, it should also be kept in mind that the lion had been a favourite theme in the iconography of Sardis from of old; no less than 22 statues of lions have been found there. Hence Trebilco's remark: 'The lion simultaneously expressed their Jewish identity and their "belongingness" in Sardis.'[40] Certainty cannot be attained in this matter, however, and more research needs to be done, but the inscription is certainly intriguing.

Intriguing as well is the inscription of no. 65. In a literal translation it says: 'Having found, having broken, read, observe' (*heurôn klasas anagnôthi phylaxon*). The imperatives 'read' and 'observe' (or 'keep') hardly leave other interpretations than that reading of the Torah is meant here and that it is inculcated in the minds of the community members that they should not only read or listen to this holy text with its commandments but also live in accordance with it.[41] Probably the plaquette with this inscription had been attached to the Torah shrine. It is not easy to say what exactly 'having broken' (*klasas*) implies, but presumably it refers to the breaking of seals or unlocking of locks on the Torah scroll.[42] Be that as it may, it is clear that the central position of the Torah was part of the identity of this community.[43]

Even though, in current interpretations, the Torah forbade the making of images, yet a Jewish family not only took upon themselves the costs of the marble

---

[39] *Donateurs et fondateurs* 27–28.

[40] *Jewish Communities* 45.

[41] Thus also L.H. Feldman, 'Diaspora Synagogues: New Light from Inscriptions and Papyri,' in S. Fine (ed.), *Sacred Realm. The Emergence of the Synagogue in the Ancient World*, New York – Oxford 1996, 64–65.

[42] Thus Trebilco, *Jewish Communities* 51; his alternative suggestion that what is meant is 'breaking open a text by discussing its meaning' seems far-fetched.

[43] See W. Ameling, 'Eine liturgische Inschrift aus der Synagoge von Sardes,' in *Klassisches Altertum, Spätantike und frühes Christentum (FS A. Lippold)*, Würzburg 1993, 495–508 [see now also his brief comments in *IJO* II 287.]

wall decoration in the great assembly hall of the synagogue ('from the gifts of God Almighty,' 29), but also the costs of the wall paintings (*zôgraphia*). These paintings are lamentably lost but in principle we could have found here a fine parallel to the famous frescoes in the synagogue of Syrian Dura-Europos (middle of the third century CE).

Herewith I want to conclude this summary survey. I hope to have made clear to readers that theologians, New Testament scholars, historians of ancient religion, and Judaic scholars can only ignore these new archaeological discoveries to their detriment, something which unfortunately still happens all too often in these fields of research. It is proper to end this survey by quoting the final sentence of Kroll's edition of these inscriptions: 'The Sardis dossier stands out for its sheer richness and scale, and for the striking vitality of late Roman Judaism that it conveys, a vitality that appears all the more remarkable because of the growing strength of Christianity at the same period in history.'[44] Of course it is hard to say whether this picture could be maintained if the whole of ancient Sardis were to be excavated, for perhaps the fact that only a small portion of this relatively large city has been brought to light conveys a slanted impression of the prominent Jewish presence there. Unfortunately we will probably never know completely for sure. But according to our present state of knowledge, it is fair to say that in the capital of ancient Lydia Jews played an important role in the cultural life of the city during at least a millennium.[45]

---

[44] Kroll, 'Greek Inscriptions' 48.

[45] The British scholar Tessa Rajak is of the opinion that what we can learn from Sardis is no more than that there Jews 'were both tolerated and tolerant' ('Jews, Pagans and Christians' 452). But although 'a little scepticism will be helpful in considering this glowing portrayal of co-existence' (453) – for even the Jewish *bouleutai* 'may in fact have had quite a mediocre ranking in the social hierarchy' (455) – her comparison with the situation in pre-war Berlin is misleading rather than elucidating. Her study of the Jews in Sardis is on the one hand a testimony to healthy reserve and restraint, but on the other hand also a proof of an inclination to skepticism in a situation where there is less reason for it than in many other cases.

Jews and Blues in Late Antiquity

From the early imperial period till the time of the Crusades circus factions played an important role in the cultural life of the Roman and Byzantine Empires. The character of these factions changed over the centuries, but their connection with the world of the athletic contests, the arenas, especially the hippodromes, remained constant. Having begun as privately run organizations of performers and supporters, in the course of the history of the Empire(s), the authorities gained more and more of a grip on them. The now publicly maintained factions were administered by a manager, the *factionarius* (whose role and function also changed over the centuries). To an increasing degree these sporting associations became political parties and pressure groups, even militias, especially in late antiquity and the early Byzantine period. The names of the four main factions were colour designations: the Greens (Πράσινοι) and Blues (Βένετοι) were the most important and influential ones; the minor ones were the Reds (Ῥούσιοι) and the Whites (Λευκοί).[1] The history and role of these factions has been excellently described by Alan Cameron (my summary of the data is based upon his monograph).[2] This short note is solely focussed on one minor aspect of this history, namely, the relationship between these factions and the Jews, about which we know little, but now somewhat more than 25 years ago thanks to recent epigraphic discoveries and new insights from social psychology.

From the beginning, the Blues and the Greens were groups that were in conflict with each other. This is clear in almost all the pagan, Jewish, and Christian sources that mention these factions. There is a long record of factional riots in the tumultuous history of Blues and Greens. The Greens, apparently always more rowdy and numerous than the Blues, were the ones who usually started the riots. They were relatively often from the lower strata of society, though not necessarily so; also the Blues were not always from the upper class, far from it. It would rather seem that most or all strata of society were represented in both factions, although the sources do give the decided impression that in general the Blues had higher social standing than the Greens. When there was fighting between Blues and Greens, however, it is usually difficult to find the cause in social or political issues. Greens hated Blues simply because they were not Greens, and

---

[1] For the astrological background of these colour designations see A. Hermann, "Farbe," *Reallexikon für Antike und Christentum* 7 (1969) 430.

[2] A. Cameron, *Circus Factions. Blues and Greens at Rome and Byzantium*, Oxford 1976.

vice versa. A comparison with modern soccer supporter groups or hooligans inevitably forces itself upon us.

There is an anonymous Jewish legend from the early Middle Ages that hints at this antagonism. In a tale called *Solomon's Throne and Hippodrome*,[3] we read that king Solomon was seated on his throne in the Jerusalem hippodrome in the style of a Byzantine Emperor. Solomon and his entourage, especially the spiritual leaders, were dressed in blue; the common people of Jerusalem were dressed in white; the people from outside Jerusalem in red; but the gentiles in green. To be sure, Jews and gentiles are here not opposed *en bloc* as Blues and Greens, but it is clear that the rabbinic author of this legend regarded the Greens as a party that was not Jewish, or not pro-Jewish, and that ranked low.

There is new epigraphic evidence as well that gives a strong impression of affinity between Jews and Blues. To begin with, there are some inscriptions from late antique Aphrodisias that point in that direction. In this Carian city, a bench in the Odeon is inscribed with two seat-markers, one of them stating that the seats there belong to the Jews (τόπος Ἑβρέων), the other one on the adjacent row that these seats belong to the elderly Jewish Blues (τόπος Βενέτων Ἑβρέων τῶν παλειῶν).[4] All the surrounding seats are for the Blues! This at least implies Jewish support for the Blues. Also in Miletus, a theatre seat is inscribed with an intriguing seat-marker Βενέτων Εἰοδέων.[5] The term 'Blue Jews' suggests clearly that they were seen by others, or saw themselves, as the enemies of the Greens. There is also epigraphical evidence from the hippodrome of late antique Tyre indicating that the Jews had their seats in the section reserved for the Blues.[6]

The question that arises automatically is whether or not it is the religious affiliations of Blues and Greens that may explain the affinity between Jews and Blues or the adversity between Jews and Greens. Cameron argued[7] that the traditional and firmly entrenched view that in the early Byzantine period (and to that period the Jewish evidence belongs) the Blues were Orthodox Christians and the Greens were Monophysites is totally wrong. What concerns him is "the conventional assumption that riots between Blues and Greens sprang from nothing so simple as the victory or defeat of this or that colour in the hippodrome;

---

[3] See the edition in A. Jellinek, *Bet ha-Midrasch. Sammlung kleiner Midraschim und vermischter Abhandlungen aus der ältern jüdischen Literatur*, vol. 5, Jerusalem 1967 (repr. of the original 1877 ed.), 34–39. English summary in L. Ginberg, *The Legends of the Jews*, vol. 4, Philadelphia 1913, 160–162 (with note 75 in vol. 6, p. 298). See the study of E. Ville-Patlagean, "Une image de Salomon en Basileus Byzantin," *Revue des Études Juives* 121 (1962) 8–33; the author mainly focusses on the dating of the original text (between the 6th and 10th century).

[4] J. Reynolds & R. Tannenbaum, *Jews and Godfearers at Aphrodisias*, Cambridge 1987, 132. Ch. Roueché, *Aphrodisias in Late Antiquity*, London 1989, 220–222, no. 180 (at pp. 218–228 Roueché deals with several other inscriptions mentioning Blues and Greens).

[5] P. Herrmann, *Inschriften von Milet*, Teil VI, Bd. 2, Berlin-New York 1998, no. 940h.

[6] J.-P. Rey-Coquais, "Tyr, fouilles récentes, ville, hippodrome et nécropole: L'apport des inscriptions," *Revue Archéologique* (1979) 166–167.

[7] Cameron, *Circus Factions* 126–153.

that factional rivalry is a direct reflection of religious rivalry. (…) [T]here is not one scrap of ancient evidence in its favour."[8] He argues on the basis of a plethora of evidence that the Greens were just as orthodox as the Blues, and that the factions did not play any role in the religious disputes because in general religious motives played no part in factional rivalry between Blues and Greens, let alone that they could be equated with moderates (Blues) and extremists (Greens). If this is correct, it becomes harder to explain the literary evidence we have to the effect that not only did the Jews usually side with the Blues but that the Greens often even initiated anti-Jewish violence. Let us review the evidence briefly.

John Malalas (first half of the sixth century, from Syrian Antioch) has several stories that give the decided impression of the existence of anti-Jewish resentment among the Greens of Antioch. The first passage is a slightly garbled notice about the reign of Caligula (37–41 CE):

From the first year of Gaius Caesar the Green faction assumed from him licence to do as they chose and rioted in Rome and in every other city for three years, till the end of his reign, for he was its supporter. In the third year of his reign, in Antioch of Syria, the supporters of the Blue faction of that city chanted in the theatre against the local Greens, "Time raises up and time casts down. The Greens are lechers!" Pronoios [read: Petronius], the consular governor, was watching at the time. There followed a great factional riot and disaster befell the city, for the Greeks of Antioch fought with the Jews of the city in a factional brawl, killed many of them, and burned their synagogues (*Chronographia* 10.20, p. 185 ed. Thurn).[9]

In another passage, dealing with the situation in the same city about 490 CE, during the reign of Zeno, Malalas writes:

Those of the Green faction in the city of Antioch started a stone fight against the Blues during a spectacle at the hippodrome, while Thalassios, the consular governor, was watching. (…) Six months later the Antiochenes of the Green faction gathered again and, during a riot at the hippodrome, killed many people. They burnt the synagogue called after Asabinos because the Jews were supporters of the Blues. They plundered all that was in the synagogue and those who lived there (*Chronographia* 15.15, p. 316 ed. Thurn).[10]

Malalas adds the lurid detail that, when Zeno was informed about the crimes of the Greens, he became angry because they had only burnt the dead Jews whereas they should have burnt the living ones as well![11] Somewhat later, in 507, Green hooligans also burned the synagogue in nearby Daphne and again killed many

---

[8] *Ibid.* 126.

[9] J. Thurn (ed.), *Ioannis Malalae Chronographia*, Berlin-New York 2000. I adapt the translation by E. Jeffreys, M. Jeffreys and R. Scott, *The Chronicle of John Malalas*, Melbourne 1986, 129–130. Cf. also M. Williams, *The Jews Among the Greeks and Romans: A Diaspora Sourcebook*, Baltimore 1998, 115. On this passage see B.J. Brooten, "The Jews of Ancient Antioch," in Chr. Kondoleon (ed.), *Antioch. The Lost Ancient City*, Princeton 2000, 31.

[10] Transl. Jeffreys, *ibid.* 218; Williams, *ibid.* 116.

[11] διὰ τί τοὺς νεκροὺς μόνον τῶν Ἰουδαίων ἔκαυσαν; ἐχρῆν γὰρ αὐτοὺς καὶ τοὺς ζῶντας Ἰουδαίους καῦσαι. Malalas, *Chron.* 15.15 (p. 317 ed. Thurn).

Jews.[12] Does all this imply that the Greens were Jew-haters and the Blues were not?

Cameron thinks this is very unlikely since "Jews were held in almost universal dislike among Christians by the fifth and sixth centuries," and he surmises that "the Blues of Zeno's day protected Jews less out of disinterested philo-Judaism than simply to annoy the Greens" (150). He points out that stories found in the *Doctrina Jacobi nuper baptizati* (mid-7th cent.) prove that either faction might persecute Jews and that Jews in turn might take their revenge on either faction. That is to say, "Jews can hardly be regarded as an issue that could be counted upon to *divide* the factions" (151). It should be added, though, that Cameron insufficiently takes into account that the *Doctrina* is a confused source on a very confused period in history.[13] He emphasizes again that the outbursts of violence were not caused by anti-Semitism; the anti-Jewish riots and outbursts of violence were always only *part* of a more encompassing agitation that had to do with factional hooliganism. "Once tempers were lost and the violence had begun, the original cause might be lost to view and (as at Antioch, and often elsewhere before and since) the unhappy Jews found themselves the victims" (151–2).

Yet we are left with the disturbing fact that, for the most part, the evidence, both literary and epigraphical, seems to suggest that to the Jews it *did* make a real difference whether they sided with the Blues or with the Greens, and that it was safer to be on the Blue side. Cameron's theory is somewhat unsatisfactory here. That the Blues protected the Jews "simply to annoy the Greens" (150), as he says, leaves unexplained why the Jews sided with the Blues. One need not follow Patricia Karlin-Hayter[14] when she suggests that the Jews had to side with the Blues because they, too, were in a sense an 'orthodox' party and because by following the less rowdy Blues they played safe. This is sheer speculation, and strange reasoning at that. Even so, one feels that Cameron's total exclusion of religious factors here has made an explanation of the Jews-Blues connection more difficult. Malalas' reports about consistent violence of Greens against Jews, *even before the Greens became Christians,* suggests that anti-Jewish sentiments did play a role here. Maybe Andrew Sharf[15] is right when he says that the Blues were usually much more likely to support the authorities and that it was, therefore, safer for the Jews to side with them.

---

[12] Malalas 16.6 (p. 324 ed. Thurn).

[13] See on Blues and Greens in the *Doctrina* G. Dagron et V. Déroche, "Juifs et Chrétiens dans l'Orient du VIIe siècle," *Travaux et Mémoires* 11 (1991) 235–237 (at pp. 70–219 of this lengthy study one finds a new critical edition and French translation of the *Doctrina Jacobi nuper baptizati*).

[14] "Les AKTA DIA KALAPODION," *Byzantion* 43 (1973) 96–97.

[15] A. Sharf, *Byzantine Jewry from Justinian to the Fourth Crusade*, London 1971, 10.

Charlotte Roueché,[16] however, more reasonably surmises that it was partly a matter of custom: Jews happened to have always had theatre or hippodrome seats in the sectors customarily occupied by the Blues. "In all these cases we have examples of pre-existing groups (the butchers, the gold-workers, the Jews, the residents of a particular area) who already had a tradition of sitting together at spectacles, becoming supporters of one colour or the other. For centuries the residents of cities all over the empire had assembled in the theatres and stadia of their cities, and had been seated according to their place in society. During those centuries, riots of one kind or another had often broken out" (131). She suggests that loyalty to the Blues and the Greens absorbed earlier forms of partisanship, and

"if such loyalties were adopted by pre-existing groups within the cities, this helps to explain why such partisanship, especially when it was suddenly empire-wide, came to seem so important and so threatening. (…) It seems likely that every auditorium became divided between Greens and Blues, and that to sit in a particular position, which may well have been the traditional seat of some particular association for centuries, was automatically to become a supporter of one colour or the other. (…) If we find, for example, Jews associated with Blues, or sail-makers associated with Greens, at more than one place in the empire, this might mean that such groups had traditionally sat in similar positions in different cities since the Roman period; such a hypothesis can only be proved or disproved as more inscriptions from auditoria are published" (*ibid.*)

Roueché's hypothesis makes sense, although it still leaves unexplained why, for example, when riots between Greens and Blues broke out, Jews were singled out for attacks. But she touches on an important point here.

As the social psychologist Muzafer Sherif has demonstrated in his influential research on intergroup relations,[17] when one has become associated with a certain group – by coincidence or, originally, for reasons that later do not matter any more – the mere awareness of other groups within the range of one's designs always generates a process of comparison between 'us' and 'the others.' In the course of time, even fundamental differences between oneself and other members of one's own group are completely overridden by the (real or presumed) differences between 'us' and these 'others.' Even great religious disagreements between members of the same group often become completely irrelevant rather soon once the overriding opposition to the others has become the dominant principle. Fidelity to one's own group and its members is then the only thing that matters, and usually this fidelity is strengthened by demonization of the others. To be a 'good' member of the group (e. g. Greens) "implies believing all the nasty qualities and practices attributed by one's group to the adversary."[18]

---

[16] Ch. Roueché, *Performers and Partisans at Aphrodisias in the Roman and Late Roman Periods*, London 1993, 130–131.

[17] See, e. g., his *Group Conflict and Co-operation. Their Social Psychology*, London 1967.

[18] Sherif, *Group Conflict* 14.

It also implies remaining deaf and blind to favourable and correct information concerning that adversary. It appears that "the *sufficient condition* for the rise of hostile and aggressive deeds (…) and for the standardization of social distance justified by derogatory images of the out-group is the existence of two groups competing for goals that only one group can attain."[19] And contact between hostile groups as equals in pleasant situations does not necessarily reduce conflict between them. Almost anyone can illustrate this kind of processes from his or her own experience.[20] And I would suggest that it is this kind of insight from social psychology, only hinted at by Roueché, that can be helpful in shedding further light on this intriguing historical problem. As the more homogeneous and, for that reason, perhaps more easily identifiable of the subgroups within the Blues, the Jews could more readily be singled out as representatives of the Blues for attacks by the Greens (we have to keep in mind that in the Roman and Byzantine periods the Jews of the greater towns and cities often tended to live in their own districts[21]). It is clear that much work remains to be done. Hopefully new sources will enable us to do that work.[22]

---

[19]   Sherif, *Group Conflict* 85 (italics his).

[20]   In the village where I live, there are two brass bands, one called 'The Royal Harmony' (De Koninklijke Harmonie) and the other 'Exercise is the Mother of Art' (Oefening Baart Kunst). Both bands comprise in equal measure an average sample of members of the village's society and they play equally well, so there are no real differences between these two groups aside from their membership of a different brass band; yet the mutual contempt and hatred is incredibly great! As Sherif, *Group Conflict* 38, remarks, "derogatory images are well documented between various groups in which cultural or national differences play little or no part."

[21]   See J. Starr, *The Jews in the Byzantine Empire*, New York 1939, 43–44.

[22]   I owe thanks to my colleague Prof. Willem Albert Wagenaar for his advice on the psychological aspects of the problem discussed.

A Note on the Evil Inclination and Sexual Desire
in Talmudic Literature

There are some factors that make it difficult to get a clear view of important aspects of rabbinic anthropology. For instance, there is as yet no critical edition of the most important literary corpus of early rabbinic Judaism, the Babylonian Talmud, and this impedes research to a considerable degree, for what solid conclusions could be based upon a not-solid textual basis? And there is also a lack of systematic thinking in Talmudic literature, which impedes us from drawing a consistent picture of rabbinic beliefs. It is, therefore, only to a limited extent that this literature gives us access to the ideas the rabbis developed about humankind.[1] Even so, it is possible to sketch some aspects of these ideas with a reasonable degree of clarity, as we will see in this short contribution.

The biblical concept that humankind's foundational distinction is that it was made in the image of God (Gen. 1:27) made R. Akiva remark: "Beloved (sc. to God) is man, in that he was created in the (divine) image; still more beloved in that it was made known to him that he was created in this image" (m. *Avoth* 3, 15). And Akiva definitely was not the only rabbi to cherish this idea. All the more striking is it that the rabbis developed the theory that an evil inclination or impulse was part of this image. The widespread Goethean concept of the existence of 'zwei Seelen in meiner Brust' was given expression by the early rabbis in a theory of two *yetsarim* ('inclinations, desires, passions, drives, impulses, bents of mind'), namely the *yetser ha-tov* (the desire to do good) and the *yetser ha-ra'* (the desire to do evil).[2]

---

[1] E. Stiegman, "Rabbinic Anthropology," *ANRW* II 19, 2, Berlin – New York 1979, 493–495.

[2] See F.C. Porter, "The Yeçer Hara: A Study in the Jewish Doctrine of Sin," in *Biblical and Semitic Studies: Yale Historical and Critical Contributions to Biblical Science*, New York 1901, 93–156 (in spite of its outdated approach, after more than a century still the best study!); S. Schechter, *Aspects of Rabbinic Theology: Major Concepts of the Talmud,* New York 1909 (repr. 1961) 242–292; E.E. Urbach, *The Sages. Their Concepts and Beliefs*, Jerusalem 1975, vol. I, 471–483; G. Cohen Stuart, *The Struggle in Man between Good and Evil. An Inquiry into the Origin of the Rabbinic Concept of Yetser Hara*, Kampen 1984; P.W. van der Horst, "Evil Inclination," in K. van der Toorn, B. Becking and P.W. van der Horst (eds.), *Dictionary of Deities and Demons in the Bible*, 2nd ed., Leiden – Grand Rapids 1999, 317–319. In these publications one finds a wealth of references to the rabbinic sources. The long passages in b. *Sukkah* 51b–52b, *Berakhoth* 60b–61b, and *Yoma* 69b–70b are among the most instructive rabbinic texts on theories about the evil inclination.

This theory may have had precursors in writings such as the pseudepigraphic *Testament of Asher* 1:3–9 and the Qumran document *1QS* 3:13–14,[3] but nowhere else do we find a comprehensive theory such as we have it in rabbinic literature. The notion of two opposing inclinations is a major feature of the anthropology of the rabbis. They found biblical support for this notion in the fact that in Gen. 2:7 ('the Lord God formed [*wayyetser*] man') the verb 'formed' is written not with one but with *two yods*, which is unusual and hence loaded with meaning:[4] It was God himself who had created humankind with *two yetsarim*, a good one and a bad one (see, e. g., b. *Berakhoth* 61a; *Sifre Deut.* 45). Moreover, Gen. 6:5 and 8:21 state explicitly that the inclination (*yetser*) of the human heart is continually evil (*ra'*), and it is so from its youth (cf. b. *Sanhedrin* 91b). Further biblical passages taken into service by the rabbis for this theory include Deut. 6:5 (and 11:13), where the Hebrew word used for 'heart,' *levav* instead of *lev*, has two *beths*, which is again taken by the rabbis as a sign that God created humankind with two inclinations (see, e. g., m. *Berakhoth* 9:5);[5] and also Gen. 4:7, Deut. 31:21 and Ps. 103:14 were interpreted accordingly.[6] Interestingly enough, according to a minority opinion (recorded in b. *Sukkah* 52b, j. *Ta'anit* III 4, 66c, and *Gen. Rabba* 27:4), God regretted having created the evil *yetser*.[7]

Even though there is some debate among the rabbis about the moment of the association of the evil inclination with humans (conception, birth, the age of ten?), the general notion seems to be that it accompanies a person from his or her earliest beginnings to old age, and for that reason it has a priority of some 13 years over the good inclination which makes its appearance only at the age of the *bar mitzwah* or puberty.[8] According to the rabbis, the good inclination induces humankind to keep God's commandments, but the evil one is the source of rebellion against God. But it is important to add that the good one never resides solely in the soul and the evil one only in the body; the seat of both of them is thought to be in the heart (*levav*!).[9] Even so the evil inclination is a necessary and even essential element in human life on earth in that it is also the source of sexual

---

[3] On which see H. Lichtenberger, *Studien zum Menschenbild in Texten der Qumrangemeinde*, Göttingen 1980, 123–142. Other possible predecessors of the concept of two *yetsarim* are discussed by Porter, "The Yeçer Hara" 136–156.

[4] G. F. Moore, *Judaism in the First Centuries of the Christian Era*, vol. I, Cambridge Mass. 1927, 484–5.

[5] Also biblical passages which use the plural of the word heart, e. g. Ps. 7:10 "For the righteous God probes the hearts," were interpreted as referring to the two *yetsarim*. See e. g. *Midrash Mishle* 12.

[6] Moore, *Judaism,* I 479–480.

[7] See Schechter, *Aspects*, 284–5; Porter, "The Yeçer Hara" 120–121.

[8] Schechter, *Aspects*, 252–255.

[9] Moore, *Judaism*, I 485, and, for the seat of both the good and the evil *yetser* in the heart, see esp. Porter, "The Yeçer Hara" 110–111. Here we observe an important difference between rabbinic Judaism and patristic Christianity; see P. Brown, *The Body and Society. Men, Women and Sexual Renunciation in Early Christianity*, New York 1988.

passion and hence of procreation (see Gen 1:28).[10] Life without the driving force of the evil inclination would be good but it would also be uncreative. For that reason the evil inclination will not be eradicated before the accomplishment of the world to come (*'olam ha-ba'*; see b. *Sukkah* 52a; cf. *Berakhoth* 17a and *Targum Ps-Jonathan* on Deut. 30:6).[11] According to a legend in b. *Yoma* 69b, the Men of the Great Synagogue wanted to kill the evil inclination, but they were warned that, if they were to do so, they would bring about the end of the world (cf. *Gen. Rabba* 9:7 quoted below). In general, however, the evil inclination is perceived as a threat to life according to God's will since, in addition to sexual desires, the concept also includes other passionate impulses, especially the passion for worshipping idols, but also anger, aggression, hatred, vanity, and unbridled ambition or lust for power (e. g., b. *Shabbath* 105b; *Gen. Rabba* 22:6; *Sifre Deut.* 33).[12]

As the originator of sin, the evil inclination is humankind's greatest and most implacable enemy. The best means of controlling this formidable tempter are the precepts of the Torah (b. *Qiddushin* 30b; *Sifre Deut.* 45; cf. Ben Sira 21:11). It is therefore incumbent upon believers to attempt to subdue it (m. *Avoth* 4:1) and to exercise severe self-control with the help of Torah study, prayer, and God's grace. They should have their good *yetser* wage war against the evil one (b. *Berakhoth* 5a; *Eccles. Rabba* 9:7). As the rabbis say in *Avodah Zarah* 5b: "As long as they [the Israelites] occupy themselves with study of the Torah and works of loving kindness, the evil inclination is mastered by them." Scholars are especially prone to submit to the evil *yetser*, since the greater the man the stronger his evil inclination, but serious study of Torah is sufficient to overcome it (b. *Sukkah* 52a).[13] The evil inclination was sometimes identified with Satan or the Angel of Death or a strange god (e. g., b. *Berakhoth* 61a; *Sukkah* 52a-b; *Bava Bathra* 16a; j. *Nedarim* 41b; *Exod. Rabba* 30:17). In parallel passages Satan and the evil impulse may be interchanged, as elsewhere are evil impulse and sin.[14] In this way it comes very close to the Pauline concept of personified Sin (e. g. Rom. 7:13–25). But in general the evil inclination is viewed as impersonal and equated with 'the heart of stone' in Ez. 36:26 (e. g., *Tanhuma* B: *Wayyikra* 12; *Cant. Rabba* I 2, 4).

All this stands in remarkable conflict with the fact that according to the biblical account the very first words God spoke to humankind were a command to

---

[10] D. Boyarin, *Carnal Israel. Reading Sex in Talmudic Culture*, Berkeley 1993, 61–67. It is obvious that angels do not have an evil inclination.

[11] More references in Porter, "The Yeçer Hara" 130–132.

[12] See Porter, "The Yeçer Hara" 111–116; Schechter, *Aspects*, 250–252; L. Jacobs, *The Jewish Religion: A Companion*, Oxford 1995, 608.

[13] Note the chapter title "Man's victory by the grace of God over the *Evil Yezer* created by God" in Schechter's *Aspects*, 264–292. For the Torah as antidote against the evil inclination see *Sifre Deut.* 45; b. *Qiddushin* 30b.

[14] See Moore, *Judaism*, I 492; Porter, "The Yeçer Hara" 121–122.

have sexual intercourse and procreate: "Be fruitful and multiply" (Gen. 1:28).[15] In rabbinic literature this biblical ideal of founding a family is fully endorsed. "Nobody may abstain from keeping the law *Be fruitful and multiply*," says the Mishnah (*Yevamot* 6:6). Rabbinic dicta to the effect that the unmarried state is disapproved of are found frequently.[16] And it is for this very reason that many Jews of the first centuries "had a sense that they were commanded by God to do that which God himself considered sinful."[17] That this is not just an exaggerated statement by a modern scholar is demonstrated by the fact that in the Talmud Resh Lakish says, "Let us ascribe merit to our ancestors for, if they had not *sinned*, we should not have come into the world" (*Avoda Zara* 5a). 'Sinned' is here the equivalent of 'had sexual intercourse.'[18] Thus by strictly obeying the first of God's commandments the Israelites sinned, because the sexual drive is inspired by the evil inclination! It is for that reason that another rabbi can say, "How can a human being escape from the evil impulse within him, when the first drop of semen a man puts into a woman is the evil impulse?" (*Avoth de Rabbi Nathan* rec. A 16).[19] The tension that is evident here is well worded by R. Acha when he says, commenting upon Ps. 51:5 ("I was brought forth in iniquity and in sin did my mother conceive me"), that in sexual intercourse, even if one is the most pious and saintly person, it is totally impossible that one should have no streak of iniquity or sin in him: "David said before the Holy one, blessed be He, 'Oh Lord of the universe, did my father Jesse have the intention of bringing me into the world?' Why, his intention was his own enjoyment; the proof for this is that after they had accomplished their desire, he turned his face in one direction and she turned her face in the opposite direction, and it was Thou that caused every single drop (of semen) to enter, and this is what David meant when he said, 'Though my father and my mother forsook me, the Lord did gather me in' (Ps. 27:10)" (*Lev. Rabba* 14:5). As Boyarin remarks, the irony that sexual desire is the agent of the first positive commandment in the Torah could not escape the

---

[15] See for the 'Wirkungsgeschichte' of this verse J. Cohen, *"Be Fertile and Increase, Fill the Earth and Master It." The Ancient and Medieval Career of a Biblical Text*, Ithaca-London 1989. According to D. Boyarin, *A Radical Jew. Paul and the Politics of Identity*, Berkeley 1994, 158–179, it is this commandment that is referred to by Paul as 'another law' when he says in Rom. 7:23: "I see in my members another law at war with the law of my mind, making me captive to the law of sin that dwells in my members."

[16] More references in Moore, *Judaism,* II 119–120, and H. McArthur, "Celibacy in Judaism at the Time of Christian Beginnings," *Andrews University Seminary Studies* 25 (1987) 163–181, esp. 164–168. Cf. P.W. van der Horst, "Celibacy in Early Judaism," *RB* 109 (2002) 390–402.

[17] Boyarin, *Radical Jew*, 159.

[18] So rightly Stiegman, "Rabbinic Anthropology" 516, and Boyarin, *Carnal Israel,*52–53, against the annotators of the Soncino translation.

[19] J. Goldin, *The Fathers According to Rabbi Nathan*, New Haven 1955, 85. Cf. also the version in *ARN* rec. B 30, and A.J. Saldarini, *The Fathers According to Rabbi Nathan*, Leiden 1975, 177–178.

rabbis.[20] Since the sexual act is usually and inevitably also performed with the purpose of satisfying physical desires, rather than solely with the purpose of begetting a child, sin is duly involved. This intractable problem could have been avoided if the rabbis had decided to attribute sexual desire to the *good yetser*. If God commands humankind to procreate, nothing would be more obvious than attributing the sexual urge that is the necessary prerequisite for this procreation, to the good impulse in humans. Why, then, did the rabbis not do that?

They did not do that because they viewed sensual pleasure with fundamental suspicion. For the very same reason why the Greeks made *eros* into a god (Eros), the rabbis degraded *eros*, in the sense of passionate desire, to the level of a dangerous and sinful affection or affliction. The overwhelming and insatiable character of *eros* induced the Greeks to deify it, because they drew no sharp distinction between the passionate desire and the deity who brought it about.[21] Some Greek authors even regarded Eros as the greatest of all gods.[22] Deification was of course not an option in the Jewish world, but demonization was. As early as the beginning of the first century CE, the Jewish wisdom poet Pseudo-Phocylides stated it clearly: "Do not deliver yourself wholly to unbridled *eros* towards your wife [or: a woman], for *eros* is not a god but a passion destructive of all!" (193–194). It is the potentially destructive character of *eros* as an unbridled and insatiable passion that made it impossible, both for Pseudo-Phocylides and for the later rabbis, to view it in a positive light. This nature of *eros* is already highlighted by the LXX translator of Prov. 30:16 (which has no equivalent in the Hebrew Bible), where the author enumerates examples of insatiability, which include Hades, fire, and also passion for a woman, *erôs gynaikos*.[23] It is this almost demonic nature of erotic desire that made it become the domain of the evil *yetser*. The demonic view is well illustrated by the story about R. Eliezer ben Hyrkanos in b. *Nedarim* 20b, where his wife says about him that when he has intercourse with her, it is as if he is compelled by a demon; he uncovers only an inch of her body and after the act he immediately covers it again. "The story represents a highly negative attitude toward sexual pleasure. Rabbi Eliezer's behavior as if driven by a demon apparently represents his conviction that he is fulfilling an obligation that should not be enjoyed but should be performed as

---

[20] Boyarin, *Radical Jew* 160.

[21] See P.W. van der Horst, "Eros," in *DDD* 304–306.

[22] For evidence see P.W. van der Horst, *The Sentences of Pseudo-Phocylides*, Leiden 1978, 240–241. There one also finds evidence of different opinions of authors who polemicized against this overrating of Eros.

[23] The Greek could also be translated as 'passion of a woman;' see D.M. d'Hamonville, *La Bible d'Alexandrie 17: Les Proverbes*, Paris 2000, 302–303. The only other occurrence of *eros* in the LXX is again in Prov., in 7:18, where a prostitute addresses a young man with the words, "Come on, let us drown ourselves in passion!" The negative overtones of *eros* are obvious here.

quickly as possible."[24] But this is a rather extreme case, and usually, certainly in the Amoraic period,[25] the rabbis stopped short of calling the evil inclination demonic or satanic (some exceptions notwithstanding)[26] for the simple reason that this *yetser* also inspired men and women to their various creative acts, including the procreation demanded by God.

It was for that reason that some of the rabbis could even say that the words "And behold, it was very good" (Gen. 1:31), spoken after the completion of the creation, refer to the evil inclination: "Can then the evil inclination be good? That is incredible! Without the evil inclination, however, no man would build a house, take a wife and beget children, or engage in trade" (*Gen. Rabba* 9:7). As Boyarin stresses, however, far from being a simple legacy of its cultural heritage, "the rabbinic insistence on the positive value of sexuality seems to have been hard won and contested."[27] If one and the same power, the evil inclination, is the driving force behind, or the source of, both idolatry and sexuality, how could the latter ever be good? One cannot have only half of this *yetser*, without its negative and destructive concomitants. If there is to be desire at all, there is bound to be also the possibility of illicit desire. But the destructive concomitants have to be, and can be, curbed and suppressed, and God, who created the evil *yetser*, gives humankind the means to do so. As part of God's creation, which is 'very good' (Gen. 1:31), the 'evil' inclination is 'good' as well. One need not resort here to the forced hypothesis of Boyarin: "My hypothesis is that the Rabbis inherited the term 'Evil Instinct' from a first-century Judaism much more averse to sexuality than they were, and unable to dispense with it, they ironized the term – 'The Evil Instinct is very good.'"[28] There is no proof whatever that the rabbis inherited a term that they actually disgreed with, on the contrary, there is clear evidence that they themselves invented and coined it. It was their concept of God as the creator of humankind in His image that forbade them to see in the 'evil inclination' nothing but evil. Most of the actions inspired by this *yetser* were evil indeed, but the act of procreation could not be evil since God himself commanded humankind to perform it, albeit only within narrowly circumscribed circumstances. The fact that *most* (though not *all*) of these actions are evil gave it its negative designation, *yetser hara'*. But that does not exclude the fact that it could incidentally be the source of a good act, namely that of procreation. "It is called the Evil Desire solely because of its destructive side, *from which it cannot escape*, but at the

---

[24] Boyarin, *Carnal Israel*, 47.

[25] In some of the later rabbinic texts there is even room for a viewpoint in which sexual intercourse that does not take place for the sake of procreation is regarded in a positive light; see Boyarin, *Carnal Israel*, 53–55.

[26] The evil inclination was sometimes identified with Satan; see above.

[27] *Carnal Israel*, 61.

[28] Boyarin, *Carnal Israel*, 63. For criticism of Boyarin's position see D. Winston, "Philo and the Rabbis on Sex and the Body," in his *The Ancestral Philosophy. Hellenistic Philosophy in Second Temple Judaism*, ed. by G.E. Sterling, Providence 2001, 199–219.

same time there is full recognition not only of the necessity for desire but of its very positive overtones."[29] For that reason it is possible to worship God not only with one's good but even with one's evil *yetser*, as is said in m. *Berakhoth* 9:5 (on the basis of the double *beth* of *levav* in Deut. 6:5 and 11:13, 'love/serve the Lord your God with all your heart'). 'Good' is here inseparable from 'evil' since they derive from one and the same source.

Inevitably, in such a 'dialectical' anthropology, tension and ambiguity remain. As Stiegman expresses it: "Sexuality is good and evil, constructive and destructive, a duty and a misfortune, beautiful and shameful."[30] In the sexual act good and evil are inextricably bound up. The joyful aspect of it is that it is done in fulfilment of a divine command; the deplorable aspect is that it is impossible to do it without lust or desire. And it is this desire that can unfold its destructive aspects as well. In a kind of prefiguration of the rabbinic view, the author of the *Testament of Reuben* had said about 'the spirit of procreation' that is given to humankind at creation that "with it sin comes in through fondness for pleasure" (2:8).[31] In practice, however, love of pleasure was not always rejected as sinful. Even in the Talmud we find some passages where non-reproductive sexual intercourse is viewed as something good. For instance, sex was permitted with pregnant wives and even encouraged with menopausal wives, and in some cases contraception was deemed permissible.[32] So the reality of life could mitigate the rabbinic principles, but the fundamental tension and ambiguity caused by the rabbis' problematic ideology of sex was never really resolved.

---

[29] Boyarin, *Carnal Israel*, 63.

[30] "Rabbinic Anthropology" 516.

[31] Cf. Philo, *Spec.* 3.313, on pleasure-lovers whose sexual activity resembles that of "pigs and goats in quest of the enjoyment that such intercourse gives."

[32] For references see the chapter entitled "The Legitimacy of Sexual Pleasure" in D.M. Feldman, *Birth Control in Jewish Law*, New York 1968, 81–105. Urbach, *Sages*, I 478.

"His Days Shall Be One Hundred and Twenty Years"

Genesis 6:3 in Early Judaism and Ancient Christianity

When mankind had become corrupted in the period preceding the flood, God said: "My spirit shall not abide in man for ever, for he is flesh; his days shall be a hundred and twenty years" (Gen. 6:3). Ancient interpreters, both Jews and Christians, did not agree about the interpretation of these words. It would seem fitting to discuss the various views of this limitation of mankind's lifespan to 120 years on the occasion of the celebration of our esteemed colleague Albert van der Heide's 60th birthday, since he has now achieved half this span.

Our earliest evidence for the interpretation of this text is to be found in the Septuagint (LXX). The Greek translation of the Pentateuch was completed somewhere in the first half of the third century BCE. This early Bible translation renders the verse as follows: "My spirit will certainly not remain in these people because they are flesh, but their days will be 120 years." Instead of the generic *'adam* of the MT, the LXX has *'these* people' and therefore also *'their* days.' By adding the demonstrative 'these' (*toutois*), the translator makes clear that he takes God's threat to apply only to the evildoers of Noah's days.[1] This interpretation most probably owes its origin to the fact that many individuals who inhabited the earth after the time of the flood are recorded as having lived longer than 120 years.[2] In Gen. 7:6, Noah is said to have been 600 years when the flood began, and in Gen. 9:29 he dies after a life of 950 years. Moreover, his son Shem dies at 600, and others exceeded the 120 years as well (see Gen. 11:11.13.15.17.19.21 etc.). Also Abraham, Isaac and Jacob exceeded the lifespan of 120 years. In Deut. 34:7, however, Moses dies at the age of 120 years and that number is probably to be viewed in the light of Gen. 6:3: Moses, the ideal man, is granted the maximum lifespan that is possible for a human being after God's decree in Gen. 6:3. But the LXX translator had to solve a difficulty that arose from the Hebrew text as it stands, so he could not take it at face value.[3] In his view, "God was talking

---

[1] See M. Harl e.a., *La Genèse* (La Bible d'Alexandrie, vol. 1), Paris 1986, 125–126.

[2] Thus A. Kamesar, *Jerome, Greek Scholarship and the Hebrew Bible. A Study of the Quaestiones Hebraicae in Genesim*, Oxford 1993, 185.

[3] In the Vulgate Jerome keeps strictly to the wording of the Hebrew text, in spite of what he writes in his *Quaestiones Hebraicae in Genesim* 6:3, quoted below in the text. The Jewish Bible translator Symmachus seems to have followed the LXX here.

only about a particular group of humans, the generation of the flood."[4] Because they are so wicked, God will destroy this antediluvial generation at an early age (relatively early, that is, for those days). For our translator, "God's words did not announce a fundamental change in human longevity."[5]

As Kugel has pointed out, the same interpretation is also found in another early document, the *Genesis Pesher* of Qumran, where we read that in the four hundred and eightieth year of Noah's life God said: "My spirit will not reside in man for ever. Their days shall be fixed at 120 years until the time of the flood" (*4Q252*, col. 1, 2–3).[6] Since Noah was 600 (480+120) years when the flood began, it is clear that the 120 years are here the time until the flood. Here it would seem that the plural 'their' in stead of 'his' has the same function as in the LXX, and this limitation of the measure to the generation of the flood is, moreover, underscored by the addition of the words 'until the time of the flood.' There can be no doubt that here we have another witness to the exegetical tradition we met first in the LXX. Also *Jubilees* 5:8 ("their days ...") implies the same interpretation.[7]

We now make a big chronological jump in order to take a look at other Jewish Bible translations from (late) antiquity, the Targums.[8] Let us begin with *Neofiti 1*, on which we now have the fine commentary by Bernard Grossfeld.[9] Our text is rendered by the meturgeman as follows: "None of the generations yet to arise will be judged according to the order of the judgment of the generation of the flood. Behold, the order of the judgment of the generation of the flood has been sealed before him: to be destroyed and blotted out from the midst of the world. Behold, I have put my spirit in the sons of man because they are flesh and their deeds are evil. Behold, I have given the span of 120 years (in the hope that) perhaps they might do repentance, but they have not done so."[10] The train of thought in this 'translation' seems to be as follows: Never again will God judge future generations in the same way as the generation of the flood. God implanted

---

[4] J. L. Kugel, *Traditions of the Bible. A Guide to the Bible As It Was at the Start of the Common Era*, Cambridge (MA) – London 1998, 184.

[5] Kugel, *Traditions* 183.

[6] See J. Maier, *Die Qumran-Essener: Die Texte vom Toten Meer* II, München-Basel 1995, 194 with n. 284, and esp. F. García Martínez, "Interpretations of the Flood in the Dead Sea Scrolls," in F. García Martínez & G.P. Luttikhuizen (eds.), *Interpretations of the Flood*, Leiden 1999, 86–108, esp. 99 ff. with extensive bibliography at 100 nn. 36–37. Also J.L. Trafton, "Commentary on Genesis A," in J.H. Charlesworth e.a. (eds.), *The Dead Sea Scrolls, vol. VIB: Pesharim, Other Commentaries, and Related Documents*, Tübingen-Louisville 2002, 207–209.

[7] See J.T.A.G.M. Ruiten, "The Interpretation of the Flood Story in the Book of Jubilees," in García Martínez & Luttikhuizen (eds.), *Interpretations* 83.

[8] For the dating of the Targums to the Torah see U. Gleßmer, *Einleitung in die Targume zum Pentateuch*, Tübingen 1995, passim.

[9] B. Grossfeld, *Targum Neofiti 1: An Exegetical Commentary to Genesis*, New York 2000.

[10] Translation by M. McNamara, *Targum Neofiti 1: Genesis* (The Aramaic Bible 1A), Edinburgh 1992, 72.

his spirit in mankind in order that they might do good, but since they are also flesh, their deeds are evil. For that reason God gave mankind 120 years, so that they might repent, but they didn't. It has to be pointed out that the words about the giving of a span of 120 years probably have to be understood as an extension, in view of the fact that in the other targumim this is explicitly indicated by the word *'rk'* (extension). Thus Targum Pseudo-Jonathan has: "I gave them an extension of 120 years that they might repent, but they have not done so."[11] The Fragment Targum has: "I gave them an extension of 120 years so that they might do repentance, but they have not done so."[12] And Targum Onkelos reads: "Let an extension be granted to them for 120 years to see if they will repent."[13] Finally we also read in a midrashic work, *Mekhilta deR. Ishmael, Beshallach* 5 (p. 38b): "For you gave an extension to the generation of the flood that they might repent, but they did not repent, as it is said, 'My spirit shall not abide in man.'" Mankind had been given by God an extra opportunity to repent, but they did not profit from this 'Gnadenzeit.'[14]

From the rabbis we now go back to earlier Jewish interpreters. Philo of Alexandria, who based his exegesis upon the LXX, remarks that the 120 years' limit was meant for Noah's contemporaries: "Why shall 'the days of man be 120 years'? By this number (Scripture) seems to limit human life. (…) But perhaps 120 years are not the universal limit of human life, but only of the men living at that time, who were later to perish in the flood after so great a number of years, which a benevolent benefactor prolonged, allowing repentance for sin" (*Quaestiones et solutiones in Genesim* I 91).[15] Here we see the rabbinic interpretation being anticipated. But half a century after Philo, the Jewish historian Flavius Josephus renders our passage as follows: "God loved this man [Noah] because of his righteousness, but did not condemn the others alone for their wickedness, it also seemed best to him to destroy all humanity, as many as there were at that time, and to create another race free of knavery, cutting short their lives and establishing their life expectancy not as formerly but at 120 years" (*Antiquitates Judaicae* I 75).[16] It is clear that Josephus interpreted Gen. 6:3 as meaning that the human lifespan had been reduced by God to 120 years for ever, not just for Noah's generation. And he was certainly not alone in that view.

---

[11] Translation by M. Maher, *Targum Pseudo-Jonathan: Genesis* (The Aramaic Bible 1B), Edinburgh 1992, 38.

[12] M. Klein, *The Fragment Targums of the Pentateuch*, vol. 2, Rome 1980, 10.

[13] A. Sperber, *The Bible in Aramaic*, vol. 1, Leiden 1992, 9.

[14] References to other passages with this motif can be found in R. Le Déaut, *Targum du Pentateuque I: Genèse*, Paris 1978, 114, and in L. Ginzberg, *The Legends of the Jews*, vol. 5, Philadelphia 1925, 174 n. 19. One might add *Avoth deR. Nathan* (A) 32 and *Bereshit Rabba* XXVI 6.

[15] Ch. Mercier (ed.), *Quaestiones et solutiones in Genesim I* (Les oeuvres de Philon d'Alexandrie 34A), Paris 1979, 165–171

[16] Translation by L.H. Feldman, *Flavius Josephus, vol. 3: Judaean Antiquities 1–4*, Leiden 2000, 28–29.

His contemporary, the anonymous author of the *Liber Antiquitatum Biblicarum* commonly called Pseudo-Philo, makes clear he was of the same opinion when he writes that the Lord said to Pinchas: "Behold you have passed the 120 years that have been established for every man" (*LAB* 48,1).[17] Of course Josephus and others with the same opinion were aware of the problem that after the flood so many persons lived much longer than 120 years. Their solution was different, however. Elsewhere Josephus says that Abraham's father Terah died at the age of 205: "For already the life expectancy was being shortened and was becoming briefer until the birth of Moses, after whom God set the limit of life at 120 years, the number that Moses also happened to live" (*Ant. Jud.* I 152). To put it in other words: God's decree to curtail human life to 120 years was carried out in stages. Only when Moses appeared on the scene was it definitive: after Moses no one ever got older than 120. This leaves room for the many biblical persons between Noah and Moses who exceeded this limit. Again a 'Gnadenzeit'![18]

Let us finally look very briefly at comparable material from early Christian sources. Julius Africanus, a Christian chronographer who was born in Jerusalem about 160 CE, writes that God decided to destroy mankind and that mankind's life would never again exceed 120 years. He then adds that one should not see a problem in the fact that after that decree people lived on for a considerable time, for the sinners of that generation were all 20 years old and the flood took place 100 years after God's decree. So they did not exceed the limit (fragm. 7 as quoted by Syncellus, *Ecloga chronographica* 38, pp. 21–2 Mosshammer). Africanus unfortunately does not address the problem of the many people who lived longer than 120 years after the flood.

The Church Father Jerome, who lived for many years in Bethlehem, does not agree, for he writes: "Lest God might seem to be cruel on the grounds that he had not given a place of repentance for sinners, he added: 'But their days shall be 120 years.' This means they shall have 120 years to do penance. So human life is not shortened to 120 years, as many mistakenly suppose, but 120 years were given to that generation for repentance. For indeed we find that after the flood Abraham lived for 175 years and others more than 200 or 300 years" (*Quaestiones in Genesim* 6:3).[19]

---

[17] Translation by H. Jacobson, *A Commentary on Pseudo-Philo's* Liber Antiquitatum Biblicarum, vol. 1, Leiden 1996, 172.

[18] In *Ant.* I 98–99, Josephus has Noah pray that the survivors of the flood may come 'to good old age and length of life similar to that of men previously,' and God promises 'that he would fulfill these prayers.' So it may be that, apart from the explanation offered in *Ant.* I 152 quoted above in the text, Josephus also believed that the longevity after the flood was due to God's promise to fulfill Noah's prayer, albeit temporarily. I owe this suggestion to my doctoral student, Tessel Jonquière.

[19] Translation by C.T.R. Hayward, *Saint Jerome's* Hebrew Questions on Genesis, Oxford 1995, 37. I owe the reference to Jerome to A. Louth (ed.), *Ancient Christian Commentary on Scripture, Old Testament, vol. I: Genesis 1–11*, Downers Grove 2001, 124–5, who also quotes Ephrem's commentary on Genesis *ad locum*.

Augustine devotes a paragraph to the problem of the 120 years in his *City of God*: "To pass to God's saying that 'their days will be a 120 years,' that is not to be taken as foretelling that after this men would not exceed 120 years, since we find that after the flood, as well as before, men surpassed even 500 years. We must realize that God said this when Noah had nearly completed 500 years, that is, he was in his 480th year, which is called the 500th year in Scripture, in accordance with its general practice of using round numbers for a total only slightly less. Now we know that the flood happened in the 600th year of Noah's life, in the second month, and thus the prediction meant that men who were going to perish would live 120 years more, and at the end of that period they would be wiped out by the flood" (*Civ. Dei* XV 24).[20]

Even from these few examples it becomes clear that in Christian sources we find the same variety of interpretation as in the Jewish material. This is not only because the Christian scholars had to face the same interpretational problems as the Jews, but also because some of them were informed about the solutions proposed by their Jewish contemporaries. Africanus and Jerome certainly had gained knowledge of Jewish biblical interpretation during their longlasting sojourns in the Holy Land.[21]

---

[20] Translation by H. Bettenson, *Augustine: Concerning the City of God*, Harmondsworth 1972, 642. Further references to Christian writers can be found in Ginzberg, *Legends* V 174.

[21] See, e. g., the evidence collected in W. Adler, *Time Immemorial. Archaic History and its Sources in Christian Chronography from Julius Africanus to George Syncellus*, Washington 1989, and A. Kamesar, *Jerome, Greek Scholarship and the Hebrew Bible. A Study of the Quaestiones Hebraicae in Genesim*, Oxford 1993.

Inscriptiones Judaicae Orientis

A Review Article[1]

The speed of recent developments in the scholarly study of early Jewish epigraphy is high. When I published my introduction to the study of Jewish inscriptions in 1991,[2] I could mention as the sources at our disposal only the outdated collection by Frey (CIJ),[3] and partial collections such as that of the inscriptions of Rome by Leon,[4] of Beth She'arim by Mazar, Schwabe, Lifshitz, and Avigad,[5] of Egypt by Lewis,[6] of the Cyrenaica by Lüderitz,[7] and of the rest of North Africa by Le Bohec.[8] Further there were of course a large number of articles with publications of inscriptions scattered over a very wide variety of journals in many languages. Now, only 13 years later, the situation has improved dramatically.

In 1992 William Horbury and David Noy published their *Jewish Inscriptions of Graeco-Roman Egypt*;[9] in 1993 Noy alone published the first volume of his *Jewish Inscriptions of Western Europe I: Italy (excluding the City of*

---

[1] The books reviewed here are the three volumes of the series *Inscriptiones Judaicae Orientis:* Vol. I, *Eastern Europe*, Texts and Studies in Ancient Judaism (TSAJ) 101, edd. David Noy, Alexander Panayotov & Hanswulf Bloedhorn, Tübingen: Mohr Siebeck, 2004; xvi+398 pp. (ISBN 3–16–148189–5); Vol. II: *Kleinasien*, TSAJ 99, ed. Walter Ameling, Tübingen: Mohr Siebeck, 2004; xviii+650 pp. (ISBN 3–16–148196–8); Vol. III: *Syria and Cyprus*, TSAJ 102, edd. David Noy & Hanswulf Bloedhorn, Tübingen: Mohr Siebeck, 2004; xvi+284 pp. (ISBN 3–16–148188–7).

[2] Pieter W. van der Horst, *Ancient Jewish Epitaphs: An Introductory Survey of a Millennium of Jewish Funerary Epigraphy (300 BCE–700 CE)*, Kampen 1991.

[3] J.-B. Frey, *Corpus Inscriptionum Judaicarum. Recueil des inscriptions juives qui vont du IIIe siècle avant Jésus-Christ au VIIe siècle de notre ère,* 2 vols., Rome 1936–1952. This work will be referred to as CIJ. Vol. 1 was reprinted in 1975 by Baruch Lifshitz, who wrote a very extensive Prolegomenon in which he proposed a considerable number of corrections and additions.

[4] H.J. Leon, *The Jews of Ancient Rome*, Philadelphia 1960, 263–346.This work was reprinted with *addenda et corrigenda* by C. Osiek, Peabody 1995.

[5] B. Mazar, *Beth She'arim I*, Jerusalem 1973; M. Schwabe – B. Lifshitz, *Beth She'arim II*, 1974; N. Avigad, *Beth She'arim III*, 1976.

[6] D.M. Lewis in an Appendix to V. A. Tcherikover – A. Fuks – M. Stern, *Corpus Papyrorum Judaicarum,* 3 vols., Cambridge (Mass.) 1957–1964, vol. III, 138–166.

[7] G. Lüderitz, *Corpus jüdischer Zeugnisse aus der Cyrenaica*, Wiesbaden 1983.

[8] Y. le Bohec, "Inscriptions juives et judaïsantes de l'Afrique Romaine," *Antiquités Africaines* 17 (1981) 165–207.

[9] Cambridge 1992. See my review in *JSJ* 25 (1994) 320–323. Abbr. *JIGRE*.

Rome), Spain and Gaul;[10] and in 1995 the second volume appeared as *Jewish Inscriptions of Western Europe II: The City of Rome.*[11] In the same period L.Y. Rahmani published his *A Catalogue of Jewish Ossuaries in the Collections of the State of Israel.*[12] In 1999 E. Leigh Gibson published *The Jewish Manumission Inscriptions of the Bosporus Kingdom.*[13] Also in 1999, E. Miranda published the Jewish inscriptions of the Jewish community in Phrygian Hierapolis.[14] And in 2001 John Kroll finally published the Greek inscriptions of the Sardis synagogue in *HTR* (they were found some 40 years before).[15] And there was of course the usual host of minor publications in various journals.[16] The zenith of this epigraphic activity, however, was reached in 2004, when the long awaited three volumes of the *Inscriptiones Judaicae Orientis* (henceforth *IJudO*) were published simultaneously.[17] It is these new volumes that will be the focus of the rest of this article.

Let me begin by stating that the name of David Noy now appears on the title page of no less than 5 volumes with Jewish inscriptions, in 2 cases as the only name, in 3 cases combined with one or two others. Noy has been the driving force behind this whole enterprise for a long time and he may rightfully be re-garded as the 'Frey' of our days, although the quality of his work surpasses that of Frey. After having covered (South-) Western Europe in the earlier volumes mentioned above, he has now turned to the Eastern part of the continent. The great extent of the progress made since Frey can be easily gauged when we see that, of the roughly 540 inscriptions published in *IJudO*, some 310 were not to be found in the old *CIJ*, *i. e.*, an impressive increase of almost 60%! In vol. 1 Noy c.s. cover ancient Pannonia, Dalmatia, Moesia, Thrace, Macedonia, Thessaly, Attica, the rest of the Greek mainland, the Greek islands (but not Cyprus), Crete,

---

[10] Cambridge 1993. See my review in *JTS* n.s. 45 (1994) 701–704. Abbr. *JIWE* I.

[11] Cambridge 1995. See my review in *JTS* n.s. 47 (1996) 256–259.Abbr. *JIWE* II.

[12] Jerusalem 1994.

[13] Tübingen 1999. See also Appendix 3 (Inscriptions from the Bosporan Kingdom) in I. Levinskaya, *The Book of Acts in Its First-Century Setting*, vol. 5: *Diaspora Setting*, Grand Rapids – Carlisle 1996, 228–246.

[14] E. Miranda, "La comunità giudaica di Hierapolis di Frigia," *Epigraphica Anatolica* 31 (1999) 109–156.

[15] John H. Kroll, "The Greek Inscriptions of the Sardis Synagogue," *HTR* 94 (2001) 5–127. See my discussion of this publication in "De synagoge van Sardis en haar inscripties," in my *Joden in de Grieks-Romeinse wereld*, Zoetermeer 2003, 40–49 [in English translation elsewhere in this volume].

[16] For short surveys see M. H. Williams, "Jewish Inscriptions of the Graeco-Roman Period – An Update," *Bulletin of Judaeo-Greek Studies* 33 (2003–2004) 40–46. For the importance of epigraphical material for the study of ancient Judaism in general see M.H. Williams, "The Contribution of Jewish Inscriptions to the Study of Judaism," in W. Horbury e.a. (eds.), *The Cambridge History of Judaism, vol. III: The Early Roman Period*, Cambridge 1999, 75–93. It may be added here that there is now also a new, third edition of the authoritative *Guide de l'épigraphiste*, edd. F. Bérard et alii, Paris 2000, but unfortunately it is very weak on Jewish epigraphy.

[17] See note 1.

and the North coast of the Black Sea. To be fair, it should be added immediately that much of the work for this volume has been done by Alexander Panayotov and, to a lesser degree, Hanswulf Bloedhorn – Noy is mainly responsible for the sections on Pannonia and the Black Sea, but he has contributed considerably to the sections covered by the two other scholars.

Noy briefly mentions the criteria for inclusion (how to tell a Jewish from a non-Jewish inscription): (i) the use of Hebrew; (ii) the use of specifically Jewish symbols; (iii) the use of Jewish terminology or designations; (iv) the use of distinctively Jewish names, in contexts where their use does not seem more likely to be Christian than Jewish; (v) provenance from a synagogue; (vi) reference to famous Jews; (vii) reference to Samaritans; (viii) some Bosporan manumissions have been included because of their similarity to Jewish manumissions from the area and the lack of indication that they are not Jewish. It is clear that some of these criteria are more decisive than others. Criteria (i), (ii), (iii), and (v) are obviously the most unambiguous and can stand on their own. As to the use of Jewish names (iv), the criterion of "contexts where their use does not seem more likely to be Christian than Jewish" is, however, much more slippery, and it is for that reason that I have advocated the position that this criterion should never be used in isolation but always in combination with one of the more solid criteria in order to be on the safe side.[18] Since Noy c.s. do not follow this advice, they include quite a number of very dubious cases (e. g., Mac14 and Mac16 are included only because of the occurrence of the names Benjamin and Abraham, which were used by Christians as well, and there is no context suggesting Jewishness; cf. also Ach15). References to famous Jews (vi) may also occur in inscriptions that are non-Jewish, but it is reasonable and useful to include them. Reference to Samaritans (vii) is to be welcomed as a criterion since there is no corpus of Samaritan inscriptions, and there probably could not be one since so often Samaritan inscriptions are impossible to distinguish from Jewish ones,[19] and for the sake of completeness they should be included. The problem here is, however, that quite often it is impossible to tell a Samaritan from a 'Samarian,' *i. e.*, a (non-Samaritan) native from Samaria (see further below). The inclusion of inscribed Samaritan amulets is most welcome (e. g. Ach50). That some non-explicitly Jewish Bosporan manumission inscriptions were included as well is reasonable, even though the lack of complete certainty about their Jewishness has to be kept in mind.

---

[18] *Ancient Jewish Epitaphs* 16–18. See also the cautions by R.S. Kraemer, "Jewish Tuna and Christian Fish: Identifying Religious Affiliation in Epigraphic Sources," *HTR* 84 (1991) 141–162.

[19] See the discussion of this problem in my "Samaritans at Rome?" in my book *Japheth in the Tents of Shem: Studies on Jewish Hellenism in Antiquity*, Leuven 2002, 257–258. On the absence of a corpus of Samaritan inscriptions see also my "The Samaritan Languages of the Pre-Islamic Period," *ibid.* 236–237.

It is striking that, whereas Noy devotes less than one page of his Preface to the problem of the criteria for inclusion,[20] Walter Ameling, the sole editor of *IJudO* II (Asia Minor), devotes a chapter of 14 pages to it (8–21). Ameling begins with a survey of ancient debates over 'who is a Jew?' The ever shifting borders of Judaism according to the different interpretations of its various groups are a source of much uncertainty in this matter. He then first lists five criteria for Jewishness which identify an inscription certainly as Jewish: (i) The identification of persons as *Ioudaioi*; Ameling rightly rejects the geographical (person from Judaea) and the onomastic (*Ioudaios* as proper name) interpretation. (ii) Mention of Jewish *realia*, such as Jewish feasts, their Holy Scriptures, synagogues, etc. Here, however, one should not rule out the possibility that Jewish-Christian groups could refer to the same *realia*. (iii) Provenance from unquestionably Jewish buildings such as synagogues or exclusively Jewish catacombs (such as Beth She'arim). (iv) Occurrence of Jewish symbols such as menorah, lulav, ethrog, shofar etc. Ameling does concede, however, that sometimes Christians used some of these symbols. (v) The use of Hebrew, which was the sacred language of none but the Jews. As we see, two of these criteria are less than 100% certain indicators of Jewishness,[21] so they might perhaps better have been included in the following list, where Ameling mentions four additional criteria of a more disputed nature. (vi) Proper names are a hard-to-use criterion, as is the designation 'Godfearers' (*theosebeis*, which can also mean 'pious').[22] Ameling also rightly rejects the inclusion of worshippers of the *Theos Hypsistos*, however great the Jewish influence may have been in this case.[23] (vii) Biblical and post-biblical Jewish expressions which may also have been used by non-Jews. (viii) Magical formulae, which often contain many Jewish elements but need not be of Jewish origin for that reason (Ameling relegates the *magika* to an Appendix). Finally (ix) the few Samaritan inscriptions, non-Jewish *stricto sensu*, but fortunately included by Ameling as well. In general it should be said that Noy's (and Panayotov's and Bloedhorn's) system of numbering the inscriptions by province (Pan 1–5, Ach 1–75, Cre 1–3) instead of numbering them through (as Ameling does for Asia Minor, 1–258), is unfortunate yet convenient: Referring to a Jewish inscription as *IJudO* I Ach 52 is cumbersome and unwieldy, but, on the other hand, when new material crops up, it can more easily be inserted into the existent collections by numbering it in this way. All entries follow the same

---

[20] This is of course to avoid repetition of what he had already said in his previous volumes (*JIGRE* and *JIWE* 1+2), but there the discussions are very brief as well.

[21] Ameling calls them 'zweifelsfrei' (13), but that is an overstatement.

[22] But one might of course ask: why include Godfearers when they were not Jews but only pagan sympathizers with Judaism?

[23] A catalogue of the inscriptions pertaining to the cult of Theos Hypsistos is to be found in S. Mitchell, "The Cult of Theos Hypsistos Between Pagans, Jews, and Christians," in P. Athanassiadi & M. Frede (eds.), *Pagan Monotheism in Late Antiquity*, Oxford 1999, 81–148, esp. 128–147.

format: Editions are listed in chronological order, followed by other bibliography and information about the place where the inscription was found, its present whereabouts, details of the material (stone, marble, bronze etc.) and the lettering, language and date. Then follows the text, with critical apparatus, accompanied by a translation; finally there are line by line comments. Many entries contain drawings or photos of the inscriptions. Brief historical information is provided on major sites and cities.

As far as the individual inscriptions are concerned, I have to restrict myself to only a few short observations on a very limited number of texts. Pan1+2[24] (from Hungaria) and Dal2 are good examples of the interesting phenomenon of a mixture of Latin and Greek (with the Latin written partly in Greek letters) that we see more often in Jewish inscriptions (we also find Hebrew inscriptions in Greek letters[25]). It is interesting that in Pan2 we find a human image on the tombstone to which later on, secondarily, the Jewish epitaphs were added and apparently the presence of human images was not felt to be a problem (4th cent. CE). Dal4 is described as an epitaph of a Samaritan, but the stone has only [….]*reitissa*, which is read as *Samareitissa*. Not only is that reading uncertain, there is also nothing that identifies the deceased woman as a Samaritan, even though the editors claim that there is "nothing inconsistent with her being a Samaritan by religion" (28). There is, moreover, no other evidence of Samaritan presence in Yugoslavia (although it cannot be ruled out altogether). Ancient terminology for 'Samarians,' natives of Samaria (whether Jews or Christians or Greeks or Phoenicians), is not differentiated from that for Samaritans by religion (*CPJ* 513 *Samaritai tên thrêskeian* [Samaritans by faith] is the only exception).[26] So, for instance, in the case of Ach35, the epitaph of Ammia Samaritis, the editors have to concede that "it is not clear whether Ammia was a Samaritan by religion or a native of Samaria" (160); and the same applies to Ach36–37, 41 (all are from Athens). In the discussion of Mac1, the famous Polycharmus inscription from the synagogue at Stobi, we learn that in recent years more inscriptions have been discovered at the site, which will be published by James Wiseman. I find it very regrettable that these new inscriptions could not be included in *IJudO*. Two fascinating and recently found Macedonian epitaphs from the 4th century CE (Mac8 and Mac9) mention a "Theodosios the Hebrew, *mellopresbyteros*, three years old (?)" and a "Geras (or: an old man), most renowned in hymns of the Hebrews." Leaving aside the fact that it remains unclear why *Hebraios* is

---

[24] Pan1 means the first inscription in the section on Pannonia. Dal stands for Dalmatia, Cre for Crete, BS for Black Sea area, Ach for Greece (mainland and islands) etc.

[25] See my *Ancient Jewish Epitaphs* 32–34.

[26] See my "The Samaritan Diaspora in Antiquity," in my *Essays on the Jewish World of Early Christianity*, Freiburg-Göttingen 1990, 137.

preferred here (and elsewhere)[27] to *Ioudaios*, it should be noticed that we have here the first attestation of *mellopresbyteros*, 'presbyter-to-be,' a person who is going to hold the office of Elder. If the reading *trietou* is correct, the designated presbyter was only three years old so that we have a nice parallel to the *mellarchôn* of 2 years (*JIWE* II 100) and the 8-years-old child *archôn* (*JIWE* II 288), both from Rome.[28] I disagree with the editors' interpretation of *propherestatos hymnois*, which they take to mean that "the deceased person was praised (i. e. commemorated) in hymns" (85). 'Most excellent in hymns' certainly must mean here that the deceased was an exceptionally able *cantor* in the synagogue services. The counter-arguments adduced are unconvincing (see *IJudO* I 85; Peek, *GV* 642 is no parallel). Could 'hymns of the Hebrews' perhaps imply the (unlikely) possibility that Geras conducted the liturgy in Hebrew?

Interesting is also the new case of a Jewish *scholastikos*, a lawyer or rhetorician, and evidence for intermarriage, both from Larissa (Ach5 and Ach6), where we also find the curious group of 'farewell-to-the-people' inscriptions (*tôi laôi chairein*, Ach1–4, 8–14). Quite extraordinary too is the manumission inscription Ach45 from Oropos, in which the (to-be-freed) slave Moschus calls himself a Jew but at the same time states that in a dream the Greek healing gods Amphiaraus and Hygieia appeared to him and commanded him to set up a *stêlê* by the altar, which he obediently did. The translation of Ach58 (from Aegina) obscures the fact that the donor here speaks in the first person (not "Theodorus built ..." but "I, Theodorus, built ...").[29] In the chapter on Delos, the five Theos Hypsistos inscriptions found in what is often assumed to be the local synagogue have been included as Ach60–64, a questionable decision since neither the precise nature of the building nor the relationship between Judaism and the cult of Theos Hypsistos can be determined with any certainty, however much ink has been spilt over these questions. Whether the dedicators were Jews or not remains an open question, as the editors themselves concede (227). These (and other) inscriptions might better have been relegated to an Appendix with *dubia*. In this same chapter, again, the two very important Samaritan inscriptions from Delos are dealt with at length (Ach66–67), but Ach 68 on the Samarian immigrant (*Praulos Samareus*) who contributed to the temple of Sarapis on Delos should have been excluded; there is nothing Jewish or even Samaritan about this man (as the editors themselves concede at p. 234). Fascinating are two new inscriptions (with *menoroth*) from Grammata Bay at the island of Syros, one with a

---

[27] See G. Harvey, "Synagogues of the Hebrews: Good Jews in the Diaspora," in S. Jones & S. Pearce (eds.), *Jewish Local Patriotism and Self-Identification in the Graeco-Roman period*, Sheffield 1998, 132–147, who collects the epigraphic evidence and concludes that the term Hebrew "consistently carries associations with piety, traditionalism and conservatism" (145). See also *IJudO* III 113–114.

[28] For more instances and discussion of this phenomenon see my *Ancient Jewish Epitaphs* 89–90.

[29] One finds the same error in *IJudO* 140 (nr. 27).

prayer for a safe sea voyage for "Eunomios and all his crew" (Ach72), the other with thanksgivings after a safe return (Ach73). Cre2, an epitaph Joseph made for his wife Berenike, is a newly discovered Cretan inscription that should now be added to the dossier I published in 1988.[30] I wonder why the inscription in *Inscr. Cret.* IV 509, mentioning a Moses (5th cent. CE), which in itself could of course be Christian, is relegated to the appendix with non-Jewish inscriptions, in view of the fact that the name of Moses is now known to have been less rare among ancient Jews than has long been assumed (see, e. g., Ach30, in spite of *IJudO* I, p. 153; also *IJudO* II 240 from Corycos).[31] Also *Inscr. Cret.* II 8 and others with names such as Sanbathis, Obadia etc. might have been mentioned here and then relegated to the category *dubia*. They may all be Christian but we simply do not know for sure. In other cases the editors do retain such dubious cases in the main corpus, but these have been put into the category 'not considered Jewish' (see App20–21).

The section on the North coast of the Black Sea [BS] contains 28 items, many of them manumission inscriptions from the Bosporan kingdom, 16 of which had also been published in 1999 by Gibson.[32] In legal form, these are entirely Greek (with close parallels in the pagan manumission inscriptions from Delphi). These often badly damaged inscriptions with their many interpretative problems[33] are discussed in rather great detail, and competently, by Noy. In BS16 we find the spelling *chithê* (χίθη) for *keitai* (κεῖται), a variant (with all four letters wrong) that can now be added to the 19 (!) different spellings of that word I listed in 1991.[34] Most interesting and controversial is BS20, an inscription with the manumission of the female slave Chrysa in 41 CE, which begins with an invocation of Theos Hypsistos, then mentions the manumission in the synagogue (*proseuchê*), and concludes with an invocation of Zeus, Gê, and Helios as overseers of the agreement. Noy sums up the debate as follows: "The most likely explanation is that, although the manumission took place in the prayer-house, the freedwoman was not put under an obligation to it in the way that other ex-slaves were; the protection of pagan gods is therefore for her benefit and irrelevant to the Jewishness of the manumittor" (307). A remarkably latitudinarian view of religious loyalty is undeniable in this inscription.[35] There are two Appendices, one containing

---

[30] "The Jews of Ancient Crete," *JJS* 39 (1988) 183–200, reprinted in my *Essays on the Jewish World* 148–165 [in abbreviated form also elsewhere in this volume].

[31] See T. Derda, "Did the Jews Use the Name of Moses in Antiquity?," *ZPE* 115 (1997) 257–260; convincingly against Derda now M. Williams, "Jewish Use of Moses as a Personal Name in Antiquity," *ZPE* 118 (1997) 274, and idem, "The case for Jewish Use of Moses as a Personal Name in Graeco-Roman Antiquity," *ZPE* 140 (2002) 279–283.

[32] See note 13.

[33] Among which the famous 'exception clause,' *chôris thôpeias kai proskarterêseôs.*

[34] *Ancient Jewish Epitaphs* 26 note 21.

[35] Note that in Ach44 from Delphi the slave-owner Ioudaios took part in a fictitious sale to Apollo.

probably medieval inscriptions (all but one in Hebrew), the other with two dozen or so inscriptions not considered Jewish (here we also find the two Cretan epitaphs mentioned above). As has already been said, I would have welcomed another Appendix with the *dubia*. After the bibliography and concordance (with *CIJ*), vol. I concludes with very useful indexes giving detailed information about the types of inscription, the languages, provenance, names, indications of age at death, vocabulary of relationships, epithets, occupations, place-names and ethnics, terms indicating Jews etc., prayers and blessings, curses, biblical quotations, dates, symbols, terms for tombs *et multa cetera*. The value of these indexes can hardly be exaggerated.

I now proceed to vol. III, Syria and Cyprus, edited as well by Noy and Bloed-horn, leaving Ameling's volume to be reviewed after the two Noy volumes. Syria (including Phoenicia) takes up the bulk of this volume with its more than 130 inscriptions, about twice as many as *CIJ* had.[36] The collection of the texts and bibliographies was done by Bloedhorn; Noy wrote the exegetical commentaries. Cyprus yields 8 inscriptions. In my forthcoming study of the Jews on ancient Cyprus[37] I deal with only 6, the difference residing mainly in the fact that *IJudO* includes three Phoenician inscriptions from as early as the 4th century BCE (Cyp6–8) which seem to contain Yahwistic names. I disagree with the remark that "Jews are unlikely to have built synagogues in Cyprus before the 3rd century CE" (220), since Acts 13:5 testifies that in Salamis, the main city on the east coast of the island, there were several synagogues as early as the middle of the first century CE. Most interesting is Cyp3 (4th–5th cent.) where we find a unique use of the expression *hê hebraïkê* for either the synagogue building or the com-munity. As to Syria,[38] the editors are too optimistic about Samaritan presence in Tyre. Such a presence is in and of itself quite possible, even probable, but two inscriptions mentioning *Samaritai* (Syr3, 11) without giving us any clue whether these were Samarians or Samaritans do not prove anything of the sort; neither does an amulet in Samaritan Hebrew (Syr6) since Samaritan amulets were often bought and used by non-Samaritans, including Christians (Syr6 comes from a tomb in the Christian necropolis). Interpreting these three inscriptions in the light of each other is unwarranted from a methodological point of view. Even so, we have to welcome the inclusion of this material. Another helpful feature is the sys-tematic inclusion of inscriptions from elsewhere pertaining to Jews of a certain place in Syria. Here, for instance, the epitaphs for Tyrian Jews buried in Beth

---

[36] This progress is of course mainly due to the big strides taken in the project *Inscriptions grecques et latines de la Syrie* (1929–....).

[37] *Zutot 2003* (Perspectives on Jewish Culture 3), Dordrecht 2004 [now also elsewhere in this volume].

[38] The inscriptions of Syrian Jewry have recently also been collected by Lea Roth-Gerson in her book *The Jews of Syria in the Light of the Greek Inscriptions*, Jerusalem 2001 [in Hebrew, *non vidi*].

She'arim and Jerusalem (Syr5–8) have been included (cf. Syr17–19, 25–26, 32, 51–52: people from Sidon, Beirut, Byblos, and Palmyra whose epitaphs were found in Beth She'arim). Fascinating is the new inscription from the circus of Tyre (Syr10), from the section reserved for the faction of the Blues, indicating the seat for a Jewish woman, Matrona the purple-fisher. For a discussion of the background of this variously attested connection between Jews and Blues I have to refer the reader to my recently published study of that subject.[39] It is very helpful to have put together here all of the twenty Greek donor inscriptions from the synagogue of Apamea with a good commentary (Syr53–72), since they yield valuable information about the social situation of the Jews in that city in the time that John Chrysostom delivered his notoriously anti-Jewish sermons in Syrian Antioch.[40] Syr58 is interesting in that it mentions an *azzana* (in Greek letters), a *hazzan* or servant (not yet cantor!)[41] of the synagogue called Nehemia, by whose term of office the donation and inscription are dated, which is highly unusual. It is amazing and instructive to see how many women there are among the donors to this rich synagogue (Syr61–71 except Syr70).

There are some fifty Jewish inscriptions from Dura-Europos, the city on the border with the Persian Empire that had an exceptionally decorated synagogue with famous wallpaintings from the middle of the 3rd century CE. These inscriptions are in Greek, Hebrew, and Aramaic, but there are also some twenty in Middle Persian. Most of the inscriptions and graffiti derive from the ancient synagogue. The Iranian inscriptions are all of them dipinti written on the wallpaintings of this synagogue.[42] They are an enigmatic group, especially because they are concentrated on two of the many panels of the paintings; the rest are in Aramaic. The Aramaic graffiti briefly explain the painted scenes, but the Persian ones usually do not, they rather look like graffiti inscribed by visitors (only Persian names are mentioned), although there are some brief remarks on the paintings (e. g., N and N "liked this picture"). Were the scribblers pagan Persian tourists who came to see the frescoes because of their great reputation? Or were they Iranian Jews who had absorbed much of Persian culture (even to the point of mentioning 'gods' in the plural (Syr121, 124–5)? Or were they Persian 'Godfearers' (pagan sympathizers with Judaism)? Are the graffiti signs of the temporary

---

[39] "Jews and Blues in Late Antiquity," in D. Accorinti & P. Chuvin (edd.), *Des Géants à Dionysos. Mélanges de mythologie et de poésie grecques offerts à Francis Vian*, Alessandria 2003, 565–572 [elsewhere in this volume].

[40] See my "Jews and Christians in Antioch at the End of the Fourth Century," in my *Japheth in the Tents of Shem* 109–118.

[41] Epiphanius, *Panarion* 30.11 explains that *azanitai* is the term used by Jews for *diakonoi* and in the inscription Syr58 *azzana* is explained as *diakonos*.

[42] The Persian graffiti are presented according to the reconstructions by Geiger but the editors unfortunately fail to mention any publication by Geiger in their bibliography. It is: B. Geiger, 'The Middle Iranian Texts,' in C.H. Kraeling, *The Excavations at Dura-Europos VIII, 1: The Synagogue*, New Haven 1956, 283–317.

occupation of Dura in 253 CE (all of them date from this year), shortly before the Persians conquered and destroyed the city in 256? And there are many more questions, to which we simply do not know the answers. I, for one, guess that the possibility that these graffiti are Jewish is small. Even so, it is very good to have all the Dura material gathered together in this volume.

There are three Appendices: one with the Jewish inscriptions in Palmyrene Aramaic from the Land of Israel, all of them epitaphs of Palmyrene Jews buried in Beth She'arim and in Jerusalem; one with Jewish inscriptions wrongly related to Syria (mainly the Jerusalem inscription with the word *Beroutos*, which is now considered to mean not 'from Beirut' but '[son] of Berous');[43] and one with 16 inscriptions not considered Jewish anymore. As a matter of fact, most inscriptions in the latter category should be classified as *dubia*, and more cases in this volume could have been included. The usual and useful indexes follow, with slight adjustment of the categories.

Volume II of *IJudO* covers Asia Minor and is the only of the three volumes that is the product of the efforts of a single scholar, Walter Ameling (professor of Ancient History in Jena). Moreover, it is by far the most voluminous of the three with its 650 pages. It is a work that deserves to be highly praised for its comprehensiveness and the judicious nature of its commentaries. Because originally Ameling's enterprise had an independent start, unrelated to Noy's project, the format is somewhat different. The other volumes have short introductions to the major sites where inscriptions were found, but not a general introduction, whereas Ameling has a useful 36-page introduction on the phenomenon of Jewish diaspora in antiquity (and there are also introductions to the individual sites). His book contains – unfortunately – no cumulative bibliography at the end[44] and, regrettably, also no map of Asia Minor with the relevant places indicated; and the indexes are arranged in a rather different way and are unfortunately less useful than those in the other volumes (no index of biblical quotations, of religious terminology, of funerary formulae etc.). As detailed and elaborated as the table of contents is, so is the table of abbreviations short and defective: e. g., for English readers it may be hard to find out that FO is 'Fundort' and AO is 'Aufbewahrungsort,' self-evident though that may be for a German classical epigraphist; too many abbreviations remain unexplained so that the reader has to be referred to other 'Abkürzungsverzeichnisse.' It was, however, a very fortunate idea to offer the reader a complete list of all ancient literary references to Jews and Judaism in Asia Minor (see Appendix I; cf. also pp. 32–36), which are mostly quoted in

---

[43] This is one of the group of epitaphs from the so-called 'Eros family' (4 persons are called Erotas), to which one may compare the name Venus, the daughter of rabbi Abundantius from Naples (*JIWE* I 36).

[44] Not many theologians or Judaic scholars will know, e. g., what is meant by "die Handbücher von Zgusta" (23), and Ameling does not make it easy to find that out (since KPN is nowhere 'aufgeschlüsselt'!; it is: *Kleinasiatische Personennamen*).

the original language in the notes to the main text. In the introduction, Ameling explains that he included the inscriptions of the islands Chios, Samos, Kos, and Rhodos since from an administrative point of view these islands before the West coast of Asia Minor often formed part of the province of Asia (the other Aegean islands were covered in *IJudO* I, Cyprus in *IJudO* II).

It is inevitable that in the commentaries on the individual inscriptions there is a lot of overlap with the two other volumes as regards the details: Again the *archisynagôgos* and the *presbyteroi* (etc.) are discussed at length; again the same personal names are dealt with; again the same deviations from the standard grammar are explained etc. But that is not something to be regretted, on the contrary, sometimes one finds here different approaches to the same questions and even additional information that sheds extra light on a problem and creates new insights. That can be seen very clearly in the section on Thrace because this province is covered in both *IJudO* I and in *IJudO* II (Thr3=12 and Thr4=13).[45] Since the much debated term *presbytera* (female elder) occurs in the first of these inscriptions, one can compare the respective commentaries, and Ameling has a better documented case here than Noy c.s., as is also the case with the comments on the *eulogia pasin* formula. But Noy is stronger in Jewish onomastics. A very telling new inscription, from the little island of Icaria, is 5a: "It is impossible that you will ever hear the truth from Jews of Icaria." This 5th or 6th century inscription was found in the local church! Nr. 11, from Rhodes, is entitled 'Ein Mann aus Samaria' by Ameling, and in his translation the man is a 'Samariter' (not: 'Samaritaner'), wisely (see above); all the more surprising is it that at nr. 24 (*Sikimitai* in Kaunos) he seems to mix up Samaritans and Samarians.

As was to be expected, the biggest chapters in the book are those dealing with Aphrodisias (70–123) and Sardis (209–297). The famous donor inscription from Aphrodisias, which is one of the most revealing epigraphic finds of a recent date,[46] is dealt with at great length and in depth. Ameling argues that the text on side A is unrelated to that on side B and that the inscriptions should not be dated in the early 3rd century CE but in the late 4th or 5th. He initially leaves unexplained, however, why, if A and B have nothing to do with each other, both texts are on the same stone, but later on he adds the observation that "die in B genannten Stifter ließen ein *mnêma* erbauen, das nach einiger Zeit – aus welchen Gründen auch immer – erneuerungsbedürftig war" (90). In contrast to Reynolds and Tannenbaum, Ameling takes *mnêma* (A 8) to have its usual meaning of 'tomb' (not 'monument' or 'memorial building') and says the inscription is

---

[45] This doublet is caused by the fact that initially the projects of Noy and his team and of Ameling were independent from each other.

[46] J. Reynolds & R. Tannenbaum, *Jews and Godfearers at Aphrodisias*, Cambridge 1987. For its significance see, e. g., my "Jews and Christians in Aphrodisias" in *Essays on the Jewish World* 166–181 (Ameling overlooks this study at 82 n. 50).

about the foundation of a collective burial place for poor Jews[47] (and not about a soup-kitchen); the *dekania* in A 3 is not a *minyan* but a funeral association.[48] The riddlesome *patellado[s]* in A 1 is interpreted as the genitive of *patellas* ('Imbißinhaber'), a word only very recently attested for the first time, and disregarded as irrelevant for the interpretation of the inscription as a whole since it is an addition by a later hand. Of the hapax legomenon *apenthêsia* (A 6) Ameling only says that "dessen Sinn klar ist" (89) and he translates it by 'Befreiung von Trauer' (75), but it is not immediately 'klar' how the foundation of a collective burial site serves to further 'Befreiung von Trauer.' Also less than clear is Ameling's remark on the name *Prounikios*, a cloth refiner (or fuller, *gnapheus*): "Der Name paßt zu einem *gnapheus*" (111). *Prounikos* often has the meaning of 'lewd,' but did cloth refiners really have a reputation of extraordinary randiness? Be that as it may, it should be said that Ameling brings forward valid reasons to differ from Reynolds' and Tannenbaum's interpretation of this inscription. It is also interesting to see how he takes issue with Charlotte Roueché's interpretation of the Jews-Blues connection in Aphrodisias and elsewhere (followed by me in the FS Vian).[49]

The five inscriptions from Ephesus are disappointingly few in number in view of the enormous scale of the excavations of this city and the many literary data about the Jewish community there. Interesting here are the two epitaphs ending with the words, "The Jews will take care of this tomb" (32, 33), and the Christian inscription in which a local bishop sneers at the "Jewish love of money" (*philargyria Ioudaïkê*, 35). It is not clear to me why *ad* nr. 36, which states that "Tation donated her house to the Jews" and was for that reason honoured by the Jewish community with a golden wreath, Ameling assumes that Tation herself was Jewish rather than an outsider (see 165 note 74). From Miletus we have the well-known theater seat inscription, "Place of the Jews who are also (called) God-fearers" (nr. 37). Ameling here pleads against the often defended metathesis of *tôn kai* into *kai tôn* (place of the Jews and the Godfearers) and argues that *theosebioi* is an honorary adjective applied by the Jewish community of Miletus to itself, a likely interpretation that is, however, not likely to end the debate. The enigmatic designation *hoi pote Ioudaioi* in nr. 40 from Smyrna ('die vormaligen Juden' or 'die vormaligen Bewohner Iudaeas' etc.) remains an unsolved problem; Ameling: *non liquet*. A special case is nr. 41, a now lost inscription from Smyrna, which was found and described in the early 18th century by my

---

[47] "Gegründet wurde ein Grabbau, der allen Mitgliedern der Gemeinde offen stand" (92); *ibid.* Ameling refers to *IJudO* III 187, 223, and 244 for parallels.

[48] The interesting implication is that three proselytes and two (pagan) 'Godfearers' were members of this Jewish burial society.

[49] See my "Jews and Blues" [in this volume] and Ch. Roueché, *Performers and Partisans at Aphrodisias in the Roman and Late Roman Periods*, London 1993. Ameling's criticism is on pp. 115–6.

near-namesake Herman van der Horst (minister of the Dutch Reformed Church in Smyrna!),[50] in which Eirenopoios, son of Jacob and "father of the tribe" (tribe = community),[51] proudly declares that he had the floor of the interior, probably of the synagogue, repaired and beautified at the cost of 7 *solidi*.

As to Sardis, we now have the second edition in a relatively short period of the many inscriptions from the giant-size synagogue that was a part of the great bathhouse-gymnasium complex.[52] Ameling rightly pays much attention to the archaeological context in which the inscriptions were found. In nr. 63 we meet the priest Samoe who calls himself *sophodidaskalos*, wisdom teacher, a hitherto unattested term that might indicate that there was a Jewish school in Sardis where Torah was taught (or was he a sort of Greek rabbi?). For the enigmatic reference to the *phylê Leontiôn* (the tribe of the Leontii, in Sardis) in nr. 69 Ameling does not come up with a new solution.[53] Interesting is the frequent occurrence in Sardis of the formula that donations to the synagogue were done *ek tôn tês pronoias* (from the [gifts] of Providence), as a variant of the more usual *ek tôn dôreôn tou theou* or *ek tôn tou theou dorêmatôn* (e. g., 71, 77. 78, 80–85).[54] The use of *Pronoia* as a term referring to God makes a very Christian impression,[55] but here we see it in an undeniably Jewish context. Curious is the speaking Torah-shrine that says, "The same Memnonius, on account of his health, had me, the Torah-shrine, decorated with marble" (nr. 129).[56] The word used here for Torah-shrine, *nomophylakion*, occurs here for the first time in this sense. The most intriguing inscription from Sardis is, however, nr. 131 ('eine liturgische Inschrift'), written on a marble plaque: "When you have found (the book and) broken (it open), read (it and) observe (it)."[57] Ameling demonstrates that with regard to the Scriptures in early Judaism and Christianity, the multiple injunction of taking, opening, reading and obeying had become almost formulaic. For that reason the 'breaking' should refer to the breaking of the seal of a book in order to open it. "Angesichts des Inhalts und der Parallelen wird man glauben dürfen, daß sich dieser Text auf die Verkündigung und Aufnahme der

---

[50] See my entry "Herman van der Horst" in the *Biografisch Lexicon voor de Geschiedenis van het Nederlandse Protestantisme*, vol. 4, Kampen 1998, 220–222.

[51] Apart from *stemma* (tribe), one finds as designations of local Jewish communities *synagôgê, ethnos, laos, genos, katoikia, hebraïkê*.

[52] One of the few Jewish inscriptions from outside this complex, a short Hebrew inscription, is unfortunately presented in a very garbled version; see nr. 56 at p. 216 (six letters have been rendered incorrectly). The same applies to the nrs. 105–108 and other Hebrew items in the volume. Especially final *mem* is consistently misprinted as *samekh*.

[53] See my discussion in "De synagoge van Sardis en haar inscripties" 47–48 [in English elsewhere in this volume].

[54] Nr. 90 has *ek tôn dôreôn tou pantokratoros theou*.

[55] See G.W.H. Lampe, *Greek Patristic Lexicon*, Oxford 1968, s.v. B 2 v.

[56] For 'speaking stones' see my *Ancient Jewish Epitaphs* 49–54.

[57] *Heurôn klasas anagnôthi phylaxon*.

Tora bezieht, also in irgendeiner Beziehung zum Toraschrein oder zu einem Lesepult stand" (287).

Of the rest of this rich volume I single out for brief mention only a few other important matters. Ameling's suggestion concerning nr. 156 (from Nicomedia), to the effect that the mention of an *anagnôstês* = *lector* (which occurs only very rarely since in principle everyone could be called upon to read Scripture in the synagogue) may be "ein Hinweis auf die niedrige Alphabetisierungsrate" of the community members, is now confirmed by the recent research of Catherine Hezser.[58] There are more than a dozen Phrygian inscription containing the formula (*eis*) *tekna teknôn*, which has often been claimed to be a shorthand reference to Exod. 34:7, but Ameling sides with J.H.M. Strubbe in rejecting this claim since the formula occurs also outside a Jewish (i.e., in a pagan) context; so these inscriptions are now excluded from the corpus. For a similar reason, but now because there are Christian parallels, inscriptions containing the so-called 'Eumeneian formula' (*estai autôi pros ton theon* = he will have to reckon with, or: answer to, God; and variants) have been excluded as well, unless there are other indications of Jewishness. It would perhaps have been better to include them in an appendix with *dubia*. Nr. 180, the epitaph of Deborah from Antioch, is metrical (disticha, hexameters and pentameters in alternation) and should have been included in my collection of metrical epitaphs;[59] I overlooked it because it is so heavily damaged that I did not notice the metre. The 23 new inscriptions from Phrygian Hierapolis are conspicuous in that they very often explicitly identify the persons mentioned on the stone as Jews. Once even a sarcophagus is called Jewish (191)![60] Also in other aspects this group of epitaphs has its specific features. In view of Acts 16:13–14 (Lydia, a Godfearer and dealer in purple-dye from Thyatira in Asia Minor) it is interesting to find in nr. 196 a clear indication of Jewish involvement in the purple industry of Hierapolis. In the same text we also find one of the very few references to the celebration of Pesach and of Shavuot in the diaspora (see also Acts 20:6 on Pesach in Philippi).[61] Nr. 213 from Laodicea is unique in that it is the only Jewish epitaph in which erasing of the inscription is also threatened with the curses in Deuteronomy 28 (usually these curses are reserved for illegal use of the tomb[62]). Nr. 218 is the inscription on the small altar from Aspendos ("For the truthful God who is not made with hands") which I have tried to demonstrate was made by a pagan sympathizer

---

[58] *Jewish Literacy in Roman Palestine*, Tübingen 2001.

[59] "Jewish Tomb Inscriptions in Verse," in my *Hellenism – Judaism – Christianity. Essays on Their Interaction*, 2nd ed., Leuven 1998, 27–47.

[60] If Ameling's interpretation is correct (see p. 407), which I think it is.

[61] The Greek terms used are *heortê tôn azymôn* and *heortê tês pentêkostês*. In an inscription from ancient Libya the feast of Booths (Sukkoth, here called *skênopêgia*) is mentioned: Nr. 71 in G. Lüderitz, *Corpus jüdischer Zeugnisse aus der Cyrenaica*, Wiesbaden 1983.

[62] See my *Ancient Jewish Epitaphs* 56–57.

with Judaism, a Godfearer.[63] Ameling is less certain about that, and after a thorough discussion he concludes: "Insgesamt bleibt der Text aber rätselhaft" (461). He interestingly speculates on a pagan oracular background but does not deny Jewish influence.[64] One of the most striking new inscriptions is nr. 222, a recently discovered new fragment of the famous inscription of Diogenes of Oenoanda. In the time of Hadrian this Epicurean philosopher Diogenes had the huge wall of the Stoa (ca. 80 x 4 meter) on the Agora of Oenoanda inscribed with a very large inscription by which, probably shortly before his death, he wanted to instruct his fellow-citizens in Epicurus' philosophy in order to dispel their fear of death and of the gods.[65] In this fragment (NF 127 in Smith's numbering) we read that the clearest sign that the gods are unable to prevent evils from happening are the Jews and the Egyptians, since "these are both the most godfearing and the most abominable of all nations." The words used here are *deisidaimonestatoi* and *miarôtatoi*. It is not easy to find an adequate translation of these terms. *Deisidaimôn* can designate not only a pious but also a superstitious person; *miaros* has both a ritual sense (impure) and a moral one (criminal). Be that as it may, it is in any case again a striking new instance of the negative view of Jews and Judaism, which had such a long history in ancient literature.[66] It is also interesting to find someone calling himself a Levite in Lycaonia (nr. 224)[67] and to meet in Corycos a goldsmith called Moses the Hebrew (nr. 240). Finally Ameling publishes some magical texts from amulets found in Asia Minor and he rightly stresses that they do prove Jewish influence but do not necessarily have to be Jewish.

Looking back upon this rich harvest we can say the following. These three works will become standard reference works for the decades to come. Noy, Panayotov, Bloedhorn, and Ameling have done the world of Judaic scholars and classical epigraphists an immense service by painstakingly collecting this material that is so widely scattered,[68] and by elucidating it by their expert comments. Even though there is much to be criticized on the level of details, in general it should be said that these volumes are excellent tools for further study of aspects of the early Jewish world that are often not mentioned at all in the literary

---

[63] "A New Altar of a Godfearer?" in my *Judaism – Hellenism – Christianity* 65–71.

[64] The entry bears the title "Jüdischer Einfluß?" (p. 458).

[65] See *Diogenes of Oinoanda. The Epicurean Inscription*, edited with introduction, translation, and notes by M. F. Smith, Napoli 1993; my review in *Mnemosyne* 48 (1995) 101–103. [See the chapter "The Most Superstitious and Disgusting of All Nations" elsewhere in this volume.]

[66] See esp. P. Schäfer, *Judaeophobia. Attitudes towards the Jews in the Ancient World*, Cambridge MA – London 1997.

[67] The only other epigraphical Levite is from Jaffa, *CIJ* II 902. It is strange that here Ameling lapses into the oldfashioned German terminology of "spätes Judentum" (483 note 6).

[68] Even publications of inscriptions in obscure journals in Russian and Turkish were traced.

sources.[69] Ameling's book is less user-friendly than the two other volumes, not only because there is no bibliography and an inadequate table of abbreviations, but also because he very frequently quotes (sometimes very long stretches of) texts in Greek (also modern Greek), Latin, Italian, French etc. without presenting a translation, which makes the book less accessible to the average Judaic scholar than the Noy volumes, but this is more than balanced by the high quality of Ameling's work.

Frey's *CIJ* has now been replaced except for ancient Palestine. For that gap we will have to await the results of the Israeli project *Corpus Inscriptionum Iudaeae/Palestinae* (CIIP), but that enterprise is still in its infancy. The CIIP will be a new corpus of all inscriptions (pagan, Jewish, Christian), in all languages, arranged topographically, found in Israel (including the West Bank, Gaza, and the Golan Heights) and dating from the 4th century BCE to the 7th century CE. The corpus will include a full re-editing of every text, a drawing or photograph, textual apparatus, English translation, and commentary. The estimate is that there will be between 6000 and 7000 texts in the corpus, some 1800 of which (perhaps more) are Jewish.[70] We will have to await the completion of that project before we can say that Frey's *CIJ* definitively belongs to the past. But even now we can say that the progress is enormous: Frey's whole corpus numbered some 1600 inscriptions, Israel included.[71] *JIGRE, JIWE* 1+2, and *IJudO* 1–3 comprise together slightly over 1600 inscriptions, Israel excluded.[72] When the 1800 or more inscriptions of the land of Israel are added, we will have almost three-and-a-half thousand Jewish inscriptions from the period between Alexander the Great and Muhammed, more than twice as many as in *CIJ*. In the last 15 years early Jewish epigraphy has put itself squarely on the map of international scholarship. Students of ancient Judaism can neglect works such as those reviewed here only to their great disadvantage.

---

[69] This can be clearly seen in the valuable book by Margaret H. Williams, *The Jews Among the Greeks and Romans. A Diasporan Sourcebook*, Baltimore 1998, where literary sources and epigraphic material play an equal role.

[70] I owe this information to Professor Jonathan Price from Tel Aviv University who initiated the enterprise together with Prof. Hannah Cotton of the Hebrew University of Jerusalem.

[71] And Lifshitz's *addenda* included.

[72] It may be interesting to notice that, while in 1991 I calculated that the epitaphs formed some 80% of the material, now a new calculation on the basis of the six above-mentioned new editions comes to some 72% (some 1150). That is mainly due to the fact that many more donor inscriptions have been found in the meantime (e. g. Sardis).

Huldah's Tomb in Early Jewish Tradition

The prophetess Huldah remains a somewhat vague but also fascinating figure in the Old Testament. In 2 Kings 22:14–20 we are told that she lived in Jerusalem at the time of king Josiah, who ruled over Judaea at the end of the seventh century BCE (ca. 640–609 BCE). After the spectacular find of the 'Book of Law' in the temple (which was the supposed reason for Josiah's reform), at the command of the king, the finders of that book approached the prophetess Huldah, the wife of Sallum who was keeper of the wardrobe, whereupon she uttered a prophecy of catastrophy (this is repeated with minor modifications in 2 Chron. 34:22–28). After this we never hear anything about this woman again.[1] In this short contribution I do not want to deal with the biblical data about this woman, but with the traditions post-biblical Judaism cherished about her, and especially about her tomb, which is not even mentioned in the Hebrew Bible.[2]

To begin with, it should be remarked that the traditions concerning Huldah's tomb are found only in rabbinic literature – in post-biblical *pre*-rabbinic literature (300 BCE – 200 CE) she is nowhere mentioned – and that all these traditions situate her tomb in Jerusalem, to be more precise, at the southern border of the Temple square. That is to say, it was situated on a piece of land that in the Second Temple period was initially still outside the Temple square, but that came to lie just inside it after the enormous expansion of the square by king Herod the Great (around the beginning of our era),[3] namely in the south-west corner. That is exactly the part in Herod's temple complex where the great gates that were named after Huldah were located, of which one can see the monumental steps and portals even today.[4]

---

[1] See C.V. Camp, 'Huldah,' in Carol Meyers (ed.), *Women in Scripture*, Boston & New York 2000, 96–97.

[2] A very succinct summary can be found in J. Jeremias, *Heiligengräber in Jesu Umwelt*, Göttingen 1958, 51–52. It is interesting to see that in a rather late (= early medieval) rabbinic midrash, Huldah's husband Sallum is said to have been the man who was revived by contact with the bones of the deceased prophet Elisha (see 2 Kings 13:21). Cf. L. Ginzberg, *Legends of the Jews*, vol. 4, Philadelphia 1913, 246, with the note in vol. 6, Philadelphia 1928, 347 n. 21.

[3] See the elaborate description by Josephus, *Antiquitates Judaicae* 15:380–425, translated and annotated in my *Bronnen voor de studie van de wereld van het vroege christendom*, deel 1: Joodse bronnen, Kampen 1997, 137–144.

[4] See e. g. B. Mazar, 'The Archaeological Excavations near the Temple Mount,' in Y. Yadin

The Mishna treatise *Middot* (early third cent. CE), which is the first to mention these gates, begins its enumeration of the five great gates of the temple square as follows: 'The two gates of Huldah on the south served for coming in and for going out (of the temple square)' (*Middot* 1:3).[5] Now it was obviously a problem that a tomb was situated inside the holy city, yes even extremely close to the temple, since it could result in corps-uncleanness (the most serious form of ritual impurity) for those who came too close to it. We see that for that reason the rabbis do their utmost to explain this situation. In the Tosefta, a rabbinic compilation of halakha that received its final redaction somewhat later than the Mishnah (around the middle of the 3rd cent. ce), we read that the rabbis state that each tomb should lie at least 50 cubits (some 25 meters) outside the city wall, and if that was not the case, it should be cleared away.[6] The Tosefta adds, however, that an exception is made for the graves of kings and prophets. But when rabbi Akiva says that such graves, too, should be emptied out, the other rabbis tell him: 'Were not the graves of the house of David and of Huldah the prophetess always in Jerusalem, and no one ever laid a hand on them?' Whereupon Akiva says that these graves had underground channels through which their uncleanness was removed to the Kidron Brook (t.*Bava Bathra* 1:11).[7] Elsewhere in the Tosefta, it is said that, although tombs are forbidden inside Jerusalem, yet there is an exception for the tombs of David and Huldah because 'these were there from the days of the former prophets' (t.*Nega'im* 6:2). Also in the tractate *Avoth de-rabbi Nathan* (recension A) 35:1 we find the same motivation.[8] Although the rabbinic explanations may be legendary and historically incorrect, yet the fact that the tombs of David and Huldah are localized so precisely at the edge of the Kidron Valley (so very close to the Huldah gates) is an unmistakable indication that even in the earliest rabbinic period (not later than the 2nd century CE, but possibly earlier) Huldah's tomb was visible at the southern side of the Temple square.[9] I will return presently to the role and function of that tomb.

In the Babylonian Talmud, *Megillah* 14a–b, a series of seven biblical prophetesses are discussed: Sarah, Miriam, Deborah, Hannah, Abigail, Hulda, and Esther.[10] As far as Huldah is concerned, the question is raised how it was possible that she dared to make her appearance as a prophetess in the same period that

---

(ed.), *Jerusalem Revealed*, Jerusalem 1976, 25–30; H. Shanks, *Jerusalem. An Archaeological Biography*, New York 1995, 142–147.

[5] Translation by H. Danby, *The Mishnah*, Oxford 1933, 590. See text and commentary in O. Holtzmann, *Middot* (Die Mischna V, 10), Giessen 1913, 48–50.

[6] See also the Babylonian Talmud, *Bava Qamma* 82b; more refernces in L. Ginzberg, *Legends* VI, 441 n. 32.

[7] See also the extra-Talmudic treatise *Semachot* 14:10.

[8] With a parallel in recension B, ch. 39.

[9] Parallel traditions are found also in the Jerusalem Talmud, *Nazir* 9, 57d.

[10] Comparable lists with female prophets are also to be found in the Christian *Constitutiones Apostolicae* VIII 2,9 and 20,1.

– *nota bene*! – the great prophet Jeremiah was prophesying. Should she not have kept silent? The school of Rav, a great Babylonian rabbi from the third century CE, adduces as an explanation that Huldah was a close relative of Jeremiah and that for that reason he did not object to her prophesying *on one occasion*! Others explain the fact that king Josiah passed over Jeremiah in favour of Huldah, by assuming that Jeremiah had just gone away on his mission to find the ten lost tribes of Israel. Rabbi Nachman, however, includes Huldah, with Deborah, among the 'shameless women': Deborah is included because it is written about her that 'she summoned Barak' (Judges 4:6), which is, of course, an unheard of insolence on the part of a woman; Huldah is included because it is written about her that she said, 'Tell the man who sent you ...' (2 Kings 22:15) instead of 'Tell the king'! Again another rabbi states that Huldah was a descendant of Rahab the whore (without making clear what that implies, but it will certainly not have been meant as a compliment).[11] Be that as it may, it is clear that many a rabbi frowned over Huldah's impertinent behaviour, as they did in Deborah's case.

A quite different note is struck in the early rabbinic midrash *Pesiqta Rabbati* 26:1–2. There we read that Jeremiah, together with Adam, Jacob, and Isaiah, was one of the four men whom God had created as perfect creatures *par excellence*. Nevertheless Jeremiah cursed the day that he was born because he had to bring such terribly bad tidings. But in cooperation with Zephaniah and Huldah he managed to fulfil his task: *he* played his part on the streets and squares of the city, Zephania did so on the Temple square, and *Huldah did so for the women*. So here she is regarded not as a competitor but as a collaborator of the great prophet. As far as I can see, this exhausts the early Jewish traditions about Huldah.[12] Altogether it is not much, but the evidence does contain some fascinating aspects that I will now briefly review.

To begin with, there is the interesting fact that in the well-known *Lives of the Prophets* (*Vitae prophetarum*) not a single word is devoted to the prophetess Huldah. At first sight that is strange since in that work not only all great prophets such as Isaiah, Jeremiah, Ezechiel, and the twelve Minor Prophets are dealt with, but also prophets who occur only as figures in biblical stories such as Elijah, Elisha, Samuel, and Nathan, No less than 23 prophets pass review here and for each of them we are told, often in detail, where their graves are to be found, but not for

---

[11] *Megillah* 14b also states that it can hardly be coincidental that both women have such ugly names: Deborah = bee, Huldah = weasel! See on this passage L.L. Bronner, 'Deborah,' in N.N. Hyman (ed.), *Biblical Women in the Midrash*, Northvale-London 1997, 109–110.

[12] Although the Targumim scarcely yield any material for our investigation, it is a nice detail that the Targum on both 2 Kings 22:14 and 2 Chron. 33:22 state that Huldah lived in a Jerusalem 'in a house of instruction.' The text of the Hebrew Bible here reads *mishneh* in the sense of 'second quarter of the city,' but because of its close resemblance to *mishnah* the translators have taken it to be a name for a rabbinic study house, which is at least meant as a positive statement. In early Christian literature, Huldah does not play any role.

Huldah. That is all the more curious since – as we have already seen – her grave in Jerusalem was well-known even in the first centuries CE. Now it should be admitted that the Jewish origin of the *Vitae prophetarum* is a matter of debate,[13] but, as I have tried to demonstrate elsewhere,[14] even if the text of this document in its present form were Christian and derived from the fourth century CE, the traditions about the tombs of the prophets it contains are certainly Jewish and date back to the beginning of the Common Era. In the light of what has been said before, the omission of Huldah may certainly be called a telling silence. Even if it cannot be strictly proved that criticism of the activity of this female prophet is the background for this omission, it is highly probable.[15]

In some (but not all) rabbinic sources we could observe an outspoken critical attitude towards Huldah: She should have kept silent during the time that Jeremiah was active, and she should not have spoken about 'that man' but, more respectfully, about 'the king.' But also in the pre-rabbinic literature of the first century CE one finds already similar sentiments, albeit not as far as Huldah is concerned but as to her match, the prophetess Deborah (Judges 4:4 explicitly calls her 'prophetess'). In his rendering of the biblical history, the historian Josephus makes no effort to conceal his disdain for this female leader figure.[16] He reduces the almost 800 words of the biblical story about Deborah (in Judges 4–5) to less than 500 (*Antiquitates Judaicae* 5:200–209), whereas his much more women-friendly contemporary, the unknown author of the Pseudo-Philonic *Liber Antiquitatum Biblicarum*, devotes more than 2500 words to this woman, and in a very positive way at that (chs. 30–33)![17] Josephus clearly wants to trivialize Deborah's role; he even makes her burst out in an indignant tone (*aganaktêsasa*) against Barak when the latter asks her to share the supreme command with him: 'You, how could you yield to a woman a rank that God has given you? Nevertheless, I do not decline it' (5.203). Deborah's famous song (Judges 5) is even completely omitted by Josephus. Louis Feldman concludes at the end of his study of Josephus' portrait of Deborah: 'Josephus (…) has, in his misogyny, both reduced

---

[13] See D. Satran, *Biblical Prophets in Byzantine Palestine. Reassessing the* Lives of the Prophets, Leiden 1995, who argues that it is a Christian document from the Byzantine period, and for the contrary position (early Jewish origin) see A. M. Schwemer, *Studien zu den frühjüdischen Prophetenlegenden* Vitae Prophetarum, 2 vols., Tübingen 1995.

[14] P.W. van der Horst, *Die Prophetengräber im antiken Judentum* (Delitzsch-Vorlesung 2000), Münster 2001. An English version in my book *Japheth in the Tents of Shem*, Leuven 2002, 119–138.

[15] Schwemer, *Studien* I 30 n. 130, remarks with regard to Huldah's absence in the *Vitae Prophetarum*: 'Weibliche Propheten standen in frühjüdischer Zeit nicht hoch im Kurs." That is an understatement.

[16] See for what follows L.H. Feldman's chapter 'Deborah' in his *Studies in Josephus' Rewritten Bible*, Leiden 1998, 153–162.

[17] See P.W. van der Horst, 'Portraits of Biblical Women in Pseudo-Philo's Liber Antiquitatum Biblicarum,' in my *Essays on the Jewish World of Early Christianity*, Fribourg-Göttingen, 1990, 111–122, esp. 114–5.

the length of the episode and the importance of Deborah, downgrading her in her role of poetess, military leader, and judge.'[18] This is not an isolated case. As in early Christian literature, one comes across a lot of denigrating language about women (biblical and non-biblical) in early Jewish sources as well.[19] The fact that, as we have seen above, Deborah and Huldah together parade as examples of 'shameless women' in later rabbinic sources is an indication that it is far from purely speculative to claim that the omission of Huldah and her tomb in the *Vitae prophetarum* may well be more than a coincidence. It is highly probable that here a conscious decision was taken.

Yet it is an established fact that Huldah's tomb, like those of the matriarchs Sarah, Rebeccah, Rachel and Leah, and Jephthah's daughter, was known to be in Jerusalem at the beginning of the Common Era and even enjoyed a certain fame. How should we interpret that? Recent research has confirmed that, even though one would not expect it from a biblical point of view, a certain veneration of saints, usually in the form of pilgrimage to and prayer at the tombs of biblical saints, had developed in the period of the Second Temple and in early Talmudic times.[20] Of course, these practices were frowned upon by scribes and rabbis, who rejected them if only because the corpse impurity one could incur at gravesites was the gravest form of ritual impurity known in ancient Judaism.[21] But, as Saul Lieberman has remarked: 'The Torah forbade a number [of these practices], and the rabbis added their own prohibitions. However, it is easier to fight wickedness than to combat the superstitions of pious people. (…) The masses had their own ways.'[22] People conceived of the biblical saints as still present in their tombs and listening to the prayers of the people who asked for intercession with God, for healing etc.[23] Not only the *Life of Isaiah* 8 makes clear that the prophet's tomb

---

[18] Feldman, 'Deborah' 162.

[19] See for a first orientation P.W. van der Horst, 'Conflicting Images of Women in Ancient Judaism,' in my *Hellenism – Judaism – Christianity: Essays on Their Interaction*, 2nd ed., Leuven 1998, 73–92.

[20] See, e. g., J.N. Lightstone, *The Commerce of the Sacred. Mediation of the Divine among Jews in the Graeco-Roman Diaspora*, Chico 1984, 70–87; W. Horbury, 'The Cult of Christ and the Cult of the Saints,' *New Testament Studies* 44 (1998) 444–469; and my above-mentioned *Prophetengräber im antiken Judentum*.

[21] The rabbinic Mishnah treatise *Ohaloth* deals with this subject. Zie W. Bunte, *Ohalot* (Die Mischna VI 2), Berlin-New York 1988, esp. 24–48.

[22] S. Lieberman, 'Some Aspects of After Life in Early Rabbinic Literature,' in his *Texts and Studies*, New York 1974, 252–253. Morton Smith rightly noticed that one should not construct a rigid opposition between 'popular religion' on the one hand and rabbinic attitudes on the other for 'even rabbinic tradition contains some elements which show an amazing indifference to this consideration [of impurity], e. g. the story that Solomon brought the coffin of David into the Temple (Pesiq. Rab. 2, ed. Friedmann 6b, & parallels): Instead of polluting it, this produced the descent of the heavenly fire' ('The Image of God,' in his *Studies in the Cult of Yahweh*, Leiden 1996, vol. 1, 131–2 n. 73).

[23] See Jeremias, *Heiligengräber* 129: '[S]ie alle waren für sie nicht tote Gestalten der Vergangenheit, sondern sie lebten in ihren Gräbern, nahmen teil am Ergehen des Volkes.' Satran, *Biblical Prophets* 111, in this connection refers to the epitaph of Saint Martin: 'Here lies Martin

was venerated in order that 'by his prayers even after his death' one could reap the fruits of his influence with God, but also the polemic against the idea that deceased persons can intercede with God, e. g. in Pseudo-Philo's *LAB* 33:4 and in other early Jewish documents,[24] strongly suggests that the tombs of biblical saints had become centres of pilgrimage where these saints were beseeched to make intercession.

That is probably also how it went in the case of Huldah. There was no denying that she played a striking role in the biblical story, however limited it was. It is quite possible that for that reason she was an inspiring role model for Jewish women. In the Hellenistic-Roman period, when the cult of biblical saints at the sites of their tombs began to develop gradually among certain sectors of the Jewish population of Palestine – a development that the rabbis could not stop, even if they tried hard – this prophetess carved out her own niche alongside all the male prophets, who *were* dealt with in the *Vitae Prophetarum*. In spite of considerable opposition, she gained a place in the very modest row of biblical women whose graves became centres of Jewish popular piety.

---

the bishop, of holy memory, whose soul is in the hand of God; but he is fully here, present and made plain in miracles of every kind' (quoted after P. Brown, *The Cult of the Saints*, Chicago 1981, 4). Cf. also John 5:28: 'All who are in the tombs will hear his voice.'

[24] See Ch. Perrot & M. Bogaert, *Pseudo-Philon: Les Antiquités Bibliques*, vol. 2, Paris 1976, 177, for references. See also J. Wilkinson, 'Visits to Jewish Tombs by Early Christians,' *Akten des XII. Internationalen Kongresses für christliche Archäologie* [= Jahrbuch für Antike und Christentum Ergänzungsband 20], 2 vols., Münster 1995, 1: 456.

Pseudo-Phocylides on the Afterlife

A Rejoinder to John Collins

In a recent publication, John Collins takes me to task for several statements I made in my commentary on Pseudo-Phocylides of 25 years ago, especially as far as this Jewish author's view of the afterlife is concerned.[1] After having carefully studied Collins' points of criticism, I had to come to the conclusion that most of them have little or no basis, as I will now demonstrate.

To begin with, I should state that the passage under discussion (vv. 103–115), in which this Jewish author sets out his view on the fate of the individual after death, is notoriously difficult and has given rise to very contradictory interpretations over the past 150 years. It is no wonder that one scholar speaks of "the unharmonized juxtaposition of contradictory ideas about afterlife" in this passage.[2] Most scholars find it very difficult, if not impossible, to interpret these 13 lines as a systematic exposition of a consistent view on life after death, especially so since, *inter alia*, the author seems to defend the immortality of the soul as much as the resurrection of the body[3] and, moreover, does not clarify the relations between body, soul, and spirit. Collins is less pessimistic, however. He concedes that Pseudo-Phocylides relied on traditional forms that "stand in some tension with each other" (85), but affirms at the same time that he "strung them together in a way that achieved a measure of coherence" (85). It may well be the case that there is more unity and coherence to this passage than I and others have been able to see,[4] but Collins' arguments are sometimes far from convincing.

I will first deal with his objections to my translation of the first line of the passage. Vv. 103–104a καὶ τάχα δ᾽ ἐκ γαίης ἐλπίζομεν ἐς φάος ἐλθεῖν / λείψαν᾽

---

[1] J.J. Collins, "Life After Death in Pseudo-Phocylides," in F. García Martínez & G.P. Luttikhuizen (eds), *Jerusalem, Alexandria, Rome. Studies in Ancient Cultural Interaction in Honour of A. Hilhorst*, Supplements to Journal for the Study of Judaism 82, Leiden 2003, 75–86. My commentary: P.W. van der Horst, *The Sentences of Pseudo-Phocylides*, Leiden 1978, 185–195.

[2] H.C.C. Cavallin, *Life After Death*, vol. I, Lund 1974, 153.

[3] See the fine discussion of this issue in the chapter "Immortality and Resurrection: Conflict or Complementarity?" in James Barr, *The Garden of Eden and the Hope of Immortality*, Minneapolis 1992, 94–116.

[4] But, as Arthur Nock said, "to press this point would be to ignore the widespread tendency of language about the afterlife to admit inconsistencies" (*Essays on Religion and the Ancient World*, vol. 1, Oxford 1972, 507 n. 19).

ἀποιχομένων was translated by me as follows: "For in fact we hope that the remains of the departed will soon come to the light again out of the earth." His own translation is rather different: "And we hope that the remains of the dead will perhaps come to the light again out of the earth" (75). Collins firstly objects (twice, 75 and 79) that 'in fact' in my translation is without any basis in the Greek. That is not true. My translation is based upon the following considerations. One has to make sense of καὶ ... δέ in the text. Usually this combination implies that the former particle denotes that something is added, and the latter that what is added is distinct from what precedes.[5] But that does not make sense here. In the preceding line (102), the author has warned against disintegrating the human frame (most probably for anatomical purposes). What follows must give the reason for this prohibition. Just as in the immediately preceding lines (100–101), the reason given for his prohibition against disturbing graves is that it may stir up divine anger, so one would expect something similar here. There can be no doubt that the prohibition against disintegrating the human frame stands in a close relationship to the immediately following remark about the hope of the resurrection of the body. Because this bodily resurrection is hoped for, one should not dissect the human frame. So one expects a word like γάρ here, not particles denoting that something is added and that what is added is different from what precedes. Now it is well-known that in Greek "δέ is not infrequently used where the context admits, or even appears to demand, γάρ."[6] Denniston lists dozens of examples, especially from poetry, and adds the observation that ancient scholia often observe: ὁ δέ ἀντὶ τοῦ γάρ (δέ is used instead of γάρ). In other words, δέ is the word indicating the causal connection that we need here.[7] So much for δέ, which is left untranslated by Collins. He does translate καί by 'and' whereas I render it by 'in fact' (which Collins says has no basis in the Greek text). Why this unusual translation? The common meanings of καί such as 'and,' 'also,' or 'even' do not make sense at all here. After a stern prohibition against disintegrating dead human bodies it would be lame to continue by saying, 'and we hope for the resurrection.' The force of καί here, however, is that of an emphatic particle. It is again discussed at length in the classic work of Denniston. He says on καί that its meaning can easily pass into 'actually' (or 'in fact'!), 'really,' 'indeed,' and that for that reason it "is often used before intensive and quantitative adverbs and adjectives,"[8] in cases such as καί λίαν, καί μάλα, καί πάνυ, καί πόλυς etc. So it makes perfect sense to translate the line as 'for in fact we hope ...' or 'for we really hope ...' or even 'for we very much hope that etc.' Another possibility is to connect καί more closely to τάχα, and to translate 'for we hope that really soon etc.'

---

[5] J.D. Denniston, *The Greek Particles*, Oxford 1954 (2nd ed.), 199.
[6] Denniston, *Particles* 169.
[7] That Ps-Phoc. does not use γάρ here is probably *metri causa*.
[8] Denniston, *Particles* 317.

This leads us immediately to another difference between Collins' and my translation. He renders τάχα by 'perhaps' as against my 'soon.' His motivation for this translation, which is in itself possible from a lexical point of view, is as follows: "Pseudo-Phocylides was no apocalyptic visionary, and there is no hint in the poem of imminent eschatology" (79); and he adds that 'perhaps' is the more appropriate translation here because "this is the only time in this passage where he speaks of hope" (79). "The resurrection of the physical body is acknowledged as a possibility to be hoped for. Presumably the author was aware that some Jews held this belief, and he affirms it tentatively. ... The tone is speculative rather than certain" (79). I find all this very unconvincing. To begin with, the fact that there is no other hint in the poem of imminent eschatology is absolutely no argument against taking τάχα to mean 'soon,' since as is the case with most other subjects broached by our author, he hardly ever devotes more than one or two lines to them, however important they may be. So this line may indeed be the only one in which the author reveals his imminent eschatology. But apart from that, 'soon' may here simply imply that the author hopes that his bodily remains will be resurrected soon after his death, so that no apocalyptic scenario of an imminent eschaton is implied at all. My above remarks about the probable meaning of καί here, especially the important observation by Denniston that it is often used before intensive and quantitative adverbs, makes it all the more probable that 'soon' and not 'perhaps' is meant here. The author's use of the verb 'hoping' (ἐλπίζειν) is not evidence of a 'speculative' tone, as Collins would have us believe, but it rather indicates that the author looks forward to something "with the implication of *confidence* about something coming to pass,"[9] as is usually the case in early Jewish and Christian literature. The whole poem speaks a strong and self-assured language, with never a trace of hesitancy, so that a lame 'perhaps,' especially in such a vital matter as the nature of life after death, would be wholly inappropriate. So Collins' translation and interpretation looks very improbable. I would even suggest that this translation is ruled out by the immediately following triumphant words ὀπίσω δὲ θεοὶ τελέθονται ('and thereafter they become gods!', 104b), which I take to express the strong conviction that the resurrected righteous will be elevated to heaven where they will shine like stars (see my commentary *ad locum*).

Let me finally add some comments about one or two other points where we disagree. Collins counters my remark about the 'very un-Greek' nature of the doctrine of the resurrection by pointing out that there are many stories in the Greek world of individuals who had returned from the dead (76). I find this irrelevant since these stories concern exceptional and individual cases and have nothing to do with shared eschatological expectations. Collins also objects to my statement that there is not the slightest hint of the use of ossuaria in the line

---

[9] *BDAG* 319 *s.v.* ἐλπίζω (italics added).

containing the prohibition against disintegrating the human frame for he finds it difficult to see "how the admonition would not apply to the practice of second-ary burial, which most certainly involved the dissolution of the human frame" (78 n. 18). As he himself concedes, however, Alexandria is still by far the most likely place of origin of the poem. Ossuaria were mainly in use in Palestine, particularly in and around Jerusalem, only occasionally elsewhere.[10] They were certainly not a common phenomenon in Alexandria but dissection of human bodies for anatomical research *was* practiced in Alexandria, and only there as far as we know. This fact makes my interpretation that 'disintegrating the human frame' refers to this practice much more feasible.

Finally, at pp. 83–84 Collins ingeniously tries to make sense of lines 105–108, where at first sight Pseudo-Phocylides seems to imply a tripartite anthropology by speaking of body, soul, and spirit. The poet says that the souls (ψυχαί) remain unharmed in the deceased (or 'among the dead,' thus Collins); that the spirit (πνεῦμα) is a loan from God to mortals and also his image; and that the body (σῶμα) comes from earth and returns again into earth, but that the air receives the spirit (πνεῦμα). Later (v. 111) he adds that God rules over the souls (ψυχαί) and that these are immortal and live forever (115). This is not the place to discuss all aspects of this seemingly confused collocation of ideas. I will again focus only on an aspect upon which Collins and I disagree. This is the question of whether or not 'soul' and 'spirit' are here distinct or identical. I argued that they are identical, as is so often the case in Jewish-Hellenistic literature (see, e. g., *Test. Abraham* [rec.A] 16–20).[11] Collins thinks they are distinct entities. He interprets the passage as follows: When we die, our body returns to dust, our soul goes to Hades, and our spirit goes up to the air. Assuming that Hades is the place is where the souls dwell after death (which is not explicit in the text!), God must rule over the souls in Hades, from where they will be again united with the spirit and the body at the resurrection. Much could be said about this reconstruction of Pseudo-Phocylides' view, but let me limit my remarks to what I think is the main point: It is said explicitly that the spirit (πνεῦμα) is a loan from God to mortals and also his image (106). In several other Graeco-Jewish texts, this is what is said about the soul (ψυχή). That does not necessarily imply that the same is meant here too, but another point should be kept in mind as well. The spirit is taken up into the air and returns to God because he had given it to humans only as a loan. It is to be assumed that from the moment of death onwards God rules over these spirits; after all they were his loan. The text, however, says that God rules

---

[10] R. Hachlili, *Ancient Jewish Art and Archaeology in the Land of Israel*, Leiden 1988, 89–119. L.Y. Rahmani, *A Catalogue of Jewish Ossuaries in the Collections of the State of Israel*, Jerusalem 1994, 21–25, 302–307. C.A. Evans, *Jesus and the Ossuaries. What Jewish Burial Practices Reveal about the Beginning of Christianity*, Waco 2003.

[11] For more instances see W. Bousset & H. Gressmann, *Die Religion des Judentums im späthellenistischen Zeitalter*, Tübingen 1966, 400.

over the souls not the spirits. Why would God rule over the souls of humans else-where (in Hades, says Collins) while the spirits of these same humans are with him in heaven (taken back again into the air)? That does not make sense. Only if one assumes that souls and spirits are identical can this anomaly be avoided. The consequence is then, however, that one has also to assume that Hades = the air (granting Collins that the souls are in Hades, which is uncertain). According to Pseudo-Phocylides' contemporary, the Stoic theologian Cornutus, in his *Compendium of Greek Theology* 35, this is precisely what was done by philosophers and theologians: τὸν δεχόμενον τὰς ψυχὰς ἀέρα "Αιδην ... προσηγόρευσαν (they called the air that receives the souls Hades). And he is not the only witness to this belief about a Hades high up in the air.[12] So an interpretation that identifies soul and spirit still seems to me to be defensible.

Much more could be said about this fascinating passage. My aim here was modest, however. I wanted to demonstrate that Collins' criticisms of my inter-pretation of Pseudo-Phocylides can in some cases be refuted and in other cases be shown to be less convincing than he thinks. I want to thank John Collins for this challenge and opportunity for debate.

Postscript

[In a postscript added to the reprint of his article in his *Jewish Cult and Hel-lenistic Culture* (Leiden 2005, 139–142), Collins tries to restate his position, but unfortunately he misrepresents one of my main points of criticism (the meaning of the combination καὶ ... δέ; apparently Collins still does not know the foun-dational work of Denniston); he ignores another (the usual sense of ἐλπίζειν); moreover, he glosses over my argument that, when the spirit is said to be a loan from God that returns to the air (= heaven) after death, it is only to be expected that God then rules over the spirits, which Pseudo-Phocylides says God does over the *souls*. Again, I am not at all convinced.]

---

[12] Many other references to where this belief is attested can be found in F. Cumont, *Lux perpetua*, Paris 1949, 189–218.

Philo's *In Flaccum* and the Book of Acts

Collecting parallels from Philo to the New Testament has been part and parcel of the Corpus Judaeo-Hellenisticum project from the beginning, and understandably so. Also apart from this project, several scholars have undertaken detailed comparisons of Philo with a specific New Testament author or corpus.[1] Much less common, however, is the comparison of one book of Philo with one New Testament book. Does a comparison between Philo's *In Flaccum* and the Book of Acts make any sense, one might ask, and the answer is yes. Both books deal for a great part with events that took place in the decades around the middle of the first century CE in a Mediterranean urban setting where diaspora Jews or Jewish communities were living. If for no other reason, this would already be enough justification for comparing these two books. Aside from that, although writing 'history,' neither of the two authors, Philo and 'Luke', were professional historiographers; they were theologians who wanted to convey a clear message and their 'histories' stood in the service of that message – however different their respective messages may have been. Both are apologetic historians of a very special sort.[2] Philo wants to demonstrate that God has never abandoned the Jewish people and will never do so.[3] Luke wants to present an apology for the main protagonist Paul and his teaching, and he wants to portray Christianity as a harmless, even beneficial religion.[4] Both of them picture their respective religions as having a positive outlook on and loyal attitude towards the Roman empire, and for that reason the apparent conflicts have to be attributed to the machinations of people with evil intent, or to misunderstanding. These are some of the more general points of contact between the two documents.

We now turn to a more detailed comparison of some elements that both writings have in common one way or another. If we look at persons, first and

---

[1] E.g., R. Williamson, *Philo and the Epistle to the Hebrews*, Leiden 1970; B.W. Winter, *Philo and Paul Among the Sophists*, Cambridge 1997.

[2] For apologetic historiography see G.E. Sterling, *Historiography and Self-Definition. Josephos, Luke-Acts and Apologetic Historiography* (Supplements to Novum Testamentum 64), Leiden 1992.

[3] See P.W. van der Horst, *Philo's Flaccus. The First Pogrom*, with Introduction, Translation, and Commentary (PACS 2), Leiden 2003, Introduction, esp. pp. 1–2, 16–17.

[4] C.K. Barrett, *The Acts of the Apostles* (ICC), vol. II, Edinburgh 1998, lxxxii–cx.

foremost to be mentioned is the Jewish puppet king Agrippa I.[5] His role in both writings is markedly and strikingly different, if not contradictory at first sight. In *In Flaccum* Philo tells us that just before the outbreak of the pogrom that took place in Alexandria in the summer of the year 38, quite unexpectedly Agrippa showed up in that city. We are informed that shortly before, the emperor Gaius gave Agrippa, the grandson of king Herod the Great, as his kingdom a third of his grandfather's inheritance, namely the part over which Philip the tetrarch, his paternal uncle, used to rule. On the way to his new kingdom in the south of Lebanon he made a stop in Alexandria and tried to remain incognito, but without success. The Jews hailed him as a king but the Greeks staged a mock ceremony in which they honoured a local Jewish lunatic by calling him *marin*, 'our Lord' in Aramaic. The importance of Agrippa's role in the events of 38 becomes apparent, however, only in the second half of the treatise. The whole treatise has been structured by Philo as a diptych: the first half is about the undeserved sufferings that the Jews underwent in the pogrom, the second half about the well-deserved sufferings of their enemy, the Roman governor Flaccus, who not only let everything run out of hand but even actively encouraged the Greeks and Egyptians to commit many atrocities against the Jews. This second half is introduced by postponed information about a declaration of loyalty that the Jewish community of Alexandria had tried to send to the new emperor, Gaius Caligula, on the occasion of his accession to the throne in 37. They had to send this declaration via the Roman governor, Flaccus, who, however, did not pass it on; he simply withheld it and put it into a drawer. As Philo says, the dramatic consequence of that was that "of all the people under the sun only the Jews would be considered enemies of the emperor" (101). But he goes on to say:

God, however, took mercy on us and saw to it that not long thereafter we had good reason to think that our hopes were not lost. For when king Agrippa visited us, we informed him of Flaccus' intrigues, *whereupon he intervened to rectify the matter*. He promised us that he would forward the decree to the emperor – which, as we later heard, is what he indeed did – with apologies for the delay, showing that we were not slow at all in understanding the duty of piety towards our benefactor and his family; that, on the contrary, we had been zealous in this respect from the very beginning, but that we had been deprived of the opportunity to demonstrate this zeal in time due to the governor's maliciousness (102–3).

What then follows is the main part of the second half of the diptych, namely the dramatic story of Flaccus' arrest, trial, condemnation, deportation and death. Philo implies here without any doubt that Agrippa's interference was instrumental in God's plan to punish Flaccus for his misdeeds.

Now, for our present purposes, we need not go into the difficult question of whether or not it was Agrippa's letter to Gaius that was the decisive factor in

---

[5] D. Schwartz, *Agrippa I: The Last King of Judaea*, Tübingen 1990, is the best monograph on this king.

Flaccus' demise – it was certainly not the only factor, to say the least – but the important point is that Agrippa is portrayed here (and elsewhere in the treatise) in a very positive way. He saved the Jews from further persecution and is the man who saw to it that the persecutor of the Jewish people was rightly punished. In the immediate sequel to *In Flaccum*, Philo's *Legatio ad Gaium*, he again presents this king as a person who went to great lengths in taking his responsibility for the safety of the Jewish people very seriously. His courageous stance in the *Legatio* is painted with fervour in a very long section of the book (see *Leg.* 261–348). As Danny Schwartz says, there we see him "as an advocate of the Jews of the Empire."[6] Philo probably knew the king very well since his brother, the alabarch Alexander, was the financier, the moneylender to Agrippa, who was a notorious spendthrift (according to Josephus, *Ant.* 19.352), and there are good reasons to surmise that, during his stay in Alexandria, Agrippa was even Philo's own guest (he says, 'king Agrippa visited *us*' [103]). How does this picture of Agrippa as a person who saved his people from (further) persecution relate to the image of Agrippa painted by Luke in the Book of Acts?

To state immediately the most obvious: Luke presents Agrippa (whom only he calls Herod) as a persecutor himself. In Acts 12 he persecutes the early church in Jerusalem: "He killed James the brother of John with the sword, and when he saw that it pleased the Jews, he proceeded to arrest Peter as well. This was done during the feast of unleavened bread" (12:2–3). At the end of the same chapter, however, we read how God punished the king for this. After having addressed a delegation of the people of Tyre and Sidon in Caesarea Maritima, "the people shouted, 'The voice of a god and not of a man!' Immediately an angel of the Lord smote him because he did not give God the glory; and he was eaten by worms and died" (12:22–23). Some remarks are in order here.[7]

Firstly, in Philo's book Flaccus took ever more severe measures against the Jews *in order to please the Jew-haters* in Alexandria, as Philo explicitly says (§ 82), and it is Agrippa who saves them; but in the Book of Acts it is Agrippa himself who takes additional measures against the Christians and has Peter put into prison *in order to please the Jews* (12:3). And secondly, while Flaccus' actions against the Jews took place partly during the feast of Sukkoth, as Philo emphatically mentions (§ 116), the one by Agrippa is emphatically said to have taken place during Pesach (12:3). It is as if Luke had read *In Flaccum* and now reverses the roles.

This impression is further strenghtened by a closer look at the fate of the main culprits of the two stories. In *In Flaccum* we see a typical example of what Lactantius would later call the *mortes persecutorum*. Almost at the end of his *De mortibus persecutorum*, written in the second decade of the 4th century CE,

---

[6] *Agrippa* 77.
[7] See also Schwartz, *Agrippa* 119–124.

Lactantius says: "In this way God vanquished all the persecutors of His Name, so that no stem or root of theirs remained" (50.1). This is the conclusion of a work in which the author describes the miserable fate of all those who tried to annihilate the adherents of the Christian faith and were consequently punished very severely by God.[8] Lactantius here stands in a long tradition: The theme of the violent death of those who fight against or resisted the (or a) deity (or its worshippers), who have been called θεομάχοι since Euripides, reaches back far into the pre-Christian period, and there can be no doubt that Philo and Luke were acquainted with it. Since Herodotus there is a long row of sinners who were punished for their impiety, quite often by being eaten by worms (σκωληκόβρωτος, cf. Acts 12:23), according to tradition; shipwreck is the favorite kind of punishment for atheists (e. g., Diagoras and Protagoras); further we come across insanity, being struck by lightning, being torn apart by wild animals or humans, being burnt etc. The motif was taken up early in Judaism and Christianity (think of the stories about the fates of Holophernes, Antiochus IV, the emperor Titus, Judas a. o.[9]), and there can be little doubt that, just like Lactantius, both Philo and Luke stood in this Graeco-Jewish-Christian tradition of what Wilhelm Nestle has called "Legenden vom Tod der Gottesverächter."[10] The significant thing is that, according to Philo, king Agrippa is the opponent of the *theomachos*, whereas according to Luke he is the *theomachos* himself, who dies a death that is typical of many 'Gottesverächter,' namely being σκωληκόβρωτος, eaten by worms.[11]

There is little reason to doubt the historicity of Agrippa's intervention on behalf of the Alexandrian Jewish community. Philo would have made a fool of himself if he had written things that many people in his environment knew had not taken place. There is no reason either to doubt that what Luke writes about Agrippa's persecution of Jerusalem Christians has a historical kernel. True, it is hard to find the reason why Agrippa engaged in persecution of the early Christians (which admittedly was very limited) because Luke does not mention any reason, thus mirroring Philo's silence on the reasons for the persecution of the Alexandrian Jews. But even so both aspects, Agrippa as opponent of a persecutor and Agrippa as a persecutor himself, are two sides of the same Agrippa-coin. It may be added that the historicity of Luke's story about Agrippa's death is more or less confirmed by Josephus (*Ant.* 19.343–352), but that Luke, unlike Josephus, stresses that he was punished this way not so much because of his persecution of the Jerusalem church but because he accepted acclamations that implied his

---

[8] J.L. Creed, (ed. and transl.), *Lactantius: De mortibus persecutorum*, Oxford 1984, xxxv–xl.

[9] Holophernes in Judith 13; Antiochus IV in 2 Macc. 9; Titus in b.*Gittin* 56b, *Bereshit Rabba* 10.7, *Vayikra Rabba* 22.3; Judas in Matt. 27:5.

[10] W. Nestle, "Legenden vom Tod der Gottesverächter," *ARW* 33 (1936) 246–269; see now esp. W. Speyer, "Gottesfeind," *RAC* 11 (1981) 996–1043.

[11] Many instances in Barrett, *Acts* I, 591.

divinity, whereas Josephus has Agrippa make critical remarks on these acclamations.[12] But in the final analysis "both Luke and Josephus agree that Agrippa died because he attempted to exceed his natural limits."[13]

When we now take another look at the Agrippa passage in *In Flaccum*, we notice a different problem, but of a minor nature, namely the king's route from Rome to Lebanon. As Philo writes, "When Agrippa was about to leave, Gaius advised him not to make the voyage to Syria via Brindisium, because that made for a long and tiresome trip, but to wait for the trade winds and then take the shorter route via Alexandria. He said that the trading vessels that departed from there were very fast and had highly experienced pilots, who guided their ships like charioteers driving their race-horses, keeping them straight and on course. Agrippa complied with this advice because Gaius was his master but also because it seemed that the advice he had been given was useful" (26). Several things may be said about this paragraph.

Strabo (*Geogr.* 6.3.7 [282]) indicates that the route via Brindisium and Greece and the Greek islands and vice versa was not uncommon at all; Philo himself describes it later on when Flaccus is deported to the island of Andros, some 100 kilometers off the coast of Athens (*Flacc.* 152–156). It was a long and arduous journey which would normally take 2 to 3 months. The route via Alexandria was not shorter – here Gaius, or Philo, is mistaken, or lying – but it is much quicker. It was, however, also more risky because one had to cross large stretches of open sea. It would usually take 2 to 4 weeks depending upon the weather and other circumstances (Pliny says that the absolute record for the passage was 9 days, *Nat. hist.* 19.1.3).

A different view of these two routes was recently proposed by the Israeli scholar Kushnir-Stein,[14] who argues that the northern route was shorter, easier and less dangerous, and that the route proposed by the emperor was longer and more difficult, thus implying that Gaius' nonsensical advice has been wholly fabricated by Philo. But Kushnir-Stein tends to overlook the problem of the quick availability of large ships on the northern route, which was no problem when travelling via Puteoli and Alexandria (because of the frequent grain transports between these two harbours), whereas on the other route it could be a real problem (even apart from the need to change ships several times). Understandably, later Christian pilgrims to the Holy Land from the West usually travelled by ship via Alexandria as well.[15]

---

[12] Barrett's remark that "Luke probably thought of him [Agrippa] as the first Gentile adversary of the church" (I, 575) is an improbable suggestion.

[13] Schwartz, *Agrippa* 149.

[14] A. Kushnir-Stein, "On the Visit of Agrippa I to Alexandria in AD 38," *JJS* 51 (2000) 232–233.

[15] E.D. Hunt, *Holy Land Pilgrimage in the Later Roman Empire, AD 312–460*, Oxford 1982, 53, 63, 72, 74.

The trading vessels mentioned by Philo were merchant ships used for the transport of a wide variety of goods such as glass, paper, linen, metals, but between Alexandria and Rome they were especially for the transportation of corn, since Alexandria was Rome's most important granary. These ships were exploited by large associations of shipowners and their *collegia*.[16] Philo says that Agrippa chose one or more of these for a quick journey to Alexandria, which sounds quite probable.

Philo also says that "Agrippa complied … because it seemed that the advice he had been given [by Gaius] was useful." One may doubt this reason, for it has rightly been suggested that Agrippa had things to do in Alexandria and that Philo had his own apologetic reasons for covering this up.[17] Kushnir-Stein points out that Philo's repeated reference to Gaius' advice (in § 31 it is even said to have been his commandment) serves to drive home the point that Agrippa's presence in Alexandria was not of his own choice, a point which seems doubtful; she suggests that his visit may have been *intended* to intervene in the Jewish-Greek conflict (see § 103!), which may have sparked the riots for that very reason.[18] But in fact there is no way of knowing the actual reason for Agrippa's visit.

Be that as it may, the short nautical excursus on the best route is illustrative, in an indirect way, for the passage on Paul's sea voyage in Acts 27–28, albeit that it was exactly the other way round, namely from a coastal town in northern Israel to Rome, but partly via the route Alexandria-Rome. A comparison with the story of Paul's stormy voyage to Rome, the final stage of which was made on a ship from Alexandria, indicates that crossing the Mediterranean was something that could not be undertaken lightly and without careful preparation both as far as the choice of the route and the vessel and as far as the time of travelling was concerned. Both passages shed mutual light upon each other as regards travel problems in the ancient Mediterranean.[19]

Finally some remarks should be made on synagogues, firstly in relation to the reference to the 'synagogue of the *Libertinoi*' in Acts 6:9. There is a passage in *Flacc.* 53 where Philo says that "his [Flaccus'] attack on our laws by means of a seizure of our synagogues, of which he had even the names removed, seemed to be succesful to him." It is hard to say what Philo has in mind when he writes about synagogues "of which he had even *the names* removed." How the removal of the synagogue names in Alexandria was brought about is uncertain. Were name plates removed, or erased (by way of *damnatio memoriae*)? Were the buildings so thoroughly destroyed that they were no longer recognizable as synagogue buildings of this or that name? We do not know. Anyway, the element

---

[16] P.W. van der Horst, *Philo's* Flaccus 117.

[17] E. g., Schwartz, *Agrippa* 74.

[18] Kushnir-Stein, "Agrippa's Visit" 230.

[19] L. Casson, *Travel in the Ancient World*, Baltimore 1974, passim.

of synagogue *names* is interesting in that both epigraphic evidence and the Book of Acts testify to this phenomenon.

From valuable epigraphic evidence in Rome we know that synagogues there had names.[20] There were synagogal communities which derived their names from prominent persons, who may or may not have been patrons of these congregations. The συναγωγὴ Αὐγουστησίων (CIJ 284, 301, 338, 368, 416, 496 = JIWE II, 547, 96, 169, 189, 194, 542)[21] was no doubt named after the first Emperor, who is known to have befriended the Jews; and the συναγωγὴ Ἀγριππησίων (CIJ 365, 425, 503 = JIWE II, 170, 130, 549) was very probably named after Augustus' son-in-law and adviser Marcus Agrippa, who was also a real friend of the Jews, as we know from literary sources. Or was it perhaps called after Agrippa I, the Jewish king just mentioned who had lived in Rome for so long?[22] The συναγωγὴ Βολουμνησίων (CIJ 343, 402, 417, 523 = JIWE II, 167, 100, 163, 577) was named after a certain Volumnius, presumably its patron, who is, however, completely unknown to us. Other communities were named after the district or area of the city where the members lived or where their house of worship was situated (or probably both). There is a synagogue of the Καμπήσιοι (CIJ 88, 319, 523, perhaps 433 = JIWE II, 288, 560, 577, 1), named after the Campus Martius; a synagogue of the Σιβουρήσιοι (CIJ 18, 22, 67, 140, 380, 35a, perhaps 37 = JIWE II, 428, 451, 452, 338, 557, 527, 488), named after the Subura, one of the most populous quarters of ancient Rome. Probably also the synagogue of the Καλκαρήσιοι (CIJ 304, 316, 384, 504, 537, perhaps 433 = JIWE II, 69, 98, 165, 558, 584, 1) belongs here: *calcar(i)enses* are lime-burners, and it seems reasonable to assume that this name derives from the quarter where the lime-burners lived and worked and where the Jewish synagogue building was situated. Further there are two synagogues named after the cities where their members originally came from: a συναγωγὴ Τριπολιτῶν (CIJ 390, 408 = JIWE II, 166, 113), probably Tripolis in Phoenicia, but possibly Tripolis in Libya being meant here; and a συναγωγὴ Ἐλέας or Ἐλαίας (CIJ 281, 509 = JIWE II, 406, 576), probably not the 'synagogue of the olive tree' (which does not make sense), but the synagogue of Elea, although it must remain quite uncertain which one of the various towns

---

[20] For the following see P.W. van der Horst, *Ancient Jewish Epitaphs. An Introductory Survey of a Millennium of Jewish Funerary Epigraphy (300 BCE – 700 CE)*, Kampen 1991, 86–89.

[21] CIJ stands for *Corpus Inscriptionum Judaicarum*, ed. J.-B. Frey, 2 vols, Rome 1936–1952. JIWE stands for *Jewish Inscriptions of Western Europe. Volume 2: The City of Rome*, ed. D. Noy, Cambridge 1995.

[22] Fergus Millar, in E. Schürer's *History of the Jewish People in the Age of Jesus Christ* III, Edinburgh 1986, 96, defends the thesis that these communities "may have originally consisted of slaves and freedmen of Augustus or of Agrippa," and he refers to οἱ ἐκ τῆς Καίσαρος οἰκίας in Phil. 4:22. This cannot be wholly ruled out. The less probable thesis that the *Agrippesioi* named themselves after the Jewish king Agrippa I (or II) is proposed, for example, by K. Galling, "Die jüdischen Katakomben in Rom als ein Beitrag zur jüdischen Konfessionskunde," *Theologische Studien und Kritiken* 103 (1931) 353.

named Elea can be meant here. Finally, there are two synagogues named after characteristics of their members. There is a συναγωγὴ Ἑβραίων (CIJ 291, 317, 510, 535 = JIWE II, 33, 2, 578, 579); here one can compare the 'synagogue of the Hebrews' in Corinth (CIJ 718), and also the one in Lydian Philadelphia (CIJ 754), the nature of which is much debated. Does it designate a synagogue of Hebrew speaking persons (but their inscriptions are mostly in Greek!), or a synagogue where the liturgy was in Hebrew (cf. Justinian's *Novella* 146!), or the synagogue of recent immigrants from Palestine, or does it simply mean: congregation of the Jews, 'Hebrews' being the self-identification of what was possibly the first community of Jews in Rome by which they distinguished themselves from other (i. e., pagan) religious or ethnic groups (note that συναγωγή was not an exclusively Jewish term!)? This last possibility seems to be favoured by the fact that Jewish communities in Greece and Asia Minor also designated themselves as συναγωγὴ (τῶν) Ἑβραίων (CIJ 718 and 754). But this, too, remains an educated guess at best. Equally debated is the nature of the συναγωγὴ Βερνακλησίων or Βερνακλώρων, 'of the *vernaculi*' (CIJ 318, 383, 398, 494 = JIWE II, 114, 117, 106, 540). It has been argued that *vernaculus* means δοῦλος οἰκογενής, houseborn slave, and that this is the synagogue of Jewish imperial slaves or freedmen. It would be very fascinating of course if there had been a separate synagogue of imperial slaves and/or freedmen. In that case it would be comparable to the συναγωγὴ Λιβερτίνων in Jerusalem mentioned in Acts 6:9.[23] This, however, is all the evidence we have for synagogue names in antiquity.[24]

Does all this shed light upon the names of the destroyed synagogues in Alexandria? Unfortunately, apart from the phenomenon of naming synagogues in itself, it does not, for we can only guess at the Alexandrian synagogue names. Were some of them called after one or the other of the Ptolemies (which is not at all improbable)? Or were they named after benefactors such as Julius Caesar and Augustus? Were some of them called 'synagogue of the Hebrews' or 'synagogue of the Ioudaioi'? Or were they named after professions or occupations such as silversmiths, ship owners, money-lenders, weavers, or other occupations that we know were held by Alexandrian Jews?[25] Or were some of them called after the city districts, such as the Delta quarter, or after the country of origin of its members? We simply do not know, unfortunately. Be that as it may, also in this minor matter the Book of Acts and *In Flaccum* confirm each other.

---

[23] For the translation problem of this verse see Barret, *Acts*, I 324; also C. Claußen, *Versammlung, Gemeinde, Synagoge. Das hellenistisch-jüdische Umfeld der frühchristlichen Gemeinden*, Göttingen 2002, 116–117. J. Leonhardt, *Jewish Worship in Philo of Alexandria*, Tübingen 2001, 94–95.

[24] Cf. the mention of 'the synagogue of the Alexandrians' in Jerusalem in Tosefta *Megillah* 2:17 (3:6).

[25] See my commentary on *Flacc.* 57.

As far as diaspora synagogues are concerned, a second aspect to be discussed
briefly is that of their location in the vicinity of water. It is not a feature mentioned directly by Philo, but he says that the Jews, after hearing that Flaccus had
been arrested, came out of the ghetto and "they poured out through the gates
and *made their way to the nearby parts of the beach, for they had been deprived
of their synagogues*. And there, standing in the purest possible place, they cried
out with one accord" (§ 122; then follows a prayer text). Apparently, in the view
of the Jews, when there is no synagogue, the beach is the next purest possible
place to pray to God. What is the background of this remark? It is notable that
Josephus mentions a decree from the city of Halicarnassus permitting the Jews
"to offer prayers near the sea *according to their custom*" (*Ant.* 14.258). And there
is also archaeological evidence for synagogues very near to the water-side, for
instance at Delos, Ostia and at the Lake of Tiberias.[26] The water was probably
needed for purificatory purposes. It would seem that "the Jews regarded the
shore as the nearest equivalent as place of worship."[27] But why is it called 'the
purest possible place' (τὸ καθαρώτατον)? It most probably refers back to § 56
where it is said that the Jews "poured out to the beaches, the *dunghills* and the
tombs," and the 'purity' of the place referred to here is no more than the fact that
the place where the Jews were praying was clear of rubbish heaps and far away
from the tombs.[28] This is confirmed by the fact that in *Mos.* 2.34 "the most pure
place (τὸ καθαρώτατον) outside the city" is chosen by the Septuagint translators for their sacred work, and *Mos.* 2.72 uses the same word for the site of the
Jerusalem temple. "In all cases, the idea of the purity of the place makes good
sense as that required for the dwelling place of God or communication with God
in a quasi-temple setting."[29] This explanation would also accord with the later
rabbinic prohibition against praying in dirty or stinking places (e. g., Babylonian
Talmud, *Berakhot* 24b). Both the people worshipping and the place of worship
have to be pure (from a ritual point of view) and clean (from a hygienic point
of view), separate though these concepts may be in principle. This is a matter
of some relevance to the passage in Acts 16:13, where it is said that in Philippi
Paul "went outside the city gate *to a river*, supposing there would be a *proseuchê*" (either a place of prayer or a synagogue[30]). Although there is no written

---

[26] A. Runesson, "Water and Worship: Ostia and the Ritual Bath in the Diaspora Synagogue,"
in B. Olsson *et al.* (eds.), *The Synagogue of Ancient Ostia and the Jews of Rome*, Stockholm
2001, 115–129; also Claußen, *Versammlung, Gemeinde, Synagoge* 116–117, 220–221.

[27] Leonhardt, *Jewish Worship in Philo* 79.

[28] For the translation problems of this passage see H. Box, *Philonis Alexandrini* In Flaccum,
Oxford 1939, 100.

[29] S. Pearce, "Belonging and Not Belonging: Local Perspectives in Philo of Alexandria,"
in S. Jones & S. Pearce (eds.), *Jewish Local Patriotism and Self-Identification in the Graeco-
Roman Period*, Sheffield 1998, 104 note 138.

[30] See on this question the recent discussion by Claußen, *Versammlung, Gemeinde, Synagoge* 118.

precept to this effect to be found in any of the ancient Jewish sources, it would seem that the combination of the texts in Acts, *In Flaccum*, and Josephus with the archaeological evidence strongly suggests the existence of a Jewish custom (even if not generally followed) of worshipping near water.[31]

Much more could be said about *In Flaccum* and Acts by way of comparison. One could deal with the role of the city theatre(s) in mob riots (§§ 41, 138 and Acts 19); with the list of countries where Jews live (in § 46, as compared to the similar list in Acts 2:11); with the traditional triad in § 158: "I, Flaccus, was born and brought up and educated etc." as compared to the same triad in Paul's statement in Acts 22:3;[32] with the role of the personified Dikê in both *Flacc.* 104 and Acts 28:4, where the pagan inhabitants of Melitê, after the shipwreck and rescue of Paul and his fellow travellers, react to Paul's being bitten by a venomous snake by saying: "No doubt this man is a murderer. Though he has escaped from the sea, Dikê has not allowed him to live."[33] And very much more.

Suffice it for the moment to say that even this superficial survey of some elements in *In Flaccum* as compared to the Book of Acts makes clear beyond doubt that Philo and Luke lived in the same world, that they not only had a common language but also a common conceptual framework, and that a New Testament scholar can only neglect Philo's historical works to his or her detriment.

---

[31] Cf. also *Ep. Arist.* 305 (about the seventy translators of the Torah): "Following the custom of all the Jews, they washed their hands in the sea in the course of their prayers to God, and then propceeded to the reading and explication of each passage."

[32] See van der Horst, *Philo's Flaccus* 228, for the details.

[33] See P.W. van der Horst, "Dike," in K. van der Toorn, B. Becking & P.W. van der Horst (eds.), *Dictionary of Deities and Demons in the Bible*, 2nd ed., Leiden – Grand Rapids 1999, 250–252.

Common Prayer in Philo's *In Flaccum* 121–124

In this paper I will deal briefly with a prayer found in Philo's *In Flaccum*. The work *In Flaccum* is one of the two so-called historical treatises of this Alexandrian Jewish philosopher. The treatise certainly describes historical events but it does so with so many novellistic embellishments and with such an obvious theological purpose that the designation 'historical treatise' needs some qualification. Apart from writing history Philo also wants to console his coreligionists by means of the conviction that God, in his benign providence, never will desert his people in times of great distress (the parallel with the book of Esther is clear). Furthermore, he is probably trying to warn the new Roman governor of Egypt not to follow in the footsteps of his predecessor. For what had happened? Philo says that in the late summer of 38, with the connivance and even the support of Flaccus, Roman governor of Alexandria and Egypt from 32–38 CE, a mob of Greeks and Egyptians began a pogrom against the large Jewish community of Alexandria. Synagogues and houses were destroyed, hundreds of Jewish men and women tortured and murdered; it was, in short, a 'Kristallnacht' exactly 1900 years *avant la date*. Soon thereafter, however, Flaccus was arrested at the command of the Roman Emperor, Gaius (Caligula), sentenced to deportation to an island, and there finally executed. In the punishment of Flaccus, Philo sees a proof of divine providence.[1]

Immediately after the news of Flaccus' arrest had spread throughout Alexandria, the Jews came together to celebrate it. This is what Philo writes about that celebration:

(121) When they heard that Flaccus had been arrested and was already within the hunter's net, they stretched out their arms to heaven and began to sing songs of praise and victory to God who oversees all human affairs. They said, "O Lord, we are not delighted at the punishment of our enemy, for we have learnt from our holy laws that we should sympathize with our fellowmen. But it is right to give thanks to you for having taken pity and compassion on us and for having relieved our constant and incessant oppression."

---

[1] For recent discussions of these events see P. Schäfer, *Judeophobia. Attitudes toward the Jews in the Ancient World*, Cambridge MA-London 1997, 136–160; and J. Mélèze Modrzejewski, *The Jews of Egypt From Rameses II to Emperor Hadrian*, Philadelphia-Jerusalem 1995, 161–183. The most recent edition of *In Flaccum* is A. Pelletier, *Contre Flaccus* (Les Oeuvres de Philon d'Alexandrie, vol. 31), Paris 1967. The most recent commentary is P.W. van der Horst, *Philo's Flaccus: The First Pogrom* (PACS 2), Leiden 2003.

(122) After they had spent all night singing hymns and other songs, at daybreak they poured out through the gates and made their way to the nearby beaches, for they were deprived of their synagogues. And there, standing in the purest place, they cried out with one accord:

(123) "O almighty King of mortals and immortals, we have come here to call on earth and sea, on air and heaven, which are the parts of the universe, and on the universe as a whole, to offer thanks to you. In these alone we can dwell, expelled as we are from all man-made buildings, deprived of the city and the public and private areas within its walls, the only people under the sun to become cityless and homeless because of the malice of their governor. (124) But you make us realize that we may be confident that what is still in need of restoration will indeed be restored, because you have already begun to answer our prayers. After all, you suddenly brought down the common enemy of our nation, who thought so highly of himself, who was the instigator of our misfortunes and expected that these things would bring him fame. And when you did so, you did not wait until he was already far away so that those who had suffered badly under him would only have learnt about it by hearsay, and hence have less satisfaction, no, you did so right here, so close by that it was almost before the very eyes of those whom he had wronged. Thus you gave them a clearer picture of your swift and unexpected intervention."

Before we take a closer look at some of the elements of this prayer, it should be noted that there is one more prayer in Philo's *In Flaccum*, and that is the one spoken by Flaccus himself. In his place of banishment he is given over to great despair and finally prays to God – the God of the Jewish people to be sure – in order to confess that he now realizes that "you are not indifferent to the nation of the Jews, nor is what they assert about your providence false, for all who say that the Jews do not have you for a champion and defender go astray from sound opinion. I am a clear proof of this, for all the mad acts that I have committed against the Jews I have now suffered myself" (170). In these final words the contents of the entire book are covered. The idea that the persecutor of God's people is punished in a commensurate way so much governs the whole treatise *In Flaccum* that Philo devotes half of the book (95 out of 191 paragraphs!) to the description of Flaccus' downfall. Therefore the treatise "may be characterized as the passion story of the justly cursed and punished governor, preceded by the story of his misdeeds and crimes against God's people."[2] Flaccus' prayer summarizes this perspective in a concise way. Although we cannot take this prayer into account as it is not a common prayer, it is worth looking at in terms of the way it mirrors the public prayer of the gathered Jews in that in this individual prayer too the enemy of the Jews emphasizes that God does not abandon his people and that it is his providence that makes things turn from evil to good.[3] This is important because

---

[2] P. Borgen, "Two Philonic Prayers and Their Contexts," *NTS* 45 (1999) 302.

[3] On providence in the ancient world in general see the short but excellent contribution by R.L. Gordon, "Pronoia," in K. van der Toorn, B. Becking and P.W. van der Horst (eds.), *Dictionary of Deities and Demons in the Bible*, Leiden-Grand Rapids 1999 (2nd ed.), 664–667. On providence in Philo P. Frick, *Divine Providence in Philo of Alexandria*, Tübingen 1999.

immediately after the prayer by the Jews, Philo says that he will present another proof that "divine providence intervened" (§ 125). Moreover, in the very last line of the whole treatise he remarks that the fate of Flaccus proved beyond doubt that "the Jewish people had not been deprived of the help of God" (191). So both prayers stand in this framework of a story about God's providential intervention in history in order to save his people from a catastrophic event and to punish its opponents. In a certain sense it is, therefore, right when the German translator of this treatise, Gerschmann, calls *In Flaccum* a 'Trostschrift.'[4] It certainly was, as we see in the opening paragraphs of the *Legatio ad Gaium*, the immediate sequel of *In Flaccum*, where Philo speaks about people who "have come to disbelieve that the deity exercises his providence for men, and particularly for the suppliant nation which the Father and King of the universe and the source of all things has taken for his portion" (*Legatio* 3), namely the people of Israel. So, Philo has to address a real and urgent pastoral need.

Philo introduces the whole scene by saying that the Jews "stretched out their arms to heaven" when they began to praise God. The raising of hands is also mentioned in the description of the Egyptian Jews in 3 Macc. 5:25, where they beseech God to save them from the king's plan to execute all Jews. In Josephus, too, we find several references to this prayer gesture, e. g. in the case of the long prayer of Moses in *Ant.* 4:40. And one is also reminded of the raised hands carved above the Jewish imprecation incised on the famous tombstone from Rheneia.[5] But the raising of hands is, of course, a widespread prayer posture in antiquity in general.[6]

Now back to the text of the public prayer itself. Actually there are two prayers, a very short one in § 121 and a longer one in §§ 123–4. The short one amounts to hardly more than a disclaimer of malicious pleasure, 'Schadenfreude.' For this reason a study by the French philonic scholar Valentin Nikiprowetzky, that examines this prayer in *In Flaccum*, bears the title '*Schadenfreude* chez Philon d'Alexandrie?'[7] The people say to God: "We are not delighted at the punishment of our enemy, for we have learnt from our holy laws that we should sympathize with our fellowmen." These are pious, perhaps all too pious words from the pen of Philo, for the whole second part of the book seems to be nothing else than a

---

[4] K.H. Gerschmann, "Gegen Flaccus," in *Philo von Alexandria, Die Werke in deutscher Übersetzung,* vol. 7, ed. W. Theiler, Berlin 1964, 124.

[5] *Corpus Inscriptionum Judaicarum* 725, with the comments by P.W. van der Horst, *Ancient Jewish Epitaphs. An Introductory Survey of a Millennium of Jewish Funerary Epigraphy (300 BCE – 700 CE),* Kampen 1991,148–149; cf. also W. Horbury, "Early Christians on Synagogue Prayer and Imprecation," in G.N. Stanton & G.G. Stroumsa (eds.), *Tolerance and Intolerance in Early Judaism and Christianity,* Cambridge 1998, 307.

[6] K. Gross, *Menschenhand und Gotteshand in Antike und Christentum,* Stuttgart 1985, 14–24; S. Pulleyn, *Prayer in Greek Religion,* Oxford 1997, 189.

[7] V. Nikiprowetzky, *Etudes philoniennes,* Paris 1996, 96–109.

glaring demonstration of 'Schadenfreude' on his part. The English translator of Philo, F.H. Colson, wryly remarks: "This is easily said but not so easily done, and if Philo believed that he himself had learned the lesson, I think he deceived himself."[8] It is true that Philo gloats upon the series of misfortunes that come over Flaccus, which he describes with obvious pleasure. Here, however, he says that the Torah of Moses teaches otherwise. Maybe Philo is thinking of the passage in Ex. 23:4–5 about bringing back the domestic animals of one's enemy when one sees them going astray or helping them when they collapse under a burden. Much more likely, however, he does not allude to a passage from the Torah, but to Prov. 24:17–18: "Do not rejoice when your enemy falls and let not your heart be glad when he stumbles, lest the Lord see it and be displeased and turn away his anger from him."[9] The fact that Philo's own 'behaviour' would seem to be so much at odds with what he says here about biblical ideas and ideals can be explained, as Nikiprowetzky suggested, on the basis of the final lines of the longer prayer where he says that "when you did so [i. e., punished Flaccus], it was not when he was already far away, so that those who had suffered badly under him would have learnt about it only by hearsay and hence have had less satisfaction, no, you did so just here, so close by that it was almost before the eyes of those whom he had wronged, and thus you gave them a clearer image of your swift and unlooked for intervention." Here the emphasis is clearly on the fact that seeing the downfall of their enemy right before their own eyes convinces the Jews that God can and will intervene quickly and effectively. So the 'Schadenfreude' – says Nikiprowetzky – is not a goal in itself, it stands in the service of the creation of hope and faith among God's people. Their joy is not about the misery of an individual person, it is about the meaning and implication of this, namely the merciful intervention of God. "Même dans ses écrits historiques, Philon ne cesse pas d'être un théologien."[10] What he aims at in his treatise is not to demonstrate a triumph of revenge but one of divine justice. That is also why at the end of the book Philo says about Flaccus' death: "Justice wanted that single body to receive the same number of wounds as that of the Jews who had been unlawfully murdered by him" (190).

The longer prayer (§§ 123–4) begins with the striking acclamation of God as "almighty King of mortals and immortals." That God is the king of humans is a current idea, but his being king of immortals is strange at first sight because it sounds

---

[8] F.H. Colson in vol. 9 of the LCL edition of Philo, Cambridge MA-London 1941, 301.

[9] I. Heinemann, *Philons griechische und jüdische Bildung*, Breslau 1932 (repr. Hildesheim-New York 1973), 526–7, explains this misattribution of a passage from the Writings to the Torah from Philo's lack of knowledge of biblical books other than those of the Pentateuch. This is hardly convincing. Also elsewhere, *nomos* is sometimes used to refer to the Jewish Bible as a whole.

[10] Nikiprowetzky, *Etudes* 102.

polytheistic. If 'immortals' means 'gods,' it would imply that God is not the only but the highest god in a pantheon. It is then a variant of the well-known Homeric formula 'father of men and gods' in pagan literature. And indeed, elsewhere Philo speaks of "Him, whom all Greeks and barbarians unanimously acknowledge, the supreme Father of gods and men and the maker of the whole universe" (*Spec. leg.* II 165). It would almost seem here as if Philo tries to blur the distinction between monotheists and polytheists. This need not be implied, however, if we take into account that Philo here may draw upon traditional prayer formulae as we come across them in Jewish prayers such as the one by Esther (addition C 23in the LXX) and the synagogal prayer incorporated in the *Apostolic Constitutions* (VII 33, 2). In both of these texts we see God invoked as 'king of the gods.' This formula is evidently patterned upon the originally polytheistic formulations such as we find in Ps. 95:3 and 82:1, where God is called 'the great king above all gods' and the like. This is no more than a verbal relic of an earlier (polytheistic) stage in the history of Israelite religion. As used by the authors of these later prayers they certainly do not imply a polytheistic stance. Philo even has Moses use this formula in a prayer in which the great Lawgiver addresses God as "Lord, King of the gods" (*Conf.* 173, in an inaccurate quote from Deut. 10:17).

Then follows the phrase, "We have come here to call on earth and sea, on air and heaven, which are the parts of the universe, and on the universe as a whole, to offer thanks to you." There has been some debate over whether or not Philo refers here to the four elements earth, water, air, and fire, which does not seem an unreasonable supposition at first sight. But there is now a growing consensus that Philo here uses a popular classification to express the four regions of the visible world. He mentions the same four in the same way as here also in *Vita Mosis* I 113 and II 37, as 'parts [=regions] of the universe' and not as elements. As a matter of fact Philo nowhere explicitly identifies heaven with fire and he never mentions heaven as the fourth element, even though he knew the theory of the four elements.[11] So what is meant here is that the whole universe is called upon to join the Israelites in thanking God for his deliverance. This is done, so the author says, because the Jews have been robbed of their homes and other private and public buildings so that only the regions of the universe are left to them as places to dwell. One should not use this, of course, to argue that Philo considered the sea and the air as places for humans to live in. The emphasis is on the homeless state of the Jews after the pogrom.

The train of thought in § 124 is not easy to follow (which is partly due to uncertainties in the translation), but it seems to be as follows: God has made a start on the fulfilling of their prayers by causing their enemy to fall down and that gives them hope that he will go on now by also restoring other things for them that they

---

[11] H. Box, *Philonis Alexandrini In Flaccum*, London 1939, 113–114. Of course, calling heaven and earth to witness is a well-known biblical theme; see Deut. 4:26; 30:19; 31:28 etc.

have lost. As is often the case in Philo, it is possible for thanksgiving to function in fact as a petition.[12] Although it is clear that Philo has the Jews urge God not to leave it at that, what exactly Philo has in mind when he speaks of the amendment of things that are still in need of restoration is uncertain. It is certainly not (only) the demolished houses and synagogues that he has in mind; there must be more, but we can only guess. Does he express here the hope for God's support in the Jewish striving for citizenship of Alexandria, that had been one of the main points of friction between Jews and non-Jews in the period preceding the pogrom? Or is it only about the restoration of the Jewish *politeuma* that Flaccus had abolished? We simply do not know. Anyway, Philo does not stress the point and makes only a vague reference. He does emphasize, however, in the remaining lines, that God has immensely consoled his people by not delaying his punishment of Flaccus till after his term, which would have given them much less pleasure, but by doing it "almost before the eyes of those whom he had wronged." That was so important because by doing so God gave them a clearer impression, and therefore a stronger conviction, of how swiftly he could and would intervene, which is of course a source of great encouragement to the Jews.[13]

In spite of several echoes from the book of Psalms, this prayer does not have close parallels elsewhere, being too much of a Philonic creation. There are also no echoes of synagogal prayers as we know them, which is to be expected since in Philo's time there was not yet any form of statutory prayer in the synagogue. That kind of prayer was a much later development. So without wanting to suggest in any way that Philo knew the synagogal Amidah (of which there were in his time at best no more than some small building blocks), in a sense we could regard this common prayer as a kind of early variant of some of the later synagogal *berakhot* of the Amidah, such as *Shomea' Tefillah* (He who listens to prayer) and *Ge'ula* (Redemption), but especially the berakhah *Avoth* in which God is praised as 'Shield of Abraham' (or 'Defender of the offspring of Abraham' as in the fourth century Graeco-Jewish prayer in the *Apostolic Constitutions* VII 33, 7, which is based upon the berakhah *Avoth*[14]). The idea of God being Abraham's shield derives from Gen. 15:1: "Do not be afraid, Abraham, I am your shield" (cf. also Sirach 51:12). This idea of God who listens to the prayers of his people, redeems them and is a shield of Abraham and his offspring, is 'translated' here by Philo into a common prayer of thanksgiving that he composed in order to bring home to his fellow Jews his belief that God's providence was, is now, and will always be active in their favour.

---

[12] C.W. Larson, "Prayer of Petition in Philo," *JBL* 65 (1946) 190; *ibid.* 201 for the importance of hope in Philo.

[13] For other Philonic prayers on behalf of Israel see Larson, "Prayer" 198.

[14] See P.W. van der Horst, "The Greek Synagogue Prayers in the Apostolic Constitutuions, book VII," in J. Tabory (ed.), *From Qumran to Cairo. Studies in the History of Prayer*, Jerusalem 1999, 19–46.

Philo and the Rabbis on Genesis

Similar Questions, Different Answers

Introduction

In the opening decades of the Common Era, the Alexandrian Jewish philosopher Philo (ca. 20 BCE–50 CE) wrote two works about the books of Genesis and Exodus in the form of questions and answers,[1] in addition to dozens of treatises with allegorical explanations of the books of Moses.[2] These two books are now known as the *Quaestiones in Genesim* and the *Quaestiones in Exodum*, of which, unfortunately, the original Greek text is lost for the most part (they have been preserved only in an Armenian translation).[3] Since both works have suffered from relative neglect by the scholarly community, David Runia has called them 'the Cinderellas of Philonic studies.'[4]

Philo was not the first biblical scholar to raise questions and formulate answers to these questions about the Holy Scriptures of the Jewish people. Neither were his Jewish predecessors the first ones to use this format for the interpretation of books regarded as holy or endowed with divine authority and canonical status in the ancient world. This literary form is commonly dubbed 'erotapokriseis,'[5]

---

[1] Only occasionally is the questions-and-answers format used by Philo also in his allegorical commentary to the Pentateuch; see P. Borgen & R. Skarsten, "*Quaestiones et solutiones:* Some Observations on the Form of Philo's Exegesis," *Studia Philonica* 4 (1976/77) 1–16, esp. 4–9.

[2] See for an introduction V. Nikiprowetzky, *Le commentaire de l'Écriture chez Philon d'Alexandrie*, Leiden 1977, or P. Borgen, *Philo of Alexandria, an Exegete for his Time*, Leiden 1997.

[3] See the edition of the Greek fragments (in the form of quotations by later Christian authors) by F. Petit, *Philo, Quaestiones in Genesim et in Exodum, fragmenta graeca*, Paris 1978. For a survey of the textual history of the *Quaestiones* see E. Hilgert, "The *Quaestiones*: Texts and Translations," in D. Hay (ed.), *Both Literal and Allegorical: Studies in Philo of Alexandria's Questions and Answers on Genesis and Exodus*, Atlanta 1991, 1–15. For reasons of time and space I leave out of account here the complicated and much debated priority question: Were the *Quaestiones* meant as Prolegomena to the allegorical treatises, or were they an 'afterthought' to them? See on this problem, *inter alios*, A. Terian, "The Priority of the *Quaestiones* Among Philo's Exegetical Commentaries," and G.E. Sterling, "Philo's *Quaestiones*: Prolegomena or Afterthought?," both in Hay, *Both Literal and Allegorical* 29–46 and 99–124. Both Terian and Sterling defend the thesis of the priority of the *Quaestiones*.

[4] D.T. Runia, "Secondary Texts in Philo's Quaestiones," in Hay, *Both Literal and Allegori-cal* 47.

[5] H. Dörrie & H. Dörries, 'Erotapokriseis,' *RAC* 6 (1966) 342–370. Their article is still a

although that is not its ancient designation (the Greeks called the genre ἀπορίαι καὶ λύσεῖ, or ζητήματα καὶ λύσεῖ [problems and solutions] or πεύσεῖ καὶ ἀποκρίσεῖ [questions and answers]).

The genre has a long pagan prehistory that goes back to the early Hellenistic period, and even further.[6] According to ancient reports, the learned tyrant of Samos called Duris wrote a book with the title Ὁμηρικὰ ζητήματα (Homeric questions), as Aristotle had done before him (Ἀπορήματα Ὁμηρικά), and this genre continued to flourish all the way down to Porphyry some six centuries later, when he wrote a work with a similar title.[7] In later antiquity the ever more prestigious, even divine, Plato underwent the same fate as we can gauge from the Πλατωνικὰ ζητήματα by Plutarch, and from other writings. Of course these treatises do not only consist of questions, they give answers as well. These two authors, Homer and Plato, or rather their writings, had acquired a sacrosanct status so as to become the 'Inbegriff', the *summum*, or repository of divine, encompassing wisdom and knowledge.[8] In order to retrieve this wisdom and knowledge, various exegetical techniques were developed, among which (in the case of Homer at least) allegory took pride of place, but the method of raising questions and giving answers was the most pedagogical. We know the titles of numerous ζητήματα commentaries which were written between the third century BCE and the second century of the Common Era, but most of them are now lost. To be sure, exegesis of Homer and Plato was not the only context in which *erotapokriseis* flourished; indeed, there is a whole range of other areas where this literary form turned out to be applicable, including the exact sciences,[9] philology,[10] philosophy[11] and jurisprudence.[12] (Note that the most probable *Sitz im Leben* of all these works is a school setting.) But for our present purposes we restrict ourselves to the genre as applied in exegetical works on authoritative or canonical scriptures, and more specifically, in commentaries on the Bible.

In the late third century BCE, the Jewish historian Demetrius, commonly called Demetrius the Chronographer, is the first traceable author who made use

very valuable survey; see, however, also the much older article by A. Gudemann, Λύσεις, *PW* 13/2 (1927) 2511–2529, and the most recent one by H.A. Gärtner, 'Zetema,' *NP* 12/2 (2002) 778–779, although both of them are restricted to pagan material. Useful bird's eye views are given by O. Dreyer, 'Lyseis,' *KP* 3 (1975) 832–833, and A. Kamesar, *Jerome, Greek Scholarship, and the Hebrew Bible. A Study of the* Quaestiones Hebraicae in Genesim, Oxford 1993, 82–86.

   [6] See Gudemann, Λύσεις 2512 and 2516; also Dreyer, 'Lyseis,' 832.
   [7] Most of these works have not been preserved; for the few fragments of Porphyry's Ὁμηρικὰ ζητήματα see A. Smith (ed.), *Porphyrius. Fragmenta*, Stuttgart-Leipzig 1993, 467–474.
   [8] See R. Lamberton, *Homer the Theologian: Neoplatonist Allegorical Reading and the Growth of the Epic Tradition,* Berkeley 1986.
   [9] E. g., Aristotle's *Problemata*.
   [10] E. g., the lost work of the grammarian Satyros.
   [11] E. g., Porphyry's *Symmikta zetemata*.
   [12] E. g., the works of Papinian.

of the Greek literary form of the *erotapokriseis* in order to deal with problems of the biblical text.[13] Five fragments of his chronicle of biblical history have been preserved in Eusebius' *Praeparatio Evangelica* (9.19.4; 9.21.1–19; 9.29.1–3; 9.29.15; 9.29.16;) and one in Clement of Alexandria's *Stromateis* (1.21.141). I cannot deal with him at length since he is not the subject of this paper, but, nevertheless, since he is a precursor of Philo, he deserves to receive at least some attention. Suffice it to say that he deals with questions such as, 'How could twelve children have been born to Jacob within seven years?,' 'How could Moses have married Zipporah, separated as they were by three generations?,' 'Why did Joseph remain in Egypt for nine years without reporting his whereabouts to his worried father in Canaan?' 'How did the Israelites who left Egypt unarmed manage to obtain weapons with which they fought after crossing the Red Sea?' What all these (and other) questions have in common is that they deal with obvious problems that present themselves upon close reading of the biblical text. Whether or not Demetrius dealt with these problems for apologetic reasons (did anti-Jewish Greeks point out inconsistencies in the Bible, as did later anti-Christian authors like Porphyry and Julian?), we do not know.[14] We do observe, however, that the Hellenistic literary form of *erotapokriseis* is here taken into Jewish service for the first time.[15] We do not know of other instances of this genre in Jewish literature in the more than two centuries between Demetrius and Philo, but it would be unwise to assume that in these centuries no other Jewish scholar made use of this literary form. The fact that Philo and, after him, other exegetes make clear that they stand in a venerable tradition makes it probable that the fact that such sources are not extant does not necessarily mean that they did not exist. They are simply lost.[16]

Biblical interpretation

We now turn to Philo and the rabbis.[17] But why the rabbis? Are they not too far removed from Philo in both time and place to make a comparison between them

---

[13] For an edition with translation and commentary of his fragments see C. R. Holladay, *Fragments from Hellenistic Jewish Authors*, vol. I, Chico 1983, 51–91.

[14] As Kamesar, *Jerome* 84, points out, Marcion's pupil Apelles employed the *quaestiones* method in his attempt to undermine the authority of the Old Testament.

[15] See E. Bickerman, 'The Jewish Historian Demetrius,' in his *Studies in Jewish and Christian History,* Leiden 1980, vol. 2, 347–358; and my article 'The Interpretation of the Bible by the Minor Hellenistic Jewish Authors,' in P.W. van der Horst, *Essays on the Jewish World of Early Christianity*, Freibourg in der Schweiz- Göttingen 1990, 187–219, here esp. 196–200.

[16] For the continuation of the genre in early Christianity see the series of six articles by G. Bardy in *RB* 41 (1932) and 42 (1933), all of them with the title "La littérature patristique des *Quaestiones et responsiones* sur l'Écriture Sainte."

[17] Unfortunately, I have not been able to consult S. Belkin, "The Earliest Source of the Rabbinic Midrash – *Quaestiones et Solutiones in Genesim et Exodum* of Philo Alexandrinus," in S. Belkin (ed.), *Abraham Weiss Jubilee Volume* (1964) 579–633 [Hebr.].

meaningful? And is there, then, any rabbinic *erotapokriseis* literature? To begin
with the last question, the answer is yes and no. The answer is yes in the sense
that from the post-Talmudic period we do have a spate of so-called *Responsa*
literature, called *She'elot u-Teshuvot*, that is 'questions and answers,'[18] but in
this case we are dealing with early medieval texts (7th century and later) in
which questions from diaspora communities all over the world were answered
by famous rabbis in Babylonia and Palestine, and these fall outside the scope
of our investigation. The answer is no in the sense that we have no rabbinic
literature in which the biblical text is discussed in the way Philo does in his
Quaestiones, namely in the form of stating a problem raised by the biblical text
as a question and presenting an answer to that question. That would seem to rule
out a comparison of Philo and the rabbis, but it rules it out only on a superficial
level. The latter point can be made clear by the simple observation that, even
though in rabbinic commentaries to the Bible, the so-called Midrashim, usually
no questions are raised explicitly, their exegetical manoeuvres are nevertheless
obviously answers to *implicit* questions, or solutions to problems, raised by the
biblical text. These cases have been termed 'versteckte ζητήματα'[19] (hidden
questions) and the phenomenon can be explained by comparing it to allegorical explanations of Homer without explicit specification of the exact nature of
the problem to be solved. "The rabbis often follow a similar procedure in their
exposition of the Old Testament. The most likely explanation for such a practice,
in both classical and rabbinic exegesis, is that some προβλήματα were either
so obvious or so well known that it became unnecessary to introduce them
explicitly."[20] The fact that midrashim often skip complete passages of Scripture
underlines that they focus not on the biblical text in all its details but rather on
the problems found there.

To illustrate my point I will give some examples that make clear that in
their midrash on Genesis, *Bereshit Rabbah*, the rabbis wrestle with questions
the biblical text throws at them.[21] The problems they see are often the same as

---

[18] See E. Fram, "Responsa," *The Oxford Dictionary of the Jewish Religion*, eds. R.J. Zwi
Werblowsky & G. Wigoder, Oxford 1997, 581–583. D. Cohn-Sherbock, *A Dictionary of Judaism and Christianity*, London 1991, 144.

[19] Gudemann, Λύσεις 2514–15.

[20] Kamesar, *Jerome* 89.

[21] For an introduction to the phenomenon of midrash see G.G. Porton, "Defining Midrash,"
in J. Neusner (ed.), *The Study of Ancient Judaism*, vol. 1, New York 1981, 55–92; idem, "Rab-
binic Midrash," in J. Neusner (ed.), *Judaism in Late Antiquity*, vol. 1, Leiden 1995, 217–236.
B.W. Holtz, "Midrash," in *idem* (ed.), *Back to the Sources. Reading the Classic Jewish Texts*,
New York 1984, 177–211; G. Stemberger, *Midrasch. Vom Umgang der Rabbinen mit der
Bibel*, München 1989. For an introduction to *Genesis Rabbah* see G. Stemberger, *Einleitung in
Talmud und Midrasch*, 8th ed., München 1992, 272–279. See further L. Haas, "Bibliography
on Midrash," in Neusner, *Study* 93–103, and the recent bibliography in G.P. Porton, 'Rabbinic
Midrash,' in A.J. Hauser & D.F. Watson (eds.), *A History of Biblical Interpretation, vol. 1: The
Ancient Period*, Grand Rapids 2003, 219–224.

the ones Philo sees, but their answers are usually quite different. It is essential to observe, however, that it is problems in the biblical text, and quite often the same problems, that both parties wish to address and solve. The chronological and geographical gap between Philo's *QG* and the rabbinic midrash on Genesis (*Bereshit Rabbah* originated in fifth-century Palestine) is an unavoidable problem, due to the fact that after Philo, *Bereshit Rabbah* is the first other Jewish commentary to Genesis we have (the ones from Qumran are by and large lost[22]). As we will see, however, in spite of this gap, the two parties address the same problems since the biblical text they dealt with was (practically) the same, with all its problematic elements.

By way of preliminary remarks, let me say something about early Jewish biblical interpretation in general. Since I am not able to do this better than James Kugel, the Harvard professor of biblical and Jewish literature, did in his wonderful book *Traditions of the Bible*, I will follow him closely in this paragraph.[23] Kugel states that, despite the great variety of styles and genres and even interpretive methods involved in the Jewish literature of the Hellenistic and Roman period, 'underlying it all is a common approach, a common set of assumptions concerning the biblical text' (14).

The first assumption is that 'the Bible is a fundamentally cryptic document' (15). All ancient Jewish interpreters 'are fond of maintaining that although Scripture may appear to be saying X, what it really means is Y' (15). Even though this may not seem a natural assumption, ancient interpreters tell us time and again that 'in place of, or beyond, the apparent meaning of the text is some hidden, esoteric message' (15). Their capability to elicit a meaning from the text that their hearers or readers would not find themselves at first glance, certainly contributed to their standing and authority in the community of believers.

Their second assumption is that 'Scripture constitutes one great Book of Instruction and as such is a fundamentally *relevant* text' (15). The lives of the great biblical figures are regarded as 'a guide given to later human beings for the leading of their own lives' (16). Biblical prophecies are relevant to the interpreter and his audience because they refer to *their* situation. This fundamental assumption 'was held to be true about *all* of the Hebrew Bible, the songs and psalms and prayers and laws and narratives it contained' (16). All of them, as the Apostle Paul says, 'were written down for *our* instruction' (1 Cor. 10:11),

---

[22] None of the passages from Genesis discussed below is commented upon in the extant Dead Sea Scrolls; see D.L. Washburn, *A Catalog of Biblical Passages in the Dead Sea Scrolls*, Atlanta 2002.

[23] *Traditions of the Bible. A Guide to the Bible As It Was At the Start of the Common Era*, Cambridge MA – London 1998, esp. 14–19. The words in the subtitle "as it was" should be understood as "as it was interpreted." A somewhat shorter and less technical version of this work was published by Kugel one year earlier as *The Bible As It Was*, Cambridge MA – London 1997.

not just so as to record events from the past, but to teach us some vital lessons for our own lives.

The third assumption is that 'Scripture is perfect and perfectly harmonious' (17). That is to say that it does not contain any mistakes, and that what might look like a mistake 'must therefore be an allusion to be clarified by proper interpretation' (17). This principle also implies that there is 'a perfect harmony between the Bible's various parts' (17). All of Scripture speaks with one voice; how could it be otherwise when God himself is the sole author? 'Taken to its extreme, this same view of Scripture's perfection ultimately led to the doctrine of 'omnisignificance,' whereby nothing in Scripture is said in vain or for rhetorical flourish: every detail is important, everything is intended to impart some teaching' (17). And since the teachings of Scripture are perfect, but sometimes the biblical heroes behave in a less than perfect way, this is an indication that 'something else *must* have been meant' (18); and the interpreters came to their heroes' 'rescue.'[24]

The fourth assumption (already hinted at) is the basic one that 'all of Scripture is somehow divinely sanctioned, of divine provenance, or divinely inspired' (18). Not only the passages in which God speaks in the first person, but also texts which speak about or to Him, or not even that, are regarded as inspired by Him and, therefore, infallible. The notion of the divine authorship of all of the Bible is not often explicitly mentioned but it underlies most if not all of ancient (Jewish and Christian) biblical interpretation. I cannot refrain from quoting in full Kugel's own summary:

Convinced that Scripture was a fundamentally cryptic document, they scrutinized its every detail in search of hidden meaning. That meaning was to be, by definition, relevant to the situation of the interpreter and his listeners, not some insight into the historical circumstances in which the text was originally written, but a message of immediate value and applicability, either a timeless moral truth or a law to be observed in one particular fashion or something bearing in some other way on the present or the immediate future. In searching for such a message, the interpreter could rest assured that no detail in Scripture's manner of speaking was insignificant, nor would there be any inconsistency between what is said in one place and what is said in another, nor any lesson that contradicted right thinking. For that reason, any apparent contradiction, or unnecessary detail or repetition or even an emphatic turn of phrase, seemed to be an invitation to the interpreter to look deeply into the text's words and so discover its *real* meaning, the hidden, relevant, perfect truth that only befit the word of God' (19).

For our present purposes it is important to emphasize that it is especially the first assumption, about the cryptic nature and the hidden meaning of the biblical text, that is relevant to our topic because it implies that the text lays a problem

---

[24] Philo himself gives a fine instance in his interpretation of Gen. 20:2, where out of fear Abraham says about his wife that she is his sister. In *QG* 4.60 he emphatically states that not a streak of impiety should come upon us by thinking unworthy things about the patriarch, whereupon he goes on to explain the deeper sense of Abraham's remark.

before or poses a question to the interpreter, which he has to solve or answer. In that sense, much of ancient Jewish interpretation of the Bible is implicitly of an *erotapokriseis* nature. Let us see if we can find out to which degree the implicit questions of the rabbis correspond to or differ from the explicit ones of Philo.[25] For practical reasons I will restrict my investigation to five illustrative passages from the first five chapters of Genesis.[26]

The texts

The first example is relatively short and simple. It concerns Gen. 2:17, where God says to Adam that, if he eats from the tree of knowledge, he will surely die. The Hebrew has *moth tamuth*, 'you will die (by) a death,' which is a current idiom in biblical Hebrew to indicate emphasis ('you will surely die'). The LXX translates rather literally with θανάτῳ ἀποθανεῖσθε. It is the occurrence of two words (instead of one) designating death or dying that is the riddle to be solved here, for it cannot be superfluous, it surely must have a deeper meaning. The rabbis are quite brief here. In *Gen.R.* 16.6 they simply state that the two words for death indicate that it is not only Adam and Eve who will die as a consequence of their transgression, but also all their descendants, *i.*e., humanity as a whole.

Philo has a more elaborate answer:

> For worthy men, death is the beginning of another life. For life is twofold: one is the corruptible life, in a body, the other the incorruptible, without a body. Consequently, only the evil man dies by death; even when he breathes, he has already been buried in advance because he did not preserve in himself any spark of the true life, that is, excellence of character (καλοκαγαθία). A meritorious and worthy man, however, does not die by death, but after a long life he passes away to eternity (*QG* 1.16).

It is clear that for Philo the two words refer to two sorts of death, a physical one and a spiritual one, the latter being wholly independant from the body. Real life is a spiritual life that can also be lived without a body. For a person who lives that life, death is not death but a transition to eternal life; a bad person, however, has already died a spiritual death, which will be followed by a physical one. These Platonic ideas are wholly absent from the sober explanation by the rabbis.

Our second example is Gen. 3:3, where according to the Hebrew text Eve says to the serpent that God had said, 'You shall not eat of the fruit of the tree that is

---

[25] For another brief comparison of Philo with rabbinic midrash, see D.T. Runia, 'Further Observations on the Structure of Philo's Allegorical Treatises,' in his *Exegesis and Philosophy. Studies on Philo of Alexandria*, Aldershot 1990, 117–119.

[26] In the following I use the translation of Philo's *QG* by R. Marcus in the first Supplement to the LCL edition, London – Cambridge MA 1953; and the French translation by Ch. Mercier in vol. 34a of the series Les oeuvres de Philon d'Alexandrie, Paris 1979. For *Gen.R.* I used H. Freedman's translation in vol. 1 of *Midrash Rabbah*, London 1939; and J. Neusner, *Genesis Rabbah. The Judaic Commentary to the Book of Genesis*, vol. 1, Atlanta 1985. All translations were slightly modified by me for clarity's sake.

in the middle of the garden, nor shall you touch it, or you shall die.' In *QG* 1.35, Philo raises the question of why, whereas God himself had only said that they should not eat from that tree (Gen. 2:17), Eve now adds the extra prohibition of not even touching the tree. Since of course that cannot be just accidental, the interpreter is bound to look for its meaning. Philo's answer is as follows:

First, because taste – and actually every sense perception – is naturally brought about by contact. Second, (she said this) for the severe punishment of those who have practised this. For if even touching (the tree) was forbidden, how much greater a crime would those have committed who, in addition to touching it, also ate of it and enjoyed it? Would they not have condemned themselves and brought punishment down upon themselves?

It is clear that according to Philo's second explanation Eve's addition to God's original prohibition was an expression of a well-known halakhic principle that the rabbis would later call *seyag la-Torah*, a fence around the Torah, i. e., an injunction in the form of a stringent intensification of the law enacted to safe-guard the observance of the commandments.[27] This principle, widely accepted in postbiblical Judaism, is here retrieved by Philo from Scripture itself.

What do the rabbis make of this verse? In *Gen.R.* 19.3 they comment upon it as follows:

It is written, 'Do not add to His words, lest He reprove you and you be found a liar' (Prov. 30:6). R. Hiyya taught, 'It means that one should not make the fence bigger than its foundation, because it may then fall and destroy the plants. The Holy One, blessed be He, had said, "For on the day on which you eat from it, you shall surely die" (Gen. 2:17), but she did not say that but "God said: You shall not eat from it and you shall not touch it." When the snake saw that she was lying, he took her and pushed here against the tree. He said to her, "Have you now died? Just as you did not die by touching it, you will not die when you eat of it."'

It is very interesting to see that the rabbis, too, see in this verse a reference to the principle of the fence around the Torah, but in quite a different way: They say that in fact Eve was lying – a traditional role of Eve in rabbinic literature[28] – and that may be seen from the fact that she made the fence bigger than its foundation. That is to say, the fact that the words 'or you shall die' follow immediately upon the words 'neither shall you touch it' suggests that Eve implied that it was not so much the eating as the touching that would entail their death, whereas God had explicitly said that it was the eating of the fruit that would do so. Thus she made the fence (not touching) bigger than the foundation (not eating). So it *was* a fence but used in a completely wrong manner by this woman who thus gave the serpent the opportunity to prove that she was mistaken: he pushed her against the tree and she did not die. Philo approves of the fact that the first woman already

---

[27] On the concept of the 'fence around the Torah' see E.E. Urbach, *The Halakhah. Its Sources and Development*, Jerusalem 1986, 7 with the notes at 361.

[28] See, e. g., N.M. Hyman, *Biblical Women in the Midrash*, Northvale 1997, 5–10.

formulated the principle of the *seyag la-Torah*, but the rabbis disapproved of the fact that she misapplied it by making it more important than the principal thing, thus opening the gate to the devil. Another midrash even goes so far as making Eve think (after she noticed that touching the tree was not lethal): 'So all the things that my husband has told me are just lies!' (*Avoth deR. Nathan* rec. A 1). Here another problem is solved, namely the fact that God gave his prohibition to eat from the tree to Adam (in Gen. 2:17) *before* the creation of Eve (in Gen. 2:22), so Eve cannot have heard it herself and hence must have heard it from Adam, who is, therefore, a liar in her view, although in the eyes of the rabbis he is the inventor of the principle of the fence around the Torah.[29]

Our third example is Gen. 3:9 where, after the fall, God called to Adam and said to him, 'Where are you?' This is at first sight an unpalatable utterance on God's part since He is supposed to be omniscient. Of course He knew where Adam was! Hence Philo raises the question, 'Why does He who knows all things ask Adam, "Where are you?", and why does he not also ask the woman?' His answer is as follows:

> The things said appear to be not a question but a kind of threat and reproach: 'Where are you *now*! From what good have you removed yourself, o man! Giving up immortality and a blessed life, you have gone over to death and unhappiness, in which you have been buried.' As to the woman, He did not consider it worthwhile to question her since she was the beginning of evil and led him (Adam) into a life of vileness (*QG* 1.45).

God is thus saved from the charge of ignorance of the whereabouts of his creatures. 'Where are you?' means actually, 'What – for God's sake – have you done?!' 'What an awful situation you have manoeuvered yourself into!' And he says this only to Adam since Eve, the source of all evil, is not even worth being spoken to by God.[30]

What do the rabbis say? In *Gen.R.* 19.9 they play with the punctuation in that the biblical *ayyekkah* ('where are you?') is read as *ekhah*, 'how,' used in exclamation: 'How are you? How is it possible that earlier you followed my will, but now the will of the serpent?!' And likewise, although slightly different, the Targum Pseudo-Jonathan translates this verse as 'How could you imagine it possible to hide from me?!' So here again we see that Philo and the rabbis tackle the same problem in the biblical text (how could God possibly say, 'Where are you?') and present solutions that are only marginally different, except for the fact that Philo here, almost in passing, solves another problem in the biblical text – why, if both Adam and Eve hide in the garden, does God talk only to Adam?

---

[29] A Christian example of this exegesis, from Ambrose of Milan, is quoted by Kugel in *Traditions* 129. For further instances see A. Louth, *Ancient Christian Commentary on Scripture. Old Testament, vol. 1: Genesis 1–11*, Downers Grove 2001, 84–85.

[30] There is a parallel to this passage in Philo's *Leg.* 3.49–50, on which see A. Méasson & J. Cazeaux, "From Grammar to Discourse: A Study of the *Quaestiones in Genesim* in Relation to the Treatises," in Hay, *Both Literal and Allegorical* 145.

– by adding the pungent comment that God did not find Eve worthwile to talk to any more, probably implying that the Bible denies that real contact between women and the divine world is possible.[31]

A fourth example: Gen. 4:15 states that the Lord said that whoever kills Cain would suffer a sevenfold punishment and that God put a mark on Cain so that no one who came upon him would kill him. It is not hard to guess which questions are raised by this text. Philo formulates the following ones (in *QG* 1.75–6):[32] Why shall anyone who kills Cain suffer sevenfold punishment? And why is a sign placed upon the fratricide so that any who meets him will not kill him, whereas it would have been fitting to do the opposite and hand him over to someone for destruction? As we will see, the rabbis deal with the same two problems.[33] Philo's answers are long and complicated and I will render them in a simplified and abbreviated form. The sevenfold punishment is explained by him as referring to the seven subdivisions of the irrational part of the soul (the five senses, the organ of speech and the sexual organ), the eighth division, however, being the (indivisible) rational part, the intellect. The seven parts, irrational as they are, are the causes of all evil and for that reason have to be punished by the highest part of the soul, the intellect.[34] This is a perfectly Greek philosophical reading of the biblical text which solves an otherwise (in Philo's eyes) insoluble problem.

The rabbis leave the problem of 'sevenfold punishment' for what it is (they did not have a typically Greek sevenfold division of the irrational part of the soul) and instead they focus on the overall theme that Cain's murderers will themselves be punished. Why is that? Here they resort to a well-known rabbinic device called *'al tiqre*: 'do not read' (*i. e.*, do not read this but read that). The biblical text has, "Therefore (*laken*), whoever kills Cain etc." In *Gen.R.* 22.12, one of the rabbis suggests, 'The cattle, beasts, and birds assembled to demand justice for Abel [the reason being that, since no other humans were there as yet, the animals would take vengeance. Cain was afraid and for that reason God said to him:] "I say to you [reading *laken* as *lakh ani* (to you I [say]), whoever kills Cain …" [thus assuring him that he need have no fear of animals]. But another rabbi read the word *laken* as *lo' ken*, 'not in this way'[35] and interpreted

---

[31] D. Sly, *Philo's Perception of Women*, Atlanta 1990.

[32] See on this passage also J. Mansfeld, 'Heraclitus, Empedocles, and Others in a Middle Platonist Cento in Philo of Alexandria,' in his *Studies in Later Greek Philosophy and Gnosticism*, Aldershot 1989, 131–156.

[33] Christian parallels in Louth, *Ancient Christian Commentary* 108.

[34] More is said by Philo on this topic but the Armenian text is so obscure (and most probably corrupt) that only the vague outlines of what he is asserting can be discerned. These are rendered in the text above.

[35] It is interesting to see that both the LXX and the Vulgate read here 'not in this way' (οὐχ οὕτως, *non sic*), as do also Symmachus and the Peshitta; see A. Salvesen, *Symmachus in the Pentateuch*, Manchester 1991, 24.

the passage as follows: Cain's judgement should *not* be like the judgement of other (future) murderers, because he killed while he had no one from whom to learn (the consequences of his deed). But from now on [people do know these consequences and for that reason] whoever kills a person shall be put to death.'[36] This is quite a different solution than Philo's but it does try to solve the same problem. It skips, however, the 'sevenfold punishment' but the solution to that problem seems to be implied.

As to the other question – why does God protect Cain with a sign instead of delivering him into the hands of his enemies?, which is what Cain would deserve – Philo offers a variety of solutions. First, he says, there are, beside a physical death, also the many deaths one can die when one has to live in fear or sorrow. So in a sense having to live on was a heavier punishment for Cain than having to die. Second, the fact that the good one (Abel) was killed whereas the bad one lived on is a clear indication that the soul is imperishable, immortal, and therefore the only thing that counts, whereas bodily life hardly deserves to be called life. In fact, Cain is dead, although physically alive, and Abel lives, although physically dead.[37] So the immortality of the soul is taught by Scripture right from the outset. Third, Cain was the first to have committed a very great crime, and by not meting out to him his deserved punishment, God sets an example of mercy to all future judges: They should hesitate in capital cases and be inclined to mercy rather than to strictness. God thus prescribes a canon of gentleness and understanding. So Philo sees here at least three important lessons being taught by God.

The rabbis are not that different here. In *Gen.R.* 22.13 they, too, offer various solutions to the scriptural riddle. One of them says that, in the light of the fact that in Ex. 4:8 leprosy is called a sign, Cain's sign was that God smote him with leprosy, thus banishing him from the community of humans. Another says that the sign was that God gave Cain a dog who would protect him against his enemies. Another sees the sign as horns that grew from Cain's head to ward off potential attackers. Then again another rabbi comes up with an original new translation of the biblical text, rendering the verse as 'God turned Cain into a sign for murderers.' The Hebrew *le-qain* ('to Cain') is here taken to be an accusative not a dative, which was possible in the eyes of the rabbis because in their daily language, Palestinian Aramaic, the preposition *le-* could denote both the direct and the indirect object.[38] In this way Cain became a terrifying example to future murderers, who would know that after such a crime they would have to live in

---

[36] The square brackets indicate that these words are not in the lapidary text of the midrash itself but have been added in order to clarify the meaning. I here follow the procedure of J. Neusner in his translation of *Genesis Rabbah*.

[37] On the Greek background of this motif see D. Zeller, 'The Life and Death of the Soul in Philo of Alexandria: The Use and Origin of a Metaphor,' *Studia Philonica Annual* 7 (1995) 19–56.

[38] See H. Odeberg, *The Aramaic Portions of* Bereshit Rabba, vol. 2: *Short Grammar of Galilaean Aramaic*, Lund – Leipzig 1939, 87.

never-ending fear. No, says another rabbi, Cain thus became an encouraging example to penitents: he showed them the saving power of repentance, for God did not punish him.[39] At least God did not punish him immediately for he gave Cain time for repentance and suspended his judgement. Cain thus signifies the possibility of forgiveness for sinners who repent. But since Cain did not repent, he was finally swept away in the flood.[40] Here we see that, as in Philo, the text gives occasion to a wide variety of explanations, not one of which is declared to be the only valid one to the exclusion of others. Again we see that the answers of Philo and the rabbis are rather different but the questions are the same.

A fifth and final instance is Gen. 5:24, the famous verse that states that 'Enoch walked with God, but then he was no more because God took him.' This verse gave rise to a spate of Enochic literature, based upon exegetical speculations about the meaning of these enigmatic words. Both Philo and the rabbis deal with it, but their explanations are glaringly different. Philo raises the simple question of what is the meaning of the words 'and then he was not because God took him away' (*QG* 1.86). His answer is as follows (in an abbreviated paraphrase): First of all, he says, the end of worthy and holy men is not death but a transfer to another place. This is what happened to Enoch, for the text implies that he was transferred from a place visible by sense perception to a place in the incorporeal and intelligible world (note the Platonic terminology!). This is what also happened to Moses (whose burial place has always remained unknown for that very reason [see Deut. 34:6]) and to Elijah (who ascended to heaven as well [see 2 Kings 2:11]).[41] These three holy men were deemed worthy by God to be taken up into the incorporeal world instead of dying. This is an utterly positive picture of Enoch, just as we find it in the Enochic literature. But now the rabbis.

One of the rabbis says (*Gen.R.* 25.1): 'He was not more' means that Enoch was not inscribed in the scroll of the righteous but in the scroll of the wicked. Another rabbi says, 'Enoch was a hypocrite, acting sometimes as a righteous, sometimes as a wicked man. Therefore the Holy One, blessed be He, said: "While he is in his righteous phase, I will take him away" (*i.e.*, when he walked with God, he died). Some sectarians[42] said to rabbi Abbahu, "We do not find that Enoch died." He asked, "Why not?" They answered: "The word 'taking' is used both here and in the case of the prophet Elijah [and since Elijah was taken up into heaven, the same applies to Enoch]." But Abbahu rejoined: "If you want to interpret the word 'taking,' then take notice of the fact that this word is used both here and

---

[39] In *QG* 1.82 Philo speaks about 'the forgiving of Cain'! Thus, e.g., also Theodoret of Cyrrhus, *Quaest. et Resp. in Genes.* 41.

[40] Kugel, *Traditions* 164, suggests that the rabbis may have read the text of Gen. 4:15 as follows: 'And the Lord said to him, "It will not be thus [that is, *lo'ken*] with any [other] killer. [But as for] Cain, punishment will be exacted from him in seven generations.'

[41] On Philo's use of 'secondary' biblical texts in his exegesis see Runia, "Secondary Texts," on this passage (*QG* I 86) esp. 51–52.

[42] Which 'sectarians' are referred to is uncertain: Christians?, Jewish mystics?, others?

in the case of Ezekiel [where it says], "Behold, I take away from you the desire of your eyes" (Ezek. 24:16 [where it definitely refers to the death of Ezekiel's wife]). Rabbi Tanhuma observed: "He refuted them well." A lady said to rabbi Jose, "One does not find that Enoch died." He said to her, "If the text had only said, 'And Enoch walked with God,' and nothing else, I would agree with you, but since it says, 'He was no more since God took him,' it means that he is not in the world anymore [because he died].'

The contrast between Enoch as Philo's holy man who was transferred by God to the heavenly realm and Enoch as the rabbis' wicked hypocrite who had to die a normal death could not be greater. This is not the place to deal with the background of these widely different interpretations. Suffice it to say here that it has much to do with the development of the traditions about Enoch in the centuries around the turn of the Common Era and the opposition to this development in the circles of rabbis who found the speculations about Enoch's ever more exalted status and authoritative revelations a dangerous threat to monotheism and saw Enoch as a rival to Moses.[43] Philo, on the other hand, welcomed the idea of Enoch's *metathesis* since it gave him the opportunity to emphasize the Platonic idea that a really holy person could be given a vision of the intelligible world. Most remarkable is that both Philo and the rabbis do note the parallel with the story of Elijah, but that Philo gladly accepts it whereas the rabbis do their utmost to reject it, even if they have to wriggle in order to avoid the obvious meaning.

Conclusion

We have selected only a very limited sample of exegetical passages, restricting ourselves to the first 5 chapters of Genesis and to passages which are covered by both Philo and the midrashic work *Genesis Rabbah*. This sample is too small to base sweeping conclusions upon. Even so, they are representative enough to warrant some provisional and tentative conclusions. We may say that, in spite of the great diversity of solutions of or answers to exegetical problems and questions, the common ground of the first century Alexandrian philosopher and the rabbis of Byzantine Palestine is to be found in the fact that they wrestled with the same questions that the biblical text put before them. Kugel's formulation of the first assumption common to all Jewish exegetes, the cryptic nature and hidden meaning of the biblical text which needs to be decoded, turned out to be at work in all cases reviewed. Also the other assumptions – the relevance to the

---

[43] See P.S. Alexander, "Enoch and the Beginnings of Jewish Interest in Natural Science," in C. Hempel a. o. (eds.), *The Wisdom texts from Qumran and the Development of Sapiential Thought*, Leuven 2003, 233–234; R. Elior, *The Three Temples. On the Emergence of Jewish Mysticism*, Oxford – Portland 2004, 205, 221; P.W. van der Horst, *Het boek der hemelse paleizen (3 Henoch)*, Kampen 1999, 11–13. On Enoch traditions in general see J.C. VanderKam, *Enoch, a Man for All Generations*, Columbia 1995.

present situation, the perfect harmony of all parts of Scripture, and its divine in-spiration were clearly discernible in the few cases that passed review. Of course, the differences in the answers are considerable, one of the most significant being that typically Greek philosophical themes such as the immortality of the soul, the noetic world, and the ascent of the soul to this world of *intelligibilia*, so prominent in Philo, are completely absent in the rabbinic sources. But such divergence is, in the final analysis, less weighty than the striking convergence in the nature of the questions. A more large-scale and detailed comparison of large parts of Philo's exegesis of Genesis, including that in many of his allegorical treatises, with not only the whole of *Genesis Rabbah* but also with the many other passages in early rabbinic literature containing exegesis of passages in Genesis, is a desideratum that I hope other scholars are willing to fill. This mod-est contribution has hopefully whetted the appetite of such scholars for tackling this fascinating enterprise.[44]

---

[44] I owe thanks to Prof. David T. Runia for his valuable comments on the first draft of this paper.

Philo of Alexandria on the Wrath of God

It was to be expected that the notion of God's wrath would constitute a problem to the Jewish philosopher Philo of Alexandria. As is well-known, the two cultural traditions that merge in his religious philosophy, the Biblical and Jewish tradition on the one hand and the Greek philosophical on the other, speak a widely different language as far as the wrath of God or the gods is concerned. Philo's ingenuity is indeed great enough to find a solution to this problem, but – as we shall see – it is a far from unproblematic enterprise. In order to make clear what the difficult task was which Philo faced, I will first present a sketch of the two diametrically opposed positions in the two traditions, and then I will show how Philo tries to create a synthesis between these antithetical positions, a task for which he was well equipped as a 'Bindeglied' *kat'exochên* between the Jewish and the Greek traditions.[1]

On the motif of God's wrath in the Old Testament I can be brief since the texts containing that motif are so numerous and well-known that a very succinct review suffices. When Moses asks God at the burning bush to send someone else to the Pharaoh, God's wrath was kindled against him (Ex. 4:14). In the story about Israel's sin with the golden calf, it is God's burning wrath that threatens to destroy the people so that Moses beseeches him to turn away from his wrath and spare the Israelites for his Name's sake (Ex. 32:10–12). God's wrath is kindled in the story of Balaam (Num. 22:22), at Israel's idolatry with Ba'al Pe'or (Num. 25:3–4), at the sin of Achan (Josh. 7:1, 26), at the worship of Ba'al en Ashera by the people (Jud. 3:8; 10:7), when Uzza took hold of the ark (2 Sam. 6:7), when Zedekiah did what was evil in the sight of the Lord (2 Kings 24:19–20) etcetera. The author of 2 Chronicles has the burning wrath of the Lord play an even more frequent role than was already the case in his sources; in the books of the great prophets, Isaiah, Jeremiah, and Ezechiel, the theme of God's wrath against Israel is a constantly recurring motif (Is. 20x, Jer. 24x, Ez. 11x); and the minor

---

[1] H. Frohnhofen, *Apatheia tou Theou. Über die Affektlosigkeit Gottes in der griechischen Antike und bei den griechischsprachigen Kirchenvätern bis zu Gregorios Thaumaturgos*, Frankfurt etc. 1987, 108, rightly remarks that Philo, in view of his boundary position, seems to be predestined "einen ersten Harmonisierungsversuch zwischen dem weitgehend apathischen Gott griechischer Provenienz und dem mitfühlenden und durch die Menschen und ihr Schicksal betroffenen jüdischen Gott andererseits vorzunehmen."

prophets also speak about God's wrath (15x in total).[2] Sometimes God's wrath is kindled spontaneously, without any discernible reason, as in 2 Sam. 24:1, where God, in seemingly unmotivated anger, incites David to count the people (it is perhaps partly the unmotivated nature of this wrath that induced the later author of Chronicles to replace 'God' here by 'Satan' in 1 Chron. 21:1). God's wrath is directed not only against his own people or members thereof, but also against the heathen nations, especially in eschatological utterances of the prophets, e. g., Is. 13:3, 5, 9, 13; Micah 5:14, Zeph. 2 (cf. in vv. 2 and 3 the expression 'the day of the wrath of the Lord'); also in Ps. 2:5, 12.[3]

The number of instances and references could be multiplied *ad libitum*, but this small selection suffices to show that the motif of God's wrath is not limited to only a handful of authors or layers of tradition in the Hebrew Bible. On the contrary, it is a conception shared by all authors: their God has the ability to get enraged about matters displeasing to him or about situations in which his love is hurt. No one denies him this emotion, or whatever other passion for that matter. Furthermore, this picture does not change essentially in post-biblical Jewish literature. In rabbinic writings God's wrath is spoken of as freely as in the Hebrew Bible, and in most of pre-rabbinic literature, including the Jewish-Hellenistic literature and the New Testament, the situation is not much different.[4]

Initially, the situation was not different in Greek culture either. In Homer, Hesiod and the early tragedians, the wrath of the gods is spoken about in a way that is not essentially different from that of the biblical authors (apart from the difference between monotheism and polytheism). But at the end of the sixth and during the fifth century BCE, in Greece a critical attitude towards the traditional stories about the Olympian gods arose, especially in philosophical circles. Xenophanes of Colophon played an important role in this movement.[5] A central element in this criticism of traditional mythology was the concept of (what would later be called) *to theoprepes*, 'that which is fitting to a god or worthy of a god' (in Latin, *dignum deo*).[6] There was a growing awareness that human affections and emotions, such as jealousy, lust, and anger, were unfittingly and unjustly ascribed to the gods in the mythological tales of the tradition (e. g., Homer and Hesiod). An

---

[2] Statistical data from G. Sauer, ''af,' in *Theologisches Handwörterbuch zum Alten Testament* 1 (1971) 221–222.

[3] For further discussion see E. Johnson, 'anaph, ' in *Theological Dictionary of the Old Testament* 1 (1974) 348–360; G.A. Herion, 'Wrath of God,' *Anchor Bible Dictionary* 6 (1992) 989–996.

[4] See the survey by E. Sjöberg and G. Stählin in the *Theologisches Wörterbuch zum Neuen Testament* V (1954) 413–419.

[5] See for his fragments H. Diels & W. Kranz, *Die Fragmente der Vorsokratiker*, vol. 1, Berlin 1951, 113–139 (nr. 21).

[6] O. Dreyer, *Untersuchungen zum Begriff des Gottgeziemenden in der Antike*, Hildesheim 1970.

effect of this idea outside of strictly philosophical circles, as far as the concept of divine wrath is concerned, can already be seen in Euripides when, in the final scene of his *Bacchae* (1348), he has one of the *dramatis personae* say that it is unseemly for gods to be like mortals in matters such as fits of anger.

It was, however, especially Plato (who wanted to banish Homer's poetry from his ideal state!) whose great influence made the idea of the *theoprepes* into a central notion in the period after him, the Hellenistic-Roman era. His theory of the essential and and absolute unchangeability of the divine world, in which there is of course no place for an emotion such as wrath, then conquers the intellectual world, albeit slowly, and becomes an unwritten dogma of the religious philosophy of later antiquity. Initially this influence will limit itself to the world of philosophical and religious thinkers, as is apparent from authors who are contemporaries of Philo in the wide sense of the word, i.e., from the third century BCE to the third century CE. For instance, Epicurus writes in the very first sentence of his *Kyriai doxai* that what is divine cannot be moved by either wrath or grace (*neque ira neque gratia*), and Cicero, who quotes this sentence, adds that if we took that into consideration, all fear of the power and anger of the gods would be banished (*De natura deorum* I 17, 45). Dispelling the fear of the wrath of the gods was one of the major motives for Lucretius to write his *De rerum natura* (cf., too, Plutarch's *De sera numinis vindicta*, esp. chs. 12 and 20). Sextus Empiricus, finally, says that it has been a dogma of all philosophers that the divine cannot be subject to emotions or passions (*apathes*, in his *Pyrrhoneiai Hypotyposeis* I 162).[7]

In a sense, Philo himself belonged to these philosophers, although one could debate the question (and it is indeed a debated question!) of whether Philo is a philosopher practicing exegesis or rather a philosophically trained exegete. Be that as it may, it is clear in what field of tension Philo had to move. It is important to see how he solved the problem of the conflict between the two traditions he stood in, not in the least because his solution will turn out to serve as a model for the way in which later philosophically trained Church Fathers would tackle the same and similar problems. To put it another way, the hermeneutical key designed by Philo would have a far-reaching influence on later Christian theology.[8]

We now find that for Philo the concept of the *theoprepes*, the *dignum deo*, had become so much of a dogma that in fact the thought that the biblical texts mentioning God's wrath could have been meant literally does not even cross his mind. To be fair, he does occasionally fall back on this biblical usage when, for

---

[7] I specifically mention here some philosophers who do not (or at least not strictly or exclusively) belong to the Platonic school in order to demonstrate that this concept was certainly not restricted to just the inner circle of Platonists.

[8] See D. T. Runia, *Philo in Early Christian Literature. A Survey*, Assen-Philadelphia 1993.

instance, he says that some people provoke God's anger by their wicked lives and that we should always avoid that (*De somniis* II 177–179), or when he says that the annual inundation of the Nile brings about a rich harvest for the inhabitants of Egypt unless God's wrath about their sinfulness prevents this from taking place (*Vita Mosis* I 6). But these are sporadic exceptions, and they are no more than concessions to biblical usage. For when the issue becomes crucial, Philo expresses himself in all clarity: "We use to think of the blessed and the immortal in terms of our own natures. For in words we do shun indeed the monstrosity of saying that God is of human form, but in actual fact we accept the impious thought that he is of human passions. And therefore we invent for him hands and feet, incomings and outgoings, enmities, aversions, estrangements, anger, in fact such body parts and passions as can never belong to the Cause" (*De sacrificiis Abelis et Caini* 95–96). For "the nature of God is without grief or fear and wholly exempt from passion of any kind, and alone partakes of perfect happiness and bliss" (*De Abrahamo* 202; cf. *Quod deus sit immutabilis* 59). Here we see Philo fully as the Greek philosopher he really is.[9]

But if this is Philo's deep conviction, how, then, does he cope with the many biblical texts that speak of God's wrath? "Why then does Moses speak of feet and hands, goings in and goings out in connexion with the Uncreated? (...) Why again does he speak of his jealousy, his wrath, his moods of anger and the other emotions similar to them, which he describes in terms of human nature?," Philo asks himself (*Quod deus sit immutabilis* 60). The answer lies in a pedagogical principle that the later Church Fathers will name *synkatabasis* or *condescensio*, that is. 'descent' (in the sense of 'accommodation') to the level of understanding of the person(s) one wants to reach.[10] In a programmatic passage, Philo formulates this principle as follows (here I briefly paraphrase *Quod deus sit immutabilis* 61–69):[11] A lawgiver who aims at the best must have only one goal before him, namely to benefit all those whom he wants to reach with his laws. Those who have a gifted nature and have had a thorough education and schooling will not feel inclined to ascribe human features to God, 'initiated in the infallible mysteries of Being' as they are. The saying that "God is not as a man" (Num. 23:19) suffices for them. There is, however, also another category of humans, those whose nature is more dull and tardy and whose education or training has been insufficient and who are for that reason incapable of a clear vision, and these are the people who need a physician who will devise a therapeutic treatment proper to their condition in order to improve them. The situation is

---

[9] Note that the title of the last mentioned treatise – *hoti atrepton to theion* – sounds like a philosophical program.

[10] On this topic see the old but still valuable study by H. Koch, *Pronoia und Paideusis. Studien über Origenes und sein Verhältnis zum Platonismus*, Berlin 1932.

[11] See the commentary by D. Winston en J. Dillon, *Two Treatises of Philo of Alexandria*, Chico 1983, 307–311.

also comparable to that of an undisciplined and foolish slave who needs a strict master who threatens him and scares him in order to keep him under control. In such situations, untruth (*ta pseudê*) is sometimes the only means to benefit them if they cannot be brought to wisdom by means of truth. When Moses ascribes to God the human attribute of anger evoked by sin, that is only a metaphor. What he wants to say is that all our deeds are reprehensible if they are the fruits of emotions and passions, but laudable if they are the products of our insight and knowledge. But it is also an elementary lesson for all those who can be brought in line only by threats. 'This is the only way in which the fool can be admonished' (68). It is for that very reason that, apart from the text about God's not being like a man (Num. 23:19), there is also another text that seems to say the opposite by stating that "the Lord your God disciplines you as a man disciplines his son" (Deut. 8:5), a saying that is directed at the 'fools.' This demonstrates that God links two principles, fear and love. "To love him is the most suitable for those into whose conception of the Existent no thought of human parts or passions enters, who pay Him the honour meet for God for His own sake only. To fear, however, is most suitable to the others" (69). [12]

It is clear that, according to Philo, quite often God, as in a pedagogical situation, has to descend to the level of children or uneducated slaves in order to bring them to insight, obedience, and the right way of life. In *De somniis* I 234–237 Philo puts it in a slightly different way: It is for those who lack the necessary wisdom that Scripture presents God in an anthropomorphic way; hence the biblical passages about His bodily parts, His movements, His anger and wrath, even His weaponry. But that is not language in which the truth is conveyed, for its aim is solely the useful effect of that language upon people who still have to learn very much. Unfortuately, there are people who cannot but imagine God as a kind of human being, with all limbs, movements, emotions, and weapons. We can only be grateful if they can be brought to lead a somewhat more sensible life by inspiring fear into them, says Philo.

Here Plato prevails over Moses. Plato's doctrine of the absolute immutability of God prevails over Moses' anthropomorphic conception of God. And it is exactly for that reason that Philo has become so influential, not in Jewish but in Christian circles. It is not a coincidence that it is two Alexandrian Christian scholars in whose works one finds the first clear traces of influence of Philo's synthesis of biblical faith and Greek philosophy, namely, Clement and Origen. [13] In Clement's *Stromateis* IV 11, 68, 3 we hear a clear echo of Philo when Clement says that no one should think that the Bible talks of real objects or events when it speaks of His limbs, movements, wrath, and threats; this is to be understood

---

[12] On this passage see also J. Dillon, 'The Nature of God in the *Quod deus*,' in Winston & Dillon, *Two Treatises* 217–228, esp. 220–2.

[13] Runia, *Philo in Early Christian Literature* 132–183.

allegorically. Philo's voice is heard even more clearly in Origen's work, in his polemics against the pagan philosopher Celsus. When Celsus ridicules the anthropomorphic ways the Bible speaks of God,[14] especially his wrath and threats, Origen argues as follows (*Contra Celsum* IV 71–72): Just as parents adapt their language to the level of their childrens' capacity of understanding, so does the Logos of God. The words that Scripture puts into God's mouth do not correspond with God's real nature but with the human capacity of understanding. The so-called wrath of God, says Origen, has in the Bible only one purpose: the correction of men's behaviour.[15] That must be clear to anyone who sees that the Bible attributes David's being instigated to count the people of Israel to God's wrath in one book (2 Sam. 24:1) but to the devil in another book (1 Chron. 21:1). That both Alexandrians knew Philo is beyond any doubt; his influence is discernible everywhere. One can gauge here how welcome Philo's solution of the problem of God's wrath was to these Platonizing Christian theologians.[16]

---

[14] On Celsus' and other anti-Christian polemicists' criticism of the biblical idea of God's wrath see J.G. Cook, *The Interpretation of the Old Testament in Greco-Roman Paganism*, Tübingen 2004, 143–5, 291–3, 302–5.

[15] In his *Homiliae in Ieremiam* XVIII – XX Origen even speaks of *apatê* (*pia fraus*, pious deceit) on God's part in this connection.

[16] See Runia, *Philo in Early Christian Literature* 176 (*et al.*); also the contributions by E. Osborn and R. Heine in P.M. Blowers (ed.), *The Bible in Greek Christian Antiquity*, Notre Dame 1997, 112–148.

Anti-Samaritan Propaganda in Early Judaism

Introduction

From a religio-historical point of view, the Samaritans should not be neglected as they were an important and large religious community in ancient Palestine, alongside the Jews, and they continue to exist to the present day, even though their community is now very small (some 675 members).[1] Samaritanism cannot be regarded as anything but a variety of Judaism.[2] Both are representatives of Israel's religion. The Samaritans worship the same God as the Jews, they have the same Torah of Moses, they keep the same laws, they have similar synagogue services etc. Samaritanism represents a conservative Yahwistic cult and cannot be regarded as a religion that is essentially different from Judaism. In practice, however, things *are* very different: Samaritans would never call themselves Jews (their self-designation is 'Israelites') and they regard Judaism as a heresy or perverted religion; similarly, in the many passages in ancient Jewish literature about the Samaritans it is far from easy to find a kind word. When the author of the Gospel of John remarks, "Jews do not share things in common with Samaritans" (4:9), it is not far from the truth. Also the passage in the Gospel of Luke in which the Samaritans refuse to receive Jesus and his disciples in one of their villages while on their way to Jerusalem (9:51–53) gives the impression of great animosity.[3] This mutual animosity is quite prominent in many of the ancient Jewish sources, and it comes almost as a surprise when in one of these sources, the extra-Talmudic treatise *Kuthim* (=Samaritans), the opening line runs as follows: "The Samaritans in some of their ways resemble the gentiles and in some resemble Israel, but in the majority they resemble Israel" (1.1).[4]

---

[1] For surveys of Samaritan research see J.D. Purvis, "The Samaritans and Judaism," in R.A. Kraft & G.W.E. Nickelsburg (eds.), *Early Judaism and its Modern Interpreters*, Atlanta 1986, 81–98, and esp. R. Pummer, "Einführung in den Stand der Samaritanerforschung," in F. Dexinger & R. Pummer (eds.), *Die Samaritaner*, Darmstadt 1992, 1–66.

[2] See the fine survey in Alan Crown's article "Samaritan Judaism," in *The Encyclopedia of Judaism*. Vol. V. Supplement Two, ed. Jacob Neusner, Alan J. Avery-Peck, and William Scott Green, New York 2004, 2241–2265.

[3] For the NT passages on Samaritans see I. Hjelm, *The Samaritans and Early Judaism. A Literary Analysis*, Sheffield 2000, 115–125.

[4] Transl. by M. Simon, "Kuthim: On the Samaritans," in A. Cohen (ed.), *The Minor Tractates of the Talmud*, vol. 2, London 1965, 615. L. Gulkowitsch, "Der kleine Talmudtraktat über die Samaritaner," *ANGELOS: Archiv für neutestamentliche Zeitgeschichte* 1 (1925) 48–56,

This relatively mild judgement is, however, certainly not the usual sentiment one finds in ancient Jewish sources because, as we will presently see, there was not much love lost between the two parties and there was a long history of mutual maligning. Because much of our data comes from Jewish sources, which are hostile, and because the Samaritan sources are generally from a late period (Byzantine and medieval) and therefore unreliable,[5] it is extremely hard to trace the history of the Samaritans, especially the early phases.[6] In this paper I am not going to search for historical facts. I will restrict myself to examining certain aspects of the history of maligning, especially the way Samaritans are portrayed in Jewish literature. Only a small selection of passages reflecting anti-Samaritan propaganda can be dealt with here.

The Hebrew Bible

The process seems already to have begun in the Hebrew Bible, where we read in 2 Kings 17 that the Assyrians deported almost all of the inhabitants of the Northern Kingdom of Israel and introduced pagans from various corners of the Assyrian Empire. These immigrants occupied Samaria and its towns. "In the early years of their settlements they did not pay homage to the Lord, so the Lord sent lions among them" (25). When the Assyrian king heard this, "he gave orders that one of the priests taken captive from Samaria should be sent back to live there and teach the people the usage of the God of the country. So one of the deported priests came back and (…) taught them how to worship the Lord" (27–28). So one could say that, according to this source, "Yahwism was introduced only as a superstitious gesture and then only by an illegitimate priest from one of the forbidden northern shrines."[7] But, the story goes on, "each of the nations went on making its own gods. They set them up in niches at the shrines which the Samaritans had made, each nation in its own settlements. (…) They keep up these old practices *to the present day*; they do not pay homage to the Lord, for they do not keep his statutes and judgements, the law and command-ment, which he enjoined on the descendants of Jacob whom he named Israel. (…) They would not listen but continued their former practices. While these nations paid homage to the Lord, they continued to serve their images, and their children and their children's children have maintained the practice of their forefathers *to this day*" (29, 34, 40–41).

---

offers a German translation. It is to be borne in mind that the closing paragraph of the same tractate says that Samaritans may only be readmitted into the Jewish community "when they have renounced Mount Gerizim and acknowledged Jerusalem and the resurrection from the dead," which of course implies that without that they are complete outsiders. The benevolent opening line of the treatise may reflect an earlier Tannaitic position (see below).

[5] See for a brief introduction to the Samaritan sources Pummer, "Einführung" 12–34.

[6] See L.L. Grabbe, *Judaism from Cyrus to Hadrian*, vol. 2, Minneapolis 1992, 503.

[7] Grabbe, *Judaism* 504.

This passage has a patently polemical nature, and it is now generally recognized that its historical accuracy and reliability is extremely dubious.[8] Modern research has demonstrated that, among other things, "only a small portion of the population (some of the upper class) were deported and the bulk of the population remained in the land."[9] Consequently, there could have been no large-scale influx of foreigners, with pagan religions, who only seemingly worshipped the God of Israel. It is obviously the biblical author's intention to convince his audience that the religious beliefs and practices of the people who lived in the northern parts of the country outside Judaea were of such a regrettably syncretistic nature that it would be best to keep them at a great distance.[10]

From its earliest known interpretations in ancient Judaism this passage was thought to describe the origins of the Samaritan religion, as we can see both in Josephus and in rabbinic literature (*Ant.* 9.277–291; b. *Qidd.* 75b).[11] Especially the men from Cutha mentioned in 2 Kings 17:30 were singled out as being Samaritan believers; hence the designation *Cuthim* in rabbinic literature and *Chouthaioi* in Josephus. But is this interpretation justified? The critical question is: Against whom was the polemic of this passage originally directed? On the basis of the reference to the *shomronim* in v. 29 it has often been assumed that it was the Samaritans whom the author had in mind. Nowadays it is assumed that 2 Kings 17 was *originally* not about the origins of the Samaritans but referred only to the syncretistic, or even gentile, population of Samaria, whom we now call 'Samarians.'[12] The final redactor, however, may have wanted to give the passage an anti-Samaritan twist. Also the passage in Ezra 4 about the opponents of the returned exiles, called 'the enemies of Judah and Benjamin' and 'the people of the land,' may not refer to the Samaritans, as it has often been taken to do, but to various groups of Samarians.[13]

---

[8] See e. g. R.J. Coggins, *Samaritans and Jews. The Origins of Samaritanism Reconsidered*, Oxford 1975, 13–18; F. Dexinger, "Limits of Tolerance in Judaism: The Samaritan Example," in E.P. Sanders et al. (eds.), *Jewish and Christian Self-Definition*, vol. 2, London 1981, 89–91; Purvis, "The Samaritans and Judaism".

[9] Grabbe, *Judaism* 504.

[10] See also M. Böhm, *Samarien und die Samaritai bei Lukas*, Tübingen 1999, 105–134.

[11] In traditional Jewish circles this is still the accepted point of view; see e. g. L.H. Schiffman, *Texts and Traditions. A Source Reader for the Study of Second Temple and Rabbinic Judaism*, Hoboken 1998, 96–98.

[12] For a survey of the debate see Dexinger, "Limits of Tolerance" 89–96, and Böhm, *Samarien* 105–134.

[13] See the observations by B. Becking, "Continuity and Community: The Belief System of the Book of Ezra," in B. Becking & M.C.A. Korpel (eds.), *The Crisis of Israelite Religion: Transformation of Religious Tradition in Exilic and Post-Exilic Times*, Leiden 1999, 272–275.

Josephus

It is striking that in his rendering of 2 Kings 17, Josephus not only does not mention any syncretism of the Assyrian colonists, he even emphasizes that after having received the necessary instruction in the true worship of God from an Israelite priest "they worshipped Him with great zeal" and that this remained the case "even to this day" (9.290). Not a single word about relapsing or about mixing this true religion with tenets or rites of their old religion! As Jürgen Zangenberg has remarked, Josephus pictures them as true proselytes: "Abwendung vom fremden Gott, Hinwendung zum wahren Gott durch Belehrung mit der Konzequenz der Treue zur angenommenen Lebensweise."[14] In rabbinic literature, the Samaritans are sometimes also presented as proselytes, but of a very suspect type, namely 'lion proselytes.'[15] They were so called because they adopted the Israelite faith only after God punished them with attacks by lions. This, of course, was not voluntary or wholehearted, so there was every reason to be suspicious of their real beliefs. There is no trace of this kind of sentiments in this passage by Josephus. On the other hand, however, Josephus does state even more emphatically than the biblical text that – contrary to what the Samaritans themselves have always maintained – there was no continuity at all between the northern Israelites and the Samaritans. The former had all been deported (see 9.278) and the latter were a new people that had adopted the religion of Israel. The only critical note that Josephus adds at the end is that these people, who he says are called *Chouthaioi* in Hebrew and *Samareitai* in Greek, are quite opportunistic in their attitude towards the Jews: "When they see the Jews prospering, they call them their kinsmen on the ground that they are descended from Joseph and are related to them through their origin from him, but when they see the Jews in trouble, they say that they have nothing whatever in common with them nor do these have any claim of friendship or kinship, and they declare themselves to be aliens of a different nation" (9.291). But aside from this, it remains remarkable and also somewhat enigmatic that Josephus alters the biblical report to make it so much more positive whereas elsewhere he is so critical of the Samarians, as we shall see presently. Was the reason that he knew the Samaritans well enough personally to be aware of the fact that they were faithful adherents of the God of Israel? Did he perhaps have a different *Vorlage* of the text of 2 Kings? Maybe Maria Böhm is right when she concludes, "So ist Ant. 9,277–291 ein Beleg dafür, daß der Erfolg der durch die Redaktion von 2Kön. 17,24–41 verbreiteten Ideologie im 1. Jh.n. noch nicht umfassend gegriffen haben kann."[16] This could be the case, but we do not know.

---

[14] J. Zangenberg, *SAMAREIA. Antike Quellen zur Geschichte und Kultur der Samaritaner in deutscher Übersetzung*, Tübingen-Basel 1994, 54.

[15] E. g., y. *Gitt.* 43c; b. *Qidd.* 75b; b. *Sanh.* 85b; b. *Niddah* 56b.

[16] *Samarien* 133.

It is only Josephus who reports the building of a Samaritan temple on Mount Gerizim (*Ant.* 11.302–347). That is not to say that we have here only a late tradition from the first century CE, for Josephus clearly used here older sources of both Jewish and Samaritan provenance.[17] The story goes as follows (the following is not a quote but a summary):

During the time that Alexander the Great was conquering the empire of the Persian king Darius, some leading Jerusalemites objected to the high priest's brother Menasseh's marriage to a non-Jewish woman and they demanded that he separate from her. When his brother, the high priest Jaddus, also supported this demand, Menasseh left Jerusalem and went to his father-in-law, Sanballat, who was the governor of Samaria, and told him that because of the priesthood he could not remain married to his daughter. Thereupon Sanballat promised Menasseh that not only could he stay married but he could also become high priest of the Samaritans. He would build a temple for him on Mount Gerizim, identical to the one in Jerusalem. As a consequence many priests and other Israelites from Jerusalem joined Menasseh and came to live in the area of Samaria. When Alexander had conquered most of Syria, he sent a message to Jaddus, the high priest of the Jews, demanding that their loyalty to Darius be replaced by loyalty to him. But the high priest wrote back that he could not break an oath of loyalty to Darius. This infuriated Alexander, who decided to punish the Jews severely. He entered Palestine and immediately Sanballat sent troops to support Alexander, telling him that he recognized him, not Darius, as his overlord. He also asked permission to build a temple, suggesting that it would create a division among the Jewish people which would make it easier to rule over them than if they were united. Alexander gave permission and Sanballat immediately started building. Alexander then went on to Jerusalem where Jaddus waited in fear and trembling. But God told him in a dream not to be afraid, to open the gates for Alexander, and to go out to meet him wearing his highpriestly gown. This is what happened, and although the Samaritans had expected him to destroy Jerusalem, Alexander, seeing the Holy Name inscribed upon the golden plaque on the high priest's mitre, prostrated himself before the Name. He greeted Jaddus and said that he had seen him in a nightly vision sent to him by God, in which Jaddus had encouraged him to undertake his great campaign because he would defeat the Persians. Thereupon Alexander sacrificed to God in the Jerusalem temple. Consequently the Samaritans, who lived in Shechem together with the Jewish apostates, decided to profess themselves Jews, seeing how kind Alexander had been to the Jews.[18] They went to meet Alexander after his departure from Jerusalem and invited him to honour their temple as well, which he promised to do only after his return from the campaign. After Alexander's death, so Josephus adds, the temple on Mount Gerizim continued to exist. "And whenever anyone was accused by the people of Jerusalem of eating unclean food or violating the sabbath or committing any other such sin, he would flee to the Shechemites" (11.346).

This story is evidently a strange mixture of legend and history, of fact and fiction. Of course Alexander the Great never worshipped God in the temple of Jerusa-

---

[17] For an analysis of the story see Dexinger, "Limits of Tolerance" 96–108; idem, "Der Ursprung der Samaritaner im Spiegel der frühen Quellen," in Dexinger-Pummer, *Die Samaritaner* 102–116; R. Egger, *Josephus Flavius und die Samaritaner*, Göttingen 1986, 65–74, 251–260.

[18] Here Josephus explicitly refers back to his earlier remarks in *Ant.* 9.291 about the opportunism of the Samaritans in this respect.

lem; it is a legend that later produced a series of even more pious varieties.[19] However, the story of building the temple on Mount Gerizim, that has often been considered a legend as well, has received increasing support from archaeology of late.[20] There is now little doubt that a rival temple was built on that mountain in the early Hellenistic period and that it remained in use until the Hasmonaean king John Hyrcanus destroyed Shechem and this temple in 110 BCE.[21] The fact that there are no biblical sources that refer to the construction of this temple is not surprising in view of the fact that "the ignoring of issues is a standard weapon in religious quarrels of all times."[22] We have to leave this historical question aside here, however.[23]

In this passage Josephus is not so much concerned with the origin of the Samaritans; this was already presented in his interpretation of 2 Kings 17 in *Ant.* 9.277–291 (partly quoted above). He is mainly concerned with "establishing the illegitimacy of the Mount Gerizim cult against competing claims from the side of the Samaritans."[24] The supposed illegitimacy of the temple does not necessarily have to do with the efforts in Jerusalem to centralize the cult. In fact we see that one and a half centuries later Jerusalem priests had no scruples about building another temple, in Leontopolis, and it remained in use without much opposition for almost two and a half centuries. So the building of the Samaritan temple was probably not the decisive factor in the break between Jews and Samaritans. Nehemiah writes that he drove away one of the sons of the high priest Joiada because that son had married a daughter of the Horonite Sanballat (another Sanballat than the one mentioned by Josephus). He regarded this as a defilement of the priesthood and of the covenant of the priests and Levites (Neh. 13:28–29). This illustrates that the issue of mixed marriages of priests or members of the high-priestly families was more significant in dividing the people into – say – an Ezra-Nehemiah party and a pro-Samaritan party in Judea. Members of the Zadokite high-priestly families had been prevented from achieving influence and

---

[19] See G. Delling, "Alexander der Große als Bekenner des jüdischen Gottesglaubens," *JSJ* 12 (1981) 1–51. Cf. also P.W. van der Horst, "De reis van Alexander de Grote naar het paradijs," in my *Studies over het jodendom in de oudheid*, Kampen 1992, 96–107, esp. 96–98.

[20] See especially a series of publications by the main excavator of Mt. Gerizim, Yitshak Magen, of which I only mention "Gerizim, Mount," in E. Stern (ed.), *The New Encyclopedia of Archaeological Excavations in the Holy Land*, Jerusalem 1993, 484–492; "Mount Gerizim – a Temple City," *Qadmoniot* 33,2 (2000) 74–118 ([Hebr.]; at pp. 119–143 of the same issue one finds more articles on Mt. Gerizim and its temple, of which Magen is a co-author).

[21] See R. Pummer, "Temple," in A.D. Crown *et al.* (eds.), *A Companion to Samaritan Studies*, Tübingen 1993, 229–231.

[22] Dexinger, "Limits of Tolerance" 98.

[23] Further discussion in Crown, "Samaritan Judaism."

[24] Dexinger, "Limits of Tolerance" 97. Dexinger adds: "Nor is he interested in describing the *first* construction of a shrine on Mount Gerizim, but only in the construction of a temple" (98), which is important in that data yielded by the excavations may be interpreted in the sense that there was an earlier sacred area.

power outside Jerusalem ever since Josiah had closed sanctuaries throughout the country. One may speculate that intermarriage with leading Samaritan families opened up this possibility again. After all, the Samaritans already claimed to possess a highpriest of Zadokite descent. The usurpation of the Jerusalem high-priesthood by the non-Zadokite Jonathan in 152 BCE ousted the Zadokites and probably confirmed the priesthood on Mount Gerizim as well as the priests who had moved to Qumran in their opposition to Jerusalem. Genealogical purity is an issue we often tend to underrate but which in ancient Jewish and Samaritan society could evoke vehement emotions and often lead to bitter rivalry. Certainly the matter described by Josephus did not lead to an immediate parting of the ways between the two groups around 300 BCE; that process was probably much slower but we do not know any details about it, although we may assume that the destruction of Gerizim and its temple by the Jewish king John Hyrcanus in 110 BCE marked a definitive break.

Chronologically in between lies the famous remark by Ben Sira that one of the nations detested by his soul, which is not a nation at all, is "the foolish people that dwell in Shechem" (50:26).[25] It is not easy to say what exactly the author is referring to here but the sense is generally taken to be anti-Samaritan. But 'foolish people' may, of course, also refer to the non-Samaritan inhabitants of Shechem, and we know there were several groups. So to say that "Ben Sira expresses his deepest contempt for the Samaritans," as Di Lella does in his commentary,[26] is definitely more than what can be inferred from this text with certainty. Also two texts in the 1st and 2nd books of the Maccabees (1 Macc. 3:10; 2 Macc. 6:2; both from the end of the second century BCE) are less than helpful, because we cannot determine whether the people spoken about are Samaritans (i. e., members of the religious community around the temple on Mount Gerizim) or Samarians (i. e., non-Samaritan inhabitants of Samaria).[27] So we must leave them aside.

Two Pseudepigrapha

Quite interesting, and hitherto somewhat neglected, evidence for the study of anti-Samaritan propaganda in Jewish sources is to be found in two pseudepigraphical

---

[25] See J.D. Purvis, "Ben Sira and the Foolish People of Shechem," *JNES* 24 (1965) 88–94; cf. also Zangenberg, *SAMAREIA* 41–43; Hjelm, *Samaritans* 138–146. There are differences between the Hebrew and Greek versions here; the Greek translation would seem to be more outspoken anti-Samaritan.

[26] P.W. Skehan & A. Di Lella, *The Wisdom of Ben Sira* (Anchor Bible 3), New York 1987, 558.

[27] See R. Pummer, "Antisamaritanische Polemik in jüdischen Schriften aus der intertesta-mentarischen Zeit," *BZ* 26 (1982) 238–242; L.L. Grabbe, "The Samaritans in the Hasmonean Period," *Society of Biblical Literature Seminar Papers 1993*, Atlanta 1993, 334–335; Hjelm, *Samaritans* 164–170.

writings, namely the *Martyrium Isaiae* and the *Paralipomena Jeremiae*. It is true that both documents have been handed down to us only in Christian adaptations and very often it is hard to pinpoint where the Jewish *Grundschrift* ends and where the Christian interpolations or rephrasings begin.[28] However, anti-Samaritan propaganda is so infinitely much more a Jewish than a Christian issue[29] that I think we can safely assume that in those passages where Samaritans negatively feature, we have hit Jewish bedrock. In the *Martyrdom of Isaiah* (3:1–12) it is a Samaritan man called Belkira[30] who plays a pivotal role in the events that lead up to the death of Isaiah. This Samaritan prophet escapes the deportation of the northern tribes by the Assyrians and flees to Jerusalem where he becomes an adept of the evil king Manasseh, inspired as he is by Beliar. He finds out where Isaiah is hiding from this king and he accuses Isaiah of false prophecies concerning the future of Israel and Judah. He also asserts that Isaiah claimed that he could see more than the prophet Moses, for Moses had said, "No man can see God and live" (Ex. 33:20), whereas Isaiah had said, "I have seen God and behold I am still alive!" (a somewhat twisted summary of Is. 6:5–7). It is this accusation of arrogance towards Moses that proves fatal for our prophet who is then tortured to death by being sawn in two with a wood-saw while Belkira stands by laughing (5:1–14).[31] It should be noted how specifically Samaritan Belkira's accusation is: According to Samaritan tradition, Moses' position is unassailable; he has reached a higher level than any other human being will ever be able to reach; he was God's only prophet and for that reason only his five books have divine authority. In contrast, the Israelite prophets can be discounted because they contradict Moses by their claim to be prophets and their talk of Jerusalem as the site of God's house. Isaiah's claim to be able to still be alive after having seen God is utterly preposterous in that he has the pretention to know better, and actually be better, than the unsurpassable Moses.[32] So, Isaiah deserves capital punishment. Here we see how a Jewish author, who probably lived in the first

---

[28] See on this hotly debated issue now the contributions in a special instalment of the *JSJ* 32,4 (2001).

[29] How little early Christian literature yields for our topic becomes apparent when one reads the chapter "Frühchristliche Literatur" in Zangenberg, *SAMAREIA*.

[30] His name is given in the various manuscripts and ancient versions as Belkira, Balkira, Bechira, Melchira etc. It has been suggested that the original Hebrew name was Bechir-ra' = the evil chosen one (or: the one chosen for evil) or Melki-ra' = evil king (cf. Melkiresha in Qumran). See my book *De Profeten. Joodse en christelijke legenden uit de oudheid*, Amsterdam 2001, 154 note 214.

[31] See for an extensive discussion of this passage M. Kartveit, "The *Martyrdom of Isaiah* and the Background of the Formation of the Samaritan Group," in V. Morabito *et al.* (eds.), *Samaritan Researches*, vol. 5, Sydney 2000, 3.15–3.28.

[32] Note that an exact rendering of Moses' words and a twisted version of the Isaian ones would certainly fit into a Samaritan milieu, as Kartveit rightly remarks (*Martyrdom* 3.24). For Samaritan views of Moses see the chapter "Moses, Lord of the World" in J. Macdonald, *The Theology of the Samaritans*, London 1964, 147–224.

century CE, viewed the Samaritans. They are followers of Beliar, that is, satanic persons. It is their disregard, their utter contempt, for the biblical prophets that turns them into persecutors of the true believers. This is interesting because this polemic takes place in exactly the same period in which the Jews gradually come to the decision that the authoritative words of God are found not only in the Torah of Moses but also in the books of the prophets and in some other writings. This position was, and is, utterly unacceptable to the Samaritans and is rejected as apostasy.[33] So, the picture really is black-and-white .

The second pseudepigraphon, *Paralipomena Jeremiae* (The Chronicles of Jeremiah),[34] is interesting from another angle, namely its view on the origins of the Samaritans which differs from that in the Bible, or at least is quite different from the way in which Jewish authors from the period (here the end of the first cent. CE or the beginning of the second cent. CE) interpreted the biblical story in 2 Kings 17. Whereas according to the latter interpretation the biblical account traces the origins of Samaritanism to the end of the eighth cent. BCE, this Jewish author puts it in the period immediately after the exile. The text (ch. 8) is so curious that it deserves to be quoted in full:[35]

The day came when God led the people out of Babylon. And the Lord said to Jeremiah: 'Get up, both you and the people, and make your way to the Jordan. Say to the people: "He that is for the Lord, let him leave behind what was done in Babylon, the men who married Babylonian wives and the women who married Babylonian husbands." And let those who listen to you cross over, and bring them to Jerusalem; but those who do not listen to you, do not bring into it.' And Jeremiah told them this; and they got up and came to the Jordan to cross over, and he repeated to them what the Lord had told him. And half of those who had married Babylonians refused to listen to Jeremiah, but they said to him: 'We will never leave our wives behind; let us take them back with us to our city.' So they crossed the Jordan and came to Jerusalem. And Jeremiah stood up (…) and said: 'No one with a Babylonian partner shall enter this city. And they said to him: 'Let us then return to Babylon, our place.' And they went away. But when they came to Babylon, the Babylonians came out to meet them and said: 'You shall not enter our city because in your hatred for us you left secretly; you shall not return to us for that reason. For we have bound ourselves by oath in the name of our god not to receive either you or your children, because you left us secretly.' And when they heard this, they turned back and came to a deserted place at some distance from Jerusalem, and there they built a city for themselves and called it Samaria. And Jeremiah sent a message to them saying: 'Repent, for the angel of righteousness is coming and will lead you to your place on high.'

---

[33] This is not to deny that the motif of a conflict between the prophets and the Torah has Jewish parallels, but in Judaism these conflicts are 'solved,' as is done for instance in b. *Yevamoth* 49b, *Menahoth* 45a, *Sanhedrin* 89a, and *Shabbath* 13b.

[34] See for this translation of the title my *De Profeten* 77.

[35] Translation by R. Thornhill in H.F.D. Sparks (ed.), *The Apocryphal Old Testament*, Oxford 1984, 831 (with some minor modifications by the present author). For an extensive discussion of this passage see J. Herzer, *Die Paralipomena Jeremiae*, Tübingen 1994, 129–143.

This is a fascinating passage that needs further discussion. Let me begin by saying once again that a striking aspect of this chapter is that it places the coming-into-being of the Samaritan community at a much later time than contemporary Jewish literature does. There is a difference of almost two centuries. But aside from that, there are some other interesting points that catch the eye.[36] Firstly, one would expect that people leaving Babylon would gather at the Euphrates, not at the Jordan. One could say, of course, that the Euphrates is merely going unmentioned because what is really important is entering the holy land. And that is right; the author's perspective is: profane land – which goes unmentioned; holy land – where there is a parting of spirits at the border; holy city – where the Jewish returnees who had married Babylonian partners do arrive but are not allowed to enter and have no choice but to return to Babylon. The Ezra-Nehemiah view of mixed marriages is decisive here. But, interestingly enough, the founders of Samaria, and for that reason of the Samaritan movement, are not the former inhabitants of the Northern Kingdom here, no, they are former Jerusalemites! They talk about 'our city' when referring to Jerusalem. As Jens Herzer says, "Anders als in der biblischen Tradition war dem Verfasser der ParJer daran gelegen, die Samaritaner hinsichtlich ihres Ursprunges mit dem Volk der Juden in Verbindung zu bringen. (…) Er stellt sich damit in bewußten Gegensatz zu den traditionellen Vorgaben, indem er die Samaritaner in einem positiveren Licht als solche darstellt, die zwar ungehorsam, aber dennoch mit Israel verwandt und durch die gemeinsame Geschichte mit ihm verbunden sind."[37] It should also be borne in mind that the final line of the passage contains a message from Jeremia to the inhabitants of the new city of Samaria to the effect that when they repent, the angel of righteousness (that is Michael, see 9.5) will come and lead them to their place on high. That is to say that they will share in the eschatological promises to Israel. And, to quote again Jens Herzer, "Dem Verfasser der ParJer scheint angesichts dieses Geschehens ein Nichtbefolgen des Umkehrrufes unmöglich zu sein, da keine weitere Gerichtsankündigung folgt."[38]

The fact that the author stresses that they were not taken back by the inhabitants of Babylonia underlines that they were not Babylonians, not pagans, they were originally inhabitants of Jerusalem who had become so inculturated into their diaspora setting, however, that they married non-Jewish partners. And this is what worked against them. So again it is the matter of intermarriage that turns out to be a major factor. As we have seen, this problem already played a significant role in Josephus' stories of the erection of a temple on Mount Gerizim. But there it was priestly purity that was defiled by mixed marriage, whereas here it is about how it affects the common people; there the story is about the foundation of a temple, whereas here no temple is mentioned at all, only the city. Although

---

[36] See my book *De Profeten* 166, notes 362–364.
[37] Herzer, *Paralipomena* 134–135.
[38] Herzer, *Paralipomena* 137.

the author does not say so explicitly, he seems to suggest that it is the idolatry of the Babylonian spouses that bars them from the holy city. So, what we see here is that the biblical chronology regarding the origins of Samaritanism is not taken into account by the author of the *Paralipomena Jeremiae* but that the biblical suggestion of syncretism is taken up by him. In the eyes of our author the Samaritans lost all claims to call themselves 'real Israelites' because they did not obey the rules of Jeremiah – read: Ezra! – which meant that they should send away any non-Jewish partners. Again, we see how the issue of mixed marriage dominated the Samaritan-Jewish debates of the time. But we can also observe that in this period, around the turn of the era, a relatively mild position vis-à-vis the Samaritans was certainly possible in Jewish circles. We had already seen this when Josephus altered the biblical report in 2 Kings 17 to take a drastically more positive position. It is clear that by the end of the first century CE the relations between Jews and Samaritans was a much debated topic. This will continue in the Tannaitic debates of the second century as we shall see.

The Samaritan Temple

But now we return for a moment to Josephus.[39] In *Ant.* XII 7–10 he tells us that Ptolemy I Soter (end of the 4th cent. B.C.) "took many captives both from the hill country of Judaea and the district round Jerusalem and from Samaria and those on Garizim and brought them all to Egypt and settled them there"(7). Later Ptolemy favoured the Jews more than others so that "their descendants had quarrels with the Samaritans because they were determined to keep alive their fathers' way of life and customs, and so they fought with each other, those from Jerusalem saying that their temple was the holy one, and requiring that the sacrifices be sent there, while the Shechemites wanted these to go to Mount Garizim" (10). This is clearly a conflict between two religious communities, a conflict that will escalate again later in Hellenistic Egypt. For in *Ant.* XIII 74–79 Josephus tells us about a violent quarrel in Alexandria during the reign of Ptolemy VI Philometor (180–145) between Jews and Samaritans over the question of whether the temple in Jerusalem or the one on Garizim was in accordance with the Law of Moses. Both parties ask the king to make the decision. Ptolemy follows the principle of *audi et alteram partem* and listens to speakers of both parties. It is the champion of the Jewish cause who is able to convince the king by using proof from the Torah and also by emphasizing that "all the kings of Asia had honoured the temple with dedicatory offerings and most splendid gifts, while none had shown any respect or regard for that on Garizim, as though it were not in existence" (78). Following the king's decision the Samaritan pleaders were put to death. It should be added here that this story is told as well in

---

[39] On the following two passages in Josephus see Zangenberg, *SAMAREIA* 64–65.

medieval Samaritan chronicles, but then with the opposite outcome![40] Be that as it may, we see here two communities in conflict over the legitimacy of their respective temples, or rather of the place where their temples were built. One is reminded of John 4:20 where the Samaritan woman says to Jesus: "Our fathers worshipped on this mountain, but you Jews say that the place where God must be worshipped is in Jerusalem."

We also see this element in two inscriptions that date from roughly the same time as the conflict in Alexandria but were found in a different region. It was a spectacular find because these two stone tablets constitute the most ancient epigraphical testimony to a Samaritan diaspora, which was much more sizeable than is generally assumed, as I have argued at length elsewhere.[41] In 1980, two Samaritan inscriptions were found on the little island of Delos.[42] Both inscriptions, dating respectively from the third to second and from the second to first century BCE, do not speak about Samaritans *expressis verbis,* but they do speak about "the Israelites on Delos who pay their first offerings to the sanctuary (of) Argarizin." The mention of *Argarizin* (= Har Garizim) leaves no room for doubt. These Delian Samaritans honour a certain Sarapion of Cnossos and Menippus of Heraclea for their benefactions towards the community, possibly the building of a synagogue.[43] The interesting thing about these inscriptions is not only that they are evidence of a very early presence of Samaritans on Delos, but also that they make it very likely that the Samaritans lived in Crete (Sarapion of Cnossos) as early as the second century BCE.[44] For our present purposes it suffices to point out that in roughly the same period to which our literary sources date a quarrel between Samaritans and Jews about the location of the temple, epigraphical evidence from elsewhere in the Samaritan diaspora gives testimony to the fact that it was precisely this 'sanctuary of Argarizin' which distinguished them from the Jews. And it is again from the same period, the second century BCE, that we have a fragment of an anonymous Samaritan author, known as Pseudo-Eu-

---

[40] See J. A. Montgomery, *The Samaritans*, Philadelphia 1907 (repr. New York 1968), 76–77; on both the Samaritan versions of this conflict and the possible reasons for it see Egger, *Josephus Flavius und die Samaritaner* 95–101.

[41] P.W. van der Horst, "The Samaritan Diaspora in Antiquity," in my *Essays on the Jewish World of Early Christianity*, Fribourg – Göttingen 1990, 136–147.

[42] See Ph. Bruneau, "'Les Israélites de Délos' et la juiverie délienne," *BCH* 106 (1982) 465–504, which is the editio princeps. An English translation of the inscriptions is given by A. T. Kraabel, "New Evidence of the Samaritan Diaspora Has Been Found on Delos," *Biblical Archaeologist* 47 (1984) 44–46.

[43] Bruneau extensively discusses all the problems. For *Argarizin* see R. Pummer, "ARGARIZIN: A Criterion for Samaritan Provenance?," *JSJ* 18 (1987) 18–25.

[44] This interpretation is not undisputed; see P. W. van der Horst, "The Jews of Ancient Crete," *JJS* 39 (1988) 183–200 [also elsewhere in this volume]. From which of the 10 known Heraclea's Menippus came is unknown. Bruneau 479 mentions in this connection an inscription (*Inscriptions de Délos* 2616) of ca. 100 BCE in which a certain *Praylos Samareus* is mentioned who has contributed to the building of the Sarapieion of Delos. This will have been a Samarian rather than a Samaritan.

polemos, where we read that after Abraham's war with the kings he was received as a guest by the city at the temple of Argarizin (or: at holy Argarizin) where he received gifts from Melchizedek (fragment 1 in Eusebius, *Praep. Evang.* 9.17.5–6).[45] A story of a visit by the great patriarch to the holy mountain of the Samaritans can only be explained as intended to reinforce the Samaritan idea that this was the place chosen by God as his dwelling.

This brings us to the debate about the original text of Deut. 27:4. In the standard versions we read: "When you have crossed the Jordan, you are to set up these stones on Mount Ebal, as I instruct you this day, and coat them with plaster. Build there an altar to the Lord your God." Instead of 'Ebal' the Samaritan Pentateuch reads 'Gerizim.' This has always been regarded by the Jews as an intentional alteration of the text by the Samaritans,[46] although the Samaritans asserted that it was the other way round: they said that the Jews had altered the original text because they were not willing to recognize that the Samaritans were right. But things are not that simple. Firstly, if it was altered by the Samaritans, it is hard to explain why the Vetus Latina also has this reading (*Gerizim*) here and why Josephus in his rendering of this passage speaks about the mountains 'Gerizim *and* Ebal' (*Ant.* 4.305). Secondly, it is well-known that there are other instances as well where Jewish scribes made anti-Samaritan changes in the biblical text.[47] In other words, it may well be that the Samaritans are right: that theirs is the original text and that the Jews changed the original for polemical or propagandistic reasons.[48] On the other hand, we know that the Samaritans themselves did not shy away from changing biblical texts. The best known example of this is the addition of the commandment to build an altar at Gerizim to the Decalogue in Exodus 20:17. So the matter is far from unequivocal.

Rabbinic views

We now turn to the rabbinic material.[49] This brief survey will cover only a few passages out of the many texts available. It begins on a gloomy note, because

---

[45] For text and translation see C.R. Holladay, *Fragments from Hellenistic Jewish Authors*, vol. 1, Chico 1983, 172–173.

[46] For this accusation in rabbinic literature see e.g. b. *Sotah* 33b, *Sifre Num.* 15:31.

[47] R. Tournay, "Quelques relectures bibliques anti-samaritaines," *RB* 71 (1964) 504–536. It is interesting that Tournay dates most of his examples to the 2nd cent. BCE. A simple instance of 'relecture anti-samaritaine' is Hos. 14:9 where the LXX and other versions have the original "Ephraim, what further dealings does it have with idols?" whereas the MT has changed the Hebrew *lo* into *li* which results in the sentence "Ephraim, what further dealings do I have with idols?"

[48] See Zangenberg, *SAMARIA* 184–185; Dexinger, "Limits of Tolerance" 108–109.

[49] For convenient collections of the relevant passages the reader is referred to [H.L. Strack &] P. Billerbeck, *Kommentar zum Neuen Testament aus Talmud und Midrasch*, vol. 1, München 1926, 538–560; Zangenberg, *SAMAREIA* 92–166. A detailed presentation of all the relevant material from the Mishna is to be found in B.W. Hall, *Samaritan Religion from John Hyrcanus*

our earliest document, called *The Scroll of Fasting* (*Megillat Ta'anit*), which probably dates to the early second century CE, lists 'the day of Gerizim' as one of the days on which it was forbidden to fast (22). This is the day on which the temple on Mount Gerizim was destroyed and rased to the ground by John Hyrcanus.[50] Because the destruction of that temple was such a joyous occasion it was forbidden to fast on that day. It is clear that in the eyes of the compilers the destruction of the temple on Mt. Gerizim (to quote Zangenberg) "nicht primär als rein militärischer Akt, sondern als besondere, heilsgeschichtlich-religiöse Tat interpretiert wurde."[51] But as so often in rabbinic literature, dissenting voices were heard.[52] Not only was there little unanimity among the rabbis but their attitudes also seem to change considerably over time.

From roughly the same period as *Megillat Ta'anit* we have a statement attributed to Rabbi Aqiva to the effect that the Samaritans are sincere proselytes, not just 'lion-proselytes,' and for that reason should be considered as Israelites (y. *Gitt.* 43c; b. *Qidd.* 75b; b. *Sanh.* 85b; b. *Niddah* 56b).[53] His near-contemporary Rabban Shimon ben Gamliel is even reported to have said that Samaritans are like Israelites in every respect, and that they are often more scrupulous in following the commandments than the Israelites (y. *Berakh.* 11b ; m. *Berakh.* 7.1; t. *Terum.* 4:14; b. *Qidd.* 76a). It is on the basis of such material that Hans Kippenberg concludes: "So findet sich im 2. Jh. n. Chr. noch gebrochen die Einsicht, daß es sich bei den Samaritanern um Israeliten handelt."[54] This is what we also saw in the perhaps slightly earlier *Paralipomena Jeremiae*. But even in the later post-Talmudic treatise, *Cuthim*, the compilers still speak of many areas in which the Samaritans can be trusted to follow the Torah carefully.[55] Yet this is not the dominant tenor in rabbinic literature of the post-Tannaitic period.

---

to Baba Rabba, Sydney 1987, 179–225. Discussions of this material also in, e. g., J. Jeremias, *Jerusalem zur Zeit Jesu*, Göttingen 1962, 387–394; H. Kippenberg, *Garizim und Synagoge*, Berlin 1971, 137–143; esp. L.H. Schiffman, "The Samaritans in Tannaitic Halakhah," *JQR* 75 (1984/85) 323–350.

[50] H. Lichtenstein, "Die Fastenrolle," *HUCA* 8–9 (1931/32) 257–352, here 288; J.A. Fitzmyer & D.J. Harrington, *A Manual of Palestinian Aramaic Texts*, Rome 1994 (2nd ed.), 186. For a discussion of this passage see Zangenberg, *SAMAREIA* 159–162; Hjelm, *Samaritans* 128.

[51] Zangenberg, *SAMAREIA* 162.

[52] A very clear case of inner-rabbinic debate and dissension is to be found for instance in b. *Hullin* 5b–6a.

[53] Aqiva also opposed the strict rulings on the Samaritans by his colleague R. Eliezer; see m. *Shev.* 8:10. The trustworthiness of the attribution of these dicta to Aqiva is doubtful, however; see Schiffman, "The Samaritans" 327.

[54] Kippenberg, *Garizim* 138.

[55] See the list in Kippenberg, *Garizim* 140–141. One may wonder whether this attitude might still have contributed to the closing of the ranks and the co-operation between Samaritans and Jews in the great anti-Byzantine revolts in sixth-century Palestine, on which see L. di Segni, "Rebellions of Samaritans in Palestine," in Crown *et al.* (eds.), *Companion* 199–201. These revolts cost the Samaritans tens of thousands of casualties.

As the final words of the treatise *Cuthim* indicate, it is only "when they have renounced Mount Gerizim and acknowledged Jerusalem and the resurrection from the dead" that they can be re-admitted into the fold of God's people.[56] That the Samaritans, like the Sadducees, rejected the idea of resurrection because it is not found in the Torah,[57] is something that must have offended the rabbis. In the Mishna, *Sanh.* 10.1, it is explicitly stated that he who denies that the Torah teaches the resurrection of the dead has no share in the world to come. That the Samaritans oppose this idea cannot be substantiated from the earliest Samaritan sources extant, but several knowledgeable Church Fathers from the third and fourth centuries confirm that the Samaritans did not believe in the resurrection of the dead.[58] However, for some reason or another, in later antiquity or early medieval times the Samaritans did adopt this idea, as the Jews did some centuries earlier.

That the Samaritan rejection of Jerusalem and the Prophets and Writings re-mained a bone of contention between the two parties should not surprise us after what we have seen. But aside from that, in the late Tannaitic and the Amoraic period we also see that the old accusation of paganism is resuscitated leading, finally, to the excommunication of the Samaritans by the rabbis. In this respect it is significant that the Samaritans receive no mention in the Mishna treatise *Avodah Zarah* (=idolatry), whereas they do in the later Gemara on this treatise in both Talmudim.[59] In the 4th century, the Church Father Epiphanius reports that Samaritans who wanted to become Jews had to be re-circumcised, and the same applied to Jews who wanted to become Samaritans (*De mensis et ponderibus* 16.7–9). This should be seen in the context of a series of rabbinic statements claiming that Samaritans are nothing but pagans: e. g., t. *Terumot* 4.14 tells us that no less a person than Rabbi (i. e., Judah ha-Nasi) decreed that Samaritans should be treated like gentiles.[60] This is a judgement that is often repeated after-wards[61] (even though it does not always go uncontested). We have to keep two things in mind here: First of all, rabbinic literature does not describe reality as it is but as the rabbis would like to have it. In other words, when the rabbis declare Samaritans to be nothing but pagans, that does not imply that the Jews in general shared this opinion and acted accordingly. We know of very many situations in

---

[56] See b. *AZ* 27a: "An Israelite may perform circumcision on a Cuthean but a Cuthean should not circumcise an Israelite, because he performs it in the name of Mount Gerizim."

[57] See J. Le Moyne, *Les Sadducéens*, Paris 1972, *passim*; G. Stemberger, *Pharisäer, Sadduzäer, Essener*, Stuttgart 1991, 68–70.

[58] Evidence in Kippenberg, *Garizim* 141–142, and in F. Dexinger, "After Life," in Crown et al. (eds.), *Companion* 9–10.

[59] Hall, *Samaritan Religion* 208.

[60] In the very same passage his father, Simeon ben Gamliel, says that Samaritans are like Jews in all respects!

[61] See the collection in Billerbeck, *Kommentar* I, 552–553, who refers to the following pas-sages from the Jerusalem Talmud: *Berakh.* 11b, *Ket.* 27a; *Dem.* 25d, *Sheq.* 36b etc.

which the common Jews simply ignored rabbinic prescripts. Secondly, even today we witness the phenomenon that strictly orthodox Jews call non-orthodox Jews simply non-Jews, whereas they know quite well that, seen from another viewpoint, this is untenable. Groups claiming exclusive rights to the epithet Jew or Israelite are very common in the history of Jewish religion. The Samaritans themselves do the same when they say that Jews are not Israelites but apostates. Again, this kind of claims often does not work on the level of practice, and this is probably why, even after the strong statements by persons like Rabbi, many Jews continued to treat the Samaritans as if they were Israelites, albeit perhaps second-rate.

But the rabbis did not give up easily. In the 4th century they started to accuse the Samaritans of worshipping a dove (y. *Av. Zar.* 44d; b. *Hull.* 6a *et al.*), so of downright idolatry.[62] This is almost certainly a completely unjustified allegation and should be seen as either a misunderstanding or, more probably, as a deliberate distortion of the Samaritan worship of *Shema* (in their language *'ashima*), the Name (i.e. YHWH). "The implication of the Jewish allegation would seem to be that the Samaritans still worshipped the goddess Ashima, whose cult is said to have been brought into the Northern Kingdom of Israel by the Assyrian colonists (2 Kings 17:29–30)."[63] There has never been the slightest evidence that the Samaritans ever worshipped this dove,[64] so here we are almost certainly in the realm of religious slander. There is little doubt that the fact that the Samaritans resolutely rejected the central rabbinic concept of Oral Torah[65] – in this respect they were again not unlike the Sadducees – was the factor that fuelled the anger of the rabbis against them. It is clear from Talmudic discussions (e.g., b. *Qidd.* 75a–76a) that, as in the pre-rabbinic material, questions of strict marriage rules, purity of lineage and related matters continued to play a large role in the rabbis' assessment of the Samaritans. The problem always was that some rabbis claimed that the *Cuthim* were not strict enough in these matters.[66] Another barometer of Jewish/non-Jewish relations was the acceptance of wine held by a group, indicating that they are considered Jews. "Until the mid-second century CE wine sealed by a Samaritan was acceptable but, in Amoraic times, it came to be forbidden (y*AZ* 5:4 (44d); b*AZ* 31a-b; cf. *Kutim* 2:9). The reason given is the corruption of the Samaritans, that is their laxity in the observance of the commandments as noted in Amoraic descriptions of them."[67] There are

---

[62] E.g., b.*Hull.* 6a: "R. Assi declared the Cuthaeans to be absolute heathens." Cf. *Gen. Rabba* 81.3.

[63] J. Fossum, "Dove," *Dictionary of Deities and Demons in the Bible* (eds. K. van der Toorn, B. Becking & P.W. van der Horst), Leiden-Grand Rapids 1999 (2nd ed.), 263.

[64] See for instance Hall, *Samaritan Religion.*

[65] See R. Bóid, "Use, Authority and Exegesis of Mikra in the Samaritan Tradition," In M.J. Mulder (ed.), *Mikra* (CRINT II,1), Assen – Philadelphia 1988, 598.

[66] Schiffman, "The Samaritans" 328–334.

[67] L.H. Schiffman, "Rabbinic Literature, Samaritans in-," in Crown, *Companion* 199.

many more early rabbinic texts on the Samaritans but for reasons of space we had to make a selection. We have seen enough, however, to be able to conclude that "the attitude of the rabbis to the Samaritans changed from one of Jewish or questionable status to the assumption that the Samaritans were like non-Jews in all halakhic matters."[68]

Conclusion

We have to draw to a close. The thread that runs throughout this story has been one of ambiguity and ambivalence. The Samaritans are at the same time both Jews and non-Jews. "They were neither in nor out."[69] The fact that the Samaritans accepted the Torah of Moses as authoritative and divine and also lived accordingly made other Jews feel that they were dealing with kinsmen. On the other hand, the fact that the Samaritans rejected some tenets that had become fundamental to post-exilic and post-biblical Judaism (i.e. the acceptance of the Prophets and Writings, the centralization of the cult in Jerusalem, the idea of a resurrection of the body) made other Jews feel that they were dealing with outsiders, beyond the pale of Judaism. Assessment of the Samaritans by individual Jews varied greatly depending on the political circumstances, how openminded or strict they were, and whether they had actual and personal knowledge of them. The Samaritans were strange coreligionists who were hard to identify and who therefore made it difficult to define the boundaries between them and the Jews. For these reasons there is no unequivocal Jewish view of the Samaritans.[70]

---

[68] Schiffman, "Rabbinic Literature" 199.

[69] Schiffman, "The Samaritans" 323.

[70] The author expresses his gratitude to the doyen of Samaritan studies, Prof. Alan Crown from Sydney, for his critical remarks on the first draft of this article. He saved me from several errors.

Jacques Basnage (1653–1723) on the Samaritans

*Or: How much did one know about the Samaritans
three centuries ago in the Netherlands?*

French Protestantism had a very difficult start. The 16th century was a period of persecution with as its most brutal zenith the so-called Massacre of St. Bartholomew's Day in August of 1572 when at the instigation of queen Catherine de' Medici between 5000 and 10000 Huguenots (as the French Protestants were called) were murdered in the cities of France. The Edict of Nance, signed in 1598 by Henri IV after the French wars of religion, formally granted the Huguenots the right of free exercise of their religion and civil equality with Catholics, but as the history of the 17th century proved, it didn't work: in fact the Huguenots hereby achieved the status of a barely tolerated minority, a status that was gradually and increasingly undermined by a long series of formal and informal encroachments of their new rights. This glaring demonstration of French intolerance reached its natural apogee in the revocation of the Edict of Nantes in 1685 by Louis XIV, the Sun King, an act which implied that the Huguenots were forced to become Catholics; otherwise they would become outlaws.[1] Although they were not allowed to leave the country, some 200,000 managed to flee from France, and a large number of Huguenots, at least one third of them, settled in the country that had the longest and strongest tradition of religious tolerance in Europe, the so-called United Republic of the Netherlands. Others went to Switzerland, England, and Germany.[2]

The most famous and illustrious of these French Protestants in the Netherlands was the writer Pierre Bayle, the tolerant skeptic who became professor of philosophy and history at Rotterdam, where he wrote his famous four-volume *Dictionnaire historique et critique* (1695–97), a man who is now generally regarded as a precursor of the Enlightenment. He is an exemplary exponent of the phenomenon that his most recent and authoritative biographer, Elisabeth Labrousse, describes to the effect that by and large the Huguenots always "were incomparably better educated and trained than the average Catholic parish

---

[1] On the serious consequences of this revocation (and its prehistory) see J. Orcibal, *Louis XIV et les protestants*, Paris 1951, *passim* but esp. 124–158.

[2] Hundreds of thousands, however, became French Catholics, of course *contre coeur*, so that in fact a kind of 'Protestant Marranos' came into being.

priest."[3] This applies *a fortiori* to his close and lifelong friend and benefactor Jacques Basnage, who played such an important role throughout his life.[4] Basnage was born in 1653 as the son of a Protestant lawyer in Rouen and a member of "one of Normandy's most celebrated dynasties, known and recognized still today for its scholarly barristers and Huguenot pastors."[5] He became a minister in his native town in 1676, but in 1685, the year of the revocation of the Edict of Nantes that marked the beginning of the so-called Second Refuge, he fled to the Netherlands where he became a minister of the French Protestant community (the Église Wallonne) in Rotterdam; since 1710 he held that position in The Hague, where – apart from being a pastor – he also played a very prominent role in Dutch affairs of state.[6] Voltaire, who was a great admirer of Basnage, wrote about him that a position of 'ministre d'État' in the Netherlands would be much more fitting to Basnage's qualities than that of Protestant pastor.[7]

Jacques Basnage was one of the most remarkable scholars of his time. His scholarship was impressively wide-ranging and his productivity was stunning. His most famous works are probably his two-volume *Histoire de la religion des églises réformées* (1690) and his general *Histoire de l'église* (1699, again two volumes). But he also wrote influential works in the field of biblical studies, pastoral theology, the history of religions, and history in general, and many polemical works against the Catholic church came from his pen as well. In total he published some 30 books, several of which were multi-volume works.[8] His most important work for our purposes is his *L'histoire et la religion des Juifs depuis Jésus-Christ jusqu'à présent* (The History and Religion of the Jews from Jesus Christ to the Present Day) of 1706–1707, which was also published in an English version in 1708 and a Dutch version in 1726 (that was reprinted as recently as 1988 in my country!).[9] In 1710 the Catholic abbot Louis Dupin published in

---

[3] E. Labrousse, *Bayle*, Oxford 1983, 5.

[4] See Labrousse, *Bayle* 18–20, 32, 45–47.

[5] G. Cerny, *Theology, Politics and Letters at the Crossroads of European Civilization: Jacques Basnage and the Baylean Huguenot Refugees in the Dutch Republic*, Dordrecht – Boston 1987, 11.

[6] See E. & E. Haag, *La France Protestante*, vol. I, Paris 1877 (2nd ed.), 930–943; Anon., "Basnage (Jacques)," in J.P. de Bie & J. Loosjes (eds.), *Biographisch Woordenboek van Protestantsche Godgeleerden in Nederland*, vol. I, Den Haag (n.d.), 334–338; B. Heurtebize, 'Basnage de Beauval, Jacques,' *Dictionnaire de la Bible* I, 2 (Paris 1926) 1495–1496; B. Dinur, 'Basnage, Jacques,' *Encyclopaedia Judaica* 4 (1972) 309–310; M. Silvera, *Jacques Basnage. Corrispondenza da Rotterdam, 1685–1709*, Amsterdam & Maarssen 2000; and esp. Cerny, *Theology, Politics and Letters* (see previous note), still the best treatment.

[7] See *Biographisch Woordenboek* I 335; Haag, *La France protestante* I 931; and Cerny, *Theology, Politics and Letters* 181. Voltaire: "[Basnage] était plus propre à être ministre d'Etat que d'une paroisse."

[8] For a bibliography of his works see *La France protestante* I 934–942; also Cerny, *Theology, Politics and Letters* 323–326.

[9] J. Basnage, *L'histoire et la religion des Juifs depuis Jésus-Christ jusqu'à present, pour servir de suplement* [sic] *& de continuation à l'Histoire de Joseph* [sic], Rotterdam: Reinier

Paris an anonymous and strictly expurgated pirate edition of the work in which everything that could be seen as damaging to the interests of the Roman Catholic Church had been removed (especially those passages in which Basnage heavily criticized the Catholic church for its many persecutions of the Jews). In 1711 an angry Basnage took revenge with his *Histoire des Juifs réclamée et rétablie par son véritable auteur contre l'édition anonyme et tronquée* (458 pages!). The *Histoire des Juifs* is a very large work that appeared in 6 volumes in the first edition of 1706–07 and in 15 in the very much enlarged second edition of 1716, in which he also replied to his critics. The Dutch translation of this latter edition is a folio-size one-volume edition of some 2000 two-column pages. The second French edition contains more than 4000 pages. The book's influence was enormous.[10]

One of the most striking aspects of this book, which is based upon a solid knowledge of the original sources of Jewish history and religion,[11] is that it also contains the first major study of the Samaritans ever to appear in the Netherlands. In its first edition some 150 pages are devoted to the Samaritans, and in the second even more; the Dutch translation of that edition contains 82 double folio-size pages in two columns on the Samaritans (in a modern standard edition that would cover between 165 and 200 pages, *i. e.*, the chapter would be monograph length). This is very striking because in the long chapter about 'Jewish sects' of which the pages on the Samaritans are a part,[12] Basnage devotes more attention to the Samaritans than to Pharisees, Sadducees, Essenes, Herodians, Karaites etc. altogether. Apart from that, he also turns out to be remarkably well-informed

---

Leers, 1706–7; new augmented ed. Den Haag: Henri Scheurleer, 1716. The English version was the translation by Thomas Taylor: *The History of the Jews from Jesus Christ to the Present Time*, London 1708 (non vidi). The Dutch version, a translation of the 1716 edition, appeared under the title *Vervolg op Flavius Josephus; of Algemene Historie der Joodsche Naatsie etc.*, Delft: Gerard onder de Linden, 1726. The book was reprinted in 1988 by publishing house De Banier in Utrecht. See my review in *Nederlands Theologisch Tijdschrift* 44 (1990) 265–266. On Reinier Leers, the famous international publisher who brought out many of Basnage's works see O.S. Lankhorst, *Reinier Leers (1654–1714), uitgever en boekverkoper te Rotterdam*, Amsterdam & Maarssen 1983.

[10] It is interesting to see that the second edition of Basnage's work inspired the Dutch Yiddish historiographer Menachem Mann to write a general history of the Jews going back to 70 CE in Yiddish, *She'erit Yisrael* (Amsterdam 1743); see L. Fuks & R. Fuks, 'Joodse geschiedschrijving in de Republiek in de 17e en 18e eeuw,' *Studia Rosenthaliana* 6 (1972) 137–165, esp. 153–156. As Cerny, *Theology, Politics and Letters* 185, remarks: "In a very real sense, it was primarily because of Basnage's *Histoire des Juifs* that Dutch Jewish scholars, Sephardim and Ashkenazim, became the first among Europe's Jews to resume what, seventeen centuries earlier, Flavius Josephus had begun."

[11] It may be added that Basnage's veneration for Josephus is somewhat excessive, no doubt because he regarded himself as this author's successor.

[12] The chapter is called "Livre second contenant l'Histoire des Sectes qui subsistoient au temps de J. Christ, et de la ruïne de Jérusalem. Les Samaritains; les Sadducécns; les Pharisicns; les Esséniens; les Hérodiens; etc. Leur origine; leurs dogmes; leurs progrés; et leur état present."

about the Samaritans.[13] To put all this into a somewhat wider framework, let me say something more about Basnage's reasons for writing this major work.

Basnage knew that one of the most famous Jewish scholars from Amsterdam, Menasseh ben Israel, had plans to write a history of the Jewish people as a sequel to Josephus' *Antiquitates Judaicae*, but that circumstances had kept him so far from completing this first Jewish history for 15 centuries. As a matter of fact, Menasseh ben Israel's unfinished manuscript was probably in Basnage's possession. Basnage, like Menasseh ben Israel a victim of Roman Catholic persecution, had a great sympathy for this project, for it was his fate as an exile that made him feel connected to the equally exiled Jews. Many Huguenots believed that they relived for themselves the Babylonian captivity of the Jews.[14] Basnage began to read widely in order to be able to write this comprehensive Jewish history which, in fact, is the first modern history of the Jews. In the list of works he consulted for this enterprise he mentions some 550 authors, from Josephus to Maimonides, and from the Mishnah to Ibn Ezra and Kabbalistic writers (although it should be added that he consulted many Hebrew works only in Latin translation); of course he also consulted non-Jewish authors.[15] Both Jewish and Christian scholars of his days praised the work as a monument of scholarship,[16] which indeed it is. That is not to say, however, that he was able to read the Jewish and Samaritan sources without the prejudices that were current in his time, also among Protestants. On the contrary: "The coexistence [in Basnage] of Baylean historical criticism and a remnant of Christian anti-Semitism that had long characterized the religious thought of Protestants and Catholics made for a curious, ambivalent hybrid that reveals much about the transition from the Age of Reason to the Age of Enlightenment."[17]

There was still another motive for him to write this work. Basnage was a Millenarian. He expected that the messianic interregnum of a thousand years would begin in the year 1716. "Basnage's ostensible reason for writing the work was Millenarian. He wanted to complete the great task Menasseh ben Israel said he was working on, the history of the Jews from the time of Flavius Josephus up to the present. It would show glaringly how God has been active in history, and would prepare mankind for the Millenium, which Basnage said would begin in

---

[13] It is a shame that Basnage does not figure among the many scholars that are dealt with in A.D. Crown, R. Pummer & A. Tal (eds.), *A Companion to Samaritan Studies*, Tübingen 1993.

[14] See M. Yardeni, 'New Concepts of Post-Commonwealth Jewish History in the Early Enlightenment: Bayle and Basnage,' *European Studies Review* 7 (1977) 245–258, esp. 246–247.

[15] His bibliography covers some 40 pages and lists titles in Hebrew, Greek, Latin, French, English, Portuguese, Italian, and Spanish. The fact that he added a bibliography at all was a *novum* in his days.

[16] Some years later, Basnage said he was very gratified by the positive reception of his work by his Jewish contemporaries; Cerny, *Theology, Politics and Letters* 186. Among his non-Jewish admirers Richard Simon takes pride of place (*La France protestante* I 938).

[17] Cerny, *Theology, Politics and Letters* 190.

1716."[18] Basnage expected that in this new era all Jews would become Christians. But in 1716 it was not the Millenium but the second edition of his *History of the Jews* that appeared, and then Basnage said that he only wrote the work to prove the truth of Christianity against the Jews (vol.I, p.v). Supersessionist though he was, he was profoundly repelled by Christian persecution of Jews.[19] We have to leave these matters, however, for what they are and we will further focus on what Basnage wrote about the Samaritans.

To begin with, it is striking that his treatment of the Samaritans is part of a long chapter on what he called the 'sects' in Judaism in the time of Jesus Christ. Even though he knew, as we shall later see, of the bitter antagonism between Samaritans and (other) Jews, from a phenomenological point of view he rightly saw that Samaritanism had to be regarded as a variant of the Israelite religion. But he also wanted to include as many sects as possible because he "found evidence for the fall of Judaism in religious schisms and heresies that arose within it."[20] And "the author prepared his reader to accept the notion that the political and religious disintegration of Palestine corroborated the displacement of Judaism by Christianity as the triumphant world religion."[21] Judaism's chief misfortune was religious factionalism, according to Basnage. One of these factions was the Samaritan movement.

After a short sketch of the vicissitudes of the city of Shechem, Basnage pays attention to the holy mountain of Garizim, its role in Samaritanism, and its precise location, partly correcting the Dutch scholar Hadrian (Adriaan) Reland who had recently published a treatise on this mountain (1706).[22] After these geographical remarks, Basnage turns to Samaritan history and opens with critical remarks on the Samaritan *Book of Joshua* which he rightly says Scaliger wrongly took to be a very ancient work, and he then presents some excerpts from the work. He also mentions the Chronicle of Abu'l Fath, that had recently been

---

[18] R.H. Popkin, "Jacques Basnage's *Histoire des Juifs* and the Bibliotheca Sarraziana," *Studia Rosenthaliana* 21 (1987) 154–162, quote on p. 161.

[19] Cerny, *Theology, Politics and Letters* 199: "Basnage reasoned that Jews should be permitted to live peacefully in order that they might study the Christian religion and, hopefully, become converted one day." *Ibid.* 200: "Jacques Basnage's censure of duress to convert Jews occupied a central position in his history." Cf. Yardeni, 'New Concepts' 252: "In the last resort Basnage is convinced that the Jews are indeed the chosen people who will yet recover the place God has destined for them." In this framework Yardeni refers to another study written by her which, unfortunately, I have not been able to consult: 'Judaism and Jews in the Eyes of the French Protestant Exiles in Holland, 1685–1715,' *Mechqarim: Studies in the History of the Jewish People and the Land of Israel* 1 (1970) 163–185 [Hebrew].

[20] Cerny, *Theology, Politics and Letters* 193.

[21] *Ibid.* 194.

[22] Reland (1678–1718) was professor of Oriental languages in Utrecht. Basnage regarded Reland as one of the greatest Orientalists of his time. His most famous work is *De religione mohammedica* of 1705. See A. Hamilton, "Adrianus Reland (1676–1718): Outstanding Orientalist," in: H. Jamin (ed.), *Zes keer zestig. 360 jaar universitaire geschiedenis in zes biografieën*, Utrecht 1996, 23–31.

exploited by Edward Bernard in his studies of the Samaritans, and other Samaritan documents, esp. letters, acquired by Huntington and published in 1704. He again quotes selected passages and adds his critical comments, pointing out the many chronological improbabilities but, in spite of that, occasionally preferring the Samaritan version of events to the Jewish one. On the whole, however, his verdict about the historical reliability of the chronicles is extremely negative, especially as far as the early origin of Samaritanism in the time of Joshua is concerned. But he wisely adds that this is a common phenomenon, also among Christian Churches: all tend to retroject their origins into times as remote in the past as possible. As to the hotly debated issue of the original text of Deut. 27:4–5, Basnage thinks it is not entirely impossible that here the Samaritans are more right than the Jews: the latter may have changed the original text, thus removing the mention of Mount Garizim. It is from several passages in the prophetic books which speak about God's love for Ephraim that Basnage concludes that God loved the Samaritans as much as the (other) Israelites. He does interpret 2 Kings 17 in the traditional way to the effect that the Samaritans had originally been Cuthaeans, but he immediately concedes that in the course of time this pagan origin had become completely obliterated since they had become Israelites, albeit erring ones. Throughout his work Basnage makes clear that his sympathies are more on the Jewish than on the Samaritan side (he repeatedly calls them 'schismatics'), even though he gives them the benefit of the doubt in the matter of the original text of Deut. 27. It should be added, however, that nowhere does he make any distinction between Samaritans and inhabitants of Samaria (Samarians) so that his picture is often blurred by irrelevant evidence. For instance, he wrongly blames it upon the Samaritans that the city of Samaria issued a coin on which the emperor Nero is called a god. It is for that reason that he devotes so much space to a host of details in the history of the city of Samaria.

In a rather longwinded survey of Samaritan history in antiquity, interrupted time and again by various excursions,[23] Basnage continuously corrects errors in Josephus, the Church Fathers, the Samaritan Chronicles and in publications by the modern scholars of his time (including Scaliger); and quite often he is right, even though he is far too much impressed by Josephus. In his treatment of the NewTestament data, he shows little critical awareness in that he takes every statement about Samaritans at face value, whereas every statement in the Samaritan Chronicles he knew was critically scrutinized and very often rejected. Even so, it is impressive to see that hardly any piece of ancient evidence for the Samaritans that was known in his time – be it Jewish, pagan, Christian, or Samaritan – escaped his eye. On the basis of this evidence he presents a summary sketch of the history of the Samaritans in antiquity. He sometimes makes mistakes, e. g.,

---

[23] For instance, a very long excursion on the double circumcision of the (supposedly) Samaritan Bible translator Symmachus.

when he situates Marinus of Neapolis, who lived in the fifth century, in the reign of Justinian, but this kind of error is an exception. For the period after Justinian, he stresses the enormous reduction in numbers of Samaritans, partly due to the devastating wars that had taken place between them and the Byzantines in the 6th century, partly due to compulsory mass conversion to Christianity and, later, Islam. He refers to the small numbers of Samaritans mentioned, among others, by Benjamin of Tudela at the end of the twelfth century.

He then jumps to his own time and provides the reader with excerpts from Huntington's recent description of the present state of the Samaritans in the Near East. He also presents a translation of the letters from the Samaritans in Nablus recently published by Huntington (1704) and addressed to "their brethren in the *city* of England." This address makes him ridicule their lack of education. The emphasis in the description is upon the very impoverished state of many Samaritans and upon the incredibility of the antiquity claimed for their Abisha Scroll. He mentions with hardly concealed amusement that several Samaritans declared they would be very happy to visit their brethren in England, but declined to do so when they heard that they would have to spend a shabbat travelling on a boat. The letter of the Samaritans, which contains a detailed description of Samaritan customs, heavily emphasizes the differences between the Samaritans and the Jews in terms of much greater or lesser strictness in keeping the commandments. For the rest it is a moving plea for contact between the Samaritans in Palestine and those in 'the city of England.'

Basnage gives elaborate comments upon the letters and in these comments he also includes other Samaritan letters sent to the scholars Job Ludolf and Joseph Scaliger. For one thing, he agrees with the Samaritans that their script is older than the Aramaic script used by the Jews. As to their strictness in keeping the shabbat, Basnage simply calls it superstition. The Jewish accusation that the Samaritans worshipped a foreign deity called Asima (cf. 2 Kings 17:34) is, however, indignantly refuted by him; he says that there is no doubt that this is a perverted interpretation of the fact that the Samaritans never pronounce the holy Tetragrammaton but instead say *Ashima*, i. e., ha-Shem (the Name). He also extensively deals with the accusation that the Samaritans worshipped a dove and analyses all the pertinent traditions, only to come to the conclusion that it is a piece of rabbinic slander.[24] He is sincerely amazed that, although the Samaritans acknowledge only one God, they ascribe such an extremely high degree of authority to their High Priest; to him, as a fervent anti-Catholic, that is an inexplicable and unacceptable attitude. He repeats that the Samaritan chronicles contain more fables and legends than historical truth.

---

[24] In this connection he also pays ample attention to the anti-Jewish slander that the Jews venerate an ass (or its head). In his view this is an equally ridiculous accusation as that of Samaritan dove worship.

He then turns to the Bible of the Samaritans and castigates them for not ac-
cepting the Prophets, not even those from the North. As to their Pentateuch,
he disagrees with those scholars who state that it is out of evil intent that they
changed both the script and the text of the books of Moses. He even believes that
they possessed the Torah of Moses in this shape as early as the times of David
and Solomon.[25] He discusses at length what he calls the errors of the Samaritans
as reported by Epiphanius and other Church Fathers. He shows how often these
Christian authors were misinformed and mixed up various groups (e. g., Sadducees and Samaritans) on the basis of second-hand reports. In this connection
he pays special attention to the fact that several Church Fathers report that the
Samaritans do not believe in the resurrection of the body, whereas the Samaritan
chronicles clearly demonstrate, says Basnage, that they *do* believe in the resurrection. Here he overlooks the possibility that in the first centuries CE this tenet
may not yet have been part of the Samaritan creed, while later on it *did* become
so.[26] He also rejects Jewish accusations of persisting animal worship among the
Samaritans, although he admits that in the beginning of Samaritan history, when
they still were Cuthaeans, idolatry may have played a role for some time but not
for long. Even though he had already refuted several stories about Samaritan
idolatry in an earlier chapter, Basnage returns to this topic in order to emphasize
again that the rabbis do serious injustice to the Samaritans by their allegations
of dove worship and of idols hidden under Mt. Garizim. He accuses the Jews
here of excessive animosity towards the Samaritans, against which he wants to
do justice to them.

He next turns to the puzzling passage in the Gospel of John, where Jesus in
his conversation with a Samaritan woman says that "salvation is from the Jews"
(John 4:22). This raises for him the intriguing question of whether Jesus meant
to exclude the Samaritans from God's salvation. His firm answer is no. And it is
interesting to see that one of the reasons for this answer is that Basnage, arguing
that the Samaritans are actually identical to the ten Northern tribes of Israel, says
that from these tribes God recruited not only several of the biblical prophets
but also the 7000 who did not bow their knees to Ba'al (1 Kings 19:18), which
would seem to rule out God's wholesale rejection of the Samaritans and their
exclusion from eternal salvation. That "salvation is from the Jews (*Ioudaioi*)"
means no more than that Jesus, the means of God's salvation, is from the tribe
of Judah. It is a rather rambling way of reasoning, but it testifies to Basnage's
fundamental tolerance. He quotes passages from Hosea 11 (esp. the verses on
Ephraim) as proof of God's tender love for the Samaritans. If there had occasionally been idolatry among the Samaritans, so there was among the Jews as well,

---

[25] In this chapter he also inserts a curious excursus on the shape(s) of the Samaritan letter
Tav.

[26] See F. Dexinger, 'Eschatology,' in Crown, Pummer & Tal (eds.), *A Companion to Samaritan Studies*, 86–90.

and God did not abandon either of them. The fact that the biblical prophets from the Northern Kingdom were God's prophets no less than those of the South is here heavily stressed by Basnage as an argument that God makes no distinction between Jews and Samaritans.

After that, with an amazing gullibility, Basnage reports as historical facts the much later Christian legend that the afore-mentioned Samaritan woman from the Gospel of John converted to Christianity together with her family and that Photina, as she is then called, together with her sisters Photo and Photis (!), preached the Gospel not only in Samaria but also in North Africa – she was the founder of the Christian Church in Carthage – and that they finally suffered martyrdom in Rome under Nero. Unfortunately, says Basnage, several of the Samaritans who had become Christians became apostates again under the influence of Simon the Magician. Here we can clearly see to which absurdities a combination of trust in the Christian tradition and inability to distinguish between Samaritans and Samarians can lead. Next he deals with the various reports about Samaritan sects. Again he is very critical of the muddle-headed report by Epiphanius and comes to the conclusion that it is only Dositheus and the Dositheans that may claim to be historical. He places Dositheus in the first century and details the problems concerning this man and his followers that are caused by the contradictory nature of our sources. And finally Basnage quotes in full the Samaritan Creed as it had been sent to Scaliger by the then High Priest Elazar from Nablus.

Looking back at what Jacques Basnage presents as a history of the Samaritans and their religion, we may single out some striking elements for our final observations. There is no denying that as an orthodox Protestant he shared in the biases and prejudices of his time and culture. His view of the biblical documents is by and large fundamentalist, though it may be called surprising that in the matter of the original text in Deut. 27 he keeps open the possibility that it is not the Jewish Masoretic text but the Samaritan Pentateuch which preserves the original reading. That was new and courageous in his time. We further observe that in the matter of the long polemical tradition about Samaritan idolatry he is conspicuously mild: he does not completely deny this possibility but he does limit it strictly to the earliest period and stresses that, if ever there has been such a thing as Samaritan idolaltry, it has been very short-lived and not really different from what could be observed in Jewish circles as well. Striking is his open-mindedness in that he is convinced that God not only continues to tolerate the Samaritans but loves them as his own children and that, therefore, tolerance on the part of non-Samaritans is a holy duty. As I said before, his picture of Samaritan history is marred at several places by the fact that he regards all information about Samaria and its inhabitants as information about Samaritans instead of about Samarians. This is regrettable, but to his great credit it must immediately be added that he has not overlooked any piece of relevant evidence, as far as I can judge. His history and religion of the Samaritans is for that reason the most comprehensive of his time. It is an impressive feat which, in spite of its many shortcomings from our modern point of view, is an important work in that in the final analysis it paints what is, for his days, a strikingly sympathetic picture of the Samaritans.

Once More: The Translation of οἱ δέ in Matthew 28:17

In view of the recent debate between K. Grayston and K.L. McKay[1] concerning the correct rendering of οἱ δέ in Mt. 28.17 (ἰδόντες αὐτὸν προσεκύνησαν, οἱ δὲ ἐδίστασαν), the following remarks are in order.

Existing translations divide roughly into three categories: (1) 'When they saw him, they worshipped him, but some doubted.' In this translation (the most usual one),[2] οἱ δέ refers to part of the disciples. (2) 'When they saw him, they worshipped him, but they doubted.' In this translation,[3] οἱ δέ refers to all of the disciples. (3) 'When they saw him, they worshipped him, but others doubted.' In this translation,[4] οἱ δέ refers to persons other than the disciples.

The problem is. of course, (a) that there is no corresponding οἱ μέν in the first half of the sentence; (b) that the following verses do not give any indication of doubt on the part of the disciples; (c) that nowhere in the context is there any indication that persons other than the disciples (who are mentioned in v. 16 and are unambiguously the grammatical subject of προσεκύνησαν in v. 17) are involved.

Grayston rightly draws Mt. 26.67 (ἐνέπτυσαν εἰς τὸ πρόσωπον αὐτοῦ καὶ ἐκολάφισαν αὐτόν, οἱ δὲ ἐράπισαν) into the discussion, but wrongly suggests the translation, 'they spat … and struck him and they slapped him,' since McKay is right when he says that the normal use of οἱ δέ involves a change of subject, whether or not οἱ μέν precedes it, for when there is no change of subject, there is normally no pronoun.[5] The change of subject may be complete or partial. Both Grayston and McKay refer to the partitive use of οἱ δέ (without a preceding οἱ μέν), but unfortunately they mention only two passages from Xenophon as illustrations of this usage (taken from Winer-Moulton's *Grammar of New*

---

[1] K. Grayston, 'The Translation of Matthew 28.17,' *JSNT* 21 (1984) 105–109; K.L. McKay, 'The Use of *hoi de* in Matthew 28.17,' *JSNT* 24 (1985) 71–72.

[2] See AV, RSV, NEB, NIV, GNB, JB, etc. and many commentaries.

[3] So Grayston, *art. cit.* (n. 1), and the commentaries of Lohmeier, Grundmann, Bonnard, and others noted by Grayston; also A.T. Robertson, *A Grammar of the Greek New Testament*, New York 1919 (3rd ed.), 694.

[4] Some mss. of the Vetus Latina; also F. Blass, A. Debrunner & F. Rehkopf, *Grammatik des neutestamentlichen Griechisch*, Göttingen 1976 (14th ed.), § 250.

[5] See, e. g., J.H. Moulton, W.F. Howard & N. Turner, *A Grammar of New Testament Greek, III: Syntax*, Edinburgh 1963, 37, referring to B.L. Gildersleeve, *Syntax of Classical Greek*, New York 1911, § 518. McKay gives no references.

Testament Greek, 1882), as if this were all the evidence. Moreover, Grayston gets rid of this evidence by means of the rhetorical question, 'But in Matthew, what reason is there for discovering separate groups?' (160). And McKay tends to be led astray by his mistaken observation that 'in view of the distance of the whole group subject from the main verbs it could be that *hoi de* were a minority of a larger group led by the eleven and did not necessarily contain any of the eleven themselves' (71).

Let it be stated clearly that it is a well known and frequently used syntactical device to *indicate a division* of a group of persons or things into two (or more) subgroups *only in the second half of the sentence* (οἱ μέν / τοὺς μέν being omitted in the first half). Instances of this usage can easily be found, e. g., in the grammar of Kühner-Gerth,[6] in Denniston's classic work on the particles,[7] or in Liddell and Scott.[8] Let me quote some examples (other than Xenophon, *Hellenica* 1.2.14 and *Cyropaedia* 3.2.12 mentioned by Grayston and McKay[9]).

Euripides, *Hercules furens* 635–636: χρήμασιν δὲ διάφοροι, ἔχουσιν, οἱ δ᾽ οὔ ('It is in respect of wealth that people are different; some have riches, some don't'). Cf. also *Hecuba* 1161–1163.

Inscriptiones Graecae II 2, 652A45 (from 397 BCE): δύο σφραγῖδε λιθίνω χρυσοῦν ἔχουσα τὸν δακτύλιον, ἡ δ᾽ ἑτέρα ἀργυροῦν ('two stone seals, one having a golden ring, the other a silver one').

Plato, *Leges* 828b–c: ὁ μὲν γὰρ δὴ νόμος ἐρεῖ δώδεκα μὲν ἑορτὰς εἶναι τοῖς δώδεκα θεοῖς, ὧν ἂν ἡ φυλὴ ἑκάστη ἐπώνυμος ᾖ, θύοντας τούτων ἑκάστοις ἔμμηνα ἱερά, χορούς τε καὶ ἀγῶνας μουσικούς, τοὺς δὲ γυμνικούς ('... dances and contests, [the latter being] both musical and gymnastic').

Andocides, *De mysteriis* 38: ...ὁρᾶν δὲ ἀνθρώπους τὸν μὲν ἀριθμὸν μάλιστα τριακοσίους, ἑστάναι δὲ κύκλῳ ἀνὰ πέντε καὶ δέκα ἄνδρας, τοὺς δὲ ἀνὰ εἴκοσιν ('... in total number about three hundred, but standing in groups, some of fifteen, some of twenty men'). *Ibid*, 105: εἰ αὐτοῖς ἔξεσται ἀδεῶς συκοφαντεῖν καὶ

---

[6] R. Kühner & B. Gerth, *Ausführliche Grammatik der griechischen Sprache* II/2, Hannover-Leipzig 1904 (3rd ed.) = repr. Darmstadt 1966, 265–266 on partial change of subject ('der Redende denkt zunächst ausschliesslich an die Mehrheit, die er als Gesamtsubjekt fasst, ohne auf die Minderheit Rücksicht zu nehmen, und fügt dann erst nachträglich mit οἱ δέ die Ergänzung oder Beschränkung hinzu'); *ibid.* 272–273 on complete change of subject ('Der Grund der Weglassung von μέν liegt teils darin, dass der Vorstellung des Redenden bei dem ersten Gliede nicht zugleich auch das entgegengesetzte Glied vorschwebte, teils darin, dass der Redende absichtlich auf den Gegensatz nicht vorbereiten will, teils darin, dass der erste Glied einen zu schwachen Gegensatz bildet').

[7] J.D. Denniston, *The Greek Particles*, Oxford 1954 (2nd ed.), 166; he remarks that in several cases the sentence with ὁ δέ / οἱ δέ 'is more or less of an after-thought.'

[8] *Greek-English Lexicon*, Oxford 1940 (9th ed.), *s.v.* δέ. See also U. von Wilamowitz-Moellendorff, *Euripides' Herakles*, III, Darmstadt 1959 (repr.), 143–144, who quotes instances from Homer to Himerius!

[9] Xenophon, *Hellenica* 1.2.14 οἱ αἰχμάλωτοι ... ἀποδράντες νυκτὸς ᾤχοντο εἰς Δεκέλειαν, οἱ δ᾽ εἰς Μέγαρα. *Cyropaedia* 3.2.12 προσάγουσι τῷ Κύρῳ τοὺς αἰχμαλώτους δεδεμένους, τοὺς δέ τινας καὶ τετρωμένους. One may also compare *Anabasis* 1.10.3; 2.3.10; 5.4.31; 7.5.2.

γράφεσθαι, τοὺς δὲ ἐνδεικνύναι (' ... whether they would be allowed to act as sycophants with impunity, and to indict some and inform against others'). Here Stephanus made the unnecessary conjecture < τοὺς μὲν > γράφεσθαι.

Lucian, *Lexiphanes* 2, clearly shows that this usage was still known in the Imperial period: κατέλαβον τοὺς ἐργάτας λιγυρίζοντας τὴν θερινὴν ᾠδήν, τοὺς δὲ τάφον τῷ ἐμῷ πατρὶ κατασκευάζοντας ('I found the labourers while some of them were singing the harvest song and others were preparing a grave for my father').

Several other instances, from Homer to late ancient times, are quoted in the works mentioned in notes 6–8, above.

That this usage is probably not wholly unknown to the other authors of the New Testament might be inferred from Acts 2.12–13: ἐξίσταντο δὲ πάντες καὶ διηπόρουν ... (13) ἕτεροι δὲ διαχλευάζοντες ἔλεγον ... The words ἕτεροι δὲ after πάντες in v. 12 indicate that the meaning is that all reacted to the phenomenon described in vv. 6–11, but that the reactions were divided: some were amazed and perplexed, others however mocked at the disciples (classical usage could have had οἱ δέ here). Cf. Acts 17.18: τινὲς συνέβαλλον αὐτῷ καί τινες ἔλεγον ...; οἱ δὲ κτλ., where it is clear that again there were different reactions to Paul's preaching.[10]

All this implies that in Mt. 28.17 οἱ δέ *cannot* mean all of the disciples, *can* mean (from a strictly grammatical point of view) other persons than the disciples, but, since no other persons are involved here at all, *must* mean part of the disciples. This motif (the doubt of some of the disciples) is not elaborated in the Matthean context, but it is well known in other post-resurrection stories (Lk. 24.22 ff., 37 ff.; Jn. 20.24 ff.). The correct translation of Mt. 28.17 is therefore most probably as follows: 'When they saw him, they (or: some of them) worshipped him, but some of them doubted.'[11]

---

[10] See also my note on Acts 2.12–3 in my 'Hellenistic Parallels to the Acts of the Apostles II,' *JSNT* 25 (1985) 49–60.

[11] [Postscriptum: In his WBC commentary on Matthew (Dallas 1995), Donald Hagner asserts that in this article I 'overstated' my case since in his view an examination of the οἱ δέ construction in Matthew mainly supports the interpretation that *all* disciples are referred to here: 'but *they* doubted' (884). This conclusion is totally unwarranted since in all instances he mentions a change of subject is unambiguously clear from the context, so all these instances are irrelevant.]

Abraham's Bosom, the Place Where He Belonged

A Short Note on ἀπενεχθῆναι in Luke 16:22

In the story of the rich man and the poor Lazarus in Luke 16, the usual translation of v. 22 is: "The poor man died and was carried away by the angels to be with Abraham," or "he was carried by the angels to the bosom of Abraham" (ἐγένετο δὲ ἀποθανεῖν τὸν πτωχὸν καὶ ἀπενεχθῆναι αὐτὸν ὑπὸ τῶν ἀγγέλων εἰς τὸν κόλπον Ἀβραάμ). None of the dozens of existing translations of Luke and commentaries on his Gospel that have I consulted offer anything other than this. There is nothing wrong with this translation, except that the verb used here for carrying away, ἀποφέρειν, can have a semantic aspect that is not captured in this rendering, an aspect which I strongly suspect is present here. I submit as a translation of the verse the following free rendition: "The poor man died and the angels carried him away to the bosom of Abraham, the place where he belonged (or: his well-deserved place)." Why do I propose this translation?

In compound verbs beginning with ἀπο-, this preposition often has the connotation of 'back to where it belongs,' or it gives the verb a notion of 'deservedness' or of what is due. To give a clear example from the New Testament: The verb ἀποδίδωμι usually means 'to give away, to give up, to yield,' but it also often has the semantic aspects of 'to meet or fulfill a contractual or other obligation, to pay out, to give back, to restore to the original possessor, to recompense, to reward.'[1] It is used in this way for paying out wages in Matt. 20.8; for paying back debts in Matt. 5.26, Luke 7.42 and elsewhere; for giving due reward in Rom. 2.6; for making 'repayments' to one's parents in 1 Tim. 5.4 etc. (see also Rev. 18.6 for a particularly good example). So time and again this verb is used for giving persons what is due to them or what they are entitled to.

Another example concerns the verb ἀπέχω: When in Matt. 6 Jesus repeatedly (vv. 2, 5, 16) says of 'the hypocrites' that they ἀπέχουσιν τὸν μισθὸν αὐτῶν, he means that they have been paid here and now what was due to them, so they cannot claim anything more in the hereafter. As has already been pointed out long ago by A. Deissmann,[2] in the immediately preceding v. 1 the author speaks of μισθὸν ἔχειν without the ἀπο-prefix, so there must be a difference. The difference is that ἀπέχειν is a technical term for getting a receipt by which debts are settled.

---

[1] BDAG 109–110.
[2] *Licht vom Osten*, Tübingen 1923 (4th ed.), 88–90.

So ἀπέχουσιν τὸν μισθὸν αὐτῶν means that they have received their due reward. Now these are very well-known instances of this usage, but it is much less well-known that other compounds with ἀπο- can have the same force.[3]

I will demonstrate this with the verb ἀπάγω. It usually means 'lead away' or 'carry off.' But it can also have the semantic aspect of 'bringing back,' 'bringing home,' 'returning,' 'rendering what one owes,' as a quick glance in LSJ shows.[4] For instance, in Xenophon, *Anabasis* 1.3.14, the soldiers say that they are going to choose other leaders as soon as possible if Clearchus is not willing to *bring them back home* (ἀπάγειν). Or Plato, *Phaedo* 58b, where in the opening scene of the dialogue the speaker recounts: "The Athenians say that this is the ship in which Theseus once sailed to Crete with the seven youths and seven maidens, and saved their lives and his own as well. The story goes that the Athenians made a vow to Apollo that if these young people's lives were saved, they would send (ἀπάξειν) a solemn mission every year to Delos, and ever since then they have kept their vow to the god, even down to the present day." This is a very illustrative example since it is the element of the vow to Apollo that makes it abundantly clear that sending a yearly mission to his sacred island was something due to be done; it was a moral obligation. Hence ἀπάγειν and not just ἄγειν or πέμπειν or the like is used here. Many more examples could be given, but a few more instances of the verb used by Luke in the verse under discussion (ἀποφέρειν) will suffice.

In Herodotus and Thucydides one finds ἀποφέρειν repeatedly used for paying taxes due to the government or for paying amounts of money that had been stipulated in a treaty (e. g., Hdt., *Hist.* 1.196.3; 4.35.1; 5.84.1; Thuc., *Hist.* 5.31). In such cases the verb undoubtedly means 'bringing [the money] to the persons entitled to it or to the bodies where it belongs.'[5] The element of belonging is also apparent in those cases in which ἀποφέρεσθαι is used for going back home or being brought home, as in Lysias, *Or.* 12.18, where it is said that a man who had died in prison was brought back home (τεθνεὼς ἐκ δεσμωτηρίου ἀπεφέρετο). And in *Leges* 910c, Plato says that worship may take place only in public temples; it is forbidden to have private shrines. If someone is found to possess such a private shrine, the governors should order it to be 'transferred' (ἀποφέρειν) to a public temple. It is clear why the verb ἀποφέρειν is used for 'transferring': the public temple is the only place where worship is due.

More instances could be quoted, but these few illustrative examples make sufficiently clear that in the case of Luke's use of ἀπενεχθῆναι in 16.22 we have to take into serious consideration that he wanted to convey the sense of Abraham's

---

[3] Even the new BDAG often does not record this semantic aspect. See for some other instances J.H. Moulton & W.F. Howard, *A Grammar of New Testament Greek*, vol. 2, Edinburgh 1929 (repr. 1963), 298.

[4] S.v. II and III.

[5] The lexicon of LSJ s.v. II 4 also lists as a meaning "to hand over as required."

bosom as the place where the poor Lazarus belonged and that he was entitled to.[6] This interpretation fits in excellently with Luke's own version of the first beatitude in Lk. 6.20: "Blessed are you who are poor, for yours is the kingdom of God."[7]

---

[6] The fact that in other places in the NT ἀποφέρειν usually has the meaning of 'carrying off, taking away' does not at all militate against this conclusion.

[7] I owe thanks to my colleagues Professors Tjitze Baarda and Maarten Menken for some critical remarks on the first version of this short note.

The Hellenistic Background of Acts 9:1

"Snorting Threat and Murder"

In this essay an attempt will be made to shed some light on an expression in Acts 9:1. It is said there of Saul that he was ἐμπνέων ἀπειλῆς καὶ φόνου εἰς τοὺς μαθητὰς τοῦ κυρίου. Firstly,the literary background of this rather unusual expression will be investigated. Secondly, the function of the genitive in ἀπειλῆς καὶ φόνου will have to be defined.

In his extraordinarily fascinating study, *The Origins of European Thought*,[1] R. B. Onians has pointed out that in archaic Greek thought breath plays a much greater role than in our modes of thinking and that breathing is connected there with all kinds of psychic functions, with emotions, wishing, thinking, even with perception in all its varieties, and procreation.[2] All kinds of Greek words that designate soul, spirit, mind, mood, and their functions appear to be connected with breathing and blowing. So ψυχή is originally breath and has an etymological connection with ψυχεῖν, to breath or to blow. And also θυμός (Latin *fumus*, Sanskrit *dhumah*) originally meant breath, vapour or smoke. Onians also convincingly demonstrates that in Homer and other early Greek writers, φρένες does not mean midriff (diaphragma, as in the classical period), but lungs, and that it designates as such the seat of emotions and thoughts.[3] (Also in later authors one still finds the lungs, πλεύμων or πνεύμων, as the seat of emotions.)[4]

So Homer says for example: δίχα δέ σφιν ἐνὶ φρεσὶ θυμὸς ἄητο, (*Iliad* 21:386), literally: 'their breath in their lungs blew in two directions', i. e. there was dissension, strife among them. Once one has read Onians' discussion of such and similar phrases, one can no longer doubt that they were meant to be taken liter-

---

[1] R. B. Onians, *The Origins of European Thought about the Body, the Mind, the Soul, the World, Time and Fate. New Interpretations of Greek, Roman, and Kindred Evidence, also of some Basic Jewish and Christian Beliefs*, Cambridge 1951 (repr. 1988).

[2] *Op. cit.* 13–122. It is well known how great the role was that breathing and air played in early Greek philosophy (Anaximenes, Diogenes of Apollonia) and also in early Greek medicine.

[3] The related φρονεῖν, later reserved especially for the intellectual faculties, is still more encompassing in Homer, "covering undifferentiated psychic activity, involving emotion and conation also" (Onians, p. 14). The same applies to οἶδα, ibid. 15 f. In early Greek thought, the various psychic and mental functions are not yet differentiated.

[4] Examples in Onians, op. cit. 37f. Striking is Hesychius: πλευμονίαν· νόσον τὴν ἐρωτικήν.

ally and not as metaphors or mere images.⁵ Also the adjective πεπνυμένος, which means 'wise, clever', should be considered to be the participle of the passive perfect of πνέω.⁶ Words and thoughts (which are not distinguished), courage and energy, are 'located in' the φρένες and the θυμός and come out of them as the situation demands. Now, if feelings and thoughts come out of the lungs, it also becomes more understandable how and why one has developed the notion of inspiration (in-breathing). The deity breathes or blows emotions, power, but also plans and thoughts into the lungs of people. See for example *Odyssey* 19:138–9 where Penelope tells about her wile: φᾶρος μέν μοι πρῶτον ἐνέπνευσε φρεσὶ δαίμων / στησαμένη μέγαν ἱστὸν ἐνὶ μεγάροισιν ὑφαίνειν (cf. *Iliad* 1:297).⁷ When in later authors these archaic forms of thought are less conscious or perhaps even no longer play any role, many expressions from this conceptual world continue to be used, but now in a metaphorical sense. It is in this framework that one has to see a whole series of expressions in Greek literature in which emotions, affections and other psychic functions are connected with verbs for breathing, snorting and blowing.⁸ How often this occurs is demonstrated by the following selection, in which I go beyond instances with πνέω and its composita in order to illustrate the phenomenon more widely.

Homer calls the Greek heroes μένεα πνείοντες Ἀχαιοί (*Iliad* 3:8; 11:508; 24:364) and similarly μένεα πνείοντες Ἄβαντες (2:536). Here belongs also *Iliad* 21:395 where it is said of the fighting Athena that she has θάρσος ἄητον, snorting courage.

Ps.-Hesiod, *Aspis* 23–5, says about men who are going to battle: τῷ δ' ἅμα ἱέμενοι πολέμοιό τε φυλόπιδός τε Βοιωτοὶ πλήξιπποι, ὑπὲρ σακέων πνείοντες ... ἕσποντο.

Sappho, fragm. 47 Lobel-Page (42 Bergk, 50 Diehl): Ἔρος δ ἐτίναξέ μοι φρένας, ὡς ἄνεμος κὰτ ὄρος δρύσιν ἐμπέτων.

Aeschylus, *Agamemnon* 187, describing Agamemnon who tries to reconcile himself with his bad fortune, ἐμπαίοις τύχαισι συμπνέων. *Ibid.* 219, on Agamemnon who sacrifices his daughter, φρενὸς πνέων δυσσεβῆ τροπαίαν (he blows from his lungs a godless wind that had veered round). *Ibid.* 374–5, on too bellicose

---

⁵ On the question of whether or not there is metaphorical language in Homer see the series of articles by W. J. Verdenius on archaic forms of thinking in *Lampas* 2 ff (1969 ff).

⁶ Onians, *op. cit.* 56ff. Contra Onians see H. Kleinknecht, *TWNT* VI 335 n.1 (not convincing).

⁷ Onians, *op. cit.* 50ff., 56. Material is also to be found in Kleinknecht, *TWNT* VI 341 ff., who, however, does not mention Onians even once in his long article on *pneuma*.

⁸ Onians writes (52): "This association of the emotion with the breathing may seem strange to us since we are in the habit of abstracting the emotion itself from its bodily expressions." How 'strange' e. g. Jackson – Lake found this becomes apparent from their comments on Acts 9:1 (*The Beginnings of Christianity* IV, London 1933, 99): "The phrase ἐμπνέων ἀπειλῆς καὶ φόνου is regular in that ἐμπνέω takes with it a genitive cause but unusual as having as its objective what must be understood quite figuratively, though such metaphors occur, esp. in poetry, with the simple πνέω".

troops, Ἄρη πνεόντων μεῖζον ἢ δικαίως. *Ibid.* 1206, Cassandra on Apollo's feelings towards her, ἐμοὶ πνέων χάριν. *Ibid.* 1235–6, Cassandra on Clytemnestra, ἄσπονδόν τ' Ἄρη φίλοις πνέουσαν.[9] *Choephoroi* 391–2, the choir, hoping that Clytemnestra and Aegisthus will be punished, says: πάροιθεν δὲ πρῴρας δριμὺς ἄηται κραδίας θυμός, ἔγκοτον στύγος (before the bow of my heart a fierce wind blows, bitter hatred). *Ibid.* 952, on the goddes Dike, ὀλέθριον πνέουσ' ἐν ἐχθροῖς κότον. *Eumenides* 840, after the choir has lost the lawsuit, it is very angry at Athena: πνέω τοι μένος ἅπαντά τε κότον. *Supplices* 26 f., the Danaides ask the land where they arrive as banished persons to accept them αἰδοίῳ πνεύματι, with respectful breathing. *Septem* 52 f., of warriors before battle, σιδηρόφρων γὰρ θυμὸς ἀνδρείᾳ φλέγων ἔπνει, λεόντων ὣς Ἄρη δεδορκότων.

Sophocles, *Electra* 610, where the choir says about Electra raging against her mother: ὁρῶ μένος πνέουσαν. *Antigone* 929 f., the choir on Antigone who is so steadfast in her opposition to Creon: ἔτι τῶν αὐτῶν ἀνέμων αὐταὶ ψυχῆς ῥιπαὶ τήνδε γ' ἔχουσαν.

Euripides, *Andromache* 189–90, Andromache on the arrogant men who have seized her: οἱ γὰρ πνέοντες μεγάλα τοὺς κρείσσους λόγους πικρῶς φέρουσι τῶν ἐλασσόνων ὕπο. *Ibid.* 326 f., Andromache reproaches Menelaos that he too easily believes the evil talk of his daughter: ὅστις θυγατρὸς ἀντίπαιδος ἐκ λόγων τοσόνδ' ἔπνευσας. *Iphigeneia Taur.* 288, in one of his attacks of madness, Orestes sees one of the Furies and calls her πῦρ πνέουσα καὶ φόνον.[10] *Phoenissai* 454, Iocaste wants to calm down her belligerent son: σχάσον δὲ δεινὸν ὄμμα καὶ θυμοῦ πνοάς.[11] *Ibid.* 876, on Oedipus who curses his son: ἐκ δ' ἔπνευσ' αὐτοῖς ἀρὰς δεινάς. *Bacchae* 620, on Pentheus, who rages at Dionysus: θυμὸν ἐκπνέων, ἱδρῶτα σώματος στάζων ἄπο. *Ibid.* 640, Dionysus says about Pentheus: ῥᾳδίως γὰρ αὐτὸν οἴσω, κἂν πνέων ἔλθῃ μέγα. *Rhesus* 785, on frightened horses: αἱ δ' ἔρρεγκον ἐξ ἀντηρίδων θυμὸν πνέουσαι κἀνεχαίτιζον φόβῳ.

There is no doubt that Aristophanes wants to make a parody of the language of the tragedians, when he writes in *Ranae* 1016 πνέοντας δόρυ καὶ λόγχας, and *Aves* 1121 οὑτοσὶ τρέχει τις Ἀλφειὸν πνέων (i. e., snorting like a runner at the Olympian games [Olympia is situated at the river Alpheios]).

Pindar, *Pythian Ode* 10:44, on Perseus who went to the Hyperboraeans θρασείᾳ δὲ πνέων καρδίᾳ μόλεν Δανάας ποτὲ παῖς. *Ibid.* 11:29–30: a woman of standing cannot conceal her lapses, everyone speaks about them immediately: ἴσχει τε γὰρ ὄλβος οὐ μείονα φθόνον, ὁ δὲ χαμηλὰ πνέων ἄφαντον βρέμει (Bowra translates: 'For bliss makes envy as big as itself; and he who breathes the dust

---

[9] In *Agam.* 1309, Cassandra says about the palace where the murder has taken place, φόνον δόμοι πνέουσιν αἱματοσταγῆ, but that probably means: the palace smells of blood.

[10] It is not certain if passages like *Hercules Furens* 862 (κεραυνοῦ τ' οἶστρος ὠδῖνας πνέων) and *Iphigeneia Aulensis* 69 (ὅτου πνοαὶ φέροιεν Ἀφροδίτης φίλαι) belong in this category.

[11] σχάσον θυμοῦ πνοάς could be compared to the Dutch expression 'stoom afblazen' (or the German 'Dampf ablassen'). But these expressions have a different background.

whispers, but is not known'). *Nemean Ode* 3:41–2, on a person of low standing: ψεφηνὸς ἀνὴρ ἄλλοτ᾽ ἀλλὰ πνέων.

Antiphon, Fragm. B 49 (Diels-Kranz), on relatives: ἴσα φρονοῦντας ἴσα πνέοντας (Diels: gleich gesinnte, gleich gestimmte Menschen).

Xenophon, *Hellenica* 7,5,12: the enemies are οἱ πῦρ πνέοντες.

Herondas, *Mimiambe* 8:58, in the middle of a lacuna, but it is certainly about a quarrel, …] τὰ δεινὰ πνεῦσαι λὰξ πατε […

Theocritus 18:54–5 says to a loving couple: εὕδετ᾽ ἐς ἀλλάλων στέρνον φιλότατα πνέοντες καὶ πόθον. Ibid. 22:82, about two fighters: φόνον ἀλλήλοισι πνέοντες.

Anthologia Palatina 2:233: a ringfighter ἔπνεεν ἠνορέης. 2:451: Vergil is πνείων εὐεπίης. 5:259: the eyes of a girl in love are πόθου πνείοντα. 7:25 Anacreon's songs are χαρίτων πνείοντα μέλη, πνείοντα δ᾽ ἐρώτων. 9:159: when a wicked person throws a stone upon the skull of a deceased man, but the stone jumps back and hits the thrower; this stone is called πνέοντα δίκης.

Dionysius of Halicarnassus, *Antiquitates Romanae* 7, 51, 3: when the revolting people see that they have no power against the Roman senate, τῆς αὐθαδείας ἧς πολὺς ἔπνει τότε, ὑφεῖται νυνί (Cary: they now abate their arrogance which then blew so strong).

Chion of Heraclea, *Epistula* 3:3: Outrageous soldiers want to destroy the city, but a philosopher calms them down so that they become μηδὲν ἔτι ἐκείνου τοῦ ἀδίκου καὶ ἁρπακτοῦ Ἄρεος πνέοντας.

Philo of Alexandria connects πνέω with the adjectives μέγας and λαμπρός, both in bonam and in malam partem. See, for example,*Vita Mosis* 1:55, Moses rejects wealth since it has such an influence upon people, τῷ παρ᾽ ἀνθρώποις μέγα πνέοντι πλούτῳ. *Ibid.* 2:240 on haughty people: οἱ μέγα πνέοντες. *De mutatione nominum* 215 πνεύσαντες μέγα, said of successful people. *De somniis* 1:107,on *paideia*, which is severe against its adversaries: μεγάλα πνεύσασα. *De Josepho* 21: Ruben says to his brothers who have sold Joseph: τραχύτατοι γὰρ (ἐστε) εἰς ὀργὴν καὶ ἀπαραίτητοι καὶ πνεῖ λαμπρὸς ἔτι ὁ ἐν ἑκάστῳ θυμός. *De congressu* 108, in its original state the soul λαμπρὸν ἔπνει. *Quod deus sit immutabilis* 174: Egypt's original power and glory is gone, ἔπνευσέ ποτε λαμπρὸν καὶ ἐπὶ μήκιστον Αἴγυπτος, ἀλλ᾽ ὡς νέφος αὐτῆς ἡ μεγάλη παρῆλθεν εὐπραγία.[12]

Pseudo-Callisthenes, *Historia Alexandri Magni* A 46 (ed. W. Kroll, 1926, p. 59), ὁ δὲ Μακεδὼν ὄμμα πρὸς αὐτὸν μηκύνας καὶ τοὺς ὀδόντας τοῖς ὀδοῦσι συντρίζων ὀργὴν ἀναπνέων τοῖον εἶπε τὸν μῦθον.

Heliodorus, *Aethiopica* 1,2,1, on a girl who behaves courageously in very difficult circumstances: τοῖς μὲν παροῦσι περιαλγοῦσα, φρονήματος δὲ εὐγενοῦς ἔτι πνέουσα.

---

[12] Josephus does not yield anything of importance for our purpose.

Aristaenetus, *Epistula* 1:5, on a husband who is angry at his wife because he suspects her of adultery· κεκραγὼς ἅμα καὶ πνέων θυμοῦ.[13]

Nonnus, *Dionysiaca* 48, 650: after the wedding night a man is ἔτι πνέων ὑμεναίων.

In order to demonstrate that this phenomenon is not limited to Greek literature, I mention briefly a few instances from Latin authors.

Cicero, *In Catilinam* 2:1 scelus inhelantem (sc. Catilinam). *Ad Herennium* 4,55,68 anhelans ex infimo pectore crudelitatem.

Lucretius, *De rerum natura* 5:392 spirantes bellum.

Propertius 1,3,7 mollem spirare quietem.

Horatius, *Carmen* 4,13,19 quae spirabat amores.

Vergil, *Aeneid* 7:510 spirans immane.[14]

As is well known, in the Old Testament, too, several words which are used to indicate the psyche and psychical functions, originally meant breath(ing) or snorting.

Nhr: Song of Songs 1:6 *bene 'immi niharu bi* = the sons of my mother were angry (orig. snorted) at me.

Pwh: Ezekiel 21:36 (31) *be'esh 'evrati 'aphiah 'alayikh* = I blow against you with the fire of my wrath. Psalm 27:12 *yepheah hamas* = he breathes out (or: snorts) violence, a striking instance since here the verb, like the Greek πνέω, has an object (cf. Proverbs 12:17 *yaphiah 'emunah*).

Nephesh is originally the throat, then also breath; it develops, like θυμός, meanings which indicate psychical functions: longing, feeling, emotions (as does Aramaic *naphsha*).[15]

Ruah is the wind, later also the spirit;[16] thus also *'aph*, originally vehement breathing or snorting (hence the meaning 'nose'), later also anger, wrath. See the accumulation of these terms in Psalm 18:16 (= 2 Sam. 22:16): *minishmat ruah appekha* in Psalm 18:16 is rendered in the LXX by ἀπὸ ἐμπνεύσεως πνεύματος ὀργῆς σου. The same expression in 2 Sam. 22:16 is rendered by ἀπὸ πνοῆς πνεύματος θυμοῦ αὐτοῦ.

---

[13] How much the original concept behind this usage has disappeared in the course of time is well demonstrated by a passage in Themistius, *Oratio* 1:7a (on the *philanthropia* of the prince): καὶ τοίνυν εἰ βασιλέως ψυχὴ μὴ κυμαίνει μηδὲ θυμοῦ καὶ ὀργῆς πνεύματα ἄγρια κυκᾷ τε αὐτὴν καὶ ταράττει ῥᾳδίως ἐξ ὀλιγῆς ἀρχῆς ῥιπιζόμενα, τότ᾽ ἔξεστιν οὐ μόνον ἐμπόροις καὶ ναύταις ἀλλὰ καὶ πᾶσιν ἀνθρώποις τὸν βίον διαπλεῖν ἀσφαλῶς.

[14] T. E. Page ad locum: *spirans* is an imitation of πνέων which is constantly used with acc. or neut. adj. of excited feeling.

[15] See L. Koehler – W. Baumgartner, *Lexicon in Veteris Testamenti Libros*, Leiden 1953, 627–8

[16] See F. Baumgärtel in *TWNT* VI 357 ff.

Although indeed "the emotion of anger was in Semitic physiology connected with breath,"[17] it should not be too easily assumed that Luke has derived his expression in Acts 9:1 from the Old Testament, i. e. the LXX, for the lack of close verbal parallels makes that very improbable.[18] Neither are there many parallels from other Jewish Greek literature, although we do find one striking instance in *Testamentum Salomonis* D 4:1 ἐμάχοντο ἀλλήλοις θυμοῦ πνέοντες ἀλλήλους διασπαράξαι βουλόμενοι. But, as has now been shown, there is overwhelmingly rich comparative material in pagan Greek literature.

We also need not look for parallels in 'non-literary sources'. Moulton and Milligan[19] mention only one instance which is not a real parallel: G. Kaibel, *Epigrammata Graeca*, Berlin 1878, no. 562, 9–10 (2nd/3rd cent. CE), ἐς δ' ὅσον ἐνπνείει βίοτόν τ' ἐπὶ ἦμαρ ἐρύκει / δύσμορος ἀντλήσει πένθος ἀεξίβιον.[20] Moreover, the whole series of parallels from Greek literature quoted above does not at all give the impression that one has to do here with an expression from colloquial speech, but rather with one from the higher literary language. Therefore we have to conclude that in Acts 9:1 Luke has taken over an expression from Greek literary tradition.

This again confirms the suspicion of several scholars that Luke must have had a certain acquaintance with Greek literature. If he were a Greek physician (as has often been concluded from Col. 4:11 and Philemon 24, wrongly so), that would not be surprising. But it is impossible to be more precise. So the debate over whether or not Luke may have known Euripides, esp. his *Bacchae*, should not be rekindled here (those interested can refer to the contributions by Nestle, Vögeli, and Hackett, none of which, curiously enough, draws Acts 9:1 into this discussion).[21] We cannot go further than stating that Luke here uses an expression that can be said with certainty to stem from Greek literary tradition.

As we have seen, when the verb πνεῖν is followed by a noun indicating an emotion (e. g. θυμός, κότος), this noun is always put in the accusative in texts dating before the hellenistic period, but in and after that period often in the genitive

---

[17] K. Lake and H.J. Cadbury, *The Beginnings of Christianity*, vol. 4, London 1933, 99.

[18] E. Preuschen no doubt is wrong in stating that Luke's source for this expression was LXX Ps. 17 (18):16 (quoted above in the text); see his *Die Apostelgeschichte* (HNT), Tübingen 1912, 54–5. The only passage in the LXX which is comparable to Acts 9:1, as far as I know, is 2 Maccabees 9:7 where Antiochus Epiphanes is said to have been πῦρ ἐμπνέων τοῖς θυμοῖς ἐπὶ τοὺς Ἰουδαίους.

[19] *The Vocabulary of the Greek Testament Illustrated from the Papyri and Other Non-Literary Sources,* London 1930, 207.

[20] They could have better referred to no. 811,7–8 where the expression χάριν ... πνέοις occurs.

[21] W. Nestle in *Philologus* 59 (1900) 46–57; A. Vögeli in *Theologische Zeitschrift* 9 (1953) 415–438; J. Hackett in *Irish Theological Quarterly* 23 (1956) 218–227 and 350–366.

case. Acts 9:1 belongs to this second group.[22] On the function of this genitive several opinions are possible.

1. Blass-Debrunner § 174 take the expression in Acts 9:1 to be constructed in analogy to ὄζειν, (ἐμ)πνεῖν τινος, 'to smell of something'. Many scholars share this opinion, e. g. A. T. Robertson in his *Grammar of the Greek New Testament in the Light of Historical Research*, New York 1914, 507, and the lexicon of Liddell-Scott-Jones, s.v. ἐμπνέω I 3.[23] How then should this genitive be considered from a grammatical point of view? Kühner-Gerth's *Griechische Grammatik* (I 356) calls the genitive after verbs meaning 'to smell of' partitive (cf. also W. W. Goodwin's *Greek Grammar* § 1102). But perhaps one should prefer H. H. Wendt's suggestion (in his commentary on Acts ad loc. p. 162) that in this case the genitive indicates that which the action indicated by the verb takes as its point of departure. Then the genitive has an ablative function.[24]

2. C. F. D. Moule, *Idiom Book of New Testament Greek*, Cambridge 1953, 36–7, takes the genitive in Acts 9:1 to be a partitive genitive which is used with "verbs connected with a portion or share", as is also the case with e. g. ἅπτομαι, μνημονεύω, ἀντέχομαι, ἐπιτυγχάνω. Thus also the *Greek-English Lexicon of the New Testament* by Grimm-Thayer (Edinburgh 1901), s.v., which translates 'inhale' and explains: "Threatening and slaughter were so to speak the elements from which he drew his breath" (thus also J. R. Lumby, *The Acts of the Apostles*, Cambridge 1904, 189). This explanation would imply that Saul did not breath all of the threatening and murder that was in him but only a part of it (cf. e. g. also Apoc. 2:17 τῷ νικῶντι δώσω αὐτῷ τοῦ μάννα τοῦ κεκρυμμένου).

3. More attractive, it would seem to me, is the opinion that in Acts 9:1 there is to be found a partitive genitive, but one that is to be understood in analogy to the genitive after verbs meaning 'to fill, to be full', etc. G. B. Winer, *Grammatik des neutestamentlichen Sprachidioms* (Leipzig 1867) § 30,9c, looks for a solution in this direction. Also E. Schweizer, in *TWNT* VI 450, takes ἐμπνέω with genitive to have the meaning of 'to be filled with'.

The interesting thing about this interpretation is that we have from antiquity itself testimonies to the effect that one has understood the genitive in Acts 9:1

---

[22] Some *Katharevousa* translations of the NT into 'modern' Greek turn it again into a classical construction: πνέων ἔτι ἀπειλὴν καὶ φόνον. The prefix εμ- in ἐμπνέειν should be connected with εἰς τοὺς μαθητάς, meaning: blowing loose on them.

[23] LSJ s.v. II 3 lists several of the passages with genitive mentioned by us under the meaning 'to smell of.'

[24] Wendt's reference to LXX Joshua 10:40 πᾶν ἐμπνέον ζωῆς is also found in several later commentaries, but it is very questionable whether this is really a parallel. Its meaning is clear: every living being (MT: *kol ha-neshamah*), but the LXX always translates that by πᾶν ἐμπνέον. R. Helbing, *Die Kasussyntax der Verba bei den Septuaginta*, Göttingen 1928, 91–2, doubts therefore whether it belongs to the text (with reference to Field's notes on the Hexapla). Preuschen *ad locum* (54–5) remarks that Joshua 10:40 is not comparable since it uses ἐμπνέον as a substantive.

in this sense. A scholion to Homer, *Iliad* 2:536 (quoted above), remarks: θυμοῦ καὶ δυνάμεως πνέοντες, τουτέστι γέμοντες.[25] Furthermore, in Hesychius we find the terse note: ἐμπνεῖ· πεπληρωμένος (ed. K. Latte II 81). And in order to prove that one has understood also Acts 9:1 in this sense, one can refer to the Peshitta and the Sahidic and Boharic versions of the New Testament; all three versions translate our verse by: "he was full of threatening and murder." Since all three versions originated independently from one another, one cannot deny them a certain interpretative value, the more so when they are viewed in combination with the Homer scholion and the Hesychius note. This explanation, that (ἐμ)πνεῖν with genitive was conceived as parallel to verbs for 'being full of' with genitive, can also be applied to other passages (quoted above), where πνεῖν is used with the genitive. So this explanation seems to have much in its favour.

4. Another theoretical possibility is to explain the genitive as being one of aiming or striving as is usual after verbs like μαιμᾶν, ὀρέγεσθαι, (ἐφ)ίεσθαι, ὁρμᾶσθαί, etc. But then (ἐμ)πνεῖν should have an element of striving or pursuit in it, which it does not. Moreover, such an explanation would fit only a few of our instances.

5. More is to be said for the explanation that we have here a genitive which designates "den Ausgangspunkt einer Handlung bei Verben der Gemütsbewegung, des Zornes".[26] This 'genitive-ablative' occurs after verbs like χολοῦσθαι, χώεσθαι, μηνίειν, θυμοῦσθαι, κοτεῖν, etc. Accordingly, it should be possible to take (ἐμ)πνεῖν to mean 'raging, being wrathful'. The above-mentioned instances from Ps-Hesiod, *Aspis* 23–4, Pindar, *Pyth.* 10:44, and Euripides, *Andromache* 326–7, prove that that is possible indeed. Moreover, we have a valuable note in Photius: πνεύσας· σφοδρῶς ὀργισθείς (ed. R. Porson II 435). However, it should be held against this explanation that in all cases of this ablative-genitive it designates the exterior motive for the emotion described, e.g., Sophocles, *Antigone* 1177 πατρὶ μηνίσας φόνου = being wrathful against her father because of the murder committed by him. In his *Syntaxe grecque*, Humbert therefore states explicitly that it is only the "cause extérieure" that can be designated by this genitive.[27] This objection is also valid against Düring's attempt to explain the genitive in Ἄρεος πνέοντας in Chio 3:3 (see above) as causative.[28]

---

[25] See H. Ebeling, *Lexicon Homericum*, Leipzig 1885, II 192.

[26] Kühner-Gerth, *Grammatik* I 388b. Schwyzer-Debrunner, *Grammatik* II 133. Blass-Debrunner § 176 state that this ablative-genitive is no longer used in Koine Greek, but that is not an objection against this explanation.

[27] J. Humbert, *Syntaxe grecque*, Paris 1960, 280. Cf. also the instances mentioned in the grammars in the previous note.

[28] I. Düring, *Chion of Heraclea. A Novel in Letters*, Göteborg 1951, 85: "ἁρπακτοῦ Ἄρεος πνέοντας, a popular flourish, inspired by well-known expressions like μένεα πνείοντες, Ἄρη πνεόντων (*Agam.* 375, parodied *Equit.* 437) but here with genitive (ablative), which sometimes implies the sense 'smelling of', as in *Anth. Pal.* XI, 240 πνεῖν τράγου, often however is used (as partitive) in the same sense as the causative, *Anth. Pal.* IX, 159 πνέοντα δίκης, II, 415 πνείων εὐεπίης Βεργίλλιος.

As one can see, most of the attempts at explanation either opt for the partitive (in various forms, see nos. 1–3) or for the ablative solution. Perhaps it is impossible to reject completely any of these proposals (except the fourth). But it would seem to me that most is to be said for the third alternative sketched above, namely to understand ἐμπνεῖν with genitive as analogous to verbs denoting 'to be full' with (partitive) genitive.[29]

---

[29] I express my gratitude to Professors W. J. Verdenius and W. F. Bakker for several valuable hints.

"Only then will all Israel be saved"

A Short Note on the Meaning of καὶ οὕτως in Romans 11:26

The problem of the meaning and translation of καὶ οὕτως in Rom 11:26 has been a matter of debate ever since the beginning of modern scholarship. The well-known question is whether this expression should be taken in a modal sense ('and so [or 'thus'] all Israel will be saved'), which is the most current translation, or in a temporal sense ('and then [or 'only then' or 'thereafter'] all Israel will be saved'), which is a much less common interpretation but one that is nevertheless defended by a handful of commentators and translators. In this short contribution to the debate I hope to prove that the temporal sense is more widespread than is commonly assumed and therefore a much more serious alternative to the modal meaning than most translations and commentaries would have us believe.[1]

It is quite understandable that most translators and commentators take οὕτως in the modal sense since it is the most current and usual meaning of the word; the temporal sense is less usual, or at least so much less frequent that several dictionaries do not even mention it. For instance, Bauer's *Griechisch-deutsches Wörterbuch zum Neuen Testament* does not mention this semantic aspect of the word and neither do Louw and Nida in their *Greek-English Lexicon of the New Testament According to Semantic Domains*. Liddell & Scott do register this meaning in their *Greek-English Lexicon*, but in such a veiled way that it is very hard to notice, since *s.v.* οὕτως I 7 they only say that οὕτως is frequently used in an apodosis after a protasis, without indicating that in several of the instances listed by them the meaning of the word is '(only) then' (moreover they deal only with cases from classical Greek). So it makes sense to present a selected number of instances which clearly indicate that οὕτως can indeed have this meaning.

That this is not superfluous is clear if one takes a look into modern commentaries. There is, for instance, the remark in an otherwise excellent commentary on Romans, the recent one by Joseph Fitzmyer, who simply states that "a tempo-

---

[1] *The Jerusalem Bible* is one of the very few translations that render: "And then after this the rest of Israel will be saved as well." The *Revised English Bible* has: "Once that has happened the whole of Israel will be saved." Cf. also *Das Neue Testament*, übersetzt und kommentiert von U. Wilckens, Hamburg 1970, 542: "Dann wird auch ganz Israel gerettet werden."

ral meaning of *houtôs* is not otherwise found in Greek."[2] Dunn is not sure about the matter and suggests that "some temporal weight cannot be excluded from καὶ οὕτως (…), but the basic sense of οὕτως is 'thus, in this manner,'"[3] without giving arguments for his non-exclusion of 'temporal weight.' Others simply deny the possibility that οὕτως could have a temporal sense (e. g., U. Luz and C.E.B. Cranfield)[4] or posit that it does have that sense here, sometimes without any references (e. g. Th. Zahn, O. Michel, C.K. Barrett), sometimes with reference to passages such as Acts 17:33 and 20:11 (e. g. E. Käsemann).

It should be pointed out that there are some publications by classical philologists on the temporal meaning of (καὶ) οὕτω(ς) which have gone unnoticed by NT scholars. As early as 1934 Kurt Latte briefly discussed this usage and demonstrated that it came to the fore more strongly in post-classical Greek,[5] and in 1961 E. Skard made some additions to Latte's dossier.[6] More recently the Dutch classical philologist D. Holwerda pointed out the importance of the observations by these two scholars for the interpretation of Romans 11:26.[7] I will discuss some of their findings and also add some important new passages to the ones they found. First some instances from pagan Greek authors will be briefly presented, thereafter some from Jewish and Christian writings.

Thucydides, *Hist.* 3.96.2 tells us that in the war against the Aetolians, the commander of the Athenian army first wanted to subdue the surrounding areas and *only then* to attack the Ophionians themselves (τὰ ἄλλα καταστρεψάμενος οὕτως ἐπὶ Ὀφιονέας … στρατεῦσαι); cf. also *Hist.* 1.37.1. In his *Charact.* 18, Theophrastus describes 'the distrustful man.' Before going to sleep, this man asks his wife whether the house-door has been bolted and the cupboard sealed etc. and, even when she has said yes, gets out of his bed in order to check everything again, καὶ οὕτω μόλις ὕπνου τυγχάνειν, 'and *only then* he goes to sleep, though with difficulty.' Here it may perhaps be possible to translate 'even so he will hardly go to sleep,' but the next instance does not leave us this escape. Plato writes in *Prot.* 314c that Socrates and Hippocrates, having arrived at Protagoras' house, decide first to finish their discussion and *only then* to go into the house (ἀλλὰ διαπερανάμενοι οὕτως ἐσίομεν). Cf. his *Gorg.* 457d, where

---

[2] *Romans* (AB 33), New York 1993, 622.

[3] *Romans* (WBC 38B), Dallas 1988, 681.

[4] Cf. also D. Sänger, *Die Verkündigung des Gekreuzigten und Israel. Studien zum Verhältnis von Kirche und Israel bei Paulus und im frühen Christentum*, Tübingen 1994, 166: "Zunächst ist negativ festzustellen, daß καὶ οὕτως keine primär temporale Bedeutung ('und dann' = καὶ τότε) in sich trägt."

[5] Review of P. Maas, *Epidaurische Hymnen* (1933) in *Göttingische Gelehrte Anzeigen* 196 (1934) 405–413, at 411.

[6] 'Zum temporalen Gebrauch von οὕτως,' *Symbolae Osloenses* 37 (1961) 151–152. Skard pays special attention to the frequent occurrence of the temporal use of οὕτως in the *Homilies* of Asterius.

[7] D. Holwerda, 'Heel Israel behouden,' in his *De Schrift opent een vergezicht*, Kampen 1998, 160–193.

Socrates says that people who start a debate often have problems in defining their subject; they first teach and instruct each other about what they know and *then* (οὕτως) bring the meeting to a close (and cf. also *Resp.* II 368d ἐκεῖνα πρῶτον ἀναγνόντες οὕτως ἐπισκοπεῖν τὰ ἐλάττω). Xenophon, *Anab.* 7.1.4, says that at a certain moment he wanted to take leave of his army but that Anaxibius urged him first to cross the Bosporus with the army and *only then* to take leave (ἔπειτα οὕτως ἀπαλλάτεσθαι)." In his *Cyrop.* 2.1.1, Xenophon writes about the Persian army: "When an eagle appeared on their right and flew on ahead of them, they prayed to the gods and heroes who watch over the land of Persia to conduct them onwards with grace and favour, and then (οὕτω) proceeded to cross the frontier." In his *Poet.* 1455b1 Aristotle states that a poet should first simplify his story and reduce it to a universal form "and only then develop the sequence of episodes" (εἶθ᾽ οὕτως ἐπεισοδιοῦν καὶ παρατείνειν). One might argue that here and in some other instances the idea of 'only then/thereafter' is expressed by εἶτα or ἔπειτα, but that is not correct: εἶτα/ἔπειτα does express that what follows is the next step, but it is only οὕτως that expresses the necessity of 'first things first' and 'only then' what follows.[8]

From the post-classical period many examples could be quoted, but two may suffice. In the *Tabula Cebetis* 19.1, the protagonist asks Heracles why (the personified) Paideia is standing outside the enclosure of the dwelling place of the happy, whereupon he answers that this happens "so that she can heal the ones arriving and give them purifying power to drink. For only then, after they have been purified, does she lead them to the virtues" (εἶθ᾽ ὅταν καθαρθῶσιν, οὕτως εἰσάγει τούτους πρὸς τὰς ἀρετάς).[9] Finally an instance from Epictetus 2.15.8: "Do you not wish to make your beginning and your foundation firm, that is, to consider whether your decision is sound or unsound, and only then (καὶ οὕτως) proceed to rear thereon the structure of your determination and your firm resolve?" More instances from Epictetus could be quoted.[10] In all these cases the emphasis is on the necessity of a certain order: first other things have to be finished and only then can the main thing be done.[11]

Now I will give some examples to demonstrate that this usage was not unknown among authors of Judaeo-Greek literature. In the *Test. of Abraham* (rec. A) 7.11 we find the archangel Michael saying to Abraham that "I have been sent to you in order to tell you not to forget death; but thereafter (εἶθ᾽ οὕτως) I will

---

[8] Another fine instance is Polybius 5.9.9.

[9] The translation by J.T. Fitzgerald and L.M. White (*The Tabula of Cebes* [Chico 1983] 91) is not correct here.

[10] In his Teubner edition of 1916 H. Schenkl lists several instances of this usage from Epictetus in his Index *s.v.*, e. g., 3.23.1–2: "Good athletes first decide what kind of athletes they want to be, only then (εἶθ᾽ οὕτως) they act accordingly."

[11] More examples in R. Kühner & B. Gerth, *Ausführliche Grammatik der griechischen Sprache* II 2, Darmstadt 1966 (= Leipzig 1904), 83.

return to him as he commanded me."[12] We see it also in the following passage in the *Vitae prophetarum*: In the *Life of Jeremiah* 6 we read that during his stay in Egypt, Jeremiah chased away the asps from the dry land and the crocodiles from the Nile, and thereafter (καὶ οὕτως) he introduced the so-called 'snakefighters.' Here it is interesting and illuminating to see that most of the manuscripts have καὶ οὕτως, but one other has καὶ τότε,[13] which indicates that this medieval Byzantine scribe knew that οὕτως here has the temporal sense of τότε (then).

In the New Testament we find, apart from Rom 11:26, some other possible instances of this usage. It is highly improbable that, when the author of Acts has Stephen say that "God gave Abraham the covenant of circumcision, καὶ οὕτως Abraham begot Isaac" (7:8), it makes sense to translate here 'and thus': Luke does not want to inform his readers about the physical condition in which Abraham begot the son that would be the heir of the covenant, but about the fact that this happened *only after* he had received the sign of this covenant! Acts 20:11 is an even clearer case, for by far the most natural translation of ἀναβὰς δὲ καὶ κλάσας τὸν ἄρτον καὶ γευσάμενος ἐφ᾽ ἱκανόν τε ὁμιλήσας ἄχρι αὐγῆς, οὕτως ἐξῆλθεν is "[Paul] went upstairs, and after he had broken bread and eaten, he continued to converse with them until dawn (!); *only then* he left." The ἄχρι αὐγῆς hardly leaves another possibility. And it also makes sense to take Acts 27:17 to mean that *only after* the sailors, who were afraid of running on to the sandbanks, had lowered the gear (or: thrown out a sea-anchor), they let the ship drift (χαλάσαντες τὸ σκεῦος, οὕτως ἐφέροντο). 1 Thess 4:16–17 is another instance: after the descent of Jesus Christ from heaven "the dead in Christ will rise *first*; *thereafter* we who are alive, who are left, will be caught up in the clouds together with them to meet the Lord in the air; *and [only] then* we will be with the Lord forever" (οἱ νεκροὶ ἐν Χριστῷ ἀναστήσονται πρῶτον, ἔπειτα ἡμεῖς οἱ ζῶντες οἱ περιλειπόμενοι ἅμα σὺν αὐτοῖς ἁρπαγησόμεθα ἐν νεφέλαις εἰς ἀπάντησιν τοῦ κυρίου εἰς ἀέρα· καὶ οὕτως πάντοτε σὺν κυρίῳ ἐσόμεθα.). This translation makes at least as much sense as the traditional one 'and so,' if only because the text so unambiguously indicates that the apostle is speaking about a temporal order: first A, therafter B, and finally (but *only then*) C. And there are more NT examples.[14]

From early Christian literature outside the New Testament I adduce only the following example to round off the picture.[15] Irenaeus tells us in *Adv. haer.* 1.30.14 that the Gnostic sect of the Ophites say that after his resurrection Jesus taught his disciples (not for 40 days, as the NT says, but) for no less than 18 months, and *only then* was he taken up into heaven: *et sic receptus est in caelum.*

---

[12] It is significant in this respect that there are manuscripts that omit εἶτα here, but none that omit οὕτως. See F. Schmidt, *Le Testament grec d'Abraham*, Tübingen 1986, 118.

[13] See A.M. Schwemer, *Studien zu den frühjüdischen Prophetenlegenden. Beiheft: Synopse zu den Vitae Prophetarum*, Tübingen 1996, 12*.

[14] E.g., 1 Cor 14:25. See Latte, *GGA* 196 (1934) 411; Holwerda, *De Schrift* 162.

[15] For instances from Asterius I refer to the article by Skard (see note 6).

Irenaeus' original Greek is lost here, but there can be no doubt at all that the Latin translation (*et sic*) reflects an original καὶ οὕτως here.[16] It is possibly under the influence of this Greek usage that in Latin Christian writers one finds this temporal use of *sic* much more frequently than in pagan Latin authors.[17]

Quite apart from the grammatical and lexical possibilities that the word οὕτως had, it is also the context in Romans 11 that makes it very probable that it was the temporal meaning of οὕτως that the author had in mind here. His whole argument is based upon the idea that it is the precedence of the gentiles which rouses Israel to jealousy. Only after the gentiles have fully entered the covenant, will Israel re-enter it, because it first has to be provoked to do so.

It is, however, not the purpose of this article to exclude the possibility that Paul used καὶ οὕτως in the modal sense in Rom 11:26.[18] What I do want to exclude, however, is the use of the false argument that it is impossible to take οὕτως in the temporal sense because this is "not found otherwise in Greek" (Fitzmyer), since our findings confirm what Kurt Latte wrote 65 years ago: "Die Wendung in der hier vorliegenden Bedeutung 'und dann' [ist] alles andere als ungewöhnlich."[19] This semantic possibility has therefore to be taken into account much more seriously than has hitherto been the case.[20]

---

[16] So Bentley Layton's translation, "And so he was taken up into heaven" (*The Gnostic Scriptures* [Garden City 1987] 180) is wrong, whereas the translation by D.J. Unger, "Then he was assumed into heaven" (*St. Irenaeus of Lyons Against the Heresies* [ACW 55; New York 1992] 102) is correct.

[17] For instances see A. Blaise & H. Chirat, *Dictionnaire latin-français des auteurs chrétiens*, Turnhout 1954, 758, where *s.v.* 3 they quote *inter alios* Filastrius 127.1: *primum erat apud Patrem et sic natus est.*

[18] Moreover, the modal and the temporal sense are not necessarily mutually exclusive.

[19] *GGA* 196 (1934) 411.

[20] I owe thanks to Professor Stephan Radt (Groningen) for his valuable suggestions.

Macarius Magnes and
the Unnamed Anti-Christian Polemicist

A review article[1]

The study of the ancient philosophical anti-Christian polemic has witnessed an upsurge of interest in the last two decades. After the sketch of the *status quaestionis* by S. Benko and A. Meredith in 1980,[2] we have seen the publication of, e. g.[3], R. Wilken, *The Christians as the Romans Saw Them* (New Haven-London 1984); R.J. Hoffmann, *Celsus: On the True Doctrine* (New York-Oxford 1987); G.B. Bozzo & S. Rizzo, *Celso: Il discorso della verità contro i cristiani* (Milano 1989); G. Rinaldi, *Biblia gentium* (Roma 1989); E. Masaracchia, *Giuliano Imperatore: Contra Galilaeos* (Roma 1990); R.J. Hoffmann, *Porphyry's "Against the Christians"* (Amherst 1994);[4] G. Rinaldi, *La Bibbia dei pagani* (2 vols.; Bologna 1997–98); J.W. Hargis, *Against the Christians. The Rise of Early Anti-Christian Polemic* (New York etc. 1999); J.G. Cook, *The Interpretation of the New Testament in Greco-Roman Paganism* (Tübingen 2000);[5] and a new edition of Porphyry's *Contra Christianos* by P.F. Beatrice has been announced for the near future.[6] To this list we can now happily add Richard Goulet's new and important critical edition, with translation, introduction, and exegetical notes, of Macarius of Magnesia's rather neglected treatise *Monogenes* (formerly *Apokritikos*), a large two-volume work of some 830 pages in French (see note 1).

---

[1] The work reviewed here is: Macarios de Magnésie, *Le Monogénès*, édition critique et traduction française par Richard Goulet, 2 vols. (Textes et traditions 7), Paris: Vrins, 2003; 383+445 pp. ISBN 2-7116-1647-9 (€ 80). Volume 1 contains the Introduction, a bibliography, a 30-page synopsis of the arguments of the anonymous philosopher and those of Celsus, Porphyry and Julian, and an index of Greek words; volume 2 contains the text, translation, and exegetical notes.

[2] See their contributions in *ANRW* II, 23, 2, Berlin-New York 1980, 1055–1149.

[3] I mention here only a selection of the most important monographs.

[4] This book has a very misleading title since it deals only with the fragments related to the unnamed opponent in Macarius Magnes' work.

[5] [Now supplemented by his *The Interpretation of the Old Testament in Greco-Roman Paganism*, Tübingen 2004.]

[6] It should be added, though, that Beatrice does not believe that a separate treatise *Against the Christians* ever existed; he rather opines that the anti-Christian arguments were part of a larger work by Porphyry to which also his *De philosophia ex oraculis haurienda* belonged. See his entry "Porphyrius" in *TRE* 27 (1997) 54–59.

The subject of this *magnum opus* is an early Christian treatise of considerable importance since it contains substantial quotations from a work in which
an anonymous Greek philosopher combats Christianity with a wide range of
arguments. It is well-known that Adolf von Harnack, as many before and after
him, regarded the unnamed opponent as none other than the Platonic philosopher
Porphyry, and more than half of the fragments in Harnack's edition of Porphyry's *Against the Christians* consist of passages from Macarius' *Monogenes*,[7] but
this did not go uncontested. The text of the treatise pretends to be a verbatim
report of a five-days public debate between Macarius and an anti-Christian philosopher whose name is not mentioned. Both the arguments of the philosopher,
who raises serious and intelligent objections to the New Testament and has sharp
criticism of both Jesus and Paul, as well as those of his Christian opponent are
often interesting and deserve closer attention than has been paid them so far.
Sadly enough, the only manuscript of the work, discovered in 1867 in Athens
and edited by Charles Blondel in 1876,[8] is now lost. Moreover, it is incomplete;
it begins somewhere in the middle of book 2 and ends before the closing chapters
of book 4; book 5 is missing as well. In addition to that, the manuscript is corrupt in many places and Goulet confesses that it has been extremely difficult and
occasionally impossible to reconstruct the original text. So many riddles remain,
but nonetheless Goulet has done us an enormous service by preparing this first
new edition after Blondel.

In an instructive 'Forschungsgeschichte' (14–40), Goulet first sketches the research on Macarius Magnes before the discovery of the manuscript, done mainly
on the basis of the few citations from the work by Nicephorus of Constantinople
(9th cent) and some others. He highlights the fact that several of these early
scholars regard 'Macarius' not as a name but an adjective (blessed) and 'Magnes'
not as a designation of his place of origin (from Magnesia) but as a proper name
(the blessed Magnes), a point he will come back to later. After the publication
of the *editio princeps* in 1876 one sees that the identification of the anonymous
adversary with either Hierocles (the target of Eusebius' *Contra Hieroclem*) or
Porphyry, or a combination of both, gains ground, although some who favour a
later date leave open the possibility that Julian the Apostate may be the unnamed
opponent. Others, such as Theodor Zahn, identify Macarius with the bishop of

---

[7] See his 'Porphyrius, "Gegen die Christen,"' in *Abhandlungen der Königlich-Preussischen
Akademie der Wissenschaften*, Jahrgang 1916, Philosophisch-historische Klasse, Berlin 1916,
3–115; and 'Neue Fragmente des Werks des Porphyrius gegen die Christen,' *Sitzungsberichte der
Preussischen Akademie der Wissenschaften 1921*, Berlin 1921, 266–284. It is amazing and also a
shame that A. Smith omitted the fragments of *Against the Christians* from his new Teubner edition of the fragments of Porphyry's works with the lame argument that they were readily available
in the recent (!) edition by Harnack; see his *Porphyrius, Fragmenta*, Stuttgart-Leipzig 1993.

[8] ΜΑΚΑΡΙΟΥ ΜΑΓΝΗΤΟΣ Ἀποκριτικὸς ἢ Μονογενής. *Macarii Magnetis quae supersunt
ex inedito codice edidit* C. Blondel, Paris 1876. Actually the book was seen through the press
by Paul Foucart after Blondel's untimely death (he died in 1873 at the age of 37).

Magnesia (in Asia Minor)[9] called Macarius who was present at the Synod of the Oak in 403; Zahn thinks this bishop wrote a refutation of 3rd and 4th century anti-Christian polemics in general around 400. T.W. Crafer, on the other hand, dates Macarius around 300 and argues that the debate took place before the Diocletian persecution; the combatants were Hierocles and Macarius.[10] Harnack sees in Macarius the bishop of Magnesia, who wrote this work in the last quarter of the 4th century, but whose target was no other than Porphyry. Since, however, Macarius knew Porphyry's work only in an anonymous and abridged form, he was not aware of the identity of his opponent (!). Others remain inclined to see either Julian or Hierocles as the anonymous opponent or to assume that the bishop indeed reacted to an anonymous anti-Christian treatise that made use of many arguments levelled by Celsus, Porphyry, Hierocles, and Julian. To date there is no consensus on any of these major issues. At the end of this survey (40) Goulet lists a dozen or so problems that still remain by and large unsolved.

The first he deals with is the title. Since the only manuscript is acephalous, we have to rely on the tables of contents of the book or references to it as we find them in some other early documents (about these see further below). This leaves us with Ἀποκριτικὸς πρὸς Ἕλληνας or Μονογενὴς πρὸς Ἕλληνας or Ἀποκριτικὸς ἢ Μονογενὴς πρὸς Ἕλληνας. Goulet rightly says that the latter double title is probably a conflation and that of the two single titles the easily understandable *Apokritikos* is more likely to have replaced the difficult *Monogenês* than the other way round. But what does *Monogenês pros Hellênas* mean as a book title? Based upon Macarius' own use of the word, it seems most feasible that *Mono-genês* (sc. *logos*) here has primarily the sense of "Discours d'un genre unique adressé aux Hellènes" but with the *double-entendre* of "Discours du Fils unique …" This seems rather odd, but I have no alternative to offer.

The second problem is the identity of the author. Goulet suggests that it is more natural to interpret *Makarios Magnês* as 'Macarius of Magnesia' than as 'the blessed Magnes,' and I fully agree. He also tends to believe Photius' report that Macarius, bishop of Magnesia, attended the Synod of the Oak in 403 and argues that nothing contradicts the identification of these two men. But he wisely adds that it is impossible to identify them "de façon incontestable" (51). Even so he thinks his position can be strengthened by geographical considerations. Many details in the text suggest a much greater acquaintance with Asia Minor than with any other geographical area. But that is, of course, not in any way a proof that our Macarius was the man of the Synod of 403.[11]

---

[9] The Greek *Magnês* can indeed mean 'living in Magnesia' (see LSJ *s.v.*).

[10] For references to publications by these and other authors I must refer the reader to Goulet's notes. Crafer published the only English translation (though an abridged one) of Macarius' work in 1919.

[11] I also do not understand how Macarius could have *borrowed* details from John Malalas (6th cent.!); see p. 52.

Another problem is the dating of the work. Here Goulet again concedes that certainty may be unattainable, but he carefully suggests, on the basis of his tentative identification of Macarius with the homonymous bishop of Magnesia who was active at the Synod of 403, that the work may have been composed in the final quarter of the 4th century rather than a century earlier. It is – *inter alia* – the christological views of the author that favour this later date. Moreover, twice in this treatise the author refers to events that have taken place more than 300 years after events in the New Testament period (4.5.1 and 4.5.2); and one has to keep in mind that these chronological remarks are made by the opponent (at least according to Macarius), *i.e.*, before Macarius wrote his refutation. Only an overly skeptical person could defend an early date around 300, then; a date after 350 is much more reasonable. Also the references to the remarkable expansion of the monastic movement in the East (2.7.10; 2.16.26–29) make sense only by the final decades of the 4th century, not much earlier (Theodoret sketches its zenit as occurring between 365 and 440).[12] This dating is further confirmed by Macarius' strikingly critical attitude towards the legitimacy of the imperial power, which – in the fourth century – is only to be explained against the background of Valens' violent rule (364–378), says Goulet, a point of view that will probably not go unchallenged.

Goulet rightly regards the public debate setting as a literary fiction but argues that there is good reason to assume that Macarius did not himself invent the objections to Christianity in order to easily refute them. It is not so much the disparity in style and diction between the unnamed opponent's objections and Macarius' responses that pleads in favour of his use of a pagan source (this disparity could still be explained as part of Macarius' technique), but it is rather what Goulet calls "le rapport dialectique entre objections et réponses," which he defines as follows: "Macarios passe systématiquement à côté des objections, il néglige la pointe philosophique d'arguments attestés par ailleurs dans la littérature antichrétienne, il laisse sans réponse certains éléments de l'objection, tandis qu'il se livre à des développements que n'appelaient pas les objections de l'adversaire" (71–72). This leaves no room for doubt: Macarius used a written source. This source, however, has ostensibly been heavily edited by him[13] so that one cannot simply use the 'quoted' objections of the pagan philosopher as 'fragments' (in the sense of *ipsissima verba*) of his original text. Even so it is clear that his work consisted primarily of sustained attacks on the person and teaching of both Jesus Christ and the apostle Paul (to a lesser degree Peter was also his target). Since the philosopher presents Christians as persons without any political power but at the same time as constructors of big churches, a tentative

---

[12] See P. Canivet, *Le monachisme syrien selon Théodoret de Cyr*, Paris 1977.

[13] For an elaborate stylistic analysis underpinning this conclusion by Goulet see pp. 76–89.

dating of his writing to the years about 300 seems defensible. Goulet does not deal with the intriguing question of why it took (almost) a century before this attack on Christianity was answered (but see below).

Before tackling the major issue of the identity of the pagan philosopher, Goulet discusses his personality and his attitude towards Christianity. Due to the heavy redactional hand of Macarius, his personality remains vague. What little can be said with certainty, however, is that the philosopher had a heart-felt disdain for Christ and his followers. Jesus is neither a sage nor a hero, let alone a god, he is a muddle-headed teacher; Paul is a great hypocrite; and Peter is an erratic personality. The New Testament testifies to the lamentably low level of its authors; much of what is said in it (e. g., about the Parousia) is irrational and absurd: "il s'en tient au choc subi par l'esprit cultivé devant le caractère parfois contradictoire, paradoxal et même brutal de certains passages du Nouveau Testament" (106).[14] The philosopher's historical and geographical knowledge is far from exceptional and does not suggest a level comparable to Porphyry's. His philosophical stance, as far as it is recoverable, is a kind of general Platonism that has no clearly Neoplatonic elements.

After all this, it comes more or less as a surprise that the long chapter on "Identification de la source païenne" (112–149) comes to the conclusion that the unnamed philosopher was, after all, no one other than Porphyry. All other possibilities are reviewed and fairly tested but all fail to pass the test. In spite of several points of contact between the unnamed philosopher and Celsus, the latter hardly focuses on the New Testament documents and – quite unlike the unnamed philosopher – he also regards Christianity as a threat to the empire and the Hellenic tradition. The unnamed philosopher refuted by Lactantius in his *Institutiones* cannot be our philosopher because of the political focus of the former and the lack of any agreements between what little we know of his arguments and those of Macarius' opponent. Hierocles, the author of the *Philalêthês* who is often seen as a good alternative to Porphyry in this respect,[15] is not our unnamed philosopher since there are too many striking differences between the tone and arguments of the two and "on ne relève pas des rapprochements suffisamment étroits pour que l'on puisse conclure à une identification des deux auteurs" (126). As to Julian the Emperor, in spite of "un grand nombre de rapprochements," which is to be expected in view of "l'existence d'un matériel polémique commun" (127), there are hardly any close parallels between the texts of the two authors. But then, there is Porphyry, and here we find "des parallèles beaucoup plus proches que ceux que nous avons rencontrés jusqu'ici" (127).

---

[14] The philosopher focuses almost exclusively on the New Testament; he has only 10 references to Old Testament passages.

[15] The most recent defense of this position is E. DePalma Digeser, 'Porphyry, Julian, or Hierokles? The Anonymous Hellene in Makarios Magnes' *Apokritikos*,' *JTS* 53 (2002) 466–502.

And indeed, with no other anti-Christian author does one find more and closer agreements than with this Platonist. What would seem to militate against the hypothesis that our unnamed philosopher is Porphyry is the fact that at a certain moment Macarius invites his opponent to have a look at a passage in Porphyry's *Philosophia ex oraculis haurienda* (3.42.6), without even hinting at the fact that this Porphyry is his opponent. But that is no serious objection because, in view of the literary fiction that the debate took place in the recent past between Macarius himself and his adversary, he simply could not tell that his opponent was Porphyry (who had already died almost a century ago).

There remain problems here, however. If Origen mentioned Celsus by name, if Eusebius mentioned Hierocles by name, if Methodius as well as Eusebius and Apollinaris mentioned Porphyry by name, and if Cyrillus mentioned Julian by name, *why*, then, would Macarius keep his opponent anonymous? Of course, one could say that only in this way could he present the debate as having taken place recently with himself as the defender of Christianity. But it is very hard to imagine that this literary fiction carried more weight with Macarius than the fact that he engaged in a battle with Christianity's most formidable opponent in antiquity, a man who wrote no less than 15 books *Contra Christianos*. And why would he engage in this battle after several others had already done so better than he ever could? And, finally, how is it to be explained that the unnamed philosopher focuses almost entirely on the New Testament, whereas we know that Porphyry also dealt critically and extensively with the Old Testament? These questions remain unanswered by Goulet's hypothesis. Although it is a subjective judgement, I for one find too much in the unnamed opponent's objections that looks non-Porphyrian. I therefore venture the hypothesis[16] that Macarius' opponent never existed but that Macarius created him in order to enable himself to write a book that refuted what he himself regarded as still the most important and threatening arguments against Christianity brought forward by its opponents in the past two centuries, from Celsus to Julian. Of course, Porphyry was one of them, indeed the most impressive one, and this explains the close parallels with Porphyry in about 50% of the fragments.[17] "Faut-il supposer plutôt que Macarios ou sa source ont compilé les objections de diverses polémistes? Aucun indice ne le suggère. On a au contraire, à la lecture des objections, l'impression d'une critique fort homogène" (135). Yes, but this homogeneity may be exactly the result of Macarius' purposeful selection and redaction. As Goulet himself says, "C'est lui qui a sélectionné, agencé et enchaîné les thèmes du discours de l'Adversaire, c'est lui qui les a mis en forme" (138). In all fairness, it should

---

[16] Not unlike the one suggested by Theodor Zahn (see above).

[17] It should be said here that Goulet's synoptic presentation of the agreements and disagreements between Porphyry and Macarius' unnamed philosopher (vol. I, 269–278) is immensely helpful.

be said to his credit that Goulet is the first to admit that there is no compelling proof of the identity of the unnamed philosopher with Porphyry. "Finalement, la question doit rester ouverte" (135; cf. 149). The main problem is that we actually know rather little about the early anti-Christian polemicists because for the most part their works were destroyed by the Christians. Goulet is well aware of this, since he says that "il faut reconnaître la possibilité que Macarios ait utilisé un traité grec aujourd'hui complètement disparu" (139).

The largest chapter of the first volume is devoted to a thorough study of Macarius as a theologian and apologist. In 80 pages (150–231) a fine and balanced sketch is presented of the accomplishments of this neglected author whose opponent has usually received much more attention than he himself. Here Goulet wants to do full justice to the man, and so he does. For reasons of space I can summarize his findings only very briefly. As an apologist, Macarius does not, or at least not always, rise to the level of his opponent – as has already been noted, he sometimes does not even fully comprehend what his opponent's argument implies (Goulet also speaks of his "incapacité à discerner le caractère propre et incommunicable de la foi religieuse;" p. 163).[18] But he does know how to apply the techniques of ancient rhetoric. As a theologian, Macarius fares better. His system of thought is coherent and can be situated very clearly in post-Nicene but pre-Constantinopolitan theological milieus, although his theology and christology is not on a par with, say, that of the great Cappadocian Fathers of this period. He should rather be seen as representing the mainstream 'popular theology' of his time. "En fait, ce document exprime très bien ce qui représentait la foi pour les hommes d'alors et il permet d'observer les corrélations qui existent entre cette foi et les désirs, les craintes et les interrogations de l'époque" (231). What I missed in this otherwise excellent chapter was a discussion of Macarius' negative attitude towards Jews and Judaism, a topic that certainly deserves closer investigation.[19]

The final chapter of vol. 1 is about the transmission of the text. Here Goulet distinguishes between extant manuscripts and those that are lost. As to the latter category, these are the manuscript reportedly found and used by Nicephorus in the 9th century, by Janos Laskaris around 1500, and by Turrianus (Torrensis) in the middle of the 16th century. It is of course especially their quotes from the now lost parts of the book that are most valuable. To this category belongs also the manuscript found and used by Blondel for the *editio princeps*, once belonging to the National Library at Athens but enigmatically lost since 1876 (it

---

[18] Sometimes Macarius bases his defence upon a wrong translation of the biblical text, as in 2.31.

[19] Unfortunately, the word index is not exhaustive (see p. 305) and the word *Ioudaios* was not included so that it is difficult to find the many places where Macarius speaks about the Jews.

dates from the 14th–15th cent.). The extant manuscripts are those miscellaneous ones which contain, *inter alia*, tables of contents of the *Monogenes*, scholia on biblical texts with passages from Macarius, or other documents containing summaries of certain passages from his text, for instance in treatises on the Eucharist. On the basis of a detailed analysis of all these data, Goulet tries to reconstruct the contents of the work in its entirety. At page 247 we finally find Goulet's stemma of all no-longer-extant codices. In this chapter he shows his mastery in the field of meticulous analysis of textual traditions.

Volume 2 contains Goulet's reconstruction of the Greek text and his French translation on facing pages. He presents this material in a very user-friendly manner. For instance, not only are the page numbers of Blondel's edition and those of the lost manuscript he used indicated *in margine*, the reader is also helped by brief marginal annotations indicating where Macarius' response to an objection by his adversary begins when there is a considerable distance between the two (as is often the case), and also the other way round in the form of references back to the place where the objection here answered can be found. In the margin one also finds the references to the numbering of the 'fragments' in Harnack's edition of Porphyry's *Contra Christianos*. In view of the high degree of corruption of the Athenian manuscript there are many places where conjectures were unavoidable; Goulet consistently alerts the readers to this by indicating conjectural readings in the text, not only in the apparatus. There are several apparatuses: On the left hand (often spilling over into the right hand) page one finds a list of sigla for the documents where the text of (parts of) the page can be found; further there is an *apparatus criticus*; an additional apparatus on *marginalia* in the Athenian ms.; and an apparatus of sources (mainly biblical). On the right hand page one finds an apparatus discussing textual problems, but in the text of the translation the reader is also referred (by means of letters) to the scriptural apparatus and (by means of asterisks) to the many exegetical notes which have been relegated to the end of the volume (pp. 377–436: Appendice exégétique). These exegetical discussions sometimes amount to very useful mini-essays (see e. g. pp. 380–382 on the problem of the delayed coming of salvation, or pp. 405–407 on objections to the doctrine of the bodily resurrection). Here one also finds a wealth of references to parrallels in early patristic sources and to scholarly literature. The translation is fluent, as far as I can judge, even though Goulet keeps rather close to the original. The constitution of the Greek text is a *tour de force* on which much could be said, but I prefer to leave that matter to more competent colleagues (although I want to say that I found Goulet's conjectures often very ingenious).

To conclude: This is a project in which a number of formidable obstacles had to be overcome, as we have seen. Goulet here presents the results of several decades of wrestling with these problems. These results are impressive. The care with which Goulet has dealt with all these often intractable matters is exemplary.

Not only students of Macarius but also those who are interested in the field of anti-Christian critique on the part of pagan Greek intellectuals owe him a great debt. Even if one is not convinced by everything Goulet proposes as a solution (as in the case of the identity of the unnamed adversary), that does not detract in the least from the great value of his work.[20]

---

[20] A good study of the interpretation of the NT by the unnamed opponent is J.G. Cook, *The Interpretation of the New Testament in Greco-Roman Paganism*, Tübingen 2000, 168–249.

A New Early Christian Poem on the Sacrifice of Isaac (Pap. Bodmer 30)

Introduction

Almost half a century ago, in 1952, several dozen papyri were discovered near the Egyptian village of Dishna (not far from Nag Hammadi, where the well-known Coptic Gnostic library was found). They were acquired by Phokion Tano, a Cypriot antiquities dealer in Cairo, who sold most of them to Martin Bodmer, the Swiss magnate and scholar who founded the famous Bibliotheca Bodmeriana in Cologny (near Geneva).

In a series of monographs that appeared from the middle of the fifties, a great number of these so-called Bodmer papyri were published (with books of the Septuagint and the New Testament, Menander, the *Pastor Hermae* etc.). The publication of Pap. Bodmer 29, some 15 years ago, was exciting news. It contained a completely new text, the early Christian *Vision of Dorotheus*.[1] This is a Greek poem from the fourth century written in Homeric language and style in which a certain Dorotheus, who had been previously unknown to us, tells about his visionary experiences.[2] On the last photo of the papyrus found in that edition, one can already see the opening lines of the next poem, again in Homeric hexametres, entitled *Pros Abra(h)am*. It took 15 years before the complete text of that poem was put at our disposal, but it is available now, in a beautiful edition, which also contains the text of six other early Christian poems from the same codex.[3] We will present here the text in an English translation and then briefly discuss the background of its contents.

---

[1] A. Hurst, O. Reverdin & J. Rudhardt, *Papyrus Bodmer XXIX: Vision de Dorothéus*, Cologny-Genève 1984.

[2] For a revised edition and English translation see A. H. M. Kessels & P. W. van der Horst, "The Vision of Dorotheus (Pap. Bodmer 29). Edited with Introduction, Translation and Notes," *VC* 41 (1987) 313–359.

[3] A. Hurst & J. Rudhardt, *Papyrus Bodmer XXX–XXXVII: "Codex des Visions." Poèmes divers*, München 1999. It should be remarked here, albeit only in passing, that actually the text of this poem had already been accessible from 1994, but that the publication that made this possible has been intentionally ignored by almost all scholars. The scandal is as follows. The Italian classicist and papyrologist Enrico Livrea was asked in 1993 by Hurst en Rudhardt, who prepared the *editio princeps*, to give them advice on certain points. He agreed and received

The papyrus itself dates from the first decades of the fifth century, but the text of the poem is certainly older, although not older than the fourth century as the editors persuasively argue in their introduction (their dating of the text and papyrus of the *Visio Dorothei* has met with only marginal criticism[4]). Their linguistic analysis of the Greek makes clear that the author of the poem *Pros Abraam* cannot be the same as Dorotheus, the author of the preceding autobiographical poem. So it is an anonymous piece. It is a poetical rendering of the story of Genesis 22, the famous narrative of the sacrifice of Isaac (or the sacrifice of Abraham, as it is often called), which, in Jewish tradition, is known as the *'Aqedat Yitschak* (litt. 'the binding of Isaac') or, more briefly, as 'the Aqedah.' The editors are not sufficiently aware of the fact that Genesis 22 had a very influential 'Wirkungsgeschichte' in the early centuries of both Judaism and Christianity (see pp. 39–40), and it is for that reason that they appeal to their colleagues to do further research to "la question de savoir s'il existe une source littéraire qui explique les écarts par rapport au texte de l'Ancien Testament ou s'il faut les attribuer à l'imagination de l'auteur" (p. 43). But there is not just one 'source littéraire' that can explain the deviations from the text of the Old Testament, there are many of them, as was to be expected.

Short though it may be (only 30 lines), the poem has a tripartite structure: Vv. 1–3 are a kind of prelude; vv. 4–27 form an acrostichon, a poem in which the opening letters of the lines form a word, in this case simply the Greek alphabet; finally an epilogue in vv. 28–30. This tripartite structure is very clearly indicated by the copyist of the papyrus in that he puts the word *hypertheta* ('placed above it') above lines 1–3; above lines 4–27 the words *kata stoicheion* ('according to the letters of the alphabet'); and above lines 28–30 the words *ta loipa prostheta* ('the rest is an addition' or epilogue).[5]

---

a copy of the Greek text and a photo of the papyrus. Shortly afterwards, Livrea himself published the papyrus with an Italian translation under the title 'Un poema inedito di Dorotheos: Ad Abramo' in the *Zeitschrift für Papyrologie und Epigraphik* 100 (1994) 175–187. It is understandable that there were furious reactions to this 'acte de piraterie littéraire'; thus, for instance, H.E. Braun, A. Hurst & J. Rudhardt in *ZPE* 103 (1994) 154 (Braun is the director of the Bibliotheca Bodmeriana).

[4] Notably J.N. Bremmer, 'The Vision of Dorotheus,' in J. den Boeft & A. Hilhorst (eds.), *Early Christian Poetry*, Leiden 1993, 253–261.

[5] In the text of the translation square brackets [...] indicate that there is a lacuna in the papyrus, and round brackets (...) that we have added one or more words for the sake of clarity. The papyrus has been preserved relatively well; the lacunae are small and especially in the acrostic part at the start of the lines they can for the most part relatively easily be filled because it is known with which letter of the alphabet each line has to begin. Only lines 13–14 (beginning with the letters *kappa* and *labda*) are completely missing because the bottom part of the papyrus is destroyed.

Text in translation

On Abraham[6]

Prelude
(1) He who put together the world and the heaven [and the s]ea
(2) sent from the ether[7] a swift an[gel] to Abraham (with the command)
(3) to sacrifice his own beloved son as a perfect offering.[8]

In alphabetical order
(4) As soon as he learnt this, he rejoiced in his willing mi[nd],
(5) and he went to see whether he could persuade his illustrious wi[fe]:
(6) 'Wife of mine, the immortal God desires that I br[ing] to Him
(7) the noble Isaac. [He was?] a great gift on the thr[eshold] of our old age,[9]
(8) (this) descendant.[10] Let him execute [God's will] (?).[11]
(9) I will bind my un[touched(?)[12] son] on the altar as an offering.'
(10) When his wife heard that, she was proud[13] [to say] (these) wise words:
(11) 'Keep cou[rage],[14] my dear child, for [you] have [been] happy in [this l]ife,
(12) Isa[ac, child] of my womb,[15] [...]
(13) {the letter *kappa*}
(14) {the letter *lambda*}
(15) Full of [sweet] joy their glorious son spoke to them:
(16) 'Parents, prepare for me a luxurious brid[al] chamber!
(17) Citizens, braid my fai[r] hair into locks,[16]

---

[6] The meaning of the Greek *pros* in this title may seem unclear at first sight since *pros* + acc. is usually an indication of direction or of address, but that does not make sense here, unless one assumes that the title refers to the fact that the final three lines (28–30) are indeed addressed *to* Abraham. The suggestion by the editors (p. 50) that the expression is comparable to the words *le-Dawid*, which are often found as a superscript to the Psalms, does not solve anything. *Pros* here has the sense of 'with regard to' (see W. Bauer – W. F. Arndt – F. W. Gingrich, *A Greek-English Lexicon to the New Testament*, Chicago & London 1979, *s.v.* 5b); hence our translation 'on.'

[7] Here for 'highest heaven.'

[8] The Greek has here *hekatombê*.

[9] 'The threshold of old age' is a well-known Homeric expression and verse-ending.

[10] One could read the word *ekgenetês* (descendant) also as *ek genetês* (from his birth).

[11] Because of the lacuna the text and meaning of this line remain uncertain. One could take the word *ekgenetês* at the beginning of the line to be the subject of the verb so as to get, 'Let (our) descendant fulfill [God's will].''

[12] The editors here read *athikton*, but that is far from certain. If correct, it could be a reference to the demand that a sacrificial animal must be completely without blemish; but it could as well refer to the fact that Isaac is still unmarried (see v. 16), 'untouched' in the sexual sense (*athiktos* can also mean 'virgin').

[13] Or 'she began' (*êrxato* instead of *êuxato*).

[14] This imperative (*tharsei*) is also often found on tombstones as encouragement for the deceased; see the discussion in P. W. van der Horst, *Ancient Jewish Epitaphs*, Kampen 1991, 120–122.

[15] Litt. 'from my limbs.' The second half of this line and the two following verses are lacking due to a large lacuna.

[16] The editors suggest that "Isaac fait peut-être allusion à (...) la flamme du sacrifice, désignée comme une chevelure tressée" (53) with reference to Bacchylides 3:56. It would

(18) tha[t] I may fulfil a [hol]y task with magnanimity."
(19) [At] once able men stirred up the f[ire] around the altar.
(20) Around the flames [rush]ed the sea that Moses
(21) would [split]. A wave lifted Abraham's son (or: Abraham lifted his son to a wave?).[17]
(22) The father brought h[im], who smelled of incense, to the altar, and (the son) rejoiced.
(23) He welcomed (?)[18] him [on top of?] the fire[19] and he hastened to
(24) strike his neck with a sharp [sword]. But God's
(25) [hand] reached out (towards him), for nearby a goat appeared.[20]
(26) Leaving his son unscathed Abra[ham plucked/sang the praise of?[21]] the fruit in the tree
(27) [so that in as]sent he chose to prepare that (goat) as a sacrificial meal (?).

[The rest i]s epilogue
(28) [...?] courageous man, could you receive another mark of honour for this (?):
(29) Thousands of flourishing [children] to make you shine (?),
(30) excellent [giver] of gifts, who has climbed the tower.[22]

Comments

The differences between this text and the biblical story are striking. To mention only the most important: (1) Not only Abraham, but Sara and Isaac as well, assent to God's command to sacrifice Isaac without any hesitation and even with enthusiasm. (2) Nothing is kept hidden from Isaac. (3) Isaac compares his imminent death to a wedding. (4) Sara is presented as speaking (whereas in the

---

seem more natural, however, to take it as a reference to the usual cosmetic preparation for a wedding.

[17] The Greek (*Abraam huia potixunaeireto kuma*) is very unclear and the whole scene is confusing in view of the fact that in the next line it is Abraham himself who brings his son to the altar.

[18] The exact meaning of the form *didisketo* is far from certain.

[19] Litt. 'Hephaistos.'

[20] The Greek here has *mêlon*, which can mean both 'goat' and 'apple.' In view of what follows (Abraham's 'plucking' of the 'fruit' [if that reading is correct]) the author seems to make a conscious play on this homophony.

[21] Both the reading and the meaning of the word *psêlen* (aorist of *psallô*) are very uncertain. In Aeschylus, *Persae* 1062, according to a scholiast, *psallein* is used in the sense of 'plucking' and that might have inspired our author, but of course the sense of '(psalm)singing' is much more current. The editors also considered the reading *psilon*, which in combination with 'son' would yield the following translation: 'Leaving unscathed his *only* son, Abraham chose the fruit in the tree to prepare as a sacrificial meal.' But it should be borne in mind that the word *psêlen* is conjectural,

[22] The final three lines are an echo of the promise of numerous offspring in Gen. 22:17, with the special twist that these offspring are the Christians, at least, if the editors are right in suggesting that climbing the tower is here equivalent to founding the church. The tower as a symbol of the church is well-known from the *Pastor Hermae*, a treatise parts of which were found in the same codex in which the present poem is to be found.

biblical story she is not even mentioned). (5) God's command is here given via an angel, but (6) the biblical angel in Gen. 22:11 here becomes God's hand. (7) The Red Sea plays an enigmatic role.[23] Many more differences in detail could be mentioned, but this short enumeration suffices to show that the biblical story has undergone some drastic modifications here. What is the background of these modifications?

It is well-known that already in the pre-Christian period and even more there-after the story of Genesis 22 gained a surplus of meaning and value in Jewish circles (and that not only in the martyrological sphere).[24] For instance, we see that Isaac's sacrifice was given a soteriological significance in the first century CE *Liber Antiquitatum Biblicarum* (*LAB*) by Pseudo-Philo. In *LAB* 18:5 we read the following utterance of God: "Because he did not object, his offering was acceptable before me, and in return for his blood (!)[25] I chose them (namely the people of Israel)." In *LAB* 40:2 Jephtha's daughter wants to emulate Isaac on a soteriological level and speaking about it to her father, she remarks: "Or have you forgotten what happened in the days of our fathers, when the father placed the son as a burnt offering, and he did not dispute with him but gladly gave his consent to him, and the one being offered was ready and the one offering was rejoicing?"[26] This joyful readiness is made even more explicit in Pseudo-Philo's rendering of Deborah's song, where he has her say (*LAB* 32:2–3):

(2) Abraham did not dispute, but set out immediately. When he set out, he said to his son, 'Behold now, my son, I am offering you as a burnt-offering and am delivering you into the hands of the one who gave you to me.' (3) The son said to the father, 'Hear me, father. If a lamb of the flock is accepted as an offering to the Lord as an odour of sweetness and if, for the sins of men, animals are appointed to be killed, but man is designed to inherit the world, how is it that you do not say to me, "Come and inherit a secure life and time without measure?" What if I had not been born into the world to be offered as a sacrifice to him who made me? Now my blessedness will be above that of all men, because there will be no other [sacrifice like this]. Through me nations will be blessed and through me the peoples will understand that the Lord has deemed the soul of a man worthy to be a sacrifice.'

Similar remarks about Isaac's heroic stance are found in Pseudo-Philo's contem-porary, the Jewish historian Flavius Josephus (*Antiquitates* I 232: 'Isaac received

---

[23] The editors are of the opinion (41) that what is meant with the reference to the sea is that Isaac, by being laid upon the altar, undergoes a symbolic baptism. In this connection they refer to Paul's allegory of the passage through the Red Sea in 1 Cor. 10:1–2. This seems somewhat forced at first sight, but it is hard to come up with a more satisfactory explanation (see, however, below in the text). Livrea (184–185) sees here a reference to a lustration ritual before sacrifice.

[24] The most exhaustive collection of material is now L. Kundert, *Die Opferung/Bindung Isaaks*, 2 vols., Neukirchen 1998.

[25] Also some medieval rabbinic midrashim speak of Isaac's blood (or ashes) as if the sacrifice had taken place in reality. See H. Jacobson, *A Commentary on Pseudo-Philo's* Liber Antiquitatum Biblicarum, Leiden 1996, vol. I, 583.

[26] Translation by Jacobson, *A Commentary on Pseudo-Philo* 582 (slightly altered).

these words [of his father] with joy'), and also in later rabbinic midrashim and in the paraphrastic Bible translations into Aramaic, the targumim.[27] For instance, *Targum Pseudo-Jonathan* renders Gen. 22:7–11 as follows:

(7) Isaac spoke to his father Abraham and said, 'Father!' And he said, 'Here I am, my son.' He said, 'Behold the fire and the wood; but where is the lamb for the burnt offering?' (8) Abraham said, 'The Lord will choose for himself the lamb for the burnt offering, my son.' And the two of them went together with a perfect heart. (9) They came to the place of which the Lord had told him, and there Abraham (re)built the altar which Adam had built and which had been demolished by the waters of the Flood. Noah rebuilt it, but it was de-molished in the generation of the Division. He arranged the wood upon it and tied Isaac his son and placed him on the altar on top of the wood. (10) Abraham put forth his hand and took the knife to slaughter his son. Isaac spoke up and said to his father, 'Tie me well, lest I struggle because of the anguish of my soul, with the result that a blemish will be found in your offering, and I will be thrust into the pit of destruction.' The eyes of Abraham were looking at the eyes of Isaac, and the eyes of Isaac were looking at the angels on high. Isaac saw them but Abraham did not see them. The angels on high exclaimed, 'Come, see two unique ones; one is slaughtering and one is being slaughtered; the one who slaughters does not hesitate, and the one who is being slaughtered stretches forth his neck.'[28]

It may be clear that the motif of Isaac's joyful willingness to be an acceptable sacrifice to the Lord already had a long tradition in Judaism by the time our anonymous author wrote his poem. The same applies also to several other non-biblical motifs in the poem. For instance, God's *hand* that restrains Abraham just in time (instead of the *angel* of the Lord in Gen. 22:11–12) is a motif that we know from ancient Jewish art: it is to be found on the wallpaintings of the Dura Europus synagogue from the middle of the third century CE, as well as in the later floor mosaic in the synagogue of Beth Alpha (but also in early Christian pictures!).[29]

---

[27] Apart from the recent and all-encompassing work by Kundert (mentioned in note 24), much material can also be found in the curious study by S. Spiegel, *The Last Trial: On the Legends and Lore of the Command to Abraham to Offer Isaac as a Sacrifice, the Akedah*, New York 1967 (repr. Woodstock 1993); also in G. Vermes, 'Redemption and Genesis xxii – The Binding of Isaac and the Sacrifice of Jesus,' in his *Scripture and Tradition in Judaism*, Leiden 1973, 193–227. See further J. Swetnam, *Jesus and Isaac. A Study of the Epistle to the Hebrews in the Light of the Akedah*, Rome 1981, 23–80; A. F. Segal, 'The Sacrifice of Isaac in Early Judaism and Christianity,' in his *The Other Judaisms of Late Antiquity*, Atlanta 1987, 109–130; J. Milgrom, *The Binding of Isaac: The Akedah – A Primary Symbol in Jewish Thought and Art*, Berkeley 1988.

[28] Translation by M. Maher, *Targum Pseudo-Jonathan: Genesis* (The Aramaic Bible 1B), Edinburgh 1992, 79–80; discussion in R. Hayward, "The Present State of Research into the Targumic Account of the Sacrifice of Isaac," *Journal of Jewish Studies* 32 (1981) 127–150.

[29] See C.H. Kraeling, *The Excavations at Dura-Europos VIII,1: The Synagogue*, New Haven 1956, Plate LI; also the discussion in R. Hachlili, *Ancient Jewish Art and Archaeology in the Diaspora*, Leiden 1998, 239–246. For other Jewish depictions of God's hand see K. Gross, *Menschenhand und Gotteshand in Antike und Christentum*, Stuttgart 1985, 354–357. Some scholars think that pictures of God's hands have a pagan or Christian origin. The Christian

At first sight it seems a strange motif that Isaac's first reaction to the message that his father is going to sacrifice him is his request to prepare a bridal chamber (the altar!) for him. This motif is not known from other sources in relation to Isaac, but it is known from Jewish traditions concerning Isaac's female counterpart, Jephtha's daughter. It is again in the pseudo-Philonic *LAB* that we read that Seila[30] – as this woman, who is anonymous in the Bible, is called here – in a reaction to the message of her father that he has to sacrifice her, says: 'The underworld has become my bridal chamber' (40:6). The motif of death as a wedding and the underworld as a bridal chamber has a long history in Greek literature. The editors of our poem rightly refer to Sophocles (*Antigone* 806 ff.) and Euripides (*Iphigeneia Aulensis* 458 ff.)[31] as possible sources for our author, but it is at least as relevant to point out that in Jewish works in which biblical stories are 'rewritten' the motif of death as marriage to the underworld had already entered into the stories about persons who had to die young by serving as sacrifices to the Lord (Isaac and Seila), albeit under Greek influence.[32] The interesting thing is, however, that in the case of Seila, as in the Greek tradition of *lamentatio*, the motif is a complaint, whereas in the case of Isaac in our poem it is a paradoxical expression of joy.

Do we have to assume now that the author of the poem was acquainted with Jewish haggada about Genesis 22? In itself that is not impossible,[33] but it would seem to be less plausible if it could be demonstrated that many of the non-biblical elements could have been known to him from his own Christian tradition. For in early Christianity, probably in reaction to soteriological elements in the Jewish haggada on Genesis 22, a Christian haggada on the same chapter began to develop. Let us therefore look for elements in these traditions about Isaac's sacrifice that may shed light on our new poem.[34]

---

depictions of the sacrifice of Isaac are discussed by I. Speyart van Woerden, 'The Iconography of the Sacrifice of Abraham,' *VC* 15 (1961) 214–255.

[30] Probably *She'ilah* = she who is demanded (by God).

[31] P. 53: 'On ne peut s'empêcher de se demander si l'Iphigenie d'Euripide n'interfère pas ici avec le modèle biblique.'

[32] See M. Alexiou & P. Dronke, 'The Lament of Jephtha's Daughter: Themes, Traditions, Originality,' *Studi medievali* (3rd series) 12 (1971) 819–863; also P.W. van der Horst, 'Portraits of Biblical Women in Pseudo-Philo's Liber Antiquitatum Biblicarum,' in my *Essays on the Jewish World of Early Christianity*, Fribourg-Göttingen 1990, 119–120. On old mural paintings in the monastery of St. Catherine in the Sinai, Isaac and Jephtha's daughter are often depicted side by side.

[33] An outdated but still useful survey of motifs borrowed by Church Fathers from Jewish haggadic tradition is L. Ginzberg, *Die Haggada bei den Kirchenvätern*, Amsterdam 1899; further, e. g., M. Hirshman, *A Rivalry of Genius. Jewish and Christian Biblical Interpretation in Late Antiquity*, Albany 1996.

[34] For what follows cf. D. Lerch, *Isaaks Opferung christlich gedeutet*, Tübingen 1950; S.P. Brock, 'Genesis 22 in Syriac Tradition,' *Mélanges Dominique Barthélémy*, Fribourg-Göttingen 1981, 2–30; R. M. Jensen, 'The Offering of Isaac in Jewish and Christian Tradition,' *Biblical Interpretation* 2 (1994) 85–110; and M.F.G. Parmentier, *Isaäk gebonden – Jezus gekruisigd:*

The new text on the sacrifice of Abraham does in fact offer possibilities for a comparison with the Christian exegetical tradition of this story. We have found eight of them:

1. Abraham is willing and he rejoices

Many Christian exegetes emphasize the human grief of the faithful Abraham. Yet there are also a number of texts that present him as not only faithful, but even as rejoicing. Evidently this joy does not originate from negative feelings towards Isaac. On the contrary, Isaac is 'the beloved son.' Abraham's joy at the sacrifice has a different background. Apart from the martyrological interpretation which we already know from Jewish sources (2 and 4 Maccabees), there is also a specifically christological one. Irenaeus (second century), for example, says that Abraham obeyed God's command to sacrifice his son, because he knew what God intended to do in the long term: "Since... Abraham was a prophet and saw in the Spirit the day of the Lord's coming, and the dispensation of his suffering, through whom both he himself and all who, following the example of his faith, trust in God, would be saved, he rejoiced exceedingly."[35] Irenaeus departs from John 8:56 here ('Abraham rejoiced that he was to see my day; he saw it and was glad'). Those who believe like Abraham are the Christians who see the life and passion of Jesus Christ prefigured in the sacrifice of Isaac. They do this in contrast to the Jews, who do not derive the meaning of Biblical texts from the life and death of Jesus Christ.

Interpreting a text from the Epistle to the Hebrews, Origen (third century) suggests that Abraham's hope did not just lie in the resurrection of Jesus Christ, but also in the resurrection of Isaac himself: "The Apostle (i. e. Heb.11:17,19)... has reported to us the thoughts of the faithful man, that belief in the resurrection began to be held already at that time in Isaac. Abraham, therefore, hoped for the resurrection of Isaac and believed in a future which had not yet happened." Immediately after this, anti-Jewish polemics follow: "How, then, are they 'sons of Abraham' who do not believe what has happened in Christ, which Abraham believed was to be in Isaac? Nay, rather, that I may speak more clearly, Abraham knew himself to prefigure the image of future truth; he knew the Christ was to be born from his seed, who also was to be offered as a truer victim for the whole world and was to be raised from the dead."[36] Athanasius (fourth century) in his sixth *Festal Letter*[37] paraphrases the exegetical starting point in the New Testament for Abraham's joy, John 8:56: "...the patriarch Abraham rejoiced not to

---

Oudchristelijke teksten over Genesis 22, Kampen 1996. [See now also E. Kessler, *Bound by the Bible. Jews, Christians and the Sacrifice of Isaac*, Cambridge 2004.]

[35] *Against the Heresies* IV,5,4–5.

[36] *Homily 8 on Genesis.*

[37] *The Festal Epistles of St. Athanasius* (*translated from the Syriac*), Oxford 1854, 50–51.

see his own day, but that of the Lord; and when he thus longed for it, he saw it, and was glad." This evokes the context of Christian-Jewish polemics about the messianic status of Jesus. Immediately after the paraphrase of John 8 Athanasius begins to discuss the meaning of Abraham's sacrifice. The context is always the dispute with the Jews. Athanasius even goes so far as to suggest that God stopped the sacrifice because otherwise the Jews would deny the prefiguration of the sacrifice of Jesus Christ, as found in Psalm 40:7 (LXX 39:6) according to the text of the Septuagint: "Sacrifice and offering Thou wouldest not, a body Thou hast prepared me." According to Athanasius, this text must be interpreted as a reference to the incomplete sacrifice of Abraham and the incarnation and death of Jesus Christ respectively. If the sacrifice of Abraham had taken place, Athanasius argues, the Jews would eliminate Psalm 39 [40] as a text in which Isaac's role and Jesus' role are put into the right perspective. Yet it was not Isaac's death but Jesus' death that liberated the world. Jesus raises us from the dead and prepares the joy of his festal banquet for us. Next, Athanasius elaborates for some time on the theme of joy. We may conclude: because he foresaw all this, Abraham rejoiced.

A sermon by the Latin author Zeno of Verona (fourth century) is an example on the Christian side in which not a typological exegesis but a martyrological motif explains Abraham's joy: "Abraham, fully devoted, shows no sad face, neither does grief persuade him to cry. No, he rejoices and is glad. And he is not afraid to risk the accusation of parricide, rather he is glad that God has commanded him to do this, so that he can satisfy his devotion.... When everything is ready for the mysterious sacrifice, the joyful father leads the joyful son, who is going to be killed by his father's right hand... In spite of the terrible situation of the son he rejoices and is glad and he jubilates that he has gained the Lord."[38]

After this, the theme of Abraham's steadfastness almost becomes an exegetical commonplace. Thus Basil of Seleucia (fifth century) writes: "How brave was his soul: he did not wail, he did not cry, he did not give in to his nature, he was not torn apart by conflicting wishes, he did not contort his face, he did not change his conviction, he did not give up his intention, he did not utter those words that can be expected from a father who is asked to butcher his child, he did not say what nature demands..."[39]

2. Abraham tries to convince Sara

Most Christian authors say that Abraham kept Sara ignorant of the command to sacrifice Isaac, because he was afraid that she would veto his plans. There are, however, quite a number of authors who record a hypothetical speech by Sara,

---

[38] *Treatise on Abraham* I 43 (II 10).

[39] J.M.Tevel, *De preken van Basilius van Seleucië*, diss. Vrije Universiteit, Amsterdam 1990, 184–185.

to show what she might have said, since Sara does not occur in Genesis 22. Even so Isho'dad of Merv, a ninth century compiler of numerous older sources, observes that opinions about the question of whether Abraham let Sara into the secret are divided.[40] In fact there are also documents that record a real discussion between Abraham and Sara. Among the descriptions of the communication between Abraham, Sara and Isaac, a large number of Syriac texts, especially the so-called "dialogue poems," a specific Syriac literary genre, catches the eye.[41] However our new text does not present a dialogue, but a monologue which Abraham holds in front of Sara. She reacts by putting heart into Isaac. An example of a real dialogue between Abraham and Sara is the anonymous Dialogue Poem on Abraham and Isaac.[42] Apparently, Sara has sensed the divine command and she asks Abraham why he is chopping wood: not by any chance to sacrifice our son? Abraham orders her to be silent, which Sara ignores of course:

> You are not aware how I have suffered
> the pains and travail through which he came to be.
> Swear to me by him that nothing will happen to him,
> for he is my hope. Then go.

To this, Abraham replies:

> The mighty God in whom I believe
> stands surety for me with you if you believe firmly
> that your son Isaac returns soon
> and remains your consolation by his youth.

3. Sara puts heart into Isaac

In our new text, Sara puts heart into Isaac. Addresses by Sara to Isaac are rare.[43] Amphilochius of Iconium (fourth century) records such an address by Sara to Isaac,[44] in which she says that she hopes that God will prevent the sacrifice at the last minute and change it into a "bloodless sacrifice." So she expects that Isaac will return alive. After this address by Sara, Abraham quickly makes off, as he is afraid that she will change her mind. Romanos the Singer (fifth-sixth century) makes Sara describe a similar feeling between hope and fear; she addresses Isaac

---

[40] J.-M.Vosté et C. van den Eynde, *Commentaire de Isho'dad de Merv sur l'Ancien Testament. I. Genèse*, in: CSCO Vol. 126 = SS Tome 67, Louvain 1950, 173 (Syriac); CSCO Vol. 156 = SS Tome 75, Louvain 1955, 187 (French).

[41] Cf. S. Brock, "Two Syriac verse homilies on the binding of Isaac", *Le Muséon* 99 (1986) 61–129; for a survey of the speeches by Sara in Syriac and Greek patristic literature, cp. *ibid.* 68.

[42] Ed. S. Brock, *Sughyotho mgabyotho (= Select Dialogue Poems)*, Glane 1982, 7–12.

[43] Brock, "Two Syriac verse homilies", 69.

[44] *On the Patriarch Abraham*, ed. L.van Rompay in: C. Datema (ed.), *Amphilochii Iconiensis Opera*, CCSG 3, Turnhout 1978, 280–281 (Coptic text with English translation).

at length.[45] An anonymous Syriac homily also allows Sara to speak. In tears, she admonishes Isaac to obey Abraham: "When you go with your father, listen and do all he tells you, and if he should actually bind you, stretch out your hands to the bonds, and if he should actually sacrifice you, stretch out your neck before his knife; stretch out your neck like a lamb, like a kid before the shearer."[46] When Isaac has returned safely, Sara addresses him once more at the end of the poem: "Welcome, my son, my beloved, welcome, child of my vows; welcome, o dead one come to life, welcome…"[47] In a reworking of his earlier sermon on the sacrifice of Abraham, Gregory of Nyssa emphasizes Sara's role more than in the earlier text.[48] This is in the year 385, in the speech that he gives on the occasion of the princess Pulcheria's death. He tries to comfort the empress Flacilla with the example of Sara's courage. In comparison with the earlier text, Sara has an unusually active role here, by means of which he hopes to set an example for the empress. After having formulated an imaginary address in which he has Sara adduce all possible kinds of objections to the sacrifice, Gregory writes: "Sara would certainly have brought forward these and similar things, if she had not seen that which is invisible to us with her own eyes. For she knew that the end of the life in the flesh is the beginning of the more divine life for those who cross over: Isaac leaves shadows behind, he reaches truth, he lets go off delusions, errors and noises and finds the good things that surpass eye and ear and heart (cf.1 Cor. 2:9). Lust will not torment him nor impure desire distract him, he will not be puffed up with pride, nor will any other of the passions that trouble the soul hinder him, but God becomes all things to him (cf. 1 Cor. 15:28). That is why she eagerly gives her son to God."[49]

4. Isaac is willing and he rejoices

There is an old and widely known tradition that Isaac himself also looked forward to the sacrifice willingly and with joy. This seems to fit in with Abraham's corresponding attitude. The idea of Abraham's joy is more or less assumed in the text of the Gospel of John (8:56); however, Isaac's quietness of mind or even joy cannot be derived so easily from Scripture. But Clement of Rome (end of the first century) already writes: "Isaac in confident knowledge of the future was gladly led as a sacrifice."[50] It is in the same vein that Melito of Sardes (second century) speaks: "…Isaac was silent, bound like a ram, not opening his mouth nor uttering

---

[45] *Kontakion on Abraham and Isaac* III 14 (in SC 99, cf. esp. 152/153 and 154/155).

[46] Brock, "Two Syriac verse homilies" 118 (Syriac) and 123 (English).

[47] *Ibidem* 122 and 125.

[48] Cp. his *On the divinity of the Son and the Spirit and on Abraham*, Gregorii Nysseni Opera [=GNO] X,2, Leiden 1996, 135 with his work *In Pulcheriam*, Gregorii Nysseni Opera IX, Leiden 1967, 469.

[49] *Ibid.* 469,10–20.

[50] 1 Clement XXXI,3.

a sound. For not frightened by the sword nor alarmed by the fire nor sorrowful at the offering, he carried with fortitude the model of the Lord."[51] Clement of Alexandria (second/third century) plays with the etymology of Isaac's name, which he interpret as "laughing,"[52] probably on the basis of the story of Isaac's birth, especially Gen. 21:6. However, Clement does not develop the theme of the laughter and joy from the birth story, but from Gen. 26:8. There Isaac's "fondling" (thus in the Hebrew) is translated into the Greek of the Septuagint as "sporting" (*paizôn*). We may wonder whether Isaac's marital bliss described here cannot also be connected somehow with his joy about the sacrifice, since precisely his wedding is used as an image for the sacrifice, both in our new text and elsewhere (see below). Moreover, Clement himself indicates the possibility that the Biblical text in question is understood as referring to the joy of the reader about his salvation (by Jesus Christ), like Isaac, who "delivered from death, laughed, sporting and rejoicing with his spouse..."[53] We conclude: Clement links a discussion of the meaning of Isaac's name with a tradition of Isaac's joy after (!) the cancellation of the sacrifice, although he finds the exegetical basis for this in the text of Genesis only four chapters further down. But a joyful Isaac before the sacrifice is of course much more remarkable. It seems feasible that this motif finds its exegetical starting point in Gen.21:6, but so far we have not found a text which explicitly makes this connection.

Amphilochius of Iconium (fourth century) in his sermon on Gen. 22 records several speeches of the actors involved, including Isaac. Abraham's son reproaches his father that he is not frank with him:

I myself, I am ready, o my father, but my mind ponders: Which is the sheep? Or what is that which will be slain? Perhaps it is me. I am the sheep! Why don't you reveal to me my killing? Why do you deceive me as if I were not willing to offer myself to God? Certainly I am willing, and I implore it, I rejoice and I take delight in it. I have become now the one whom you hide from me; for after a while God will reveal everything to me. And now, build a place of sacrifice, and this will become a tomb for me, for your son, and I shall ascend it well. I myself, my father, I shall help you eagerly to build my tomb. I shall heap up the stones. May my tomb resemble a temple, and guide me thereto. Slay me for the One who has called you.[54]

Once again we have a passage here without a typological perspective: its scope seems to be purely martyrological. The same goes for a passage in the sermon by Zeno of Verona (fourth century) already referred to above,[55] which explains Isaac's joy as a joy about the faith of Abraham, who is frank with Isaac: "The father, who felt safe about the faith of his offspring, revealed to his son, concern-

---

[51] Fragment 9.
[52] *Paidagogos* I,5,22,3.
[53] *Paidagogos* I,5,22,2.
[54] CCSG 3, 286/287.
[55] See note 38.

ing whom he had no doubts, what the Lord had required from him, and made clear to him what he himself had promised to the Lord. The boy rejoiced about the faithful father, being strongly faithful himself, and he did not refuse the death which the God who had given life had ordered. The father rejoices about the joyful boy and he joyfully binds the hands of the only pledge of his love, who offers them willingly to have them cuffed."[56]

5. *Isaac regards the sacrifice as a wedding*

In the new text, Isaac makes a speech before his parents and he compares the sacrifice with a wedding. Apart from the Greek tradition referred to above that death is regarded as a wedding with the god of the underworld (Hades), the background of this comparison is the incompatibility of the sacrifice of his only son with the promise to Abraham that his descendants would be numerous. By this comparison, Isaac shows that he continues to have faith in God's promise. We have found no other address of Isaac to both his parents, but his wedding is discussed a few times, also as an image of the sacrifice. Thus a sermon of Gregory of Nyssa (fourth century) that contains a section which looks like a paraphrase of a poem by Pseudo-Ephrem[57] on Abraham and his sacrifice, tells us that initially Abraham thought that God would order him to let Isaac marry: "For without doubt he expects something like the command to let his son marry and to prepare the bridal chamber quickly, so that the blessing on his seed could take effect."[58] In an imaginary speech, Abraham reacts to God's command: "Is this the bridal chamber I am to build? Is this the marital bliss for which I am to make preparations? Am I to light a funeral pyre for him instead of a wedding lamp? Is it for this purpose that I shall put on a wreath? Shall I be a father of many nations in this way, when no child is conceded to me?"[59] Equally in an imaginary speech by Abraham, this time addressed to Isaac, Basil of Seleucia (fifth century) writes: "But I, my child, was already thinking about your wedding suite and bridal chamber. But unwittingly I have raised my dearest for the fire and the sword: instead of a wedding suite there is an altar, instead of the wedding torch there is the altar flame."[60]

6. *Around the flames the Red Sea roars*

According to the editors of the papyrus, Isaac underwent a symbolic baptism at the moment of his sacrifice (cf. above, n. 23). We have found this motif nowhere

---

[56] CCSL XXII, 115.
[57] *On the divinity...*, cf. note 48 above and GNO X,2, 109–113.
[58] GNO X,2 133,7–10.
[59] GNO X,2 134,15–19.
[60] Tevel, *Preken* 184–185.

else in this form. In some explications of Gen. 22 baptism is discussed, however.. Clement of Alexandria (second/third century) makes a connection between Abraham's three days journey (Gen. 22:3–4) and baptism ("the seal") in the name of the Trinity.[61] Cyril of Jerusalem (fourth century) writes that, because Abraham was prepared to sacrifice his son, he received circumcision as the seal of his faith. Now the Christians, who follow the faith of Abraham, become children of Abraham and "receive like him the spiritual seal, being circumcised by the Holy Spirit through baptism, not in the foreskin of the body, but in the heart."[62] Since Isaac was only eight days old when he was circumcised (cf. Gen. 21:4), our text cannot refer to his circumcision (which might then have been linked with Christian baptism). It would seem highly likely that we have here some kind of *prefiguration* of Christian baptism. The Red Sea is a very common type of baptism in patristic texts, as Daniélou has shown.[63] Is this what the new text hints at? Daniélou also demonstrates that some Jewish and some Christian sources link the sacrifice of Abraham and the exodus from Egypt together. The Paschal Lamb and Abraham's sacrifice both have atoning value.[64]

7. God's hand holds Abraham back

The text of Gen. 22 says clearly that the angel of the Lord called Abraham and made him change his mind at the last minute. In the new text, however, it is God's hand that holds him back. Brock has edited a Syriac homily that says that "the Lord's right hand overshadowed as a voice came from on high."[65] The phraseology is taken from Ps.138:7–8. We already referred above to ancient depictions of Abraham's sacrifice like those in the Dura-Europos synagogue, the synagogue mosaic of Beth Alpha and many Christian sarcophagi and other artefacts that represent God's hand in this scene.[66] We probably have here a Jewish motif that apparently influenced Christian tradition.

8. A goat/apple as fruit in the tree serves as an alternative

The typological link between the near-sacrifice of Isaac and the complete sacrifice of Jesus Christ leads to different designations in Greek of the ram which is substituted for Isaac in the Genesis story. Those designations come close to the notion of "sacrificial lamb." "Ram" in Greek is *krios*. From the catena tradition it

---

[61] *Stromateis* V,11,73.

[62] *Catechesis* V,5–6.

[63] Cp. J. Daniélou, *From Shadows to Reality. Studies in the Typology of the Fathers*, London 1960, 175–201.

[64] *Ibid.* 119–120.

[65] "Two Syriac verse homilies" 127, at line 77.

[66] Cp. E.Lucchesi Palli in E. Kirchbaum (Hrsg.), *Lexikon der christlichen Ikonographie* I, Freiburg 1968, col.24.

is evident how the church fathers wrestled to make sense of the typology. Melito of Sardes (second century) says: "The Lord was a lamb (*amnos*) like the ram (*krios*) which Abraham saw caught in a Sabek-tree."[67] Eusebius of Emesa (fourth century) contradicts Melito when he says that the ram (*krios*) was precisely not a young lamb (*amnos neos*) like Isaac, but a ram (*krios*) that was full-grown like the Lord; no doubt he once again refers to the difference in value between the two sacrifices.[68] Severian of Gabala (fourth/fifth century)[69] uses the term *probaton* ("sheep," referring to Is. 53:7); the same is true of the sermon by Basil of Seleucia. Lastly, Melito of Sardes, speaking about Jesus in comparison to Isaac, brings all terms together: "As a ram he was bound.... as a lamb he was shorn, as a sheep he was led to slaughter, and as a lamb he was crucified..."[70] Nowhere in the context of the exegesis of Gen. 22 have we come across the word *mèlon* ("goat") that is used in the new text. In fact, this term is not found anywhere in the Greek Old Testament. It looks as if the author consciously chose an unusual term, perhaps because of the poetic effect or because of the play on words with "the fruit in the tree" (more specifically an apple, also named *mèlon* in Greek).

However, something is the matter with the tree, at least in the Syriac tradition. Thus Ephrem the Syrian (fourth century) in his commentary on Gen. 22:13 writes: "Abraham saw a ram in a tree and he took him and offered him as a sacrifice instead of his son. That there was no ram there is proved by Isaac asking for the lamb. And that there was no tree there is confirmed by the wood on Isaac's shoulders. The mountain spat out the tree and the tree the ram, in order that in the ram that was hung and that was made into a sacrifice for Abraham's son, the day would be prefigured of him who was hung on the wood like a ram and who tasted death for the sake of the whole world."[71] The dialogue poem referred to above equally speaks of "the tree that has not been conceived, which bears a fruit that has not been received."[72] Sebastian Brock points out that, according to a Jewish tradition, the ram was one of the ten things created at the beginning of creation;[73] he also shows how the "virgin birth" of the ram came to lead its own life in Syriac tradition. Could it be that our new text with its play on words with "goat" and "apple" is indebted to this Syriac tradition?

---

[67] Fragment 10.

[68] Petit, *La chaîne* 236, frg.1277.

[69] Petit, *La chaîne* 232, frg.1271.

[70] Fragment 9.

[71] R.M.Tonneau, *Sancti Ephraem Syri in Genesim et in Exodum commentarii*, in: *CSCO* 152, *SS*71, Louvain 1955, 84. The "day" is of course a reference to John 8:56. Edward G.Matthews, Jr., *The Armenian Commentary on Genesis Attributed to Ephrem the Syrian*, CSCO 573, Leuven 1998, p. XXXI, ranges the fact that Abraham finds a ram in "a tree" and not in "a bush" among "Jewish readings or ideas" that can be found in both the Pseudo-Ephremitic work he edits and also in Ephrem's genuine works: he emphasizes (note 70) that "tree" is the reading of all the Targums, against the reading of the Peshitta.

[72] *Sughyotho* 10.

[73] "Genesis 22 in Syriac Tradition" 28 n. 72.

Conclusions

The new poem offers the following points of contact with the Christian exegetical tradition of Gen. 22: Abraham's joy, a well-known motif that is connected with John 8:56; the dialogue between Abraham and Sara (in the tradition mostly imaginary); the dialogue between Sara and Isaac (in the tradition rarely attested); Isaac's joy, departing from the etymology of "Isaac" and from Gen. 26:8; the wedding as an image of the sacrifice; the linking of the sacrifice with baptism; the hand of God instead of the voice of the angel; the ram (goat) as fruit in the tree.

But there are also differences which seem to indicate a certain originality of our Christian poet: the dialogues are more like monologues; Isaac addresses both his parents; Isaac asks to have his hair plaited; there are active bystanders at the sacrifice; the unsacrificed Isaac smells of incense (as if the sacrifice had been completed in some sense); the play on words with goat/apple. These motifs deserve further research. Thus it seems that we have here a literary product that stands within the Greek poetic tradition,[74] but that has been influenced by other, probably Syriac, traditions: especially the presence of speeches and the "fruit in the tree" seem to point into that direction.

---

[74] J.B.Glenthøj, *Cain and Abel in Syriac and Greek Writers (4th–6th centuries)*, CSCO 567, Leuven 1997, p. 275 indicates that just as in the homiletic tradition related to Gen.4, dialogue is also more characteristic of Syriac than of Greek homilies on Gen.22.

The Role of Scripture in Cyril of Scythopolis' Lives of the Monks of Palestine

Studying the role of Scripture in the writings of Cyril of Scythopolis turned out to be a less easy enterprise than I had anticipated. The reasons for that are the following. In his edition of Cyril's Greek text, Eduard Schwartz included an appendix with a list of biblical references ('Zitate und Anspielungen');[1] and in his annotations to Price's translation of the work, John Binns has duly listed the biblical quotations and allusions at the bottom of the pages.[2] So at first sight it would seem that the ground had been well prepared for the kind of research I wanted to undertake. On closer scrutiny, however, that turned out not to be the case, for these two lists are far from being identical.[3] To mention only the most important differences: Schwartz has references that one does not find in Binns; Binns has references that Schwartz does not have; and sometimes their references differ for one and the same passage in the text. Moreover, there are dozens of passages in Cyril with unmistakably biblical allusions where neither Schwartz nor Binns notes any reference. So in order to provide the present investigation with the basis it needs, the whole of Cyril's text had to be read all over again in search of biblical quotations and allusions.[4]

---

[1] E. Schwartz, *Kyrillos von Skythopolis* (TUGAL 49/2), Leipzig 1939, 254–256. For serious criticisms of Schwartz's edition see P. Thomsen, "Kyrillos von Skythopolis," *OLZ* 43 (1940) 457–463; cf. also E. Stein, "Cyrille de Scythopolis. A propos de la nouvelle édition de ses oeuvres," *Analecta Bollandiana* 62 (1944) 169–186; and F. J. Dölger, "E. Schwartz, *Kyrillos von Skythopolis* [TUGAL IV 49,2]," *Byz. Ztschr.* 40 (1940) 474–484. As these critical reviews show, a new edition of Cyril based on all the evidence is a strongly felt desideratum. Important data about manuscripts and versions are to be found in H.-G. Beck, *Kirche und theologische Literatur im byzantinischen Reich*, München 1959, 410.

[2] *Cyril of Scythopolis: The Lives of the Monks of Palestine*, translated by R.M. Price with an Introduction and Notes by J. Binns, Kalamazoo 1991.

[3] A.-J. Festugière's annotated French translation proved to be less helpful in tracing biblical quotes and reminiscences; see his *Les moines d'Orient* III 1–3, Paris 1962–1963. In his introduction to Cyril, however, he claims to have found "216 citations de l'Écriture" (III 1, 43). I have not been able to consult the Italian translation by R. Baldelli & L. Mortari, *Cirillo di Scitopoli. Storie monastiche del deserto di Gerusalemme*, Bresseo di Teolo 1990.

[4] For Cyril's use of non-biblical sources the best survey to date is B. Flusin, *Miracle et histoire dans l'oeuvre de Cyrille de Scythopolis*, Paris 1983, 41–86.

Let us begin with some dry statistics. Altogether I found 275 biblical refer-ences[5] in Cyril's *Lives*: 133 from the (Greek) Old Testament and 142 from the New Testament.[6] By 'reference' I mean both quotations and allusions.[7] On the 243 pages of Greek in Schwartz's edition this is slightly over one reference a page on average.[8] This distribution is also more or less reflected in the individual *Lives*: Euthymius has 107 references on 80 pages; Sabas 117 on 116 pages; John the Hesychast 23 on 22 pages; Cyriacus 21 on 13 pages; Theodosius 6 on 5,5 pages; Theognius 4 on 2 pages; only the poor Abraamius has 0 references on 4 pages (but, admittedly, this *Vita* is not complete). The New Testament is referred to slightly more often than the Old (142 versus 133) from an absolute point of view, but in view of the fact that the New Testament is much smaller than the Old, it may be said from a relative point of view that it is much more referred to than the Old Testament. On the other hand, the biblical book that is most often quoted or alluded to is a book from the Old Testament, namely the book of Psalms. With its 40 references it is good for almost 15% of all quotations and allusions, in the *Life of Sabas* even for 20%: that *Vita* contains no less than 22 references to the book of Psalms. In another respect, too, the book of Psalms stands out among the biblical books in Cyril's writings. What I call 'favorite quotes' (or allusions), *i.e.* quotes that occur more than once, derive from 16 biblical books, 4 Old Testament and 12 New Testament books, but it is only the book of Psalms that has 4 passages that are quoted more than once and even some verses that are quoted 3 or 4 times: Ps. 4:8(9) and Ps. 144[145]:9.[9] Genesis with 18 references and Isaiah with 12 (9 of them in the *Life of Sabas*!), further Matthew with 25 references, Luke with 18, and Paul's Letter to the Romans with 13 are also great favorites, but they all lag far behind the book of Psalms.

Now it must be added immediately that in this respect Cyril does not deviate from other early monastic writers or writings, as some random comparisons make clear. If one takes, for instance, the *Historia monachorum in Aegypto*, one will find that the book of Psalms is most often referred to, immediately followed by the Gospel of Matthew, then the book of Genesis, and then the prophet Isaiah.[10] In Theodoret of Cyrrhus' work on the Syrian monks (*Philotheos*

---

[5] Schwartz has 240 references; Binns 182. For Festugière see note 3.

[6] Although I do realize the inadequacy of the terminology when speaking of 'Old Testa-ment' and 'New Testament,' for reasons of convenience I retain this traditional terminology.

[7] I found what I think are 115 quotations and 160 allusions, but I will come back later in this article to the problematic nature of this distinction.

[8] In practice, one page sometimes contains a whole cluster of citations and/or allusions, whereas sometimes these are completely or almost completely absent in a large number of con-secutive pages (e. g. *Sab*. 33–38 [pp. 118–128 Schw.]). Especially in the long passages that Cyril devotes to the christological controversies, scriptural references are completely lacking (which might be indicative of the lack of biblical support for the positions of the warring parties).

[9] Only Gen. 25:8 is referred to 4 times as well.

[10] See the Index of biblical passages in P. W. van der Horst, *Woestijn, begeerte en geloof. De Historia monachorum in Aegypto (ca. 400 na Chr.)*, Kampen 1995, 124–126.

historia), the picture is only slightly different: Again the book of Psalms is way out in front, followed by Genesis and Matthew, but this time the Gospel of John scores higher than Isaiah.[11] In John Cassian's *Conlationes* the book of Psalms easily wins over all other biblical books in terms of frequency of quotes and allusions, followed by Matthew, Isaiah and Genesis, but this time Paul's epistle to the Romans scores as high as Isaiah.[12] In Palladius' *Historia Lausiaca*, however, the Gospels of Matthew and Luke score highest, followed by the book of Psalms and Genesis (Isaiah being almost absent).[13] And, finally, a quite different example: in an anthology of texts about the desert fathers in Dutch translation that I compiled recently and which comprises a wide variety of material from the fourth through sixth centuries, we find a situation that is, interestingly enough, completely parallel to what we find in Cyril: there are 290 quotations and allusions in some 280 pages of text (so again approximately one reference a page); the highest score is that of the book of Psalms, followed by the Gospels of Matthew and Luke, then by Isaiah and Genesis.[14] And a look at other works from the world of early monasticism almost invariably yields the same or at least a very similar picture.[15]

Now it should not surprise us that Matthew is the Gospel that is most often referred to. Being the first Gospel in the canonical order, it was read most often in services and hence became the best known and most frequently quoted of the four Gospels in the ancient church, to begin with.[16] Moreover, it is especially the Sermon on the Mount, with its high demands – which only Matthew has – that was an enormous source of inspiration for the early monks; hence the number of quotations from Matthew 5–7 in our sources is relatively large.[17] And it stands to reason that in general a Gospel with stories about Jesus was more of a favorite and therefore better known among the desert fathers and their biographers than

---

[11] See the Index in P. Canivet & A. Leroy-Molinghen (edd.), *Théodoret de Cyr: Histoire des moines de Syrie* II (SC 257), Paris 1979, 319–322.

[12] See B. Ramsey, *John Cassian: The Conferences*, New York 1997, 861–882.

[13] See G.J.M. Bartelink, *Palladio: La storia lausiaca*, Milan 1974, 407–408.

[14] See P. W. van der Horst, *De woestijnvaders*, Amsterdam 1998, 281–285.

[15] D. Burton-Christie, *The Word in the Desert. Scripture and the Quest for Holiness in Early Christian Monasticism*, New York – Oxford 1993, 97: "All agree that the most frequently cited Old Testament texts are the Psalms, followed by the books of Genesis and Isaiah." Cf. H. Bacht, "Vom Umgang mit der Bibel im ältesten Mönchtum," *Theologie und Philosophie* 41 (1966) 558–559: Psalms, Isaiah, and Matthew are the top three in the *Apophthegmata patrum*. It should be added here that already in the New Testament the books of Psalms, Isaiah and Genesis are the most often quoted books from the Old Testament, although the differences with other books are far less outspoken than in the literature of the desert fathers.

[16] E.g., E. Romero Pose, "Matthieu," in *Dictionnaire encyclopédique du christianisme ancien*, ed. A. di Berardino, vol. 2, Paris 1990, 1589–1590.

[17] See K. McVey, "The *Chreia* in the Desert: Rhetoric and the Bible in the *Apophthegmata Patrum*," in A.J. Malherbe *et al.* (eds.), *The Early Church in Its Context. Essays in Honor of Everett Ferguson*, Leiden 1998, 245, who refers to L. Regnault, "The Beatitudes in the *Apophthegmata Patrum*," *Eastern Churches Review* 6 (1974) 23–43 (non vidi).

the more 'theoretical' writings of the New Testament. But what made the books of Genesis, Psalms and Isaiah to be preferred to other biblical books?

As for the book of Genesis, there can be little doubt that, apart from its being best known due to its position as the first book in the Bible, it was especially the stories about the pioneers of faith, the Patriarchs, that made this book a particular favorite with the early monks. The Patriarchs' roaming through the Near Eastern deserts at God's command cannot have failed to make impact on the minds of the desert fathers and their admirers. The fact that Cyril repeatedly alludes to the wording of Gen. 25:8, where Abraham's death is described, when he writes about the death of Sabas (*Sab*. 70 [171,29]),[18] of Euthymius (*Euth*. 39 [59,14]), and of Theodosius (*Theod*. 4 [239,26]), makes clear that he regarded these saints as worthy followers of this great Patriarch. In this connection John Binns rightly speaks of "the importance of demonstrating that the lives of the saints conform to biblical models."[19]

As far as Isaiah is concerned, we should remind ourselves of the fact that "the concept of the wilderness blossoming like the rose is developed in Isaiah as nowhere else."[20] Both at the beginning and at the end of the *Life of Sabas* (*Sab*. 6 [90,9] and 90 [200,6]) famous Isaianic passages such as "Let the desert rejoice and blossom like the lily" (Is. 35:1) and "the Lord will make her wilderness like Eden and her desert like the garden of the Lord" (Is. 51:3) are quoted or alluded to.

Now most of the desert fathers will not have possessed a Bible.[21] Books were expensive and scarce items, usually only accessible in libraries,[22] and possession of books in general was often frowned upon by these monks.[23] But they certainly knew these texts from their weekly gatherings where the Scriptures were read. And that applies *a fortiori* to the book of Psalms. Psalms were often learnt by heart in order to be sung in the weekly services,[24] but not only that. Psalms were

---

[18] Numbers between brackets after the chapter number refer to page and line in Schwartz's edition.

[19] J. Binns, *Ascetics and Ambassadors of Christ. The Monasteries of Palestine, 314–631*, Oxford 1994, 61. See also D. Krueger, "Typological Figuration in Theodoret of Cyrrhus's *Religious History* and the Art of Postbiblical Narrative," *JECS* 5 (1997) 393–419.

[20] J.F.A. Sawyer, *The Fifth Gospel. Isaiah in the History of Christianity*, Cambridge 1996, 56.

[21] See Y. Hirschfeld, *The Judean Desert Monasteries in the Byzantine Period*, New Haven and London 1992, 96.

[22] H. Y. Gamble, *Books and Readers in the Early Church*, New Haven & London 1995, 170–174, on early monastic libraries.

[23] Burton-Christie, *The Word in the Desert* 115–116. H. Dörries, "Die Bibel im ältesten Mönchtum," *TLZ* 72 (1947) 217 (215–222).

[24] Burton-Christie, *The Word in the Desert* 117–118. See on this aspect now especially the most important monograph on Sabas ever, namely J. Patrich, *Sabas, Leader of Palestinian Monasticism. A Comparative Study of Eastern Monasticism, Fourth to Seventh Centuries*, Washington 1995, 229–239 and 264.

also memorized because the desert fathers (and also the other monks) used them for their meditations.[25] What is important is that

"[f]irstly it was the Psalter alone that they used, not because they lacked anything else but because there was a growing conviction in the fourth century in both secular and monastic circles that the 'songs of the Spirit,' as they were considered to be, were to be preferred to mere ecclesiastical compositions. (...) Secondly, this attitude towards the inspiration of the Psalter coupled with the fact that the aim was to fill day and night with unbroken prayer meant that, whereas previously it had been used selectively, appropriate psalms for different occasions and situations being drawn from it, it was now to be committed to memory and for the first time used in its entirety, and it came to be regarded as a great and worthy accomplishment to go through the whole Psalter in the space of twenty-four hours: in effect, the hymn book of the secular church became the prayer book of monasticism."[26]

This made the book of Psalms not only the best known book of the Bible in these circles but also the most beloved, since it played such a pivotal role in their struggle for spiritual growth. For our purposes it is not irrelevant to note that, as far as Cyril himself is concerned, in an autobiographical note in the *Vita* of Sabas he tells us that the great saint urged his [Cyril's] father: "Teach him the Psalter, for I need him!" (*Sab.* 75 [180,23]).[27]

Cyril uses a remarkably wide variety of formulas to introduce quotations from Scripture, which include "that text of Scripture says ..." (*Euth.* 35 [53,14]), "Scripture calls such a person ..." (*Sab.* 28 [113,14]), "the Gospel saying of the Lord that runs ..." (*Sab.* 2 [88,8–9]), "that terryfing threat that runs ..." (*Sab.* Prol. [86,14], introducing Mat. 25:26–27), "the curse of the Prophet who says ..." (*Sab.* 2 [88,15]), "the Davidic saying ..." (*Sab.* 12 [95,13]), "in accordance with what is written ..." (*Sab.* 12 [95,17]), "with the words of the prophet ..." (*Sab.* 16 [99,15]), "what the prophet advises ..." (*Sab.* 39 [129,18]), "as the apostle says ..." (*Sab.* 40 [131,15]), "the precept that says ..." (*Sab.* 47 [138,3]), "it is well said in divine Scripture that ..." (*Sab.* 52 [144,25]), "David says ..." (*Cyr.* 10 [228,29]), "the Gospel says ..." (*Cyr.* 3 [224,4–5]) etc.[28] What is striking here is that words for 'saying' are used much more frequently than words for 'writing' ('it is written' occurs only very rarely). Is this a reflection of the fact that the early monks were exposed to Scripture more often by hearing than by reading it? Most probably so.[29]

---

[25] Burton-Christie, *The Word in the Desert* 97, 112–113.

[26] P. F. Bradshaw, *Daily Prayer in the Early Church,* London 1981, 94.

[27] Biblical books completely absent from Cyril's writings are, from the Old Testament, Leviticus, 2 Samuel, 1 and 2 Chronicles, Ezra, Nehemia, Esther, Lamentations, and 7 of the 12 Minor Prophets (Hosea, Obadiah, Micha, Nahum, Zephaniah, Haggai, Malachi); from the New Testament, the Epistles to Titus and Philemon, 1+2+3 John, and the Apocalypse of John.

[28] Cf. Bacht, "Vom Umgang mit der Bibel" 559–560, who deals with the various quotation formula's in the *Apophthegmata patrum.*

[29] It should be borne in mind that many monks were illiterate as most other people of their times; see Gamble, *Books and Readers in the Early Church* 1–41. Deviations from the biblical

More often, however, biblical quotations are not marked as such, but are interwoven with Cyril's text. For instance, in his farewell address on his death bed Euthymius says: "While humility exalts to a height, love prevents falling from this height, since he who humbles himself will be exalted and love never fails" (*Euth.* 39 [58,9–10]), the latter part of this saying being nothing else than literal quotes from Luke 18:14 and 1 Cor. 13:8. In another story an angel appears to Sabas, shows him a cave and says: "Make it your home and he who gives food to the animals and to the young ravens that invoke him will himself take care of you" (*Sab.* 15 [98,4–6]), which is for the most part a literal quote from Psalm 146[147]:9. Once Sabas said to his disciple Agapetus, who had fallen asleep: "Drive heavy sleep from your eyes and carelessness from your heart to save yourself as a gazelle from the snares and as a bird from the trap" (*Sab.* 23 [107,20]), again half of the saying being a quote from Prov. 6:5 (LXX). And many more examples could be given.

This brings us to the slippery area of allusions. Making a hard and fast distinction between quotations and allusions is notoriously difficult. As the examples just mentioned make clear, it is too simple to state that only citations that are marked off clearly from their context by quotation formulas count as quotations. But then the question arises: When does a quotation that is not preceded by a quotation formula cease to be a quotation and become an allusion? That is often hard to say, partly because there is so far no generally accepted definition of what an allusion is. This problem is strikingly demonstrated by Douglas Burton-Christie in his important book *The Word in the Desert*.[30] In this study on the role of Scripture in the sayings of the desert fathers (*Apophthegmata Patrum*), he lists in a very revealing appendix the numbers of biblical quotations and allusions as noted in four editions and translations of the *apophthegmata*. There one can see that Cotelier noted 145 of them, Ward 93, Regnault 224, and Mortari no less than 832! To give one more concrete example: Cotelier noted 6 references to the book of Genesis, Ward 4, Regnault 20, and Mortari 52. Now, fortunately, for our present purpose it is not necessary to go into the details of the debate about what an allusion is. Suffice it to say that allusions – whether broadly or narrowly defined – far outnumber the quotations in Cyril's work. His language is imbued with biblical diction, phraseology, imagery, and all sorts of reminiscences. "The Bible is used consistently and frequently in all parts of his Lives."[31] As if to make this programmatically clear, in the opening paragraph of his work Cyril makes use of a long concatenation of five biblical passages without marking them as such (except for one element).

---

text in Cyril may partly be due to quoting from memory, partly also to changing the text on purpose. Of the latter we find a fine instance in *Theogn.* 1 (243,1–2) where a reference to the cross of Jesus is inserted into an otherwise literal quotation from Job 38:11.

[30] Burton-Christie, *The Word in the Desert* 301–303.
[31] Binns, *Ascetics and Ambassadors of Christ* 60.

Let me give one or two other examples, the first one borrowed from John Binns' book on the Judaean desert fathers.[32] In his story of the foundation of Castellion, Cyril notes that there were large numbers of demons lurking there that Sabas had to struggle with. Some shepherds were witnesses to this struggle: "There were shepherds in the desert round that mountain, who were out in the fields keeping watch over their flock; marking the tumult (...) they were extremely frightened and said to each other: '(...) Let us make our way to the hill and see what has happened'" (*Sab.* 27 [111,6–11]). The extremely close verbal similarity with the scene of the shepherds in the fields of Bethlehem in the Gospel of Luke 2:8–15 cannot escape one's notice and it is clear that purposefully Cyril has shaped the narrative after this biblical model. The second example is quite different. The opening line of the *Life of Sabas* (Prol. [85,12]) runs, "Blessed be the God and Father of our Lord Jesus Christ," which is a literal quote of the opening line of both Paul's Second Letter to the Corinthians (1:3) and his Epistle to the Ephesians (1:3). So right from the start of this work on Cyril's favorite saint a biblical or apostolic note is sounded.

Let us now have a closer look at some of the passages in the *Life of Sabas* where Cyril quotes explicitly from Scripture to see how biblical material functions in this important document. The first passage is somewhat ambiguous since here Cyril does explicitly refer to the Bible but it is not a real quote. The passage runs as follows: "Sabas [was] predestined by God from the womb and foreknown before his creation like the great prophet Jeremiah" (2 [87,21–23]). There is little verbal overlap here with the Greek text of Jer. 1:5, but the reference is made explicit enough, as if Cyril wants to make sure that the reader will take notice of the parallel between Sabas and 'the great prophet Jeremiah.' Maybe, however, the implication is also that, just as the apostle Paul draws a parallel between his own vocation and that of Jeremiah in Gal. 1:15, the same can be claimed for Sabas as well.[33] Be that as it may, here again we observe "the importance of demonstrating that the lives of the saints conform to biblical models."[34] This motif is also clearly to be seen in the story of Sabas' healing of the woman with a haemorrhage (*Sab.* 62 [163,14–164,10]) which is so evidently patterned on the Gospel story of Jesus' healing of the woman who suffered from the same ailment (Mat. 9:20–22). The same applies to the story of Euthymius' successful prayer for rain during a long period of drought (*Euth.* 25 [38,1–39,17]) which is modelled upon the story of Eliah's prayer for rain in 1 Kings 18:41–45.[35]

---

[32] Binns, *Ascetics and Ambassadors of Christ* 62.

[33] Cf. the references to the birth of Samuel in the birth stories of Euthymius (*Euth.* 2 [8–9]) and Sabas (*Sab.* 1 [87,4]), with the comments by Flusin, *Miracle et histoire* 91–92.

[34] Binns, *Ascetics and Ambassadors of Christ* 61. Krueger, "Typological Figuration in Theodoret of Cyrrhus's *Religious History*" 393–394, states: "Theodoret's primary tool for placing the local saints into a context comprehensible to his readers was the device of biblical typology, the linking of his modern-day heroes with biblical figures."

[35] See Flusin, *Miracle et histoire* 155–158.

In the same chapter Cyril has Sabas think of "the Gospel saying of the Lord (*tên euangelikên apophasin tou Kyriou*) who says, 'No one who puts his hand to the plough and turns back is fit for the kingdom of heaven,'" which is from the Gospel of Luke 9:62 (albeit with some variants[36]), and Sabas also thinks: "I am afraid (...) of earning the curse of the prophet that runs, 'Accursed are they who turn from Thy commandments'" (2 [88,8–15]), a curse which is a quote not from a prophetic book but from a Psalm (Ps. 118[119]:21). However, on the very next page Cyril mentions David by name as the author of the Psalms, where Ps. 24[25]:18 is introduced as a 'Davidic song' (*Davitikê melôdia*, in *Sab.* 4 [89,8]; further *Sab.* 12 [95,13], *Cyr.* 10 [228,30]), so either he mistakenly thinks that the passage derives from one of the prophetic books of the Bible or, more probably, he regards David as a prophet, which is also a New Testament motif: for instance, in Acts 2:30 David is explicitly called 'a prophet,' and in Mark 12:36 (cf. Mat. 22:43–45) David is said to have spoken 'through the Holy Spirit,' which qualifies him as a prophet.[37] Again some chapters later, when Cyril describes Sabas' solitary life in the Coutila and Rouba desert, Ps. 54[55]:8 ("Behold, I have wandered afar and lodged in the desert") is introduced as a 'Davidic saying' (*Davitikon logion*), whereas some lines further on in the same chapter Ps. 45[46]:11 ("Be still and know that I am God") is just called 'what is written' (*to gegrammenon*; 12 [95,13–17]). As to the latter case, however, it has to be remarked that the LXX text of Ps. 54 does mention the name of David in v.1, whereas that name is lacking in Ps. 45. Still in the same paragraph there is again a quote from Luke, now not introduced as a 'Gospel saying of the Lord' but as something "God has said" (*ho theos ... eipôn*), whereas what follows is Jesus' word, "Behold, I have given you authority to tread underfoot snakes and scorpions and (authority) over all the power of the enemy" (Luke 10:19 in *Sab.* 12 [95,25–27]). Now Jesus is more often called God by Cyril, so 'God' may refer to Jesus here, but it is also possible to see here a reference to the idea that God himself is the one who inspired the biblical authors. All this evidence, however, also seems to point to a certain penchant for stylistic variation with Cyril.

Be that as it may, what is common to all these quotes and their contexts is the eminently practical orientation in the use that is made of Scripture. Exegetical debates are avoided, interpretive subtleties eschewed, theoretical exercises rejected, for the only thing that counts is a strong practical and ethical commitment to Scripture, "doing the Word."[38] As Burton-Christie has said: "Interpretation for the desert fathers always involved the possibility of personal and communal

---

[36] Schwartz prints the following text of the quote in Cyril: οὐδεὶς ἐπιβαλὼν τὴν χεῖρα αὐτοῦ ἐπ' ἄροτρον καὶ στραφεὶς εἰς τὰ ὀπίσω εὔθετός ἐστιν εἰς τὴν βασιλείαν τῶν οὐρανῶν, whereas Luke 9:62 according to the Nestle-Aland reconstruction runs: οὐδεὶς ἐπιβαλὼν τὴν χεῖρα ἐπ' ἄροτρον καὶ βλέπων εἰς τὰ ὀπίσω εὔθετός ἐστιν τῇ βασιλείᾳ τοῦ θεοῦ.

[37] On David as a prophet see also *Barnabas* 12:10.

[38] Burton-Christie, *The Word in the Desert* 151–152.

transformation. Holiness in the desert was defined, finally, by how deeply a person allowed himself or herself to be transformed by the words of Scripture."[39] That is what Scripture was meant for first and foremost.

The hermeneutics of the desert fathers also implied that "only those with experience could adequately interpret the sacred texts. (...) Because the texts are holy, only a holy one – the one with experience – can properly interpret them."[40] This is well illustrated by the role Scripture plays in the *Life of Sabas*. Most of the biblical quotes seem to aim at making the solitary and often dangerous life in the desert possible as a profound spiritual experience, and at the same time it is this experience that makes it possible to discover the riches of the words of Scripture. For example, after having fought the demons for many years and defeated them, Sabas received the insight that the word of Isaiah 2:4, "Beat your swords into plowshares and your spears into pruning hooks," was to be implemented as follows: "He was now (...) entrusted by God with the charge of souls; he was persuaded by the word of God not to devote time pointlessly to enemies who had been defeated but to transfer his spiritual energies from a war-like disposition to husbanding those who had grown rank with evil thoughts, for the benefit of the many" (*Sab.* 16 [99:10–15]). But later, in one of the conflicts about the Great Laura, it is the opposite word from the prophet Joel (3:10LXX), "Beat your plowshares into swords and your pruning hooks into spears," that is applied as follows by Sabas to those who want to found a laura of their own: "What is the advantage in agriculture when the land is in the grip of war? How can you, who have not yet overcome the passions of flesh and soul, undertake the formation of others, when you are still under the sway of pleasure and vain-glory?" (*Sab.* 39 [129,21–23]). It is his own long ascetic struggle that has opened his eyes for what he sees as the deeper sense of these words of Scripture and its value for the spiritual formation of a monk.

Among the desert fathers and their biographers there is a pervading sense of the need to apply Scripture to one's own life in the desert and also a strong conviction that that was what Scripture was written for. Sabas did not allow new-comers to live in a cell in the laura, but had them first stay in a small cenobium, until they had learnt the psalter and received a strict monastic formation. He said: "A monk enclosed in a cell must be gifted with discernment and be zealous, a combatant, sober, self-controlled and disciplined, a teacher not needing teaching, capable of curbing all the members of his body and of keeping a secure watch on his mind. I know that such a man is called single-minded by the scriptural saying, "The Lord gives the single-minded a home to dwell in" (Ps. 67[68]:7, in

---

[39] Burton-Christie, *The Word in the Desert* 23. Cf. Dörries, "Die Bibel" 218: "Die Schrift-auslegung der Wüste müht sich ja nicht um den ursprünglichen Sinn eines Schriftworts, gar in seinem geschichtlichen Zusammenhang, sondern paßt es seinem Verständnis an, darin freilich bestrebt, es im eigenen Leben zu voller Geltung zu bringen."

[40] Burton-Christie, *The Word in the Desert* 23.

Sab. 28 [113,15–16]).' The text of this Psalm-verse is here reinterpreted in a very characteristic way. In its original setting, as the context makes unambiguously clear, the passage in this Psalm praised God for being the helper of persons who against their will had come to live in solitude, for instance orphans, widows, prisoners, and other abandoned people. God will see to it, the Psalm says, that they will get a home again so as to make an end to their solitude. Now the Hebrew text of Ps. 68:7 speaks about these lonely persons as *yechidim* who are given a home by God to dwell in. The text that Cyril used, the LXX, renders this by *monotropos*,[41] which is also a common term in pre-Christian Greek for a person who lives alone. In Christian Greek the word begins to develop the sense of 'single-minded person,' as a glance in Lampe's lexicon shows.[42] It is this semantic development, fruitfully combined with his own 'desert hermeneutics,' that enables Sabas (or Cyril for that matter) to read this verse in a strikingly new way: It is not about persons who are alone *against their will*, it is about persons who are given by God a home, *i. e.* a cell in a laura, because they *really want* to live a solitary life and they are completely single-minded in that respect, because it's all they have learned to want. Only if one has reached that stage of discipline, one is deemed worthy of a God-given cell. To us modern readers it may seem as if the original sense of the text is stood upon its head here, but that has always been the fate of the Bible and we should not blame the desert fathers for that.[43] "They saw the sacred texts as projecting worlds of possible meaning that they were called upon to enter. (…) It also meant opening oneself to the new possibilities of meaning offered by these texts, realizing this meaning within oneself, and being transformed by this realization. (…) The ultimate expression of the desert hermeneutic was a *person*, one who embodied the sacred texts and who drew others out of themselves into a world of infinite possibilities."[44] Cyril's *Lives of the Monks of Palestine* illustrates this very well.

---

[41] ὁ θεὸς κατοικίζει μονοτρόπους ἐν οἴκῳ. *Monotropos* is a hapax legomenon in the Greek Bible.

[42] G.W.H. Lampe, *A Patristic Greek Lexicon*, Oxford 1968, 884a. See also M. Harl, *La langue de Japhet*, Paris 1992, 207 (= *REG* 73 [1960] 468).

[43] Bacht, "Vom Umgang mit der Bibel" 561, rightly notes that the basic conviction of the desert fathers was that the addressees of the Bible are *we*.

[44] Burton-Christie, *The Word in the Desert* 299, 300.

Twenty-Five Questions to Corner the Jews

A Byzantine Anti-Jewish Document from the Seventh Century

Introduction

Probably in the second quarter of the seventh century CE, in the time that witnessed the rise of Islam, an anonymous Christian somewhere in the Byzantine Empire wrote a small manual aimed at helping his coreligionists to gain the upper hand over Jews in religious disputations. The manual has the form of 25 arguments phrased as questions. This little treatise had gone entirely unnoticed until it was recently published by a French scholar.[1] The modest aim of this contribution is to present an English translation of the Greek text (without commentary), and thereafter to attempt to situate this document in its historical context.

The title of the treatise is not easy to translate: Ἐπαπορητικὰ κεφάλαια κατὰ τῶν Ἰουδαίων. It is clear that it is a treatise against (κατά) the Jews which is intended to bring them into an 'aporetic' situation (ἐπαπορητικά), *i. e.*, a situation from which there is no way out (hence the verb 'to corner' in the title). But what exactly is meant by κεφάλαια? The current meaning of the word is 'chapters,' but it can also be used for parts or components of a chapter, hence 'topics' or 'subjects' or 'passages from Scripture' etc.[2] In certain contexts κεφάλαιον can develop the sense of 'argument on a specific subject,' as here.

Translation

Arguments to corner the Jews

(1) If the Law is a universal good, why then was it not given to every nation but to only one? And if it is not a universal good, then obviously it is a partial good.

---

[1] V. Déroche, "La polémique anti-judaïque au VIe et au VIIe siècle: Un mémento inédit, Les Képhalaia," *Travaux et Mémoires* 11 (1991) 275–311. This edition is based upon nine textual witnesses from the 10th–14th centuries. It is on account of the publication date of this edition (1991) that one does not find a reference to this treatise in the otherwise comprehensive work by H. Schreckenberg, *Die christlichen Adversus-Judaeos-Texte und ihr literarisches und historisches Umfeld (1.–11. Jh.)*, Frankfurt 1990 (2. Aufl.).

[2] See G.W.H. Lampe, *A Patristic Greek Lexicon*, Oxford 1968, 748, and H.D. Saffrey & A.-Ph. Segonds, *Marinus: Proclus ou sur le bonheur*, Paris 2001, 64 note 15.

And if it is a partial good, it is clear that it was given because of a certain need, I mean because of the one who was to arise from the people of Israel. If the promise to Abraham, "In you and in your offspring all nations will be blessed,"[3] is not a universal good, is it not obvious then that the promise to the nations will not be realized through the Law but through the coming of him who was expected, namely Christ? So it is of necessity that the Law comes to an end and the promise becomes reality when Christ appears.

(2) If God is the God of all people and wants all people to be saved,[4] whereas according to you it is through the Law that salvation has been given to all, why then has He not given the Law to every nation instead of only to one?

(3) If the Anointed One, *i. e.* the Christ,[5] is, as is written, "the expectation of the nations,"[6] then it is obviously through him that there will be blessing for the nations. But if it is through him, then it is not through the Law; and if that is the case, then with the coming of the Anointed One the Law and the Jewish way of life necessarily come to an end.

(4) If it is impossible for the nations, especially for those who live far away, to come thrice yearly to Jerusalem, as the Law decrees,[7] is it not evident then that the Law is unable to bless the nations but rather declares them to be cursed? For (Scripture) says, "Cursed is everyone who does not remain in all that is written in the book of the Law in order to do that."[8]

(5) If it is impossible that all the nations of the world, from East and West, from North and South, should live in the promised country from Dan to Berseba, is it not obvious then that the nations cannot live in accordance with the Law? And if that is the case, is it not obvious as well that the promise for the nations is not realized through the Law but through a way of life in accordance with Christ?

(6) If the Anointed One whom you await – whoever he may be – again proclaims the Law of Moses at his coming, is he not bound to be a figure less than Moses to whom the Law was given? In which respect does this figure, who has been proclaimed by so many prophets, differ from the man who is now your teacher, who explains and proclaims the Law,[9] but who has never been able to save or bless any of you or of the nations through the Law?

---

[3] Gen. 12:3 LXX with some modifications, notably the addition of 'and in your offspring.'

[4] See 1 Tim. 2:4.

[5] The first Greek word is Ἠλειμμένος, the second one Χριστός.

[6] Gen. 49:10 LXX. The Greek has ἔθνη, so the semantic aspect of 'gentiles' is present as well. In what follows, though, ἔθνη will consistently be translated by 'nations.'

[7] Deut. 16:16.

[8] Deut. 27:26, freely quoted.

[9] Who is meant here is unclear. Déroche surmises it is the Babylonian exilarch of the Jews (308).

(7) If at every banishment God has ordained a fixed period for the exile of the Jews, such as 215 years in Egypt, 70 years in Babylon, and – let us say – some three and a half years during the reign of Antiochus,[10] periods in which they would suffer terrible things but were still considered worthy (to receive) the prophets and divine oracles, what is it that would now prevent God from promising you to call back your compatriots? But lo, 600 years and more have passed since you were driven from the promised land during which you remain bereft of prophets and divine oracles.[11]

(8) If it is necessary that at the coming of the Anointed One the Law should disappear and 'the expectation of the nations'[12] come true, how then is it possible that at the coming of the one who is called the Christ among you – I mean Zerubbabel – he himself (re)built the temple and validated the Jewish laws whereas no 'expectation of the nations' came true at all but rather he himself put his hope in the nations by requesting them to (help him) (re)build the temple?[13]

(9) If Moses announces, "God will raise up for you from among your brethren a prophet like me,"[14] who is that prophet like Moses, I mean a prophet and lawgiver and miracle worker from the people of Israel? Those who say it is Zerubbabel are mistaken, for he was neither a prophet nor a miracle worker nor a lawgiver, even though he was a Jew.

(10) If Moses announces, "God will raise up for you from among your brethren a prophet like me; listen to him in everything that he will say to you,"[15] how could the one who does not accept this prophet not be a sinner?

(11) If Moses announces, "Everyone who will not listen to this prophet will be extirpated from the nation,"[16] how is it possible that a people that pre-eminently has not listened to Isaiah, Jeremiah and the other prophets, has not been extirpated, whereas in the time of our Christ those who did not believe in him were extirpated, all of them indeed? They have been deprived of their country, their city, their temple, their priests, their sacrifices, their prophets, their scholars,[17] and of all other institutions of their laws, so much so that they could not demonstrate in any respect any more that they were Jews. So sober up and learn by

---

[10] Antiochus IV Epiphanes; the author refers to the years 167–164 BCE.

[11] Probably the author reckons the expulsion from the promised country to have taken place not after the fall of Jerusalem in 70 but after the crucifixion of Jesus in 30, as was often done in Byzantine literature.

[12] Gen. 49:10 LXX.

[13] Cf. Ezra 6.

[14] Deut. 18:15.

[15] Deut. 18:15, with a very free rendering of the final words (the LXX only has αὐτοῦ ἀκούσεσθε).

[16] Deut. 18:19, again very freely quoted.

[17] Or: scribes.

what cause you have been bereft of these things, instead of fooling yourselves with idle hopes.

(12) If God declares under oath, whoever it may be He is talking to, "You are a priest for eternity according to the order of Melchizedek,"[18] and not according to the order of Aaron, how could the order of Aaron be anything but temporary and that of Melchizedek eternal?[19]

(13) If then the priesthood according to Melchizedek and the one according to Aaron are different in kind, let them explain to us how it is possible that the two are identical. And since that is impossible, let them explain to us which of the two is temporary and which is eternal. It is of course obvious that the priesthood according to Aaron, which by reason of its hereditary nature was preserved among the sons of priests, was of a temporary nature because of the dying out of those to whom (this task) was entrusted; whereas the priesthood according to Melchizedek was promised to only one person because of its eternal nature.[20]

(14) If it is impossible that God should lie and if it is possible to hear him saying under oath, "You are a priest for ever according to the order of Melchizedek," whereas the priesthood according to Aaron is derived from the Law, isn't it absolutely inevitable then that a change of priesthood necessarily implies a change of the Law as well?

(15) If God declares to David, again under oath, that his offspring and the throne of his kingship are eternal,[21] then show us or tell us where we have to look for David's offspring and throne so that, after such a long time, we will not surmise that this prediction was a lie.

(16) If, as you say, all nations will perish with Gog[22] in the final days before the coming of the Christ you expect, which then are the nations whose expectation is the Christ for their salvation,[23] and not for their perdition?

(17) If, because of Israel's exodus from Egypt, the Egyptians were destroyed by the supremely heavy punishment of drowning, and if you, after having received the Law, have totally extirpated many nations as well, and if you have done the same thing again during the reigns of Hizkia and Zerubbabel and also during the rule of the Macedonians and the Maccabees and on many other occasions with very many nations, apparently because of the customs in your Law and traditions, is it not overly clear on the basis of such deeds that it is not so much

---

[18] Ps. 110:4 (109:4 LXX).
[19] Cf. Hebr. 7:11.
[20] Ps. 110[109]:4 with Hebr. 7:23.
[21] Ps. 89:4.
[22] Ezek. 38.
[23] Cf. Gen. 49:10.

a promise that is realized for the nations through the Law but rather a multitude of torments?

(18) If God has ordered that in the desert there would come a first and a second tabernacle,[24] and the first one is a representation[25] of this world but the second one a representation of the heavenly world,[26] then is it not obvious that when the first one disappears the second would appear that had always remained inaccessible and invisible for the priests of the Law?

(19) If all impiety and injustice done by people is directed against either God or one's neighbour, is it not obvious then that the commandments in the Law which do not pertain to this[27] – for example, circumcision, abstention from work on the sabbath, the rules for food and dress, purity regulations, sacrifices and the like – have been given for another purpose? And if that is true, which it is, it is obvious that they were not given because of God or one's neighbours but – as has already been said – in order to confine and safeguard the nation until the coming of the one who is expected to arise from its midst. Now that he has come, of necessity those rules of the Law stop being valid and only faith and love of God and one's neighbour remain,[28] that is to say, all that is more pleasing to God and does not abolish a life in accordance with Christ.

(20) If the Christ who had been prophesied by the Law and the prophets, is the expectation of the nations and their rule[29] and hope, how is it possible that you do not see that now all the nations have bowed down before the Christ worshipped by us, thrown away their idols because of him while sending up their Amen to God, since all of them regard Abraham as their father and – in accordance with what is written, "The whole world is filled with the knowledge of the Lord"[30] – read Moses and the prophets, and on the basis of these writings depend on Christ since they have distanced themselves from their old superstition?

(21) If in every of your captivities each of your tribes has been preserved, how is it possible that now, after the coming of him whom we believe to be the Christ,

---

[24] Ex. 26:33; Lev. 16.

[25] Gr. *typos*.

[26] Hebr. 8–9.

[27] The Greek has τὰ περιττὰ τοῦ νόμου, which is hard to render adequately. The adjective *perittos* can mean 'superfluous, unnecessary,' hence Déroche's translation "les superfluités de la Loi" (306). But that is not what the author wants to say here, for he immediately adds that these laws served to safeguard the people of Israel till Christ's coming. What he means is that these rules do not pertain to, and hence go beyond, the sins people commit against God or their fellow humans. Only after Christ's coming do they become 'superfluous' indeed. At the background is Gal. 3:23–29.

[28] Cf. 1 Cor. 13:13.

[29] Here ἀρχή is *abstractum pro concreto* in the sense of ἄρχοντες, rulers.

[30] Is. 11:9, quoted freely.

not a single one (of your tribes) has been preserved and you have also lost all the institutions of your Law?

(22) If according to you the Christ from the tribe of Judah who was proclaimed by the Law and the prophets[31] has not come, why do you go on expecting him now that not even one tribe has been preserved or can be preserved any more?

(23) If it is impossible for mules to know by themselves to which donkey and which horse they owe their existence, then similarly you cannot know (who your forebears are) after having been fused and mixed for thirty or more generations.

(24) If it is because of your individual sins that you have been made bereft of your country, city, temple, priests, prophets, sacrifices, and the whole worship according to the Law, how then could it be that previously, when you – aside from other individual sins – surrendered yourselves to idolatry, both privately and collectively, and openly demonstrated your impiety towards God by slaughtering your own children for idols, you were not then deprived completely of all these things, but only partially and temporarily, whereas now, now that you no longer slaughter your children nor murder each other or commit idolatry, you have been completely deprived of these things because of your individual sins?

(25) If we have been led to Christ by the Law and the prophets as if by a pedagogue,[32] then it is a good thing that the Law has been given by a good God who has turned out to be a pedagogue for leading the Jews towards the one who has been raised from their midst and who turned out to be the salvation not only for the nations but for the whole world.[33]

Context

This is not the place for an in-depth study of this document, but some provisional remarks are in order here. The hey-day of early Christian *Adversus Judaeos* literature was the three centuries between 150 and 450 CE.[34] In those centuries, from Justin's *Dialogus cum Tryphone Judaeo* to Evagrius' *Altercatio inter Simonem Judaeum et Theophilum Christianum*,[35] anti-Jewish polemics is very

---

[31] Gen. 49:10 and Micah 5:1.

[32] Gal. 3:24–25.

[33] *I.e.*, including the Jews.

[34] See on this, apart from Schreckenberg's *magnum opus* (note 1), also the still fundamental study by Marcel Simon, *Verus Israel. A Study of the Relations Between Christians and Jews in the Roman Empire (AD 135–425)*, Oxford 1986 (French original: Paris 1948), esp. 135–178. The first important instance of this type of literature is of course Justin's *Dialogue with the Jew Trypho*.

[35] See on this author (not to be confused with Evagrius Ponticus or Evagrius of Antioch) C. Kasper, "Evagrius, antijüdischer Polemiker," in S. Döpp & W. Geerlings (eds.), *Lexikon der*

much in the air. Thereafter, when Christianity has become the dominant power in the late-antique and early Byzantine world, the church can afford to be less worried about the Jews whose rights had in the meantime been drastically curtailed and whose position had for that reason become much weaker.[36] Anti-Jewish polemics then decreases (although it never disappears).[37]

There is, however, a clearly discernible revival of Christian anti-Jewish literature in the second half of the sixth and the first half of the seventh century, the period to which our *Kephalaia* belong. From that period we have, for instance, the *Dialogus Timothei et Aquilae* (second half of the sixth cent.), the *Dialogus Athanasii et Zacchaei* (also second half of the sixth cent.), the *Disputatio Gregentii cum Herbano Judaeo* (probably about 600), the *Disputatio de religione* (also about 600), the *Doctrina Jacobi nuper baptizati* (circa 635), the *Apologia contra Judaeos* written by Leontius of Neapolis on Cyprus (circa 640),[38] the *Dialogus Papisci et Philonis* (the middle of the seventh cent.), and several other less well-known works of a similar nature.[39] It has, moreover, to be kept in mind that probably for the most part this literature has not been preserved.[40] What is the *Sitz im Leben* of these writings?

It should not be assumed that these texts, mostly dialogues, are verbatim reports of disputations that had really taken place. What militates against that assumption is, *inter alia*, the endless repetition in all these works of the same arguments and the same biblical 'prooftexts.' These are manuals or textbooks for interreligious polemics, in this case of Christians against Jews, although it has to be added that the ever recurring arguments and prooftexts must inevitably have derived from the practice of really conducted debates if such manuals were to make any sense.

Given that the later works stem from the second quarter and the middle of the seventh century, one could surmise their background to have been the decree

---

antiken christlichen Literatur, Freiburg 1998, 223.

[36] See A. Linder, *The Jews in Roman Imperial Legislation*, Detroit-Jerusalem 1987, and K.L. Noethlichs, *Die Juden im christlichen Imperium Romanum (4.–6. Jahrhundert),* Berlin 2001.

[37] It is illustrative of the changed situation that in Schreckenberg's large survey (see note 1) the discussion of anti-Jewish literature from the three centuries between 150 and 450 takes more than 200 pages whereas the discussion of this literature in the three centuries between 450 and 750 takes less than 100 pages.

[38] This is the only work in this series of which we know the author.

[39] In his Introduction to the edition of the Greek text Déroche gives a much more detailed enumeration with bibliography (for the latter see also H.G. Beck, *Kirche und Theologische Literatur im byzantinischen Zeitalter*, München 1959, 332–333 n. 1). Information also in S. Krauss & W. Horbury, *The Jewish-Christian Controversy*, vol. 1, Tübingen 1996, 46–50. Schreckenberg's work (note 1) is more informative than most other works. The later character of these works in comparison with earlier ones is most apparent in the greater role of Jewish polemics against veneration of the cross, of relics, of tombs of saints, of icons etc., which was regarded by Jews as idolatry (graven images).

[40] See B. Blumenkranz, "Vie et survie de la polémique anti-juive," *Studia Patristica* I,1, Berlin 1957, 460–476.

which the Emperor Heraclius (who ruled from 610–641) issued in 632 to the effect that all Jews had to be baptized and convert to Christianity.[41] In such a situation many Christians inevitably came into contact with Jews who, after their compulsory baptism, still had to be talked out of their old beliefs and practices (in fact many of them became Marranos *avant la date*).[42] But that does not explain the instances of anti-Jewish disputes from the period before Heraclius.

It is important to state that at the beginning of the period discussed here, namely in 553 CE, the Emperor Justinian issued his famous *Novella* 146 (entitled *De Hebraeis*). In this edict Justinian decrees that in their synagogue services the Jews are allowed, yes even encouraged, to use Greek Bible translations instead of the Hebrew original, preferably the Septuagint since these translators were heralds of the coming of Christ, but if need be, also the translation by Aquila.[43] Moreover the Emperor prohibits the use of the primary text of the rabbinic movement, the Mishnah (here called *deuterôsis*, which probably also included the Talmud, which was based upon the Mishnah), and in other edicts he also deprived them of their few remaining rights within the state. Under the emperors after Justinian, "the Jews were increasingly reduced to the position of a very marginalised social and cultural element within a predominantly Christian society."[44] These measures could not but provoke a strong reaction, if not a counterattack, on the part of the Jews (as they did on the part of the Samaritans as well). From several sources of this period we learn that indeed it was often Jews who initiated debates in which Christians were challenged, especially as regards their untenable interpretations of the Jewish Bible. Exactly in the period in which the Church, by means of the Christian Emperors, curtailed the Jews more and more and cornered them, the Jews launched a counterattack.

As early as the beginning of the fifth century CE, Jerome already pointed out the intensity of Jewish attacks on Christian exegesis of the Jewish Bible (*Comm. in Isaiam* 7.14), for example when it concerned the explanation of the prophetic text about the 'virgin' (*parthenos*) who would bear a son, where according to the Jews the original text simply spoke about a 'young woman' (*'almah*). And not long after the Council of Chalcedon, in 452 CE, the Emperor Marcianus issued a decree that the decisions taken at that council should not become a matter of

---

[41] See A.N. Stratos, *Byzantium in the Seventh Century, vol. 1: 602–634*, Amsterdam 1968, 305–307; G. Dagron & V. Déroche, "Juifs et chrétiens dans l'Orient du VIIe siècle," *Travaux et Mémoires* 11 (1991) 28–32. cf. A. Sharf, *Byzantine Jewry from Justinian to the Fourth Crusade*, London 1971, 53–56.

[42] Maximus Confessor (c. 580–662) already stated clearly in his *Epistula* 8 (*in fine*) that he feared that this compulsory baptism would lead to very insincere 'conversions' on the part of the Jews.

[43] Text, translation and commentary in Linder, *Jews* 402–411. See also M. Avi-Yonah, *Geschichte der Juden im Zeitalter des Talmud in den Tagen von Rom und Byzanz*, Berlin 1962, 250.

[44] J.F. Haldon, *Byzantium in the Seventh Century. The Transformation of a Culture*, Cambridge 1990, 346.

public debate because such discussions would only lead to profanization of the Christian mysteries by the Jews.[45]

It is also in the period under consideration here (sixth-seventh cent.) that one finds very outspoken anti-Christian polemics in Jewish liturgical poetry.[46] The continuous attacks on 'Edom' in these synagogal poems are very clearly meant as polemics against the church of Rome (= Edom = Constantinople). Also some passages in rabbinic literature point in the direction of not only active Jewish participation but also of initiation of debates with Christians.[47] The Talmud tells us that a rabbi in Caesarea Maritima said to his Christian fellow citizens, in a setting of a debate about the meaning of biblical texts, that he and his coreligionists had so much to do with Christians that they studied thoroughly the Christian interpretation of the Holy Scriptures.[48] That Christians did not always prevail in such circumstances stands to reason, in spite of what the Christian *Adversus Judaeos*-tractates would have us believe.

At the beginning of the seventh century, John Moschus tells in his famous *Pratum spirituale*, ch. 172, that the Alexandrian monk Cosmas Scholasticus, who owned the greatest private library in the city, spent his days in writing polemical treatises against the Jews, but John remarks that Cosmas himself never embarked upon or exposed himself to actual debates with Jews in the city but sent out others to perform this task, in which they could gratefully make use of the arguments penned by Cosmas. This man could in theory have been the author of our *Kephalaia*. The Byzantine patriarch Photius records that in the same city even Samaritans engaged in debate with Christians with an array of anti-Christian arguments.[49] This and other material[50] strongly suggests that it was exactly the weakened position of the Jews within the Christian Byzantine Empire that induced them to challenge the Christians in matters of interpretation of the Bible. It is in this framework that our little treatise with 25 questions to corner the Jews gets a credible context, certainly if it could be dated to the years after Heraclius' edict of 632. It cannot be proved, but nor is it to be excluded, that the problem of the attractiveness of the Jewish religion, as we know it so well especially from

---

[45] Text and translation in Linder, *Jews* 337–355.

[46] See W.J. van Bekkum, "Anti-Christian Polemics in Hebrew Liturgical Poetry (*Piyyut*) of the Sixth and Seventh Centuries," in J. den Boeft & A. Hilhorst (eds.), *Early Christian Poetry*, Leiden 1993, 297–308; and *idem*, "Jewish Messianic Expectations in the Age of Heraclius," in G.J. Reinink & B.H. Stolte (eds.), *The Reign of Heraclius (610–641): Crisis and Confrontation*, Leuven 2002, 95–112.

[47] Simon, *Verus Israel* 179–201.

[48] B. *Avoda Zara* 4a.

[49] Photius, *Bibliotheca* cod. 230 (= vol. V, pp. 60–64 Henry). See R. Pummer, *Early Christian Authors on Samaritans and Samaritanism*, Tübingen 2002, 425–429.

[50] *Inter alia* from writings of the famous abbott of the St. Catharina monastery in the Sinai, Anastasius Sinaita (seventh cent.); see Déroche, 'La polémique' 284–285.

the anti-Jewish sermons John Chrysostom held in Antioch in the years 386–387 CE,[51] still played a significant role in the decades around 600 CE.

Further, it has to be noted that, even if the anti-Jewish polemics in these treatises did not serve the practical purpose of beating the Jews in debate, they were useful within he Church, specifically serving to confirm the beliefs and identity of Christians who came into contact with Jews. Demarcation is, and was, always essential for self-identification.[52]

The document discussed here, 'un petit manuel offensif,'[53] makes clear that Christians tried to be as well prepared as they could for possible controversies with Jews. It is unique in so far as it is the only treatise known to us in which only the questions not the answers are given. This feature is telling, for the implication is of course that there are no possible answers (N.B.: *epaporêtika*!). That is also indicated by the frequently recurring formula that introduces the actual question: "..., is it not obvious then that ...?"[54] The Greek formulation indicates even more clearly (by means of the negative particle *ou*) than the English translation that any other answer than 'yes' is impossible: the Christian is 100% right, the Jew can only say Amen and convert.

The questions do not display a clear principle of ordering, but there is a certain clustering. Questions 1–5 deal with the inability of the Law to realize the salvation that was promised to the gentiles. Questions 6–11 argue that it is only Christ who meets the definition of 'a prophet like Moses.' Questions 12–15 posit that the temporary priesthood of Aaron and the eternal one of Melchizedek are mutually exclusive. Questions 16–20 emphasize again that the Law does not bring salvation to the gentiles whereas Christian faith does. Questions 21–24 state that in its present situation the people of Israel cannot fulfill the Law any longer and that the Messiah cannot arise from the tribe of Judah because that tribe cannot be distinguished from other Israelite tribes any more. Question 25 is the crowning conclusion.

Biblical verses from the Old Testament playing a key role are Gen. 49:10, Deut. 18:15, 18 and Ps. 110:4. (From the New Testament especially Paul and the Letter to the Hebrews play an important role.) The well-known Shiloh-passage in Gen. 49:10 about the ruler from Judah that will not fail and will be the 'expectation of the Gentiles' (thus the Septuagint version that was used by the author[55])

---

[51]   See P.W. van der Horst, 'Jews and Christians in Antioch at the End of the Fourth Century,' in S.E. Porter & B.W.R. Pearson (eds.), *Jewish-Christian Relations Through the Centuries*, Sheffield 2000, 228–238. The author of the *Kephalaia* borrowed heavily for his anti-Jewish argumentation from Chrysostom's sermons.

[52]   The invariable conversion of the Jewish interlocutor at the end of the debates serves of course exactly that purpose.

[53]   Déroche, "La polémique" 297.

[54]   Greek: *pôs ou prodêlon hoti* ...; a real 'bluff formula.'

[55]   For the significant differences between the Hebrew and the Greek text here see M. Harl

was interpreted in a messianic sense by both Jews and Christians in antiquity, and the same applied to Deut. 18:15–18 (a prophet like Moses) and Psalm 110[109]:4 (You are a priest for ever according to the order of Melchizedek). It is no wonder that exactly those texts that both parties interpreted as predictions of the messiah became a source of controversy over the question who this messiah was. In questions 8 and 9 the author assumes, rather unexpectedly, that from the Jewish point of view Zerubbabel would turn out to be the messiah or the prophet like Moses in Deut. 18. This interpretation of the figure of Zerubbabel, based upon Haggai 2:22–24, is not to be found explicitly in Jewish sources, but the fifth-century Christian exegete Theodoret of Cyrrus also polemicizes against the Jewish opinion that (a second) Zerubbabel would turn out to be the messiah.[56] And it will certainly not be sheer coincidence that precisely in the seventh century a Byzantine Jew wrote the *Sefer Zerubbabel* in which Zerubbabel, though not a messiah, is a great apocalyptic visionary,[57] which could be interpreted by malevolent and ill-informed Christian contemporaries as being about a person with a great role in the eschaton, that is, a messiah. Since, however, the author of our treatise seems to be rather well-informed, we certainly cannot exclude the possibility, confirmed by Theodoretus, that this idea was favoured in certain Jewish circles.[58]

Much more remains to be said about the *Kephalaia epaporêtika*. In fact the study of this treatise is still in its infancy. In this contribution, my modest aim was to enable readers who may not be familiar with this text to make a first acquaintance with a small but fascinating chapter in the history of Jewish-Christian relations in the early Byzantine era.

---

e.a., *La Bible d'Alexandrie, 1: La Genèse*, Paris 1986, 308–309, and J.W. Wevers, *Notes on the Greek Text of Genesis*, Atlanta 1993, 826.

[56] See, e. g., his *Comm. in Isaiam* 11.10 (PG 81, 1872). Other passages from his and Jerome's works are mentioned by R.L. Wilken, "The Restoration of Israel in Biblical Prophecy: Christian and Jewish Responses in the Early Byzantine Period," in J. Neusner & E.S. Frerichs (eds.), *"To See Ourselves As Others See Us." Christians, Jews, 'Others' in Late Antiquity*, Chico 1985, 454 note 17.

[57] See M. Himmelfarb, "Sefer Zerubbabel," in D. Stern & M.J. Mirsky (eds.), *Rabbinic Phantasies. Imaginative Narratives from Classical Hebrew Literature*, Philadelphia-New York 1990, 67–90. Further Wilken, "The Restoration of Israel," 443–471, esp. 453–461; R.L. Wilken, *The Land Called Holy. Palestine in Christian History and Thought*, New Haven-London 1992, 207–214; and Van Bekkum, "Jewish Messianic Expectations" 104–106.

[58] That the interpretation of Gog and Magog plays a role in both our document (Question 16) and the *Sefer Zerubbabel*, as well as in other Jewish and Christian sources from this period, corroborates the impression that the themes broached by the anonymous author of the *Kephalaia* played a role in real life debates. See also on this Wilken, "The Restoration of Israel," 459.

"The Most Superstitious and Disgusting of All Nations"

Diogenes of Oenoanda on the Jews

Sometime during Hadrian's reign, probably in the twenties of the 2nd century CE, a wealthy inhabitant of the city of Oenoanda (in Lycia) called Diogenes had the huge wall of the Stoa on the Agora inscribed with a gigantic inscription (ca. 80 x 4 meter). His intention was to instruct his fellow-citizens, probably shortly before his death, in Epicurus' philosophy in order to dispel their fear of death and of the gods. About a century and a half later this building was dismantled and many blocks of the inscription were re-used for the construction of a new fortification wall and other buildings. In 1884 the first fragments of this inscription were discovered in the city. The excavations have continued at that site since then, albeit very intermittently, for some 120 years, and time and again new fragments of this curious text were found. The by then complete and well-known Teubner edition of 1967 by C. W. Chilton included 88 fragments. But British investigations at Oenoanda from 1968 till 1983 more than doubled the number of known fragments, increasing it from 88 to no less than 212. (It should be added in parentheses, however, that the 88 fragments already known contain some 3550 words, whereas the 124 new fragments have only some 2350). These new fragments were discovered and published in a long series of articles by Martin F. Smith. He finally published a new edition of all the fragments, the fullest ever, in 1993.[1]

Ten years later, in 2003, Smith published a supplement because, due to his own industrious search for new fragments, he was able to present eleven more new pieces, including the largest piece found so far.[2] Most of these new fragments yield little new information, but N[ew] F[ragment] 126 is of importance. NF 126, the most substantial and best preserved of all the fragments, is engraved

---

[1] M. F. Smith, *Diogenes of Oinoanda. The Epicurean Inscription*, edited with introduction, translation and notes, Napoli 1993 (see my review in *Mnemosyne* 48 (1995) 101–103). In this book one also finds the remarkable story of the gradual discovery of the text of this treatise on stone.

[2] M. F. Smith, *Supplement to Diogenes of Oinoanda, The Epicurean Inscription*, Napoli 2003. As a matter of fact Smith had already published most of this new material, which was discovered in 1997, in 1998; see his 'Excavations at Oinoanda 1997: The New Epicurean Texts,' *Anatolian Studies* 48 (1998) 125–170. The full commentary on these new fragments is to be found in the 1998 article, not in the book of 2003.

on a block of marble with a width of 165 cm. and it has 5 columns of text. It discusses matters of theology and religion such as that 'the Epicurean conception of the gods as living a life of complete self-sufficiency and tranquillity and not concerning themselves with our world is beneficial to human beings, whereas the conception of them as beings who created the world and human beings and interfere with our affairs, punishing the wicked and rewarding the righteous, is harmful.'[3] All of this is well-known, of course, but one of the more novel aspects of NF 126 is that Diogenes here attacks the Jews and Egyptians. He states the following:

A clear indication of the inability of the gods to prevent wrongdoings is provided by the nations of the Jews and Egyptians, who, as well as being the most superstitious (*deisid-aimonestatoi*) of all peoples, are also the most disgusting (*miarôtatoi*) of all peoples (NF 126 III 8–IV 1).

Some remarks are in order here.[4] Let me begin by saying something more about the immediate context of the statement within the document itself and then add some observations about the wider context in terms of Greek and Roman views of Judaism. NF 126 belongs to the section on Epicurean physics of which theology was a part.[5] Diogenes here argues that evil-doers apparently are not afraid of the gods, otherwise they would not commit their evil acts. Really righteous people, on the other hand, are not righteous out of fear of the gods but because they have the right set of ideas; it is their ethical convictions that keep them from doing evil. Even ordinary people are righteous, 'in so far as they are righteous' (II 7–8), on account of the laws and the penalties imposed by the laws; and even if some of them do keep away from evil on account of the gods, they form only a handful. 'Hardly two or three (of such) individuals are to be found among great segments of the masses, and not even these are steadfast in acting righteously, for they are not fully persuaded about Providence' (II 13 – III 7). Then follow the lines about the Jews and Egyptians quoted above, and after that a *vacat* indicates the beginning of a new paragraph.

First it has to be said that this remark about Jews and Egyptians has no parallels in Epicurean literature. In spite of the many critical remarks on traditional religious beliefs in the writings of Epicurus and his followers, we do not find

---

   [3] Smith, *Supplement to Diogenes of Oinoanda* 75.

   [4] 'Excavations at Oinoanda 1997,'140–142, has some useful comments on these lines, but Diogenes' remarks deserve closer investigation. For some additional comments see also W. Ameling, *Inscriptiones Judaicae Orientis II: Kleinasien*, Tübingen 2004, 472–477, who reprints part of the new fragment, offers a German translation, and adds two pages of comments.

   [5] See J.M. Rist, *Epicurus. An Introduction*, Cambridge 1972, 140–163; A.A. Long, *Hellenistic Philosophy*, London 1974, 41–49. A good selection of Epicurean texts on the gods is to be found in A.A. Long & D.N. Sedley, *The Hellenistic Philosophers*, vol. 1, Cambridge 1987, 139–149.

such snide remarks on the Jews (or Egyptians[6]), as far as the fragmentary state of preservation of Epicurean literature permits us to see. As both Smith and Ameling remark, it cannot be ruled out that the great Jewish revolt of 115–117 CE in Egypt and the Cyrenaica and also the Bar Kochba war of 132–135 CE had a negative influence upon Diogenes' attitude towards the Jews.[7] That may be the case, but there is no way of confirming that (but see further below). We will now have to take a closer look at the two qualifications of the Jews as both *pantôn deisidaimonestatoi* and *pantôn miarôtatoi*.

As to the use of *deisidaimôn* for Jews, we have to keep in mind the semantic range of that word. As is well-known, *deisidaimôn* has the dual aspect of 'religious, devout' on the one hand, and of 'excessively scrupulous in religious matters, superstitious' on the other.[8] Both the positive and the negative connotations of the word were in evidence already in classical times, as is clearly demonstrated by a comparison of, e. g., Aristotle's use of the term in a context of words denoting respect for the gods (in *Pol.* 5.11.25 [1315a1–3]), and Theophrastus' use of it in a context of words denoting fear and cowardice (in his famous *Character* 16). That the same semantic duality still applied in the period much closer to the time of Diogenes of Oenoanda is proved by, for example, Diodorus Siculus 1.70.8, where *deisidaimonia* is equated to a *theophilês bios* (a god-loving life)[9] on the one hand and Plutarch's critical treatise *Peri deisidaiminias* (*De superstitione*) on the other.[10] The usage in the Jewish historian

---

[6] I will leave the Egyptians out of account here in order to focus on the Jews. I am aware of the risk that, by doing so, I create the impression that Diogenes singles out the Jews for vituperation, which he does not, and the reader is requested to keep this in mind. That both Jews and Egyptians (and others) were often the victims of ethnic biases and stereotypes is well illustrated by G. Bohak, 'The Ibis and the Jewish Question: Ancient "Anti-Semitism" in Historical Perspective,' in M. Mor *et al.* (eds.), *Jews and Gentiles in the Holy Land in the Days of the Second Temple, the Mishnah and the Talmud*, Jerusalem 2003, 27–43. For Greek and Roman criticism of the Egyptian religion see, e. g., K.A.D. Smelik & E.A. Hemelrijk, '"Who Knows Not What Monsters Demented Egypt Worships?" Opinions on Egyptian Animal Worship in Antiquity as Part of the Ancient Conception of Egypt,' in *Aufstieg und Niedergang der Römischen Welt* II 17, 4, Berlin 1984, 1852–2000.

[7] Smith, 'Excavations at Oinoanda 1997,' 142; Ameling, *Inscriptiones Judaicae Orientis II* 474 n. 14.

[8] See the two books of 75 years ago by my fellow-countrymen H. Bolkestein, *Theophrastos' Charakter der deisidaimonia als religionsgeschichtliche Urkunde*, Giessen 1929, and P.J. Koets, *Deisidaimonia. A Contribution to the Knowledge of the Religious Terminology in Greek*, Purmerend 1929. For more recent literature see P.B. Colera, & J.R. Somolinos, *Repertorio bibliográfico de la lexicografía griega*, Madrid 1998, 231. A very useful short discussion is C. Spicq, *Notes de lexicographie néotestamentaire. Supplément*, Fribourg: Editions universitaires – Göttingen 1982, 113–117. By far the most extensive recent treatment to date is D.B. Martin, *Inventing Superstition: from the Hippocrates to the Christians*, Cambridge MA – London 2004.

[9] But Diodorus uses it occasionally also in a negative sense; see Martin, *Inventing Superstition* 79–92.

[10] For references to passages in the works of Plutarch apart from *De superstitione* see Spicq, *Notes de lexicographie néotestamentaire* 114–115, and Martin, *Inventing Superstition*

Flavius Josephus, a near-contemporary of Diogenes, is illustrative in that he employs the word *deisidaimonia* in both senses: for 'religion, system of cultic belief and practice, faithfulness' (referring to the Jewish faith) on the one hand, and for 'religious fanaticism, bigotry, superstition' on the other.[11] Even though the denigrating sense becomes dominant in later antiquity, the positive or neutral sense is still alive in the time of Diogenes. [12]

But in what sense did Diogenes use the word *deisidaimôn*? Contrary to what one would expect, there are no other occurrences of this word (or of *deisidaimonia*) in the extant fragments, so that one will have to take a decision about the sense of the word solely on the basis of this passage. One might argue that a positive sense would enhance the contrast between piety and disgusting or even criminal behaviour. But one might argue as well that it is exactly an extreme scrupulosity in things religious that would lead one to expect that transgressions of generally accepted rules of conduct will be avoided by the persons concerned out of fear of divine punishment. It may be helpful in this respect to cast a glance at Greek attitudes towards Jewish religion and see how the *deisidaimonia* motif is used in the traditions concerning these attitudes.

All the relevant material has been helpfully collected by the late Menachem Stern (of the Hebrew University in Jerusalem) in his massive and magisterial three-volume work *Greek and Latin Authors on Jews and Judaism* (henceforth *GLAJJ*).[13] The first ancient author to be mentioned here is the second century BCE historian Agatharchides of Cnidus who, in order to illustrate the stupidity of all sorts of superstition, mentions the fact that by abstaining from work on every sabbath the Jews once lost the city of Jerusalem during a war because they were unwilling to defend it during the seventh day. He ridicules their behaviour as a glaring case of *deisidaimonia* (*ap*. Josephus, *Contra Apionem* 1.205–11 = *FGH* A86 F20a–b = *GLAJJ* no. 30).[14] About a century later the geographer Strabo castigates Moses' successors (not Moses himself; see *Geogr*. 16.2.35–36)[15] for having introduced a wide variety of superstitious practices, such as circumcision and abstaining from the meat of certain animals (*Geogr*. 16.2.37 = *GLAJJ*

93–108.

[11] See K.H. Rengstorf (ed.), *A Complete Concordance to Flavius Josephus*, vol. 1, Leiden 1973, 418.

[12] See also the material collected in F.W. Danker, *A Greek-English Lexicon of the New Testament and Other Early Christian Literature* (based on W. Bauer), third ed., Chicago 2000, 216.

[13] M. Stern, *Greek and Latin Authors on Jews and Judaism*, 3 vols., Jerusalem 1974–1984. In vol. 3, 156, one finds the references to passages with the *deisidaimonia* motif. The motif of 'Jewish superstition' is discussed also by P. Schäfer, *Judeophobia. Attitudes Towards the Jews in the Ancient World*, Cambridge MA 1997, index s.v.

[14] The same story is also to be found in Josephus, *Ant. Jud.* 12.6.

[15] Contrast Quintilian, *Inst*. 3.7.21: 'Founders of cities are detested for concentrating a race which is a curse to others, as for example the founder of the Jewish superstition [=Moses]' (GLAJJ no. 230).

no. 115). Erotianus, a first century CE glossator of Hippocrates, also mentions abstention from pork as a sign of Jewish *deisidaimonia* in a clearly derogatory sense (*GLAJJ* no. 196). In Plutarch's *De superstitione* the Jews are mentioned twice as examples of a reprehensible *deisidaimonia*: in 3 (166A; *GLAJJ* no. 255) their keeping of the sabbath is singled out as such; in 8 (169C; *GLAJJ* no. 256) it is said that 'because it was the sabbath, the Jews sat immovable in their places while the enemy were planting ladders against the walls and capturing the defenses, and they did not get up but remained there, bound in *deisidaimonia* as in one great net.' In *Stoic. repugn.* 38 (1050E; *GLAJJ* no. 257) the opinions held by Jews and Syrians about gods are categorized by Plutarch as *deisidaimonia*. More instances could be given, but these few may suffice to show that Jewish *deisidaimonia* in Greek eyes was almost always something to be despised or ridiculed. Most of the Greek (and Roman)[16] intellectuals had little or no appreciation for the religious ideas and customs of the Jews; they could see little else than superstition in what they regarded as the excessive scrupulosity that this religion entailed. In their eyes, Judaism was religion carried to its extremes. It is very probable that Diogenes of Oenoanda stands in this tradition.[17]

But why does Diogenes say of the Jews: *pantôn eisi miarôtatoi*? Several earlier authors do state that the Jewish religion is a specimen of *deisidaimonia*, but even so they refrain from describing the Jews in such negative terms as Diogenes does. What is the meaning of *miarôtatoi* here? *Miaros* can be said of anything or anyone stained, defiled, or polluted in the literal sense, but more often it denotes immoral behaviour or it pertains to 'something that [or someone who] violates cultic or moral canons to such an extent as to invite revulsion, [hence] abominable, wretched, foul, depraved, disgusting.'[18] Parker says about the related word *miainô* that 'it can be used for the pollution of a reputation through unworthy deeds, or of truth through dishonesty; justice, law, and piety are in danger of defilement.'[19] The author who emphasizes the motif of the Jews' *miaria* or *miarotês* more than anyone else is the Graeco-Egyptian priest Manetho (ca. 300 BCE). This early representative of Jew-hatred pictures the Jews as originally a bunch of lepers and otherwise polluted (*miaroi*) persons in Egypt who had to be expelled from the country at divine command because they ritually defiled the country, whereafter they founded their rogue-state in and around Jerusalem (*ap.* Josephus, *Contra Apionem* 1.228–252 = *FGH* C609 F10 = *GLAJJ* no. 21). That this anti-Jewish version of Jewish beginnings, a perverted version of the exodus story with a strong emphasis on Jewish impurity and defilement, survived till the

---

[16] For similar Roman views on Jewish *superstitio* see Schäfer, *Judeophobia* 180–195.

[17] This conclusion is corroborated by Dale Martin's observation that since Theophrastus, in philosophical writings *deisidaimonia* is always used in a negative sense; see *Inventing Superstition* 21–35.

[18] See Danker (Bauer), *Greek-English Lexicon* 650.

[19] R. Parker, *Miasma. Pollution and Purification in Early Greek Religion*, Oxford 1983, 3.

time of Diogenes is proved by the spiteful caricature of the Jews and their origins in Tacitus, *Hist.* 5.3–5 (*GLAJJ* no. 281).[20] However, in the development of this anti-Jewish story between Manetho and Tacitus the emphasis is put more and more on the immoral character of the Jews.[21] They are increasingly blackened in a process of demonization that finds its (provisional) climax in the work of the first century CE Alexandrian grammarian Apion.[22] He tells a story about an annual cannibalistic ritual in which the Jews slaughter, sacrifice and eat a Greek who has been fattened for that very purpose (*ap.* Josephus, *Contra Apionem* 2.91–96 = *FGH* C616 F4i = *GLAJJ* no. 171).[23] This utter moral depravity with its extremely disgusting manifestations, a widespread motif in the anti-Jewish literature of Hellenistic and early Roman times,[24] is what justified more than anything else calling the Jews *miaroi*, or rather *miarôtatoi pantôn*. Acts of cannibalism, and eating a Greek at that, proved beyond doubt that the Jews were the most abominable and depraved of all nations, so it was believed.[25] More than one ancient author, therefore, condemns the Jews as the worst possible atheists and misanthropes. Even though the word *miaros* does not occur often in this context, the idea is expressed in a wide variety of other derogatory terms as well. It is highly unlikely, in my view, that Diogenes of Oenoanda was wholly unaware of all this, and for that reason it seems very probable that what he had in mind was exactly the moral depravity of the Jews. This also fits in with the context, in which he speaks about his conviction that the gods do not punish evildoers.

In addition to that, if the above mentioned suggestion that Diogenes' attitude towards the Jews may have been influenced by reports about the war between Jews and Romans and Greeks in Cyrene and Egypt in the years 115–117 has any merits, it may be the following. Less than a century after Diogenes, the historian Cassius Dio relates that the Jews of Cyrene had put a certain Andreas at their head in 115 CE and were destroying Greeks and Romans. 'They would eat the flesh of their victims, make belts for themselves of their entrails, anoint themselves with their blood, and wear their skins for clothing; many they sawed in two, from the head downwards; others they gave to wild beasts, and still others they forced to fight as gladiators' (*Hist.* 68.32.1–2 = *GLAJJ* no. 437). However much of this report may have been exaggerated, as is to be expected

---

[20] On which see now esp. R.S. Bloch, *Antike Vorstellungen vom Judentum. Der Judenexkurs des Tacitus im Rahmen der griechisch-römischen Ethnographie*, Stuttgart 2002.

[21] For a brief sketch of this development see P.W. van der Horst, *Philo's Flaccus. The First Pogrom*. Introduction, Translation and Commentary, Leiden 2003, 18–34.

[22] See the chapter 'Who Was Apion?' in P.W. van der Horst, *Japheth in the Tents of Shem. Studies on Jewish Hellenism in Antiquity*, Leuven 2002, 207–222.

[23] Note that *miaros* often has the connotation of 'defiled by blood;' see Parker, *Miasma* 104–143.

[24] Tacitus, *Hist.* 5.5.1, speaks about the *pravitas* of the Jewish *ritus*.

[25] See Schäfer, *Judeophobia* 58, 203. Also E. Bickermann, 'Ritualmord und Eselskult,' in his *Studies in Jewish and Christian History*, vol. 2, Leiden 1980, 225–255.

of wartime rumors, if even part of this kind of stories had reached the inhabitants of Oenoanda, Diogenes would have seen reasons enough to make his statement about the *miaria* of the Jews. As Smith says, if the news of this revolt 'were fresh in Diogenes' mind when he was writing the present passage, and reports about atrocities, including acts of cannibalism, allegedly committed by the rebels, had been part of the news, this would help to explain his strong words about the Jews.'[26] This becomes even more probable if one takes into account that these war rumors fitted in with a tradition of stereotypes of the Jews as cruel cannibals.[27]

Even though we do not have any evidence of Jewish presence in Oenoanda itself, it should be borne in mind that in the imperial period Asia Minor harboured a great many Jewish communities.[28] Lycia, too, had Jewish communities as early as the second century BCE according to a literary source (see *1 Maccabees* 15.23), and there is also epigraphic evidence for Jews in Lycia, in both Limyra and Tlos, from the early Roman period.[29] So there is some reason to believe that Diogenes had some, even if only a distant, acquaintance of Jews. As we all know from modern experience, 'knowing' some Jews never suffices to rid people of long-standing anti-Semitic stereotypes and prejudices. So even if Diogenes had known Jews himself, it is fully within the range of what is possible that he still regarded them as the most superstitious and abominable of all nations. Nonetheless, it is revealing that such an eminently rational and otherwise sympathetic personality as Diogenes was not able to rise above the level of the worst anti-Jewish clichés of his time.[30]

---

[26] 'Excavations at Oinoanda 1997,' 142.

[27] Pagan critics of early Christianity repeated the same motif; see A. McGowen, 'Eating People: Accusations of Cannibalism Against Christians in the Second Century,'*JECS* 2 (1994) 413–442.

[28] See P.R. Trebilco, *Jewish Communities in Asia Minor*, Cambridge 1991.

[29] All the relevant evidence is collected in Ameling, *Inscriptiones Judaicae Orientis II* 470–480.

[30] The same applies to Tacitus and other ancient (and modern!) intellectuals.

The Shadow in Hellenistic Popular Belief

From cultural anthropologists we learn that it is a well known fact that in many cultures the shadow plays a much more important role than in our modern society, especially in what used to be called 'primitive' cultures, but not only there.[1] The shadow is not so much the place where the light cannot penetrate, so not just *privatio*, but it has a very specific meaning and function of its own: the shadow of a human being or an animal (sometimes also of an object such as a tree) is his/her/its soul, vital power, double, or *alter ego*.[2] It is potent enough to exert a powerful influence upon whom it falls or with whom it comes into contact. One can harm or damage someone if one deals with his shadow violently; and it can be dangerous, or beneficial, if one is 'touched' by the shadow of certain humans or animals. Shadow and life are seen as identical to such a degree that many are afraid of noon time because at that moment one's shadow is at its smallest. When one's shadow disappears, one dies. Many magical practices are based upon this belief. The children's game in which they try to trample upon each other's shadow has its background in this belief (often children's games retain elements of old popular beliefs). In many cultures and among numerous nations, anthropologists have observed this phenomenon and described it, and

---

[1] See J.G. Frazer, *The Golden Bough III: Taboo and the Perils of the Soul*, London 1911 (3rd ed.), 77–100 ('The Soul as a Shadow and a Reflection'); J. von Negelein, 'Bild, Spiegel und Schatten im Volksglauben,' *Archiv für Religionswissenschaft* 5 (1902) 1–37; F. Pradel, 'Der Schatten im Volksglauben,' *Mitteilungen der schlesischen Gesellschaft für Volkskunde* 12 (1904) 1–36; B. Ankermann, 'Totenkult und Seelenglaube bei afrikanischen Völkern,' *Zeitschrift für Ethnologie* 50 (1918) 89–153; M. Bieler, 'Schatten,' *Handwörterbuch des deutschen Aberglaubens* 9, Berlin 1940, 126–142; H. Fischer, *Studien über Seelenvorstellungen in Ozeanien*, München 1965, *passim*; for Western Europe see the chapter 'Ohne Schatten, ohne Seele' in E.L. Rochholz, *Deutscher Glaube und Brauch im Spiegel der heidnischen Vorzeit* I, Berlin 1867, 59–130. One also finds some relevant material in H.B. Alexander, 'Soul (Primitive),' *Encyclopedia of Religion and Ethics* 11 (1920) 727; W. Brede Kristensen, *The Meaning of Religion*, The Hague 1960, 410–1; G. van der Leeuw, *Phänomenologie der Religion*, Tübingen 1956 (2nd ed.), 324–5, 328–9.

[2] I. Lévy-Bruhl, *L'âme primitive*, Paris 1927, 161: "Très souvent, dans les représentations collectives des primitifs, le 'principe vital' ou 'vie' de l'individu ne se distingue pas de son ombre, de son image ou de son reflet (reflection). Les observateurs rapportent constamment qu'au dire des indigènes leur ombre est leur 'âme.'" Bieler, 'Schatten' 127: "Der Schatten gilt einer Person oder Sache als wesentlich zugehörig. Das äussert sich in dem Glauben, der Schatten habe dieselbe Macht zu wirken wie sein Träger, umgekehrt aber widerfahre dem Menschen, was seinem Schatten widerfährt."

also for ancient cultures scholars have been able to point to literary sources which testify to this belief. For ancient Greek and Roman culture, however, the relevant material has never been collected, as far as I know.[3] Some years ago I published a modest collection of this evidence, but that was done from a very specific angle and at a place where classical philologists are not likely to look for it.[4] In this short contribution, I will present this material anew, but now both sifted and with some new material added, and hopefully in a place that is more accessible to classicists and historians of religion.

Let us begin with a series of texts that all deal with the curious topic of the hyena's shadow:[5]

Aristotle, fr. 369 Rose (= Aelian, *Nat. anim.* 6:14): τοῖς κυσὶ δὲ ἐπιτίθεται ἡ αὐτὴ (sc. ἡ ὕαινα) τὸν τρόπον ἐκεῖνον· ὅταν ᾖ πλήρης ὁ τῆς σελήνης κύκλος, κατόπιν λαμβάνει τὴν αὐγὴν καὶ τὴν αὑτῆς σκιὰν ἐπιβάλλει τοῖς κυσί, καὶ παραχρῆμα αὐτοὺς κατεσίγασε καὶ καταγοητεύσασα ὡς αἱ φαρμακίδες εἶτα ἀπάγει σιωπῶντας καὶ κέχρηται ὅ τι καὶ βούλεται αὐτοῖς.[6]

Ps-Aristotle, *De mirab. auscult.* 145: ἐν δὲ τῇ Ἀραβίᾳ ὑαινῶν τι γένος φασὶν εἶναι, ὃ ἐπειδὰν προΐδῃ τὸ θηρίον ἢ ἄνθρωπον, ἐπιβῇ ἐπὶ τὴν σκιάν· ἀφωνίαν ἐργάζεται καὶ πῆξιν τοιαύτην ὥστε μὴ δύνασθαι κινεῖν τὸ σῶμα.[7] Τοῦτο δὲ ποιεῖν καὶ ἐπὶ τῶν κυνῶν.

Pliny the Elder, *Nat. hist.* 8:106 ... *umbrae eius* (sc. *hyaenae*) *contactu canes obmutescere et quibusdam magicis artibus omne animal quod ter lustravit in vestigio haerere.*

Solinus, *Coll.* 27:24 *qui forte si venantes umbram eius* (sc. *hyaenae*) *dum sequuntur contigerint, latrare nequeant voce perdita.*

Geoponica 15, 1, 10 (p. 433 ed. Beckh): ὕαινα φυσικῷ τινι λόγῳ τῇ ἀπὸ σελήνης νυκτερινῇ σκιᾷ τοῦ κυνὸς ἐπιβᾶσα ὥσπερ διὰ σχοίνου ἀπὸ ὕψους κατάγει αὐτόν.

Proclus, *In Rempublicam* I (p. 290 ed. Kroll): καὶ γὰρ αἱ σκιαί, αἷς τὰ εἴδωλα συζυγεῖν φησι (sc. Plato), τοιαύτην ἔχουσι φύσιν· καὶ γὰρ αὗται σωμάτων εἰσὶ καὶ

---

[3] One finds some short remarks in Frazer, *Golden Bough* III (see n. 1); M.P. Nilsson, *Geschichte der griechischen Religion*, München 1955 (2nd ed.), 398 n. 3; E. Stemplinger, *Antiker Volksglaube*, Stuttgart 1948, 182. J. C. Lawson, *Modern Greek Folklore and Ancient Greek Religion. A Study in Survivals,* New York 1964 (=1910), 289. In the great encyclopaedias (e. g., Pauly-Wissowa), however, one will look in vain for an entry on the shadow [*Der Neue Pauly* does not contain one either]. The book by V. Hölzer, *Umbra. Vorstellung und Symbol im Leben der Römer*, diss. Marburg 1965 (typewritten), is disappointing in that the evidence is treated unsatisfactorily and from too rationalistic an angle.

[4] P.W. van der Horst, 'Peter's Shadow. The Religio-Historical Background of Acts V 15,' *New Testament Studies* 23 (1976/77) 204–212. [See now also my entry 'Shadow' in the *Anchor Bible Dictionary* 5 (1992) 1148–1150.]

[5] See also Steier in *Pauly-Wissowa Suppl.* IV (1924) 765.

[6] In *Nat. anim.* 3:7, Aelius draws on the same tradition: κύνας δὲ ἀφώνους ἀποφαίνειν ταῖς ὑαίναις ἡ αὐτὴ πάρεσχε (sc, ἡ φύσις). There is a *varia lectio* here: ... τὰς ὑαίνας ὅταν αὐταῖς τὴν σκιὰν ἐπιβάλῃ.

[7] The text is somewhat uncertain here, but that does not affect the meaning of the passage.

σχημάτων εἰκόνες, καὶ παμπόλλην ἔχουσι πρὸς τὰ ἀφ' ὧν ἐκπίπτουσιν συμπάθειαν, ὡς δηλοῖ καὶ ὅσα μάγων τέχναι πρός τε τὰ εἴδωλα δρᾶν ἐπαγγέλλονται καὶ τὰς σκιάς. Καὶ τί λέγω τὰς ἐκείνων δυνάμεις; ἃ καὶ τοῖς ἀλόγοις ἤδη ζώοις ὑπάρχει πρὸ λόγου παντὸς ἐνεργεῖν. ἡ γὰρ ὕαινα, φασι, τὴν τοῦ κυνὸς ἐν ὕψει καθημένου πατήσασα σκιὰν ἐπιβάλλει καὶ θοίνην ποιεῖται τὸν κύνα.[8]

Timotheus of Gaza, in M. Haupt, *Opuscula* III, Leipzig 1876, 279: ὅτι ἐν σελήνῃ ἐρχομένῃ ἐὰν κυνὸς ὄντος ἐπὶ στέγους λάβηται κάτωθεν τῆς αὐτοῦ σκιᾶς, αὐτὸν καταφέρει ἄνωθεν τὸν κύνα.[9]

Although there are minor variants in this hyena tradition – sometimes the hyena tramples upon the dog's shadow, sometimes it casts its own shadow upon the dog – one nevertheless sees here a more or less uninterrupted chain of traditions on the magical power of an animal's shadow from the 4th century BCE till far into the Middle Ages.

We also have unambiguous testimonies about the powers of human shadows from the Hellenistic and Roman periods:

Ennius, *ap.* Cicero, *Tusc. Disp.* 3, 12, 26 (Thyestes, who has committed a serious crime, says:) *Nolite, hospites, ad me adire, ilico istic, ne contagio mea bonis umbrave obsit. Tanta vis sceleris in corpore haeret.*[10]

Pliny the Elder, *Nat. hist.* 28:69 *magi vetant eius causa contra solem lunamque nudari aut umbram cuiusquam ab ipso respergi* (one should not urinate on someone's shadow).

In the New Testament we find in Acts 5:15 (on the inhabitants of Jerusalem): … ὥστε καὶ εἰς τὰς πλατείας ἐκφέρειν τοὺς ἀσθενεῖς καὶ τιθέναι ἐπὶ κλιναρίων καὶ κραβάττων ἵνα ἐρχομένου Πέτρου κἂν ἡ σκιὰ ἐπισκιάσῃ τινὶ αὐτῶν.[11]

Defixionum Tabellae 190, 4 ff. (ed. A. Audollent, Paris 1904, 249): *Dii inferi, vobis commendo illius membra, colorem, figuram, caput, capillos, umbram, cerebrum, fruntem, supercilia, os* etc.

---

[8] See the short note in A.-J. Festugière, *Proclus. Commentaire sur la République* II, Paris 1970, 98–9 n. 3.

[9] Timotheus is also the source of the *Aristophanis Historiae Animalium Epitome* (ed. Sp. Lambros, *Supplementum Aristotelicum* I, Berlin 1885) 2:320 where we find a very similar story.

[10] See H.D. Jocelyn, *The Tragedies of Ennius*, Cambridge 1967, 421.

[11] In this connection, another passage in the works of Luke deserves our attention as well, although it is not about a shadow of a human being but of God. In Luke 1:35, the angel Gabriel answers Mary's question of how she could become pregnant without a man as follows: πνεῦμα ἅγιον ἐπελεύσεται ἐπὶ σέ, καὶ δύναμις ὑψίστου ἐπισκιάσει σοι· διὸ καὶ τὸ γεννώμενον ἅγιον κληθήσεται, υἱὸς θεοῦ. This is to say that Mary's pregnancy is due to her being overshadowed by God's shadow. For this idea there is no parallel in the immediate 'Umwelt' of the NT, but there is one in ancient Egypt: an old Egyptian text speaks of the seminal emission of a deity's shadow(!); see the text and translation in B. George, *Zu den altägyptischen Vorstellung vom Schatten als Seele*, Bonn 1970, 113–6. See on this text also my essay in *NTS* 23 (1976/77) 204–212.

A curious passage is Dio Chrysostom 67:4–5, because here Dio describes as too ridiculous for words the belief that someone's health and power are dependent upon the length of his shadow, which as a matter of fact is a conception that is current among many nations including the ancient Greeks. He says: εἰ οὖν τις εἴη τοιοῦτος ἄνθρωπος οἷος ζῆν πρὸς τὸ αὑτοῦ σκιάν, ὥστε αὐξομένης μὲν αὐτῆς ἐπαίρεσθαι καὶ μεγαλαυχεῖσθαι καὶ τοῖς θεοῖς θύειν αὐτός τε καὶ τοὺς φίλους κελεύειν, βραχυτέρας δὲ γιγνομένης λυπεῖσθαί τε καὶ ὁρᾶσθαι ταπεινότερος, καὶ τοσούτῳ μᾶλλον ὅσῳπερ ἂν ἐλάττων γίγνηται, καθάπερ αὐτὸς φθίνων, θαυμαστὴν ἄν, οἶμαι, παρέχοι διατριβήν. .... τῆς γὰρ αὐτῆς ἡμέρας ὁτὲ μὲν λυποῖτ' ἄν, ὁτὲ δὲ χαίροι. πρωὶ μὲν ἐπειδὰν ἴδη τὴν σκιὰν ἑωθινὴν πάνυ μακράν, τῶν τε κυπαρίττων καὶ τῶν ἐν τοῖς τείχεσι πύργων σχεδὸν μείζω, δῆλον ὅτι χαίροι, ἂν ὡς αὐτὸς ἐξαπίνης γεγονὼς τοῖς Ἀλωάδαις ἴσος καὶ εἰς τὴν ἀγορὰν βαδίζοι ἂν καὶ εἰς τὰ θέατρα καὶ πανταχόσε τῆς πόλεως ὅπως ἂν ὑπὸ πάντων βλέποιτο. Περὶ δὲ πλήθουσαν ἀγορὰν ἄρχοιτ' ἂν σκυθρωπότερος αὑτοῦ γίγνεσθαι καὶ ἀναχωροίη. Τῆς δὲ μεσημβρίας αἰσχύνοιτ' ἂν ὀφθῆναι ἀνθρώπῳ τινὶ καὶ ἔνδον μένοι ἂν ἐγκλεισάμενος, ἐπειδὰν ἐν τοῖς ποσὶ βλέπη τὴν σκιάν. Πάλιν δὲ περὶ δείλην ἀναλαμβάνοι ἂν αὐτὸν καὶ γαυρότερος φάνοιτ' ἂν ἀεὶ πρὸς ἑσπέραν.[12]

In this context one could also list those texts which, although they do not mention shadows explicitly, express the fear of noon or the midday hour (when the shadow is small), e.g., Lucan, *Phars.* 3:423 ff.; Philostratus, *Heroicus* 1:3; Porphyry, *De antro nymph.* 26; etc.[13]

There are four passages which are sometimes adduced in this connection but of which the interpretation is a matter of debate.[14] These texts all state that (there is a tradition to the effect that) one loses one's shadow the moment one enters the temple of Zeus on Mount Lykaion in Arcadia:

Polybius 16, 12, 7: τὸ γὰρ φάσκειν ἔνια τῶν σωμάτων ἐν φωτὶ τιθέμενα μὴ ποιεῖν σκιὰν ἀπηληγκυίας ἐστὶ ψυχῆς. ὃ πεποίηκε Θεόπομπος, φήσας τοὺς εἰς τὸ τοῦ Διὸς ἄβατον ἐμβάντας κατ' Ἀρκαδίαν ἀσκίους γίνεσθαι.

Pausanias 8, 38, 6: τὸ δὲ ὄρος παρέχεται τὸ Λύκαιον καὶ ἄλλα ἐς θαῦμα καὶ μάλιστα τόδε· τέμενός ἐστι ἐν αὐτῷ Λυκαίου Διός, ἔσοδος δὲ οὐκ ἔστιν ἐς αὐτὸ ἀνθρώποις· ὑπεριδόντα δὲ τοῦ νόμου καὶ ἐσελθόντα ἀνάγκη πᾶσα αὐτὸν ἐνιαυτοῦ πρόσω μὴ βιῶναι. Καὶ τάδε ἔτι ἐλέγετο, τὰ ἐντὸς τοῦ τεμένους γενόμενα ὁμοίως πάντα καὶ θηρία καὶ ἀνθρώπους οὐ παρέχεσθαι σκιάν. Καὶ διὰ τοῦτο ἐς τὸ τέμενος

---

[12] On this passage see Frazer, *Golden Bough* III 87: 'The rhetorician who thus thought to expose the vanity of fame as an object of human ambition by likening it to an ever-changing shadow, little dreamed that in real life there were men who set almost as much store by their shadows as the fool whom he had conjured up in his imagination to point a moral. So hard is it for the straining wings of fancy to outstrip the folly of mankind.'

[13] More passages in W. Drexler, 'Meridianus Daemon,' in W.H. Roscher (ed.), *Ausführliches Lexikon der griechischen und römischen Mythologie* II (1897) 2832 ff. (who, however, proposes a different interpretation).

[14] Nilsson, *Geschichte* I 398 n. 3; also Th. H. Gaster, *Myth, Legend, and Custom in the Old Testament*, New York 1969, 791.

θηρίου καταφεύγοντος οὐκ ἐθέλει συνεσπίπτειν ὁ κυνηγέτης ἀλλὰ ὑπομένων ἐκτὸς καὶ ὁρῶν τὸ θηρίον οὐδεμίαν ἀπ' αὐτοῦ θεᾶται σκιάν. χρόνον μὲν δὴ τὸν ἴσον ἔπεισί τε ὁ ἥλιος τὸν ἐν τῷ οὐρανῷ καρκίνον καὶ ἐν Συήνῃ τῇ πρὸ Αἰθιοπίας οὔτε ἀπὸ δένδρων οὔτε ἀπὸ τῶν ζῴων γενέσθαι σκιὰν ἔστι. Τὸ δὲ ἐν τῷ Λυκαίῳ τέμενος τὸ αὐτὸ εἰς τὰς σκιὰς ἀεί τε καὶ ἐπὶ πασῶν πέπονθε τῶν ὡρῶν.

Plutarch, *Quaest. Graec.* 39 (300C): τὸ μέντοι σκιὰν μὴ πίπτειν ἀπὸ τοῦ ἐμβάντος εἰς τὸ Λύκαιον λέγεται μὲν οὐκ ἀληθῶς, ἔσχηκε δὲ πίστιν ἰσχυράν. Πότερον τοῦ ἀέρος εἰς νέφη τρεπομένου καὶ σκυθρωπάζοντος ἐπὶ τοῖς εἰσιοῦσιν, ἢ ὅτι θανατοῦται μὲν ὁ ἐμβάς, τῶν δ' ἀποθανόντων οἱ Πυθαγορικοὶ λέγουσι τὰς ψυχὰς μὴ ποιεῖν σκιὰν μηδὲ σκαρδαμύττειν.

Finally, a scholion to Callimachus' *Hymn to Zeus* (1:13, p. 42 ed. Pfeiffer): πᾶν ζῷον εἰσιὸν ἐκεῖ (into Zeus' temple) μεμολυσμένον ἄγονον ἐγίνετο καὶ σκιὰν τὸ σῶμα αὐτοῦ οὐκέτι ἐποίει.

In none of these four texts is it stated unambiguously that it was the loss of one's shadow that caused the noxious effects mentioned. It might be, therefore, that we are dealing with two different traditions here, one about the harmful effects of entering this temple of Zeus (death, infertility), another about the loss of one's shadow upon entering this sanctuary. Nevertheless it seems more logical to assume a certain interconnectedness between these two elements, so that what is meant is that the loss of one's shadow consequent upon entering Zeus' temple entailed such disastrous effects as death or infertility. Apparently entering this temple was believed to cause a person to be robbed of his or her vital power. The shadowless creature would, on this showing, be the human being or animal already marked out for death. 'But, if the ultimate explanation of the shadowless precinct on Mount Lykaion lies in the connexion once thought to exist between shadow and soul, it by no means follows that this was the explanation given by the Greeks of the classical period. They may well have forgotten the real meaning of a belief to which they still clung and have attributed it to some irrelevant cause.'[15]

There are some other passages of which it is uncertain whether or not they belong in this context. I refer to those texts which speak of the favourable or unfavourable influence of the shadow of certain trees. Pliny the Elder, *Nat. hist.* 17:18, extensively discusses the qualities of the shadows of various trees, in which the 'Leitprinzip' is: *umbra aut nutrix aut noverca est.* Lucretius, *De rer. nat.* 6:783–5, says: *arboribus primum certis gravis umbra tributa / usque adeo, capitis faciant ut saepe dolores / siquis eas subter iacuit prostratus in herbis.*

---

[15] A.B. Cook, *Zeus. A Study of Ancient Religion* I, Cambridge 1914, 67. See also the discussion by W.H. Roscher, 'Die Schattenlosigkeit des Zeus-Abatons auf dem Lykaion,' *Jahrbücher für classische Philologie* 38 [145] (1892) 701–709 (702: 'hier weicht … der schutzende dämon von der person des gottentweihenden eindringlings und überlässt ihn den schrecken des todes'). It should be borne in mind that many Arcadians regarded Mount Lykaion as the Olympos (Pausanias VIII 38, 2).

One may compare Virgil, *Ecloga* 10:75–6: *surgamus, solet esse gravis cantantibus umbra, / iuniperi gravis umbra, nocent et frugibus umbrae.*[16] In the light of the texts already discussed, it is not implausible that the same magical ideas are in the background here as well, although I am not wholly certain.[17]

There are three other texts that *stricto sensu* do not belong here but do mention a σκιά in an unusual sense. First, *Papyrus Maspéro* II 67188 παραφύλαξόν με ἀπὸ παντὸς πονηροῦ πνεύματος, ὑπόταξόν μου πᾶν πνεῦμα δαιμονίων φθειροποιῶν … καὶ πᾶσα(ν) σκιά(ν).[18] Cf. also *Hippiatrica Berolinensia* 130:135 βοήθημα πρὸς πάθη διάφορα καὶ πρὸς τὸ σκιὰς ἐκ τῶν στάβλων διῶξαι. Probably, in these two cases σκιά means 'evil spirit,' a sense that derives from the designation of the deceased as 'shadows' as found in Homer.[19] The shadow as the (evil) spirit of the deceased has, however, a different background from the shadow concept that is the topic of this article. Finally, there is a curious passage in Philostratus, *Vita Apoll.* 3:15 (on the Brahmans): ὑπαίθριοι … δοκοῦντες αὐλίζεσθαι σκιάν τε ὑπεραίρουσιν αὐτῶν, καὶ ὕοντος οὐ ψεκάζονται, καὶ ὑπὸ τῷ ἡλίῳ εἰσίν, ἐπειδὰν αὐτοὶ βούλονται. It is very hard to imagine what is meant by their raising their own shadow above themselves (as a cover) so that they do not get wet when it rains.[20]

The relevant Graeco-Roman material, as far as it is known to me,[21] has been presented now. It can still be supplemented somewhat from Jewish sources of the Hellenistic-Roman period. The Old Testament has some elements, albeit very few, that seem to reflect the idea of the shadow as power.[22] In most OT passages the Hebrew word for shadow (*tsel*) simply means 'protection,' also when it is used of persons. But when in Num. 14:9 the Israelites are spoken to about the Canaanites, "Do not fear the people of the land, for they are bread for us; their shadow has been removed from them," it probably means that their power

---

[16] Other Latin passages in Hölzer, *Umbra* 61–3. See also Plutarch, *Quaest. Conv.* 3:1 (647F).

[17] But see Pradel, 'Schatten' 29–31, and Bieler, 'Schatten' 129–133.

[18] Quoted from J.H. Moulton & G. Milligan, *The Vocabulary of the Greek New Testament*, London 1930, 578.

[19] E.g., *Od.* 10:495, 11:207. Cf. Pradel, 'Schatten' 3–5.

[20] Another enigmatic passage is Herondas, *Mime* 1:15–6 τὸ γὰρ γῆρας ἡμέας καθέλκει κή σκιὴ παρέστηκεν. Perhaps the idea is here one of a shadow as protective spirit (as in modern Greek folklore; see Pradel, 'Schatten'13–4), for which one can also have fear; cf. the expression 'to fear one's shadow' in Plato, *Phaedo* 101d; Aristophanes, fragm. 77 (more passages in Pradel 13).

[21] [The reader should realize that the search for this material was done in the mid-seventies when the CD-ROM of the Thesaurus Linguae Graecae was not yet available.]

[22] As such the OT does not stand isolated in the Ancient Near East. The role of this shadow-concept in the Babylonian-Assyrian Empires can be seen in the entry *tsillu* in *The Assyrian Dictionary* 16 (1962) 189–192. The Old-Egyptian material has been collected in George, *Zu den altägyptischen Vorstellungen* (see n. 11). All OT passages about the *tsalmawet* (shadow of death) are left out of account here because this expression means 'deep darkness.' See D. Winton Thomas, 'Salmawet in the Old Testament,' *Journal of Semitic Studies* 7 (1962) 191–200.

has gone (although the meaning of 'protection' can definitely not be ruled out; they hang together anyway).[23] At any rate, it is interesting to see that two early Targums (Aramaic Bible translations) translate this passage exactly in this way and hence were familiar with this concept: Both Onkelos and Pseudo-Jonathan render this verse as follows: "Their strength is departed from them."[24]

It is also striking that the LXX version of Job 15:29 (where the Hebrew text is quite unclear) says about the wicked, who will not flourish: οὐ μὴ βάλῃ ἐπὶ τὴν γῆν σκιάν. Here, too, one may surmise that the concept under discussion is in the background.[25] Perhaps a connection between power and shadow is also presupposed in LXX Psalm 139:8: κύριε κύριε, δύναμις τῆς σωτηρίας μου, ἐπεσκίασας ἐπὶ τὴν κεφαλήν μου ἐν ἡμέρᾳ πολέμου. Here one finds almost the same connection between δύναμις and ἐπισκιάζειν that one sees in Luke 1:35 (quoted above). Whether the element of power or rather that of of protection is dominant in passages such as Deut. 33:12 (ὁ θεὸς σκιάζει ἐπ᾽ αὐτῷ πάσας τὰς ἡμέρας), is hard to say.

In rabbinic sources one does not find very much of relevance. In the Mishnah treatise *Avodah Zarah* 3:8, it is said that one is not allowed to sit in the shadow of an Ashera (i. e. a tree that is worshipped as the statue of a female divinity); and in the Gemara (the rabbinic discussion of this passage in the Babylonian Talmud), this topic is elaborated upon (*Avodah Zarah* 48b–49a). But the very same text also states that the one who does sit there does not become ritually impure, which makes it uncertain whether this passage belongs here. Anyway it is striking that in Mishnah *Oholoth* ch. 2 (cf. also chs. 5 and 11) it is said that everyone who is overshadowed by something that also overshadows a corpse, becomes impure; so a shadow can make one impure after all.[26] What makes the difference between standing in the neighbourhood of a corpse in the open air on the one hand and the same situation in a tent on the other is the fact that *via its shadow* the tent creates contact between the person concerned and the corpse.[27]

---

[23] See Gaster, *Myth* 301

[24] See A. Díez Macho (ed.), *Biblia Polyglotta Matritensia. Series IV: Targum Palaestinense in Pentateuchum, L. 4, Numeri*, Madrid 1977, 128–129.

[25] Thus at least Gaster, *Myth* 791.

[26] The underlying principle is formulated as follows by H. Danby, *The Mishnah*, Oxford 1933, 649 note 3: "From Num. 19,14 it is inferred that all (men and utensils) who are under the same tent or roof as a corpse (i. e. a dead human body or a part of it), or who are overshadowed by something which also overshadows a corpse (…) suffer corpse-uncleanness and remain unclean for seven days."

[27] [For further discussion see my essay 'Two Short Notes on Josephus,' in my *Hellenism – Judaism – Christianity: Essays on Their Interaction*, Louvain 1998 (2nd ed.), 60–62. Also J. Finkel, 'The Guises and Vicissitudes of a Universal Folk-Belief in Jewish and Greek Tradition,' in H. A. Fischel (ed.), *Essays in Greco-Roman and Related Talmudic Literature*, New York 1977, 344–365, with some dubious interpretations (but Finkel rightly stresses the Greek influence upon the rabbis in this matter)].

In Talmud Bavli there are passages (*Horayoth* 12a, *Keritoth* 5b–6a; cf. also *Yevamoth* 122a) where it is stated explicitly or implicitly that the loss of one's shadow indicates the loss of one's soul. In the midrashic work *Mekhilta, Wayassa'* on Ex. 15:22, the text says that 'when a viper looks upon the shadow of a flying bird, this bird immediately is whirled around and falls in pieces' (vol. II p. 88 ed. Lauterbach), thus rivaling the paradoxographic accounts in Graeco-Roman literature. Also in the Talmud, *Pesachim* 111b, there is a passage on the harmful effects of the shadow of certain trees, again paralleled in pagan sources (see the passage from Pliny's *Nat. hist.*, above). Though few in number, these Jewish texts do not leave us in any doubt that in ancient Judaism, too, this concept of the shadow as an influential power was well known.[28] The fact that most of the Jewish evidence is from the post-biblical period strongly suggests that Hellenistic influence is at work here.

It would take us too far to also present here the material on shadow concepts in Gnosticism. Suffice it to say that the idea of the shadow as an *alter ego* plays a role here as well; see, e.g., two passages in the *Hypostasis of the Archons* 137,23 ff and 142,11 ff.[29] The Gnostic material, especially in the Nag Hammadi codices, deserves a closer investigation in this respect than is possible here.

The material from Graeco-Roman and Jewish sources presented here has made sufficiently clear that the concept of a shadow as a vital power, widespread as it is all over the world, was also current in the Hellenistic and Roman periods in both pagan, Jewish, and Christian circles.[30]

---

[28] This is confirmed by the NT text in Acts 5:15 (quoted above) which speaks about the beliefs of the inhabitants of Jerusalem. For material in later (medieval) rabbinic texts see J.D. Eisenstein, 'Death,' *Jewish Encyclopedia* IV (1903) 486; also M. Gaster in *Germania* 26 (1881) 210 ff. (non vidi).

[29] See R. Bullard, *The Hypostasis of the Archons*, Berlin 1970, 24–5, 34–5. For some remarks (though insufficient) see J.P. Culianu, 'La femme céleste et son ombre,' *Numen* 23 (1976) 191–209.

[30] The texts cited from Polybius and Plutarch demonstrate that there was also strong criticism of this idea.

The First Atheist

There was a time when the life of human beings was disordered and beastly, and life was ruled by force, when there was no reward for the virtuous nor any punishment for the wicked. It was then, I think, that humans decided to establish laws to punish [wrongdoers] so that justice might rule and be master over crime and violence. And they punished anyone who did wrong. Then, since the laws held public deeds in check and prevented men from open acts of violence, but they committed them secretly, then it was, I believe, that a shrewd and clever-minded man invented for mortals fear of the gods, so that there might be a deterrent for the wicked, even if they act or say or think anything in secret. Hence from this source the divine was introduced [with the claim] that there is a deity who enjoys imperishable life, hearing and seeing with his mind, his thought and attention on all things, his nature so divine that he will hear whatever is said among mortals and be able to see whatever is done. If ever you plot some evil deed in silence, even this will not escape the gods, for they have knowledge.

It was such stories that he told when he introduced this most delightful teaching and hid the truth with a false tale. He said the gods dwell there and placed them where they might make the greatest impression upon human beings, there where he knew that fears come to mortals and benefits also [to relieve] the miseries of life, from the vault on high, where they beheld the shafts of lightning and fearful blows of thunder and star-filled gleam of heaven, the beautiful design of Time, that clever builder, parade-ground for the brilliant mass of the sun and source of rainfall moistening the earth below. Such were the fears with which he surrounded humans and by which this clever man established the deity in the proper place, with a handsome story, and extinguished lawlessness by means of laws. (…) It was thus, I think, that someone first persuaded mortals to believe that there is a race of gods.[1]

This striking atheist manifesto does not come from an 18th or 19th century intellectual, as one might be inclined to expect. No, it is from the second half of the fifth century BCE! As a matter of fact, this text is one of the earliest atheist documents in world history, if not the very first. In this short contribution I want to elucidate the historical context of this text fragment in order to shed some light on a lasting contribution of ancient Greece to modern culture. For, whether one

---

[1] Greek text in H. Diels & W. Kranz, *Die Fragmente der Vorsokratiker*, II, Berlin 1960 (10th ed.), 386–389 (fr. 88B25; henceforth the abbreviation D–K will be used to refer to this work); also, with an improved text, in B. Snell (ed.), *Tragicorum graecorum fragmenta* I, Göttingen 1971, 180–182 (fr. 43F19). The translation is by Ch. H. Kahn, "Greek Religion and Philosophy in the Sisyphus Fragment," *Phronesis* 42 [1997] 247–262, at 247–8 (slightly modified by me); Kahn translates Snell's text. The Greek text consists of 42 iambic trimeters.

rejects or accepts atheism, no one can deny that in the phenomenon of atheism we have received a lasting challenge from classical Athens.[2] For it is in Athens that we have to situate the origin of this fragment and probably also of atheism. I will now sketch briefly the historical situation in which this text came into being.

The author of the text is Critias.[3] Critias was born in the fifties of the fifth century BCE into a family that belonged to the aristocratic circles of Athens.[4] He was a nephew of Plato's mother. Anti-democratic sentiments were part of the family tradition – his father and he himself participated in 411 in the oligarchic revolution of the Council of Four Hundred.[5] The gifted boy received a very good education, with a heavy accent on (the by that time still relatively new) philosophy, and he became a pupil of Socrates and the Sophists.[6] He was also artistically gifted; he played the flute very well. After the fall of the oligarchic council, he managed to stay in Athens for some time thanks to his political shrewdness, but a couple of years later, in 406, he was dragged along in the downfall of his friend, the opportunistic politician Alcibiades, and he went into exile (in Thessaly). After the capitulation of Athens in 404 (the end of the Peloponnesian War with Sparta), he returned to his home town and was even made a member of the governing council of the Thirty, which was presided over by the Spartan conqueror of Athens, Lysander. During the administrative reformation of the city he very soon turned out to be one of the most rabid adversaries of democracy

---

[2] For that reason A. Lesky, *Geschichte der griechischen Literatur*, Bern-München 1963 (2. Aufl.), 393 rightly calls our text "ein geistesgeschichtlich wichtiges Fragment."

[3] Much ink has been spilled over the question of whether or not Euripides was the author of this so-called Sisyphus-fragment since in antiquity some aired that view (see Aëtius I 7,2); on that matter M. Winiarczyk, "Nochmals das Satyrspiel 'Sisyphos'," *Wiener Studien* 100 (1987) 35–45, is very informative. For several reasons this seems unlikely. For a balanced discussion (and refutation) of Euripidean authorship see especially M. Davies, "Sisyphus and the Invention of Religion," *Bulletin of the Institute of Classical Studies* 36 (1989) 16–32. Charles Kahn's recent attempt to defend again Euripides' authorship has not convinced me (see his "Greek Religion and Philosophy in the Sisyphus Fragment," *Phronesis* 42 [1997] 247–262); cf. now also D. T. Runia, "Atheists in Aetius," *Mnemosyne* 49 (1996) 554 (542–576).

[4] One of the most elaborate studies of Critias is still W. Nestle, "Kritias. Eine Studie," *Neue Jahrbücher für das klassische Altertum* 11 (1903) 81–107 and 178–199, reprinted in his *Griechische Studien. Untersuchungen zur Religion, Dichtung und Philosophie der Griechen*, Stuttgart 1948, 253–320; from the same author also *Vom Mythos zum Logos. Die Selbstentfaltung des griechischen Denkens von Homer bis auf die Sophistik und Sokrates*, Aalen – Stuttgart 1966 (reprint of the edition Stuttgart 1942), 400–420; see also M. Untersteiner, *The Sophists*, Oxford 1954, 313–320; B. Zimmermann, "Kritias," *NP* 6 (1999) 851–2.

[5] See, e.g., J. B. Bury, *A History of Greece*, London 1963, 489–493.

[6] The fact that Critias was a student of Socrates was not favourable for the latter in the trial of Socrates in 399. See W. K. C. Guthrie, *Socrates*, Cambridge 1971, 60–63, 94–95. A contemporary called Critias "the layman among the philosophers and the philosopher among the laymen" (fragm. 88A3 D–K).

and he had hundreds of his political opponents murdered.[7] When, in 403, he was engaged in battle with one of them (Thrasybulus) at Mounichia, he himself was killed. He was hated by almost everyone as a calculating, inhuman tyrant with a ruthless personality. In spite of all that, Plato had a great admiration for his uncle (he even named one of his dialogues after him), and Aristotle followed him in that respect.[8]

Critias was also a many-sided and fairly good writer.[9] He composed elegies and wrote philosophical aphorisms and treatises (*inter alia* on epistemological problems), even a work on the nature of love(!), as well as descriptions of the various forms of government (*Politeiai*), and tragedies, too. Of all these works, however, very little has been preserved, only a few dozen of fragments. The fragment translated at the beginning of this article – actually one of the largest we have – comes from Critias' satyr play *Sisyphus*, at least according to the ancient author who quotes it.[10] In Greek mythology, Sisyphus was a shrewd and sly archvillain who often outwitted the gods but even so ended up in Hades, where by way of punishment he had to roll a heavy boulder uphill and every time he had almost reached the hilltop, the boulder rolled down so that he had to start all over again.[11] This is the only fragment we have of Critias' play,[12] so we do not have the context of the fragment and do not even know who the speaker is, although it is not improbable that it is Sisyphus himself who speaks here. Be that as it may, the ideas in the text had been developed and written down by Critias and it is reasonable to assume that they reflect his own convictions.[13] The question that arises then is how it can be explained that someone in the final decades of the fifth century BCE could develop such ideas. What was the cultural context in which such theories about the invention of religion could be developed?

---

[7] In the less than eight months of their terror regime the Thirty killed some 1500 citizens, all of them advocates of democracy; see Nestle, *Griechische Studien* 262 with n. 51.

[8] For references see Nestle, *Vom Mythos zum Logos* 400–401 nn. 5–7, *Griechische Studien* 254 n. 5, and Untersteiner, *Sophists* 316–317. In Xenophon's *Memorabilia Socratis* and *Hellenica*, however, Critias gets a very negative press (e. g.. *Mem.* I 2,12 πάντων κλεπτίστατός τε καὶ βιαιότατος καὶ φονικώτατος ἐγένετο; cf. also *Hell.* II 3,47); see Nestle, *Mythos* 400 n. 4 and *Griechische Studien* 253. Critias' later biographer Philostratus calls him κάκιστος ἀνθρώπων ξυμπάντων (*Vitae sophistarum* I 16). The famous orator Lysias also has nothing positive to say about Critias.

[9] See A. von Blumenthal, *Der Tyrann Kritias als Dichter und Schriftsteller*, Berlin 1923. Cf. also W. Schmid & O. Stählin, *Geschichte der griechischen Literatur* I/3, München 1940, 170–185, and Lesky, *Geschichte der griechischen Literatur* 393–394.

[10] Sextus Empiricus, *Adversus Mathematicos* IX 54.

[11] For references see P. Grimal, *The Dictionary of Classical Mythology*, Oxford 1986, 510.

[12] It is also unknown in which year he wrote the play, although it must have been between 415 and 405 BCE.

[13] P. Decharme, *La critique des traditions religieuses chez les Grecs*, Paris 1904 (repr. Brussel 1966), 123: "Sisyphe (...) avait plus d'une fois exprimé les idées personnelles du poète." Nestle, *Griechische Studien* 279: "... die offenbar seine eigene Überzeugung wiedergeben."

The history of philosophy has from the beginning always been a history of criticism of religion as well. In the writings of almost all Presocratics we find implicit or explicit criticism of the traditional, often all too human conceptions of the gods in Greek mythology and religion.[14] From the sixth century BCE onwards, the gods of popular religion were subjected to a process of drastic re-interpretation by the Greek philosophers, but all these early thinkers maintained one form or another of divine principle. A radical or fundamental atheism is not yet found among them.[15] But when in the course of the fifth century the movement of the Sophists (originally chiefly a rhetorical movement that focused on the art of debating and persuading) began to spread and to be influenced by the Ionian philosophers of nature, matters began to change. The Sophists were not in and of themselves enemies of religion, but their strongly relativizing approach to ethics and law[16] extended also to religion in the long run.

The most famous of the Sophists, Protagoras, became well-known, even notorious, for his book *On the gods* in which the opening sentence already declares that one cannot know whether or not gods exist and, if gods did exist, of what nature they would be, because it is too difficult to find that out and life is too short for it (fr. 80B4 D-K).[17] Here we see already a form of agnosticism that resulted from the insight that had been gained by the Presocratic philosophers to the effect that the traditional gods (and, for that matter, religion) were created by humans after their own image. If the theory of a 'contrat social' which the Sophists had developed on the basis of their philosophical theories concerning the origins and development of laws was extrapolated to religion, which is what we see happen in the fragment of Critias, then the step from an agnostic to an atheistic point of view seems inevitable. It was, however, not a necessary step. For we see that, despite their scepticism and relativism, only very few of the Sophists became radical atheists. Of course that may be due to the fact that possibly many a sceptic was careful not to proclaim his conviction loudly, for a lawsuit based on a charge of *asebeia* was easily incurred, as a number of Athenians had experienced (Anaxagoras, Protagoras, Diagoras, Socrates

---

[14] Decharme, *La critique des traditions religieuses* 39–179. W.K.C. Guthrie, *A History of Greek Philosophy*, vol. III, Cambridge 1969, 226–249; W. Fahr, ΘΕΟΥΣ NOMIZEIN. *Zum Problem der Anfänge des Atheismus bei den Griechen*, Hildesheim 1969, *passim*.

[15] See R.C.T. Parker, "Atheism," *The Oxford Classical Dictionary* (3rd ed.), Oxford 1996, 201, and Kahn, "Greek Religion and Philosophy in the Sisyphus Fragment" 250. Xenophanes of Colophon (ca. 570–470 BCE) combated the polytheism of his day and advocated a doctrine with one god, as did a century later Socrates' pupil Antisthenes, although perhaps these ideas should be seen as henotheistic rather than monotheistic.

[16] See the so-called *physis-nomos* controversy, on which F. Heinimann, *Nomos und Physis. Herkunft und Bedeutung einer Antithese im griechischen Denken des 5. Jahrhunderts*, Basel 1945, is still the standard work .

[17] See Guthrie, *History of Greek Philosophy* III 234–235.

etc.).[18] But we do indeed see that in the last decades of the fifth century unbelief became more widespread in intellectual circles, especially in Athens.[19] The poet Cinesias even seems to have founded a club of infidels who convened on a regular basis in order to ridicule the gods during their symposia,[20] and several Greek authors from the decades around the year 400 make clear that they knew persons who cherish the conviction that gods do not exist at all (see, e. g., Plato, *Leges* X 908b-e). Scholars have also repeatedly pointed at the striking fact that the great historian Thucydides (a contemporary of Critias) banished each and every supernatural element from his historiography, unlike all his predecessors. And his famous fellow townsman, the tragedian Euripides, has always been suspected to have been a crypto-atheist.[21] The comedian Aristophanes did not fail to caricaturize this philosophical-theological modernism, especially in his play *The Clouds* (from 423). If this topic was even raised in such popular stage forms as the comedy, it is clear that atheism was in the air. The political and social circumstances in Athens were conducive to it. The long and devastating war with Sparta, the catastrophic Sicilian expedition,[22] the outbreak of a plague in Athens, and other factors, created scepticism as regards the traditional beliefs, so attacks on these beliefs were well received by many.[23]

It may be clear now that Critias did not write in a cultural vacuum. Even so he differs from his rationalist allies. While Protagoras views religion as a product that has been brought about gradually but inevitably by the imperfect human brain, while Prodicus sees religion as a psychological result of human gratitude for the gifts of life, and while Democritus explains the phenomenon of religion as a consequence of human fear of natural phenomena,[24] Critias takes up a much more malicious and cynical model of explanation.

---

[18] See Nestle, *Mythos* 476–485. Fahr, ΘΕΟΥΣ NOMIZEIN 181–182, enumerates at least 12 lawsuits for *asebeia* between 433 and 350.

[19] See M.P. Nilsson, *Geschichte der griechischen Religion*, vol. I, München 1967 (3rd ed.), 770. P. A. Meijer, "Philosophers, Intellectuals and Religion in Hellas," in H. Versnel (ed.), *Faith, Hope and Worship. Aspects of Religious Mentality in the Ancient World*, Leiden 1981, 216–232. J. N. Bremmer, *Greek Religion*, Oxford 1994, 90–91. R. Parker, *Athenian Religion*, Oxford 1996, 208 with n. 37. Rich bibliography in M. Winiarczyk, *Bibliografie zum antiken Atheismus 1700–1990*, Bonn 1994.

[20] See E. R. Dodds, *The Greeks and the Irrational*, Berkeley 1966, 188–189.

[21] E.g., M. Lefkowitz, "Was Euripides an Atheist?," *Studi italiani di filologia classica* 5 (1987) 149–166.

[22] See Bury, *History of Greece* 466–489.

[23] W. Nestle, *Griechische Religiosität vom Zeitalter des Perikles bis auf Aristoteles,* Berlin-Leipzig 1933, 79–83.

[24] Fahr, ΘΕΟΥΣ NOMIZEIN 92–101. Decharme, *La critique des traditions religieuses* 113–120. On Prodicus especially Guthrie, *History* III 238–242. Democritus' theory was elaborated later by Epicurus and reaches its apotheosis in the great didactic poem *De rerum natura* of the Latin poet Lucretius. But note that Critias' views were criticized in Epicurean circles; see K. Kleve, *Gnosis Theon. Die Lehre von der natürlichen Gotteserkenntnis in der epikureischen Theologie*, Oslo 1963, 104–108.

He views religion as a deceitful invention of a person who wants to keep the masses in check. It is a theory that suits Critias better than other explanations, for *he himself* could have been the deviser of this 'noble lie' (the γενναῖον ψεῦδος of the closing paragraphs of Plato's *Respublica* III) in his antidemocratic mindset and heartfelt disdain for common people. He combined elements of the theories of his predecessors and contemporaries with the cold psychological calculation that was part of his own character. He was someone for whom his aim, the repression of the masses, justified any means. The sly inventor of religion in the Sisyphus fragment almost certainly stands for Critias himself. There is here a unity of life and doctrine that even induced Wilhelm Nestle to speak in this case "von einem in seiner Art harmonischen Ganzen."[25]

Was it indeed Critias himself who thought up this theory on the invention of religion? I raise this question because Wilhelm Nestle has argued that Critias borrowed this theory from Diagoras of Melos. Nestle's reasoning is as follows. Cicero says that "there are people who have asserted that the whole idea of immortal gods was invented by wise men in the interest of the state, so that people who are impervious to reason could be brought to the fulfillment of their duties by means of religion" (*De natura deorum* I 118.)[26] The phrase 'people who have asserted' could of course be a vague reference to Critias and those who share his opinion but it could also be that Cicero has more persons in mind who have formulated such theories. In the immediately preceding paragraph (I 117), Cicero mentions Diagoras of Melos and Theodorus of Cyrene, the two most proverbial atheists in antiquity, the first of whom – like Critias – lived in the second half of the fifth century.[27] One and a half centuries after Cicero, Plutarch writes in a discussion of Carthaginian child sacrifices, "Would it not have been far better for the Carthaginians to have taken Critias or Diagoras to draw up their law code at the very beginning, and so not to believe in any divine power or god, rather than to offer such sacrifices as they used to offer to Cronos?" (*De*

---

[25] *Mythos* 419. Cf. also his *Griechische Studien* 319. In both publications by Nestle on Critias one can discern a somewhat reserved but certainly present admiration for this tyrant who regarded himself as an *Übermensch*. Elsewhere Nestle calls him "ein geborener Herrenmensch" (written in 1944!); see his *Griechische Geistesgeschichte von Homer bis Lukian*, Stuttgart 1944, 195. On Nestle's outspoken sympathy for Nazism see now the revealing opening paragraph in J. N. Bremmer, "Rationalization and Disenchantment in Ancient Greece: Max Weber among the Pythagoraeans and Orphics?," in R. Buxton (ed.), *From Myth to Reason? Studies in the Development of Greek Thought*, Oxford 1999, 71–83.

[26] See the excellent commentary on this passage in A.S. Pease, *M. Tulli Ciceronis de natura deorum libri tres*, Darmstadt 1968 (=1955), 513–4.

[27] The few fragments of their lost works and the ancient *testimonia* about both authors have been conveniently collected in a new Teubner edition by the greatest expert on ancient atheism: M. Winiarczyk, *Diagoras Melius. Theodorus Cyrenaeus*, Leipzig 1981. Theodorus lived sometime between 350 and 250 BCE. The best monograph on Diagoras is still F. Jacoby, *Diagoras ὁ ἄθεος*, Abhandlungen der deutschen Akademie der Wissenschaften zu Berlin 1959:3, Berlin 1959, now to be supplemented by M. Winiarczyk, "Diagoras von Melos – Wahrheit und Legende," *Eos* 67 (1979) 191–213 and 68 (1980) 51–75.

superstitione 12, 171C). Nestle says with reference to both of these passages: "Wenn nun so Critias und Diagoras in der Überlieferung nebeneinander stehen, so werden wir annehmen dürfen, daß sie nicht nur in ihrem Atheismus, sonder auch in dessen Begründung einig waren."[28] Nestle then assumes that Critias has borrowed several arguments from a work by Diagoras with the enigmatic title Ἀποπυργίζοντες λόγοι. 'Entfestigenden Reden' is Nestle's translation. The verb ἀποπυργίζειν does not occur elsewhere, neither does the simplex πυργίζειν, but the related verb πυργοῦν means 'to fortify, defend, fence round,' (litt. 'to surround with towers'). In Nestle's view, the neologism ἀποπυργίζειν must have the opposite meaning, so in this context Ἀποπυργίζοντες λόγοι must mean something like 'destructive arguments' or 'conquering reasonings,' or the like.[29] Another explanation is possible as well, however. Felix Jacoby interprets the expression as "'Fortifying Arguments' – having as their object either mankind or gods and meaning respectively either 'defending mankind by (a wall with) towers' or 'inclosing the gods, hemming them in, blockading them by (a wall with) towers'."[30]

Be that as it may, this much seems to be clear that in that work Diagoras, probably as the first but in any case as one of the very first in history, presented a systematic argument against beliefs in god(s). The work is lost (apart from five lines that do not exhibit any atheism), but on the basis of ancient testimonies about the author (and we have more than hundred of these) we can conclude that Diagoras, because of the total arbitrariness and great injustice in the ins and outs of world history as he saw it, could no longer believe in the governing hand of a deity or of gods and, for that very reason, also not in their existence.[31] His ideas led to an *asebeia* lawsuit against him in 415 in Athens in which, because he had already fled the city, he was sentenced by default and outlawed.[32] Also, a price was put on his head because he was said to have desecrated the Eleusinian mysteries (see Tatian, *Oratio ad Graecos* 27). That Diagoras and Critias knew each other cannot be doubted. For a long time they were fellow townsmen – between 435 and 415 Diagoras spent many years in Athens – and they lived and worked in the same milieus. But that does not constitute any proof that Diagoras was the *auctor intellectualis* of Critias' theory on the invention of religion. It would

---

[28] Nestle, *Mythos* 416.

[29] See also Winiarczyk's edition p. 30.

[30] Jacoby, *Diagoras* 30.

[31] That the riddle of the prosperity of the wicked (the theme of Psalm 73) could in this period bring people to atheism is apparent from fragment 286 of Euripides' *Bellerophon*, on which see Guthrie, *History* III 229, and C. Riedweg, "The 'Atheistic' Fragment from Euripides' *Bellerophontes*," *Illinois Classical Studies* 15 (1990) 39–53. One should keep in mind that in 416 BCE, the total male population of Melos, the island where Diagoras was born, was slaughtered by the Athenian army because the Melians refused to become members of the Attic sea-league led by Athens

[32] H. Dörrie, "Diagoras," *Der Kleine Pauly* I (1975) 1507; Fahr, ΘΕΟΥΣ ΝΟΜΙΖΕΙΝ 89–92; Winiarczyk, "Diagoras von Melos," *passim*.

seem to me that the motives of Diagoras' atheism were different from those of Critias. Diagoras was a deeply disillusioned man, Critias an unscrupulous cynic.[33] Both of them did not believe in the gods, but it is never said of Diagoras in the ancient sources that a politically motivated deceit intended to intimidate the common people played a role in his theory, not even in texts where both men are mentioned in one breath, as in Plutarch (see above).

As far as this first historical generation of atheists is concerned, we can cautiously draw the following conclusions. Even though Diagoras was the first outspoken atheist,[34] it was in all probability Critias who first invented a theory of the origin of religion that was based on a cynical lust for power,[35] an explanation that would play an important part in later history, albeit only after the Middle Ages.[36]

---

[33] I agree with Schmid, *Geschichte* 180 n. 6: "D[iagoras]' Gottesleugnung hatte einen ganz persönlichen Grund, und wie er sich positiv die Entstehung der Religion dachte, darüber wissen wir nichts." Also Guthrie, *History* III 244 n. 3, disagrees with Nestle in this respect. Cf. Jacoby, *Diagoras* 26: "The book of Diagoras was of a purely negative (or, perhaps, we had better say polemical) character, confining itself to attacking the belief in the existence of god(s), and not developing a theory of his own about the origin of this belief."

[34] Winiarczyk, "Diagoras von Melos," is here too sceptic.

[35] Schmid, *Geschichte* 180: "Der erste, der es wagte, nicht im Affekt, sondern in kühler Überlegung die φύσις der Götter in Frage zu stellen, war der Verfasser des Sisyphos." Kahn, "Greek Religion and Philosophy" 259, speaks of an 'atmosphere of moral cynicism' in the fragment of Critias.

[36] See Nestle, *Mythos* 419, *Griechische Geistesgeschichte* 198–199; Fahr, ΘΕΟΥΣ NOMIZEIN 101; and esp. Davies, "Sisyphus" 30–32. One could think of, e. g., Machiavelli, Hume, Gibbon, Holbach and Fichte. On the reasons why atheism could not be developed further in antiquity see J. N. Bremmer, "Literacy and the Origins and Limitations of Greek Atheism," in J. den Boeft & A. H. M. Kessels (edd.), *Actus. Studies in Honour of H. L. W. Nelson*, Utrecht 1982, 43–55, esp. 51–52.

I thank Jan Bremmer (Groningen) and David Runia (Leiden) for their valuable criticisms of the first draft of this article. To Charles Kahn (Philadelphia) I am grateful for sending me a copy of his recent article on the Sisyphus fragment (see note 3).

Subtractive Versus Additive Composite Numerals
in Ancient Languages

1. Introduction

The numeral systems all over the world have the common characteristic that the lowest numbers are referred to by a basic set of (different) words which bear no formal likeness to one another, but which can be grouped in a series in such a way that the minimal difference in meaning between the successive numbers is 'one.' This basic set may run to 'ten' or 'five,' even to 'two' or 'three' only, but once it is exhausted, the universal method to make further numerals is to combine the members of the basic series or to form derivatives of them.

In the Indo-European languages, this procedure starts with numbers higher than 'ten,' or can be shown to have started there in former times, because phonetic change may have blurred the original coherence: 'eleven' and 'twelve' were once derivatives of 'one' and 'two,' but these pairs have phonetically drifted apart. The connection, however, between, e. g., 'six,' 'sixteen,' 'sixty' and 'seven,' 'seventeen,' 'seventy' is clear: Compounds like 'sixteen' have a meaning in which the numerical values of the components 'six' and 'teen' (a variant form of 'ten') have been added together and are therefore termed *additive* numerals, while in the *multiplicative* numeral 'sixty' the value of 'six' is multiplied by 'ten' ('-ty' being originally a variant form of 'ten').

On the other hand, there are languages in which the basic set of numerals is much earlier exhausted. In Wolof, a language spoken in modern Senegal, 'six' is 'five-one,' 'seven' is 'five-two,' etc., 'ten' being a totally different word; and the same holds good of ancient Sumerian.[1]

Addition and multiplication, however, are not the only arithmetical procedures used in forming further numerals from the basic set. A third method is *subtraction*. In Yoruba, one of the languages of modern Nigeria, 'eleven' up to 'fourteen' are referred to by compounds meaning 'one over ten,' 'two over ten' etc., 'twenty' by a new word which bears no likeness to any members of the basic set of numerals, while 'fifteen' up to 'nineteen' are compounds meaning

---

[1] A. Falkenstein, *Das Sumerische*, Leiden 1959, 40–41. The notable instance of languages not having numerals other than the basic set are those of the natives of the Australian Continent. They either count 'one, two, many' or 'one, two, three, many.' See R.M.W. Dixon, *The Languages of Australia*, Cambridge 1980, 107–8, 120.

literally 'five short of twenty,' 'four short of twenty' etc. These latter five are, then, *subtractive* numerals This subtractive procedure is followed not only in 25 to 29, 35 to 39, but also for the uneven tens 50, 70, 90 up to 170, which can be analyzed as 10 short of three times 20, 10 short of four times 20 etc.[2] Just as the additional method, subtraction is in some languages operative already between 'five' and 'ten.' In modern Finnish, the numerals for 'eight' and 'nine' are derivatives of the words for 'two' and 'one' respectively, and are therefore subtractive from the numerical value of 10.

In the modern Germanic, Romance, and Slavic languages, subtraction is not employed, but the English way of indicating the time combines addition and subtraction: 'A quarter past nine' and 'half past nine' are additive, but 'a quarter to ten' is subtractive.

In the following survey of the most important and best known ancient languages around the Mediterranean Sea, we shall also introduce a further distinction between systematical and incidental subtractives, for it is clear that the additive 'twenty nine' is part of the numeral system of the English language, while subtractive expressions like 'thirty less one' and 'one short of thirty' are not.

2. Latin

The numeral systems of the Romans contained both additives and subtractives: *undecim, duodecim* up to *septendecim* on the one hand, and *duodeviginti, undeviginti* on the other; *viginti-unus* up to *viginti-septem*, then *duodetriginta, undetriginta* and so on in the further tens, the highest subtractive actually recorded being *undecentum* (Pliny, *Nat. hist.* 7.214).

The Roman figures used to indicate these subtractive numerals do not normally correspond with the linguistic peculiarity of the latter. *Duodeviginti* is written as XVIII or XIIX (so *CIL* V 4299) which are additions of X and VIII or IIX. *Undeviginti* is XVIIII or XIX (Dessau nos. 1999 and 2000), likewise additions of X and VIIII or IX. An example of a Roman subtractive figure actually reflecting the subtractive value of the numeral for which it stands is IIL for *duodequinquaginta* in *CIL* X 3427. Note that the basic numerals *quattuor* and *sex* up to *novem* are likewise incongruously represented by the subtractive and/or additive figures IV, VI, VII, VIII/IIX, VIIII/IX.[3]

---

[2] E.C. Rowlands, *Yoruba*, London 1969, 106–7. The word for 200 is a new word and not 20 x 10; consequently, 190 is 'ten short of 200.'

[3] This shows by the way the danger of making inferences about the linguistic nature of a numeral system from its graphic representation by numerical symbols. In the same way the Maya figures for 6, 7, 8, 9 are combinations of a horizontal stroke and one dot, two dots etc. The corresponding numerals, however, are four mutually different prefixes which in their turn bear no formal likeness to those for 'five and one,' 'five and two' etc. either; see A.M. Tozzer, *A Maya Grammar*, New York 1977, 98–99.

This rather striking characteristic of Latin, which distinguishes it from most of the other Indo-European languages, is not commented on by Leumann in his historical grammar,[4] although Sanskrit offers a close parallel. For by the side of the additive *navadasa*, 19, there also occurred the subtractive *unavimsatih*, 'twenty less one,' in which *una-* is short for *ekona*, 'less one.' This alternative method could be used for all the tens plus nine up to 99, and has survived, apparently as the only method, in a number of modern Indian languages.[5]

Incidentally, Latin authors used, instead of the additive *undecim* up to *septendecim* and the subtractive *duodeviginti* and *undeviginti*. numerals formed in a different way. As the series 11–19 was in itself heterogeneous, there were attempts to replace the two subtractives (18 and 19) by numerals formed on the analogy of *undecim – septendecim*; and so Livy uses *octodecim* in 39.5.14 (*tetrachma Attica centum octodecim milia*) as does Scaevola in *Digesta* 33.2.37 (*usque dum filia mea annos impleat octodecim*).

The Latin dictionary of Lewis and Short also contains a lemma *novendecim* with references to Livy 3.24 and Livy, *Epitome* 18: *cum annos novendecim haberet*. However, at 3.24 the editions have *undeviginti*, while the 18th periocha does not contain the passage quoted. It is found in the 119th, in which it is said that Octavian was appointed consul *cum XVIIII annos haberet*. The lemma is no longer present in Glare's new *OLD*.[6]

More often the whole series 11–19 was replaced by numerals of the types *decem (et) ...* or *... (et) decem*, both being used, for instance, by Cicero in his *Pro Roscio Amerino* 7.20 *fundos decem et tris* and 35.99 *tribus et decem fundis*. Most probably these numerals were formed in imitation of the compounds with *viginti*, *triginta* etc., such as *viginti et septem ... tabulas* (Cic., *Verr.* 4.123), *septem et viginti* (Plautus, *Merc.* 430), *tres et viginti pondo* (Varro, *De re rustica* 2.4.11). Further instances up to 19 are:

13: *decem tres/tria* in Livy 29.2.17; 37.30.8; 37.46.3; 45.43.5 (at 36.45.3, however, he uses *tredecim*).

17: *decem septemque* in Nepos, *Cato* 1.2; Vulg. 2 Chron. 12.13; *decem et septem* in Vulg. 3 Reg. 14.21; 4 Reg. 13.1 etc.; *decem septem* in a bilingual Latin-Greek inscription from Ephesus of AD 103/4: *sestertia decem septem milia nummum*; the amount is expressed otherwise in the Greek part: δηνάρια τετρακισχείλια διακόσια πεντήκοντα (Dessau no. 7193); *septem decem* in Aulus Gellius 10.28, perhaps quoted from Tubero, *Hist.* I.

---

[4] M. Leumann, J.B. Hofmann & A. Szantyr, *Lateinische Grammatik*, I, München 1963, 293.

[5] M. Monier-Williams, *A Sanskrit-English Dictionary*, Oxford 1964, 221a. Cf. J. Beames, *A Comparative Grammar of the Modern Aryan Languages, to Wit, Hindi, Panjabi, Sindhi, Gujarati, Oriya and Bangali*, Delhi 1966, vol. II, 36.

[6] Ch.T. Lewis & Ch. Short, *A Latin Dictionary*, Oxford 1962 (=1879), 1219b; P.G.W. Glare, *Oxford Latin Dictionary*, Oxford 1982, 1194c, 2092a s.v. *undeviginti* (Livy 3.24.10).

18: *decem et octo* in Caesar, *Bell. Gall.* 4.19.4 (but *duodeviginti* at 2.5); Eutropius 1.1; Vulg. Judices 3.14; 10.8; 20.25 etc.; Luke 13.4, 11, 16.

19: *decem et novem* in Livy 40.40.13; 45.43.5 (he uses *undeviginti*, however, at 3.24.10; 23.46.4; 34.10.4); Vulg. Jos. 19.38; 2 Sam. 2.30; etc. *decem novem* in Caesar, *Bell. Gall.* 1.8; Tacitus, *Hist.* 2.59 (but *undeviginti* at *Ann.* 12.56).

It is difficult to say to what extent the manuscripts represent in this respect the original wording of the authors. During the manuscript tradition, fully written numeral words may have been copied as figures or vice versa, but if the manuscripts were reliable here, our instances seem to indicate that some authors used different types side by side. The reason for doing so may have been their desire of stylistic variation. One passage, however, points rather to the opposite inclination: in 45.43.5 Livy combines within one passage *decem tria, decem et novem* and *viginti et septem*, probably for uniformity's sake, instead of the rather dissimilar *tredecim, undeviginti* and *viginti et septem*.

The new formations did not succeed in supplanting the series *undecim* up to *quindecim*, which have survived, be it in a modified form, in Italian, French, Spanish, and Portuguese, *sedecim* also in Italian and French. Only *septendecim* and both subtractives *duodeviginti* and *undeviginti* are no longer extant in the Romance languages and were definitely replaced by the newer compounds. The Vulgate version of the Bible has *undecim* up to *sedecim*, then *decem et septem, decem et octo, decem et novem*,[7] and in old French likewise *dis e set, dis e uit, dis e nuef* (ca. 1190 CE) occur. Apparently these new formations were not popular for 11 to 15/16; they may have sounded somewhat learned because of their likeness to Greek τρεισκαίδεκα (classical Attic) or δέκα καὶ τρεῖς and δεκατρεῖς (both Hellenistic).[8] It is, however, difficult to say why then exactly *septendecim*, which is no longer present in the Vulgate, was the exception. Only in Rumanian the complete series 11–19 has been given up and replaced by compounds meaning 'one above ten,' 'two above ten' etc., which are, moreover, usually shortened to 'one above,' 'two above' etc.

The replacement of the subtractives for 28, 38, ..., 98, and 29, 39, ..., 99 is certainly to be explained from the analogy of the numerically preceding *viginti-unus* ... *viginti-septem* etc. An instance outside of the Vulgate is present in Seneca, *Epist.* 77.20 (*Sattia*) *quae inscribi monumento suo iussit annis se nonaginta novem vixisse*, whereas *undecentum* is used once by his contemporary

---

[7] *Duodeviginti* at 2 Sam. 8.13 is present only in the edition of the Abbey of St. Jerome (*Biblia sacra iuxta latinam vulgatam versionem ad codicum fidem cura et studio monachorum Pont. Abbatiae S. Hieronymi in urbe*, Rome 1926–1972). The Sixto-Clementina has *decem et octo*; see B. Fischer, *Novae concordantiae ...*, Stuttgart – Bad Cannstatt 1977, 1669.

[8] E. Schwyzer & A. Debrunner, *Griechische Grammatik*, München 1968 (4th ed.), 594; F. Blass & A. Debrunner, *Grammatik des neutestamentlichen Griechisch*, Göttingen 1965 (12th ed.), § 63.

Pliny the Elder (*Nat. hist.* 7.214). The Vulgate does not contain any subtractives between 20 and 100.[9]

Another kind of subtractives could be used when one wanted to express that a specific number, usually a 'round number,' that is a multiple of tens, was almost but not wholly involved. These were no compounds but word groups as appears from the varying order of the constituent elements, and consisted of (a) the numeral not attained, (b) the word *minus*, and (c) a second numeral expressing the shortage.

A well-known instance is found in the Vulgate version of Paul's Second Letter to the Corinthians 11.24: *A Iudaeis quinquies quadragenas una minus accepi*, 'Five times I have received at the hands of the Jews the forty [lashes] less one.' As this instance goes back via the Greek to a Hebrew-Aramaic expression ensuing from a rather specific motive, it will be discussed below in § 5.2. Ovid, however, offers a less complex example in *Met.* 12.553–5, where Nestor, the son of Neleus, relates that his eleven brothers had all been killed by Hercules, but does so as follows:

Bis sex Nelidae fuimus, conspecta iuventus!
Bis sex Herculeis ceciderunt me minus uno
Viribus

This is a poetical way of saying what Apollodorus elsewhere phrased in prose as: 'He killed Neleus and his sons, except Nestor' (*Bibl.* 2.7.3.). The phenomenon can be paralleled by many modern instances. But why is it done? Because psychologically it is not the same to say 'ninety-nine' or 'a hundred less one.' The former is certainly less impressive, as shopkeepers know by instinct that an article sells more easily at the price of 99 cents than for one dollar.[10] For that reason alone it is less correct to translate the passage from Paul quoted above as the New English Bible does: 'Five times the Jews have given me *thirty-nine* strokes'; but see § 5.2.

3. Greek

About the numerals in the oldest Greek that we have – Mycenaean – nothing can be said because in the Linear B script all numbers (and there are many of them) are written in figures. As soon as numbers were written as words, that is in Homer, it appears that there are additives for numbers between tens, not only for the lower up to 'seven and ...' (ἕνδεκα *Il.* 2.713; δώδεκα *Il.* 1.25; δυώδεκα *Il.* 2.637; δυοκαίδεκα *Il.* 2.557; ἐκκαιδεκάδωρος *Il.* 4.109; ἑπτὰ δὲ καὶ δέκα *Od.* 5.278; ἓν καὶ εἴκοσι *Il.* 2.748; πίσυρές τε καὶ εἴκοσι *Od.* 16.249; etc.), but also

---

[9] See Fischer, *Novae concordantiae* 1669 and 5293.
[10] See the remarks by J. Gonda, 'Varia over indonesische telwoorden,' *Bijdragen tot de taal-, land- en volkenkunde* 109 (1953) 25–27.

for those that contain 'eight and ...,' 'nine and ...' (ὀκτωκαιδεκάτη *Od.* 5.279; ἐννεακαίδεκα *Il.* 24.496). Perhaps the latter instance should be read as ἐννέα καὶ δέκα since one may indeed ask the question whether composite cardinals in Homer are compound words already or word groups yet. Passages like *Od.* 5.278–9 (ἑπτὰ δὲ καὶ δέκα μὲν πλέεν ἤματα ποντοφορεύων, ὀκτωκαιδεκάτη δ᾽ ἐφάνη ὄρεα σκιόεντα) rather seem to indicate the latter (cf. *Od.* 16.249).

Subtractives are, on the other hand, wholly lacking in Homer, and so likewise in Hesiod, Pindar, the Tragedians, and Aristophanes. This does not imply, however, that they did not exist, because poets abandon sometimes the current ways of expressing numbers by using circumscriptions. Hesiod, for instance, uses τρισεινάδα, '27th day,' instead of ἑπτακαιεικοστήν (*Op.* 814; cf. τρεισκαιδεκάτην *Op.* 780). Aeschylus paraphrases τριακόσιαι by τριακάδας δέκα and διακόσιαι καὶ ἑπτά by ἑκατὸν δὶς ἑπτά θ᾽ (*Pers.* 339, 343). So when Pindar uses τεσσαράκοντα καὶ ὀκτώ (*Pyth.* 9.113), this may be the numeral he used in his spoken language, but it is also possible that he has rephrased here a subtractive numeral, and the same may be said here for Homer's ἐννεακαίδεκα (*Il.* 24.496), for as soon as we turn to prose writers it appears that subtractive numerals did exist as well.

If we leave aside subtractive expressions which contain indefinite elements, such as '1000 drachmae but for a trifle' (Isaeus 11.43), 'all but one' (Herodotus 1.202), 'all but a few' (Plutarch, *Caesar* 30.3), we may discern within the exact subtractions three types which differ a little in meaning:

(A) pure subtractives: 'forty ships less one': the things subtracted and those from which they are subtracted belong to the *same* kind.
(B) impure subtractives: 'three drachmae less two obols': the things subtracted are of a *different* kind.
(C) combinations of A and B: e. g., Herodotus 9.30 ἕνδεκα μυριάδες ἦσαν, μιῆς χιλιάδος πρὸς δὲ ὀκτακοσίων ἀνδρῶν δέουσαι, 'there were eleven myriads of men less one thousand and eight hundred.' This subtraction is pure because ultimately men are subtracted from men, but impure because formally a chiliad is subtracted from myriads which are different things, although the whole is semantically equivalent to '110.000 less (1.000 + 800).'

In the majority of the cases, except those of class B, the subtracted numeral (e. g. 2) is smaller than the one that otherwise would have had to be added (8 in this case). Only once, in '300 less 8' (Thucydides 4.38.5), is the subtracted number larger, and in '120 less 5' (Diodorus Sic. 13.14.4) the numbers would be equal. In all cases, however, the speaker/author takes care to mention provisionally a round number which is higher than the one he would have mentioned otherwise, according to the additive method, that is. But this does not imply that in the sentence the round number always precedes the subtracted number. Both orders occur: in Aristotle, *Rhet.* 2.14.4 περὶ τὰ ἑνὸς δεῖν πεντήκοντα (sc. ἔτη) the round number follows the small subtracted one.

Formally, that is, according to the terminology which is used, the subtractives show the following diversity:

1. Verbs (ἀπο-, κατα-)δεῖν, almost always a participle with the shortage in the genitive case, e.g. Plutarch, *Pomp.* 79.4 ἑξήκοντα μὲν ἑνὸς δέοντα βεβιωκὼς ἔτη. Aristotle, *Rhet.* 2.14.4, quoted above, is the only instance of an infinitive construction.
2. Verb δεύειν: Apollonius Rhod. 2.974–5 τετράκις εἰς ἑκατὸν δεύοιτό κεν εἴ τις ἕκαστα πεμπάζοι (sc. ῥέεθρα), 'four times would one miss in a hundred if one would count each of the streams.'
3. Verbs (ἀπο-)λείπειν, participles, but in different constructions. With genitive in Diodorus Sic. 13.14.4 τριήρεις μὲν ἐπλήρωσαν πέντε λειπούσας τῶν ἑκατὸν εἴκοσι, 'they manned triremes five missing of the 120' (the same in Isocrates 12.270 γεγονὼς μὲν ἔτη τρία μόνον ἀπολείποντα τῶν ἑκατόν). With dative in Josephus, *Ant.* 4.238 πληγὰς μιᾷ λειπούσας τεσσαράκοντα, litt. '40 stripes falling short by one' (the same in *Ant.* 4.248).
4. Preposition πλήν· Herodotus 1.202 τὰ πάντα πλὴν ἑνός.
5. Preposition παρά with accusative: Paul, 2 Cor. 11.24 ὑπὸ Ἰουδαίων πεντάκις τεσσεράκοντα (sc. πληγὰς) παρὰ μίαν ἔλαβον, 'five times I have received at the hands of the Jews the forty (lashes) less one.' Although this passage will be dealt with in a special paragraph (5.2) because of its Jewish background – together with Josephus, *Ant.* 4.238 and 248 quoted above – some remarks are to be made here as to the way it is treated in Walter Bauer's lexicon to the New Testament.[11] The parallel material there adduced consists of quotations from classical authors which are *impure* examples because 'days' are subtracted from 'years' etc. (Herodotus 9.33; Josephus, *Ant.* 4.176; P.Oxy. 264.4 [see below]); or there are no definite cardinal numerals involved (Plutarch, *Caes.* 30.3; see above). Of course, they do illustrate the use of παρά in subtractive constructions, but there is a better parallel which matches Paul's wording in every respect: Cassius Dio 58.20.5 τῷ γοῦν ἐπιόντι ἔτει,(…), πεντεκαίδεκα στρατηγοὶ ἐγένοντο· καὶ τοῦτο καὶ ἐπὶ πολλὰ ἔτη συνέβη, ὥστε ἔστι μὲν ὅτε ἑκκαίδεκα, ἔστι δ' ὅτε παρ' ἕνα ἢ καὶ δύο χειροτονεῖσθαι, 'next year there were 15 praetors, (…), and for many years the following also happened, (namely) that at one time 16 praetors but at another time one or even two fewer were chosen.' A comparable remarks is made by Dio at 59.20.5, but there it runs: ἔστι δ' ὅτε ἑνὶ πλείους ἢ καὶ ἐλάττους.

With regard to the motivation of the subtraction, the different kinds that we distinguished above (indefinite, pure, impure, combined) are not alike. The cases in which either the round number or the subtracted number or both are rendered by an indefinite numeral or adjective are always clearly motivated: 'all but a few' (Plutarch, *Caes.* 30.3), 'one thousand drachmae but for a trifle' (Isaeus 11.43), 'fifteen talents but for a trifle' (Lysias 19.43), 'not much short of ninety years' (Polybius 12.16.13). In these latter three the shortage is considered to be so insignificant that it is not deemed worth to be specified.

Likewise, when dissimilar things are subtracted (class B), these things are always in themselves relatively small fractions of the units from which they are

---

[11] W. Bauer, *Griechisch-Deutsches Wörterbuch zu den Schriften des Neuen Testaments*, Berlin 1958 (5th ed.), s.v. παρά. English version in W. Bauer, W.F. Arndt, F.W. Gingrich, F.W. Danker, *A Greek-English Lexicon of the New Testament*, Chicago & London 1979.

subtracted, so that the motivation of the subtraction is self-evident. Herodotus 2.134 'He (Pharaoh Mycerinus) left a pyramid as well but one much smaller than that of his father (Cheops); each of its sides falls 20 feet short of three plethora (*i. e.* 300 feet).' Josephus, *Ant.* 4.176 'When forty years but for thirty days had passed, …' Especially in Graeco-Egyptian accounts and contracts on papyrus these subtractions – usually by παρά with accusative – are very frequent: 'I agree that I have sold to you the weaver's loom belonging to me measuring three weaver's cubits less two palms' (P.Oxy. 264.2–4; 54 CE); this cubit, γερδιακὸς πῆχυς, probably equalled five palms.[12] The method is almost normal in the Byzantine period in prices expressed in (x) νομίσματα (χρυσοῦ) παρὰ (y) κεράτια, '(x) golden solidi less (y) siliquae' (i. e. 1/24 solidus), of which Preisigke listed selection-wise over a hundred instances.[13] The *keration* was both a coin and a weight, and at least in a number of these cases the subtraction is not so much motivated by the wish to mention an amount in round numbers as by the fact that nominally the number of solidi was correct indeed but that these golden coins through abrasion no longer had their correct weight. This appears from P.Cairo Masp. 70.2 which contains the line, 'the solidi were found to be seven keratia less' (6th cent. CE).

A very special instance of dissimilar subtraction, also quoted by Bauer, is Herodotus 9.33 ἀσκέων δὲ πεντάεθλον παρὰ ἕν πάλαισμα ἔδραμε νικᾶν Ὀλυμπιάδα. At first sight this seems to suggest that the man won in four events (jumping, running, throwing the discus and the javelin) but lost in the wrestling and hence was no Olympic victor. The parallel version in Pausanias 3.11.6–8, however, states clearly that he (Teisamenos) had won in two events (running and jumping), which implies that his opponent (Hieronymus) had won in the other two. On the other hand, it is known that in the final event, the wrestling, one had to be floored thrice to be the looser, and since *palaisma* also means 'wrestling bout' the meaning of the whole is not so much that he won in two events, like his opponent, and lost in the final one, but rather that he won in two events and two wrestling bouts, like his opponent, but lost only the third decisive wrestling bout.

The passages in which numerical substantives are subtracted from numerical substantives or from numerals (class C) are formally not different from the kind which we have just discussed, but as, for instance, μία χιλιάς and χίλιοι are semantically hardly different, we shall discuss these cases together with the pure subtractions (class A).

The motivation of the following subtractions of small numbers from large numbers in classes A and C seems evident, also to our modern mind: 110.000 but for 1.800 (Herodotus 9.30); 20.000 less 2.000 (Dionysius Halic. 7.3.2.);

---

[12] That is, if it was the same as the linen weaver's cubit; see F. Preisigke, *Fachwörter des öffentlichen Verwaltungsdienstes Ägyptens*, Göttingen 1915, 118.

[13] F. Preisigke, *Wörterbuch der griechischen Papyrusurkunden* …, vol. 3, Berlin 1931, 348a–b.

10.000 less 300 (Thucydides 2.13.3.); 1.500 less 15 (Herodotus 2.7); 300 less 8 (Thucydides 4.38.5); 160 less 2 (Aristotle in Diogenes Laert. 5.27); 130 less 2 (Herodotus 1.130); 120 less 5 (Didodorus Sic. 13.14.4); 100 less 4 (Apollonius Rhod. 2.974–5); 100 less 3 (Isocrates 12.270).

The most natural motivation is, of course, always that one which is provided by the context itself, as in Herodotus 9.70, 'the Greeks were in a position to kill in such a way that of the 300.000 men of the (Persian) army – less the 40.000 with whom Artabazus had fled – not even 3.000 of the remaining soldiers survived.' The above quoted instance of '130 less 2' (Herodotus 1.130), although its motivation seems clear, may nevertheless belong rather to the category with which we will deal now, that of 'tens less two/one.' For although the total number of occurrences is rather small, Herodotus – in compound numerals above 20 – appears to have a slight predilection for using subtractives with 'less two/one,' of which he has nine instances,[14] instead of additives with 'and eight/nine' which he uses only five times. If we assume the subtractives to be the rule here, we can offer reasonable explanations for at least four out of these five 'additive exceptions.'

Two of the occurrences of ὀκτὼ καὶ εἴκοσι ἔτεα (1.106; 4.1) happen to refer to the same span of time in history, to wit the number of years that the Scythians were ruling in the Near East. In 1.106, where he mentions those 28 years for the first time, he expresses them by an additive numeral because their mention happens consciously in anticipation of 4.1 – the first paragraph of his *Logos Skythikos* – where the 28 years will get a very specific illustration. He mentions these years twice there, first by using the subtractive ἔτεα δυῶν δέοντα τριήκοντα, with the reference ὡς καὶ πρότερόν μοι εἴρηται back to 1.106, next by using again the additive ὀκτὼ καὶ εἴκοσι ἔτεα, and telling us what was so curious about these years, namely that the Scythian wives, who had stayed at home, had meanwhile had intercourse with their slaves and given birth to a new generation of men; and when the Scythians returned from Asia, they were met by an army consisting of these young men. The alternating use of subtractive and additive constructions here is no coincidence; note also the shift in the position of the substantive ἔτεα in these three phrases. A comparable situation is present in 6.27, where he tells that the inhabitants of Chios had sent a company of a hundred young men to Delphi of whom only two returned. Next he goes on to explain what had happened to the ἐνενήκοντα καὶ ὀκτώ, an additive construction because the subtractive is already implied in the foregoing. These cases then betray a reluctance to repeat identical expressions, which is certainly also responsible for the varying order of τεσσεράκοντα καὶ τριηκόσια καὶ χίλια ἔτεα versus μυρίοισί τε ἔτεσι καὶ χιλίοισι καὶ πρὸς τριηκοσίοισί τε καὶ τεσσεράκοντα in 2.142, and of ἑξήκοντα καὶ τριηκόσιοι versus τριηκόσια καὶ ἑξήκοντα in 3.90. In short, it seems that in the context of

---

[14] 1.14, 16, 130, 214; 2.157; 4.1, 90; 5.52; 6.57.

these subtractives it is stylistic variation that was responsible for the use of the additives.

In 7.186, however, this explanation does not work. We read there that the total number of the Persian army resulting from the foregoing addition amounted to πεντακοσίας τε μυριάδας καὶ εἴκοσι καὶ ὀκτὼ καὶ χιλιάδας τρεῖς καὶ ἑκατοντάδας δύο καὶ δεκάδας δύο ἀνδρῶν, or 5.283.220 men. Although it would have been possible to use here καὶ δυῶν δεούσας τριάκοντα, this subtraction is probably avoided because the result would not be a round number – as in 9.30 – since there are still three additions to be made here. No explanation at all can be given for 8.48 ἀριθμὸς δὲ ἐγένετο ὁ πᾶς τῶν νεῶν, πάρεξ τῶν πεντηκοντέρων, τριηκόσιαι καὶ ἑβδομήκοντα καὶ ὀκτώ. The exception introduced by πάρεξ did certainly not prevent the subtraction here because πάρεξ and subtraction are found together elsewhere (1.130); this passage must remain an exception.[15]

With '18,' however, the usage seems to be the opposite of the foregoing: Herodotus uses six times ὀκτωκαίδεκα,[16] while δυῶν δέοντα εἴκοσι is found only once (1.94). Neither the additives nor the subtractives seem to be used for a special reason, except perhaps ὀκτωκαίδεκα σταδίους ἢ εἴκοσι in 1.126, where variation may have been the reason for suppressing another εἴκοσι (δυῶν δέοντας).

In the work of his younger contemporary Thucydides, the use of subtractives is still more pronounced. Additives with 'eight' or 'nine' are not found at all, and instead subtractives with 'two' or 'one' are used eleven times, six of which are '20 less two/one;'[17] '300 less 1' (in 4.102.3) is of course an instance which is very clearly motivated.

Further instances from prose are: Hippocrates, *Aff.* 9 and *Loc. hom.* 6, both '20 less 2;' *IG* I 374.405–17 (=*CIA* I 325) '20 less 1,' '30 less 1,' although the figures added have an additive structure; Xenophon, *Hell.* 1.1.5 '20 less 2,' although on the basis of Thuc. 8.108.1–2 one would expect here '22' instead, so there may be an error here; Xenophon has ὀκτωκαίδεκα in *Anab.* 3.4.5 and 7.4.16; Plato, *Leg.* 5, 738a has '670 less 1,' but ὀκτωκαίδεκα in *Leg.* 2, 666a and 8, 833d (the latter, however, in the close vicinity of εἴκοσι; cf. on Herodotus 1.126 above); Aristotle, *Rhet.* 2.14.4 (1390b10–1) '50 less 1,' *Hist. anim.* 3.20 (522a30–1) '20 less 1,' *Polit.* 5.9.23 (1315b36) δυοῖν δέοντα εἴκοσι is preceded in the same paragraph by ὀκτωκαίδεκα (cf. Herodotus 4.1. above); Plutarch, *Pomp.* 79.4 '60 less 1.'

As compared to the language of the poets, in which as far as '18' and '19' are concerned additive constructions occur right from the start and subtractives are absent, it is a remarkable fact that so many of the latter are found in prose, and

---

[15] Herodotus 3.89: 70 <+ 8> μνέας has been left out because it is a conjecture; it rather had to be <8 +> 70; cf. J. Enoch Powell, *A Lexicon to Herodotus*, Hildesheim 1960, 100 *s.v.* εἴκοσι.

[16] 1.126; 2.100, 111, 175; 3.50; 8.1; the numeral for 19 does not occur.

[17] 5.16.3; 7.31.4; 7.53.3; 8.6.5; 8.17.3; 8.102.1; the remaining are found at 2.2.1; 5.68.3; 8.7.1; 8.25.1.

that some of the additive competitors can be shown to occur there in stylistic opposition to subtractives.

This raises, of course, the question of which of the two is to be considered to represent the more original situation. In view of the rather low frequency of additives for '18' and '19' etc., one wonders at least why so many grammars in their survey tables of the numerals suggest that addition was the norm here and subtraction the exception. Only Jannaris presents both as equivalent possibilities for older Greek,[18] but adds that subtraction formed no part of the spoken language.[19]

Especially with regard to subtractions from lower tens such as '20' and '30,' of which the motivation is no longer apparent in contexts where much higher numbers play a role, we may also reckon with the possibility that in prose some of them were replaced in the course of the long manuscript tradition, first by figures which were later reworded as additives, or immediately by the latter. This assumption seems quite plausible in view of the variation of numeral versus figure which occurs, for instance, in the manuscripts of the Greek New Testament.

An intermediate stage is to be seen in *IG* I 374, in which the subtractions '20 less 1' and '30 less 1' are accompanied by figures which in Greek always have an additive structure. For that reason we believe that some cases of ὀκτωκαίδεκα and ἐννεακαίδεκα in earlier prose are not original but due to the replacement process just sketched, either immediately or indirectly via the stage of figure notation. Only when a subtractive was motivated, as in 2 Cor. 11.24, could it resist such a rewording, and at best the higher numeral was written as a figure, in this case in mss. F and G: μ̄ παρὰ μίαν. In other cases, however, replacements are not exceptional in the New Testament. At John 5.5, the readings of the numeral vary between τριάκοντα καὶ ὀκτώ, τριάκοντα ὀκτώ, and λη´, and instead of the frequent δώδεκα, some mss. have δεκαδύο at Luke 9.17, Acts 19.7; 24.11 etc.[20]

Although this cannot be proved by textual variants, it seems not farfetched to assume that in early prose these lower subtractives were slightly more frequent than it appears from the present state of the mss., also because the uncial (stage of the) tradition of these works must have been twice as long as that of the New Testament writings.

With regard to the subtractives in Classical Attic, Jannaris remarks: 'This clumsy circumlocution was hardly proper to popular speech even in A [*i. e.*, Classical Attic] times. As a matter of course it is unknown to N [*i. e.*, Neohel-

---

[18] A.N. Jannaris, *An Historical Greek Grammar Chiefly of the Attic Dialect*, Hildesheim 1968 (= 1898) §§ 642, 643, 645 (pp. 172–3).

[19] *Historical Greek Grammar* § 643.

[20] Xenophon has the Koine form δέκα πέντε only in *Anab.* 7.8.26, elsewhere he uses πεντεκαίδεκα (4.7.16 etc.). *Anab.* 7.8.25–6, however, is generally considered to be an appendix added by a later editor.

lenic].'[21] This conclusion does not seem to follow with necessity from the facts as described above and is therefore not very convincing. It is equally well possible that the use of subtractives for '18,' '19' etc. was the original situation which was kept up in the everyday spoken language and in prose up to the beginning of the fourth century BCE, parallel to the situation in Latin up to the Principate.

The motivation for these subtractions from 20 may originally have been the same as that illustrated above for other numerals. In a very simple society, '20' may have been at first a relatively high number; not many persons owned that much cattle. But '20' lost this connotation, of course, as soon as situations arose in which higher numbers were involved. The subtractives once formed may have persisted for a very long time, as Latin shows.

The spoken language as well as prose writing was probably much more conservative in this respect than the poets, who can be shown to have been innovative in specific areas of style and language. They increased, for instance, their means of varying their usage by admitting elements from other dialects, such as Aeolic πίσυρες by the side of Ionic τέσσαρες, and they were also responsible for the birth of many new compounds, like those beginning with ποικιλο-, etc. They may have been the first to replace the 'clumsy' subtractives, and then it is no coincidence that, for all we know, the first additives with '8' and '9' occur in poetry: τεσσεράκοντα καὶ ὀκτώ in Pindar, *Pyth.* 9.113 (474 BCE), and ἔννεα καὶ δέκα in Homer, *Il.* 24.496.

The gradual substitution of the subtractives, which is halfway in Herodotus, would then be comparable to what happened to the ordinal numerals. In the Attic inscriptions up to the time of Augustus,[22] the compound ordinals consisted of two ordinals with intervening καί: τρίτος καὶ δέκατος, 'thirteenth.' This, too, is a rather 'clumsy' way of formulating, which again had its exact parallel in Latin *tertius decimus* etc. and was henceforward substituted by the type τρεισκαιδέκατος. This latter type, however, was already used by Homer, *Od.* 5.279 ὀκτωκαιδεκάτη. Herodotus made use of both types, at least according to the mss. tradition: in 3.93–4 he has in a series the ordinals from τρίτος καὶ δέκατος up to εἴνατος καὶ δέκατος, but elsewhere τεσσερεσκαιδέκατος (1.84) and ἑκκαιδέκατος (2.143 twice). Thucydides likewise has the double ordinals, nine times,[23] and ἑπτακαιδέκατος only twice, at 4.101.1 and 7.28.3, but here several editions nevertheless read ἑβδόμη καὶ δεκάτη and ἑβδόμῳ καὶ δεκάτῳ, just as elsewhere, following Krüger's conjecture; these two exceptions may indeed be due to later copyists. So if we assume that the 'clumsy' double ordinal type was the original construction which was kept up in the spoken language, in prose

---

[21] *Historical Greek Grammar* 172.

[22] At least according to K. Meisterhans & E. Schwyzer, *Grammatik der attischen Inschriften*, Berlin 1900 (3rd ed.), 163. We are, of course, waiting for Threatte'svolume on morphology to appear.

[23] 1.87.6; 2.2.1; 5.56.5; 5.81.2; 5.83.4; 6.7.4; 6.93.4; 7.18.4; 8.58.1.

writings and in inscriptions, it again seems likely that the type τρεισκαιδέκατος was introduced by the poets; Pindar's ἑβδόμᾳ σὺν καὶ δεκάτῃ (*Pyth*. 4.10) shows, however, that they could use the older type as well. Herodotus' use of both types of ordinals, like his use of both subtractives and additives, either reflects a transitory stage in the spoken language, or it is a conscious enlargement of his stylistic repertoire.

4. Coptic

During the greater part of its literary existence, the Egyptian language was written in various consonant scripts. First in the picture-like hieroglyphs, later also in hieratic, the cursive form of the hieroglyphs, still later also in demotic, which in its turn was a more cursive form of hieratic. These three writing systems were used side by side as late as the Roman period. Only when, by the side of these, a fourth system, the Greek alphabet, also began to be used for writing Egyptian, which probably was the case already in the second century CE, this language showed for the first time its vowels. It is therefore only from Coptic, as Egyptian in Greek letters is called, that one can get a clear vision of the structure of the numeral system.

The basic set of numerals ran from 'one' to 'ten' and included also the tens for 'twenty,' 'thirty,' and 'forty' as they bear no likeness at all to 'two,' 'three,' and 'four;' the tens for 'fifty' to 'ninety,' it is true, bear some likeness to the numerals from 'five' up to 'nine' but not systematically, and it is best, therefore, to consider them as basic numerals, too, just as the words for '100,' '1.000,' and '10.000.' Alternatively, '80' was sometimes expressed or circumscribed as '4(x)20' (cf. quatre-vingts) or '50(+)30' (cf. soixante-dix) and '100' as '5(x)20.'[24]

The numbers between the tens were formed in two different ways. First, there were compounds consisting of a ten (10–90) and a basic numeral (1–9); in these formations the tens 10, 20, 30, 80, 90 and the basic numerals 1–8 had special variant forms. For instance, 'ten' was *mêt*, and 'seven' was *sashf*, but 'seventeen' was *mnt-sashfe*. Second, it was also possible to make word groups consisting of a ten + 'and' + a unit, such as *maabe mn psite*, '39,' by the side of the compound *mabpsite*. In these word groups the constituent numerals had no special variant forms. A third, alternative method was to juxtapose a ten and a compound. In this way were formed '50(+)22' for '72,' and '50(+)29' for '79' (cf. '50(+)30' for '80' above).[25]

Of the Old-Egyptian numerals only the basic units as well as those for '100,' '1.000,' '10.000,' and '100.000' were sometimes spelled in full and are therefore known to us, that is to say of course, only their consonantal skeleton. All other

---

[24] See W.C. Till, *Koptische Grammatik*, Leipzig 1955, 84 (§ 167).
[25] Till, *Kopt. Gramm.* 84.

numbers were indicated by figures, '93' for instance by repeating 9 times the sign for '10' followed by three vertical strokes for '3.' The historical grammar of Coptic makes it clear, however, that the Old-Egyptian words to be postulated for '50' up to '90' were derivations of some kind from the basic numerals for '5' up to '9,' possibly plurals from the formal point of view, as in the Semitic languages.[26]

The numeral system of the Coptic language did not contain any subtractive formations; of Old-Egyptian nothing is known in this respect. Incidentally, however, there occur in Coptic subtractive expressions, one of them being, as might be expected, 2 Cor. 11.24, which is present in both major Coptic versions of the New Testament (in the Sahidic and Boharic dialects). We refer again to § 5.2 for the treatment of this passage.

In the Greek papyri found in Egypt, prices, weights, and other measures are often expressed as a whole with a shortage, especially prices in the 5th–8th centuries. Lists and accounts drawn up in Coptic show this phenomenon too. Two instances are found on ostraca unearthed at Wadi Sarga and dating from about the same period, the 6th–7th centuries.[27]

The first is a shipment account of wine and runs as follows: 'The list of the wines. We shipped from Tuho ten *hands* and six *simpula*, which make seven hundred and seventy less one.'[28] Apparently the 'hands' and 'simpula' were larger wine measures, adding up to almost the round number of 770 of a much smaller measure, which number was then preferred to the less surveyable 769, or else '770 less 1' might indicate the price, and in that case 'one' probably rather represents a smaller unit of currency subtracted from an amount expressed in larger units, comparable to what happens in our second ostracon.

This is likewise an account of a shipment, this time of fodder and barley: 'Lo, nineteen *artabae* of fodder less one *oipe*, and nineteen *artabae* of wheat less two *oipe* have I sent southward. Written 10th of Mesore, 6th Indiction.'[29] Of the same kind are two more instances: 'Fifteen years less three months' (*RNC* 40) and 'seven *holokottina* (*i. e.* solidi) less one *trimesion* (i. e. 1/3 solidus)' (P. Jkôw).[30] These four instances all betray the same preference for mentioning rather a higher number less something than a lower number plus something.

---

[26] A. Gardiner, *Egyptian Grammar*, Oxford 1957 (3rd ed.), § 260; E. Edel, *Altägyptische Grammatik*, Rome 1955–1964, § 395; C.E. Sander-Hansen, *Ägyptische Grammatik*, Wiesbaden 1963, § 219.

[27] F. Preisigke, *Wörterbuch der griechischen Papyrusurkunden* ...II, Berlin 1927, 232b–233a, *s.v.* παρά.

[28] W.E. Crum & H.I. Bell, *Wadi Sarga. Coptic and Greek Texts,* Copenhagen 1922, 118 (no. 133).

[29] Crum & Bell, *Wadi Sarga* 150 (no. 191).

[30] Both instances taken over from W.E. Crum, *A Coptic Dictionary*, Oxford 1939, 593.

5. Hebrew and Aramaic

The numeral systems of the West-Semitic languages (Hebrew and the various Aramaic dialects, including Syriac) were all of the same structure. The basic set of numerals ran up to 'ten;' the words for 'eleven' to 'nineteen' were additive compounds of the basic numerals and 'ten;' 'twenty' was formally the masculine plural of 'ten,' which is supposed to have replaced an earlier dual of 'ten.'[31] The further tens were formally masculine plurals of the basic numerals from 'three' to 'nine;' the numerals in between were additive word groups consisting of a ten + 'and' + a basic, in which the 'higher' usually preceded the 'lower' element. Apparently the system did not contain subtractive formations. Nevertheless, in post-biblical Hebrew and Jewish Aramaic literature one does find a number of instances of subtractive numerals, mostly with the formula 'less one.' These instances can be divided into two categories: (1) Cases in which there is a deviation, in the sense of a diminution, from a round number given in the Bible or from an otherwise normative count. (2) Cases based upon the principle of the 'fence around the Law' (*seyag la-Torah*), developed in post-biblical Judaism.

5.1. Clear instances of deviations from a biblical number: In Exod. 16.35, Num. 13.33–4, Deut. 8.2, 29.5, and Joshua 5.6, it is stated that after the exodus the people of Israel wandered through the desert for forty years. In the Babylonian Talmud (= Bavli), *Zevahim* 118b, the rabbis say: 'The duration of the Tent of Meeting (*i. e.* the Tabernacle) in the wilderness was forty years less one. How do we know that? Because a master said: In the first year (*sc.* of the exodus) Moses made the Tabernacle; (only) in the second year the Tabernacle was set up' (cf. the similar passage *ibid.* 119a).[32] A comparable case is Bavli, *Arakhin* 13a: 'Whence do we know that it took seven years to conquer the land? Caleb said: "Forty years old was I when Moses, the servant of the Lord, sent me from Kadesh-Barnea to spy out the land (Joshua 14.7) … and now lo, I am this day four-score and five years old (Joshua 14.10)." And a master said: "In the first year Moses built the Tabernacle, in the second the Tabernacle was put up, then he sent out the spies. When Caleb passed over the Jordan, how old therefore was he? He was two years less than eighty years old.[33] When he distributed the inheritances, he said: "Now lo, I am this day four-score and five years old" (Joshua 14.10). Whence it follows that it took seven years for them to conquer the land.'

---

[31] H. Bauer & P. Leander, *Historische Grammatik der hebräischen Sprache des Alten Testaments*, Hildesheim 1965, vol. I, 626.

[32] Cf. Josephus, *Ant.* 4.176 τῶν δὲ τεσσεράκοντα ἐτῶν παρὰ τριάκοντα ἡμέρας συμπεπληρωμένων κτλ.

[33] Allowing forty years for the sojourn of Israel in the wilderness. It should be noted here that when the same passage recurs in *Zev.* 118b the printed editions have '78' but codex Munich reads 'eighty less two.'

An instance of deviation from a round number within Scripture itself is mentioned by the rabbis in Talmud Bavli, *Bava Bathra* 123a: 'Why do you find the number seventy in their total (*sc.* of Jacob's sons and grandsons in Gen. 46.27) and only seventy less one in their detailed enumeration (in Gen. 46.8 ff.)?' This problem was solved by later rabbis as follows. *Pirqe de-Rabbi Eliezer* 39 reads: 'When they (*sc.* Jacob and his descendants) came to the border of Egypt, all the males were enrolled (in genealogical tables, to the number of) sixty-six; Joseph and his two sons in Egypt (made a total of) sixty-nine.[34] But it is written: "With seventy persons your father went down into Egypt" (Deut. 10.22). What did the Holy One, blessed be He, do? He entered into the number with them and the total became seventy, to fulfil that which is said: 'I will go down with thee into Egypt' (Gen. 46.4). When Israel came up from Egypt, all the mighty men were enrolled (amounting to) six hundred thousand less one. What did the Holy One, blessed be He, do? He entered into the number with them and their total amounted to six hundred thousand, to fulfil that which is said: 'I will go down with thee into Egypt and I will also surely bring thee up again' (Gen. 46.4).'[35]

Instances with deviations from round numbers not from Scripture but from tradition include Talmud Bavli. *Yevamoth* 64a: 'The divine presence does not rest on less than two thousand and two myriads of Israelites. Should the number of Israelites happen to be two thousand and two myriads less one, and any particular person has not engaged in the propagation of the race, does he not thereby cause the divine presence to depart from Israel?' (cf. a very similar passage in *Bava Qamma* 83a). Also Talmud Bavli, *Sotah* 36b: '(It was stated above that on the stones of the ephod) there were fifty letters, but there were fifty less one! Rabbi Isaac said: One letter was added to the name of Joseph, as it is said: "He appointed it in Joseph for a testimony, when he went out over the land of Egypt" (Psalm 81.6, where Joseph's name is spelt with five letters instead of the usual four: *yhwsp* instead of *ywsp*). Talmud Bavli, *Nedarim* 38a: 'Fifty gates of understanding were created in the world, all but one were given to Moses.' Very curious is Talmud, *Sanhedrin* 95b: 'The length of his (Sanherib's) army was four hundred parasangs, the horses standing neck to neck formed a line forty parasangs long, and the grand total of his army was two million six hundred thousand less one. Abaye inquired: Less one *ribbo* (ten thousand), one thousand, one hundred, or one? The question stands over.' Not in every case it is clear how a tradition of these round numbers (22.000; 50; 2.600.000) has come into being, but for our purposes that is not important.[36]

---

[34] So the extant mss.; the early editions, however, read 'seventy less one' probably on the basis of mss. now lost.

[35] G. Friedlander's translation of *Pirke de-Rabbi Eliezer*, London 1916, 304, slightly revised.

[36] For other instances see b.*Niddah* 30a (sixty less one) and *Eruvin* 83a (seventy less one).

It should be added here that in some isolated instances in the Aramaic dialect of the Jerusalem Talmud (*Yerushalmi*) the Greek loanword παρά is used in its subtractive meaning. *Eruvin* 20b *shov'in min shov'in chamishah 'alafin para' me'at*: 70 x 70 = 5.000 – 100. *Demai* 24c *chada' para' tsivchad*: one minus a little bit. Cf. *Ketuvoth* 30d.[37]

In general the principle is clear: a given round number, mostly either biblical or traditional, is the point of departure, and deviations from it to below are indicated by a subtractive way of counting.

5.2. The same holds for the category to be discussed now, but nevertheless it is dealt with separately because the relevant material is concerned with the principle of 'a fence around the Torah.' This principle (formulated in Mishnah, *Avot* 1.1) can be described as follows: In order to avoid that a commandment in the Torah be transgressed, rules are developed that create a margin of safety (a 'fence') around the commandments.[38] This can best be illustrated by presenting the material under discussion. In the Torah, in Deuteronomy 25.3, it is said: 'They may give him forty strokes, but not more. Otherwise, if they go further and exceed this number, your fellow-countryman will have been publicly degraded.' The explicit and emphatic injunction 'not more,' and the reasons given for it, made people be aware that it would constitute a serious transgression if the person concerned would receive more than forty strokes. Hence, as a 'fence' it was ordained in post-biblical Judaism that, for safety's sake, the punishment would consist of 'forty less one' strokes, so that, even if the executor would make a mistake in counting and inflict a stroke too much, the man or woman would not get more than forty strokes or stripes. Hence the Mishnah, *Makkot* 3.10, states: 'How many stripes do they inflict on a man? Forty less one (*'arba'im chaser 'achat*), for it is written: "by number forty,"(that is) a number near to forty.'[39]

For the same reason the apostle Paul writes in 2 Cor. 11.24: ὑπὸ Ἰουδαίων πεντάκις τεσσεράκοντα παρὰ μίαν ἔλαβον,[40] which shows that the principle is

---

[37] See G. Dalman, *Grammatik des jüdisch-palästinischen Aramäisch*, Leipzig 1905 (repr. Darmstadt 1960), 134.

[38] G.F. Moore, *Judaism in the First Centuries of the Christian Era*, 3 vols., Cambridge MA 1927, I 259: 'Avoth I 1, "Make a fence for the Law," that is, protect it by surrounding it with cautionary rules to halt a man like a danger signal before he gets within breaking distance of the divine statute itself.'

[39] This 'by number forty' is arrived at by the rabbis by linking up the final word of Deut. 25.2 *b^emispar*, 'by number,' with the first word of Deut. 25.3 *'arba'im*, 'forty.' Thus they tried to give a biblical basis to their deviation from the biblical number. See S. Krauss, *Sanhedrin – Makkot* (Die Mischna IV 4–5), Giessen 1933, 369–70. Cf. the Talmudic discussion of this mishnah in *Makkot* 22b: 'If it were written "forty in number," I should have said it means forty in number, but as the wording is "by number forty," it means a number coming up to the forty' (Soncino translation).

[40] On the question of how Paul could have incurred this maximum penalty see A.E. Harvey, 'Forty Strokes Save One,' in A.E. Harvey (ed.), *Alternative Approaches to New Testament Studies*, London 1985, 79–96.

older than the Mishnah, as can also be inferred from Josephus, *Ant.* 4.238 ὁ
δὲ παρὰ ταῦτα ποιήσας πληγὰς μιᾷ λειπούσας τεσσαράκοντα τῷ δημοσίῳ σκύτει
λαβὼν κτλ. Cf. *ibid.* 4.248 πληγὰς τεσσαράκοντα μιᾷ λειπούσας λαμβάνων κτλ.
(and note that in *Ant.* 10.77 and *Bell.* 6.270 Josephus uses τριακονταεννέα!).
Targum Pseudo-Jonathan (an Aramaic paraphrastic translation of the Hebrew
Bible) renders Deut. 25.3 as follows: 'Forty (stripes) may be laid upon him, but
with one less shall he be flogged, (the full number) shall not be completed, lest
he flog him more than these thirty-nine (lashes), excessively, and he be in danger
and your brother be despised while you see him.'[41]

There is another instance in the Mishnah that is sometimes referred to in this
context, wrongly in our opinion.[42] In *Shabbath* 7.2 the context is a discussion
of the types of work forbidden on Sabbath. The text runs as follows: 'The main
classes of work are forty less one (*'arba'im chaser 'achat*).' The same tradition
is found in the Midrash, *Numbers Rabba* 18.21: 'The principal categories of
work (forbidden on Sabbath) are forty less one.' At first sight one would expect
that there is a fixed number 40 in either Scripture or tradition relating to this
issue. But there is no such number, and if it were there, the Mishnah would make
no sense, for the principle of 'a fence around the Torah' would demand in that
case *more*, not *less* than 40 kinds of forbidden work. So this principle cannot be
at work here, and it is very hard to say what is the reason for this specific way
of counting here.

Sidney Hoenig's suggestion, 'The 40 mentioned biblically in the case of
malkot (punishment by lashes) was utilized for application in a parallel manner
for the sabbatical prohibitions,'[43] is not and cannot be proved. Even if that would
apply to the use of the number 40, it definitely does not apply to the formula '40
less 1,' since the 'fence-principle' is operative in only one of the two cases, not
in both. One might, however, suggest that the use of '40 less 1' instead of 'thirty-
nine' in the case of forbidden kinds of work may have been a rather mechanical
transfer of terminology which existed already longer (for the 39 strokes) to a dif-

---

[41] See also H.L. Strack & P. Billerbeck, *Kommentar zum Neuen Testament aus Talmud
und Midrasch* III, München 1926, 527–8. J. le Moyne, *Les Sadducéens*, Paris 1972, 239. G.F.
Moore, *Judaism* II-III, Cambridge MA 1927–30, II 27–8, III 171. Characteristically, the later
Syriac version (Peshitta) of 2 Cor. 11.24 uses about the same words as the Mishnah (*'arba'in
chasir chada'*). It is uncertain whether the terminology in *Acta Pilati* (*Evang. Nicodemi*) 4.3
(λέγουσιν οἱ Ἰουδαῖοι τῷ Πιλάτῳ· ὁ νόμος ἡμῶν περιέχει· ἄνθρωπος εἰς ἄνθρωπον ἐὰν ἁμαρτήσῃ,
ἄξιός ἐστιν λαμβάνειν τεσσαράκοντα παρὰ μίαν, ὁ δὲ εἰς θεὸν βλασφημῶν λιθοβολίᾳ λιθοβολεῖσθαι
αὐτόν) depends upon 2 Cor. 11.24 or shows independent knowledge of Jewish usage.

[42] E. g., W.H. Roscher, *Die Zahl 40 im Glauben, Brauch und Schrifttum der Semiten* (Abh.
der phil.-hist. Klasse der kön. sächs. Akad. der Wiss. 27:4), Leipzig 1909, 25. This study by
Roscher is a supplement to his *Die Tessarakontaden und Tessarakontadenlehren der Griechen
und anderer Völker* (Berichte über die Verhandl. der kön. sächs. Ges. der Wiss., phil.-hist.
Klasse 61), Leipzig 1909.

[43] S.B. Hoenig, 'The Designated Number of Kinds of Labor Prohibited on the Sabbath,'
Jewish Quarterly Review 68 (1978) 205.

ferent situation in which the same number (39) played a role, albeit without the same background. It is, therefore, interesting to see that in the midrashic work *Mekhilta de-Rabbi Yishmael*, Shabbata 2 (III p. 206 ed. Lauterbach), it is stated in connection with Exod. 35.1 ('And he said to them: These are the words etc.'): 'Rabbi says: This includes the laws about the thirty-nine (*sheloshim we-tesha*) categories of work prohibited on the sabbath which Moses gave them orally.' The fact that in this passage the usual additive number is used makes clear that 'forty less one' had not become a fixed expression in relation to the types of work forbidden on the Sabbath, unlike the forty less one strokes. Also clear is the fact that the forty less one types of work are later than the forty less one strokes (Paul precedes the Mishnah by at least one and a half century). One might suggest that the number of types of work prohibited on the Sabbath – performance of which made one liable to beating[44] – was worked out to match the number of blows in the beating and therefore the same form of numeral was used. But this is no more than an educated guess.[45] It seems to be impossible to state with certainty what was the background in this case.

6. Conclusion

It may have become clear that the principles operative behind the use of sub-tractive numerals are definitely not the same in all languages discussed in this article. For Latin it was already known that subtractives were very old elements that remained in use for a long time (till the first centuries of our era) but then gradually disappeared and hence are no longer part of the Romance languages. As to Greek, subtractives have either been totally neglected by modern scholars or considered to be a rare and clumsy irregularity in the otherwise additive sys-tem. Now, however, it turns out to have been a usage of much wider currency than has always been assumed. Most probably it was, as in Latin, an element of the early spoken language that has persisted in prose writings till the end of the Classical period. Contrary to the classical languages, in Semito-Hamitic languages (Egyptian, Coptic, Hebrew, Aramaic) subtractives have never been part of the numeral system. Hence there are considerably fewer instances, but, as far as Hebrew and Aramaic are concerned, in almost all these cases it could be demonstrated that the use of subtractives was caused by the existence of a normative round number from which there is a deviation to below. To this cat-egory, and only to this, belongs the only passage in the Bible where a subtractive numeral is used, 2 Cor. 11.24.

---

[44] Flogging is the punishment for all kinds of violation, by overt act, of negative biblical injunctions (Mishnah, *Makkot* 3.1–9); see H.H. Cohn in *Encyclopaedia Judaica* 6 (1972) 1349; Z.W. Falk, *Introduction to the Jewish Law of the Second Commonwealth* II, Leiden 1978, 160.

[45] We owe this suggestion to Prof. Morton Smith (letter of Sept. 25, 1985).

The Great Magical Papyrus of Paris (PGM IV) and the Bible

The so-called 'Great Magical Papyrus of Paris' or P(apyrus) G(raeca) M(agica) IV is a Greek manuscript in the Bibliothèque Nationale, where it is catalogued as *Supplément grec* 574 (or Anastasi 1073). It is a large manuscript, containing 36 leaves from a codex, and its text runs to 3274 lines in total.[1] It was acquired in Egypt in the early 19th century by the famous collector of antiquities, Giovanni Anastasi, and bought by the Bibliothèque Nationale at an auction in Paris in 1857.[2] This and the other Anastasi papyri probably come from Thebes where they were discovered in a grave sometime around 1825, as Anastasi was told, although we cannot be completely certain about this. Be that as it may, it was certainly written in Egypt in the Roman period. The papyrus contains a handbook for a practicing magician that was 'compiled from many sources.'[3] As Hans-Dieter Betz has suggested, the compiler probably travelled around Egypt to visit temple libraries which often served as depositories of magico-religious literature,[4] and to exchange materials with other magicians; he assembled documents over a period of time and successively or finally copied them all into a handbook.[5] With its more than 50 documents PGM IV is the single most comprehensive handbook for magical practices known from the ancient world.[6] Papyrologists agree that the manuscript was written in the early fourth century, but the documents contained in it may of course be older, some of them even much older. It is clear that each and every document or tradition found in this compilation has a prehistory of its own, and it is now generally agreed that

---

[1] In Karl Preisendanz's edition the Greek text covers 57 pages; see K. Preisendanz (hrsg.), *Papyri Graecae magicae. Die griechischen Zauberpapyri*, vol. 1, Stuttgart 1973 (reprint of the Leipzig 1928 edition, revised by A. Henrichs), 66–180. The present author examined the manuscript in the Bibliothèque Nationale on April 12–13, 2000.

[2] Almost 30 years earlier, Anastasi had sold a larger lot of these papyri to the Dutch archaeologist C.J.C. Reuvens, the founder and first director of the Oudheidkundig Museum in Leiden.

[3] H.D. Betz, *The 'Mithras Liturgy,'* Tübingen 2003, 7.

[4] See G. Fowden, *The Egyptian Hermes. A Historical Approach to the Late Pagan Mind*, Cambridge 1986, 57–58.

[5] Betz, *The 'Mithras Liturgy'* 7–8.

[6] For the wide variety of practices dealt with in PGM IV see W. Brashear, 'The Greek Magical Papyri: An Introduction and Survey; Annotated Bibliography (1928–1994),' *ANRW* II 18,5, Berlin & New York 1995, 3497–3498.

PGM IV contains material that has a chronological range from the first through the third centuries CE. The scribe is certainly not the author but he is not just a mechanical compiler either. He makes it clear that he has sometimes examined more than one copy of his documents and hence notes textual variants, and he also inserts marginal comments and cross-references,[7] but he makes no effort to edit or rewrite the procedures collected, on the contrary, he was concerned about accuracy. PGM IV is the best possible illustration of the kind of books that, according to Acts 19:19, were publicly burned in Ephesus after the apostle Paul had unmasked the Jewish magicians in that city.

After the *editio princeps* by Carl Wessely in 1888,[8] the whole document was reprinted with several necessary corrections and emendations by Preisendanz in 1928 as nr. IV in his *PGM*,[9] accompanied by a German translation. The first English translation, by a team of American scholars, was published in 1986 in *The Greek Magical Papyri in Translation*, edited by Hans-Dieter Betz.[10] In 1987 a Spanish translation appeared.[11] An anonymous French translation was published in 1995.[12] And I myself published parts of the papyrus text in a Dutch translation in 1997.[13] The secondary literature on this papyrus is enormous. In a book-length article of more than 300 pages published in 1995, the late William Brashear lists hundreds of publications (between 1928 and 1994) dealing either with PGM IV as a whole or with documents contained in it or with individual passages.[14] A century ago the study of the Greek magical papyri still had to be justified and defended against the scorn of worthies such as Wilamowitz-Moellendorff,[15] but in the meantime the climate has changed drastically: the study of ancient magic is now not only a respected scholarly enterprise, it has even become part and parcel of the study of ancient religions.

Most of the compilations or anthologies of Graeco-Roman magical formularies were produced in the first three centuries C.E., although the papyri which preserved them mostly date from the third to sixth centuries. Their disparate

---

[7] Betz, *ibid.* 8 for examples. See, e.g., lines 500 and 2427. Many more examples in A.D. Nock, 'Greek Magical Papyri,' in his *Essays on Religion and the Ancient World*, vol. I, Oxford 1972, 178–179.

[8] C. Wessely, 'Griechische Zauberpapyri von Paris und London,' *Denkschrift der Kaiserlichen Akademie der Wissenschaften in Wien*, Phil.-hist. Klasse 36 (1888) 44–126. It is a rather sloppy edition with many errors.

[9] See note 1.

[10] Chicago 1986, 36–101.

[11] J.L.C. Martínez & M.D.S. Romero, *Testos de magia en papiros griegos*, Madrid 1987 (non vidi).

[12] *Manuel de magie égyptienne: Le papyrus magique de Paris*, Paris 1995.

[13] P.W. van der Horst, *Bronnen voor de studie van de wereld van het vroege christendom*, 2 vols., Kampen 1997, II 100–112.

[14] W. Brashear, 'The Greek Magical Papyri: An Introduction and Survey; Annotated Bibliography (1928–1994),' *ANRW* II 18,5, Berlin & New York 1995, 3380–3684, esp. 3516–3527 on PGM IV.

[15] See Brashear, 'The Greek Magical Papyri' 3410.

contents betray their checkered development every few lines, as Brashear has noticed: "Recipes and instructions for making gems, charms, amulets, figurines, and potions are intermingled with divination by numbers, dice or Homeric verses. Amatory magic follows hard on execration, exorcism or magico-medical recipe. Hecate, Kore, Apollo, Aphrodite, and Athena are invoked along with Ereschigal, Adonai, Jehovah and Jesus. Suddenly there appears a snatch of classical Greeek poetry, but it is interlarded with *voces magicae*. A Coptic section succeeds a Greek one. It is sometimes difficult to find any unifying principle whatsoever."[16] Although this is meant as a description of Greek magical formularies in general, it applies perfectly to PGM IV.

That the recipes and prescriptions of PGM IV were indeed put into practice is shown by several recent finds. For instance, a find in Egypt of a jar containing a lead foil inscribed with a charm and a clay figurine of a kneeling woman with her hands bound behind her back and her body pierced by thirteen nails corresponds rather closely to the procedures prescribed in PGM IV 296–434, in spite of a number of deviations in both the *praxis* and the *logos*. Also other love charms on lead *lamellae* follow parts of this text.[17] The fact that of some formularies we have parallel versions in two or three different languages (e. g., Greek, Coptic and Aramaic)[18] is also an indication that they were meant for practical purposes and that a diversified clientele was served with them.[19]

An interesting feature of PGM IV (and of other magical papyri) is the insertion of metrical hymnic passages into the formularies. So we find a hymn to the Moon (2241–2347), to the Sun (436–461 and 1957–1981), to Aphrodite (2902–2939) and several more (in total 15 hymns).[20] The sometimes poor linguistic and metrical qualities of these hymns are indicative of a non-classical provenance and nowadays most scholars assume that they originated in the early imperial period, i. e., in the first two centuries C.E., maybe some of them somewhat earlier. Although much in the magical papyri has an Egyptian or otherwise Oriental background, these hymns are certainly of Greek provenance. As Brashear says, "They hearken back to the days when the Olympian and chthonian deities reigned supreme, when Iao, Baal, Ereschigal, Nebutosualeth and their likes were hundreds of miles away and still unheard of."[21] In earlier scholarship it was often assumed that the magical papyri were, apart from some Greek influence,

---

[16] Brashear, 'The Greek Magical Papyri' 3414.

[17] Brashear, 'The Greek Magical Papyri' 3416–17 with notes, and cf. 3446. Also Nock, 'Greek Magical Papyri' 179–80.

[18] Brashear, 'The Greek Magical Papyri' 3405, 3419. Cf. also the almost identical text on the lead tablet SB IV 7452 and the formulae prescribed in PGM IV 341 ff.

[19] On the magical papyri as "the actual working copies of practical magicians" see Nock, 'Greek Magical Papyri' 177.

[20] For a complete survey see A. Henrichs (following E. Heitsch, *Die griechischen Dichterfragmente der römischen Kaiserzeit*, Göttingen 1963) in *PGM*, vol. 2, 266.

[21] Brashear, 'The Greek Magical Papyri' 3421.

"a hodge-podge of oriental, Gnostic, Mithraic and Babylonian elements."[22] But in our days it is only Greek, Egyptian, and Jewish (with perhaps some Christian) elements that are seen as the main components.[23]

As is well-known, the importance of Jewish elements in the Greek magical papyri should not be underrated: in approximately one third of the rites and charms Jewish elements are detectable.[24] Not only are Iao and Adonai and Sabaoth invoked more frequently than most other deities except Helios, but also Moses, Solomon and the Patriarchs Abraham, Isaac, and Jacob figure in several passages in the papyri, and "angels, archangels, cherubim and seraphim abound."[25] All these biblical names seem to have become elements of a "trans-cultural magical lingo," as Morton Smith has dubbed it.[26] Also many of the strange sounding *voces magicae* or *nomina barbara*,[27] may have a Hebrew or Aramaic background.[28] Even if that is not the case, sometimes alliterative hocus-pocus of several hundred words long is simply called Hebrew by the magicians themselves.[29] This has to do with the great reputation of Jewish magicians and magic in late antiquity.[30] Jewish and biblical elements, names, motives and formulas were borrowed freely because they were believed to be exceptionally potent and effective. It is, therefore, not strange that, if one moves from pagan magical texts to Jewish ones, one often does not have the feeling of moving to a different world. If syncretism is to be found anywhere, it is in the world of ancient magic.[31]

---

[22] Brashear, 'The Greek Magical Papyri' 3422.

[23] On the paucity of Latin and Roman elements see Brashear, 'The Greek Magical Papyri' 3425–3426.

[24] See M. Smith, 'The Jewish Elements in the Magical Papyri,' in his *Studies in the Cult of Yahweh*, vol. 2, Leiden 1996, 246–247. Note that this implies that in two thirds of the material no Jewish influence at all is to be detected. See on the importance of Jewish elements also Th. Hopfner, *Griechisch-ägyptischer Offenbarungszauber*, 2 vols., Amsterdam 1974–1983 (corrected reprint of the edition of 1921–1924), II 31–33.

[25] Brashear, 'The Greek Magical Papyri' 3427. On the patriarchs also M. Rist, 'The God of Abraham, Isaac, and Jacob: A Liturgical and Magical Formula,' *JBL* 57 (1938) 289–303.

[26] Smith, 'The Jewish Elements' 245.

[27] For an extensive list see Brashear, 'The Greek Magical Papyri' 3576–3603.

[28] For instances see C. Bonner, *Studies in Magical Amulets, Chiefly Graeco-Egyptian,* Ann Arbor 1950, 187.

[29] In PGM V 115–6 even the Egyptian name Osoronnophris (= Osiris Wennefer) is said to be 'the true name which has been transmitted to the prophets of Israel'! For Hebrew in Coptic magical papyri see M. Kropp, *Ausgewählte Koptische Zaubertexte*, vol. 3, Brussels 1930, 218.

[30] See for literature Brashear, 'The Greek Magical Papyri' 3426 note 222. M. Simon, *Verus Israel. A Study of the Realtions Between Christians and Jews in the Roman Empire (AD 135–425)*, Oxford 1986, 339–368. J. Gager, *Moses in Greco-Roman Paganism*, Nashville 1972, 134–161.

[31] Sometimes it is impossible to decide whether a magical papyrus is of Christian or Jewish provenance; e. g., P.IFAO iii 50 in R.W. Daniel & F. Maltomini (eds), *Supplementum Magicum I*, Opladen 1990, 49–52 (no. 19).

In this framework it is worthwile to take a closer look at a famous passage in PGM IV, the so-called 'Hebrew formula' (*logos hebraïkos*, 3007–3086).[32] It is a charm of 80 lines in which a spell to be used in case of demonic possession is presented. Although the recipe is attributed to the legendary Egyptian magician Pibechis, it teems with Jewish elements. After having listed the ingredients of a magic potion, the text states it should be prepared while saying a formula that begins with the word Joel, a composite of the Hebrew Jeho- (= YHWH) and -El (God), that we find elsewhere in the form Jael and Jaoel.[33] In the same formula also the variant forms Jaba, Jôê and Jaêô occur (elsewhere we find Jabe, Jaoue, Jao, Jaou, Ja etc.).[34] This indicates how important the invocation of the name of the God of Israel was considered,[35] even though it is here part of a string of *nomina barbara* that concludes with the name of the Egyptian creator god Ptah. It should also be noted that in the next line we find the well-known string of the seven vowels of the Greek alphabet (a, e, ê, i, o, u, ô),[36] of which Eusebius, a contemporary of the scribe of the papyrus, says that its power is thought to be equivalent to that of the Tetragrammaton YHWH (*PE* 11.6.36); and he is right, as is testified by several passages in other magical papyri and in the Nag Hammadi codices as well.[37] The formula ends with the imperative "come out of NN" (3013: *exelthe apo tou deinos*), using the same terminology as in the story of Jesus' exorcism in Luke 4:35 (*exelthe ap' autou*). And after having spelled out the *nomina barbara* to be written on the amulet, the author adds that it is a formula "terrifying every demon" (3017: *pantos daimonos phrikton*), which is

---

[32] For bibliography see Brashear, 'The Greek Magical Papyri' 3526–3527. I single out for mention A. Deissmann, *Licht vom Osten*, Tübingen 1923, 214–228; W.L. Knox, 'Jewish Liturgical Exorcism,' *HTR* 31 (1938) 191–203; S. Eitrem, *Some Notes on the Demonology in the New Testament*, Oslo 1966, 15–30; for parallels in Jewish mystical texts see J.-H. Niggemeyer, *Beschwörungsformel aus dem "Buch der Geheimnisse"*, Hildesheim 1975, *passim*; P.S. Alexander, 'Jewish Elements in Gnosticism and Magic c. CE 70 – c. CE 270,' in W. Horbury a. o. (eds.), *The Cambridge History of Judaism*, vol. 3, Cambridge 1999, 1073–1074. Further the publications mentioned in notes 10–13 are relevant.

[33] See, e. g., *Vita Adae et Evae* (Greek version) 29:4; 33:5; *Apoc. Abraham* 10:3; 13:1 etc. with the comments in R. Rubinkiewicz, *L'Apocalypse d'Abraham en vieux slave*, Lublin 1987, 127–129.

[34] See on these and other transcriptions of the Tetragrammaton A. Deissmann, *Bibelstudien*, Hildesheim – New York 1977 (repr. of the Marburg 1895 ed.), 1–20 ('Griechische Transsskriptionen des Tetragrammaton'). Note that sometimes Iao is equated with Aion; see H. Lewy, *Chaldaean Oracles and Theurgy*, new ed. by M. Tardieu, Paris 1978, 409 n. 32. Quite popular is the palindrome *iaôai*.

[35] See D. Aune, 'Iao,' *RAC* 17 (1996) 1–12, esp. 5–6.

[36] See H. Leclercq, 'Amulettes,' *Dictionnaire d'archéologie chrétienne et de liturgie* I 2 (1907) 1794–95 (1784–1860); F. Dornseiff, *Das Alphabet in Mystik und Magie*, Leipzig 1925, 35–60 ('Die Vokalreihen im Zauber').

[37] See for the evidence P. Cox Miller, 'In Praise of Nonsense,' in A.H. Armstrong (ed.), *Classical Mediterranean Spirituality: Egyptian, Greek, Roman*, London 1986, 481–505, esp. 482–4. Also R. Kotansky, *Greek Magical Amulets*, Opladen 1993, 41–53, no. 9.

of course strongly reminiscent of James 2:19, "The demons too believe this and they are terrified (*phrissousin*)."

The conjuration itself begins with the striking opening line, 'I conjure you by the God of the Hebrews, Jesus!' (3019–20). The fact that the God of the Hebrews[38] is invoked is not in itself something extraordinary, as we have already seen. A deity who liberates his people from bondage, who splits the sea for that very reason and destroys their enemies by that very measure, is without doubt a god who is able to chase out a demon from a possessed person. But why is that god called Jesus, of all names? This sounds as un-Jewish as it could be. And, of course, several scholars, among which even Preisendanz, have suggested that the word 'Jesus' is an interpolation.[39] But that is a futile observation, for even it that were true, it still should be said that the scribe of the papyrus – if he was the interpolator, otherwise it was his predecessor – found it suitable to give the god of the Hebrews the name of Jesus. This is remarkably reminiscent of the passage in the Book of Acts (19:13) where it is Jews in Ephesus, the sons of the high-priest Sceva, who conjure evil spirits in the name of Jesus; and they are not Christians! In that story, however, the evil spirit says: 'I don't know Jesus', and he does not leave his victim (Acts 19:16). But one could also refer to the freelance Jewish exorcists who drive out demons in the name of Jesus in Mark 9:38 and Lk. 9:49, who were apparently more successful.[40] Be that as it may, Irenaeus informs us that by the end of the second century CE Jews were still using the name of Jesus in exorcisms (*Adv. Haer.* 2.6.2).

The text goes on by saying about this God that he "appears in fire" (3023), which seems to be a reference to the role of fire in theophanies as they are depicted in Old Testament texts such as Ex. 3:2, 13:21, 19:18 etc. This deity is told to send down an implacable angel "to bind [litt. 'cause to enter into its proper place'] the demon flying around this creature that God formed in his holy paradise" (3026–27). It is interesting to see that the demon that was first ordered to go out of the possessed is now said to be flying around him. According to Luke 11:24–26, Jesus said that when an unclean spirit (a demon) has gone out of a man, he passes through waterless areas (no doubt flying around there) and finding no rest so that finally it says, "I will return to my house from which I came," and then things get even worse. Such a demon has to be bound in order to prevent it from causing greater damage to the human creature.[41] This creature

---

[38] For this biblical expression see Exod. 3:18; 7:16; 9:1.

[39] For a discussion of this issue see J.M. Hull, *Hellenistic Magic and the Synoptic Tradition*, London 1974, 71. Hull compares a passage earlier in the same papyrus where we find, "Hail, God of Abraham, hail, God of Isaac, hail, God of Jacob, Jesus Chrestus [sic] etc." (PGM IV 1228–29).

[40] See D.E. Aune, 'Magic in Early Christianity,' *ANRW* II 23,2 (1980) 1545–1549 (The Magical Use of the Name of Jesus).

[41] Ph. S. Alexander in E. Schürer, *The History of the Jewish People in the Age of Jesus Christ*, III/1, Edinburgh 1986, 357 compares this passage to *Tobith* 8:2–3: when Tobias had

"God formed in his holy paradise," an unmistakable reference to Genesis 2 of which we find another one later on in the phrase "who formed from dust the race of humans" (3047). The function of this element is that of a *historiola*, a reference to a piece of (usually foreign) mythology that serves to underline the invincible power of the deity invoked and hence to frighten the demon.[42] We find such a reference again some lines further when the spell goes on: "I conjure you by the one who appeared to Israel[43] in a shining pillar and a cloud by day, who saved his people from the Pharaoh and brought upon Pharaoh the ten plagues because of his disobedience" (3033–38). In this *historiola* the most powerful scenes from Israel's history are evoked and the idea behind it is that such archetypal events "retain their supernatural force and can be reactivated at any given time by the simple act of recounting them."[44] It is interesting to notice that in the middle of the third century CE the great Christian scholar Origen remarks that "'the God of Israel,' and 'the God of the Hebrews,' and 'the God who drowned the king of Egypt and the Egyptians in the Red Sea' are formulae which are often used [by non-Jews] to overcome demons or certain evil powers" (*Contra Celsum* 4.34).[45]

The spell continues by ordering the demon to reveal its identity and to tell whatever sort it is (*lalêsai hopoion kai an êis*), whether it is "heavenly or aerial, terrestrial or subterranean, or netherworldly or Ebousaeus or Chersaeus or Pharisaeus" (3043–44). This firstly reminds us of the story of the Gerasene demoniac in which Jesus' question, "What is your name?" (Mk. 5:9; Lk. 8:30), is answered with the name *Legion*. Knowledge of the nature or name of the demon is a prerequisite for its expulsion. But perhaps a better interpretation is to take *lalêsai* (3038) and *lalêson* (3042, 3044) as used absolutely, without combining it with the following *hopoion ktl*. The sense then is that the demon has made its victim dumb and we should translate as, "speak, of whatever nature you may be."[46] This would constitute a striking parallel to the story of the *pneuma alalon*, the mute spirit who robs persons of their speech, in Mark 9:17. The demon must be made to speak, and its victim will follow suit.[47] Secondly, the 'heavenly or aerial' demon suggests comparison with what Pseudo-Paul writes on the evil spirits which he calls 'the prince of the power of the air' and 'powers in the

---

smoked the demon out of his bridal chamber, the angel Raphael pursued it to Upper Egypt and bound it to stop it from returning. Cf. *Jub.* 10:5.

[42] On *historiolae* see Brashear, 'The Greek Magical Papyri' 3438–40; F. Graf, 'Historiola,' *NP* 5 (1998) 642. Aune, 'Magic in Early Christianity' 1547, coined the term 'magical *Heilsgeschichte*' in this connection.

[43] The papyrus has 'Osrael' but the context leaves no doubt about the correct reading.

[44] Brashear, 'The Greek Magical Papyri' 3439. Cf. Knox, 'Jewish Liturgical Exorcism' 195. Aune, 'Magic in Early Christianity' 1547.

[45] [See my "The God Who Drowned the King of Egypt," the next essay in this volume.]

[46] Eitrem, *Some Notes* 18–19.

[47] See Hull, *Hellenistic Magic* 68–69.

heavenly places' (Eph. 2:2; 3:10). The most interesting feature here, however, is the three names or categories at the end. There is no doubt that these are borrowed from Gen. 15:20–21, where the ten nations living in Canaan in Abraham's days are mentioned, among which are the Jebusites, the Girgashites, and the Perizzites. In the the LXX version these have become *Iebousaioi, Gergesaioi* and *Pherezaioi*. These have here been garbled into *Ebusaios* (well recognizable), *Chersaios* (possibly an amalgam of *Gergesaios* and *Chettaios*, Hittite, also in the list), and *Pharisaios*, 'Pharisee' thus becoming the name of a demon class! The latter designation of course also suggests familiarity with New Testament stories about inimical Pharisees.[48]

Another interesting feature is that the magician tries to force the demon to reveal its identity be conjuring it "by the seal which Solomon placed on the tongue of Jeremiah" (3039–40). The *Seal of Solomon* was the name of a famous amulet in antiquity, often in the form of a signet ring.[49] Of course Solomon's reputation as magician was widespread in antiquity, as the stories about him in Josephus (*Ant.* 8.44–49) and the *Testament of Solomon* demonstrate,[50] but the story of the seal or ring being placed on Jeremiah's tongue is an otherwise unknown haggadic motive. Deissmann[51] surmises that it derives from Jer. 1:6–10 LXX where the prophet protests to the Lord that he is too young for his task and that he cannot speak, whereupon the Lord stretches out his hand, touches Jeremia's mouth, and says, "Look, I have put my words into your mouth" (1:9). This passage certainly has some connection with the remark in our papyrus, but there is still a long way between the Lord touching the prophet's mouth and Solomon putting his seal on the prophet's tongue. *Non liquet*, but again we can observe how biblical or post-biblical Jewish motives are here taken into service by a non-Jewish magician.

The magician continues conjuring the demon by the one "whom every heavenly power of angels and archangels praises" (3050–52), which may be a vague echo of Isaiah 6 or rather a motif taken over from Jewish mystical traditions as we find them in the earliest strata of Hekhalot literature. He also calls the divinity "the great god Sabaoth" (3052), taking the second element in *YHWH Tseva'oth* to be a divine name, as was (and still is) so often done. Then follows another

---

[48] Deissmann, *Licht vom Osten* 223 n. 12. Cf. Knox, 'Jewish Liturgical Exorcism' 196: "The change of Perizzites to Pharisees suggests that the papyrus has been edited by someone who knew that the Pharisees figure as the villains of the N.T." Eitrem, *Some Notes* 23, suggests that John 8:48 ("are you a Samaritan and do you have a demon?") implies that 'Samaritan' may also have become a designation of a class of demons.

[49] Many ancient amulets are inscribed with *sphragis Solomônos*. See K. Preisendanz, 'Salomo,' *PW* Suppl. 8 (1965) 660–704 (on the *Seal* 670–676). Also A. Jacoby, 'Clavicula Salomonis,' *Handwörterbuch des deutschen Aberglaubens* 2 (1930) 88–93.

[50] See, apart from Preisendanz's article in Pauly-Wissowa, A.B. Kolenkow, 'Relationships Between Miracle and Prophecy in the Greco-Roman World and Early Christianity,' *ANRW* II 23,2 (1980), 1471–1506, esp. 1489–91.

[51] Deissmann, *Licht vom Osten* 223 n. 11.

historiola when he calls this god the one "through whom the Jordan river drew back and the Red Sea, which Israel crossed, became impassable" (3053–55), with clear references to Joshua 3 and Exodus 14, although perhaps Ps. 114:3 ("The sea looked and fled, the Jordan turned back") is a more likely candidate because of the collocation of the two events. These impressive miracles testify to such a great power in the divinity that the demon cannot but surrender. God is then called "the one who revealed the 140 languages and distributed them by his own command" (3056–58). This is a nice example of magical bluffing out a demon. The Jewish tradition recognizes 70 languages (on the basis of the table of 70 nations in Gen. 10), but the magician doubles the number in order to impress the evil spirit. Or – another intriguing possibility – did the author know about another Jewish tradition, that one finds only occasionally in rabbinic literature (e. g., *Sifre Deut.* 311), to the effect that there were 140 nations in the world?[52] That would imply an even more intimate knowledge of Jewish traditions than we have seen hitherto.

The remark that God is the one "whom the wings of the cherubim praise" (3061) betrays knowledge of Ezek. 10:5 or, more probably, of a Hekhalot tradition,[53] but the unexpected combination *tou cherubin* (singular article with the noun in a Hebrew or Aramaic plural) suggests that it is a distant acquaintance. The text goes on: "I conjure you by the one who put the mountains around the sea [or] a wall of sand and commanded the sea not to overflow; and the abyss obeyed" (3062–64). Here we see clear echoes of Jer. 5:22 and Job 38:10–11, and it should be noticed that "the power of God to set bounds to the sea is again suitable to overawe demons who are afraid of water."[54] In the following lines we read about "the one in holy Jerusalem before whom the unquenchable fire burns for all time, with his holy name" (3069–70). The fact that the name of Jerusalem is in the unusual spelling of *Hierosolymos* (instead of *Hierosolyma*) suggests again that the author of the spell is not a Jew himself, and the mention of the *ner tamid* in the Jerusalem temple[55] does not contradict that suggestion since that undying light "was legendary in antiquity,"[56] and we find it mentioned several times by pagan authors (in PGM IV it is also mentioned in line 1219).[57] At the end the author urges the magicians who want to put this spell into practice not to eat pork and to keep themselves pure, "for this charm is Hebraic (*ho logos estin Hebraïkos*) and is preserved among pure men" (3084–86). Here one of the

---

[52] See L. Ginzberg, *The Legends of the Jews*, vol. 5, Philadelphia 1925, 195 for further references.

[53] See Alexander in Schürer, *The History of the Jewish People* 357 n. 27

[54] Knox, 'Jewish Liturgical Exorcism' 199.

[55] Deissmann, *Licht vom Osten* 224 n. 11, thinks the reference is to the never ending burnt offering mentioned in Lev. 6:8–13, which is less likely.

[56] W.C. Grese in Betz (ed.), *Greek Magical Papyri* 97 n. 407.

[57] E. Schürer, *History of the Jewish People in the Age of Jesus Christ*, vol. 2, Edinburgh 1979, 297 n. 18.

most important dietary rules of the Jewish people is inculcated because the spell is Jewish, says the author. Is that really true?[58]

It is tempting to say yes because of the abundance of biblical and post-biblical Jewish motifs in this document. But we should not lose sight of the fact that the document also contains indications of a relatively distant acquaintance with these traditions, as we have seen. Even though the name of Jesus could be used by Jews for exorcistic purposes, that is still a far cry from calling Jesus the God of the Hebrews. That seems to be far too much against the very nature of Judaism for us to be able to maintain a Jewish authorship. But what, then, of the Jews in Elephantine, who worshipped several Gods alongside YHWH? One could also say that making Pharisees into a class of demons is too much of an anti-Jewish statement to make Jewish authorship of the spell possible. But then, could we expect a Jewish magician of the Egyptian countryside in the second or third century CE to know what a Pharisee is? He would certainly have never met one! Even so, I am inclined to think that we have here a rather extreme case of pagan borrowing of Jewish motifs. Perhaps we have here the product of a close cooperation between a pagan and a Jewish magician. The reputation of Jewish magicians was so great, as we know from several sources,[59] that one can imagine very well that a pagan magician tried to incorporate as many Jewish elements in his own spells as possible, possibly with the help of a Jewish colleague. But it cannot be ruled out entirely that, after all, the spell was written indeed by a syncretistic Jew who had no qualms about calling Jesus the god of the Jews.[60] The only thing that mattered to him was that his spell worked. It is fitting to conclude with two characteristic quotes from the late and unforgettable Morton Smith's study of the Jewish elements in the magical papyri:

> To speak of the Jewish elements in the magical papyri is to beg the question, what was Judaism in the times and places where the papyri were written? This question cannot be answered precisely. We know from preserved evidence that Judaism took many different forms, some of them surprising (primitive Christianity, for instance), but we don't know what more surprising forms may have been represented by the great majority of the evidence – that [is] now lost.[61]

And on our spell (3007–3086) Morton Smith says:

---

[58] See for the following Smith, 'The Jewish Elements' 242–256.

[59] The same applies to Samaritans.

[60] That he composed the charm originally in Hebrew is untenable; *contra* M. Gaster, 'The Logos Ebraikos in the Magical Papyrus of Paris and the Book of Enoch,' in his *Studies and Texts*, vol. I, New York 1971 (repr. of 1928), 356–364. It must be conceded, however, that "knowledge of Hebrew was surely behind this stuff, though far behind" (Smith, 'The Jewish Elements' 249). For a comparable case from Hadrumetum (near Carthage) see A. Bernand, *Sorciers grecs*, Paris 1991, 299–302.

[61] Smith, 'The Jewish Elements' 242.

The conjuration is probably the work of a pagan who uses a Jewish text – carelessly. "The god of the Hebrews, Jesus" seems unlikely for either a Jew or a Christian, and the many historical mistakes also favor pagan authorship, though only slightly; the biblical ignorance of both Jews and Christians should not be underestimated. Again the unquenched fire in Jerusalem suggests a date prior to 70 for the text the pagan used.[62] So does the description of Jesus, reflecting a pagan's impression of Christianity in its first appearance, and so does the favorable attitude of an Egyptian towards Jews, unlikely after 115–117.[63]

It is not difficult to agree. Much more could and should be said of this charm and its relation to biblical materials, but time and space forbid. Hopefully the few data presented suffice to give an adequate impression of the problems involved.

---

[62] Further on the same page Smith suggests that "its extinction would have been a considerable embarrassment and would have discouraged reference to it after it had been so conspicuously discredited." Nock, 'Greek Magical Papyri' 183, says, "the writer's Jerusalem may well be a Jerusalem of the imagination," which I find less convincing.

[63] Smith, 'The Jewish Elements' 250. Cf. also R. Kotansky, 'Greek Exorcistic Amulets,' in M. Meyer & P. Mirecki (eds.), *Ancient Magic and Ritual Power*, Leiden 1995, 262–266.

"The God Who Drowned the King of Egypt"

A Short Note on an Exorcistic Formula

In the middle of the third century CE, the Christian scholar Origen wrote in his apologetic work *Contra Celsum* that 'the formula "the God of Abraham, the God of Isaac, and the God of Jacob" is used not only by members of the Jewish nation in their prayers to God and in their exorcisms of demons, but also by almost all others who deal in magic and spells. For in magical treatises it is often to be found that God is invoked by this formula' (4.33).[1] He then goes on to say that 'furthermore, "the God of Israel," and "the God of the Hebrews," and "the God who drowned the king of Egypt and the Egyptians in the Red Sea," are formulae which are often used to overpower demons and certain evil powers' (4.34).[2] Pagan use of originally biblical or Jewish formulae, including the above-mentioned, is indeed widely attested.[3] It is upon the formula last mentioned by Origen, 'the God who drowned the king of Egypt and the Egyptians in the Red Sea,' that I want to focus here.

To begin with, it is to be observed that this is not a literal quote from Scripture. In Ex. 15:4 LXX we read that God 'cast Pharaoh's chariots and his army into the sea, he sunk (κατεπόντισεν) his picked officers in the Red Sea.' And in Deut. 11:3–4 LXX Moses says to the people of Israel that they have to remember 'all [God's] signs and the miracles that he did in Egypt to Pharaoh, the king of Egypt, and to all his land, and what he did to the army of the Egyptians, to

---

[1] As a matter of fact, the formula "the God of Abraham, the God of Isaac, and the God of Jacob" indeed occurs more often in the Greek Magical Papyri than the other formulae mentioned by Origen (see below in the text). For references and literature see R. Kotansky, *Greek Magical Amulets. The Inscribed Gold, Silver, Copper, and Bronze Lamellae; Part I: Published Texts of Known Provenance*, Opladen 1993, 291.

[2] Translation (slightly modified) by H. Chadwick, *Origen: Contra Celsum*, Cambridge 1965, 209–210. On Origen's own belief in the efficacy of magic see G. Bardy, 'Origène et la magie,' *Recherches de science religieuse* 18 (1928) 126–142, and N. Brox, 'Magie und Aberglauben an den Anfängen des Christentums,' *Trierer Theologische Zeitschrift* 83 (1974) 157–180, esp. 161–166.

[3] See, *inter multos alios*, W.L. Knox, 'Jewish Liturgical Exorcism,' *Harvard Theological Review* 31 (1938) 191–203, and idem, *St. Paul and the Church of the Gentiles*, Cambridge 1939, 208–211 ('Jewish Influences on Magical Literature') and M. Smith, 'The Jewish Elements in the Magical Papyri,' in his *Studies in the Cult of Yahweh*, vol. 2 (ed. by S.J.D. Cohen), Leiden 1996, 242–256.

their chariots and their cavalry, how he made the water of the Red Sea flow over (ἐπέκλυσεν) them as they pursued you.' All the ingredients of the formula are found in these two biblical passages, so although it is not a quote, the contents are there. The wording of the formula – ὁ θεὸς ὁ καταποντώσας ἐν τῇ ἐρυθρᾷ θαλάσσῃ τὸν Αἰγυπτίων βασιλέα καὶ τοὺς Αἰγυπτίους – is reminiscent of both passages, καταποντώσας being closer to κατεπόντισεν in Ex. 15:4 than to ἐπέκλυσεν in Deut. 11:4, but 'the king of the Egyptians' being closer to 'the king of Egypt' in Deut. 11:3 than to 'Pharaoh' in Ex. 15:4. Be that as it may, the important thing is that the formula captures in a nutshell the essence of the most dramatic story of Israel's past, its liberation by God from Egypt and the consequent destruction of its enemies.

In the framework of a magical spell such a formula has the function of a *historiola*, a mini-history[4] about the great deeds of a deity in the past, told in order to induce the deity concerned to remain true to its reputation and repeat its powerful act(s) in the present. As Fritz Graf has aptly said about *historiolae*, they are 'in magische Rezepte eingebaute knappe Erzählungen (…), die einen mythischen Präzedenzfall für eine magisch wirksame Handlung liefern.'[5] And in the same framework David Frankfurter writes about *historiolae* in terms of 'the idea that the mere recounting of certain stories situates or directs their "narrative" power into this world.'[6] Of this phenomoneon we have many pagan, Jewish, and Christian instances.[7]

In the famous exorcistic charm called the *Hebraïkos logos* in the great magical papyrus from Paris (PGM IV 3007–3086), we find the following adjuration: 'I adjure you by the great god Sabaoth, through whom the Jordan river drew back and the Red Sea, which Israel crossed, became impassable' (3053–3055).[8] This passage makes reference to both Joshua 3:13–14 (or Ps. 113:3) and Exod. 14:27. Here we do not find the exact formula 'the god who drowned the king of Egypt' but the idea is implied clearly in the words about the Red Sea becoming impassable. In spite of the biblical language and echoes, this spell most probably is not of Jewish origin but is a case of pagan borrowing of Jewish motifs.[9] This

---

[4] D. Aune, 'Magic in Early Christianity,' *Aufstieg und Niedergang der Römischen Welt* II 23, 2 (1980) 1547, aptly calls it a 'mini-aretalogy.'

[5] F. Graf, 'Historiola,' *NP* 5 (1998) 642.

[6] D. Frankfurter, 'Narrating Power: The Theory and Practice of the Magical *Historiola* in Ritual Spells,' in M. Meyer & P, Mirecki (eds.), *Ancient Magic and Ritual Power*, Leiden 1995, 457–476, here 457.

[7] See Th. Hopfner, 'Mageia,' *Pauly-Wissowa* 14,1 (1928) 343, and A.A. Barb, 'The Survival of Magic Arts,' in A. Momigliano (ed.), *The Conflict Between Paganism and Christianity in the Fourth Century*, Oxford 1963, 122. Frankfurter's is the best treatment to date.

[8] Translation by W.C. Grese in H.D. Betz (ed.), *The Greek Magical Papyri in Translation*, Chicago & London 1986, 97. For the Greek text see K. Preisendanz (& A. Henrichs), *Papyri Graecae Magicae. Die griechischen Zauberpapyrae*, vol. 1, Stuttgart 1973, 170–172.

[9] See my 'The Great Magical Papyrus of Paris (PGM IV) and the Bible' (forthcoming [elsewhere in this volume]), and Smith, 'Jewish Elements' 250.

pagan magician had no qualms about evoking powerful biblical scenes; the only thing that mattered to him was that his spell was effective. What could be more effective in chasing away a demon than invoking the deity who made the Red Sea impassable to the king of Egypt and drowned him in it? One can observe that in general the imagery of the plagues of the exodus is strongly emphasized in this spell. This should not surprise us. Morton Smith has figured out that out of the roughly 560 spells found in the corpus of pagan Greek magical papyri, some 200 show biblical or Jewish material one way or another.[10] This is strong evidence of the pervasive influence of biblical and post-biblical Jewish traditions in the international and interdenominational world of late ancient magic. A striking instance, which is very similar to the case under discussion, is PGM XXXVI 295–311, a love spell in which the magician evokes the image of the angels of God descending and overturning the five cities of Sodom, Gomorrah, Admah, Zeboim, and Segor, and of the God who rained down sulphur on these cities. Here Genesis 19 is taken into service in order that the woman desired by the client may come to him and 'fulfil the mystery rite of Aphrodite' (306), *i. e.*, have sex with him!

Although it is to be expected that the magical use of the motif of 'the God who drowned the king of Egypt' started its career in Jewish circles, there are hardly any Jewish examples prior to the pagan ones attested by Origen (third cent.).[11] From the third century CE we have a Jewish lead tablet from Hadrumetum in Tunisia containing a love charm in which the sorcerer casts a spell in the name of him 'who created the heaven and the sea' (10) and 'who split the sea with his staff' (12).[12] In view of the parallellism with 'who created the heaven and the sea,' there can be no doubt that the subject of 'who split ... the sea' is here God, not Moses. Here we do not find the drowning of the pharaoh explicitly mentioned, but it is certainly implied. Also from later centuries we only find

---

[10] Smith, 'Jewish Elements' 246–7. The only 'purely Jewish' spell found in PGM is nr. XXIIb 1–26, the 'Prayer of Jacob.'

[11] Those scholars who regard the 'Hebrew logos' as a Jewish document dating from before 70 CE, will of course take exception to this. On that matter see my forthcoming 'The Great Magical Papyrus of Paris (PGM IV) and the Bible' [see the previous chapter].

[12] For the text see G. Maspéro, 'Sur deux *tabellae devotionis* de la nécriopole romaine d'Hadrumète,' *Bibliothèque Égyptologique* 2 (1893) 303–311. It is also to be found in A. Deissmann, 'Ein epigraphisches Denkmal des alexandrinischen Alten Testaments,' in his *Bibelstudien*, Marburg 1895 (repr. 1977), 29; L. Blau, *Das altjüdische Zauberwesen*, Westmead 1970 (= Budapest 1898), 97; A. Audollent, *Defixionum tabellae*, Paris 1904, 373–377, no. 271 (cf. *ibid.* 323, no. 241, line 26 *chôrisas tên thalassan Iaô*); and R. Wünsch, *Antike Fluchtafeln*, Bonn 1912, 21–26, no. 5. For an English translation and commentary see J.G. Gager, *Curse Tablets and Binding Spells from the Ancient World*, New York – Oxford 1992, 112–115 (no. 36). Gager doubts its Jewish provenance, unrightly so; see R. Kotansky, 'Greek Exorcistic Amulets,' in M. Meyer & P, Mirecki (eds.), *Ancient Magic and Ritual Power*, Leiden 1995, 274. Literally the text reads, 'who split his staff with the sea,' but this is obviously an error; so rightly Deissmann 38, and P.S. Alexander, 'Jewish Elements in Gnosticism and Magic,' in W. Horbury a. o. (eds.), *The Cambridge History of Judaism*, vol. 3, Cambridge 1999, 1075 with note 51.

instances that do contain the motif but not the exact wording of the formula, as was also the case in PGM IV (4th cent.).

Among the magic bowls from late ancient Babylonia we find a few instances. In bowl 21 published by Naveh and Shaked,[13] we read the following adjuration: 'He who places a crown for the kingship, and makes dominion in the sky, and who has subdued Goliath by the hand of David, and Pharaoh by the hand of Moses, and Egypt by the hand of Joseph, and the wall of Jericho by the hand of Joshua bar Nun, may he ...' (10–11). This string of *historiolae* briefly lists some of the main mighty deeds of the God of Israel, of which the drowning of the king of Egypt is only one in a series. In the second instance, the largest Aramaic incantation bowl known so far,[14] the exorcism starts with the words, 'In the fulness of thy triumph thou overthrowest thy adversaries, thou sendest forth thy fury, it consumes them like stubble' (Exod. 15:7). To be sure the pharaoh and his army are not mentioned here explicitly, but these words, quoted from the Song at the Sea, are almost a direct continuation of the words 'Pharaoh's chariots and his army he cast into the sea' (Exod. 15:4), and there is no doubt that it was exactly these adversaries the magician had in mind. So again we see how important the evocation of this mighty deed of God was for exorcists, just as Origen mentioned, the parallel between the two – exorcism and exodus – of course residing in the element of liberation from an evil power.[15]

No wonder that in Christian circles, both in Egypt and elsewhere, many of these originally Jewish elements were adopted for exorcistic purposes.[16] Typically Christian elements were added, however, the cross and the resurrection of course foremost among them, being the Christian counterparts of the exodus from Egypt. Hence they could serve the same purpose.[17] In his *Dialogue with Trypho* 85.2 Justin quotes a summary of the Creed which has been taken over from an exorcistic formula, as Knox has convincingly argued.[18] And in *Contra Celsum* 1.6, Origen says that Christian exorcists subdue demons 'by the name of Jesus with the recital of the histories about him.' What else is the Creed than

---

[13] J. Naveh & Sh. Shaked, *Magic Spells and Formulae. Aramaic Incantations of Late Antiquity*, Jerusalem 1993, 127–130.

[14] J. Naveh & Sh. Shaked, *Amulets and Magic Bowls. Aramaic Incantations of Late Antiquity*, Jerusalem – Leiden 1985, 198–199, nr. 13 line 2.

[15] I did not find any instances in the three volumes *Magische Texte aus der Kairoer Geniza* edited by P. Schäfer & Sh. Shaked, Tübingen 1994–1999.

[16] E.g, the death of the Egyptians at the exodus is mentioned (as part of a long series of *megaleia tou theou*, all from the OT) in an exorcistic formula said to have been composed by Gregory Thaumatourgos; see for the Greek text Th. Schermann, *Griechische Zauberpapyri und das Gemeinde- und Dankgebet im 1. Klemensbrief*, Leipzig 1909, 20. Note that the motif occurs also in Hebrews 11:29; and cf. Justin, *Dialogus* 131.3, and the prayer in *Constitutiones Apostolicae* 8.12.12.

[17] See K. Thraede, 'Exorzismus,' *RAC* 7 (1969) 44–117, esp. 109–114.

[18] *St. Paul* 209. After the quote it is added that in this name (sc. of Jesus Christ whose life has just been summarized) every demon will be defeated and conquered.

a recital of the histories (*historiolae*) about Jesus? 'These credal exorcisms are surely formed on the earlier Jewish model of reciting the *historia* of the God of Israel.'[19] There is abundant evidence indeed that in exorcistic formulae Christian *historiolae* very soon began to be added to those of Jewish origin, or to supplant them.[20] But that is another story.

---

[19] Kotansky, 'Greek Exorcistic Amulets,' in Meyer & Mirecki (eds.), *Ancient Magic and Ritual Power*, 263 n. 47. Also Kotansky, *Greek Magical Amulets* 174–180.

[20] See Aune, 'Magic' 1547–8. See also W. Heitmüller, *"Im Namen Jesu": Eine sprach- und religionsgeschichtliche Untersuchung zum Neuen Testament, speziell zur altchristlichen Taufe*, Göttingen 1903, 334–336 ('Die Entstehung des Tauf-Symbols').

Original places of publication

'The Jews of Ancient Crete,' *Journal of Jewish Studies* 39 (1988) 183–200
'The Jews of Ancient Cyprus,' *Zutot: Perspectives on Jewish Culture* 2003 [published in 2004] 110–120
'The Jews of Ancient Sicily,' *Zutot: Perspectives on Jewish Culture* 2004 [published in 2005] 54–59
'The Synagogue of Sardis and Its Inscriptions.' Dutch original in *Nederlands Theologisch Tijdschrift* 56 (2002) 16–26
'Jews and Blues in Late Antiquity,' in D. Accorinti & P. Chuvin (eds.), *Des Géants à Dionysos. Mélanges de mythologie et de poésie grecques offerts à Francis Vian*, Alessandria: Edizioni dell' Orso, 2003, 565–572
'A Note on the Evil Inclination and Sexual Desire in Talmudic Literature,' in U. Mittmann-Richert, F. Avemarie & G.S. Oegema (eds.), *Der Mensch vor Gott. Forschungen zum Menschenbild in Bibel, antikem Judentum und Koran (Festschrift für Hermann Lichtenberger zum 60. Geburtstag)*, Neukirchen: Neukirchener Verlag, 2003, 99–106
'His Days Shall Be One Hundred and Twenty Years': Genesis 6:3 in Early Judaism and Ancient Christianity,' *Zutot: Perspectives on Jewish Culture* 2002 [published in 2003] 18–23
'*Inscriptiones Judaicae Orientis:* A Review Article,' *Journal for the Study of Judaism* 36 (2005) 65–83
'Huldah's Tomb in Early Jewish Tradition.' Dutch original in *Nederlands Theologisch Tijdschrift* 55 (2001) 91–96
'Pseudo-Phocylides on the Afterlife: A Rejoinder to John J. Collins,' *Journal for the Study of Judaism* 35 (2004) 70–75
'Philo's *In Flaccum* and the Book of Acts,' in: R. Deines & K.-W. Niebuhr (eds.), *Philo und das Neue Testament. Wechselseitige Wahrnehmungen* (Wissenschaftliche Untersuchungen zum Neuen Testament 172), Tübingen: Mohr Siebeck, 2004, 95–105
'Common Prayer in Philo's *In Flaccum* 121–124,' *Kenishta: Studies of the Synagogue World*, ed. J. Tabory, vol. 2, Bar Ilan University Press, 2003, 21–28
'Philo and the Rabbis on Genesis: Similar Questions, Different Answers,' in: A. Volgers & C. Zamagni (eds.), *Erotapokriseis. Early Christian Question-and-Answer Literature in Context* (Contributions to Biblical Exegesis and Theology 37), Leuven: Peeters, 2004, 55–70
'Philo of Alexandria on the Wrath of God.' Dutch original in A. de Jong & A. de Jong (eds.), *Kleine encyclopedie van de toorn*, Utrecht: Universitaire pers, 1993, 77–82
'Anti-Samaritan Propaganda in Early Judaism,' in P.W. van der Horst, M.J.J. Menken, J.F.M. Smit & G. van Oyen (eds.), *Persuasion and Dissuasion in Early Christianity, Ancient Judaism, and Hellenism* (Contributions to Biblical Exegesis and Theology 33), Leuven: Peeters, 2003, 25–44

'Jacques Basnage (1653–1723) on the Samaritans. Or: How much did one know about the Samaritans three centuries ago in the Netherlands?' (unpublished)

'Once More: the Translation of οἱ δέ in Matthew 28:17,' *Journal for the Study of the New Testament* 27 (1986) 27–30

'Abraham's Bosom, the Place Where He Belonged. A Short Note on ἀπενεχθῆναι in Luke 16:22,' *New Testament Studies* 52 (2006) [forthcoming]

'"Snorting Threat and Murder." The Hellenistic Background of Acts 9:1,' German original in *Novum Testamentum* 12 (1970) 257–269

'"Only Then Will All Israel Be Saved": A Short Note on the Meaning of καὶ οὕτως in Romans 11:26,' *Journal of Biblical Literature* 119 (2000) 521–525

'Macarius Magnes and the Unnamed Anti-Christian Polemicist. A Review Article,' *Vigiliae Christianae* 58 (2004) 332–341

'A New Early Christian Poem on the Sacrifice of Isaac (Pap. Bodmer 30),' in A. Hurst & J. Rudhardt (eds.), *Le Codex des Visions* (Recherches et rencontres 18), Genève: Librairie Droz, 2002, 155–172

'The Role of Scripture in Cyril of Scythopolis' *Lives of the Monks of Palestine*,' in J. Patrich (ed.), *The Sabaite Heritage in the Orthodox Church from the Fifth Century to the Present*, Leuven: Peeters, 2001 [published in 2002], 127–145

'Twenty-Five Questions to Corner the Jews: A Byzantine Anti-Jewish Document from the Seventh Century,' in E.G. Chazon, D. Satran & R.A. Clements (eds.), *Things Revealed. Studies in Early Jewish and Christian Literature in Honor of Michael E. Stone* (Supplements to the Journal for the Study of Judaism 89), Leiden: Brill, 2004, 289–302

'"The Most Superstitious and Disgusting of All Nations." Diogenes of Oenoanda on the Jews' in: A. P. M. H. Lardinois e. a. (edd.), *Land of Dreams. Greek and Latin Studies in Honour of A. H. M. Kessels,* Leiden: Brill, 2006, 291–298

'The Shadow in Hellenistic Popular Belief.' German original in M. J. Vermaseren (ed.), *Studies in Hellenistic Religions* (Etudes Préliminaires des Religions Orientales dans l'Empire Romain 78), Leiden: Brill, 1979, 27–36

'The First Atheist.' Dutch original in *Nederlands Theologisch Tijdschrift* 53 (1999) 42–49

'Subtractive Versus Additive Composite Numerals in Antiquity,' *Illinois Classical Studies* 13 (1988) 183–202

'The Great Magical Papyrus of Paris (PGM IV) and the Bible' (unpublished)

'"The God Who Drowned the King of Egypt." A Short Note on an Exorcistic Formula,' in A. Hilhorst & G.H. van Kooten (eds.), *The Wisdom of Egypt. Jewish, Early Christian, and Gnostic Studies in Honour of Gerard P. Luttikhuizen*, Leiden: Brill, 2005, 135–140

Bibliography of Pieter W. van der Horst, 1970–2005

A. *Articles and books*

1970
1. 'Drohung und Mord schnaubend (Acta IX 1),' *Novum Testamentum* 12 (1970) 257–269

1971
2. 'A Pagan Platonist and a Christian Platonist on Suicide,' *Vigiliae Christianae* 25 (1971) 282–288

1972
3. 'Can a Book End With ΓAP?,' *Journal of Theological Studies* n.s. 23 (1972) 121–124
4. 'A Wordplay in 1 John 4:12?,' *Zeitschrift für die neutestamentliche Wissenschaft* 63 (1972) 280–282

1973
5. 'Observations on a Pauline Expression,' *New Testament Studies* 19 (1972/73) 181–187
6. 'Macrobius and the New Testament. A Contribution to the Corpus Hellenisticum,' *Novum Testamentum* 15 (1973) 220–232

1974
7. (with J. Mansfeld) *An Alexandrian Platonist Against Dualism. Alexander of Lycopolis' Treatise "Critique of the Doctrines of Manichaeus" Translated with an Introduction and Notes,* Leiden: Brill, 1974; 99 pp.
8. 'Musonius Rufus and the New Testament. A Contribution to the Corpus Hellenisticum,' *Novum Testamentum* 16 (1974) 306–315

1975
9. 'Hierocles the Stoic and the New Testament. A Contribution to the Corpus Hellenisticum,' *Novum Testamentum* 17 (1975) 156–160

1976
10. 'Peter's Shadow. The Religio-Historical Background of Acts V 15,' *New Testament Studies* 23 (1976/77) 204–212

1977
11. 'Rabbi Dow Marmur over het christendom,' *Ter Herkenning* 5 (1977) 125–127
12. 'A Classical Parallel to Isaiah 5:8,' *The Expository Times* 89 (1977/78) 119–120

1978
13. 'In Memoriam Prof. Dr. W. C. van Unnik,' *Areopagus* 11, 3 (1978) 24
14. *The Sentences of Pseudo-Phocylides with Introduction and Commentary* (Studia in Veteris Testamenti Pseudepigrapha 4), Leiden: Brill, 1978; 296 pp.
15. 'Is Wittiness Unchristian? A Note on εὐτραπελία in Eph. V 4,' in T. Baarda, A.F.J. Klijn, W.C. van Unnik (edd.), *Miscellanea Neotestamentica* II, Leiden: Brill, 1978, 163–177
16. 'Pseudo-Phocylides and the New Testament,' *Zeitschrift für die neutestamentliche Wissenschaft* 69 (1978) 187–202
17. 'Seven Months' Children in Jewish and Christian Literature from Antiquity,' *Ephemerides Theologicae Lovanienses* 54 (1978) 346–360

1979
18. 'Het 'geheime Markusevangelie'. Over een nieuwe vondst,' *Nederlands Theologisch Tijdschrift* 33 (1979) 27–51
19. 'Der Schatten im hellenistischen Volksglauben,' in M. J. Vermaseren (ed.), *Studies in Hellenistic Religions*, EPRO 78, Leiden: Brill, 1979, 27–36
20. 'Jezus in de joodse literatuur van de oudheid,' *Kerk en Theologie* 30 (1979) 105–114
21. 'Some Late Instances of Inceptive ΔΕ,' *Mnemosyne* (ser. IV) 32 (1979) 377–379

1980
22. *Aelius Aristides and the New Testament* (Studia ad Corpus Hellenisticum Novi Testamenti 6), Leiden: Brill, 1980, X+115 pp.
23. 'Notes on the Aramaic Background of Luke II 41–52,' *Journal for the Study of the New Testament* 7 (1980) 61–66

1981
24. 'Cornutus and the New Testament. A Contribution to the Corpus Hellenisticum,' *Novum Testamentum* 23 (1981) 165–172
25. 'Chaeremon, Egyptisch priester en antisemitisch Stoïcijn in de tijd van het Nieuwe Testament,' *Nederlands Theologisch Tijdschrift* 35 (1981) 265–272

1982
26. 'De joodse toneelschrijver Ezechiel,' *Nederlands Theologisch Tijdschrift* 36 (1982) 97–112
27. 'The Secret Hieroglyphs in Classical Literature,' in J. den Boeft and A.H.M. Kessels (edd.), *Actus. Studies in Honour of H.L.W. Nelson,* Utrecht: Instituut voor Klassieke Talen, 1982, 115–123
28. 'De correspondentie van Hans Lietzmann,' *Kerk & Theologie* 33 (1982) 291–300
29. 'The Way of Life of the Egyptian Priests According to Chaeremon,' in M. Heerma van Voss e.a. (edd.), *Studies in Egyptian Religion in Honour of Professor Jan Zandee*, Leiden: Brill, 1982, 61–71

30. (with T. Baarda) *De spreuken van Pseudo-Phocylides. De spreuken van Pseudo-Menander*, Kampen: Kok, 1982, 90 pp.

1983

31. 'Het eerste congres van de European Association for Jewish Studies,' *Ter Herkenning* 11,2 (1983) 28–29
32. 'Moses' Throne Vision in Ezekiel the Dramatist,' *Journal of Jewish Studies* 34 (1983) 21–29
33. 'Hellenistic Parallels to the Acts of the Apostles: I 1–26,' *Zeitschrift für die neutestamentliche Wissenschaft* 74 (1983) 17–26
34. 'Openbaring,' *Moderne Encyclopedie van de Wereldliteratuur* 7 (1983) 78
35. 'Philo van Alexandrië,' *Moderne Encyclopedie van de Wereldliteratuur* 7 (1983) 228–229
36. 'Chariton and the New Testament. A Contribution to the Corpus Hellenisticum,' *Novum Testamentum* 25 (1983) 348–355

1984

37. *Chaeremon, Egyptian Priest and Stoic Philosopher. The Fragments Collected and Translated with Explanatory Notes* (EPRO 101), Leiden: Brill, 1984; XX + 80 pp.
38. 'Nieuwe Keulse en Weense publicaties over het vroege jodendom,' *Kerk en Theologie* 35 (1984) 129–137
39. 'Some Notes on the *Exagoge* of Ezekiel,' *Mnemosyne* (ser. IV) 37 (1984) 354–375
40. 'Hiërogliefen in de ogen van Grieken en Romeinen,' *Phoenix* 30 (1984) 44–53

1985

41. 'Het heidense antisemitisme in de oudheid,' *Ter Herkenning* 13,1 (1985) 45–53
42. 'Korte notities over vroeg-joodse epiek,' *Nederlands Theologisch Tijdschrift* 39 (1985) 102–109
43. 'Pseudo-Phocylides,' in J. H. Charlesworth (ed.), *The Old Testament Pseudepigrapha* II, New York: Doubleday, 1985, 565–582
44. 'Hellenistic Parallels to the Acts of the Apostles (2:1–47),' *Journal for the Study of the New Testament* 25 (1985) 49–60
45. 'Schriftgebruik bij drie vroege joods-hellenistische historici: Demetrius, Artapanus, Eupolemus,' *Amsterdamse Cahiers voor exegese en bijbelse theologie* 6 (1985) 144–161

1986

46. (with A.H.M. Kessels) 'Het Visioen van Dorotheüs (Papyrus Bodmer XXIX),' *Nederlands Theologisch Tijdschrift* 40 (1986) 97–111
47. 'Het christendom in het Romeinse rijk in de eerste eeuw: Enkele sociale en godsdiensthistorische aspecten,' *Hermeneus* 58 (1986) 58–67
48. 'Once More: The Translation of οἱ δέ in Matthew 28:17,' *Journal for the Study of the New Testament* 27 (1986) 27–30
49. 'The Role of Women in the Testament of Job,' *Nederlands Theologisch Tijdschrift* 40 (1986) 273–289
50. 'Het oorlogsvraagstuk in het christendom van de eerste drie eeuwen,' *Lampas* 19 (1986) 405–420

1987

51. 'De *Birkat ha-minim* in het recente onderzoek,' *Ter Herkenning* 15, 1 (1987) 38–46
52. '"Lord, Help the Rabbi." The Interpretation of SEG XXXI 1578b,' *Journal of Jewish Studies* 38 (1987) 102–106
53. 'Profetisch charismaticus met farizeese inslag,' in: *Wie is Jezus?* Themanummer van *Rondom het Woord* 28/29 (1987) 17–21
54. *Joods-hellenistische poëzie*, Kampen: Kok, 1987; 90 pp.
55. 'Addenda et Corrigenda to the first edition,' in P. W. van der Horst, *Chaeremon, Egyptian Priest and Stoic Philosopher*, second edition, Leiden: Brill, 1987, 81–85
56. 'Een merkwaardige anti-joodse legende in een middeleeuws lexicon,' *Ter Herkenning* 15 (1987) 185–192
57. 'The Measurement of the Body. A Chapter in the History of Ancient Jewish Mysticism,' in D. van der Plas (ed.), *Effigies Dei. Essays on the History of Religions* (Supplements to Numen 51), Leiden: Brill, 1987, 56–68
58. (with A.H.M. Kessels) 'The Vision of Dorotheus (Pap. Bodmer 29). Edited with Introduction, Translation and Notes,' *Vigiliae Christianae* 41 (1987) 313–359

1988

59. 'Novum Testamentum et Orbis Antiquus. Notities bij een nieuwe serie,' *Nederlands Theologisch Tijdschrift* 42 (1988) 60–66
60. *De onbekende god. Essays over de joodse en hellenistische achtergrond van het vroege christendom* (Utrechtse Theologische Reeks 2), Utrecht: Universiteitsdrukkerij, 1988; 285 pp.
61. 'De Samaritaanse diaspora in de oudheid,' *Nederlands Theologisch Tijdschrift* 42 (1988) 134–144
62. 'Hoe leesbaar moet een wetenschappelijke publicatie zijn?,' *Areopagus* 21,2 (1988) 11–12
63. 'The Unknown God (Acts 17:23),' in R. van den Broek, T. Baarda, J. Mansfeld (edd.), *Knowledge of God in the Graeco-Roman World* (EPRO 112), Leiden: Brill, 1988, 19–42
64. 'The Interpretation of the Bible by the Minor Hellenistic Jewish Authors,' in M. J. Mulder (ed.), *Mikra. Text, Translation, Reading and Interpretation of the Hebrew Bible in Ancient Judaism and Early Christianity* (Compendia Rerum Iudaicarum ad Novum Testamentum II 1), Assen – Philadelphia: Van Gorcum – Fortress, 1988, 519–546
65. 'The Jews of Ancient Crete,' *Journal of Jewish Studies* 39 (1988) 183–200
66. 'Ezechiel Tragicus en Anonymus,' in H. Warren, M. Molegraaf (edd.), *Spiegel van de Griekse poëzie van de oudheid tot heden*, Amsterdam: Meulenhof, 1988, 195–197
67. 'Gustaaf Adolf van den Bergh van Eysinga,' *Biografisch Lexicon voor de geschiedenis van het Nederlandse Protestantisme* III, Kampen: Kok, 1988, 37–39
68. (with G. Mussies) 'Subtractive Versus Additive Composite Numerals in Antiquity,' *Illinois Classical Studies* 13 (1988) 183–202

1989

69. 'Mijn vijf favoriete romans,' *Areopagus* 22, 1 (1989) 48–50.
70. 'Hellenistic Parallels to Acts (Chapters 3 and 4),' *Journal for the Study of the New Testament* 35 (1989) 37–46

71. 'Jews and Christians in Aphrodisias in the Light of Their Relations in Other Cities of Asia Minor,' *Nederlands Theologisch Tijdschrift* 43 (1989) 106–121

72. 'De reis van Alexander de Grote naar het Paradijs. Een middeleeuws-joodse legende over Alexander de Grote,' *Ter Herkenning* 17 (1989) 16–24

73. 'The Altar of the 'Unknown God' in Athens (Acts 17:23) and the Cult of 'Unknown Gods' in the Hellenistic and Roman Periods,' in *Aufstieg und Niedergang der Römischen Welt* II 18, 2, Berlin-New York: W. de Gruyter, 1989, 1426–1456

74. 'Pseudo-Phocylides Revisited,' *Journal for the Study of the Pseudepigrapha* 3 (1988 [appeared in 1989]) 3–30

75. 'Nieuwe literatuur over het jodendom,' *Nederlands Theologisch Tijdschrift* 43 (1989) 229–236

76. 'Introduction,' in M. A. Knibb and P. W. van der Horst (edd.), *Studies on the Testament of Job* (SNTS Monograph series 66), Cambridge, Cambridge University Press, 1989, 1–6

77. 'Images of Women in the Testament of Job,' *ibidem* 93–116

78. 'Geen ander evangelie? Notities over verdeeldheid in het oudste christendom,' in A. Houtepen (ed.), *Breekpunten en keerpunten. Beslissende historische momenten en factoren in het oecumenische proces*, Leiden – Utrecht, IIMO, 1989, 55–70.

1990

79. (with G. Mussies), *Studies on the Hellenistic Background of the New Testament* (Utrechtse Theologische Reeks 10), Utrecht: Rijksuniversiteit, 1990; 242 pag.

80. 'Het onderzoek van de vroege joodse mystiek sinds Scholem,' *Nederlands Theologisch Tijdschrift* 44 (1990) 121–138

81. 'Sara's zaad,' *MARA* 3 (1990) 44–52

82. *De Bijbelse Geschiedenis van Pseudo-Philo; een joodse hervertelling van de Bijbel uit de eerste eeuw van onze jaartelling* (Na de Schriften 7), Kampen: Kok, 1990; 174 pag.

83. *Essays on the Jewish World of Early Christianity* (NTOA 14), Fribourg-Göttingen: Universitätsverlag – Vandenhoeck & Ruprecht, 1990; 255 pag.

84. 'Zoek de Wijsheid. Een nieuw vroeg-joods Wijsheidsgeschrift uit het Hebreeuws vertaald,' *Ter Herkenning* 18 (1990) 174–194

85. 'Diplomatie in de antieke wereld,' *BZ: maandblad van het ministerie van buitenlandse zaken*, jrg. 17 no. 7, sept.1990, 9–10

86. 'Sarah's Seminal Emission. Hebrews 11:11 in the Light of Ancient Embryology,' in D. L. Balch – E. Ferguson – W. A. Meeks (edd.), *Greeks, Romans, and Christians (Essays in Honor of Abraham J. Malherbe)*, Minneapolis, Fortress Press, 1990, 287–302

87. 'Juden und Christen in Aphrodisias im Licht ihrer Beziehungen in anderen Städten Kleinasiens,' in J. van Amersfoort – J. van Oort (edd.), *Juden und Christen in der Antike*, Kampen, Kok, 1990, 125–143

88. 'Portraits of Biblical Women in Pseudo-Philo's *Liber Antiquitatum Biblicarum*,' *Journal for the Study of the Pseudepigrapha* 5 (1989 [appeared in 1990]) 29–46

89. 'Nimrod in Early Jewish Haggada,' in A. Kuyt – E.G.L. Schrijver – N.A. van Uchelen (edd.), *Variety of Forms. Dutch Studies in Midrash*, Amsterdam: Palache Instituut, 1990, 59–75

90. (with K. van der Toorn) 'Nimrod Before and After the Bible,' *Harvard Theological Review* 83 (1990) 1–29

1991

91. '"De waarachtige en niet met handen gemaakte God": naar aanleiding van een nieuwe inscriptie,' *Nederlands Theologisch Tijdschrift* 45 (1991) 177–182
92. *Ancient Jewish Epitaphs. An Introductory Survey of a Millennium of Jewish Funerary Epigraphy (300 BCE – 700 CE)*, Kampen: Kok-Pharos, 1991; 180 pag.
93. *Het Nieuwe Testament en de Joodse grafinscripties uit de hellenistisch-romeinse tijd* (Utrechtse Theologische Reeks 12), Utrecht: Rijksuniversiteit, 1991; 30 pag.
94. 'Jacob Frank: de bizarre ware Jacob,' *Trouw* 10 december 1991, 10
95. 'Willem Cornelis van Unnik,' *Rondom het Woord* 33,4 (1991) 30–34

1992

96. 'Did Sarah Have a Seminal Emission?,' *Bible Review* 8,1 (1992) 35–39
97. 'Israel, de Bijbel en de hellenistische cultuur en instituties,' *Schrift* 139 (1992) 26–30
98. 'A New Altar of a Godfearer?,' *Journal of Jewish Studies* 43 (1992) 32–37
99. 'Notities bij het thema: vrouwen in het vroege jodendom,' *Kerk & Theologie* 43 (1992) 113–129
100. 'Gij zult van goden geen kwaad spreken.' De Septuaginta-vertaling van Exodus 22:27 (28), haar achtergrond en invloed,' *Nederlands Theologisch Tijdschrift* 46 (1992) 192–198
101. 'Jewish Funerary Inscriptions: Most are in Greek,' *Biblical Archaeology Review* 18,5 (1992) 46–57
102. 'Corpus Hellenisticum Novi Testamenti,' *The Anchor Bible Dictionary* (= *ABD*) I (1992) 1157–1161
103. 'Ezekiel the Tragedian,' *ABD* 2 (1992) 709
104. 'Phocylides, Pseudo-,' *ABD* 5 (1992) 347–348
105. 'Shadow,' *ABD* 5 (1992) 1148–1150
106. 'Das Neue Testament und die jüdische Grabinschriften aus hellenistisch-römischer Zeit,' *Biblische Zeitschrift* NF 36 (1992) 161–178
107. 'Het recept van Gamaliel,' *Ter Herkenning* 20 (1992) 118–122
108. 'Deborah and Seila in Ps-Philo's Liber Antiquitatum Biblicarum,' in I. Gruenwald, S. Shaked, G. Stroumsa (edd.), *Messiah and Christos. Studies in the Jewish Origins of Christianity Presented to David Flusser*, Tübingen 1992, 111–118
109. *Studies over het jodendom in de oudheid*, Kampen: Kok, 1992; 224 pp.
110. '"I Gave Them Laws That Were Not Good.' Ezekiel 20:25 in Ancient Judaism and Early Christianity,' in J. N. Bremmer & F. García Martínez (edd.), *Sacred History and Sacred Texts in Early Judaism. A Symposium in Honour of A. S. van der Woude*, Kampen, Kok Pharos, 1992, 94–118
111. 'Wat moeten wij met Paulus?,' in H. Pool e.a. (edd.), *Honderd vragen over homoseksualiteit en kerk*, Gorinchem 1992, 13–14
112. 'Two Short Notes on Josephus,' *Studia Philonica Annual* 4 (1992) 59–64

1993

113. Vorwort, Einleitung, Fußnoten, Appendizes und Register in: Willem Cornelis van Unnik, *Das Selbstverständnis der jüdischen Diaspora in der hellenistisch-römischen Zeit*, aus dem Nachlaß herausgegeben und bearbeitet von P. W. van der Horst (Arbeiten zur Geschichte des Antiken Judentums und des Urchristentums XVII), Leiden: Brill, 1993; 200 pag.

114. 'How Many Jews Spoke Greek? A Reply to Mr. Chapman,' *Biblical Archaeology Review* 19 (1993) 70–72
115. (under pseudonym [Wim Slenk]) *Epafras. Het verhaal van een vreemde bekering*, Gorinchem: Narratio, 1993; 48 pag.
116. 'Einige Beobachtungen zum Thema 'Frauen im antiken Judentum',' *Berliner Theologische Zeitschrift* 10 (1993) 77–93
117. 'Tamar in Pseudo-Philo's *Biblical History*,' in A. Brenner (ed.), *A Feminist Companion to Genesis* [The Feminist Companion to the Bible 2], Sheffield: Sheffield Academic Press, 1993, 300–305
118. 'A Note on the Judas Curse in Early Christian Inscriptions,' *Orientalia Christiana Periodica* 59 (1993) 211–215
119. 'Jesus and the Jews according to the Suda,' *Zeitschrift für die neutestamentliche Wissenschaft* 84 (1993) 268–277
120. 'Philo Alexandrinus over de toorn Gods,' in A. de Jong & A. de Jong (edd.), *Kleine encyclopedie van de toorn*, Utrecht: Universitaire pers, 1993, 77–82
121. '"Thou shalt not revile the gods." The LXX-translation of Ex. 22:28 (27), its background and influence,' *Studia Philonica Annual* 5 (1993) 1–8
122. 'Johann Jakob Wettstein nach 300 Jahren: Erbe und Auftrag,' *Theologische Zeitschrift* 49 (1993) 267–281
123. 'Hellenism,' in A. D. Crown, R. Pummer & A. Tal (edd.), *A Companion to Samaritan Studies*, Tübingen: Mohr, 1993, 117–118
124. 'Jewish Metrical Epitaphs,' in J. den Boeft & A. Hilhorst (edd), *Early Christian Poetry*, Leiden: Brill, 1993, 1–14.
125. 'De pelgrim van Bordeaux: het oudste verslag van een christelijke pelgrimage naar het Heilige Land (AD 333),' *Ter Herkenning* 21 (1993) 217–225
126. 'Women in Ancient Judaism,' *Theology Digest* 40 (1993) 211–216

1994

127. 'Introduction,' in J. W. van Henten & P. W. van der Horst (edd.), *Studies in Early Jewish Epigraphy* (AGAJU 21), Leiden: Brill, 1994, 1–8
128. 'Jewish Poetical Tomb Inscriptions,' in J. W. van Henten & P. W. van der Horst (edd.), *Studies in Early Jewish Epigraphy* (AGAJU 21), Leiden: Brill, 1994, 129–147
129. 'Silent Prayer in Antiquity,' *Numen* 41 (1994) 1–25
130. 'Johann Jakob Wettstein na 300 jaar: erfenis en opdracht,' *Nederlands Theologisch Tijdschrift* 48 (1994) 1–11
131. 'Het lot van Judas in vroegchristelijke grafinscripties,' *Kerk en Theologie* 45 (1994) 138–142
132. 'Ontwikkelingen in de vroege joodse angelologie,' *Nederlands Theologisch Tijdschrift* 48 (1994) 141–150
133. 'Two Notes on Hellenistic Lore in Early Rabbinic Literature,' *Jewish Studies Quarterly* 1 (1993/94) 252–262
134. *Hellenism – Judaism – Christianity. Essays on Their Interaction* (Contributions to Biblical Exegesis and Theology 8), Kampen: Kok Pharos, 1994; 300 pp.
135. *Gebeden uit de antieke wereld. Grieks-Romeinse, Joodse en Christelijke gebedsteksten in het Nederlands vertaald en toegelicht*, Kampen: Kok, 1994; 115 pp.
136. 'The Birkat ha-minim in Recent Research,' *The Expository Times* 105 (1994) 363–368

137. 'Theologie als niet-kerkelijke wetenschap,' in F.G.M. Broeyer & T. van Willigenburg (red.), *Facultas Theologica: soror sororum! Opstellen over theologie en universiteit* (Utrechtse Theologische Reeks 27), Utrecht: Universiteit, 1994, 73–85.
138. 'Samaritans and Hellenism,' *Studia Philonica Annual* 6 (1994) 28–36

1995
139. 'Sex, Birth, Purity and Ascetism in the *Protevangelium Jacobi*,' in *Neotestamentica: Journal of the New Testament Society of South Africa* 28,3 (1994/5) 205–218
140. 'Maximus van Tyrus' tractaat over het gebed,' *Hermeneus* 67 (1995) 11–16
141. 'Hermias' satire op de Griekse filosofie. Een Nederlandse vertaling van de *Irrisio gentilium philosophorum*,' *Kerk en Theologie* 46 (1995) 155–164
142. 'Maximus van Tyrus over het gebed,' *Nederlands Theologisch Tijdschrift* 49 (1995) 12–23
143. 'Images of Women in Ancient Judaism,' in: R. Kloppenborg & W. J. Hanegraaff (edd.), *Female Stereotypes in Religious Traditions* (Studies in the History of Religions 66), Leiden: Brill, 1995, 43–60
144. *Het leven van Simeon de pilaarheilige. De twee Griekse levensbeschrijvingen vertaald, ingeleid en toegelicht* (Utrechtse Theologische Reeks 30), Utrecht: Universiteit, 1995; 60 pag.
145. 'Gebeden uit de antieke wereld,' *Rondom het Woord* 37,2 (1995) 21–25
146. 'De Joden van Napels in de Romeinse keizertijd,' *Ter Herkenning* 23 (1995) 55–64
147. *Woestijn, begeerte en geloof. Het leven van de eerste monniken in Egypte.* De Historia monachorum in Aegypto (ca. 400 na Chr.) vertaald en toegelicht (Christelijke bronnen 8), Kampen: Kok, 1995; 126 pp.
148. 'Ananke,' in K. van der Toorn, B. Becking & P. W. van der Horst (edd.), *Dictionary of Deities and Demons in the Bible* (= *DDD*), Leiden: Brill, 1995, 60–62
149. 'Chaos,' *DDD* 354–356
150. 'Dike,' *DDD* 476–480
151. 'Dominion,' *DDD* 498–500
152. 'Father of the Lights,' *DDD* 620–621
153. 'God (II),' *DDD* 692–699
154. 'Hosios kai Dikaios,' *DDD* 810–812
155. 'Hyle,' *DDD* 819–820
156. 'Lamb,' *DDD* 938–941
157. 'Mammon,' *DDD* 1012–1014
158. 'Thanatos,' *DDD* 1609–1613
159. 'Themis,' *DDD* 1613–1614
160. 'Unknown God,' *DDD* 1664–1670
161. 'Introduction,' in P. W. van der Horst (ed.), *Aspects of Religious Contact and Conflict in the Ancient World* (Utrechtse Theologische Reeks 31), Utrecht: Theologische Faculteit, 1995, 11–15
162. 'Jewish Self-Definition by Way of Contrast in *Oracula Sibyllina* III 218–247,' *ibidem* 147–166
163. 'Gottesfürchtige,' *Lexikon für Theologie und Kirche* 4 (1995) 914–915

1996
164. (with G. Mussies) 'A Greek Christian Epitaph in Utrecht,' *Zeitschrift für Papyrologie und Epigraphik* 110 (1996) 285–289
165. 'Sarah's Seminal Emission: Hebrews 11:11 in the Light of Ancient Embryology,' in A. Brenner (ed.), *A Feminist Companion to the Hebrew Bible in the New Testament*, Sheffield: Sheffield Academic Press, 1996, 112–134 [see no. 86]
166. 'Exegetische notities over Maria in het *Protevangelium Jacobi*,' *Nederlands Theologisch Tijdschrift* 50 (1996) 108–121
167. 'Niezen als omen in de antieke wereld,' *Hermeneus* 68 (1996) 179–181
168. 'Korte notities over het godsbegrip bij Grieken en Romeinen en de vergoddelijking van Jezus in het Nieuwe Testament,' *Bijdragen: tijdschrift voor filosofie en theologie* 57 (1996) 149–157
169. '"A Simple Philosophy." Alexander of Lycopolis on Christianity,' in K. A. Algra, P. W. van der Horst & D. T. Runia (edd.), *Polyhistor. Studies in the History and Historiography of Ancient Philosophy Presented to Jaap Mansfeld on his Sixtieth Birthday* (Philosophia Antiqua 72), Leiden-New York-Köln: Brill, 1996, 313–329
170. 'Inscriptions (Greek),' in: J. Neusner and W.S. Green (edd.), *Dictionary of Judaism in the Biblical Period*, 2 vols., New York: Macmillan, 1996, 1:315–316
171. 'The Distinctive Vocabulary of Josephus' *Contra Apionem*,' in L.H. Feldman & J.R. Levison (edd.), *Josephus' Contra Apionem: Studies in its Character and Context* (AGAJU 34), Leiden: Brill, 1996, 83–93
172. 'Johannes von Gischala,' *Lexikon für Theologie und Kirche* 5 (1996) 910
173. 'Judas der Galiläer,' *Lexikon für Theologie und Kirche* 5 (1996) 1024
174. 'Maximus of Tyre on Prayer. An Annotated Translation of Εἰ δεῖ εὔχεσθαι (Dissertatio 5),' in H. Cancik, H. Lichtenberger & P. Schäfer (edd.), *Geschichte – Tradition – Reflexion: Festschrift für Martin Hengel zum 70. Geburtstag*, 3 vols., Tübingen: Mohr, 1996, Vol. 2: 323–338

1997
175. 'Plato's angst als motief in de oudchristelijke apologetiek,' *Nederlands Theologisch Tijdschrift* 51 (1997) 1–12
176. *Bronnen voor de studie van de wereld van het vroege christendom, deel 1: Joodse bronnen*, Kampen: Kok, 1997; 268 pp.
177. *Bronnen voor de studie van de wereld van het vroege christendom, deel 2: Pagane bronnen*, Kampen: Kok, 1997; 272 pp.
178. 'De hel: een proces van loutering,' *Rondom het Woord* 39 (1997) 34–39
179. 'Hellenistic Parallels to the Acts of the Apostles,' in: C. A. Evans & S. E. Porter (edd.), *New Testament Backgrounds. A Sheffield Reader*, Sheffield: Sheffield Academic Press, 1997, 207–229
180. 'Notes on the Aramaic Background of Luke 2:41–52,' in: S. E. Porter & C. A. Evans (edd.), *New Testament Text and Language. A Sheffield Reader*, Sheffield: Sheffield Academic Press, 1997, 235–240
181. 'Het gebed in het vroege jodendom,' *Nieuwsbulletin van de Willem C. van Unnik Stichting 1997*, 4–15
182. 'Pseudo-Philo,' *Theologische Realenzyklopädie* XXVII (1997) 670–672
183. 'The Finger of God. Miscellaneous Notes on Luke 11:20 and its *Umwelt*,' in: W. L. Petersen, J. S. Vos, H. J. de Jonge (edd.), *Sayings of Jesus: Canonical & Non-*

Canonical. Essays in Honour of Tjitze Baarda (Supplements to Novum Testamentum 89), Leiden: Brill, 1997, 89–104

1998

184. 'Plato's Fear as a Topic in Early Christian Apologetics,' *Journal of Early Christian Studies* 6 (1998) 1–14
185. 'Het Achttiengebed in het Grieks?,' *Nederlands Theologisch Tijdschrift* 52 (1998) 124–138
186. 'Herman van der Horst,' *Biografisch Lexicon voor de Geschiedenis van het Nederlandse Protestantisme* 4, Kampen: Kok, 1998, 220–221
187. 'Papyrus Egerton 5: Christian or Jewish?,' *Zeitschrift für Papyrologie und Epigraphik* 121 (1998) 173–182
188. *Hellenism – Judaism – Christianity: Essays on Their Interaction*, second enlarged edition, Leuven: Peeters, 1998; 342 pp. [see no. 134]
189. 'Neglected Greek Evidence for Early Jewish Liturgical Prayer,' *Journal for the Study of Judaism* 29 (1998) 278–296
190. 'Laat staan de hartstochten,' *Trouw* 5 sept. 1998, 19
191. *De Woestijnvaders. Levensverhalen van kluizenaars uit het vroege christendom*, Amsterdam: Prometheus, 1998; 285 pp.
192. 'Maria, de joodse alchemiste,' *Areopagus* n.s. 2,3 (1998) 13
193. 'De Septuaginta,' *Hermeneus* 70 (1998) 266–271
194. 'Agnostos Theos,' *Religion in Geschichte und Gegenwart*, Band I, 4. Aufl. (=*RGG* I⁴), Tübingen 1998, 188
195. 'Alexander von Lykopolis,' *RGG* I⁴, 288
196. 'Aphrodisias,' *RGG* I⁴, 584
197. 'Apologetik (Judentum, hellenistisch),' *RGG* I⁴, 612
198. 'Areopagrede,' *RGG* I⁴, 718–719
199. 'Aristeas (Exeget),' *RGG* I⁴, 726
200. 'Aristobul,' *RGG* I⁴, 728
201. 'Artapanos,' *RGG* I⁴, 797
202. '*Sortes*: Sacred Books as Instant Oracles in Late Antiquity,' in L.V. Rutgers, P.W. van der Horst, H.W. Havelaar, L. Teugels (eds.), *The Use of Sacred Books in the Ancient World* (Contributions to Biblical Exegesis and Theology 22), Leuven: Peeters, 1998, 143–174
203. 'Hoe Henoch god werd,' *Prana: tijdschrift voor spiritualiteit en de randgebieden der wetenschappen* 110 (december 1998) 58–60

1999

204. 'Adam,' in K. van der Toorn, B. Becking & P. W. van der Horst (eds.), *Dictionary of Deities and Demons in the Bible,* second extensively revised edition (= DDD²), Leiden: Brill – Grand Rapids: Eerdmans, 1999, 5–6
205. 'Amazons,' DDD², 27–28
206. 'Eros,' DDD², 304–306
207. 'Evil Inclination,' DDD², 317–319
208. 'Hypnos,' DDD², 438–439
209. 'De eerste atheïst,' *Nederlands Theologisch Tijdschrift* 53 (1999) 42–49

210. *Het Boek der Hemelse Paleizen (3 Henoch): een joods mystiek geschrift uit de late oudheid*, uit het Hebreeuws vertaald en toegelicht (Joodse Bronnen 2), Kampen: Kok, 1999; 116 pp.
211. 'Weg van de wereld,' *Rondom het Woord* 41,1 (1999) 47–57
212. 'The Greek Synagogue Prayers in the Apostolic Constitutions, book VII,' in J. Tabory (ed.), *From Qumran to Cairo. Studies in the History of Prayer*, Jerusalem: Orchot, 1999, 19–46
213. *Sortes: het gebruik van heilige boeken als lotsorakels in de oudheid* (Mededelingen van de Afdeling Letterkunde van de Koninklijke Nederlandse Akademie van Wetenschappen, Nieuwe reeks, deel 62, no. 3), Amsterdam: KNAW, 1999; 40 pp.
214. 'Was the Synagogue a Place of Sabbath Worship Before 70 CE?,' in S. Fine (ed.), *Jews, Christians, and Polytheists in the Ancient Synagogue. Cultural Interaction during the Graeco-Roman Period*, London-New York: Routledge,1999, 18–43
215. 'Was de synagoge vóór 70 een plaats van eredienst op sabbat?,' *Bijdragen* 60 (1999) 125–146
216. 'De woestijnvaders: spiritualiteit, begeerte en ascese in de vroege kerk,' *Kunst en wetenschap* 8, nr.3 (1999) 9–10
217. (with J. Laenen) 'De hemelse reis,' *Rondom het Woord* 41, nr.3 (1999) 38–43
218. '"Leer hem de Psalmen, want ik heb hem nodig!" De Bijbel in het werk van Cyrillus van Skythopolis,' *Nederlands Theologisch Tijdschrift* 53 (1999) 274–285

2000

219. 'Ancient Jewish Bibliomancy,' *Journal of Graeco-Roman Christianity and Judaism* 1 (2000) 9–17
220. *Mozes, Plato, Jezus. Studies over de wereld van het vroege christendom*, Amsterdam: Prometheus, 2000; 282 pp.
221. 'Messianisme en gebed in de rollen van de Dode Zee. Een bespreking,' *Nederlands Theologisch Tijdschrift* 54 (2000) 35–47
222. 'Jozef en Asenet,' *Schrift* 187 (2000) 25–27
223. 'Eve in the New Testament,' 'Rebekah in the New Testament,' 'Wife of Lot,' 'Prophesying Daughters,' in C. Meyers e.a. (eds.), *Women in Scripture*, Boston – New York: Houghton Mifflin Company, 2000, 84, 144–5, 448, 457–8
224. (with L. Teugels) 'De toekomst van de joodse studiën aan Nederlandse theologische faculteiten,' *Areopagus* 4,2 (2000) 18–20
225. 'Christelijke woestijnheiligen in het antieke Nabije Oosten,' *Phoenix* 46 (2000) 26–37
226. '"Pas dan zal heel Israël gered worden." Hoe moet Romeinen 11:26 vertaald worden?,' *Kerk en Theologie* 51 (2000) 183–188
227. 'Jews and Christians in Antioch at the End of the Fourth Century,' in S.E. Porter & B.W.R. Pearson (eds.), *Christian-Jewish Relations Through the Centuries*, Sheffield: Sheffield Academic Press, 2000, 228–238
228. 'Telkens nieuwe vormen,' *Rondom het Woord* 42, 2 (2000) 50–55
229. '"Only Then Will All Israel Be Saved": A Short Note on the Meaning of καὶ οὕτως in Romans 11:26,' *Journal of Biblical Literature* 119 (2000) 521–525
230. 'Wisdom From Time Immemorial: Ancient Speculations About Antediluvian Knowledge,' in: C. Kroon & D. den Hengst (eds.), *Ultima Aetas: Time, Tense and Transience in the Ancient World. Studies in Honour of Jan den Boeft*, Amsterdam: VU University Press, 2000, 95–106

231. 'Bibliomancy,' in C.A. Evans & S.E. Porter (eds.), *Dictionary of New Testament Background*, Downers Grove & Leicester: InterVarsity Press, 2000, 165–167
232. 'Jewish Literature: Historians and Poets,' in C.A. Evans & S.E. Porter (eds.), *Dictionary of New Testament Background*, Downers Grove & Leicester: InterVarsity Press, 2000, 580–584
233. 'Maria the Jewish Alchemist,' in C.A. Evans & S.E. Porter (eds.), *Dictionary of New Testament Background*, Downers Grove & Leicester: InterVarsity Press, 2000, 679–680
234. (with M.F.G. Parmentier) 'Een nieuw oudchristelijk geschrift over het offer van Izaäk,' *Bijdragen* 61 (2000) 243–260
235. 'De toekomst van de joodse studiën aan Nederlandse theologische faculteiten,' in R. Fontaine, E. Schrijver & I. Zwiep (red.), *De toekomst van de joodse studies in Nederland*, Amsterdam: Menasseh ben Israël Instituut, 2000, 29–37

2001
236. 'Celibaat in het vroege jodendom,' *Kerk & Theologie* 52 (2001) 22–32
237. 'Vroegjoodse mystieke interpretaties van motieven in Exodus,' *Schrift* 194 (2001) 56–58
238. 'Het graf van de profetes Hulda in de joodse traditie,' *Nederlands Theologisch Tijdschrift* 55 (2001) 91–96
239. 'Willem Cornelis van Unnik,' *Biografisch Lexicon voor de Geschiedenis van het Nederlandse Protestantisme* V, Kampen: Kok, 2001, 514–516
240. *De profeten. Joodse en christelijke legenden uit de oudheid*, Amsterdam: Athenaeum – Polak & van Gennep, 2001; 188 pp.
241. 'The Samaritan Languages in the Pre-Islamic Period,' *Journal for the Study of Judaism* 32 (2001) 178–192
242. 'Greek in Jewish Palestine in Light of Jewish Epigraphy,' in J.J. Collins & G.E. Sterling (eds.), *Hellenism in the Land of Israel*, Notre Dame: University of Notre Dame Press, 2001, 154–174
243. *Die Prophetengräber im antiken Judentum* (Franz-Delitzsch-Vorlesung 2000), Münster: Institutum Judaicum Delitzschianum, 2001; 28 pp.
244. 'Judaica en Samaritana: een besprekingsartikel,' *Nederlands Theologisch Tijdschrift* 55 (2001) 328–332
245. 'De Magistro: Willem Cornelis van Unnik (1910–1978),' *Areopagus* 5, 4 (dec. 2001) 26–28

2002
246. 'De synagoge van Sardis en haar inscripties,' *Nederlands Theologisch Tijdschrift* 56 (2002) 16–26
247. 'The Role of Scripture in Cyril of Scythopolis' *Lives of the Monks of Palestine*,' in J. Patrich (ed.), *The Sabaite Heritage in the Orthodox Church from the Fifth Century to the Present*, Leuven: Peeters, 2001 [published in 2002], 127–145
248. 'Jezus in de joodse literatuur van de oudheid,' *Spiegel Historiael* 37 (2002) 122–127
249. *Japheth in the Tents of Shem. Studies on Jewish Hellenism in Antiquity* (Contributions to Biblical Exegesis and Theology 32), Leuven: Peeters, 2002; 272 pp.
250. 'Who Was Apion?,' in *Japheth in the Tents of Shem* 207–221
251. 'Samaritans at Rome?,' in *Japheth in the Tents of Shem* 251–260

252. (with M.F.G. Parmentier) 'A New Early Christian Poem on the Sacrifice of Isaac,' in A. Hurst & J. Rudhardt (eds.), *Le Codex des Visions* (Recherches et rencontres 18), Genève: Librairie Droz, 2002, 155–172

253. 'Apion, 'cimbaal van de wereld',' *Lampas* 35 (2002) 228–241

254. 'Celibacy in Early Judaism,' *Revue Biblique* 109 (2002) 390–402

255. 'Celibato en el Judaísmo Antiguo,' *Sefarad* 62 (2002) 85–98

256. 'Shomronim we-hityawanut' [Hebr.], in E. Stern & H. Eshel (eds.), *Sefer ha-Shom-ronim* [Book of the Samaritans], Jerusalem: Yad Ben-Zvi Press, 2002, 184–191

257. 'Maria Alchemista, the First Female Jewish Author,' *Zutot: Perspectives on Jewish Culture* 2001 [published in 2002], 44–47

258. 'Antediluvian Knowledge: Jewish Speculations About Wisdom From Before the Flood in Their Ancient Context,' in H. Lichtenberger & G.S. Oegema (eds.), *Jü-dische Schriften in ihrem antik-jüdischen und urchristlichen Kontext*, Gütersloh: Gütersloher Verlagshaus, 2002, 163–181

259. 'Mammon,' *Religion in Geschichte und Gegenwart*, Band V, 4. Aufl., Tübingen: Mohr Siebeck, 2002, 720–721

260. 'Joden en hooligans in de late oudheid,' *Nederlands Theologisch Tijdschrift* 56 (2002) 273–279

261. 'The First Pogrom: Alexandria 38 CE,' *European Review* 10 (2002) 469–484

2003

262. 'Het grafschrift van Jakobus, de broer van Jezus?,' *Nederlands Theologisch Tijd-schrift* 57 (2003) 1–9

263. 'The Last Jewish Patriarch(s) and Greco-Roman Medicine,' in M. Mor a. o. (eds.), *Jews and Gentiles in the Holy Land in the Days of the Second Temple, the Mishnah and the Talmud*, Jerusalem: Yad Ben-Zvi Press, 2003, 87–96

264. 'Nova Judaica. Een overzicht van enkele belangrijke recente publicaties,' *Kerk en Theologie* 54 (2003) 143–159

265. 'Common Prayer in Philo's *In Flaccum* 121–124,' *Kenishta: Studies of the Syn-agogue World*, ed. J. Tabory, vol. 2, Bar Ilan University Press, 2003, 21–28

266. 'Anti-Samaritan Propaganda in Early Judaism,' in P.W. van der Horst e.a. (eds.), *Persuasion and Dissuasion in Early Christianity, Ancient Judaism, and Hellenism* (Contributions to Biblical Exegesis and Theology 33), Leuven: Peeters, 2003, 25–44

267. "His Days Shall Be One Hundred and Twenty Years': Genesis 6:3 in Early Judaism and Ancient Christianity,' *Zutot: Perspectives on Jewish Culture* 2002 [published in 2003] 18–23

268. 'A Note on the Evil Inclination and Sexual Desire in Talmudic Literature,' in U. Mittmann-Richert, F. Avemarie & G.S. Oegema (eds.), *Der Mensch vor Gott. Forschungen zum Menschenbild in Bibel, antikem Judentum und Koran (Festschrift für Hermann Lichtenberger zum 60. Geburtstag)*, Neukirchen: Neukirchener Verlag, 2003, 99–106

269. 'Jews and Blues in Late Antiquity,' in D. Accorinti & P. Chuvin (edd.), *Des Géants à Dionysos. Mélanges de mythologie et de poésie grecques offerts à Francis Vian*, Alessandria: Edizioni dell' Orso, 2003, 565–572

270. *Philo's Flaccus: The First Pogrom. Introduction, Translation and Commentary* (Philo of Alexandria Commentary Series 2), Leiden: Brill, 2003; XII+278 pp.

271. *Joden in de Grieks-Romeinse wereld. Vijftien miniaturen* (Utrechtse Studies 5), Zoetermeer: Meinema, 2003; 170 pp.

272. 'Der Zölibat im Frühjudentum,' in W. Kraus & K.-W. Niebuhr (hrsgg.), *Frühjudentum und Neues Testament im Horizont Biblischer Theologie* (Wissenschaftliche Untersuchungen zum Neuen Testament 162), Tübingen: Mohr Siebeck, 2003, 3–14

2004

273. 'Nogmaals: het grafschrift van Jakobus, de broer van Jezus,' *Nederlands Theologisch Tijdschrift* 58 (2004) 18–27

274. 'Pseudo-Phocylides on the Afterlife: A Rejoinder to John J. Collins,' *Journal for the Study of Judaism* 35 (2004) 70–75

275. 'De studie van het jodendom en het Nieuwe Testament,' *Areopagus* 8,1 (2004) 39–41

276. 'Vijfentwintig vragen om joden in het nauw te drijven: Een Byzantijns anti-joods document uit de zevende eeuw,' *Nederlands Theologisch Tijdschrift* 58 (2004) 89–99

277. 'Ha-nasi' ha-acharon weha-rephu'ah ha-yewanit-romit,' in Lee I. Levine (ed.), *Retsef u-temunah: Yehudim we-yahaduth be'erets Yisra'el ha-byzantit-notsrit* [Continuity and Renewal. Jews and Judaism in Byzantine-Christian Palestine], Jerusalem: Yad Ben-Zwi & The Jewish Theological Seminary of America, 2004, 233–241

278. 'Eén mei in Litouwen,' *Nieuw Israëlitisch Weekblad* 14 mei 2004, 14

279. 'Joodse miniatuurtjes (1): Gezondheid!,' *Chadashot. Maandblad van de Liberaal Joodse Gemeente Utrecht* 6, nr. 7 (sept. 2004) 19–21

280. *De Samaritanen. Geschiedenis en godsdienst van een vergeten groepering*, Kampen: Kok, 2004; 128 pag.

281. 'The Jews of Ancient Cyprus,' *Zutot: Perspectives on Jewish Culture* 2003 [published in 2004] 110–120

282. 'Vertaling komt rabbijnen slecht uit,' *Trouw* 1 okt. 2004, 15

283. 'Philo's *In Flaccum* and the Book of Acts,' in: R. Deines & K.-W. Niebuhr (eds), *Philo und das Neue Testament. Wechselseitige Wahrnehmungen* (Wissenschaftliche Untersuchungen zum Neuen Testament 172), Tübingen: Mohr Siebeck, 2004, 95–105

284. Review article on R. Goulet, (ed.), *Macarios de Magnésie: Le Monogénès* (2003), *Vigiliae Christianae* 58 (2004) 332–341

285. 'Joodse miniatuurtjes (2): Amuletten,' *Chadashot. Maandblad van de Liberaal Joodse Gemeente Utrecht* 6, nr. 8 (okt. 2004) 23–25

286. 'Philo and the Rabbis on Genesis: Similar Questions, Different Answers,' in: A. Volgers & C. Zamagni (eds.), *Erotapokriseis. Early Christian Question-and-Answer Literature in Context* (Contributions to Biblical Exegesis and Theology 37), Leuven: Peeters, 2004, 55–70

287. 'Joods in Litouwen,' *Areopagus* 8,3 (oct. 2004) 17–18

288. 'Joodse miniatuurtjes (3): NBV en NIK,' *Chadashot. Maandblad van de Liberaal Joodse Gemeente Utrecht* 6, nr. 9 (nov. 2004) 23–25

289. 'Twenty-Five Questions to Corner the Jews: A Byzantine Anti-Jewish Document from the Seventh Century,' in E.G. Chazon, D. Satran & R.A. Clements (eds.), *Things Revealed. Studies in Early Jewish and Christian Literature in Honor of Michael E. Stone* (Supplements to the Journal for the Study of Judaism 89), Leiden: Brill, 2004, 289–302

290. 'De oorsprong van het kwaad volgens een vroegjoodse visie,' in: C. van der Burg & L. Minnema (eds.), *In de ban van het kwaad. Het kwaad in religieuze verhalen wereldwijd*, Zoetermeer: Meinema, 2004, 113–120

291. 'Joodse miniatuurtjes (4): Tiberius Julius Alexander,' *Chadashot. Maandblad van de Liberaal Joodse Gemeente Utrecht* 6, nr. 10 (dec. 2004) 23–25

2005

292. 'De ontwikkeling van het Grieks en het Nieuwe Testament. Opmerkingen naar aanleiding van een recente publicatie,' *Nederlands Theologisch Tijdschrift* 59 (2005) 21–30

293. 'Joodse miniatuurtjes (5): Het grafschrift van Regina,' *Chadashot. Maandblad van de Liberaal Joodse Gemeente Utrecht* 7, nr. 1 (febr. 2005) 9–11

294. 'Joodse miniatuurtjes (6): Jacob Frank: verlossing door zonde,' *Chadashot. Maandblad van de Liberaal Joodse Gemeente Utrecht* 7, nr. 2 (mrt. 2005) 9–12

295. 'Jannes Reiling (1923–2005): een persoonlijke herinnering,' *Areopagus* 9,1 (2005) 7

296. '*Inscriptiones Judaicae Orientis:* A Review Article,' *Journal for the Study of Judaism* 36 (2005) 65–83

297. 'Joodse miniatuurtjes (7): Waarom engelen niet eten,' *Chadashot. Maandblad van de Liberaal Joodse Gemeente Utrecht* 7, nr. 3 (apr. 2005) 25–27

298. '"Vroom maar misdadig.' Een Griekse filosoof over het joodse volk,' *Kerk & Theologie* 56 (2005) 143–150

299. '"The God Who Drowned the King of Egypt.' A Short Note on an Exorcistic Formula,' in: A. Hilhorst & G.H. van Kooten (eds.), *The Wisdom of Egypt. Jewish, Early Christian, and Gnostic Studies in Honour of Gerard P. Luttikhuizen*, Leiden: Brill, 2005, 135–140

300. 'Joodse miniatuurtjes (8): Serveerde Abraham een niet-kosjere maaltijd?, ' *Chadashot. Maandblad van de Liberaal Joodse Gemeente Utrecht* 7, nr. 4 (mei 2005) 7–11

301. 'Joodse miniatuurtjes (9): Joodse 'feestnamen',' *Chadashot. Maandblad van de Liberaal Joodse Gemeente Utrecht* 7, nr. 5 (juni 2005) 9–11

302. 'Sex, Birth, Purity and Ascetism in the *Protevangelium Jacobi*,' in Amy-Jill Levine (ed.), *A Feminist Companion to Mariology* (Feminist Companion to the New Testament and Early Christian Writings 10), London – New York: T. & T. Clark, 2005, 56–66 [see no. 139]

303. 'Aan Abrahams dis: Joodse interpretaties van Genesis 18:8,' *Nederlands Theologisch Tijdschrift* 59 (2005) 207–214

304. 'Unnik, Willem Cornelis van,' *Religion in Geschichte und Gegenwart* (4. Aufl.) 8 (2005) 794–795

305. 'De hellenistische cultuur en de Joden,' *Lampas* 38 (2005) 214–225

306. 'Joodse miniatuurtjes (10): 'Joodse tempels,' *Chadashot. Maandblad van de Liberaal Joodse Gemeente Utrecht* 7, nr. 6 (september 2005) 9–11

307. *Het vroege jodendom van A tot Z. Een kleine encyclopedie over de eerste duizend jaar (350 v.C. – 650 n.C.)*, Zoetermeer: Meinema (forthcoming in 2006)

308. *Paula in Palestina. Hiëronymus' biografie van een rijke Romeinse christin (rond 400)* (forthcoming in 2006)

B. Book reviews

1. W. Hamm, *Der Septuaginta-Text des Buches Daniel* (1969), *Mnemosyne* (ser. IV) 26 (1973) 194–195
2. H.C.C. Cavallin, *Life After Death. Paul's Argument for the Resurrection of the Dead in 1 Cor. 15,* Part I (1974), *Bijdragen* 36 (1975) 330–331
3. R. Kieffer, *Essais de méthodologie néotestamentaire* (1972), *Mnemosyne* (ser. IV) 28 (1975) 432–434
4. H. Jagersma, *Ten derden dage* (1976), *Areopagus* 9,5 (1976) 30
5. F. O. van Gennep, *School voor koningen* (1976), *Areopagus* 10,1 (1977) 52–53
6. W. H. Zuidema, *God's partner* (1977), *Areopagus* 10,5 (1977) 62
7. N. Baumert, *Täglich sterben und auferstehen. Der Literalsinn von 2 Kor. 4,12–5,10* (1973), *Mnemosyne* (ser. IV) 30 (1977) 322–324
8. B.M.F.van Iersel, M. de Jonge, J. Nelis (edd.), *Van Taal tot Taal. Opstellen over het vertalen van de Schriften aangeboden aan W. K. Grossouw* (1977), *Areopagus* 11,1 (1978) 62
9. L. Grollenberg, *Die moeilijke Paulus* (1977), *Areopagus* 11,1 (1978) 62–64
10. H. W. Attridge, *First-Century Cynicism in the Epistles of Heraclitus* (1977), *Journal for the Study of Judaism* 9 (1978) 90–91
11. G. H. ter Schegget, *Het lied van de Mensenzoon* (1975), *Nederlands Theologisch Tijdschrift* 32 (1978) 334–336
12. B. Vuysje, *De nieuwe jazz* (1978), *Areopagus* 11,5 (1978) 62
13. D. Kaimakis, *Der Physiologus nach der ersten Redaktion* (1974), *Mnemosyne* (ser. IV) 31 (1978) 319–320
14. L. van Hartingsveld, *Het huwelijk in het Nieuwe Testament* (1977), *Areopagus* 12,1 (1979) 55–56
15. *Plato. Verzameld werk*, vertaald door X. de Win (1978), *Areopagus* 12,1 (1979) 56–57
16. U. Fischer, *Eschatologie und Jenseitserwartung im hellenistischen Diasporajudentum* (1978), *Nederlands Theologisch Tijdschrift* 33 (1979) 244–245
17. B. Jongeling, *Een Aramees boek Job* (1974), *Religious Studies Review* 5 (1979) 221–222
18. G. Quispel, *Het Geheime Boek der Openbaring* (1979), *Areopagus* 12,5 (1979) 79–81
19. E. Verhoef, *Er staat geschreven ...De oudtestamentische citaten in de brief aan de Galaten* (1979), *Nederlands Theologisch Tijdschrift* 34 (1980) 326–327
20. *Text and Interpretation.* FS M. Black (1979) en *Text-Wort-Glaube.* FS K. Aland (1980), *Nederlands Theologisch Tijdschrift* 35 (1981) 244–245
21. J. Hani, *La religion égyptienne dans la pensée de Plutarque* (1976), *Mnemosyne* (ser. IV) 34 (1981) 165–166
22. B. van Ginkel – J. A. Picard, *Het Evangelie van Jezus* (1980), *Nederlands Theologisch Tijdschrift* 35 (1981) 342–343
23. H. M. Matter, *Wederkomst en wereldeinde* (1980), *Nederlands Theologisch Tijdschrift* 35 (1981) 343
24. F. Siegert, *Drei hellenistisch-jüdische Predigten* (1980), *Kerk en Theologie* 32 (1981) 315–316
25. W. S. Vorster, *Wat is 'n Evangelie?* (1981), *Gereformeerd Theologisch Tijdschrift* 82 (1982) 97–98

26. B. M. Metzger, *New Testament Studies. Philological, Versional, and Patristic* (1980), *Theologische Literaturzeitung* 107 (1982) 511–513

27. G. W. Bowersock, *Julian the Apostate* (1978), *Mnemosyne* (ser. IV) 35 (1982) 207–208

28. P. Schäfer, *Synopse zur Hekhalot-Literatur* (1981), *Nederlands Theologisch Tijdschrift* 36 (1982) 338–339

29. V. Messori, *Wat te zeggen van Jezus*; B. Giertz, *Met eigen ogen;* W.S. Duvekot, *Jezus Messias*; W.G. Overbosch, *De Messias en zijn stad;* L. van Hartingsveld, *Jezus de Messias;* J.P. Versteeg, *Evangelie in viervoud;* P.A. Elderenbosch, *Israel, Kerk, Oecumene*; (all from 1980 and 1981), *Nederlands Theologisch Tijdschrift* 37 (1983) 69–71

30. C. H. Lindijer, *De armen en de rijken bij Lucas* (1981), *Kerk en Theologie* 34 (1983) 59–60

31. H. van Vliet, *Did Greek-Roman-Hellenistic Law Know the Exclusion of the Single Witness?* (1980), *Kerk en Theologie* 34 (1983) 60

32. M. Simon, *Le christianisme antique et son contexte religieux* (1981), *Kerk en Theologie* 34 (1983) 60–61

33. L. Prijs, *Inleiding in de joodse godsdienst* (1980), *Nederlands Theologisch Tijdschrift* 37 (1983) 155

34. R. Riesner, *Jesus als Lehrer* (1981), *Kerk en Theologie* 34 (1983) 238–239

35. J. J. Collins and G. W. E. Nickelsburg (edd.), *Ideal Figures in Ancient Judaism* (1980), *Bibliotheca Orientalis* 40 (1983) 443–445

36. J. Swetnam, *Jesus and Isaac* (1981), *Journal for the Study of Judaism* 14 (1983) 225–227

37. H. Jacobson, *The Exagoge of Ezekiel* (1983), *Nederlands Theologisch Tijdschrift* 38 (1984) 238

38. M. J. Vermaseren (ed.), *Die orientalischen Religionen im Römerreich* (1981), *Mnemosyne* (ser. IV) 37 (1984) 252–256

39. W. Speyer, *Büchervernichtung und Zensur des Geistes bei Heiden, Juden und Christen* (1981), *Nederlands Theologisch Tijdschrift* 38 (1984) 241

40. A. Casurella, *The Johannine Paraclete in the Church Fathers*; D. Brady, *The Contribution of British Writers Between 1560 and 1830 to the Interpretation of Revelation 13:16–18*; A. H. Jones, *Independence and Exegesis. The Study of Early Christianity in the Work of A. Loisy, Ch. Guignebert and M. Goguel* (all from 1983), *Kerk en Theologie* 35 (1984) 340–341

41. D. Winston and J. Dillon (edd.), *Two Treatises of Philo of Alexandria* (1983), *Journal for the Study of Judaism* 15 (1984) 214–217

42. R.-A. Turcan, *Mithra et le mithriacisme* (1981), *Mnemosyne* (ser. IV) 37 (1984) 460–461

43. N.A. van Uchelen, *Joodse mystiek. Merkawa, tempel en troon* (1983), *Studia Rosenthaliana* 17 (1984) 189–191

44. D. Flusser (red.), *De laatste dagen in Jeruzalem* (1983), *Nederlands Theologisch Tijdschrift* 39 (1985) 60–61

45. C. Verhoeven e.a., *Porphyrius, De grot van de nimfen* (1984), *Areopagus* 18,1 (1985) 61

46. E. Lohse, *Het getuigschrift van de christenen* (1982), *Nederlands Theologisch Tijdschrift* 39 (1985) 142

47. P. *Cornelius Tacitus, Die Historien* V, Kommentar von H. Heubner und W. Fauth (1982), *Nederlands Theologisch Tijdschrift* 39 (1985) 145–146

48. P. Schäfer, *Geniza-Fragmente zur Hekhalot-Literatur* (1984), *Nederlands Theologisch Tijdschrift* 39 (1985) 146–147

49. Th. C. de Kruijf – M.J.H.M. Poorthuis, *Abinoe – Onze Vader* (1984) and F. de Grijs, *Het Onzevader uitgelegd aan Peter B.* (1984), *Nederlands Theologisch Tijdschrift* 39 (1985) 243–244

50. D. T. Runia, *Philo of Alexandria and the Timaeus of Plato* (1983), *Nederlands Theologisch Tijdschrift* 39 (1985) 247

51. H. Bietenhard, *Der tannaitische Midrasch Sifre Deuteronomium übersetzt und erklärt* (1984), *Nederlands Theologisch Tijdschrift* 39 (1985) 247–248

52. P. Athanassiadi-Fowden, *Julian and Hellenism* (1981), *Mnemosyne* (ser. IV) 38 (1985) 218–220

53. M. van Loggem, *Paulus* (z.j.), *Areopagus* 18,4 (1985) 51–52

54. R. Bultmann, *Der Stil der paulinischen Predigt und die kynisch-stoische Diatribe* (repr. 1984), *Nederlands Theologisch Tijdschrift* 39 (1985) 341–342

55. M. S. Cohen, *The Shi'ur Qomah: Texts and Recensions* (1985), *Nederlands Theologisch Tijdschrift* 39 (1985) 343–344

56. H. Hommel, *Sebasmata. Studien zur antiken Religionsgeschichte und zum frühen Christentum* (1983–84), *Kerk en Theologie* 36 (1985) 336–337

57. H. Cancik (ed.), *Markus-Philologie* (1984) and M. Reiser, *Syntax und Stil im Markusevangelium* (1984), *Kerk en Theologie* 36 (1985) 337–338

58. J. Neusner, *Das pharisäische und talmudische Judentum* (1984), *Kerk en Theologie* 37 (1986) 76

59. C. A. Wauters, *Mithras* (1985), *Nederlands Theologisch Tijdschrift* 40 (1986) 174

60. W. S. Duvekot, *De Pastorale Brieven* (1984) and Th. Naastepad, *Jacobus* (1984), *Nederlands Theologisch Tijdschrift* 40 (1986) 243

61. H. J. Eckstein, *Der Begriff Syneidesis bei Paulus* (1983) and U. Wegner, *Der Hauptmann von Kafarnaum* (1985), *Kerk en Theologie* 37 (1986) 270–272

62. J. Jervell, *The Unknown Paul* (1984), *Nederlands Theologisch Tijdschrift* 40 (1986) 336–337

63. M. Himmelfarb, *Tours of Hell* (1985) and M. Dean-Otting, *Heavenly Journeys* (1984), *Nederlands Theologisch Tijdschrift* 40 (1986) 339–340

64. P. Fornaro, *La voce fuori scena* (1982), *Mnemosyne* (ser. IV) 39 (1986) 482–483

65. R. Radice, *Filone di Alessandria. Bibliografia generale 1937–1982* (1983), *Mnemosyne* (ser. IV) 39 (1986) 496

66. T. Rajak, *Josephus* (1983), *Mnemosyne* (ser. IV) 39 (1986) 497–499

67. D. Sperber, *A Dictionary of Greek and Latin Legal Terms in Rabbinic Literature* (1984), *Mnemosyne* (ser. IV) 39 (1986) 568–569

68. G. Luck, *Arcana Mundi* (1985), *Mnemosyne* (ser. IV) 39 (1986) 569–570

69. A.F.J. Klijn (red.), *Apokriefen van het Nieuwe Testament* (1984–85), *Nederlands Theologisch Tijdschrift* 41 (1987) 78–79

70. A.R.C. Leany, *The Jewish and Christian World 200 BC to AD 200* (1984); M. Whittaker, *Jews and Christians: Graeco-Roman Views* (1984); M. de Jonge (ed.), *Outside the Old Testament* (1985); J. R. Bartlett, *Jews in the Hellenistic World* (1985), *Nederlands Theologisch Tijdschrift* 41 (1987) 81–82

71. Y. van der Goot – K.A.D. Smelik (red.), *Joods leven in Nederland* (1986), *Nederlands Theologisch Tijdschrift* 41 (1987) 84

72. B. Chiesa – B. Lockwood, *Ya'qub al-Qirqisani on Jewish Sects and Christianity* (1984), *Nederlands Theologisch Tijdschrift* 41 (1987) 158

73. K. Beyer, *The Aramaic Language* (1986), *Kerk en Theologie* 38 (1987) 172–173

74. H. W. Hollander and M. de Jonge, *The Testaments of the Twelve Patriarchs. A Commentary* (1985), *Nederlands Theologisch Tijdschrift* 41 (1987) 243–244

75. H. Engel, *Die Susanna-Erzählung* (1985), *Nederlands Theologisch Tijdschrift* 41 (1987) 244–245

76. A. Kasher, *The Jews in Hellenistic and Roman Egypt* (1985), *Nederlands Theologisch Tijdschrift* 41 (1987) 245–246

77. R. Kuntzmann – J. Schlosser (edd.), *Études sur le judaïsme hellénistique* (1984), *Bibliotheca Orientalis* 43 (1986) 477–479

78. T. V. Smith, *Petrine Controversies in Early Christianity* (1985), *Nederlands Theologisch Tijdschrift* 41 (1987) 320–321

79. A. Uleyn, *Psychoanalytisch lezen in de Bijbel* (1985), *Nederlands Theologisch Tijdschrift* 41 (1987) 321–322

80. N. de Lange, *Atlas van de joodse wereld* (1986), and idem, *Judaism* (1986), *Nederlands Theologisch Tijdschrift* 41 (1987) 324–325

81. G. A. Wewers, *Terumoth – Priesterhebe* (1985), and idem, *Pea – Ackerecke* (1986), *Nederlands Theologisch Tijdschrift* 41 (1987) 325–326

82. J. van Laarhoven, *Wijsheid per post* (1986), *Nederlands Theologisch Tijdschrift* 41 (1987) 329

83. H. C. Kee, *Miracle in the Early Christian World* (1983), *Mnemosyne* (ser. IV) 40 (1987) 467–469

84. J. H. Charlesworth, *The Old Testament Pseudepigrapha and the New Testament* (1985), *Nederlands Theologisch Tijdschrift* 42 (1988) 73–74

85. E. J. Schnabel, *Law and Wisdom from Ben Sira to Paul* (1985) and G. Schimanowski, *Weisheit und Messias* (1985), *Nederlands Theologisch Tijdschrift* 42 (1988) 74–76

86. G. Schwarz, *'Und Jesus sprach'. Untersuchungen zur aramäischen Urgestalt der Worte Jesu* (1985), *Nederlands Theologisch Tijdschrift* 42 (1988) 76–77

87. G. Fowden, *The Egyptian Hermes* (1986), *Nederlands Theologisch Tijdschrift* 42 (1988) 147

88. R. Beckwith, *The Old Testament Canon of the New Testament Church* (1985) and B. M. Metzger, *The Canon of the New Testament* (1987), *Nederlands Theologisch Tijdschrift* 42 (1988) 154–156

89. C. J. den Heyer, *Marcus* (1985), *Nederlands Theologisch Tijdschrift* 42 (1988) 157

90. E. Bammel, *Judaica* (1986), *Nederlands Theologisch Tijdschrift* 42 (1988) 159–160

91. G. Reeg, *Die Geschichte von den Zehn Märtyrern* (1985), *Nederlands Theologisch Tijdschrift* 42 (1988) 160–161

92. S. Safrai, *Een volk met een land* (1986), *Nederlands Theologisch Tijdschrift* 42 (1988) 161

93. P. Lapide, *Het leerhuis van de hoop* (1986), *Nederlands Theologisch Tijdschrift* 42 (1988) 161

94. J. J. Petuchowski, *Zoals onze meesters leerden ...* (1986), *Nederlands Theologisch Tijdschrift* 42 (1988) 161–162

95. I. B. H. Abram, *Joodse traditie als permanent leren* (1986), *Nederlands Theologisch Tijdschrift* 42 (1988)162

96. R. Naftaniël – S. Schoon, *De zaak Goeree* (1986), *Nederlands Theologisch Tijdschrift* 42 (1988) 162

97. G. J. M. Bartelink, *Het vroege christendom en de antieke cultuur* (1986), *Nederlands Theologisch Tijdschrift* 42 (1988) 163–164

98. P. M. M. Geurts, *Plutarchus van Chaeronea: Waarom God zo lang wacht met straffen. Over godsdienstige angst,* (1986), *Nederlands Theologisch Tijdschrift* 42 (1988) 246

99. B. Palmer (ed.), *Medicine in the Bible* (1986), *Nederlands Theologisch Tijdschrift* 42 (1988) 258

100. D. S. Russell, *The Old Testament Pseudepigrapha* (1987), *Nederlands Theologisch Tijdschrift* 42 (1988) 263

101. J. Neusner, *De joodse wieg van het christendom* (1987), *Nederlands Theologisch Tijdschrift* 42 (1988) 263–264

102. D. Mendels, *The Land of Israel as a Political Concept in Hasmonean Literature* (1987), *Nederlands Theologisch Tijdschrift* 42 (1988) 342

103. M. Lattke, *Die Oden Salomos in ihrer Bedeutung für Neues Testament und Gnosis* III (1986), *Nederlands Theologisch Tijdschrift* 42 (1988) 343

104. L. B. Schelhaas, *Wie 't kleine niet eert ... Het gebruik van het lidwoord bij persoonsnamen in het Nieuwe Testament* (1987), *Kerk en Theologie* 39 (1988) 355

105. F. Watson, *Paul, Judaism and the Gentiles* (1986), *Nederlands Theologisch Tijdschrift* 43 (1989) 58–59

106. S. Schoon, *Leven in één wereld, een uitdaging voor joden en christenen* (1987) and D. Cohn-Sherbock, *Jews, Christians, and Liberation Theology* (1987), *Nederlands Theologisch Tijdschrift* 43 (1989) 63

107. J. Verkuyl, *Antroposofie en het Evangelie van Jezus Christus* (1986), *Nederlands Theologisch Tijdschrift* 43 (1989) 71

108. G. Schwarz, *Jesus und Judas* (1987), *Kerk en Theologie* 40 (1989) 76–77

109. B. Engelhart – J. W. Klein, *50 eeuwen schrift. Een inleiding tot de geschiedenis van het schrift* (1988), *Rondom het Woord* 31,1 (1989) 77–79

110. *Die Religion in Geschichte und Gegenwart* (1986³) and *The Encyclopedia of Religion* (1987), *Nederlands Theologisch Tijdschrift* 43 (1989) 238–240

111. J. T. Sanders, *The Jews in Luke-Acts* (1987), *Nederlands Theologisch Tijdschrift* 43 (1989) 248–249

112. L. Moraldi, *Nach dem Tode. Jenseitsvorstellungen von den Babyloniern zum Christentum.* (1987), *Nederlands Theologisch Tijdschrift* 43 (1989) 331

113. O. Schwankl, *Die Sadduzäerfrage (Mk. 12:18–27 parr)* (1987), *Nederlands Theologisch Tijdschrift* 43 (1989) 335–6

114. W. Pratscher, *Der Herrenbruder Jakobus und die Jakobustraditionen* (1987), *Nederlands Theologisch Tijdschrift* 43 (1989) 336–337

115. G. Röhser, *Metaphorik und Personifikation der Sünde. Antike Sündenvorstellungen und paulinische Hamartia* (1987), *Nederlands Theologisch Tijdschrift* 43 (1989) 337–338

116. G. Mayer, *Die jüdische Frau in der hellenistisch-römischen Antike* (1987), *Nederlands Theologisch Tijdschrift* 43 (1989) 339–340

117. R. H. Popkin – M. H. Signer, *Spinoza's Earliest Publication?* (1987), *Nederlands Theologisch Tijdschrift* 43 (1989) 340–341

118. D. Gooding, *According to Luke* (1987), *Kerk en Theologie* 40 (1989) 345–346

119. G. J. M. Bartelink, *De geboorte van Europa* (1989), *Vrienden van het gymnasium* 29 (maart 1990) 7

120. M. N. Ebertz, *Das Charisma des Gekreuzigten. Zur Soziologie der Jesusbewegung* (1987), *Nederlands Theologisch Tijdschrift* 44 (1990) 162–3

121. P. Schäfer, *Übersetzung der Hekhalot-Literatur* II (1987), *Nederlands Theologisch Tijdschrift* 44 (1990) 168–9

122. *Concordantie op de Bijbel in de Nieuwe Vertaling van het NBG* (tweede druk, 1988), *Nederlands Theologisch Tijdschrift* 44 (1990) 255

123. L. Portefaix, *Sisters Rejoice; Paul's Letter to the Philippians and Luke-Acts as Received by First-Century Philippian Women* (1988), *Nederlands Theologisch Tijdschrift* 44 (1990) 257–258

124. R. Radice & D. T. Runia, *Philo of Alexandria: An Annotated Bibliography 1937–1986* (1988); F. Siegert, *Philon von Alexandrien. Über die Gottesbezeichnung 'wohltätig verzehrendes Feuer' (De Deo)* (1988); R. Williamson, *Jews in the Hellenistic World: Philo* (1989), *Nederlands Theologisch Tijdschrift* 44 (1990) 262–264

125. R. Hachlili, *Ancient Jewish Art and Archaeology in the Land of Israel* (1988), *Nederlands Theologisch Tijdschrift* 44 (1990) 264–265

126. J. Basnage, *Vervolg op Flavius Josephus; Of Algemeene Historie der Joodsche Naatsie* (1726=1988), *Nederlands Theologisch Tijdschrift* 44 (1990) 265–266

127. H. Frohnhofen, *Apatheia tou theou. Über die Affektlosigkeit Gottes in der griechischen Antike und bei den griechischsprachigen Kirchenvätern* (1987), *Nederlands Theologisch Tijdschrift* 44 (1990) 268–269

128. D. A. Carson – G. M. Williamson (edd.), *It Is Written: Scripture Citing Scripture* (FS B. Lindars, 1988), *Nederlands Theologisch Tijdschrift* 44 (1990) 340–1

129. W. van Bekkum, *Mozes onze leraar. Mozes in de rabbijnse traditie* (1988), *Nederlands Theologisch Tijdschrift* 44 (1990) 342

130. C. Marcheselli-Casale, *Risorgeremo, ma come?* (1988), *Nederlands Theologisch Tijdschrift* 44 (1990) 342–343

131. J. A. van Belzen – J. M. van der Lans (edd.), *Rond godsdienst en psychoanalyse* (1987), *Nederlands Theologisch Tijdschrift* 44 (1990) 356–7.

132. A. Caquot – M. Hadas-Lebel – J. Riaud (edd.), *Hellenica et Judaica* (1986), *Bibliotheca Orientalis* 46 (1989) 447–8 [published in 1990]

133. L. H. Feldman, *Josephus. A Supplementary Bibliography* (1986), *Bibliotheca Orientalis* 46 (1989) 448–449 [published in 1990]

134. E. Will – C. Orrieux, *Ioudaïsmos-Hellènismos. Essay sur le judaïsme judéen à l'époque hellénistique* (1986), *Mnemosyne* 43 (1990) 268–270

135. A. Linder, *The Jews in Roman Imperial Legislation* (1987), *Mnemosyne* 43 (1990) 270–272

136. S. C. Reiff, *Published Material from the Cambridge Genizah Collection* (1988), *Nederlands Theologisch Tijdschrift* 45 (1991) 70–71

137. T. S. Beall, *Josephus' Description of the Essenes Illustrated by the Dead Sea Scrolls* (1988), *Nederlands Theologisch Tijdschrift* 45 (1991) 71–72

138. H. Gross, *Tobit. Judit* (1987), *Bibliotheca Orientalis* 47 (1990) 203–204

139. D. Zeller (ed.), *Menschwerdung Gottes – Vergöttlichung von Menschen* (1988), *Nederlands Theologisch Tijdschrift* 45 (1991) 149–150

140. B. Ego, *Im Himmel wie auf Erde. Studien zum Verhältnis von himmlischer und irdischer Welt im rabbinischen Judentum* (1989), *Nederlands Theologisch Tijdschrift* 45 (1991) 150–151

141. I. Shamir – Sh. Shavit (edd.), *Encyclopedie van de joodse geschiedenis* (1989), *Nederlands Theologisch Tijdschrift* 45 (1991) 151–152

142. N. Smart, *The World's Religions* (1989), *Nederlands Theologisch Tijdschrift* 45 (1991) 242

143. M. Küchler – Chr. Uehlinger (edd.), *Jerusalem. Texte-Bilder-Steine* (1987), *Nederlands Theologisch Tijdschrift* 45 (1991) 251–252

144. *La Bible d'Alexandrie 2: L'Exode*, edd. A. le Boulluec et P. Sandevoir (1989), *Nederlands Theologisch Tijdschrift* 45 (1991) 252–253

145. M. Hengel, *The Zealots* (1989), *Nederlands Theologisch Tijdschrift* 45 (1991) 254–255

146. M. E. Mills, *Human Agents of Cosmic Power in Hellenistic Judaism and the Synoptic Tradition* (1990), *Theologische Literaturzeitung* 116 (1991) 431–432

147. A. D. Crown (ed.), *The Samaritans* (1989), *Nederlands Theologisch Tijdschrift* 45 (1991) 341–342

148. P. Trebilco, *Jewish Communities in Asia Minor* (1991), *Journal for the Study of Judaism* 22 (1991) 292–295

149. M. Frey, *Untersuchungen zur Religion und zur Religionspolitik des Kaisers Elagabal* (1989), *Bibliotheca Orientalis* 48 (1991) 268–270

150. H. Schwier, *Tempel und Tempelzerstörung* (1989), *Nederlands Theologisch Tijdschrift* 46 (1992) 65–66

151. D. Trobisch, *Die Entstehung der Paulusbriefsammlung* (1989), *Nederlands Theologisch Tijdschrift* 46 (1992) 67

152. T. Onuki, *Gnosis und Stoa* (1989), *Nederlands Theologisch Tijdschrift* 46 (1992) 67–68

153. G. Theissen, *Lokalkolorit und Zeitgeschichte in den Evangelien* (1989), *Nederlands Theologisch Tijdschrift* 46 (1992) 68–69

154. E. Levine, *The Aramaic Version of the Bible* (1988), *Nederlands Theologisch Tijdschrift* 46 (1992) 71–72

155. P. Schäfer, *Übersetzung der Hekhalot-Literatur III* (1989), *Nederlands Theologisch Tijdschrift* 46 (1992) 72–73

156. G. J. Baudy, *Die Brände Roms* (1991), *Numen* 39 (1992) 150–151

157. D. Kosch, *Die eschatologische Tora des Menschensohnes* (1989), *Nederlands Theologisch Tijdschrift* 46 (1992) 162–163

158. M.J.H.M. Poorthuis, *De joodse groeperingen ten tijde van Jezus* (1989), *Nederlands Theologisch Tijdschrift* 46 (1992) 163–164

159. P. Kuhn, *Offenbarungsstimmen im antiken Judentum* (1989), *Nederlands Theologisch Tijdschrift* 46 (1992) 167–168

160. J.-C. Kaiser & M. Greschat (edd.), *Der Holocaust und die Protestanten* (1988), *Nederlands Theologisch Tijdschrift* 46 (1992) 169–170

161. *Flavius Josephus, De Joodse Oorlog & Uit mijn leven*, vertaald, ingeleid en van aantekeningen voorzien door F.J.A.M. Meijer en M.A. Wes (1992), *Hermeneus* 64 (1992) 218–19

162. J. Ernst, *Johannes der Täufer* (1989), *Nederlands Theologisch Tijdschrift* 46 (1992) 234

163. C. J. Hemer, *The Book of Acts in the Setting of Hellenistic History* (1989), *Nederlands Theologisch Tijdschrift* 46 (1992) 234–5

164. A. J. Droge, *Homer or Moses? Early Christian Interpretations of the History of Culture* (1989) and P. Pilhofer, *Presbyteron kreitton. Der Altersbeweis der jüdischen und christlichen Apologeten und seine Vorgeschichte* (1990), *Nederlands Theologisch Tijdschrift* 46 (1992) 239–41

165. J. Murphy-O'Connor, *The École Biblique and the New Testament: A Century of Scholarship (1890–1990)* (1990), *Nederlands Theologisch Tijdschrift* 46 (1992) 241

166. A. Kuyt & N. A. van Uchelen, *History and Form: Dutch Studies in the Mishnah* (1988), *Nederlands Theologisch Tijdschrift* 46 (1992) 241–2

167. S. Beller, *Vienna and the Jews, 1867–1938* (1989), *Nederlands Theologisch Tijdschrift* 46 (1992) 242–3

168. A. G. Hamman, *Das Gebet in der alten Kirche* (1989), *Nederlands Theologisch Tijdschrift* 46 (1992) 245

169. A. Strotmann, *Mein Vater bist Du! (Sir 51, 10). Zur Bedeutung der Vaterschaft Gottes in kanonischen und nichtkanonischen frühjüdischen Schriften* (1991), *Tijdschrift voor Theologie* 32 (1992) 309–310

170. M. de Jonge, *Jewish Eschatology, Early Christology and the Testaments of the Twelve Patriarchs* (1991), *Nederlands Theologisch Tijdschrift* 46 (1992) 344–5

171. H. Schreckenberg, *Die christlichen Adversus-Judaeos-Texte* (2 vols., 1988–1990), *Nederlands Theologisch Tijdschrift* 46 (1992) 346–7

172. J. H. Charlesworth, *Graphic Concordance to the Dead Sea Scrolls* (1991), *Nederlands Theologisch Tijdschrift* 46 (1992) 347–8

173. C. A. Brown, *No Longer Be Silent: First Century Jewish Portraits of Biblical Women* (1992), *Journal for the Study of Judaism* 33 (1992) 249–250

174. D. B. Garlington, *'The Obedience of Faith'. A Pauline Phrase in Historical Context* (1991); W. T. Wilson, *Love without Pretence. Romans 12, 9–21 and Hellenistic Jewish Wisdom Literature* (1991); C. C. Newman, *Paul's Glory-Christology. Tradition and Rhetoric* (1992), *Journal for the Study of Judaism* 33 (1992) 257–260

175. A. F. J. Klijn, *Jewish Christian Gospel Tradition* (1992), *Vigiliae Christianae* 46 (1992) 435–437

176. C. Hezser, *Lohnmetaphorik und Arbeitswelt in Mt 20,1–16* (1990), *Nederlands Theologisch Tijdschrift* 47 (1993) 65

177. I. Taatz, *Frühjüdische Briefe* (1991), *Nederlands Theologisch Tijdschrift* 47 (1993) 67

178. M. Lattke, *Hymnus. Materialien zu einer Geschichte der antiken Hymnologie* (1991), *Nederlands Theologisch Tijdschrift* 47 (1993) 68–9

179. M. van Loopik, *The Ways of the Sages and the Way of the World* (1991), *Nederlands Theologisch Tijdschrift* 47 (1993) 69–70

180. M. D. Swartz, *Mystical Prayer in Ancient Judaism* (1991) and P. Schäfer, *Übersetzung der Hekhalot-Literatur IV* (1991), *Nederlands Theologisch Tijdschrift* 47 (1993) 164–165

181. D. S. Potter, *Prophecy and History in the Crisis of the Roman Empire. A Historical Commentary on the Thirteenth Sibylline Oracle* (1990), *Numen* 40 (1993) 198

182. J. Cohen, *"Be Fertile and Increase, Fill the Earth and Master It". The Ancient and Medieval Career of a Biblical Text* (1992), *History of European Ideas* 17 (1993) 394–395

183. G. E. Sterling, *Historiography and Self-Definition. Josephos, Luke-Acts and Apologetic Historiography* (1992), *Vigiliae Christianae* 47 (1993) 203–206

184. E. Ruckstuhl & P. Dschulnigg, *Stilkritik und Verfasserfrage im Johannesevangelium* (1991), *Nederlands Theologisch Tijdschrift* 47 (1993) 318–319

185. F. Siegert, *Drei hellenistisch-jüdische Predigten II* (1992), *Studia Philonica Annual* 5 (1993) 219–222

186. D. I. Brewer, *Techniques and Assumptions in Jewish Exegesis Before 70 CE* (1992), *Nederlands Theologisch Tijdschrift* 48 (1994) 71–72.

187. C. Dogniez & M. Harl, *La Bible d'Alexandrie 5: Le Deutéronome* (1992), *Nederlands Theologisch Tijdschrift* 48 (1994) 161–162.

188. M Franzmann, *The Odes of Solomon* (1991), *Nederlands Theologisch Tijdschrift* 48 (1994) 163–164

189. L. P. Hogan, *Healing in the Second Temple Period* (1992), *Nederlands Theologisch Tijdschrift* 48 (1994) 167–168

190. D. Noy, *Jewish Inscriptions of Western Europe*, vol. 1 (1993), *Journal of Theological Studies* n.s. 45 (1994) 701–704

191. W. Horbury & D. Noy, *Jewish Inscriptions of Graeco-Roman Egypt* (1992), *Journal for the Study of Judaism* 25 (1994) 320–323

192. A. Pietersma, *The Apocryphon of Jannes and Jambres the Magicians* (1994), *Journal for the Study of Judaism* 25 (1994) 328–330

193. W. Schottroff, *Das Reich Gottes und der Menschen. Studien zum Verhältnis der christlichen Theologie zum Judentum* (1991), *Nederlands Theologisch Tijdschrift* 48 (1994) 340

194. M. F. Smith, *Diogenes of Oenoanda. The Epicurean Inscription* (1993), *Mnemosyne* 48 (1995) 101–103

195. S. J. Friesen, *Twice Neokoros. Ephesus, Asia and the Cult of the Flavian Imperial Family* (1993), *Mnemosyne* 48 (1995) 254–256

196. R. Feldmeier & U. Heckel (edd.), *Die Heiden. Juden, Christen und das Problem des Fremden* (1994), *Vigiliae Christianae* 49 (1995) 93–95

197. E. Testa, *The Faith of the Mother Church* (1992), *Bibliotheca Orientalis* 52 (1995) 121–123

198. E. Grässer, *Aufbruch und Verheissung. Gesammelte Aufsätze zum Hebräerbrief* (1992), *Nederlands Theologische Tijdschrift* 49 (1995) 75

199. K. Ch. Wong, *Interkulturelle Theologie und multikulturelle Gemeinde im Matthäusevengelium* (1992), *Nederlands Theologisch Tijdschrift* 49 (1995) 163–164

200. W. T. Wilson, *The Mysteries of Righteousness. The Literary Composition and Genre of the* Sentences *of Pseudo-Phocylides* (1994), *Journal for the Study of Judaism* 26 (1995) 231–234

201. R. Eisenman & M. Wise, *De Dode-Zeerollen onthuld* (1993), *Nederlands Theologisch Tijdschrift* 49 (1995) 240–241

202. Y. Liebes, *Studies in Jewish Myth and Jewish Messianism* (1993), *Nederlands Theologisch Tijdschrift* 49 (1995) 242–243

203. Uriel da Costa, *Examination of Pharisaic Traditions* (1993), *Nederlands Theologisch Tijdschrift* 49 (1995) 329–330

204. H. Vorgrimler, *Geschichte der Hölle* (1993) and A. E. Bernstein, *The Formation of Hell* (1993), *Numen* 42 (1995) 319–321

205. T. Ilan, *Jewish Women in Graeco-Roman Palestine* (1995), *Journal for the Study of Judaism* 26 (1995) 364–366

206. J. N. Bremmer, *Greek Religion* (1994), *Nederlands Theologisch Tijdschrift* 50 (1996) 66

207. G. H. Twelftree, *Jesus the Exorcist* (1993), *Nederlands Theologisch Tijdschrift* 50 (1996) 71–72

208. K. P. Donfried & I. H. Marshall, *The Theology of the Shorter Pauline Epistles* 1993) and J.D.G. Dunn, *The Theology of Paul's Letters to the Galatians* (1993), *Nederlands Theologisch Tijdschrift* 50 (1996) 160–161

209. H. A. McKay, *Sabbath and Synagogue. The Question of Sabbath Worship in Ancient Judaism* (1994), *Nederlands Theologisch Tijdschrift* 50 (1996) 161–162

210. D. Noy, *Jewish Inscriptions of Western Europe, Vol. 2: The City of Rome* (1995), *Journal of Theological Studies* n.s. 47 (1996) 256–259

211. R. Liebers, *'Wie geschrieben steht': Studien zu einer besonderen Art frühchristlicher Schriftbezuges* (1993), *Nederlands Theologisch Tijdschrift* 50 (1996) 246.

212. G. van Oyen, *De studie van de Marcusredactie in de twintigste eeuw* (1993), *Nederlands Theologisch Tijdschrift* 50 (1996) 246–7

213. M.C. de Boer (ed.), *From Jesus to John* (1993), *Nederlands Theologisch Tijdschrift* 50 (1996) 247.

214. J. C. Thom, *The Pythagorean Golden Verses* (1995), *Mnemosyne* 49 (1996) 351–352

215. L. Boffo, *Iscrizioni greche e latine per lo studio della Bibbia* (1994), *Mnemosyne* 49 (1997) 511–512

216. O. Cullmann, *Das Gebet im Neuen Testament* (1994), *Nederlands Theologisch Tijdschrift* 50 (1996) 335–336

217. R.E. DeMaris, *The Colossian Controversy* (1994), *Nederlands Theologisch Tijdschrift* 50 (1996) 336–337

218. J.H. Charlesworth (ed.), *The Dead Sea Scrolls: Hebrew, Aramaic, and Greek Texts with English Translation*, vols. 1+2 (1994–1995), *Nederlands Theologisch Tijdschrift* 50 (1996) 339–340

219. S.A. Takács, *Isis and Sarapis in the Roman World* (1995) and W. Fauth, *Helios Megistos. Zur synkretistischen Theologie der Spätantike* (1995), *Nederlands Theologisch Tijdschrift* 51 (1997) 50–51

220. G. Dorival e.a., *La Bible d'Alexandrie 4: Les Nombres* (1994), *Nederlands Theologisch Tijdschrift* 51 (1997) 59–60

221. A.F.J. Klijn, *De brieven van Paulus aan Timoteüs, Titus en Filemon* (1994); H.J. Kouwenhoven, *De brief aan de Colossenzen* (1995); W. Weren, *Matteüs* (1994); C.A. Newsom & S.H. Ringe (red.), *Met eigen ogen: Commentaar op de bijbel vanuit het perspectief van vrouwen* (1995), *Nederlands Theologisch Tijdschrift* 51 (1997) 60–61

222. J. Wijchers & S. Kat, *Bijbels namenboek* (1994), *Nederlands Theologisch Tijdschrift* 51 (1997) 61

223. R. Riesner, *Die Frühzeit des Apostels Paulus* (1994), *Nederlands Theologisch Tijdschrift* 51 (1997) 61–62

224. L. Borman, K. del Tredici, A. Standhartinger (eds.), *Religious Propaganda and Missionary Competition in the New Testament World* (1994), *Nederlands Theologisch Tijdschrift* 51 (1997) 62–63

225. D. Sänger, *Die Verkündigung des Gekreuzigten und Israel. Studien zum Verhältnis von Kirche und Israel bei Paulus und im frühen Christentum* (1994), *Nederlands Theologisch Tijdschrift* 51 (1997) 65–66

226. P. Schäfer & K. Herrmann (edd.), *Übersetzung der Hekhalot-Literatur, Band I: §§ 1–80* (1995), *Nederlands Theologisch Tijdschrift* 51 (1997) 66

227. G. S. Oegema, *Der Gesalbte und sein Volk* (1994), *Nederlands Theologisch Tijdschrift* 51 (1997) 149–150

228. A. Chester & R. P. Martin, *The Theology of the Letters of James, Peter, and Jude* (1994); D. Moody Smith, *The Theology of the Gospel of John* (1995), *Nederlands Theologisch Tijdschrift* 51 (1997) 151

229. J. Ysebaert, *Die Amtsterminologie im Neuen Testament und in der Alten Kirche* (1994), *Nederlands Theologisch Tijdschrift* 51 (1997) 151–152

230. V.M. Fiddelaar, *Israël in religieus perspectief* (1995), *Nederlands Theologisch Tijdschrift* 51 (1997) 155

231. H.-J. Becker, *Der Jerusalemer Talmud: Sieben ausgewählte Kapitel* (1995), *Nederlands Theologisch Tijdschrift* 51 (1997) 155–156

232. J. Schaper, *Eschatology in the Greek Psalter* (1995), *Journal for the Study of Judaism* 28 (1997) 123–124

233. Chr. Riedweg, *Ps.-Justin (Markell von Ankyra?), Ad Graecos de vera religione (bisher "Cohortatio ad Graecos")* (1995), *Mnemosyne* 50 (1997) 366–367

234. L. T. Stuckenbruck, *Angel Veneration and Christology* (1995), *Nederlands Theologisch Tijdschrift* 51 (1997) 238–239

235. W. R. Baker, *Personal Speech-Ethics in the Epistle of James* (1995), *Nederlands Theologisch Tijdschrift* 51 (1997) 239–240

236. K. Elliott & I. Moir, *Manuscripts and the Text of the New Testament* (1995), *Nederlands Theologisch Tijdschrift* 51 (1997) 240

237. U. Gleßmer, *Einleitung in die Targume zum Pentateuch* (1995), *Nederlands Theologisch Tijdschrift* 51 (1997) 242

238. M. Jacobs, *Die Institution des jüdischen Patriarchen: Eine quellen- und traditionskritische Studie zur Geschichte der Juden in der Spätantike* (1995), *Nederlands Theologisch Tijdschrift* 51 (1997) 242–243

239. N. G. Cohen, *Philo Judaeus: His Universe of Discourse* (1995), *Nederlands Theologisch Tijdschrift* 51 (1997) 243–244

240. R.M. Grant & G. W. Menzies, *Joseph's Bible Notes (Hypomnesticon)* (1996), *Bibliotheca Orientalis* 54 (1997) 195–197

241. J.A. Harrill, *The Manumission of Slaves in Early Christianity* (1995), *Kerk & Theologie* 48 (1997) 168–169

242. P. Borgen & S. Giversen (eds.), *The New Testament and Hellenistic Judaism* (1995), *Journal for the Study of Judaism* 28 (1997) 323–324

243. L. Schottroff & M.T. Wacker (eds.), *Von der Wurzel getragen. Christlich-feministische Exegese in Auseinandersetzung mit Antjidaismus* (1996), *Journal for the Study of Judaism* 28 (1997) 348–349

244. E.N. Lane (ed.), *Cybele, Attis, and Related Cults: Essays in Memory of M.J. Vermaseren* (1996), *Nederlands Theologisch Tijdschrift* 51 (1997) 317

245. N. de Lange, *Greek Jewish Texts from the Cairo Genizah* (1996), *Nederlands Theologisch Tijdschrift* 51 (1997) 328–329

246. L. Fine, *Kabbala: verkenning in joodse mystiek* (1996), and W. Zuidema, *Lucht, water, Vuur. Kabbalà: Twee tractaten en een catechismus* (1996), *Nederlands Theologisch Tijdschrift* 51 (1997) 329–330

247. M. Hengel, *Judaica et hellenistica: Kleine Schriften* I (1996), *Nederlands Theologisch Tijdschrift* 52 (1998) 56

248. H. Botermann, *Das Judenedikt des Kaisers Claudius* (1996), *Nederlands Theologisch Tijdschrift* 52 (1998) 56–57

249. G. Strecker, *Theologie des Neuen Testaments* (1996), *Nederlands Theologisch Tijdschrift* 52 (1998) 57–58

250. B.H. McLean, *The Cursed Christ. Mediterranean Expulsion Rituals and Pauline Soteriology* (1996), *Nederlands Theologisch Tijdschrift* 52 (1998) 58–59

251. C.J. den Heyer, *Opnieuw: Wie is Jezus. Balans van 150 jaar onderzoek naar Jezus* (1996), *Nederlands Theologisch Tijdschrift* 52 (1998) 59

252. W.J. van Bekkum e.a. (edd.), *Jeruzalem in jodendom, christendom an islam* (1996), and M. Poorthuis e.a. (edd.), *The Centrality of Jerusalem* (1996), *Nederlands Theologisch Tijdschrift* 52 (1998) 59–60

253. Flavius Josephus, *De oude geschiedenis van de Joden*, deel I, vertaald door F.J.A.M. Meijer en M.A. Wes (1996), *Nederlands Theologisch Tijdschrift* 52 (1998) 60–61

254. C.E. Arnold, *The Colossian Syncretism* (1995), *Nederlands Theologisch Tijdschrift* 52 (1998) 159–160

255. M.C. de Boer, *Johannine Perspectives on the Death of Jesus* (1996), *Nederlands Theologisch Tijdschrift* 52 (1998) 160–161

256. R. Strelan, *Paul, Artemis, and the Jews in Ephesus* (1996), *Nederlands Theologisch Tijdschrift* 52 (1998) 161–162

257. F. Neirynck (ed.), *Q-Synopsis* (1995) and M. Borg (ed.), *Het verloren evangelie Q* (1997), *Nederlands Theologisch Tijdschrift* 52 (1998) 247

258. M. de Groot, *Het evangelie naar Maria* (1996), *Nederlands Theologisch Tijdschrift* 52 (1998) 247

259. J. D. G. Dunn, *The Epistles to the Colossians and to Philemon* (1996), *Nederlands Theologisch Tijdschrift* 52 (1998) 247–248

260. Ch. Burchard, *Gesammelte Studien zu Joseph und Asenath* (1996), *Nederlands Theologisch Tijdschrift* 52 (1998) 249–250

261. A.M. Schwemer, *Vitae prophetarum* (1997), *Nederlands Theologisch Tijdschrift* 52 (1998) 250

262. W. Fenske, *'Und wenn ihr betet ...' (Mt. 6,5): Gebete in der zwischenmenschlichen Kommunikation der Antike als Ausdruck der Frömmigkeit* (1997), *Nederlands Theologisch Tijdschrift* 52 (1998) 324–325

263. B. Gerhardsson, *The Shema in the New Testament* (1996), *Nederlands Theologisch Tijdschrift* 52 (1998) 325

264. P. J. Tomson, *'Als dit uit de hemel is ...' Jezus en de schrijvers van het Nieuwe Testament in hun verhouding tot het jodendom* (1997), *Nederlands Theologisch Tijdschrift* 52 (1998) 325–326

265. Y. Shavit, *Athens in Jerusalem: Classical Antiquity and Hellenism in the Making of the Modern Secular Jew* (1997), *Nederlands Theologisch Tijdschrift* 52 (1998) 327–328

266. B. van Iersel, *Marcus uitgelegd aan andere lezers* (1997), and J. Reiling, *De eerste brief van Paulus aan de Korintiërs* (1997), *Nederlands Theologisch Tijdschrift* 52 (1998) 328–329

267. G. Stanton, *Dichter bij Jezus? Nieuw licht op de evangeliën* (1997), *Nederlands Theologisch Tijdschrift* 52 (1998) 329

268. C. M. Tucket (ed.), *The Scriptures in the Gospels* (1997), *Nederlands Theologisch Tijdschrift* 52 (1998) 330

269. W. R. G. Loader, *Jesus' Attitude Towards the Law: A Study of the Gospels* (1997), *Nederlands Theologisch Tijdschrift* 52 (1998) 330–331

270. S. Meißner, *Die Heimholung des Ketzers: Studien zur jüdischen Auseinandersetzung mit Paulus* (1996), *Nederlands Theologisch Tijdschrift* 52 (1998) 331–332

271. J. Moatti-Fine, *La Bible d'Alexandrie 6: Jésus (Josué)* (1996), *Nederlands Theologisch Tijdschrift* 52 (1998) 332

272. P. Schäfer & H.-J. Becker (edd.), *Synopse zum Talmud Yerushalmi III: Ordnung Nashim* (1998), *Nederlands Theologisch Tijdschrift* 52 (1998) 332–333

273. Flavius Josephus, *De oude geschiedenis van de joden,* deel II: Boek VIII-XIII, vertaald door F.J.A.M. Meijer en M.A. Wes (1997), *Nederlands Theologisch Tijdschrift* 52 (1998) 333–334

274. M. van Loopik (red.), *Tweespalt en verbondenheid: Joden en christenen in historisch perspectief* (1998), *Nederlands Theologisch Tijdschrift* 52 (1998) 334

275. G. Wöhrle, *Hypnos der Allbezwinger* (1995), *Mnemosyne* (ser. iv) 51 (1998) 760

276. W. Zager, *Gottesherrschaft und Endgericht in der Verkündigung Jesu* (1996), *Nederlands Theologisch Tijdschrift* 53 (1999) 55–56

277. R.D. Anderson, *Ancient Rhetorical Theory and Paul* (1996), *Nederlands Theologisch Tijdschrift* 53 (1999) 56–57

278. E. Bammel, *Judaica et Paulina* (1997), *Nederlands Theologisch Tijdschrift* 53 (1999) 57–58

279. J.T. Fitzgerald (ed.), *Friendship, Flattery, and Frankness of Speech. Studies on Friendship in the New Testament World* (1996), *Mnemosyne* (ser. iv) 52 (1999) 226–227

280. H. Meisinger, *Liebesgebot und Altruismusforschung. Ein exegetischer Beitrag zum Dialog zwischen Theologie und Naturwissenschaft* (1996), *Nederlands Theologisch Tijdschrift* 53 (1999) 143–144

281. P. Balla, *Challenges to New Testament Theology* (1997), *Nederlands Theologisch Tijdschrift* 53 (1999)144–145

282. J.J. Kanagaraj, *Mysticism in the Gospel of John* (1998), *Nederlands Theologisch Tijdschrift* 53 (1999) 145–146

283. J.D.G. Dunn, *The Theology of Paul the Apostle* (1998), *Nederlands Theologisch Tijdschrift* 53 (1999) 146–147

284. N. Walter, *Praeparatio Evangelica. Studien zur Umwelt, Exegese und Hermeneutik des Neuen Testaments* (1997), *Nederlands Theologisch Tijdschrift* 53 (1999) 147–148

285. Th. Silverstein & A. Hilhorst, *Apocalypse of Paul* (1997), *Nederlands Theologisch Tijdschrift* 53 (1999) 148

286. L.T. Stuckenbruck, *The Book of Giants from Qumran* (1997), *Nederlands Theologisch Tijdschrift* 53 (1999) 148–149

287. R. Hachlili, *Ancient Jewish Art and Archaeology in the Diaspora* (1998), *Nederlands Theologisch Tijdschrift* 53 (1999) 150–151

288. W. Hansen, *Phlegon of Thralles' Book of Marvels* (1997), *Mnemosyne* 52 (1999) 382

289. A. Keller, *Translationes Patristicae Graecae et Latina* (1997), *Mnemosyne* 52 (1999) 480–481

290. A.W. Zwiep, *The Ascension of the Messiah in Lukan Christology* (1997), *Nederlands Theologisch Tijdschrift* 53 (1999) 249–250

291. G. Theissen & D. Winter, *Die Kriterienfrage in der Jesusforschung* (1997), *Nederlands Theologisch Tijdschrift* 53 (1999) 250–251

292. S. Krauss – W. Horbury, *The Jewish-Christian Controversy* (1996), *Bijdragen* 59 (1998) 462

293. M. Bar-Ilan, *Some Jewish Women in Antiquity* (1998), *Journal for the Study of Judaism* 30 (1999) 325–327

294. D.K. Falk, *Daily, Sabbath, and Festival Prayers in the Dead Sea Scrolls* (1998), *The H-Judaic Jewish Studies Book Review* 21 Sept. 1999, 1–5 (online)

295. E. Trocmé, *De vroege jaren van het christendom* (1999), *Nederlands Theologisch Tijdschrift* 53 (1999) 317–318

296. E.S. Gruen, *Heritage and Hellenism: The Reinvention of Jewish Tradition* (1998), *Journal of Biblical Literature* 119 (1999) 729–731

297. R. Brändle & V. Jegher-Bucher, *Johannes Chrysostomus: Acht Reden gegen Juden*(1995), *Zeitschrift für Antikes Christentum* 3 (1999) 307–308

298. R. Kieffer & J. Bergman (eds.), *La main de Dieu. Die Hand Gottes* (1997), *Nederlands Theologisch Tijdschrift* 54 (2000) 71–72

299. P.J. Madden, *Jesus' Walking on the Sea* (1997), *Nederlands Theologisch Tijdschrift* 54 (2000) 72

300. B.M. Winter, *Philo and Paul Among the Sophists* (1997), *Nederlands Theologisch Tijdschrift* 54 (2000) 72–73

301. Flavius Josephus, *De Oude Geshiedenis van de Joden*, vol. III (1998), and Flavius Josephus, *Tegen de Grieken* (1999), vert. door F.J.A.M. Meijer & M.A. Wes, *Nederlands Theologisch Tijdschrift* 54 (2000) 76–77

302. H. Schreckenberg, *Die christlichen Adversus-Judaeos-Bilder* (1999), *Nederlands Theologisch Tijdschrift* 54 (2000) 77

303. S. Fine, *This Holy Place. On the Sanctity of the Synagogue During the Greco-Roman Period* (1997), *Biblical Archaeology Review* 26, 1 (2000) 58–60

304. H.D. Betz, *Antike und Christentum: Gesammelte Aufsätze* IV (1998), *Journal for the Study of Judaism* 31 (2000) 69–70

305. L.I. Levine, *The Ancient Synagogue: The First Thousand Years*(1999), *The H-Judaic Jewish Studies Book Review* 17 April 2000, 1–4 (on line)

306. P. Harlé, *Les Juges* (1999), and M. Harl e.a., *Les douze prophètes* (1999) [La Bible d'Alexandrie 7 and 23], *Nederlands Theologisch Tijdschrift* 54 (2000) 165–166

307. E.J. Vledder, *Conflict in the Miracle Stories* (1997), *Nederlands Theologisch Tijdschrift* 54 (2000) 168–169

308. W. Aalders, *De Septuaginta* (1999*)*, *Nederlands Theologisch Tijdschrift* 54 (2000) 171–172

309. M. Fiedrowicz, *Prinzipien der Schriftauslegung in der Alten Kirche* (1998), *Nederlands Theologisch Tijdschrift* 54 (2000) 173

310. W. Reinbold, *Propaganda und Mission im ältesten Christentum* (2000), *Tijdschrift voor geschiedenis* 113 (2000) 396–397

311. H. Hübner, *Vetus Testamentum in Novo*,vol. 2 (1997), *Nederlands Theologisch Tijdschrift* 54 (2000) 255–256

312. S.E. Porter (ed.), *Handbook to Exegesis of the New Testament* (1997), *Nederlands Theologisch Tijdschrift* 54 (2000) 256

313. M. Schneemelcher (ed.), *Neutestamentliche Apokryphen*, 2 vols. (1997/99). *Nederlands Theologisch Tijdschrift* 54 (2000) 257

314. Chr. Böttrich (ed.), *Tischendorf-Lesebuch. Bibelforschung in Reiseabenteuern* (1999), *Nederlands Theologisch Tijdschrift* 54 (2000) 257

315. M. Goodman (ed.), *Jews in a Graeco-Roman World* (1998), *Mnemosyne* 53 (2000) 494–497

316. E. Verhoef, *De Brieven aan de Tessalonicenzen* (1998). and G. Haufe, *Der erste Brief des Paulus an die Thessalonicher* (1999), *Nederlands Theologisch Tijdschrift* 54 (2000) 348

317. S. Bieberstein, *Verschwiegene Jüngerinnen – vergessene Zeuginnen: Gebrochene Konzepte im Lukasevangelium* (1998), *Nederlands Theologisch Tijdschrift* 54 (2000) 349

318. G.N. Stanton & G.G. Stroumsa (eds.), *Tolerance and Intolerance in Early Judaism and Christianity* (1998), *Nederlands Theologisch Tijdschrift* 54 (2000) 349–350

319. S.M. McDonough, *YHWH at Patmos. Rev. 1:4 in its Hellenistic and Early Jewish Setting* (1999), *Nederlands Theologisch Tijdschrift* 54 (2000) 353

320. D. Holwerda, *De Schrift opent een vergezicht* (1998), *Nederlands Theologisch Tijdschrift* 55 (2001) 75

321. N.A. Beck, *Mündiges Christentum im 21. Jahrhundert. Die antijüdische Polemik des Neuen Testaments und ihre Überwindung* (1998), *Nederlands Theologisch Tijdschrift* 55 (2001) 76–77

322. H.-J. Becker, *Die großen rabbinischen Sammelwerke Palästinas* (1999), *Nederlands Theologisch Tijdschrift* 55 (2001) 77–78

323. R. Baumgarten, *Heiliges Wort und Heilige Schrift bei den Griechen* (1998), *Mnemosyne* 54 (2001) 235–237

324. J.S. Park, *Conceptions of Afterlife in Jewish Inscriptions* (2000), *Nederlands Theologisch Tijdschrift* 55 (2001) 160

325. D.N. Freedman (ed.), *Eerdmans Dictionary of the Bible* (2000), *Nederlands Theologisch Tijdschrift* 55 (2001) 161

326. E. van Diggele, *Een volk dat alleen woont. De strijd om de joodse identiteit van de staat Israël* (2000), *Nederlands Theologisch Tijdschrift* 55 (2001) 162

327. Chr. Fahner (transl.), *Eusebius' Kerkgeschiedenis* (2000) and P.L. Maier (transl.), *Eusebius: The Church History* (1999), *Nederlands Theologisch Tijdschrift* 55 (2001) 164

328. L. Wells, *The Greek Language of Healing from Homer to New Testament Times* (1998), *Nederlands Theologisch Tijdschrift* 55 (2001) 256

329. Randall Stewart (ed.), *Sortes Astrampsychi*, vol. II (2001), *Bryn Mawr Classical Review* of 1 Oct. 2001 on Internet (http://ccat.sas.upenn.edu/bmcr/)

330. G.W. Dawes (ed.), *The Historical Jesus Quest: A Foundational Anthology* (1999), *Nederlands Theologisch Tijdschrift* 55 (2001) 342–343

331. A. Lehnardt, *Rosh ha-Shana: Neujahr* (2000), *Nederlands Theologisch Tijdschrift* 55 (2001) 346

332. P. Leupen, *Het meetlint over Jerusalem. De fatale mythe van een heilige stad* (2001), *Nederlands Theologisch Tijdschrift* 55 (2001) 349–350

333. P. Pilhofer, *Philippi, Band II: Katalog der Inschriften von Philippi*, (2000), *Biblical Interpretation* 9 (2001) 444–446

334. D.H. Hannah, *Michael and Christ* (1999), *Nederlands Theologisch Tijdschrift* 56 (2002) 70

335. J.N. Bremmer, *The Rise and Fall of the Afterlife* (2002), *Tijdschrift voor Geschiedenis* 115 (2002) 276–278

336. E. Hornung, *The Secret Lore of Egypt. Its Impact on the West* (2001), *Bryn Mawr Classical Review* 18.04.2002 (http://ccat.sas.upenn.edu/bmcr/)

337. S.E. Porter (ed.), *Diglossia and Other Topics in New Testament Lingistics* (2000), *Nederlands Theologisch Tijdschrift* 56 (2002) 150–151

338. N. Förster, *Marcus Magus* (1999), *Nederlands Theologisch Tijdschrift* 56 (2002) 155–156

339. J.C. O'Neill, *The Point of It All: Essays on Jesus Christ* (2000), *Nederlands Theologisch Tijdschrift* 56 (2002) 156–157

340. H.W. Basser, *Studies in Exegesis. Christian Critiques of Jewish Law and Rabbinic Responses 70–300 CE* (2000), *Nederlands Theologisch Tijdschrift* 56 (2002) 157–158

341. J.C. VanderKam, *An Introduction to Early Judaism* (2001), *Nederlands Theologisch Tijdschrift* 56 (2002) 158

342. K.L. Noethlichs, *Die Juden im christlichen Imperium Romanum (4.–6. Jahrhundert)*, Berlin 2001, in *Bryn Mawr Classical Review* 11–06–2002 (http://ccat.sas.upenn. edu/bmcr/)

343. Chr. Burchard, *Der Jakobusbrief* (2000), *Nederlands Theologisch Tijdschrift* 56 (2002) 261–262

344. M. Fieger, K. Schmid & P. Schwagmeier (edd.), *Qumran – Die Schriftrollen vom Toten Meer* (2001), *Nederlands Theologisch Tijdschrift* 56 (2002) 262–263

345. M. Lattke, *Oden Salomos. Text, Übersetzung, Kommentar,* vol. 1 (1999), *Nederlands Theologisch Tijdschrift* 56 (2002) 263

346. M. Winiarczyk, *Euhemeros von Messene. Leben, Werk und Nachwirkung* (2002), *Bryn Mawr Classical Review* of 21/07/02 (http://ccat.sas.upenn.edu/bmcr/)

347. P. Schubert (ed.), *Vivre en Égypte gréco-romaine. Une sélection de papyrus* (2000), *Bryn Mawr Classical Review* of 06/09/02 ((http://ccat.sas.upenn.edu/bmcr/)

348. A.F. Norman, *Antioch as a Centre of Hellenic Culture as Observed by Libanius* (2000) and M. Edwards, *Neoplatonic Saints: The Lives of Plotinus and Proclus by Their Students* (2000), *Bijdragen* 62 (2001) 471–472

349. R.D. Anderson, *Glossary of Greek Rhetorical Terms* (2000), *Nederlands Theologisch Tijdschrift* 56 (2002) 342

350. Ch. Hempel, *The Damascus Texts* (2000), and J.R. Davila, *Liturgical Works* (2000), *Nederlands Theologisch Tijdschrift* 56 (2002) 344–345

351. D.-M. d'Hamonville, *La Bible d'Alexandrie 17: Les Proverbes* (2002), and E. Bons e.a., *La Bible d'Alexandrie 23.1: Osée* (2002), *Nederlands Theologisch Tijdschrift* 56 (2002) 345–346

352. S.T. Kat, *Kontinuität und Diskontinuität zwischen christlichem und nationalsozialistischem Antisemitismus* (2001), *Nederlands Theologisch Tijdschrift* 56 (2002) 346

353. R.S. Bloch, *Antike Vorstellungen vom Judentum. Der Judenexkurs des Tacitus im Rahmen der griechisch-römischen Ethnographie* (2002), *Bryn Mawr Classical Review* of 1 Nov. 2002 (http://ccat.sas.upenn.edu/bmcr/)

354. H.W. Basser, *Studies in Exegesis: Christian Critiques of Jewish Law and Rabbinic Responses 70–300 CE* (2000), *Vigiliae Christianae* 56 (2002) 319–321

355. W.D. Furley & J.M. Bremer, *Greek Hymns* (2001), *Nederlands Theologisch Tijdschrift* 57 (2003) 66–67

356. S. Byrskog, *Story as History – History as Story: The Gospel Tradition in the Context of Ancient History* (2000), *Nederlands Theologisch Tijdschrift* 57 (2003) 76–77

357. B.T. Viviano, *Trinity – Kingdom – Church. Essays in Biblical Theology* (2001), *Nederlands Theologisch Tijdschrift* 57 (2003) 77–78

358. Azariah de' Rossi, *The Light of the Eyes,* transl. by J. Weinberg (2001), *Nederlands Theologisch Tijdschrift* 57 (2003) 79–80

359. H.D. Saffrey & A.-P. Segonds (edd.), *Marinus: Proclus ou sur le bonheur* (2001), *Mnemosyne* 56 (2003) 97–99

360. N. Belayche, *Iudaea-Palaestina: The Pagan Cults of Roman Palestine* (2001), *Nederlands Theologisch Tijdschrift* 57 (2003) 153–154

361. T. Eskola, *Messiah and the Throne. Jewish Merkabah Mysticism and Early Christian Exaltation Discourse* (2001), *Nederlands Theologisch Tijdschrift* 57 (2003) 159–160

362. A. Samellas, *Death in the Mediterranean – The Christianization of the East* (2002), *Nederlands Theologisch Tijdschrift* 57 (2003) 160–161

363. J. Leonhardt, *Jewish Worship in Philo of Alexandria* (2001), *Nederlands Theologisch Tijdschrift* 57 (2003) 161–162

364. M. Niehoff, *Philo on Jewish Identity and Culture* (2001), *Frankfurter Judaistische Beiträge* 29 (2002 [publ. in 2003]) 155–157

365. H. Görgemanns (ed.), *Plutarch. Drei religionsphilosophische Schriften* (2003), in *Bryn Mawr Classical Review* 2003.06.09 (online: http://ccat.sas.upenn.edu/bmcr/)

366. M. Hengel, *Paulus und Jakobus. Kleine Schriften III* (2002), *Nederlands Theologisch Tijdschrift* 57 (2003) 243–244

367. A. Lehnardt, *Besa. Ei (Übersetzung des Talmud Yerushalmi II.8)* (2001), *Nederlands Theologisch Tijdschrift* 57 (2003) 245–246

368. J.R. Bartlett (ed.), *Jews in the Hellenistic and Roman Cities* (2002), *Nederlands Theologisch Tijdschrift* 57 (2003) 246–247

369. C. Claußen, *Versammlung, Gemeinde, Synagoge. Das hellenistisch-jüdische Umfeld der frühchristlichen Gemeinde* (2002), *Nederlands Theologisch Tijdschrift* 57 (2003) 247–248

370. M. Lattke, *Oden Salomos. Text, Übersetzung, Kommentar, Teil 2* (2001), *Nederlands Theologisch Tijdschrift* 57 (2003) 248–249

371. M. Finkelberg, G.G. Stroumsa (edd.), *Homer, the Bible, and Beyond. Literary and Religious Canons in the Ancient World* (2003), *Bryn Mawr Classical Review* of 13 Sept. 2003 (online: http://ccat.sas.upenn.edu/bmcr/)

372. D.J. van Uden e.a., *Sjabbat: een dag apart* (2002), *Nederlands Theologisch Tijdschrift* 57 (2003) 342

373. C. Hempel, A. Lange & H. Lichtenberger (eds), *The Wisdom Texts from Qumran and the Development of Sapiential Thought* (2002), *Nederlands Theologisch Tijdschrift* 57 (2003) 343–344

374. R. Pummer, *Early Christian Authors on Samaritan and Samaritanism* (2002), *Nederlands Theologisch Tijdschrift* 57 (2003) 344–345

375. F. Jung, *SOTÊR. Studien zur Rezeption eines hellenistischen Ehrentitels im Neuen Testament* (2002), *Mnemosyne* 56 (2003) 745–747

376. H.D. Betz, *The 'Mithras Liturgy'* (2003), *Nederlands Theologisch Tijdschrift* 58 (2004) 160–161

377. F. Vinel, *La Bible d'Alexandrie, 18: L'Ecclésiaste* (2002), *Nederlands Theologisch Tijdschrift* 58 (2004) 165

378. G.W.E. Nickelsburg, *Ancient Judaism and Christian Origins: Diversity, Continuity, and Transformation* (2003), *Review of Biblical Literature* 6 July 2004 (http://www.bookreviews.org/bookdetail.asp?TitleId=3956); also in *Journal of Biblical Literature* 124 (2005) 176–178

379. W. Deming, *Paul on Marriage and Celibacy* (2004), *Bryn Mawr Classical Review* 23.08.2004 (on internet: http://ccat.sas.upenn.edu/bmcr/)

380. V.D. Arbel, *Beholders of Divine Secrets: Mysticism and Myth in the Hekhalot and Merkavah Literature* (2003), in: *Review of Biblical Literature* Oct. 3, 2004 (see http://www.bookreviews.org/BookDetail.asp?TitleId=4078)

381. J.E. Taylor, *Jewish Women Philosophers in First-Century Alexandria* (2003), in: *Gnomon* 76 (2004) 634–635

382. S. Liekis, *A State within a State? Jewish Autonomy in Lithuania 1918–1925* (2003), and H. Kruk, *The Last Days of the Jerusalem of Lithuania. Chronicles from the Vilna Ghetto and the Camps 1939–1944* (2003), in *Nederlands Theologisch Tijdschrift* 58 (2004) 343–344

383. C. Colpe, *Iranier – Aramäer – Hebräer – Hellenen* (2003), in *Nederlands Theologisch Tijdschrift* 58 (2004) 344–345

384. H. Löhr, *Studien zum frühchristlichen und frühjüdischen Gebet* (2003), *Nederlands Theologisch Tijdschrift* 58 (2004) 349–350.

385. N. de Lange, *Judaism* (2003), *Nederlands Theologisch Tijdschrift* 58 (2004) 350–351

386. A.-M. Denis e.a., *Introduction à la littérature religieuse judéo-hellénistique* (2000), *Vigiliae Christianae* 58 (2004) 452–455

387. U. Hackl e.a., *Quellen zur Geschichte der Nabatäer* (2003), *Nederlands Theologisch Tijdschrift* 59 (2005) 61–62

388. I. Peres, *Griechische Grabinschriften und neutestamentliche Eschatologie* (2003), *Nederlands Theologisch Tijdschrift* 59 (2005) 71–72

389. M. Hadas-Lebel, *Philon d'Alexandrie: un penseur en diaspora* (2003), *Nederlands Theologisch Tijdschrift* 59 (2005) 72

390. E. Kessler, *Bound by the Bible: Jews, Christians and the Sacrifice of Isaac* (2004), *Bryn Mawr Classical Review* 2.03.2005 (on internet: http://ccat.sas.upenn.edu/bmcr/)

391. F. Blanchetière, *Les premiers chrétiens étaient-ils missionaries (30–135)?* (2002), *Journal for the Study of Judaism* 36 (2005) 89–90

392. P. J. Williams a. o. (eds.), *The New Testament in Its First Century Setting: Essays on Context and Background in Honour of B. W. Winter on His 65th Birthday* (2004), *Review of Biblical Literature* 13 April 2005 (at: http://www.bookreviews.org/BookDetail.asp?TitleId=4424)

393. George H. van Kooten (ed.), *The Creation of Heaven and Earth. Re-interpretations of Genesis 1 in the Context of Judaism, Ancient Philosophy, Christianity, and Modern Physics*. Themes in Biblical Narrative 8 (2005), *Bryn Mawr Classical Review* 31–04–2005 (on internet at: http://ccat.sas.upenn.edu/bmcr/)

394. R. Ferwerda, *Keizer Julianus en Saloustios: Over de wereld en haar goden* (2003), *Nederlands Theologisch Tijdschrift* 59 (2005) 158

395. W. Harmless, *Desert Christians: An Introduction to the Literature of Early Monasticism* (2004), *Nederlands Theologisch Tijdschrift* 59 (2005) 166–167

396. R. Kalmin & S. Schwartz (eds.), *Jewish Culture and Society Under the Christian Roman Empire* (2003), *Mnemosyne* 58 (2005) 153–156

397. A.J. Hauser & D.F. Watson (eds.), *A History of Biblical Interpretation, vol. 1: The Ancient Period* (2003), *Nederlands Theologisch Tijdschrift* 59 (2005) 252–253

398. P.J. Tomson & D. Lambers-Petry (eds.), *The Image of the Judaeo-Christians in Ancient Jewish and Christian Literature* (2003), *Nederlands Theologisch Tijdschrift* 59 (2005) 258–259

399. J. Taylor, *Pythagoreans and Essenes: Structural Parallels* (2004), *Nederlands Theologisch Tijdschrift* 59 (2005) 260–261

400. F.G. Hüttenmeister, *Shabbat – Schabbat* (2004), and A. Lehnardt, *Pesahim – Pesachopfer* (2004), *Nederlands Theologisch Tijdschrift* 59 (2005) 261–262

401. S. Krauter, *Bürgerrecht und Kultteilnahme. Politische und kultische Rechte und Pflichten in griechischen Poleis, Rom und antikem Judentum* (2004), *Journal for the Study of Judaism* 36 (2005) 355–358

402. J.W. Hargis, *Against the Christians. The Rise of Early Anti-Christian Polemic* (2001), *Vigiliae Christianae* 59 (2005) 205–207

403. A.P. Hayman, *Sever Yetsira: Edition, Translation, and Text-Critical Commentary* (2004), *Nederlands Theologisch Tijdschrift* 59 (2005) 349–350

404. R.G. Kratz, *Das Judentum im Zeitalter des zweiten Tempels* (2004), *Nederlands Theologisch Tijdschrift* 59 (2005) 350

405. M.F. Smith, *Supplement to Diogenes of Oenoanda, The Epicurean Inscription* (2003), *Mnemosyne* ser. IV 58 (2005) 603–605

406. J.G. Cook, *The Interpretation of the Old Testament in Greco-Roman Paganism* (2004), *Vigiliae Christianae* 59 (2005) 465–467

407. P. Pilhofer, M. Baumbach, J. Gerlach & D.U. Hansen, *Lukian: Der Tod des Peregrinos* (2005), *Bryn Mawr Classical Review* on line of 16-11-2005 (http.//ccat.sas.upenn.edu/bmcr/)

Index of passages

Old Testament

New Testament

Rabbinic literature

Early Christian Literature

Pagan Greek and Latin Literature

Inscriptions and Papyri

JIWE I 155	38	JIWE II 577	104
JIWE I 156	38, 40	JIWE II 578	105
JIWE I 157	38, 41	JIWE II 579	105
JIWE I 158	38	JIWE II 584	104
JIWE I 159	38	KAI 260	44
JIWE I 160	38	Naveh-Shaked I 13	283
JIWE I 161	38, 41	Pap. Maspéro 70:2	257
JIWE II 1	104	Pap. Maspéro 67188	239
JIWE II 2	105	Pap. Oxyrrhynchus	
JIWE II 33	105	264:2–4	256, 257
JIWE II 69	104	Pap. Bodmer 30	190–205
JIWE II 96	104	PGM IV	269–279
JIWE II 98	104	PGM IV 296–434	271
JIWE II 100	76, 104	PGM IV 436–461	271
JIWE II 106	105	PGM IV 1219	277
JIWE II 113	104	PGM IV 1957–1981	271
JIWE II 114	105	PGM IV 2241–2347	271
JIWE II 117	105	PGM IV 2902–2939	271
JIWE II 130	104	PGM IV 3007–3086	273, 281
JIWE II 163	104	PGM IV 3013	273
JIWE II 165	104	PGM IV 3017	274
JIWE II 166	104	PGM IV 3019–20	274
JIWE II 167	104	PGM IV 3023	274
JIWE II 169	104	PGM IV 3026–7	274
JIWE II 170	104	PGM IV 3033–8	275
JIWE II 189	104	PGM IV 3038	275
JIWE II 194	104	PGM IV 3039–40	276
JIWE II 288	76, 104	PGM IV 3042	275
JIWE II 338	104	PGM IV 3043–4	275
JIWE II 406	104	PGM IV 3044	275
JIWE II 428	104	PGM IV 3047	275
JIWE II 451	104	PGM IV 3050–1	276
JIWE II 452	104	PGM IV 3052	276
JIWE II 488	104	PGM IV 3053–5	277, 281
JIWE II 527	104	PGM IV 3056–8	277
JIWE II 540	105	PGM IV 3061	277
JIWE II 542	104	PGM IV 3062–4	277
JIWE II 547	104	PGM IV 3069–70	277
JIWE II 549	104	PGM IV 3084–6	277
JIWE II 557	104	PGM XXXVI 295–311	282
JIWE II 558	104	PGM XXXVI 306	282
JIWE II 560	104	SEG 8:269	13
JIWE II 576	104		

Index of modern authors

Index of names and subjects

Wissenschaftliche Untersuchungen zum Neuen Testament

Alphabetical Index of the First and Second Series

Bøe, Sverre: Gog and Magog. 2001. *Volume II/135.*
Böhlig, Alexander: Gnosis und Synkretismus. Volume 1 1989. *Volume 47* – Volume 2 1989. *Volume 48.*
Böhm, Martina: Samarien und die Samaritai bei Lukas. 1999. *Volume II/111.*
Böttrich, Christfried: Weltweisheit – Menschheitsethik – Urkult. 1992. *Volume II/50.*
Bolyki, János: Jesu Tischgemeinschaften. 1997. *Volume II/96.*
Bosman, Philip: Conscience in Philo and Paul. 2003. *Volume II/166.*
Bovon, François: Studies in Early Christianity. 2003. *Volume 161.*
Brocke, Christoph vom: Thessaloniki – Stadt des Kassander und Gemeinde des Paulus. 2001. *Volume II/125.*
Brunson, Andrew: Psalm 118 in the Gospel of John. 2003. *Volume II/158.*
Büchli, Jörg: Der Poimandres – ein paganisiertes Evangelium. 1987. *Volume II/27.*
Bühner, Jan A.: Der Gesandte und sein Weg im 4. Evangelium. 1977. *Volume II/2.*
Burchard, Christoph: Untersuchungen zu Joseph und Aseneth. 1965. *Volume 8.*
– Studien zur Theologie, Sprache und Umwelt des Neuen Testaments. Ed. by D. Sänger. 1998. *Volume 107.*
Burnett, Richard: Karl Barth's Theological Exegesis. 2001. *Volume II/145.*
Byron, John: Slavery Metaphors in Early Judaism and Pauline Christianity. 2003. *Volume II/162.*
Byrskog, Samuel: Story as History – History as Story. 2000. *Volume 123.*
Cancik, Hubert (Ed.): Markus-Philologie. 1984. *Volume 33.*
Capes, David B.: Old Testament Yaweh Texts in Paul's Christology. 1992. *Volume II/47.*
Caragounis, Chrys C.: The Development of Greek and the New Testament. 2004. *Volume 167.*
– The Son of Man. 1986. *Volume 38.*
– see *Fridrichsen, Anton.*
Carleton Paget, James: The Epistle of Barnabas. 1994. *Volume II/64.*
Carson, D.A., O'Brien, Peter T. and *Mark Seifrid* (Ed.): Justification and Variegated Nomism.
Volume 1: The Complexities of Second Temple Judaism. 2001. *Volume II/140.*
Volume 2: The Paradoxes of Paul. 2004. *Volume II/181.*
Ciampa, Roy E.: The Presence and Function of Scripture in Galatians 1 and 2. 1998. *Volume II/102.*

Classen, Carl Joachim: Rhetorical Criticsm of the New Testament. 2000. *Volume 128.*
Colpe, Carsten: Iranier – Aramäer – Hebräer – Hellenen. 2003. *Volume 154.*
Crump, David: Jesus the Intercessor. 1992. *Volume II/49.*
Dahl, Nils Alstrup: Studies in Ephesians. 2000. *Volume 131.*
Deines, Roland: Die Gerechtigkeit der Tora im Reich des Messias. 2004. *Volume 177.*
– Jüdische Steingefäße und pharisäische Frömmigkeit. 1993. *Volume II/52.*
– Die Pharisäer. 1997. *Volume 101.*
Deines, Roland and *Karl-Wilhelm Niebuhr* (Ed.): Philo und das Neue Testament. 2004. *Volume 172.*
Dettwiler, Andreas and *Jean Zumstein* (Ed.): Kreuzestheologie im Neuen Testament. 2002. *Volume 151.*
Dickson, John P.: Mission-Commitment in Ancient Judaism and in the Pauline Communities. 2003. *Volume II/159.*
Dietzfelbinger, Christian: Der Abschied des Kommenden. 1997. *Volume 95.*
Dimitrov, Ivan Z., James D.G. Dunn, Ulrich Luz and *Karl-Wilhelm Niebuhr* (Ed.): Das Alte Testament als christliche Bibel in orthodoxer und westlicher Sicht. 2004. *Volume 174.*
Dobbeler, Axel von: Glaube als Teilhabe. 1987. *Volume II/22.*
Dryden, J. de Waal: Theology and Ethics in 1 Peter. 2006. *Volume II/209.*
Du Toit, David S.: Theios Anthropos. 1997. *Volume II/91.*
Dübbers, Michael: Christologie und Existenz im Kolosserbrief. 2005. *Volume II/191.*
Dunn, James D.G.: The New Perspective on Paul. 2005. *Volume 185.*
Dunn , James D.G. (Ed.): Jews and Christians. 1992. *Volume 66.*
– Paul and the Mosaic Law. 1996. *Volume 89.*
– see *Dimitrov, Ivan Z.*
–, *Hans Klein, Ulrich Luz* and *Vasile Mihoc* (Ed.): Auslegung der Bibel in orthodoxer und westlicher Perspektive. 2000. *Volume 130.*
Ebel, Eva: Die Attraktivität früher christlicher Gemeinden. 2004. *Volume II/178.*
Ebertz, Michael N.: Das Charisma des Gekreuzigten. 1987. *Volume 45.*
Eckstein, Hans-Joachim: Der Begriff Syneidesis bei Paulus. 1983. *Volume II/10.*
– Verheißung und Gesetz. 1996. *Volume 86.*
Ego, Beate: Im Himmel wie auf Erden. 1989. *Volume II/34.*
Ego, Beate, Armin Lange and *Peter Pilhofer* (Ed.): Gemeinde ohne Tempel – Community without Temple. 1999. *Volume 118.*

– and *Helmut Merkel* (Ed.): Religiöses Lernen in der biblischen, frühjüdischen und früh-christlichen Überlieferung. 2005. *Volume 180.*

Eisen, Ute E.: see *Paulsen, Henning.*

Elledge, C.D.: Life after Death in Early Judaism. 2006. *Volume II/208.*

Ellis, E. Earle: Prophecy and Hermeneutic in Early Christianity. 1978. *Volume 18.*

– The Old Testament in Early Christianity. 1991. *Volume 54.*

Endo, Masanobu: Creation and Christology. 2002. *Volume 149.*

Ennulat, Andreas: Die 'Minor Agreements'. 1994. *Volume II/62.*

Ensor, Peter W.: Jesus and His 'Works'. 1996. *Volume II/85.*

Eskola, Timo: Messiah and the Throne. 2001. *Volume II/142.*

– Theodicy and Predestination in Pauline Soteriology. 1998. *Volume II/100.*

Fatehi, Mehrdad: The Spirit's Relation to the Risen Lord in Paul. 2000. *Volume II/128.*

Feldmeier, Reinhard: Die Krisis des Gottessohnes. 1987. *Volume II/21.*

– Die Christen als Fremde. 1992. *Volume 64.*

Feldmeier, Reinhard and *Ulrich Heckel* (Ed.): Die Heiden. 1994. *Volume 70.*

Fletcher-Louis, Crispin H.T.: Luke-Acts: Angels, Christology and Soteriology. 1997. *Volume II/94.*

Förster, Niclas: Marcus Magus. 1999. *Volume 114.*

Forbes, Christopher Brian: Prophecy and Inspired Speech in Early Christianity and its Hellenistic Environment. 1995. *Volume II/75.*

Fornberg, Tord: see *Fridrichsen, Anton.*

Fossum, Jarl E.: The Name of God and the Angel of the Lord. 1985. *Volume 36.*

Foster, Paul: Community, Law and Mission in Matthew's Gospel. *Volume II/177.*

Fotopoulos, John: Food Offered to Idols in Roman Corinth. 2003. *Volume II/151.*

Frenschkowski, Marco: Offenbarung und Epiphanie. Volume 1 1995. *Volume II/79* – Volume 2 1997. *Volume II/80.*

Frey, Jörg: Eugen Drewermann und die biblische Exegese. 1995. *Volume II/71.*

– Die johanneische Eschatologie. Volume I. 1997. *Volume 96.* – Volume II. 1998. *Volume 110.* – Volume III. 2000. *Volume 117.*

Frey, Jörg and *Udo Schnelle (Ed.):* Kontexte des Johannesevangeliums. 2004. *Volume 175.*

– and *Jens Schröter* (Ed.): Deutungen des Todes Jesu im Neuen Testament. 2005. *Volume 181.*

Freyne, Sean: Galilee and Gospel. 2000. *Volume 125.*

Fridrichsen, Anton: Exegetical Writings. Edited by C.C. Caragounis and T. Fornberg. 1994. *Volume 76.*

Gäckle, Volker: Die Starken und die Schwachen in Korinth und in Rom. 2005. *Volume 200.*

Garlington, Don B.: 'The Obedience of Faith'. 1991. *Volume II/38.*

– Faith, Obedience, and Perseverance. 1994. *Volume 79.*

Garnet, Paul: Salvation and Atonement in the Qumran Scrolls. 1977. *Volume II/3.*

Gemünden, Petra von (Ed.): see *Weissenrieder, Annette.*

Gese, Michael: Das Vermächtnis des Apostels. 1997. *Volume II/99.*

Gheorghita, Radu: The Role of the Septuagint in Hebrews. 2003. *Volume II/160.*

Gräbe, Petrus J.: The Power of God in Paul's Letters. 2000. *Volume II/123.*

Gräßer, Erich: Der Alte Bund im Neuen. 1985. *Volume 35.*

– Forschungen zur Apostelgeschichte. 2001. *Volume 137.*

Green, Joel B.: The Death of Jesus. 1988. *Volume II/33.*

Gregg, Brian Han: The Historical Jesus and the Final Judgment Sayings in Q. 2005. *Volume II/207.*

Gregory, Andrew: The Reception of Luke and Acts in the Period before Irenaeus. 2003. *Volume II/169.*

Grindheim, Sigurd: The Crux of Election. 2005. *Volume II/202.*

Gundry, Robert H.: The Old is Better. 2005. *Volume 178.*

Gundry Volf, Judith M.: Paul and Perseverance. 1990. *Volume II/37.*

Häußer, Detlef: Christusbekenntnis und Jesusüberlieferung bei Paulus. 2006. *Volume 210.*

Hafemann, Scott J.: Suffering and the Spirit. 1986. *Volume II/19.*

– Paul, Moses, and the History of Israel. 1995. *Volume 81.*

Hahn, Ferdinand: Studien zum Neuen Testament. Volume I: Grundsatzfragen, Jesusforschung, Evangelien. 2006. *Volume 191.* – Volume II: Bekenntnisbildung und Theologie in urchristlicher Zeit. 2006. *Volume 192.*

Hahn, Johannes (Ed.): Zerstörungen des Jerusalemer Tempels. 2002. *Volume 147.*

Hamid-Khani, Saeed: Relevation and Concealment of Christ. 2000. *Volume II/120.*

Hannah, Darrel D.: Michael and Christ. 1999. *Volume II/109.*

Harrison; James R.: Paul's Language of Grace
in Its Graeco-Roman Context. 2003.
Volume II/172.
Hartman, Lars: Text-Centered New Testa-
ment Studies. Ed. von D. Hellholm. 1997.
Volume 102.
Hartog, Paul: Polycarp and the New Testa-
ment. 2001. *Volume II/134.*
Heckel, Theo K.: Der Innere Mensch. 1993.
Volume II/53.
– Vom Evangelium des Markus zum vierge-
staltigen Evangelium. 1999. *Volume 120.*
Heckel, Ulrich: Kraft in Schwachheit. 1993.
Volume II/56.
– Der Segen im Neuen Testament. 2002.
Volume 150.
– see *Feldmeier, Reinhard.*
– see *Hengel, Martin.*
Heiligenthal, Roman: Werke als Zeichen.
1983. *Volume II/9.*
Hellholm, D.: see *Hartman, Lars.*
Hemer, Colin J.: The Book of Acts in the
Setting of Hellenistic History. 1989.
Volume 49.
Hengel, Martin: Judentum und Hellenismus.
1969, ³1988. *Volume 10.*
– Die johanneische Frage. 1993. *Volume 67.*
– Judaica et Hellenistica.
Kleine Schriften I. 1996. *Volume 90.*
– Judaica, Hellenistica et Christiana.
Kleine Schriften II. 1999. *Volume 109.*
– Paulus und Jakobus.
Kleine Schriften III. 2002. *Volume 141.*
– and *Anna Maria Schwemer:* Paulus zwi-
schen Damaskus und Antiochien. 1998.
Volume 108.
– Der messianische Anspruch Jesu und
die Anfänge der Christologie. 2001.
Volume 138.
Hengel, Martin and *Ulrich Heckel* (Ed.):
Paulus und das antike Judentum. 1991.
Volume 58.
– and *Hermut Löhr* (Ed.): Schriftauslegung
im antiken Judentum und im Urchristen-
tum. 1994. *Volume 73.*
– and *Anna Maria Schwemer* (Ed.): Königs-
herrschaft Gottes und himm-lischer Kult.
1991. *Volume 55.*
– Die Septuaginta. 1994. *Volume 72.*
–, *Siegfried Mittmann* and *Anna Maria
Schwemer* (Ed.): La Cité de Dieu / Die Stadt
Gottes. 2000. *Volume 129.*
Herrenbrück, Fritz: Jesus und die Zöllner.
1990. *Volume II/41.*
Herzer, Jens: Paulus oder Petrus? 1998.
Volume 103.
Hill, Charles E.: From the Lost Teaching of
Polycarp. 2005. *Volume 186.*

Hoegen-Rohls, Christina: Der nachösterliche
Johannes. 1996. *Volume II/84.*
Hoffmann, Matthias Reinhard: The Destro-
yer and the Lamb. 2005. *Volume II/203.*
Hofius, Otfried: Katapausis. 1970. *Volume 11.*
– Der Vorhang vor dem Thron Gottes. 1972.
Volume 14.
– Der Christushymnus Philipper 2,6-11.
1976, ²1991. *Volume 17.*
– Paulusstudien. 1989, ²1994. *Volume 51.*
– Neutestamentliche Studien. 2000.
Volume 132.
– Paulusstudien II. 2002. *Volume 143.*
– and *Hans-Christian Kammler:*
Johannesstudien. 1996. *Volume 88.*
Holtz, Traugott: Geschichte und Theologie des
Urchristentums. 1991. *Volume 57.*
Hommel, Hildebrecht: Sebasmata. Volume 1
1983. *Volume 31* – Volume 2 1984.
Volume 32.
Horbury, William: Herodian Judaism and New
Testament Study. 2006. *Volume 193.*
Horst, Pieter W. van der: Jews and Christians in
Their Graeco-Roman Context. 2006.
Volume 196.
Hvalvik, Reidar: The Struggle for Scripture
and Covenant. 1996. *Volume II/82.*
Jauhiainen, Marko: The Use of Zechariah in
Revelation. 2005. *Volume II/199.*
Johns, Loren L.: The Lamb Christology of the
Apocalypse of John. 2003. *Volume II/167.*
Joubert, Stephan: Paul as Benefactor. 2000.
Volume II/124.
Jungbauer, Harry: „Ehre Vater und Mutter".
2002. *Volume II/146.*
Kähler, Christoph: Jesu Gleichnisse als Poesie
und Therapie. 1995. *Volume 78.*
Kamlah, Ehrhard: Die Form der
katalogischen Paränese im Neuen Testa-
ment. 1964. *Volume 7.*
Kammler, Hans-Christian: Christologie und
Eschatologie. 2000. *Volume 126.*
– Kreuz und Weisheit. 2003. *Volume 159.*
– see *Hofius, Otfried.*
Kelhoffer, James A.: The Diet of John the
Baptist. 2005. *Volume 176.*
– Miracle and Mission. 1999. *Volume II/112.*
Kieffer, René and *Jan Bergman (Ed.):* La Main
de Dieu / Die Hand Gottes. 1997. *Volume 94.*
Kim, Seyoon: The Origin of Paul's Gospel.
1981, ²1984. *Volume II/4.*
– Paul and the New Perspective. 2002.
Volume 140.
– "The 'Son of Man'" as the Son of God.
1983. *Volume 30.*
Klauck, Hans-Josef: Religion und Gesellschaft
im frühen Christentum. 2003. *Volume 152.*
Klein, Hans: see *Dunn, James D.G.*

Kleinknecht, Karl Th.: Der leidende Gerecht-
fertigte. 1984, ²1988. *Volume II/13.*

Klinghardt, Matthias: Gesetz und Volk Gottes.
1988. *Volume II/32.*

Kloppenborg, John S.: The Tenants in the
Vineyard. 2006. *Volume 195.*

Koch, Michael: Drachenkampf und Sonnen-
frau. 2004. *Volume II/184.*

Koch, Stefan: Rechtliche Regelung von Kon-
flikten im frühen Christentum. 2004.
Volume II/174.

Köhler, Wolf-Dietrich: Rezeption des
Matthäusevangeliums in der Zeit vor
Irenäus. 1987. *Volume II/24.*

Köhn, Andreas: Der Neutestamentler Ernst
Lohmeyer. 2004. *Volume II/180.*

Kooten, George H. van: Cosmic Christology
in Paul and the Pauline School. 2003.
Volume II/171.

Korn, Manfred: Die Geschichte Jesu in verän-
derter Zeit. 1993. *Volume II/51.*

Koskenniemi, Erkki: Apollonios von Tyana in
der neutestamentlichen Exegese. 1994.
Volume II/61.

– The Old Testament Miracle-Workers in
Early Judaism. 2005. *Volume II/206.*

Kraus, Thomas J.: Sprache, Stil und histori-
scher Ort des zweiten Petrusbriefes. 2001.
Volume II/136.

Kraus, Wolfgang: Das Volk Gottes. 1996.
Volume 85.

Kraus, Wolfgang and *Karl-Wilhelm Niebuhr*
(Ed.): Frühjudentum und Neues Testament
im Horizont Biblischer Theologie. 2003.
Volume 162.

– see *Walter, Nikolaus.*

Kreplin, Matthias: Das Selbstverständnis Jesu.
2001. *Volume II/141.*

Kuhn, Karl G.: Achtzehngebet und Vaterunser
und der Reim. 1950. *Volume 1.*

Kvalbein, Hans: see *Ådna, Jostein.*

Kwon, Yon-Gyong: Eschatology in Galatians.
2004. *Volume II/183.*

Laansma, Jon: I Will Give You Rest. 1997.
Volume II/98.

Labahn, Michael: Offenbarung in Zeichen und
Wort. 2000. *Volume II/117.*

Lambers-Petry, Doris: see *Tomson, Peter J.*

Lange, Armin: see *Ego, Beate.*

Lampe, Peter: Die stadtrömischen Christen in
den ersten beiden Jahrhunderten. 1987,
²1989. *Volume II/18.*

Landmesser, Christof: Wahrheit als Grundbe-
griff neutestamentlicher Wissenschaft.
1999. *Volume 113.*

– Jüngerberufung und Zuwendung zu Gott.
2000. *Volume 133.*

Lau, Andrew: Manifest in Flesh. 1996.
Volume II/86.

Lawrence, Louise: An Ethnography of the
Gospel of Matthew. 2003. *Volume II/165.*

Lee, Aquila H.I.: From Messiah to Preexistent
Son. 2005. *Volume II/192.*

Lee, Pilchan: The New Jerusalem in the Book
of Relevation. 2000. *Volume II/129.*

Lichtenberger, Hermann: Das Ich Adams und
das Ich der Menschheit. 2004. *Volume 164.*

– see *Avemarie, Friedrich.*

Lierman, John: The New Testament Moses.
2004. *Volume II/173.*

Lieu, Samuel N.C.: Manichaeism in the Later
Roman Empire and Medieval China.
²1992. *Volume 63.*

Lindgård, Fredrik: Paul's Line of Thought in
2 Corinthians 4:16-5:10. 2004.
Volume II/189.

Loader, William R.G.: Jesus' Attitude Towards
the Law. 1997. *Volume II/97.*

Löhr, Gebhard: Verherrlichung Gottes durch
Philosophie. 1997. *Volume 97.*

Löhr, Hermut: Studien zum frühchristlichen
und frühjüdischen Gebet. 2003. *Volume 160.*

– see *Hengel, Martin.*

Löhr, Winrich Alfried: Basilides und seine Schu-
le. 1995. *Volume 83.*

Luomanen, Petri: Entering the Kingdom of
Heaven. 1998. *Volume II/101.*

Luz, Ulrich: see *Dunn, James D.G.*

Mackay, Ian D.: John's Raltionship with
Mark. 2004. *Volume II/182.*

Maier, Gerhard: Mensch und freier Wille.
1971. *Volume 12.*

– Die Johannesoffenbarung und die Kirche.
1981. *Volume 25.*

Markschies, Christoph: Valentinus Gnosticus?
1992. *Volume 65.*

Marshall, Peter: Enmity in Corinth: Social
Conventions in Paul's Relations with the
Corinthians. 1987. *Volume II/23.*

Mayer, Annemarie: Sprache der Einheit im
Epheserbrief und in der Ökumene. 2002.
Volume II/150.

Mayordomo, Moisés: Argumentiert Paulus
logisch? 2005. *Volume 188.*

McDonough, Sean M.: YHWH at Patmos:
Rev. 1:4 in its Hellenistic and Early Jewish
Setting. 1999. *Volume II/107.*

McGlynn, Moyna: Divine Judgement and
Divine Benevolence in the Book of
Wisdom. 2001. *Volume II/139.*

Meade, David G.: Pseudonymity and Canon.
1986. *Volume 39.*

Meadors, Edward P.: Jesus the Messianic
Herald of Salvation. 1995. *Volume II/72.*

Meißner, Stefan: Die Heimholung des Ketzers. 1996. *Volume II/87.*

Mell, Ulrich: Die „anderen" Winzer. 1994. *Volume 77.*

Mengel, Berthold: Studien zum Philipperbrief. 1982. *Volume II/8.*

Merkel, Helmut: Die Widersprüche zwischen den Evangelien. 1971. *Volume 13.*
- see *Ego, Beate.*

Merklein, Helmut: Studien zu Jesus und Paulus. Volume 1 1987. *Volume 43.* – Volume 2 1998. *Volume 105.*

Metzdorf, Christina: Die Tempelaktion Jesu. 2003. *Volume II/168.*

Metzler, Karin: Der griechische Begriff des Verzeihens. 1991. *Volume II/44.*

Metzner, Rainer: Die Rezeption des Matthäusevangeliums im 1. Petrusbrief. 1995. *Volume II/74.*
- Das Verständnis der Sünde im Johannesevangelium. 2000. *Volume 122.*

Mihoc, Vasile: see *Dunn, James D.G.*

Mineshige, Kiyoshi: Besitzverzicht und Almosen bei Lukas. 2003. *Volume II/163.*

Mittmann, Siegfried: see *Hengel, Martin.*

Mittmann-Richert, Ulrike: Magnifikat und Benediktus. 1996. *Volume II/90.*

Mournet, Terence C.: Oral Tradition and Literary Dependency. 2005. *Volume II/195.*

Mußner, Franz: Jesus von Nazareth im Umfeld Israels und der Urkirche. Ed. von M. Theobald. 1998. *Volume 111.*

Mutschler, Bernhard: Das Corpus Johanneum bei Irenäus von Lyon. 2005. *Volume 189.*

Niebuhr, Karl-Wilhelm: Gesetz und Paränese. 1987. *Volume II/28.*
- Heidenapostel aus Israel. 1992. *Volume 62.*
- see *Deines, Roland*
- see *Dimitrov, Ivan Z.*
- see *Kraus, Wolfgang*

Nielsen, Anders E.: "Until it is Fullfilled". 2000. *Volume II/126.*

Nissen, Andreas: Gott und der Nächste im antiken Judentum. 1974. *Volume 15.*

Noack, Christian: Gottesbewußtsein. 2000. *Volume II/116.*

Noormann, Rolf: Irenäus als Paulusinterpret. 1994. *Volume II/66.*

Novakovic, Lidija: Messiah, the Healer of the Sick. 2003. *Volume II/170.*

Obermann, Andreas: Die christologische Erfüllung der Schrift im Johannesevangelium. 1996. *Volume II/83.*

Öhler, Markus: Barnabas. 2003. *Volume 156.*
- see *Becker, Michael*

Okure, Teresa: The Johannine Approach to Mission. 1988. *Volume II/31.*

Onuki, Takashi: Heil und Erlösung. 2004. *Volume 165.*

Oropeza, B. J.: Paul and Apostasy. 2000. *Volume II/115.*

Ostmeyer, Karl-Heinrich: Taufe und Typos. 2000. *Volume II/118.*

Paulsen, Henning: Studien zur Literatur und Geschichte des frühen Christentums. Ed. von Ute E. Eisen. 1997. *Volume 99.*

Pao, David W.: Acts and the Isaianic New Exodus. 2000. *Volume II/130.*

Park, Eung Chun: The Mission Discourse in Matthew's Interpretation. 1995. *Volume II/81.*

Park, Joseph S.: Conceptions of Afterlife in Jewish Insriptions. 2000. *Volume II/121.*

Pate, C. Marvin: The Reverse of the Curse. 2000. *Volume II/114.*

Peres, Imre: Griechische Grabinschriften und neutestamentliche Eschatologie. 2003. *Volume 157.*

Philip, Finny: The Origins of Pauline Pneumatology. 2005. *Volume II/194.*

Philonenko, Marc (Ed.): Le Trône de Dieu. 1993. *Volume 69.*

Pilhofer, Peter: Presbyteron Kreitton. 1990. *Volume II/39.*
- Philippi. Volume 1 1995. *Volume 87.* – Volume 2 2000. *Volume 119.*
- Die frühen Christen und ihre Welt. 2002. *Volume 145.*
- see *Becker, Eve-Marie.*
- see *Ego, Beate.*

Pitre, Brant: Jesus, the Tribulation, and the End of the Exile. 2005. *Volume II/204.*

Plümacher, Eckhard: Geschichte und Geschichten. 2004. *Volume 170.*

Pöhlmann, Wolfgang: Der Verlorene Sohn und das Haus. 1993. *Volume 68.*

Pokorný, Petr and *Josef B. Souček:* Bibelauslegung als Theologie. 1997. *Volume 100.*

Pokorný, Petr and *Jan Roskovec* (Ed.): Philosophical Hermeneutics and Biblical Exegesis. 2002. *Volume 153.*

Popkes, Enno Edzard: Die Theologie der Liebe Gottes in den johanneischen Schriften. 2005. *Volume II/197.*

Porter, Stanley E.: The Paul of Acts. 1999. *Volume 115.*

Prieur, Alexander: Die Verkündigung der Gottesherrschaft. 1996. *Volume II/89.*

Probst, Hermann: Paulus und der Brief. 1991. *Volume II/45.*

Räisänen, Heikki: Paul and the Law. 1983, ²1987. *Volume 29.*

Rehkopf, Friedrich: Die lukanische Sonderquelle. 1959. *Volume 5.*

Rein, Matthias: Die Heilung des Blindgeborenen (Joh 9). 1995. *Volume II/73.*

Reinmuth, Eckart: Pseudo-Philo und Lukas. 1994. *Volume 74.*

Reiser, Marius: Syntax und Stil des Markusevangeliums. 1984. *Volume II/11.*

Rhodes, James N.: The Epistle of Barnabas and the Deuteronomic Tradition. 2004. *Volume II/188.*

Richards, E. Randolph: The Secretary in the Letters of Paul. 1991. *Volume II/42.*

Riesner, Rainer: Jesus als Lehrer. 1981, ³1988. *Volume II/7.*

– Die Frühzeit des Apostels Paulus. 1994. *Volume 71.*

Rissi, Mathias: Die Theologie des Hebräerbriefs. 1987. *Volume 41.*

Roskovec, Jan: see *Pokorný, Petr.*

Röhser, Günter: Metaphorik und Personifikation der Sünde. 1987. *Volume II/25.*

Rose, Christian: Die Wolke der Zeugen. 1994. *Volume II/60.*

Rothschild, Clare K.: Baptist Traditions and Q. 2005. *Volume 190.*

– Luke Acts and the Rhetoric of History. 2004. *Volume II/175.*

Rüegger, Hans-Ulrich: Verstehen, was Markus erzählt. 2002. *Volume II/155.*

Rüger, Hans Peter: Die Weisheitsschrift aus der Kairoer Geniza. 1991. *Volume 53.*

Sänger, Dieter: Antikes Judentum und die Mysterien. 1980. *Volume II/5.*

– Die Verkündigung des Gekreuzigten und Israel. 1994. *Volume 75.*

– see *Burchard, Christoph*

Salier, Willis Hedley: The Rhetorical Impact of the Se-meia in the Gospel of John. 2004. *Volume II/186.*

Salzmann, Jorg Christian: Lehren und Ermahnen. 1994. *Volume II/59.*

Sandnes, Karl Olav: Paul – One of the Prophets? 1991. *Volume II/43.*

Sato, Migaku: Q und Prophetie. 1988. *Volume II/29.*

Schäfer, Ruth: Paulus bis zum Apostelkonzil. 2004. *Volume II/179.*

Schaper, Joachim: Eschatology in the Greek Psalter. 1995. *Volume II/76.*

Schimanowski, Gottfried: Die himmlische Liturgie in der Apokalypse des Johannes. 2002. *Volume II/154.*

– Weisheit und Messias. 1985. *Volume II/17.*

Schlichting, Günter: Ein jüdisches Leben Jesu. 1982. *Volume 24.*

Schnabel, Eckhard J.: Law and Wisdom from Ben Sira to Paul. 1985. *Volume II/16.*

Schnelle, Udo: see *Frey, Jörg.*

Schröter, Jens: see *Frey, Jörg.*

Schutter, William L.: Hermeneutic and Composition in I Peter. 1989. *Volume II/30.*

Schwartz, Daniel R.: Studies in the Jewish Background of Christianity. 1992. *Volume 60.*

Schwemer, Anna Maria: see *Hengel, Martin*

Scott, Ian W.: Implicit Epistemology in the Letters of Paul. 2005. *Volume II/205.*

Scott, James M.: Adoption as Sons of God. 1992. *Volume II/48.*

– Paul and the Nations. 1995. *Volume 84.*

Shum, Shiu-Lun: Paul's Use of Isaiah in Romans. 2002. *Volume II/156.*

Siegert, Folker: Drei hellenistisch-jüdische Predigten. Teil I 1980. *Volume 20 –* Teil II 1992. *Volume 61.*

– Nag-Hammadi-Register. 1982. *Volume 26.*

– Argumentation bei Paulus. 1985. *Volume 34.*

– Philon von Alexandrien. 1988. *Volume 46.*

Simon, Marcel: Le christianisme antique et son contexte religieux I/II. 1981. *Volume 23.*

Snodgrass, Klyne: The Parable of the Wicked Tenants. 1983. *Volume 27.*

Söding, Thomas: Das Wort vom Kreuz. 1997. *Volume 93.*

– see *Thüsing, Wilhelm.*

Sommer, Urs: Die Passionsgeschichte des Markusevangeliums. 1993. *Volume II/58.*

Souèek, Josef B.: see *Pokorný, Petr.*

Spangenberg, Volker: Herrlichkeit des Neuen Bundes. 1993. *Volume II/55.*

Spanje, T.E. van: Inconsistency in Paul? 1999. *Volume II/110.*

Speyer, Wolfgang: Frühes Christentum im antiken Strahlungsfeld. Volume I: 1989. *Volume 50.*

– Volume II: 1999. *Volume 116.*

Stadelmann, Helge: Ben Sira als Schriftgelehrter. 1980. *Volume II/6.*

Stenschke, Christoph W.: Luke's Portrait of Gentiles Prior to Their Coming to Faith. *Volume II/108.*

Sterck-Degueldre, Jean-Pierre: Eine Frau namens Lydia. 2004. *Volume II/176.*

Stettler, Christian: Der Kolosserhymnus. 2000. *Volume II/131.*

Stettler, Hanna: Die Christologie der Pastoralbriefe. 1998. *Volume II/105.*

Stökl Ben Ezra, Daniel: The Impact of Yom Kippur on Early Christianity. 2003. *Volume 163.*

Strobel, August: Die Stunde der Wahrheit. 1980. *Volume 21.*

Stroumsa, Guy G.: Barbarian Philosophy. 1999. *Volume 112.*

Stuckenbruck, Loren T.: Angel Veneration and Christology. 1995. *Volume II/70.*

Stuhlmacher, Peter (Ed.): Das Evangelium und die Evangelien. 1983. *Volume 28.*
- Biblische Theologie und Evangelium. 2002. *Volume 146.*
Sung, Chong-Hyon: Vergebung der Sünden. 1993. *Volume II/57.*
Tajra, Harry W.: The Trial of St. Paul. 1989. *Volume II/35.*
- The Martyrdom of St.Paul. 1994. *Volume II/67.*
Theißen, Gerd: Studien zur Soziologie des Urchristentums. 1979, ³1989. *Volume 19.*
Theobald, Michael: Studien zum Römerbrief. 2001. *Volume 136.*
Theobald, Michael: see *Mußner, Franz.*
Thornton, Claus-Jürgen: Der Zeuge des Zeugen. 1991. *Volume 56.*
Thüsing, Wilhelm: Studien zur neutestamentlichen Theologie. Ed. von Thomas Söding. 1995. *Volume 82.*
Thurén, Lauri: Derhethorizing Paul. 2000. *Volume 124.*
Tolmie, D. Francois: Persuading the Galatians. 2005. *Volume II/190.*
Tomson, Peter J. and *Doris Lambers-Petry* (Ed.): The Image of the Judaeo-Christians in Ancient Jewish and Christian Literature. 2003. *Volume 158.*
Trebilco, Paul: The Early Christians in Ephesus from Paul to Ignatius. 2004. *Volume 166.*
Treloar, Geoffrey R.: Lightfoot the Historian. 1998. *Volume II/103.*
Tsuji, Manabu: Glaube zwischen Vollkommenheit und Verweltlichung. 1997. *Volume II/93.*
Twelftree, Graham H.: Jesus the Exorcist. 1993. *Volume II/54.*
Urban, Christina: Das Menschenbild nach dem Johannesevangelium. 2001. *Volume II/137.*
Visotzky, Burton L.: Fathers of the World. 1995. *Volume 80.*
Vollenweider, Samuel: Horizonte neutestamentlicher Christologie. 2002. *Volume 144.*
Vos, Johan S.: Die Kunst der Argumentation bei Paulus. 2002. *Volume 149.*
Wagener, Ulrike: Die Ordnung des „Hauses Gottes". 1994. *Volume II/65.*
Wahlen, Clinton: Jesus and the Impurity of Spirits in the Synoptic Gospels. 2004. *Volume II/185.*
Walker, Donald D.: Paul's Offer of Leniency (2 Cor 10:1). 2002. *Volume II/152.*

Walter, Nikolaus: Praeparatio Evangelica. Ed. von Wolfgang Kraus und Florian Wilk. 1997. *Volume 98.*
Wander, Bernd: Gottesfürchtige und Sympathisanten. 1998. *Volume 104.*
Watts, Rikki: Isaiah's New Exodus and Mark. 1997. *Volume II/88.*
Wedderburn, A.J.M.: Baptism and Resurrection. 1987. *Volume 44.*
Wegner, Uwe: Der Hauptmann von Kafarnaum. 1985. *Volume II/14.*
Weissenrieder, Annette: Images of Illness in the Gospel of Luke. 2003. Volume II/164.
- , *Friederike Wendt* and *Petra von Gemünden* (Ed.): Picturing the New Testament. 2005. *Volume II/193.*
Welck, Christian: Erzählte ‚Zeichen'. 1994. *Volume II/69.*
Wendt, Friederike (Ed.): see *Weissenrieder, Annette.*
Wiarda, Timothy: Peter in the Gospels. 2000. *Volume II/127.*
Wifstrand, Albert: Epochs and Styles. 2005. *Volume 179.*
Wilk, Florian: see *Walter, Nikolaus.*
Williams, Catrin H.: I am He. 2000. *Volume II/113.*
Wilson, Walter T.: Love without Pretense. 1991. *Volume II/46.*
Wischmeyer, Oda: Von Ben Sira zu Paulus. 2004. *Volume 173.*
Wisdom, Jeffrey: Blessing for the Nations and the Curse of the Law. 2001. *Volume II/133.*
Wold, Benjamin G.: Women, Men, and Angels. 2005. *Volume II/2001.*
Wright, Archie T.: The Origin of Evil Spirits. 2005. *Volume II/198.*
Wucherpfennig, Ansgar: Heracleon Philologus. 2002. *Volume 142.*
Yeung, Maureen: Faith in Jesus and Paul. 2002. *Volume II/147.*
Zimmermann, Alfred E.: Die urchristlichen Lehrer. 1984, ²1988. *Volume II/12.*
Zimmermann, Johannes: Messianische Texte aus Qumran. 1998. *Volume II/104.*
Zimmermann, Ruben: Christologie der Bilder im Johannesevangelium. 2004. *Volume 171.*
- Geschlechtermetaphorik und Gottesverhältnis. 2001. *Volume II/122.*
Zumstein, Jean: see *Dettwiler, Andreas*
Zwiep, Arie W.: Judas and the Choice of Matthias. 2004. *Volume II/187.*

For a complete catalogue please write to the publisher
Mohr Siebeck • P.O. Box 2030 • D–72010 Tübingen/Germany
Up-to-date information on the internet at www.mohr.de